HOLLYWOOD CINEMA

An Introduction

Richard Maltby

and
Ian Craven

BLACKWELL
Oxford UK & Cambridge USA

First published 1995

Blackwell Publishers Ltd
108 Cowley Road
Oxford OX4 1JF
UK

Blackwell Publishers Inc.
238 Main Street
Cambridge, Massachusetts 02142
USA

British Library Cataloguing in Publication Data

A CIP catalogue record for this book is available from the British Library.

Library of Congress Cataloging-in-Publication Data

Maltby, Richard, 1952–
    Hollywood cinema: an introduction / Richard Maltby and Ian Craven.
      p. cm.
    Includes bibliographical references and index.
    ISBN 0-631-15706-9 (alk. paper). – ISBN 0-631-15732-8 (pbk.: alk. paper)
    1. Motion pictures – United States – History.   2. Motion picture industry – United States – History. I. Craven, Ian. II. Title.
    PN1993.5.U6M2296   1995
    791.43'0973 – dc20
                                             94-3794
                                              CIP

Typeset in 11 on 12^1/$_2$ pt, Palatino
by Best-set Typesetters Ltd, Hong Kong
Printed in Great Britain by Hartnolls Limited, Bodmin, Cornwall

This book is printed on acid-free paper

15.99

HOLL

This book is to be returned on or before the last date stamped below or you will be charged a fine

New City College – Redbridge campus
Library and Learning Centre
Barley Lane
Romford RM6 4XT
https://towham.cirqahosting.com
Redbridge: 020 8548 7118

for our students

Contents

Illustrations

Preface

The title of this book sounds preposterous: who needs to be introduced to anything so familiar, so much a part of the world's daily life, as Hollywood? But however well acquainted we are with Hollywood's stars and movies, few of us actually spend much time thinking seriously about what they mean, or about how they mean what they mean. This book aims to introduce – perhaps better to *re*-introduce – its readers to Hollywood: to the cultural and commercial institution that is Hollywood, and also to the critical study of the products of that institution: the movies. As importantly, it also aims to provide its readers with the critical tools to articulate everything you already know about Hollywood, but have not had the means to express. We would have called it *How to Take Hollywood Seriously*, if that title itself had not sounded too frivolous.

Our book is as concerned with the idea of Hollywood as it is with individual movies. It starts from the proposal that in order to understand how movies work, we have first to consider what they are for. Why do people go to the movies, and what place do these mass-produced fictions have in our lives? What exactly do we mean when we talk of Hollywood as a source of entertainment or escapism? What do we escape from, and where do we escape to? These introductory questions about entertainment lead us into a discussion of the forces that have shaped Hollywood as a cultural institution. Chapter 2 looks at the American cinema as an industry engaged in the production and sale of a commercial commodity, and at some of the ways in which the commercial considerations of the "show business," such as the star system, have shaped the aesthetic organization of its products. That theme is pursued in chapter 3, which considers how Hollywood's generic conventions operate as a system of product differentiation, to standardize and regulate the industry's output according to the expectations of audiences and producers. Chapter 4 examines the influence of technological change on Hollywood. It looks at how relatively minor developments in the technology of lenses or film processing have produced significant changes in what movies look and sound like, as well as at the effects of the introduction of sound, widescreen, and video.

The next four chapters examine the formal properties of Hollywood movies, and the ways in which a movie's manipulation of space, time, and movement can affect the audience's relationship to the cinema screen. Chapter 5 discusses how movies use the spatial conventions of Hollywood's continuity system to express emotions as well as to represent events. Chapter 6 looks at a number of different senses in which a movie can be considered a performance, examining different styles of Hollywood acting and the relationship between stars and the characters they embody. Chapter 7 considers ideas of time, tense, and history in Hollywood, and the way in which a movie's duration governs the construction of its narrative. Chapter 8 explores how the kinds of stories that Hollywood shows to its viewers are affected by the formal considerations discussed in earlier chapters. It analyzes the relationship between narrative and other sources of audience pleasure, and the importance of ambiguity in the organization of Classical Hollywood narrative.

The final two chapters provide overviews of Hollywood's relationship with the institutions of American politics, and of the development of the critical machinery used to dismantle and assess the products of the dream factory. Chapter 9 considers a number of different senses in which movies can be considered political, from questions of censorship to the representation of social problems. It explores the concept of ideology, and the uses to which it has been put in the critical analysis of Hollywood. Chapter 10 outlines the history of film criticism and discusses how different critical and theoretical traditions, from newspaper reviews to poststructuralist theory, have understood Hollywood. Like each of the earlier chapters, it contains an extended analysis of an individual movie as an illustration of the chapter's argument.

Several critical assumptions underlie the book's approach to its topic. One is that Hollywood is different from other national cinemas or film movements, primarily because of its commercial scale. We assume that Hollywood movies are determined, in the last instance, by their existence as consumable goods in a capitalist economy. Throughout the book we place the movies that we discuss within the economic and historical context of their production and consumption. Only by thinking about the way Hollywood movies are used by their audiences can we understand what we have called Hollywood's commercial aesthetic. The stress we place on considering a movie's context also leads us to argue that to understand Hollywood cinema fully we must understand it historically. Although the book is not organized chronologically, we argue throughout that Hollywood's audiences, its genres, its technology and even its formal properties have histories and are best understood through those histories. The examples we discuss cover almost the whole of Hollywood's history, from 1915 to the present. In addition, there is a Chronology at the back of the book, as well as a Glossary of critical and technical terms. Finally, in thinking about how Hollywood movies work, we assume that far from being passive recipients of a finished "text," the cinema audience plays an active role in the construction of a movie's meaning.

Acknowledgments

Since its inception, this book has been a collaborative project, and many people have helped it along its journey. Ian Craven and I began the book as a joint project, and shared the construction of its conceptual framework. Ian also wrote early versions of some sections, including several of the case studies. In the event, the work of completing the book fell to me. Although I am responsible for the final text, the book retains the evidence of our original plan in referring to us both as its authors.

This book benefited greatly from the critical assessments of Blackwell's anonymous readers, who forced us to reconsider a number of our assumptions. The issues explored here have also been examined and refined by several generations of our students. Through their questioning and debate, they have added to our understanding of Hollywood cinema in a myriad ways. If they read this, many of them will recognize an idea or a phrase that first saw the light of day in their seminar. The dedication, I hope, is some recognition of their many contributions.

At a crucial moment in the book's writing, Kate Bowles brought order to an unruly text, and insisted that its authors actually say what they meant. When all else failed, Kate found ways of saying it for us, especially in chapter 8, where she recast much of the argument. Kate is properly this book's third author as well as its first editor. Ruth Vasey has read and corrected half-a-dozen versions of the text and improved it on every occasion. Readers who wish this book were shorter will never know how grateful they should be to Ruth for insisting that it not get any longer. To properly express my gratitude to Ruth would take another book, so I just thank her for everything.

Friends at Exeter have read and listened to some of the arguments in this book, advised and supported me through the tribulations of authorship, and just generally tolerated its production beyond the calls of collegiality. I thank, sincerely, Stuart Murray, Karen Edwards, Anthony Fothergill,

Judith Higginbottom, Jo Seton, Michael Wood, Richard Bradbury, Bob Lawson-Peebles, Peter Quartermaine, Ron Tamplin, and most especially Mick Gidley, for his friendship, his guidance, and his example as scholar and teacher. I am also grateful to the School of English and American Studies at Exeter for a study leave that allowed me to complete the writing. For trading ideas that have become central to this book, I happily acknowledge my gratitude to Tino Balio, David Bordwell, Mary-Beth Haralovich, Lea Jacobs, Steve Neale, Janet Staiger and Kristin Thompson. Douglas Martin helped prepare the Chronology.

Other intellectual debts are legion, as the book's voluminous endnotes reveal. The collaborative nature of this project is most clearly visible in those pages, at the end of each chapter, which record the contributions of the scholars whose ideas this book discusses, borrows and argues with. Thanks are also due to the librarians and archivists who helped me discover the primary documents cited here: Sam Gill, Howard Prouty and the staff at the Margaret Herrick Library of the Academy of Motion Picture Arts and Sciences in Los Angeles, Maxine Fleckner-Ducey and the staff of the Wisconsin Center for Film and Theater Research in Madison, Gillian Hartnoll and the staff of the British Film Institute Library in London. In chapter 1 the lyrics of 'Moses' (Roger Edens/Betty Comden/Abel Green; 1952 EMI Catalogue Partnership/EMI Robbins Catalog Inc.) are reprinted by permission of CPP/Belwin Europe, Surrey, England.

At Blackwell's, Simon Prosser has kept faith with the project for longer than he or I would care to remember, and guided it to completion. Hazel Coleman and Emma Gotch have skillfully turned the manuscript into a book, and Fiona Sewell's copy-editing has unobtrusively added clarity and consistency to what the book says. Ginny Stroud-Lewis's picture research and Frances Tomlinson's illustrations have enhanced the book's argument as well as its appearance. My thanks to them all. Whatever faults remain here are mine.

Richard Maltby
December 1994

Introduction: Taking Hollywood Seriously

> You can take Hollywood for granted like I did, or you can dismiss it with the contempt we reserve for what we don't understand. It can be understood too, but only dimly and in flashes. Not half a dozen men have ever been able to keep the whole equation of pictures in their heads.
>
> F. Scott Fitzgerald[1]

"Metropolis of Make-Believe"[2]

> Welcome to Hollywood, what's your dream? Everyone comes here. This is Hollywood, land of dreams. Some dreams come true, some don't, but keep on dreamin'. This is Hollywood, always time to dream, so keep on dreamin'.
>
> Happy Man (Abdul Salaam El Razzac) in *Pretty Woman* (1990)

> You can't explain Hollywood. There isn't any such place.
>
> Rachel Field[3]

The sign said "HOLLYWOODLAND." A real estate company put it up in 1923, to advertise a housing development in Beechwood Canyon. Each letter was 50 feet tall, 30 feet wide, and studded with electric light bulbs. It cost $21,000. Most of it is still there, though the "land" went in 1949. On its fiftieth anniversary, the sign became an historic-cultural monument. But as anyone who has visited Los Angeles will tell you, if you go looking for Hollywood, the sign won't help you find it, because the place you're looking for isn't really there. In Raymond Chandler's novel, *The Little Sister*, private detective Philip Marlowe observes that "you can live a long time in Hollywood and never see the part they use in pictures."[4] The entertainment capital of the world, the Metropolis of Make-Believe, turns out to be more difficult to locate than simply by following directions to Schwab's drugstore on Sunset Boulevard.

Instead, you will find Hollywood much closer to home, in the familiar surroundings of the neighborhood movie theater, the back seat of the family car at the local drive-in, and now most often in your living room, on video or television. With every viewing, these mundane places are transformed into Hollywood, the movies, a never-never land of wish-fulfillment, fantasy, and immediate gratification, where, as the song says, "every shop girl can be a top girl" and every typist fulfill her dream of being, for a while, Joan Crawford or "the wrenchingly beautiful Winona Ryder in everything she ever was cast in."[5] Hollywood is a state of mind, not a geographical entity. You can visit it in the movies, and make it part of the soap opera of your own life. But as anyone who has walked down Hollywood Boulevard after dark will tell you, you wouldn't want to live there.

This introduction to Hollywood cinema does not try to introduce you to the art of film. Film is a material and a medium. Cinema is a social institution, and the concerns of this book are primarily with questions of culture rather than of Art. Indeed, Art is not a word that we shall employ too many times in the following pages. There is a critical tradition that makes significant claims for Hollywood cinema as an art practice comparable to the practice of literature or painting. This tradition has many strengths. Its weakness lies in its tendency to take movies out of the context of their production and consumption as objects in an industrial and commercial process. This book argues that we can only understand Hollywood's movies by examining that context. Most introductions to film studies argue that the common technological and aesthetic properties of film mean that the various forms of cinema can be treated as a single subject for study. Our more limited focus concentrates exclusively on mainstream American cinema, but within that narrower perspective we shall look not only at how movies work in terms of their formal and aesthetic properties, but also at their function as consumable goods in a capitalist economy. It is implicit in our argument that Hollywood differs in distinct and definable ways from other national cinemas or international film movements. Two Hollywood movies separated by 70 years, such as *Way Down East* (1920) and *Pretty Woman* (1990), have more in common with each other than either does with contemporary European art cinema, documentary, or avant-garde film. Throughout this book, we make a distinction in the way we use the two terms film and movie. We use **film** to mean the physical, celluloid material on which images are registered and a soundtrack recorded, and **movie** to refer to the stream of images that we consume as both narrative and spectacle when the material is projected. This distinction between film and movie is broadly comparable to the distinction between print and literature: the material and the experiential forms have different properties.[6]

In 1968, as film studies began to appear on the curricula of American universities, the *New Yorker*'s film critic Pauline Kael complained about classes in which students who interpreted a movie's plot as a mechanism for producing audience response were corrected by teachers who explained it in terms of a creative artist working out a theme, "as if the conditions under which the movie is made and the market for which it is designed were irrelevant, as if the latest product from Warners or Universal should be analyzed like a lyric poem."[7] Kael wanted to preserve Hollywood from the excesses of academicization. *Morocco* (1930), she thought, was "great trash," and "trash doesn't belong to the academic tradition." Part of the pleasure in trash was "that you don't have to take it seriou¡sly, that it was never meant to be any more than frivolous and trifling and entertaining."[8] What draws us to movies, she argued, is the opening they provide "into other, forbidden or surprising, kinds of experience," "the details of crime and high living and wicked cities . . . the language of toughs and urchins . . . the dirty smile of the city girl who lured the hero away from Janet Gaynor." Unlike Kael, we do want to take entertainment seriously. But in doing so, we want to bear in mind her stricture that "If we always wanted works of complexity and depth we wouldn't be going to movies about glamorous thieves and seductive women who sing in cheap cafes."[9]

Writer Ross Wills explained the elusive relationship between Hollywood and the nation it represents when he observed that Hollywood "is not America at all, but it is all America" – to which Carey McWilliams added that it is "America in flight from itself."[10] In *The Wizard of Oz* (1939),

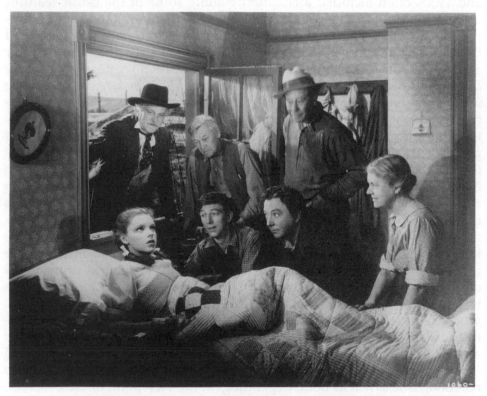

At the end of *The Wizard of Oz* (1939), Dorothy (Judy Garland) wakes up to discover that her journey to Oz took her no further than her own back yard. Aquarius Picture Library

when the screen turns from black-and-white to Technicolor, Dorothy (Judy Garland) tells her little dog, "I don't think we're in Kansas any more, Toto." It turns out, of course, that she is both right and wrong. The inhabitants of Oz are all familiar figures from the midwest farm she left, and when Dorothy finally achieves her ambition to get back to Kansas, she realizes that "If I ever go looking for my heart's desire again, I won't go looking any further than my own back yard, because if you can't find it there, then you probably never lost it in the first place." Dorothy's inscrutable observation encapsulates the relationship Hollywood proposes between itself and the everyday world of its audience: Oz is Kansas, but in Technicolor. It has, at the same time, the familiarity of home and the exoticism of a foreign country. In the very notion that it gives its audiences what they want, Hollywood proposes itself as a benevolent institution, much as the Wizard of Oz himself turns out to be.[11] Hollywood – the movies – is the place this happens, a place of refuge from the everyday, the place where dreams come true, time after time after time.

Many people who have visited Los Angeles to look for Hollywood have written about their encounters as if they were discovering a familiar foreign land. European writers of travel books about America in the 1920s and 1930s often included a chapter detailing some of the exotic features of the place, and in due course it fell prey to the investigations of anthropologists. In 1946 Hortense Powdermaker, whose previous fieldwork had been among the Melanesian peoples of the south Pacific, spent a year among the natives of Hollywood. The book she then wrote, *Hollywood the Dream Factory: An Anthropologist Looks at the Movie-makers*, provided the intellectual model for a stream of later journalistic and sociological investigations. In it she frequently compared ex-cannibal chiefs and magicians to front-office executives and directors. In Hollywood's atmosphere of permanent crisis and its belief in "the breaks" as the cause of success, she found elements of magical thinking that might have been recognizable in New Guinea: "Just as the Melanesian thinks failure would result from changing the form of a spell, so men in Hollywood consider it dangerous to depart from their formulas. . . . The Melanesian placates hostile supernatural forces through a series of taboos; Hollywood attempts to appease its critics and enemies with the [Production] Code."[12] Stressing the absence of planning on the part of studio executives ("The god is profits, and opportunism the ritual of worship"), Powdermaker found Hollywood to be a fundamentally irrational place, a place of irretrievable contradictions, whose inhabitants "all move within an orbit of love and hostility, competitiveness and dependency," where a "pseudo-friendliness and show of affection cover hostility and lack of respect." While to some Hollywood "may be considered a hotbed of Communism or the seat of conservative reaction," she saw it as both, depending on the viewpoint of the observer. The Hollywood she observed was a site of contradictions, both "a center for creative genius" and "a place where mediocrity flourishes;" at the same time "an important industry with worldwide significance" and "an environment of trivialities characterized by aimlessness."

For Powdermaker, the contradictory nature of the place revealed itself most vividly in one essential opposition: "Making movies must be either business *or* art, rather than both." For many filmmakers, she suggested, "there seems to be a continuous conflict, repeated for each picture, between making a movie which they can respect and the 'business' demands of the front office. It is assumed . . . that a movie which has the respect of the artist cannot make money." This opposition also structured her own account of Hollywood, as it has structured so many other writers' tales. Describing one of her informants, "Mr Literary," a successful writer of A-features, she suggested that:

> He regards his work at the studio as a form of play and rather enjoys it as such. He uses the word "play" because he says that he cannot take it seriously. . . . He has never worked on any movie which has even moderately satisfied him. Each time he starts with high hopes that this one will be different, but each time it is the same: so many interferences, so many changes, that the final script is not his, although he has far more influence over it than do most writers. He does not have this attitude of "play" toward writing a novel or a short story. That is deadly earnest. Then he is concerned with working out a real problem and any interference with it he would regard as a real crisis.[13]

Powdermaker saw the contradiction between business and art as ordinarily resolved only in failure, when business and aesthetic weakness combine to produce "the confusion, wastefulness and lack of planning . . . which is taken for granted in Hollywood."[14] Writing three decades later, Steven Bach echoed Powdermaker's criticism, suggesting that the "art versus business" conflict "has remained stubbornly resistant to resolution and remains the dominating central issue of American motion pictures to the present day." Bach's book, *Final Cut*, is an account of the production of *Heaven's Gate*, a Western directed by Michael Cimino in 1979 that went catastrophically over budget. Intended to be "a blockbuster with 'Art' written all over it," the movie's epic failure in fact led directly to the sale of United Artists, the company which had financed it. Bach, head of production at United Artists at the time, argues that the movie's commercial failure was inextricably interwoven with its aesthetic pretensions. Characters and story were sacrificed to the director's indulgence in "an orgy of brilliant pictorial effects." *Heaven's Gate* failed, according to Bach, not because its budget escalated to $44 million, way beyond any hope of profit, but because it failed as entertainment: it did not "engage audiences on the most basic and elemental human levels of sympathy and compassion."[15]

Bach's definition of Hollywood's entertainment purpose was little different from that of successful screenwriter Frances Marion in 1937. What the audience wanted, she argued, was to have its emotions aroused:

it wants something that will pleasantly excite it, amuse it, wring it with suspense, fill it with self-approval, or even arouse its indignation . . . above all things, it wants to be "sent home happy." It looks to the photoplay to provide it with a substitute for actual life experience, and to function in such fashion the screen story must contain elements that are emotionally satisfying. Something approaching the ideal life is what this audience prefers to see, rather than life as it actually knows it. It wants to see interesting things which, within the limits of possibility, might happen to it; preferably things to which its own day dreams turn.[16]

A Classical Cinema?

The very name Hollywood has colored the thought of this age. It has given to the world a new synonym for happiness because of all its products happiness is the one in which Hollywood – the motion-picture Hollywood – chiefly interests itself.

Carl Milliken, 1928[17]

If Hollywood is not a place it is also not a time. Since the 1960s Hollywood has persistently been described as not being "what it was," and a succession of both journalistic and critical works have talked of *The Fifty-year Decline of Hollywood, Hollywood in Transition, The New Hollywood*, or *Hollywood and After*.[18] But as well as changing, Hollywood has also remained the same, at least in the sense of remaining in the same business of entertaining its audience, of producing the maximum pleasure for the maximum number for the maximum profit. If we are to take Hollywood seriously and understand its business, the first thing we must do is to "describe the way American films *work*."[19] The most important and influential critical work written on Hollywood in the last twenty years is *The Classical Hollywood Cinema: Film Style and Mode of Production to 1960*, by David Bordwell, Janet Staiger, and Kristin Thompson. In it, they delineate the formal features of what they call the **Classical Hollywood** style, and trace its evolution, along with the organizational history of Hollywood's production practices. By 1917, the authors argue, the essential features of the Classical style were in place. Since then, these features – the way that a movie organizes narrative time and space, the continuity script, the management structure, and the division of labor in production – have remained fundamentally unchanged. It is this historical continuity that enables us to make generalizations about Hollywood over a period that spans most of this century.

Published in 1985, *The Classical Hollywood Cinema* set new standards for historical research in film studies, and also gave a new precision to ideas of "the Classical" in relation to Hollywood. The French critic, André Bazin (whose work is discussed on a number of occasions in the following pages), first described Hollywood as "a classical art," arguing that it should be admired for "the richness of its ever-vigorous tradition, and its fertility when it comes into contact with new elements." He also suggested that the genius of the Hollywood system should be analyzed via a socio-logical approach to its production, since a crucial element of that system was the way in which it "has been able, in an extraordinarily competent way, to show American society just as it wanted to see itself."[20] The idea of a classical cinema has remained in play as part of most critical accounts of Hollywood, although it has most frequently been invoked as a background against which exceptional works could be defined and distinguished. Bordwell, Staiger, and Thompson investigated the formal organization of the "ordinary film," basing their account of Classical style on an analysis of a randomly selected sample of Hollywood movies. Their analysis of style thus addressed what Bazin had suggested was most admirable about Hollywood, with a precision that had been largely absent from previous descriptions of "classic narrative film" or "classic realism." The idea of "the classical" implies the observance of rules of composition and aesthetic organization that produce unity, balance, and order in the resulting art-work. "Classical" works conform. They are bound by rules that set strict limits on innovation. The authors of *The Classical Hollywood Cinema* regard the style they describe as classical because "the principles which Hollywood claims as its own rely on notions of decorum, proportion, formal harmony, respect for tradition, mimesis, self-effacing craftsman-ship, and cool control of the perceiver's response – canons which critics in any medium usually call 'classical.'"[21]

In this book we argue that Hollywood functions according to what we have called a **commercial aesthetic**, one that is essentially opportunist in its economic motivation. This argument sits uneasily with the stylisti-cally determined view of a movie's organization implicit in the idea of classicism. The assumption that Hollywood movies are determined, in the last instance, by their existence as commercial commodities is central to our understanding of what Hollywood is. Bordwell, Staiger, and Thompson conclude that, although economic factors have strongly af-fected the development of the classical style, in their final analysis "stylistic factors can explain the most specific and interesting aspects of Hollywood filmmaking." For them, a set of formal conventions of narrative construc-tion, spectacle, verisimilitude, and continuity "constituted Hollywood's very definition of a movie itself."[22] From the critical perspective we have adopted in this book, these investigations of Hollywood's formal conven-tions can address one of the two sets of questions we can ask about the way movies work: the way in which Hollywood is, in David Bordwell's phrase, "an excessively obvious cinema."[23] But there is another set of questions, dealing with the relationships that exist between movies and their audi-ences, that needs to take into account other considerations than those examined in *The Classical Hollywood Cinema*. A history of Hollywood's stylistic evolution cannot fully acknowledge the sociological approach that Bazin argued for, or describe the wider external pressures and forces at work in the Hollywood system. The first four chapters of this book discuss these external pressures as influences regulating the final product.

Answers to questions about what Hollywood is for must be sought not only in its movies but also in the social, cultural, and institutional contexts that surround it. The approach that we have called "consumerist criticism" aims to answer these questions by examining Hollywood's commercial aesthetics. At one level, we shall be concerned with what viewers use movies for: "to learn how to dress or how to speak more elegantly or how to make a grand entrance or even what kind of coffee maker we wish to purchase, or to take off from the movie into a romantic fantasy or a trip."[24] At another level, we shall examine how Hollywood movies are organized to deliver pleasure to their audiences. Take something as obvious as Hollywood's happy endings. The authors of *The Classical Hollywood Cinema* found that 60 percent of the movies they analyzed "ended with a display of the united romantic couple – the cliché happy ending, often with a 'clinch' – and many more could be said to end happily."[25] In contrast to a strictly formal analysis that sees classical movies as driven by the logical progression of their narratives, Rick Altman has pointed out that the similarity of Hollywood happy endings suggests that classical narrative "reasons backward." A movie's beginning, he argues, must be "retro-fitted" so that it appears to lead logically to the predetermined happy ending. "The end is made to *appear* as a function of the beginning in order better to disguise the fact that the beginning is actually a function of the ending."[26] More generally, movies are engineered to produce a sequence of audience responses, "thrilling us when we should be thrilled," as a writer in the *Nickelodeon* put it in 1910, "making us laugh or cry at the appointed times, and leaving us, at the end of the film, in a beatific frame of mind."[27] Screenwriting manuals and practicing screenwriters alike emphasize that scripts are engineered to maintain a level of engagement on the part of the audience. John Sayles describes the concise discussions he had with the producers of *Piranha* (1978):

> They said, "You're going to rewrite *Piranha*. Make sure you keep the main idea, the idea of piranhas being loose in North American waters." I said, "Okay, how often do you want an attack? About every fifteen minutes?" They said, "Yeah, but it doesn't have to be an attack. Maybe just the threat of an attack – but some sort of action sequence about that often to keep the energy going." I said, "Anything else?" They said, "Keep it fun."[28]

As a final level of its inquiry, consumerist criticism examines the institutional and ideological constraints on Hollywood. Movies, we shall argue, have happy endings because part of their cultural function is to affirm and maintain the culture of which they are part. That cultural function was, for instance, inscribed in the industry's Production Code, which regulated the content and treatment of every Hollywood movie between 1931 and 1968. The fact that 85 percent of Hollywood movies feature heterosexual romance as their main plot device needs to be seen in the context of this regulatory framework. And if, as we shall suggest, the movie theater is a site in which cultural and ideological anxieties can be aired in the relative safety of a well-regulated fiction, we might well ask why we need quite so much reassurance that heterosexual romance is supposed to end happily. These issues are discussed in chapters 1 and 8. The set of questions that consumerist criticism addresses indicates that the Hollywood of our inquiry is different from that uncovered by *The Classical Hollywood Cinema*. At a practical level, however, this disagreement is a matter of emphasis, and the two kinds of analysis complement each other.

One further question about Classical Hollywood has to do with whether it still exists. Bordwell, Staiger, and Thompson end their book in 1960, a date that they acknowledge is "somewhat arbitrary."[29] By then, Classical Hollywood's mode of production, the vertically integrated company operating a studio, had come to an end, but the style it produced persisted. Although the style altered after 1960, it had also altered before, and the style of the new Hollywood of the 1970s can best be explained, they suggest, by the same process of stylistic assimilation that had operated throughout Hollywood's history: "As the 'old' Hollywood had incorporated and refunctionalized devices from German Expressionism and Soviet montage, the 'New' Hollywood has selectively borrowed from the international art cinema."[30] We take up the issue of whether Hollywood after the 1960s should be considered Classical or post-Classical in our discussion of space in chapter 5. As a synonym for the "studio system" of production, "Classical Hollywood cinema" has become a conventional usage in film criticism. At times in this book, we shall take issue with conventions of critical usage, but not here. In this book, Classical Hollywood cinema is taken to be a period of Hollywood's history, and refers to the style, the mode of production, and the industrial organization under which movies were made from the early 1920s to the late 1950s.

Hollywood and its Audiences

The last couple of years, I thought that a large proportion of the American public wanted to see blood or breasts. Now I think they want to see cars. Our biggest film to date, *Eat My Dust!*, just piles up one car after another.
Roger Corman, 1977[31]

Our dream was to make a movie about how movies screw up your brain about love, and then if we did a good job, we would become one of the movies that would screw up people's brains about love forever.
Nora Ephron on *Sleepless in Seattle* (1993)[32]

Although Hollywood's goal of entertainment has remained constant, the audience it has sought to entertain has changed as many times in the 80 years of Hollywood's existence as have the ways of producing and packaging movies.[33] Since 1950, moviegoing has been a minority activity. In 1946, one third of the American public went to a movie every week. By 1983, fewer than a quarter went once a month, but that group accounted for 85 percent of all movie admissions.[34] As significantly, the industry's idea of its audience has changed. In the late 1920s, the industry estimated that between three quarters and four fifths of its audience were women.[35] Although the reliability of this estimate is open to question, for most of the 1930s and 1940s there was a widespread assumption among production and distribution personnel that the large majority of movie audiences in the US and Europe were female. At a story conference during the production of *Snow White* in 1936, Walt Disney argued that the dream sequence in which Snow White sings "Some Day My Prince Will Come" would appeal particularly to the female audience. "After all," he said, "80 percent of our audience are women."[36] In 1939 a sociologist reported that "it is really that solid average citizen's wife who commands the respectful attention of the industry."[37]

From about 1955, however, the industry's conception of its audience shifted. In the mid-1960s, American-International Pictures (AIP), an independent company specializing in "exploitation" pictures (its first major success was in 1957 with *I Was a Teenage Werewolf*), codified the strategy behind its production and distribution policy in what it called "the Peter Pan Syndrome": younger children would watch anything older children would watch, and girls would watch anything boys would watch, but not vice versa; therefore, "to catch your greatest audience you zero in on the 19-year-old male."[38] The industry began to pursue the teenage audience because they were "the best picture-goers in the country at this time – the most consistent, the best equipped with leisure time and allowance money, the most gregariously inclined, and to be sure the most romantic." This led to what Thomas Doherty has called "a progressive 'juvenilization' of movie content and the movie audience that is today the operative reality of the American motion picture business."[39]

Because of its professed commitment to providing universal entertainment for an undifferentiated audience, the industry made relatively few systematic attempts to inquire into the composition or preferences of that audience in the studio period. In the late 1960s, however, Hollywood's relation to its audience underwent a substantial revision when the industry trade association, the Motion Picture Association of America, established a ratings system, classifying certain movies as unsuitable for sections of the potential audience. Censor boards in many foreign countries had long prohibited children from attending some movies, but American distributors had always resisted proposals for similar schemes in their domestic market. Instead they preferred to use the Production Code as a system of regulation to ensure that all Hollywood movies would only offer entertainment that would prove harmless to all their audiences. (We discuss the operation of the Production Code in chapter 1.) By the mid-1960s, however, shifts in American cultural values had undermined the credibility of the Production Code, and it was abandoned in 1968. The industry's decision to introduce a ratings system was immediately provoked by two decisions of the US Supreme Court, upholding the rights of local governments to prevent children being exposed to books or movies considered suitable only for adults. In the wake of these decisions the industry faced a flood of state and municipal legislation establishing local schemes for film classification, and the introduction of a ratings system was an attempt to outmaneuver that legislation.[40]

The Code and Ratings Administration (CARA) divided movies into four categories: G, suitable for general admission; M, allowing unrestricted admission, but suggesting that parents should decide whether the movie was suitable for children under 16; R, restricting attendance by requiring children under 16 to be accompanied by an adult; and X, restricting attendance to those over 16. Since 1968, the system has been modified several times. In 1970 the M category became GP, when the age restriction was raised to 17; in 1972 GP was renamed PG (for parental guidance suggested); and CARA itself was renamed the Classification and Rating Administration in 1977, abandoning any reference to the existence of a Code governing movie production as well as the practice of vetting scripts in advance of production. In 1983, CARA added another category, PG-13, providing a "strong caution" to parents of children under 13. In 1990, CARA renamed the X category NC-17 in an attempt to create a category for art movies restricted to the over-17s, since X had become generally understood as referring to pornography. The ratings system has imposed few actual limitations on attendance, but it has required producers to conceive of their audiences differently, engineering their movies to achieve a particular rating – a requirement often built into a movie's finance agreements. Distributors will not handle X-rated movies, and movies such as *Dressed to Kill* (1980) and *Angel Heart* (1987) have been re-edited to qualify for an R. The G rating has been almost equally firmly avoided. Of 336 films rated in 1981, only seven were rated G, and it has been common industry practice to insert swearing, nudity, or violence to ensure a PG or R rating.[41]

In a further move away from the commercial assumptions underlying the operation of the studio system, the industry started to make more use of market research in attempts to target movies more effectively at particular audiences at the same time as the ratings system was introduced. By the late 1980s, marketing strategists in the major companies were reconsidering the assumption that their movies should appeal primarily to teenage boys, in recognition of the "greying of the movie-going audience." In 1984, only 15 percent of the audience was over 40. In 1990, the over-40s made up 24 percent of the audience, providing a more viable target market. Fox production chief Roger Birnbaum suggested that these changes in audience composition meant that "a studio can develop a slate of pictures that doesn't just cater to one demographic." In a return to much earlier assumptions, he reported that "the demographic on women, today, is very strong."[42]

However, Hollywood's notion of its audience has always had to remain very generalized, because of the size of a movie's market. Hollywood movies have always been made for an international audience, and since the early 1920s, between a third and half of Hollywood's earnings have come from audiences outside the United States. Much of the cultural power of Hollywood and other artifacts of American mass culture has lain in the fact that they were designed "for universal exhibition."[43] Several times in this book we describe these values as Utopian. As our description of its immaterial geography suggests, Hollywood itself is a Utopia, a nowhere that has also been America to most of the rest of the world for much of this century. For the citizens of Manchester, Melbourne, and Mombassa, Westerns have provided the most recognizable American landscape. The most familiar American cityscapes may even have been shot on a studio backlot. Hollywood has exported an image of the United States that has become so much a part of everyday life in even distant and scarcely westernized areas as to seem, paradoxically, less an *American* product and more a part of an international mass culture in which we all share. At the center of this empire, Americans can become too possessive of their cultural capital. In a recent history of the American musical, Rick Altman claims that however much non-American critics may understand "the context and meaning" of a movie such as *Singin' in the Rain* (1952), they will inevitably lack the familiarity with American culture that equips them to translate the movie's "raw thematic material into . . . the culture's master themes."[44] Altman argues that:

> The culture's master themes are not actually *in* the text, yet the text is produced in such a way as to evoke them for a particular interpretive community. Perception of the relationship is a more important cultural phenomenon than any actual relationship that might exist. It is through the spectator's knowledge and perception that culture and cinema interact in a reciprocal relationship.[45]

While not questioning Altman's general proposition about the relationship between cinema and culture, we would point out that because Hollywood movies have never been made only for an American audience, they have also been part of the other cultures they have visited. An Austrian audience watching *The Sound of Music* (1965) or an Australian audience watching *The Sundowners* (1960) saw their national histories Americanized. In movies like these, audiences outside the United States have viewed their own cultural pasts through a filter in which their domestic environment has been represented as exotic, while the "domestic market" addressed by the movie has not been theirs but that of North America. In such circumstances, it is hardly surprising that Hollywood should have become an imaginative home to many of its foreign audiences. In a 1989 article about the effect of new communications technologies on cultural identity, David Morley and Kevin Robins suggested that "American culture repositions frontiers – social, cultural, psychic, linguistic, geographical. America is now within."[46] But for much of the world, American popular culture had become part of their cultural identity by 1926, when a State Department official observed that "If it were not for the barrier we have established, there is no doubt that the American movies would be bringing us a flood of the immigrants. As it is, in vast instances, the desire to come to this country is thwarted, and the longing to emigrate is changed into a desire to imitate."[47] Two years later, a film industry representative declared that motion pictures "color the minds of those who see them. They are demonstrably the greatest single factors in the Americanization of the world and as such fairly may be called the most important and significant of America's exported products."[48] Less enthusiastically, the *Daily Express* complained that British cinemagoers "talk America, think America, and dream America. We have several million people, mostly women, who to all intent and purpose are temporary American citizens."[49] They were, of course, not American citizens at all, but citizens of Hollywood's imagined Utopian community. But for many people who visit the familiar foreign territory of Hollywood in the movies and in their imagination, Hollywood is what they imagine America to be.

Our discussions of Hollywood's audience and of Classical Hollywood will have already alerted you to our concern with questions of history. This book is not a history of Hollywood so much as a thematic investigation of what Hollywood is, and what Hollywood movies are. It is, however, informed by the belief that we need to understand Hollywood from a range of historical perspectives. Hollywood has at least three separate but overlapping histories. The history of production, the story of the studios and their stars, has preoccupied the majority of movie historians. Much less notice tends to be taken of movie reception, but Hollywood's audience has a history, too, and that history – the history of the box-office – has had a determining influence on the history of production. Thirdly, Hollywood has a critical history: a history of the changes in what critics have understood Hollywood to be. Most critical histories of Hollywood are descriptive, charting its high and low points, although different critics, of course, describe that history differently. The book's final chapter discusses the history of criticism of Hollywood, and aspects of this critical history arise in several other places, such as the discussion of auteurist criticism in chapter 1.

These three overlapping accounts of Hollywood are narratives of continuity as well as change. All are in competition with Hollywood's history of itself, projected in fan magazines, star biographies, and "exposés," as well as in movies about Hollywood. Much of what passes for Hollywood's history has been written as if it were itself a Hollywood story and as if the history of entertainment were under an obligation to be entertaining. *Singin' in the Rain*, for instance, provides us with a history of Hollywood's introduction of sound, during the course of which Cosmo Brown (Donald O'Connor) discovers the principles of sound dubbing by standing in front of Kathy Selden (Debbie Reynolds) and moving his mouth while she sings; a much more entertaining version of history than a mundane account of the development of multiple channel recording and post-synchronization would be. The most common explanation for the introduction of sound, that it was a last desperate gamble by an almost bankrupt Warner Bros., is likewise a Hollywood fantasy, discredited by research that has shown that the major companies' transition to sound was a much more orderly and considered process.[50] Nevertheless, it is still widely reproduced, because its story of the kids from the ghetto making good with an invention the big studios had turned down fits in with the mythological history of Hollywood, the *Singin' in the Rain* history of the place, which proposes that the history of Hollywood must conform to the conventions of its own narratives. This Hollywood was the invention of press and publicity agents. It served as a disguise for the American film industry, the means by which public attention was diverted away from the routine, mechanical, standardized aspects of the industry's central operations toward its more attractive, glamorous periphery. That disguise has worked almost as well for many of Hollywood's critics and historians as it did for the readers of its fan magazines in the 1930s, since all the pressures of the industry act against the displacement of Hollywood as "Metropolis of Make-Believe" by a more prosaic description of the economic forces and business practices involved in selling entertainment.

Taking Hollywood seriously can often seem like a perverse activity, because the institutions of high culture and popular culture alike actively discourage us from doing so. Students of Hollywood resemble those cartoon characters who, when making a decision, find themselves being offered self-interested advice by a miniature angel perched on one shoulder and a tiny devil on the other. The angelic ghost of high cultural values whispers in the critic's right ear that something so frivolous doesn't deserve so much attention, while the demonic and demotic voice of commercial culture whispers in the other ear that taking it seriously will take all the fun out of it. Throughout this book we will argue against the angel, that entertainment is too important and too complex not to be taken seriously. But we will also argue against the devil that thinking seriously about the pleasure in entertainment doesn't prevent you experiencing it – at least, not in Hollywood's benign Utopia.

Notes

1   F. Scott Fitzgerald, *The Last Tycoon* (Harmondsworth: Penguin, 1974), pp. 5–6.
2   Description of Hollywood in the opening sequence of *A Star is Born* (1937).
3   Rachel Field, *To See Ourselves*, quoted in Carey McWilliams, *Southern California: An Island on the Land*, 1st pub. 1946 (Santa Barbara: Peregrine Smith, Inc., 1973), p. 330.

4   Raymond Chandler, *The Little Sister*, 1st pub. 1949 (Harmondsworth: Penguin, 1973), p. 109.

5   "Hooray for Hollywood," composed by Richard Whiting and Johnny Mercer, from *Hollywood Hotel* (1937); Caitlin Moran, "The Day We Spent Granny's Lolly," *The Observer* (July 26, 1992), p. 47.

6   Although this technical distinction is particularly useful to us here, most critical writing uses the two terms "film" and "movie" interchangeably.

7   Pauline Kael, "Trash, Art, and the Movies," in *Going Steady* (Boston: Little, Brown, 1970), p. 93.

8   Kael, pp. 112–13.

9   Kael, pp. 104–5, 113–14.

10 McWilliams, p. 342.

11 The author of the Oz stories, L. Frank Baum, himself moved from Chicago to Hollywood in 1910, two years after the first movie company arrived. All of the Oz stories except the first, *The Wonderful Wizard of Oz*, were written in southern California, and California historian Kevin Starr suggests that Los Angeles was the Emerald City, that southern California "was Baum's Oz dream materialized . . . the Garden of the West so long struggled for on the prairies of the Midwest." Oz was "America transformed, made magic . . . a tidy, prosperous utopia, recognizably mid-American in its benevolent technology and bourgeois prosperity," where its citizens could concentrate "on the business of living, which for them was the life of emotion and imagination – and having adventures." Kevin Starr, *Material Dreams: Southern California through the 1920s* (New York: Oxford University Press, 1990), pp. 65–7.

12 Hortense Powdermaker, *Hollywood the Dream Factory: An Anthropologist Looks at the Movie-makers* (Boston: Little, Brown, 1950), p. 285.

13 Powdermaker, pp. 313, 169, 16, 27, 142–3.

14 Powdermaker, p. 166.

15 Steven Bach, *Final Cut: Dreams and Disaster in the Making of Heaven's Gate* (London: Faber, 1986), pp. 195, 338, 416. Not everyone, however, regards *Heaven's Gate* as an aesthetic failure. Robin Wood is one of several critics who have argued that it is "one of the few authentically innovative Hollywood films" and "among the supreme achievements of the Hollywood cinema." Robin Wood, "*Heaven's Gate* Reopened," *MOVIE* 31/32 (1986), pp. 73, 83.

16 Frances Marion, *How to Write and Sell Film Stories* (New York: Covici Friede, 1937), quoted in Frank H. Ricketson, *The Management of Motion Pictures* (New York: McGraw-Hill, 1938), p. 13.

17 Lamar Trotti, "The Motion Picture as a Business," delivered as a speech by Carl E. Milliken, April 1928. Motion Picture Association Archive, New York.

18 Ezra Goodman, *The Fifty-year Decline of Hollywood* (New York: Simon and Schuster, 1961); Richard Dyer McCann, *Hollywood in Transition* (Boston: Houghton Mifflin, 1962); Jim Hillier, *The New Hollywood* (London: Studio Vista, 1993); Jerzy Toeplitz, *Hollywood and After: The Changing Face of Movies in America* (London: Allen and Unwin, 1974).

19 Thomas Elsaesser, "Why Hollywood?," *Monogram* 1 (1971), p. 6.

20 André Bazin, "La Politique des Auteurs," in Peter Graham, ed., *The New Wave* (London: Secker and Warburg, 1968), pp. 143–4, 154.

21 David Bordwell, Janet Staiger, and Kristin Thompson, *The Classical Hollywood Cinema: Film Style and Mode of Production to 1960* (London: Routledge and Kegan Paul, 1985), p. 4.

22 Bordwell et al., p. 367.

23 Bordwell et al., p. 3. Part One of *The Classical Hollywood Cinema* provides an analysis of

the formal properties of classical Hollywood style.

24   Kael, p. 101.

25   David Bordwell, *Narration in the Fiction Film* (London: Methuen, 1985), p. 159.

26   Rick Altman, "Dickens, Griffith, and Film Theory Today," in Jane Gaines, ed., *Classical Hollywood Narrative: The Paradigm Wars* (Durham, NC: Duke University Press, 1992), p. 32.

27   H. Kent Webster, "Little Stories of Great Films," *Nickelodeon* 3:1 (January 1, 1910), p. 13, quoted in Bordwell et al., p. 195.

28   Quoted in Hillier, p. 44.

29   Bordwell et al., p. 10.

30   Bordwell et al., p. 373.

31   Quoted in Hillier, p. 41.

32   Quoted in Kathryn Hughes, "Crocodile Tears from Hollywood," *Observer* (September 5, 1993), p. 43.

33   Contemporary Hollywood makes made-for-TV movies and television mini-series, for instance, but most critical and historical accounts have ignored them, limiting their discussion of Hollywood's output to feature-length motion pictures.

34   Bruce A. Austin, *Immediate Seating: A Look at Movie Audiences* (Belmont, CA: Wadsworth, 1989), pp. 44, 90.

35   In 1929, the industry's trade association suggested that 75 percent of its audience were women. Two years earlier, *Moving Picture World* had suggested women had an 83 percent majority in the audience. In 1928, an *Exhibitors Herald* article asserted that "Woman has, in the last ten years at least, become the objective in the [theater] manager's planning, because it has become an established fact that women fans constitute the major percentage of patronage or at least cast the final vote in determining the majority patronage." *The Film in National Life: Being the Report of an Enquiry Conducted by the Commission on Educational and Cultural Films into the Service which the Cinematograph may Render to Education and Social Progress* (London: Allen and Unwin, 1932), p. 35. This report led to the establishment of the British Film Institute; Beth Brown, "Making Movies for Women," *Moving Picture World* (March 26, 1927), p. 34, quoted in Gaylyn Studlar, "The Perils of Pleasure? Fan Magazine Discourse as Women's Commodified Culture in the 1920s," *Wide Angle* 13:1 (January 1991), p. 7; Jeanne Allen, "The Film Viewer as Consumer," *Quarterly Review of Film Studies* 5:4 (Fall 1980), p. 486.

36   Walt Disney, Disney studio story conference, December 8, 1936, quoted in Robin Allen, "European Influences on the Animated Feature Films of Walt Disney," PhD thesis, University of Exeter, 1992.

37   Margaret Thorp, *America at the Movies* (London: Faber, 1946), p. 17.

38   Robin Bean and David Austen, "U.S.A. Confidential," *Films and Filming* 215 (November 1968), pp. 21–2. Quoted in Thomas Doherty, *Teenagers and Teenpix: The Juvenilization of American Movies in the 1950s* (Boston: Unwin Hyman, 1988), p. 157.

39   William R. Weaver, "AIP Heads Set Sight on Teenage Patron," *Motion Picture Herald* (May 25, 1957), p. 20. Quoted in Doherty, p. 156; Doherty, p. 3.

40   Douglas Ayer, Roy E. Bates, and Peter J. Herman, "Self-Censorship in the Movie Industry: An Historical Perspective on Law and Social Change," *Wisconsin Law Review* 3 (1970), pp. 791–838; Austin, pp. 106–16.

41   Aljean Harmetz, "Rating the Ratings," in *Rolling Breaks and Other Movie Business* (New York: Knopf, 1983), p. 96; Georgia Jeffries, "The Problem with G," *American Film* (June 1978), p. 51.

42   Quoted in Hillier, p. 31.

43 From 1913, the British Board of Film Censors categorized movies as being suitable either for exhibition to adult audiences, or "for universal exhibition."

44 Rick Altman, *The American Film Musical* (Bloomington: Indiana University Press, 1989), p. 340.

45 Altman, *American Film Musical*, p. 340.

46 David Morley and Kevin Robins, "Spaces of Identity: Communications Technologies and the Reconfiguration of Europe," *Screen* 30:4 (Autumn 1989), p. 21.

47 James True, *Printer's Ink* (February 4, 1926), quoted in Charles Eckert, "The Carole Lombard in Macy's Window," *Quarterly Review of Film Studies* 3 (Winter 1978), pp. 4–5.

48 "Certain Factors and Considerations Affecting the European Market," internal MPPDA memo, October 25, 1928, Motion Picture Association of America Archive, New York (hereafter MPA).

49 Quoted in Jeffrey Richards, *The Age of the Dream Palace: Cinema and Society in Britain 1930–1939* (London: Routledge and Kegan Paul, 1984), p. 63.

50 Douglas Gomery, "The Coming of Sound: Technological Change in the American Film Industry," in Tino Balio, ed., *The American Film Industry*, revised edn (Madison: University of Wisconsin Press, 1985), pp. 229–51.

1 Entertainment

To recapture the active response of the film-fan is the first step toward intelligent appreciation of most pictures . . . One cannot profitably stop there, but one cannot sensibly begin anywhere else.

V.F. Perkins[1]

Escape

My mother obtained a job at the State cinema when I was ten. For me that meant a ticket to Paradise, and regularly I worshipped at the shrine of the gods and goddesses. I couldn't wait for the moment to come when the velvet curtains would sweep apart, the lights dim, and a shared intimacy would settle on the hushed audience.

British movie fan, describing cinemagoing in the 1940s[2]

Truly, a great picture. A rousing, stirring picture. A romantic picture. A story that sweeps you out of your humdrum life and carries you off to sea – to fight with strong, silent Elmo Lincoln against the perils of mutiny on the high seas – to fall in love with a beautiful woman and sacrifice liberty for her sake – to make a miraculous escape from the fetid dungeon of a southern republic and become master of a colony of beach-combers, conquering them by might of fist and brain and then – to save the one woman from a terrible fate in the midst of red revolution.

Advertisement for *Under Crimson Skies* (1920)[3]

We have all grown up with Hollywood as an important but usually unconsidered part of our lives. From the games of cowboys and Indians we play as children to our first date at the movies, from the way we hold a beer glass or style our hair after our favorite movie star to the way we think about love and heroism, we could all trace Hollywood's influence on us. But usually we don't bother. For the most part we barely acknowledge the cultural influence of the movies in an apologetic tone of voice. If we are ever asked to do more than take Hollywood for granted, we are likely to say that the movies are not serious enough to be taken seriously. They are, after all, only entertainment, and the whole point about entertainment is that we are not supposed to take it seriously. To describe an experience as "entertaining" often seems to have said all that needs to be said about it.

What entertainment is, and what the word "entertainment" means, seems self-evident. What makes a movie entertaining is apparently so obvious as to need no explanation, and whatever entertainment is, it is obvious. Experience tells us that something is obviously entertaining – or else, equally obviously, not. Entertainment is . . . what we find entertaining.

Although we recognize entertainment easily enough when we experience it, we generally have difficulty in defining it. The dictionary is no help, for there the word seems self-explanatory: entertainment is "that which entertains . . . amusement; a performance or show designed to give pleasure."[4] Instead of defining it, we tend to describe the satisfactions we expect from entertainment. We say that we want our entertainment to be "diverting" or "amusing," or to "hold our attention." But this language circles around the object of our concern, rather than taking us any closer to it, and in popular use, the word almost seems to defy our attempts to analyze or enlarge upon its meaning. The adjectives most often attached to the noun "entertainment" are dismissive: "just," "mere," "only," "light." It is hard to imagine alternatives: what would "heavy entertainment" be like? These problems of definition are symptomatic of the place entertainment occupies in our lives. What we recognize as entertainment is something that provides a pleasurable distraction from our more important concerns – of work, of politics, of Art – and therefore something to which it is inappropriate to apply the more rigorous intellectual criteria that we employ in other areas of our lives – including those of definition.

The vexed questions of what entertainment is and why no one takes it seriously will haunt us throughout this book. But it is important to recognize at the outset how distinctive the experience of entertainment is. Entertainment presents itself to us as almost wondrously benign. It offers us pleasure, and makes no demands on us, except that it asks us not to think about it. It justifies itself, in the very notion that it gives its audiences what we want. If we sometimes feel uneasy, even guilty, about taking entertainment seriously, we are merely responding to the forces in our culture that tell us that if we are going to devote our energies to thinking, we should be thinking about something more serious, more difficult. The forces impelling us into this attitude are twofold. One is the attitude of the entertainment industry itself, which has consistently sought to describe the cultural effects of its products as trivial, and has thus contributed to the treatment of the products as trivial. In 1992, Peter Hoffman, president of Cinemavision, announced plans to distribute Hollywood movies in India and Eastern Europe. Asked about the cultural impact of his proposals, he responded, "US culture is not pernicious. I'm only talking leisure, entertainment, here."[5]

The other force governing our attitudes to entertainment is the practice of criticism. We shall discuss the institutions and ideologies of criticism later in this chapter, and again in the last chapter of the book, but for now we need simply to note that the principal cultural function of criticism is to make judgments of value, and that the most authoritative forms of criticism in our culture have not valued entertainment highly. For most of the twentieth century, critical authority saw movies as part of a mass culture it condemned as vulgar, philistine, or lacking in moral seriousness. More recently, Hollywood has become an acceptable object of study (on university film studies courses, for instance), but as Richard Dyer has pointed out, entertainment cinema is seldom studied as entertainment. Instead, elaborate academic discourses explain that as well as being entertaining, entertainment movies deal with "history, society, psychology, gender roles, indeed, the meaning of life," and these concerns can be discussed with much the same seriousness previous generations of critics brought to the study of literature.[6]

In their different ways, industrial and critical discourses both place entertainment in a curious cultural limbo, where it is simultaneously disregarded and protected. Because we do not have to take it seriously (or if we are taking it seriously, we treat it as something else), we also do not have to worry about it. Because it is somehow not fully part of "culture," entertainment exists in a separate, self-contained, social space, where the fact that we consider it unimportant protects it from scrutiny. Our everyday experience of moviegoing is not so different. The movie theater, the great dark room where the dream factory's dreams are sold, permits its audiences the intensity of privacy in a public space. Our eyes, our minds, and sometimes our hands are permitted to wander, perhaps into forbidden places in an exploration of self, of other, of difference. We know – perhaps we remember – that the great dark room is a site of Eros: at the most banal level one of our culture's places for adolescent sexual discovery, but also a place for **public fantasy**, for the public expression of ideas and actions we must each individually repress in our everyday behavior.

The price of admission to this everyday place of refuge from the everyday is our knowledge that what happens inside the great dark room has nothing to do with what happens outside. No matter how vividly we have experienced its imaginary landscapes and Utopian possibilities, we leave the theater reminding ourselves that what we have seen was "only a movie." That is the hidden reason why Hollywood movies have happy endings. The re-establishment of order renders the viewer's experimentation with expressive behavior a matter of no consequence, contained within the safe, unexplored, unconsidered, and trivialized space of entertainment. In that space, stories are governed not by their own developmental logic, but by the logic of a conventionalized, generic morality, which ensures that entertainment functions as a process of "recreation," by which, as the authors of the Production Code put it, "a man rebuilds himself after his work, after his labor, during which he gets the chance to rebuild himself physically . . . morally, spiritually and intellectually."[7] Others, as we shall see, have viewed this machine for the production of pleasure as much less benevolent. But for both its creators and its detractors, Hollywood's most profound significance lies in its ability to turn pleasure into a product we can buy. We need to attend closely to the industrial and economic processes involved in the manufacture and marketing of these transient images, as well as to their content, if we are to appreciate the full complexity of our relationship to Hollywood, and Hollywood's relationship to American culture. But however we come to view Hollywood, we should begin in the place where we view it, in the great dark room.

Watching Bruce Willis in *Die Hard* (1988) on video both is and is not like the experience our grandparents (or great-grandparents) had watching Douglas Fairbanks in *The Black Pirate* (1926) in an "atmospheric theater," decorated to create the illusion that its patrons were watching the movie and listening to the 50-piece orchestra in an ancient, moonlit Italian garden.[8] Some of the technological changes in production are obvious, but equally important are changes in the conditions in which movies are consumed. The picture palaces of the 1920s invited their audiences into the temporary occupation of a gilded mansion more lavishly decorated and staffed than the finest hotels. When New York's Roxy Theater, "The Cathedral of the Motion Picture," opened in 1927, the souvenir book commemorating the event declared that "when you enter its portals you step magically from the drab world of confusion and cares into a fairy palace . . . with all the allurements that art, science and music can offer."[9] Very little of that goes on when you put the cassette in the video-recorder and watch *Die Hard* in "the drab world of confusion" that is your living room.[10] Critic Roy Armes has argued that cinema's uniqueness really derives from the fact that, unlike the other entertainment media innovated at the same time or since – the still camera, the gramophone, radio, and television – it was not designed for consumption at home.[11]

But if we think about what pleasures and satisfactions the movies offer their audiences, we can find a consistency beneath the obvious variations. A 1925 Paramount advertisement encouraged audiences to:

> Go to a motion picture . . . and let yourself go. Before you know it you are *living* the story – laughing, loving, hating, struggling, winning! All the adventure, all the romance, all the excitement you lack in your daily life are in – Pictures. They take you completely out of yourself into a wonderful new world. . . . Out of the cage of everyday existence! If only for an afternoon or an evening – escape![12]

Hollywood's product, the experience of escape packed into a two-hour story in which a sympathetic character overcomes a series of obstacles to achieve his or her desire, has consistently provided the basis of Hollywood's appeal to its audiences. Like 1920s audiences in the palaces of fantasy, video viewers in the 1990s can become part of the high life they watch in a darkened room; for an hour or two, the happy ending can be theirs, too.[13]

The idea of "escape" is still central to popular accounts of contemporary Hollywood, but this term, too, has received little serious critical attention.

In examining what satisfactions entertainment offers its audience, Richard Dyer has suggested that the appeal of what is usually called "escapism" is better understood as "Utopian." He argues that the movies provide a Utopianism of the feelings, presenting, "head on as it were, what Utopia would feel like, rather than how it is organized." Entertainment's escape is to a revised, Utopian version of the audience's own world: Utopian both in the sense that it is a place of more energy and more abundance than the "real" world, and also in the sense that its issues, problems, and conflicts are clearer and more intense than those we experience in our day-to-day reality. Dyer argues that entertainment can thus be seen to respond to "real needs created by society," although, importantly, it only responds to some needs – broadly, to the needs of its audience as individuals, rather than as members of social groups or classes. So while entertainment responds to real social needs, it also defines what people's legitimate social needs are understood to be. As Dyer suggests, "the ideals of entertainment imply wants that capitalism itself promises to meet."[14]

Dyer was not the first person to suggest that Hollywood provides Utopian solutions to everyday desires. In the late 1940s, two sociologists, Martha Wolfenstein and Nathan Leites, looked at all the A-features with a contemporary urban setting released in the production season of 1945–6, and at a more selected sample released over the subsequent two years.[15] Their conclusions dealt not so much with the kinds of issue that were likely to arise in a Hollywood thriller or comedy as with the way their stories unfolded and the range of events that occurred. Unconcerned with the artistic status of the movies they studied, Wolfenstein and Leites saw them as a reservoir of common, ready-made daydreams that were "not merely escapes from the routines of daily life." Because movies were shared public experiences, and therefore less embarrassing than the "more fugitive, private, home-made day-dreams" of individuals, members of their audience could more easily incorporate the accounts they offered of emotional problems into their own lives.[16] In such a scenario, the movies engaged their audience in an interplay between experience and wish, and it was in these terms that Wolfenstein and Leites reached their conclusions about what happened in Hollywood. While their study was confined to a narrow period, some of their comments could just as well describe how Hollywood movies of the 1930s or the 1980s worked.

American movies, they suggested, do not try to reconcile their audiences to the disappointments and complications of life by dramatizing them. Characters with antisocial motives are seldom presented as sympathetic, while Hollywood's heroes and heroines are absolved from both guilt and responsibility for what they do. The destructive impulses in a plot are externalized, most likely to be embodied in unsympathetic characters who are eventually safely defeated.[17] What we wish for the hero and heroine is accomplished less often by their own actions than by the world around them, a world ultimately served by benevolent coincidence, "the car that gets out of control, the ticket agent who assigns the hero and heroine the same berth." Hollywood movies provide solutions to emotional problems in which "wish-fulfillments can occur without penalties. . . . The contention of American films is that we should not feel guilty for mere wishes." In keeping with this world without consequences, love in American films rarely involves suffering, since "whenever life may look discouraging, a beautiful girl turns up at the next moment." Hollywood movies "express confidence both in the plenitude of opportunities and in the adequate strength of impulses. . . . the lost opportunity is comic rather than tragic in American films."[18]

Heroes and heroines are seldom made vulnerable by emotional susceptibility; objects of affection are easily replaced. Love tends to be reasonable and righteous, and, of course, ends happily. Defining an unhappy ending as involving the death or defection of one partner, Wolfenstein and Leites discovered that only one Hollywood movie in six had such an ending; French films, on the other hand, "show love turning out unhappily half the time." Violence and romance share many of the same properties in Hollywood. Violence may be fast moving, noisy, or technically intricate but it is unlikely to be emotionally involved. People are most likely to be murdered in Hollywood to get them out of the way when they become obstacles to the achievement of some goal. The murder victim thus tends to be reduced to a thing, a block in the path, rather than an object of intense feelings and possible regret. In American movies, Wolfenstein and Leites suggested, "men and women may, and often do shoot each other. They do not break each other's hearts."[19]

Such an account of Hollywood emotions might describe *Fatal Attraction* (1987) or *Basic Instinct* (1992) as well as it described *The Big Sleep* (1946) or *The Mask of Dimitrios* (1944), but it also comes close to describing Hollywood emotions as superficial, stereotyped, and dishonest. Similarly, in *Hollywood the Dream Factory*, Hortense Powdermaker maintained that no one in Hollywood was concerned with "the reality of emotions and with truthfulness of meaning."

> Man, according to Hollywood, is either completely good, or bad. His personality is static, rarely showing any development either in growth or in regression. The villain is a black-eyed sinner who can do no good and who cannot be saved; while the hero is a glamorous being, who can do no wrong of his own volition, and who is always rewarded. Missing is a realistic concept of the human personality, a complex being who can love and hate, who has human frailties and virtues.[20]

Only the exceptional movie showed "real human beings living in a complicated world" with any truthfulness or understanding, but audiences, she feared, had been conditioned by years of viewing not to expect anything different.

Such charges against Hollywood movies persist; director Henry Jaglom, for instance, decries contemporary Hollywood movies because they "lie to you so overwhelmingly; they never talk back to people about their real lives."[21] The charges are fundamentally aesthetic ones, part of a more general accusation that Hollywood's output is banal, repetitive, and predictable. Often they are linked to a social agenda, a complaint that the movies either exploit their audiences or pander to their baser instincts. One of the most devastating critiques of Hollywood's escapist aesthetics was written in the late 1940s by two emigré members of the Frankfurt School for Social Research, Theodor Adorno and Max Horkheimer:

> Amusement under late capitalism is the prolongation of work. It is sought after as an escape from the mechanized work process, and to recruit strength in order to be able to cope with it again. But at the same time mechanization has such power over a man's leisure and happiness, and so profoundly determines the manufacture of amusement goods, that his experiences are inevitably after-images of the work process itself. . . . what happens at work, in the factory, or in the office can only be escaped from by approximation to it in one's leisure time. All amusement suffers from this incurable malady. Pleasure hardens into boredom because, if it is to remain pleasure, it must not demand any effort and therefore moves rigorously in the worn grooves of association. No independent thinking must be expected from the audience: the product prescribes every reaction . . . Any logical connection calling for mental effort is painstakingly avoided.[22]

Not every hostile critic of Hollywood would share Adorno and Horkheimer's political opinions, but the accusation that the "escapism" offered by the movies is shallow because it is aesthetically deficient is a critical commonplace. Writing at the same time as Adorno and Horkheimer, art critic Clement Greenberg denounced what he called "kitsch" and others called "mass culture" on the grounds that it "predigests art for the spectator and spares him effort, provides him with a shortcut to the pleasures of art that detours what is necessarily difficult in genuine art." Kitsch, claimed Greenberg, "provides vicarious experience for the insensitive with far greater immediacy than serious fiction can hope to do."[23] Such critical attitudes have lost little of their conviction in the intervening years, and continue to present an obstacle to the task of taking Hollywood seriously, since by their predetermined criteria Hollywood is not serious, except perhaps as a symptom of a social condition in need of diagnosis.

Money on the Screen

The budget *is* the aesthetic.

James Schamus[24]

"You know what prestige means, don't you?" "Sure, pictures that don't make money."

Steve Canfield (Fred Astaire) and Peggy Dainton (Janis Paige) in *Silk Stockings* (1957)

When I was at Bennington some of the English teachers who pretended an
indifference to Hollywood or its products, really *hated* it. Hated it down deep
as a threat to their existence.

F. Scott Fitzgerald[25]

The obstacles to our thinking critically about Hollywood have as much to
do with a set of prevailing attitudes toward the movies' cultural status as
with anything intrinsic to its products. Before we can begin to take Hollywood seriously we first have to reconsider our conventional expectations
of it, and the tradition of criticism that has produced these attitudes. In
unpacking that tradition we can start to account for our often automatic
responses to Hollywood and to question both their origin and their
appropriateness.

Many of our reactions to Hollywood movies are grounded in "common-
sense" assumptions about the place of art, and of criticism, in our culture.
Reading a daily newspaper will tell you that Art is a separate sphere,
located in its own discrete section away from the concerns of "the real
world" on the news pages. A newspaper's arts pages also inform us that
the primary function of criticism is evaluative. Whether it is deciding
which play is worth going to see, or if a novel can enter the canon of great
works to be studied on university literature courses, common-sense criticism is judgmental. The privileges of Art – immunity from the laws of
obscenity as well as from the demands of commerce, for instance – are
valuable enough for common sense to remind us that they should not be
given out indiscriminately. As part of the shared "common sense" that
enables us to function on a daily basis in our culture, we acquire a set of
assumptions that help us to recognize Art when we see it.

A first principle of this knowledge is that, like gold, Art must be scarce
and difficult to get if it is to retain its value. Common sense tells us,
perhaps a little perversely, that Art is never commonplace. We are encouraged to recognize an opposition between "High" Art and that which is
merely "popular," as though aesthetic quality were inversely proportional
to the scale of a work's appeal. Although the detailed criteria by which
"high" culture is distinguished from "popular culture" are subject to variation, they are grounded in three familiar assumptions. To qualify as Art
within the conventions of traditional western aesthetics, the thing in question must be a specific, definable object: a poem, a painting, but first of all
a distinct "*work* of art." Secondly, the "work" must express the sensibility
of the artist who produced it, and thirdly, it must also require "work" from
its viewer or reader before he or she can appreciate it. As Robert Allen
says, by these criteria, "the greater the art, the more difficult it is for the
uninitiated to understand."[26]

Some cinema, distanced from the more recognizable forms of
Hollywood, can be constructed as Art, but traditional criticism has always
found Hollywood more difficult to take seriously than European or
Third World cinema. "The main stumbling block for film aesthetics," suggests Peter Wollen, "has not been Eisenstein, but Hollywood. There is no
difficulty in talking about Eisenstein in the same breath as the poet

Mayakovsky, a painter like Malevich, or a theatre director like Stanislavsky. But John Ford or Raoul Walsh?"[27]

One of the main differences between Hollywood and the most widely recognized tradition of European filmmaking has been that European films have displayed a much closer alliance to the other arts, in both their narrative and pictorial structures. While the history of the American cinema is normally understood in terms of its genres, the history of the European film is conventionally written as a series of movements: German expressionism, Italian neo-realism, the French New Wave, for example. In their content, but even more importantly in the framework that they provide for criticism, these movements correspond to similar movements in literature or painting. We recognize a movie such as Ingmar Bergman's *Persona* (1966) as having aesthetic worth: it *looks* like Art, and as we watch it we *work* at understanding what it is "about." Its themes, which express the sensibility of an individual author, are serious enough to grace a work of literature: the boundary between sanity and madness, the illusion of human personality. Its mimetic performances (mimetic in that they offer a recognizable imitation of behavior that we might encounter outside the cinema) are augmented by a self-consciously expressive visual style. David Cook summarizes the critical consensus on Bergman in terms that could equally well describe the thematic preoccupations of Samuel Beckett, T.S. Eliot, or Franz Kafka. Bergman is "essentially a religious artist whose films concern the fundamental questions of human existence: the meaning of suffering and pain, the inexplicability of death, the solitary nature of being, and the difficulty of locating meaning in a seemingly random and capricious universe."[28]

As an equally archetypal work within its own tradition, *The Wizard of Oz* (1939) makes rather different claims on our attention. With the utter implausibility of its storyline, the tendency of its characters to burst into song-and-dance routines at the drop of a hat, the presence of its stars, and the artificial intensity of its color and special effects, it almost defies us to take it seriously. It seems primarily intent only on celebrating its own status as entertainment. If we start talking about what *The Wizard of Oz* is "about," we are more likely to recapitulate the plot than discover themes suitable to literary or pictorial Art. Trying to argue for an interpretation of *The Wizard of Oz* that makes it seem intellectually complex will probably make us feel uncomfortably pretentious. The movie is patently more concerned with its **production values** than with symbolism, suggestive ambiguity, and psychologically dense characterization. By production values, Hollywood publicity usually meant those elements of a movie designed to appeal to an audience independently of the story: the sets, the costumes, the star performances, the "quality" of the product visible on the screen. In a more critical language, they represent areas of pleasure offered to the viewer incidental to, and separate from, the plausibility of the fiction. In contrast to the authenticity and organic unity cherished in *Persona*, *The Wizard of Oz* is characterized more by its synthetic quality, and by its opportunist aggregation of elements designed to appeal to a range of different viewers. The commercial motivation underlying its organization is apparent and inescapable.

To stress economics so early in an account of Hollywood runs the risk of encouraging the belief that, because all movies are made for profit, they are all equally tarred with the same brush of impurity, whether we call it commercialism or capitalism. In this book, we shall try to define what we have called Hollywood's "commercial aesthetic," but first we must deal with the fundamental incompatibility that traditional criticism has constructed between the commercial and the aesthetic. For many academic critical practices, evaluating a work aesthetically requires the exclusion of questions of money. This is one function of the art gallery. If you want to see Botticelli's *Birth of Venus*, you can go to the Uffizi gallery in Florence, fight your way through the other tourists and stand in front of it for ten seconds, before turning to look at all the other Botticellis in the Botticelli room. You might ruminate on its rediscovery of classical subject-matter in the Renaissance, perfectly fused with the remnants of high Gothic style. But the *Birth of Venus* was not originally painted to hang in a museum for the edification of tourists with a smattering of art history in their education. It was commissioned by an Italian nobleman for his private contemplation at his country villa, where he "escaped from the business, heat or plague of the town to recreate himself with the tranquillity and pleasures of a rural retreat."[29] Insofar as the painting's Neo-Platonic allegory expresses a thematic purpose, that purpose belonged not to Botticelli but to his patron, Lorenzo di Pierfrancesco de' Medici.[30] The painting expresses Botticelli's craft skills, and it is the celebration of those skills that draws crowds to the Uffizi. What Botticelli had to do with the construction of the painting's allegorical meaning is another question; at most, he was one participant in a negotiation between patron, writer, and artist. Like all commissioned art, *Venus* is the site of that negotiation, a compromise between diverse motives.

By taking *Venus* out of the grand-ducal wardrobe and putting her in the gallery, the academicians have literally transported the picture out of the material world in which it was produced and perceived, and placed it in another, altogether more sanitized and abstracted context, in which it can be studied without reference to the economics of its production.[31] Preserved in conditions designed to minimize the physical effects of the passage of time, the painting has become a definable aesthetic object and ceased to be a commodity. A financial valuation of it would have little meaning; possessing an aesthetic value but not an exchange value, it has become "priceless." Most textual criticism – whether of paintings, writing, or movies – performs a comparable act of dematerializing the text it criticizes. Questions of money have been seen as the specialized interests of economic historians or systems analysts, separate from the loftier business of analyzing texts. In talking about books, we seldom discuss the processes of a book's production or the commercial transactions involved in its transmission from author to reader. The book as a material object is only a necessary vessel, in which the text's abstract ideas are carried. Money may affect its manufacture but does not impinge on its meaning.

Extracting the text from its context can be immensely productive. Such criticism focuses with clarity on the object for analysis. It may be the prelude to very precise acts of interpretation and evaluation; it may allow real pleasure to be taken in the text. Abstraction frees the reader to encounter the text – that is, the process of making meaning through a work – without distracting questions of origin or intended destination. But it also tends to treat the text entirely as something "found," finished and complete, its meaning intrinsic and only awaiting release, and that militates against giving readers much authority in this relationship, since they are limited by their sensitivity to a nuance of meaning already inscribed there, usually by its author.[32] As readers, we begin by seeking the author's voice as a name to give to the unifying thematic and stylistic patterns in the text. But once launched on this quest, we find ourselves bound by the obligations of a critical contract to the belief that the text has such patterns, placed there by the author, to communicate his or her ideas. By such devices, we construct the book as the expression of the author's sensibility. Our competence as critical readers comes to be judged on our ability to discover the author's intentions. In our invention of an intending author, we construct a criticism that resembles a game of hide-and-seek. The more cleverly the secret meaning of a text is buried, the better we are as critics if we can unearth it, and the greater the artistry of the author in his or her act of concealment.

Few Hollywood movies respond well to this critical treatment; it is more likely to expose their relative thematic banality. But it is the fact that Hollywood movies cost money, and are often formally organized in the interests of profit, that does most to disqualify them as objects of critical scrutiny. The very things that most emphatically define Hollywood cinema's commercial function as entertainment – musical routines, car chases, screen kisses, the spectacular, the star presence – become the greatest obstacles to dealing critically with the movies themselves. For many critics, where the operation of money cannot be suppressed, Hollywood must be abandoned; it cannot function as art because it is a commodity. Publicists in the 1920s had often described Hollywood as an "art industry," but Adorno and Horkheimer ironically called it a "culture industry" because they believed the concept to be an oxymoron, a contradiction in terms. Dwight MacDonald's 1953 denunciation of mass culture shared their contempt:

> It is fabricated by technicians hired by businessmen; its audiences are passive consumers, their participation limited to the choice between buying and not buying. The Lords of *kitsch*, in short, exploit the cultural needs of the masses in order to make a profit and/or to maintain their class rule. . . . Like nineteenth-century capitalism, Mass Culture is a dynamic, revolutionary

force, breaking down the old barriers of class, traditions, taste, and dissolving all cultural distinction. It mixes and scrambles everything together, producing what might be called homogenized culture. . . . It thus destroys all values, since value judgments imply discriminations. Mass Culture is very, very democratic: it refuses to discriminate against, or between, anything or anybody. All is grist to its mill, and all comes out finely ground indeed. . . . It is a debased, trivial culture that voids both the deep realities (sex, death, failure, tragedy) and also the simple, spontaneous pleasures . . . the unsettling and unpredictable (hence unsalable) joy, tragedy, wit, change, originality and beauty of real life. The masses, debauched by several generations of this sort of thing, in turn come to demand trivial and comfortable cultural products.[33]

MacDonald's position combined an elitist cultural conservatism with political radicalism; he argued that mass culture was an instrument of political domination, differentiated from both High and Folk Culture by being mechanical, commercial, imitative, vulgar, bureaucratic, and centralized, and appealing to its audiences' worst instincts – all negative qualities to be denigrated against the positive values of High or Folk Art.[34] Both politically and culturally, this is an extremely pessimistic position: mass culture, as represented by Hollywood, is seen to be aesthetically banal and conservative in its inherent support for the status quo. Although this position acknowledges the revolutionary force of mass culture, Hollywood's is not a revolution of which it approves.

For the vulgar Romantic in us all, Hollywood is not Art because it is commercial. For the vulgar Marxist in us all, Hollywood's enslavement to the profit system means that all its objects can do no other but blindly reproduce the dominant ideology of bourgeois capitalism. We wish to avoid both these simplifications by suggesting that Hollywood's status as a commodity, the very thing that usually frustrates a more detailed understanding of it, can provide a starting point for its analysis. Far from disqualifying movies from consideration as "art" objects worthy of serious consideration, an emphasis on Hollywood in commercial terms may begin a debate about the critical assumptions that underpin our expectations of what constitutes art and culture as a whole. More than any other cinema, Hollywood makes its industrial and economic negotiations with its audience explicit. Precisely because of that, Hollywood can become the paradigm for an examination of the material relationships between texts and the audiences and critics who encounter and engage them, not just in cinema, but in other media and other historical moments.

A starting point for a more positive response to Hollywood and its commercial aesthetics is offered by a colleague of Adorno and Horkheimer at the Frankfurt School who had proposed a more optimistic view of the aesthetic and political possibilities of new technologies like the cinema. Far from seeing the cinema negatively as something opposed to the true values of High Art, Walter Benjamin enthused over its ability to overturn earlier hierarchies of value in art by mass producing the artistic object. Abolishing the scarcity of the art object, mechanical reproduction also abolished the power which that scarcity placed in the hands of its owners. An elite class was thus deprived of its traditional ability to determine artistic value and so encourage dominant forms of representation. Mechanical reproduction robbed the aesthetic object, in Benjamin's terms, of its "aura"; the aesthetic object became more familiar and less intimidating in its reproducibility.[35] To an even greater extent than photography, cinema minimized the value of the unique original by requiring the production of large numbers of identical objects, none of which could be seen as more original, and therefore more valuable, than any of the others. The economics of Hollywood rely expressly upon this technical possibility, since any number of prints can be struck from an original master negative and exhibited simultaneously.

Benjamin was, however, concerned more with political and ideological questions than with the economics of the motion picture industry. He stressed that the mechanical reproducibility of art made important shifts in the traditional power relationships between producers and consumers, granting more authority over the use and possible meanings of an art object to the consumer. Rather than approaching the art object with reverence, the movie spectator approaches it with demands and expectations. As a result, Benjamin suggested, the mechanical reproducibility of art, as most clearly represented by the cinema, changed the relationship between art, artists, and society in fundamental ways. However, although Benjamin applauded the radically democratic possibilities of cinema, he was no more enthusiastic about what Hollywood actually produced than were Adorno and Horkheimer.

The most frequently voiced criticism of Benjamin's argument is that he failed to acknowledge the economic power of the culture industries, which have simply demonstrated a greater inventiveness in commodifying art in new ways. Now you can buy a T-shirt with Van Gogh's *Sunflowers* on it, but such irreverence has done nothing to diminish the market value of the scarce original. The problem, however, may lie as much with the critical assumptions involved in the separation of culture and industry as it does in the objects produced by the culture industries. Hollywood movies are everything Dwight MacDonald said they were, but if we are to examine the revolutionary force that they represent, we need to do more than declare that, according to an aesthetic regime to which they have never conformed, they are vulgar and banal. Instead, we must find ways of approaching Hollywood that recognize Hollywood's commercial aesthetic for what it is.

The Multiple Logics of Hollywood Cinema

We were witnessing a mute struggle between Von Sternberg and his actors. . . . the stars could not afford to think exclusively of the artistic merits of the final picture. . . . The director wanted to create a masterpiece of unrelenting reality; the stars had to avoid shocking their public. Yet they were conscious that, on the wings of a real masterpiece (that is, a masterpiece measured as masterpieces of the films are measured, by box-office receipts), they, as actors, might mount yet higher in the salary scale . . . on the other hand, to sacrifice ever so small a section of their public esteem for a poor picture would be mere folly. . . . Miss Compson did not mind acting the part of an immoral woman; indeed, she rather specialized in prostitute parts . . . But she did not like being exhibited as a wretched and unsuccessful prostitute.

Jan and Cora Gordon[36]

Rather than recognize Hollywood's commercial aesthetic, film criticism has frequently attempted to reconstruct its products in terms more amenable to traditional criticism. At a relatively early point in the development of an academically respectable version of film criticism, there emerged an authorial criticism that became known as the *"politique des auteurs"* because of its origins in French critical theory and the group of writers clustered around the journal *Cahiers du Cinéma*. When it was adopted by Anglo-American critics, it was half-translated by one of its early proponents, Andrew Sarris, as "the *auteur* theory." It attempted to retain individual creativity as the source of value in Hollywood. Sarris argued that a "premise of the *auteur* theory is the distinguishable personality of the director as a criterion of value." The auteur theory, he claimed, "values the personality of the director precisely because of the barriers to its expression. It is as if a few brave spirits had managed to overcome the gravitational pull of the mass of movies."[37]

This celebration of individual directorial genius valorized the work of ostentatiously rebellious Hollywood figures such as Orson Welles, whose career was marked by confrontations with "the system." An expectation still active in the criticism of literature and the visual arts, of artists as figures outside and largely unaffected by their surrounding society, was transported into film criticism. By contrast, what André Bazin called "the genius of the system," and the achievements of those who functioned competently within it, were denigrated.[38] Michael Curtiz, the senior contract director at Warner Bros. in the 1930s and 1940s, is a case in point. Movies like *The Adventures of Robin Hood* (1938) and *Mildred Pierce* (1945) are marked by a consistently detailed visual style, and the head of production at Warner Bros., Hal Wallis, insisted that "you couldn't mistake a Curtiz setup, that it had a stamp as clearly marked as a Matisse."[39] **Auteurist** criticism, however, paid more attention to a director's thematic consistency than to the craft skills for which they were employed, and cast Curtiz as a craftsman "blessed with talent but not genius."[40] Sarris categorized Curtiz as "lightly likable" and considered him an "amiable technician": "If many of the early Curtiz films are hardly worth remembering, none of the later ones are even worth seeing. . . . The director's one enduring masterpiece is, of course, *Casablanca*, the happiest of happy accidents, and the most decisive exception to the auteur theory."[41]

It is not difficult to see why industry practitioners should have been so resistant to a critical approach that suggested that a single individual – the director – should be credited with the creation of a movie. The multiplicity of people involved in a production and the multiplicity of different pressures exerted upon it make the negotiations surrounding a commissioned painting seem relatively straightforward. The individual intentions of a director or writer may conflict with a corporate interest; the producer's desire to spend money on lavish production values may be set against the accountants' desire to save money; the belief that the exploitation of sex and violence onscreen maximize profits has to negotiate with the institutions of censorship; the dictates of genre may square uncomfortably with a studio style.

On the other hand, it is not difficult to see the appeal of the auteur theory, and its emergence as a response to changes in the structure of Hollywood itself. The economic crisis of the late 1960s was at the time seen as evidence that "Old Hollywood" had lost its ability to anticipate the tastes of its audience. As early as 1954 it had been suggested the "lost audience," "mature, adult, sophisticated people who read good books and magazines, who attend lectures and concerts, who are politically and socially aware and alert," might be attracted back to the theaters by a more sophisticated cinema, or at least a cinema with greater pretensions, such as that which played in the art-house circuit.[42] The identification of an individual artist as a movie's responsible creator was a valuable element in the establishment of such a cinema, as it was in the establishment of cinema as a subject of academic study.

A critical model of the director-as-author had developed in more high-toned American reviewing during the 1960s. If this approach found little favor with the older generation whose artistry it sought to recognize, it did provide a model by which Hollywood could be discussed as art, and a new generation of directors, many of them educated in its precepts at film schools or university film courses, could see themselves in the role of artist. The "movie brat" directors who emerged during the short-lived "Hollywood Renaissance" of 1971–4 – Francis Coppola, Martin Scorsese, Brian De Palma, Steven Spielberg, George Lucas – found obvious material benefits in the enhanced industrial status of the director, in part because they became marketable commodities, even stars, in their own right. "Steven Spielberg" is as much, and as valuable, a brand name as "Arnold Schwarzenegger," as a critical as well as a commercial commodity.[43] Moreover, the much greater instability of contemporary studio management has increased both the practical authority of the director and his or her relative permanence within the system. The director now assumes many of the functions previously undertaken by a studio producer. According to Pandro S. Berman, a producer at RKO and MGM:

My greatest contribution was to find the story material, develop it into a screenplay, cast it, and make the picture, usually using other studio personnel for all those jobs. To make a distinction between the producer I am describing and the producer of today, the producer of today is more of an agent, a packager, a promoter, or a financial man who will put things together and take them to a studio, a distribution company, or a bank and get financing. That method has had a very great effect in that the producer has abdicated his function as the creative man in the set-up. He has gone to other business activities, leaving the director as the creative influence.[44]

Of course, variations in practice between different studios, and the variable influence of individuals, make all generalizations about the role and influence of producers, directors, actors, and technical personnel tendentious. The hierarchy of the industry was never immutable, and there were major shifts with the growth of independent production from the 1940s on. By the 1980s, authorship in Hollywood had become a commercially beneficial fiction, indicated by the opening credits of movies that declared themselves to be "a Taylor Hackford film" or "a Robert Zemeckis film." But the multiple logics and intentions that continue to impinge on the process of production ensure that authorship remains an inadequate explanation of how movies work.

In his history of Hollywood filmmaking in the studio period, Thomas Schatz has castigated auteur criticism for "stalling film history and criticism in a prolonged state of adolescent romanticism," by misdescribing the actual relations of power, creative control, and expression within Hollywood, and by denying the material and the economic at the base of production.[45] Hollywood is inescapably a film *industry*, the show *business*, the dream *factory*. As Harry Cohn, head of Columbia Studios, explained to Robert Parrish:

> Let me give you some facts of life. I release fifty-two pictures a year. I make about forty and buy the rest. Every Friday, the front door of this studio opens and I spit a movie out onto Gower Street . . . If that door opens and I spit and nothing comes out, it means a lot of people are out of work – drivers, distributors, exhibitors, projectionists, ushers, and a lot of other pricks. . . . I want one good picture a year. That's my policy. Give me a *Mr Deeds* or a *Jolson Story* or an *All the King's Men* or a *Lost Horizon* and I won't let an exhibitor have it unless he takes the bread-and-butter product, the *Boston Blackies*, the *Blondies*, the low-budget westerns, and the rest of the junk we make. I like good pictures too, but nobody knows when they're going to be good, so to get one, I have to shoot for five or six, and to shoot for five or six, I have to keep the plant going with the program pictures.[46]

The "other pricks" Cohn mentioned included directors, writers, actors – the people usually seen as being central to the creative process. Cohn relegated them to areas incidental to the industrial and commercial process he described. His economic logic also made the symbiotic relationship between the "good" pictures and "the rest of the junk we make" inescapably clear.

Every area of the Hollywood cinema is determined, in the last instance, by economic considerations. As *Sullivan's Travels* (1941), a "screwball" comedy set in Hollywood, explains, purely aesthetic questions cannot be separated from economic issues. At the start of the movie, successful (i.e. profitmaking) director John L. Sullivan (Joel McCrea), grown tired of making formula entertainment like *Ants in Your Pants of 1939*, announces his desire to make *Oh Brother, Where Art Thou?*, a prestige message-picture about contemporary social conditions. Studio executives Lebrand (Robert Warwick) and Hadrian (Porter Hall) attempt to dissuade him. They remind him prestige pictures do not make money. Failing to put him off, they seek a compromise:

Sullivan: I want this picture to be a commentary on modern conditions, stark realism, the problems that confront the average man.
Lebrand: But with a little sex in it.
Sullivan: A little, but I don't want to stress it. I want this picture to be a document. I want to hold a mirror up to life. I want this to be a picture of dignity, a true canvas of the suffering of humanity.
Lebrand: But with a little sex in it.
Sullivan: With a little sex in it.
Hadrian: What about a nice musical?

And so the debate continues, with Sullivan arguing for something that will "realize the potentialities of film as the sociological and artistic medium that it is," and the executives arguing the profitability of entertainment. Partly through the power that his position as a successful director allows him, partly through sheer stubbornness, Sullivan eventually gets his way, and, disguised as a tramp, he embarks on a trip to gather material for his picture at first hand. An unlikely chain of events leads him to confront contemporary social conditions rather more forcefully than he had anticipated, as a prisoner on a chain gang. A night at a picture show, the prisoners' only form of "escape" from their imprisonment, convinces Sullivan of the importance of entertainment cinema. He eventually returns to Hollywood with a renewed commitment to musicals and comedies.

Sullivan's Travels is a product of the multiple logics that shape Hollywood's commercial aesthetic, as well as a discourse upon them. It is, therefore, an instructive movie about the appropriateness of critical responses to Hollywood. It rationalizes a commitment to entertainment cinema as socially responsible. It acknowledges the world of the audience's response while framing that world within its own conventions. In the same way as Sullivan does, it enacts a compromise, and ends up operating somewhere between social commentary and slapstick comedy. It is neither slavishly "escapist" nor unremittingly dedicated to the social realism toward which it intermittently gestures. Its drive toward profitability has to be balanced against any social statement it wishes to make.

As a network of competing and conflicting impulses, *Sullivan's Travels* helps to break down our more monolithic conceptions of Hollywood. The institution is seen as divided against itself, its various agents in competi-tion and conflict with each other. As Lebrand, Hadrian, and Sullivan debate the most appropriate social role for Hollywood, contradictions are raised and explored, and aspirations set against each other. The resonances of these multiple logics inform our understanding of the subsequent story at every level. At the end of the plot the contradictions are tidied up, and Sullivan returns to making *Ants in Your Pants of 1941*. But we are still left with an image of the institution as a dynamic matrix of conflicting voices, held together in tension by the forces that cross it. In this complex network, a movie is most usefully understood as a site crossed and shaped by many (often contradictory) intentions and logics, each transforming it more or less visibly and more or less effectively. As opposed to auteurism, which supposes and expects a movie to be coherent – narratively, thematically, formally – a view of the production process that recognizes its multiple logics and voices will recognize that Hollywood's commercial aesthetic is too opportunistic to prize coherence, organic unity, or even the absence of contradiction among its primary virtues. Within such a system, the most interesting products are likely to be those in which "the story is simple but the subtexts are disturbingly complex."[47]

The Play of Emotions

The paradox is that because the American cinema is so commercial, because the pressure of money is so strong, everything in a film has to be the very best. That means the most expensive, but it also means the most authentic, the most honest. No half measures, everything on the edge of excess . . . The amount the Americans are prepared to spend on making their films is in a way a sign of respect for the audience.

Andrej Wajda[48]

It seems to me that seduction can only take place when one is willing.
Nina Yuvshenko (Cyd Charisse) in *Silk Stockings* (1957)

In *The Courtship of Eddie's Father* (1962) Tom Corbett (Glenn Ford) and Elizabeth Marten (Shirley Jones) have an argument over the aesthetic sensibilities of "people who cry at sad movies." Tom, dismissing such behavior in terms Dwight MacDonald would find familiar, is rounded on by Elizabeth, who demands to know "why do you think people go to cry at sad movies?" The question is one of some critical significance, since Elizabeth's proposition, that the tears may be triggered by the movie but are given substance by the viewer's life outside the cinema, has implica-tions for what we include in our critical concerns. Hollywood relies for much of its aesthetic effect on its affective qualities, on the emotional engagement of its audience with the text – on the tears, laughter, fear, and erotic arousal it provokes in its viewers. In the experience of its audience, a movie is the emotional equivalent of a roller-coaster ride at least as much as it is a thematically significant story: borrowing a term, we might call the combination a "story-ride."[49]

Hollywood companies have always pre-tested their product by showing it to preview audiences prior to its final editing and release, as a means of attempting to ensure that the movie provides a maximum of audience pleasure and therefore a maximum profit. In the 1940s this pre-testing progressed in complexity from simply asking viewers to fill in cards at the end of the movie to employing devices, such as the Televoting Machine and the Reactograph, that required preview audiences to monitor their engagement with a movie during its screening by turning a dial graded from "very dull" to "like very much." Synchronized to the projector, these devices literally produced a continuous graph of audience response.[50] In adjusting the final release version of a movie to the results of these preview tests, what was being altered was what Thomas Elsaesser terms "the rhythm of the action" rather than the action of the movie itself.[51] The endings of *Blade Runner* (1982) and *Fatal Attraction* (1987), for instance, were modified on the strength of preview audience demands for an upbeat coda in one case and vengeance in the other. If such changes did modify the story or thematic structure of the movies, they did so in response to what the producers perceived as the higher commercial priority of providing an "entertaining" emotional pattern.[52]

What exactly are we buying when we go to the movies? What does Hollywood sell us as entertainment? In a recent screenwriting manual, Michael Hauge argues that audiences go to the movies not to see characters laugh, cry, or get frightened, but to have those experiences themselves; movies attract us because they provide "an opportunity to experience emotion."[53] Popular evaluative criticism – the reviews of Gene Siskel and Roger Ebert, for example – concur. Much in the manner of a screenwriting manual, they emphasize the presence or absence of emotionally engaging characters about whom it is possible to "care." Siskel's comment on *Unforgiven* (1992) – "great to look at but stuffed with unimportant characters and told at a much too slow pace" – does not so much summarize the movie as articulate the essence of a commercial aesthetic, one that concurs with Steven Bach's final opinion on *Heaven's Gate* (1980), which we discussed in the introduction. The generation of audience emotion substitutes for "Art" in Hollywood's commercial aesthetic. Story construction and "realism" in character consistency or setting are vehicles by which that goal is achieved, but they can also be sacrificed to a movie's larger purpose of entertaining its audience in the safe public space of the cinema.

Our reasons for going to the movies may be only tangentially related to the featured picture being shown. The Paramount chain advertised itself in 1929 by telling its customers, "You don't need to know what's playing at a Publix House. It's bound to be the best show in town."[54] Surveys taken in the 1920s indicated that 68 percent of the audience went to the movies for the "event," while only 10 percent went specifically to see the featured movie. The scheduling of "continuous performances" also worked to undermine the centrality of the main feature to the experience of moviegoing. Advertising campaigns for even a prestige movie such as *Gone with the Wind* (1939) found it necessary to remind exhibitors to stress start and intermission times, to ensure that audiences missed no part of the movie. In 1960 *Psycho* advertised itself with directives that insisted that "No one . . . BUT NO ONE . . . will be admitted to the theater after the start of each performance."[55] As part of the academization of cinema, film criticism has centered its concern on the individual feature movie as a text, and has largely ignored the conditions under which its audiences experienced it.

The picture palaces offered entry into a luxurious environment that in itself was an "escape" from the oppressions of metropolitan life. In the 1930s, the installation of air-conditioning in American movie theaters turned the summer months from the worst-attended to the best-attended season; for many Americans, the movie theater was the only cool place available on hot summer evenings. For a substantial part of the audience, a principal attraction of the cinema has always been the dark itself, the fact that it offers a public privacy to groups who have no other legitimate access to a comfortable, unchaperoned space. The movies' preoccupation with heterosexual romance may not be unconnected to the place of the cinema as a prime site for courtship rituals in western culture.[56] A 1933 investigation into the relationship between movies and the conduct of adolescents reported anxiously that the majority of them admitted imitating the forms of love-making they saw on the screen. As one 15-year-old girl explained, "What movie does not offer pointers in the art of kissing? I do not think that it is surprising that the younger generation has such a fine technique. . . . A young couple sees the art of necking portrayed on the screen every week for a month or so, and is it any wonder that they soon develop talent?" A 21-year-old male college junior explained that in his experience, movies played upon their viewers' emotions, puting them "in a particularly sensitive and weakened mood in relation to that emotion which the movie most stressed . . . so a highly charged sex movie puts many girls in an emotional state that weakens, let us say, resistance. . . . I generally pick the movies we attend with that point in mind."[57] For some audiences, at least, watching the screen to construct hypotheses about characters, narrative, and theme has not always been the primary purpose in attending the cinema.

As a preliminary definition to guide our consideration of the way movies entertain and the things they entertain us with, we can suggest that entertainment is best defined as a commercial commodity, produced and consumed as part of a capitalist industrial system. In return for the price of admission to an entertainment, we expect to witness some kind of performance produced by people who make their living performing for paying audiences. We might be watching professional football, a highwire act in the circus, or operatic recitals instead of going to the movies. What links all of these activities is the conditions of their consumption. In each, paying customers form themselves as an audience, to be served by specialist entertainers who are paid to perform. Hollywood's commercial aesthetic addresses us as consumers as well as spectators, and we commonly describe our encounter with cinema in monetary terms. A "good" movie is one that gives us our "money's worth," a return in pleasure for the money we have invested in the ticket price. Hollywood manufactures a non-durable consumer commodity, which is the experience of "going to the movies" rather than the more discrete experience of any particular movie. We experience cinema entertainment as an alternative leisure-time experience to eating at a restaurant or spending an evening with friends in a bar or pub. Like food or drink, but unlike a book or record, the entertainment of "going to the movies" is a transient experience; when we finish consuming a movie, we have only a ticket stub to show for our transaction. What we really buy at the cinema is time; our tickets grant us access to the viewing space for a fixed duration, while we rent the apparatus of cinema.

The buying and selling of time is the central activity of the leisure industries in a capitalist economy. Leisure time is most comprehensively understood as time that is not obligated, by either work or other social obligations.[58] Entertainment is one of the commodified forms that leisure can take. The notion that leisure is a prerogative of everyone, and not just the wealthy few, belongs to industrial societies. The factory system organized and disciplined the hours of work to a much greater extent than had happened in pre-industrial cultures, establishing a more rigid distinction between time spent working and time spent doing something else. In a way that had not occurred in pre-industrial societies, time-not-working – leisure time – became an empty period that needed to be occupied. In our leisure time, within economic and legal constraints, we can choose and control our activity.

Leisure time is bought by time spent at work, where we normally act under instruction or from some sense of obligation. The metaphors used to discuss leisure time link it specifically to commercial processes; we talk of "spending time" or of "time-consuming" activities. We expect to occupy much of our leisure time as consumers of commercial commodities: sports equipment or children's toys, for example. Nevertheless, we can detect the vestigial presence of a nineteenth-century producer ethic in the moral preference we recognize for "direct" or participatory leisure activities like playing a sport or practicing a craft over those "vicarious" experiences that involve us as paying customers to professional performances. It is often suggested that the best use of leisure time is in a form of production, when we "amuse ourselves" by "making our own entertainment." This hierarchical distinction between "direct" activity and "vicarious" passivity is one source of the idea that entertainment involves no work on the part of its consumer, no expenditure of energy, but only of money. Unlike folk culture, which is something you make, entertainment is something you buy.

Hollywood seduces us. The movie theater is a place where we are encouraged to accept the fantasies we see in front of us as a substitute for other realities. By its framing devices, from the entrance lobby to the dimming of the lights just before the movie starts, the building is designed to cut us off from the world outside, and propel us into the alternative world on the screen – perhaps no longer as effectively as the picture palaces of the 1920s and 1930s, but the mechanisms and the intent are the same. From the moment the lights go down and we are transported into the other world on the screen, the movie seeks our cooperative involvement in its fantasy. Midway through *Silk Stockings* (1957), Fred Astaire, playing movie producer Steve Canfield, and Cyd Charisse, as Soviet commissar Ninotchka, perform a dance routine that could stand as a metaphor for Hollywood's relation to its audience. The scene is the culmination of Canfield's sexual and political seduction of Ninotchka, both for himself and for capitalism. As the routine develops, she is slowly, and at first reluctantly, pulled into Astaire's dance until eventually, they dance together. By the end of the dance, she is in love.

This process of seduction that comes with the purchase of the commodity is more visible in the musical than elsewhere in Hollywood, because musical numbers represent a world of fantasy more explicitly. The change into the world of fantasy is signalled by changes in the way characters move and behave. For them, numbers represent an escape from the more pressurized world of the movie narrative, just as the cinema offers its audience the same opportunity for escape from the everyday. Hollywood movies present themselves to us as effortless, both in their production and in our consumption of them. When we watch Gene Kelly and Donald O'Connor improvise the "Moses Supposes" dance routine in *Singin' in the Rain* (1952) with whatever props happen to be available, we are unlikely to think about the amount of rehearsal-time required to make their performance look so spontaneous. The active participation of the audience, its involvement in its own seduction, is a primary goal of Hollywood cinema; for without this participation the audience may well not return to the movie theater. In economic terms we might justifiably see the consumer as both the source and object of Hollywood cinema, because unless we continue to engage Hollywood and take pleasure from it, production will cease.

Given the place entertainment occupies in our culture, to study Hollywood is to perform a perverse, unnatural act, to turn amusement into work. Inevitably, it involves reading movies "against the grain" of their declared absence of seriousness. Some critics have sought to demonstrate that movies which seem on the surface to be lighthearted, sentimental, and frivolous are covertly complex, serious, and responsible works of major artistic importance. Others have argued that the most characteristic of Hollywood movies – *The Beautiful Blonde from Bashful Bend* (1948), for example, whose very title encapsulates its industrial ambition to entertain – are symptoms of American culture and essentially interesting, as

Canfield puts it to Ninotchka in *Silk Stockings*, as "a sociological study" in a textual form. We do not want to deny either possibility, but our emphasis on money and the way that it determines Hollywood production values lead us to believe that the study of Hollywood requires a movement away from more familiar models of artistic production and how texts produce meaning. We are concerned to account for Hollywood in the terms in which the movies themselves operate, and to avoid critical reconstructions of Hollywood movies that overlook their commercial status. In the remainder of this chapter, we want to point to some of the defining characteristics of Hollywood entertainment as a commodity.

Regulated Difference

> Griffin (Tim Robbins): [The story] lacked certain elements that we need to market a film successfully.
>
> June (Greta Scacchi): What elements?
>
> Griffin: Suspense, laughter, violence, hope, heart, nudity, sex, happy endings. Mainly happy endings.
>
> *The Player* (1992)

Hollywood movies are frequently accused of being formulaic; a marginally less hostile way of making the same point is to say that they are conventional.[59] A movie is designed for consumption in a single act of viewing. One reason you only need to see a movie once is that movies are so like each other, and that is part of the pleasure they offer their audiences.[60] If a movie conforms to systems of convention with which viewers are familiar, the viewers' prior knowledge is both activated and guaranteed by their being able to predict the movie's development or outcome. Describing the Western in terms that might apply much more generally to Hollywood's product, Robert Warshow suggested that it "is an art form for connoisseurs, where the spectator derives his pleasure from the appreciation of minor variations within the working out of a pre-established order."[61] Echoing the economic system by which the movies were manufactured, Hollywood's commercial aesthetic extends the principles of standardization, interchangeability, minor variation, and market placement that underlie the consumer industries of fashion and cosmetics into the cultural form of entertainment fiction. Steve Neale has described this system of product differentiation as "an aesthetic regime based on regulated difference, contained variety, pre-sold expectations, and the re-use of resources in labour and materials."[62] Repetition and variation are central to Hollywood's commercially motivated aim of providing the maximum pleasure for the maximum number, to ensure a maximum profit.

Interchangeability, standardization: the terminology of industrial manufacture is not a metaphor, but a description of a production process. In place of the ideas of uniqueness and organic forms that are commonly applied to more traditional aesthetic objects, a Hollywood movie can be thought of as a manufactured assembly of component parts. These parts may function harmoniously, like a well-designed machine, but they are also visible as separate elements: we may dislike the story but love the costumes, think the co-star is terrible but really enjoy the bit where her grandfather tells the story about the frog – and, of course, we would watch it again anyway just for Keanu Reeves, or Winona Ryder, or even Gary Cooper. A Hollywood movie is an aggregation of familiar parts, and its individuality results from its particular combination of stand-ardized elements. As a mode of production, aggregation relies on the interchangeability of these elements, and the connoisseur's pleasures in an aesthetic of aggregation involve a strong sense of **intertextuality**: of a movie's inheritance from, and resemblance to, other similarly styled aesthetic objects.

Historically, Hollywood's commercial aesthetic has been a regime of regulated difference in several senses. Economically, the flow of product through the production and distribution system was regulated in ways we shall discuss in chapter 2. Production was also socially and morally regu-lated. The movies were a form of public culture, and until 1952 they were explicitly denied the freedom of expression guaranteed the press under the First Amendment. In 1915 the Supreme Court had ruled that motion pic-tures were "mere representations of events, of ideas and sentiments, pub-lished and known"; the motion picture industry was "a business, pure and simple . . . not to be regarded . . . as part of the press of the country, or as organs of public opinion."[63] This judgment established the legality of state movie censorship, and its consequences obliged the industry to make sure that their product was acceptable not only to their customers but also to the guardians of American public culture. As the president of the industry's trade association, Will Hays, told producers in 1932, "Whether we like it or not, we must fact the fact that we are *not* in that class of industries whose only problem is with the customer. Our public problem is greater with those out of than those in the theater." It was not the people who fre-quented saloons, he reminded them, who had enforced prohibition upon the country.

To counter the threat of regulation imposed from outside by censorship, the industry devised mechanisms of self-regulation to ensure that the content of its movies proved acceptable to "the classes that write, talk, and legislate" as well as to their audiences.[64] The most important of these mechanisms was the Production Code of 1930, which had a determining effect on movie content throughout the Classical period of studio produc-tion. Aside from its fabled trivial requirements that, for instance, one of the four participating feet remain on the floor during a love scene (to avoid what was delicately known as the "horizontal embrace"), the Production

Code contributed significantly to Hollywood's avoidance of contentious subject-matter, and was a determining force on the construction of narrative and character in every studio-produced movie after 1931. The agreements that underlay the Code amounted to a consensus over what constituted appropriate entertainment for an undifferentiated mass audience in America and, by default, the rest of the world.

Quite overtly at issue in the industry's internal discussions about self-regulation was a definition of entertainment as a social function, and when the industry implemented the Production Code, it acquiesced in the suggestion that entertainment had a moral obligation to its consumers, to provide them with what the Code called "correct entertainment . . . which tends to improve the race, or at least to re-create and rebuild human beings exhausted with the realities of life."[65] Movies were thus endowed with an affirmative cultural function that was dramatically at odds with a view of art as a vehicle of social criticism or negation. This affirmation was most clearly articulated in one of the Code's two governing principles, that "No picture shall be produced which will lower the moral standards of those who see it." This was the law by which a strict moral accountancy was imposed on Hollywood's plots, through which the guilty were punished and the sympathetic were found to be innocent.

But self-regulation had other and in some ways opposite effects, too. As Will Hays was fond of saying, show business was everybody's business. In a speech his association often quoted, Hays told a group of clubwomen, "the fact is, motion pictures are yours rather than ours. It is for you indeed to say what they shall be like and how far forward they may go toward their limitless possibilities."[66] Hollywood has constantly asserted that the movies belong to their public rather than their producers. As Irving Thalberg, head of production at MGM, put it in 1930, "we do not create the types of entertainment; we merely present them":

> The motion picture does not present the audience with tastes and manners and views and morals; it reflects those they already have. . . . People see in it a reflection of their own average thoughts and attitudes. If the reflection is much lower or much higher than their own plane they reject it. . . . The motion picture is literally bound to the mental and moral level of its vast audience.[67]

The producers consciously sought to deny authorial responsibility for whatever moral or political intent was imputed to their product. In part their attitude arose from the movies' legal status as unprotected speech, but it also had to do with the perception of movies as commodities. The Production Code became the industry's guarantee that it manufactured "pure" entertainment, amusement that was not harmful to its consumers, in much the same way that the purity of meat or patent medicines was guaranteed by the US Food and Drug Administration. What constituted purity in entertainment was never defined solely by the producers themselves. Throughout Hollywood's history, the press, religious, educational, and civic groups, and state and national legislatures have expressed their opinions and exercised their authority over what is harmful in entertainment.

The producers' attitude also denied responsibility for the meaning of any movie. They saw themselves manufacturing a product that was used by its consumers. Responsibility for its use resided with the purchaser rather than the seller. In keeping with the ideological assumptions surrounding the circulation of money in the cultures that have produced and consumed Hollywood movies, the viewer may reasonably demand to do what he or she likes with the movie he or she has paid to watch. Literary texts and paintings assert authorship as a principle of creativity. Hollywood's commercial aesthetic, on the other hand, not only advertises its products as being created by a multiplicity of personnel, but also concedes the authority to decide what a movie's content means to the individual viewer, who is provided with a host of opportunities to exercise that authority to maximize his or her pleasure from the movie. Within limits, Hollywood movies are constructed to accommodate, rather than predetermine, their audiences' reactions, and this has involved devising systems and codes of representation that permit a range of interpretations and a degree of instability of meaning.

What Ruth Vasey has called the producers' "principle of deniability" resulted in a particular kind of ambiguity and textual uncertainty in movies regulated by the Production Code.[68] As Colonel Jason S. Joy, the Code's first administrator, explained, to entertain its undifferentiated audience, the movies needed a system of representational conventions "from which conclusions might be drawn by the sophisticated mind, but which would mean nothing to the unsophisticated and inexperienced."[69] Once the limits of explicit "sophistication" had been established, the production industry had to find ways of appealing to both "innocent" and "sophisticated" sensibilities in the same object without transgressing the boundaries of public acceptability. This involved devising systems and codes of representation in which "innocence" was inscribed into the text while "sophisticated" viewers were able to "read into" movies whatever meanings they pleased to find, so long as producers could use the Production Code to deny that they had put them there. This requirement was perhaps most obvious in dealing with representations of sexuality, but it applied equally to Hollywood's representation of other subjects – particularly the treatment of crime, which was often merely suggested rather than detailed on the screen.

Some of its consequences in terms of conventions of representation were explored by Martha Wolfenstein and Nathan Leites. What interested them was not the dismissive recognition that people in Hollywood movies only really behaved like people in Hollywood movies, but rather what the implications of that behavior, or that representation of behavior, were.[70] Hollywood movies, they suggested, above all involve a play with appearances; they are, repeatedly, dramas of false appearances, in which we see the hero and heroine enacting forbidden desire, but in the end escaping any penalty for it because the enactment is revealed as only a false appearance. In particular, they drew attention to a character they called "the good-bad girl," who attracts the hero by an appearance of wickedness, but whom, in the end, he discovers "he can take home and introduce to Mother." Lauren Bacall as Vivian Sternwood in *The Big Sleep* (1946) or Julia Roberts as Vivian Ward in *Pretty Woman* (1990), are instances of the type, which Wolfenstein and Leites identified as specifically American.[71] The double aspect of the character of her partner, the good-bad man, is more concerned with violence than sex, since he is likely to be suspected of crimes he did not commit.

> The theme of looking guilty but being innocent, recurs persistently in various forms throughout American films. . . . A young couple may spend a night innocently alone together or pose as husband and wife, but only to get a tourist cabin or serve some equally non-sexual exigency. . . . In such scenes

Rita Hayworth, "the good-bad girl" in *Gilda* (1946). Columbia (courtesy Kobal)

the audience knows that the couple are innocent, but onlookers in the film regard them as guilty. The appearances tell a falsely accusing story. There is much less than meets the eye; and it is not always easy to prove it. . . . The older drama of conscience, where the conflict is internal and the individual suffered from feelings of guilt, has been transformed into a conflict between the individual and the world around him. Self-accusations have become accusations of others, directed against the self from outside. . . . The movie hero, warding off false accusations, suffers almost as much as if he were guilty; his feeling of relief in the end, and the freedom he wins, are in part paid for by this suffering.[72]

A number of functions are achieved by this structure of projection and denial. It is through the false appearance of the hero or heroine's guilt that the forbidden desires that the viewer has on their behalf are enacted, but the unfolding of the plot demonstrates that the hero and heroine never imagined those forbidden desires. The movie's happy ending tells us that social sanctions to enforce good behavior are superfluous, since people are inherently good, and would behave impeccably if left to themselves.

What the plot unfolds is a process of proof. Something is undone rather than done: the false appearance is negated. The hero and heroine do not become committed to any irretrievable act whose consequences they must bear. Nor do they usually undergo any character transformation, ennoblement or degradation, gain or loss of hope, acceptance of a new role of the diminution and regrets of age. They succeed in proving what they were all along. They emerge from the shadow of the false appearance.[73]

Finally, Wolfenstein and Leites' analysis points to another recurrent feature of Hollywood movies: their self-reflectivity. "The drama of false appearance" might summarize the opinion of Hollywood's strongest critics as well as it describes its most recurrent plots. We know that Hollywood is Tinseltown, constructed by gossip columnists, studio publicists, and special effects technicians whose profession is the manufacture of deceptive illusion – because Hollywood tells us so. It is one expression of the "art versus business" dichotomy discussed in the introduction, and its contradictions and intricacies manifest themselves most clearly in Hollywood movies about Hollywood. Hollywood's entertainment, we have suggested, is self-explanatory, self-contained (in the safe space of the movie theater), self-justifying ("it's only entertainment"), and self-regulated. It is, then, hardly surprising that Hollywood represents itself so often in its movies.

Silk Stockings is a musical remake of an earlier comedy, *Ninotchka* (1939), that plays with questions of art and entertainment, value and pleasure. Among its subjects are the production of Hollywood cinema, the need for entertainment, and the values that entertainment is to endorse. On the surface the movie's values could hardly be more straightforward: it seems to present a Cold War celebration of the "American way." The evolution of the lovers' relationship allows for the presentation of a series of crude oppositions between "east" and "west." The east is cold, austere, its people subject to material deprivation and the dictates of autocratic government; the west is warm, beautiful, and the people live happy and free in material abundance. The east aspires to the values of High Art while the west is committed to the values of entertainment. Even this interpretation, however, suggests that entertainment has a political function, meeting the deep-rooted "universal" and "human" needs that can find expression in its forms. Ninotchka's "liberation" insists that these needs can be suppressed but never ultimately destroyed by the repressions of a social system antithetical to them. Hollywood can help us to liberate ourselves too; as in *Sullivan's Travels*, entertainment is sanctioned as both humanizing and pleasurable.

But Hollywood's multiple logics ensure that the movie will equivocate in its statement of values; the movie's self-reflectivity means that *Silk Stockings* cannot take itself too seriously, so it qualifies its overtly political, even propagandist effect. The movie's representation of Hollywood is persistently ironic: movie producer Canfield wants to turn Tolstoy's *War and Peace* into a musical titled *Not Tonight Josephine*. The adaptation is presented as a debasement. As well as a basis for liberation, entertainment is presented as hallucination and narcotic. However lightheartedly and affirmatively, the movie remains troubled with the Hollywood it has imagined. Although it celebrates entertainment for its own sake, it is also clear that if we wish to read it in other terms, the movie will justify and help generate that reading. Its commercial status as entertainment does not close off our critical activity so much as challenge it to explain the relationship between the movie's simultaneous operation as both a representation and a commodity form.

How to Take Gene Kelly Seriously

Hollywood, we are suggesting, is playfully complex. Its representation of its own complexity, like its representation of sexuality, is often only there if the "sophisticated" viewer chooses to see it, and the complexity it represents is introverted. Much of Hollywood's product is about itself; the world represented in Hollywood movies is an enclosed world, no matter how distant its back-lots may be disguised as being. Perhaps the extent of Hollywood's self-reflectivity has been overlooked by critics because it is one of the ways in which Hollywood advertises its lack of seriousness: it seems at times to be *only* about itself. As we noted in the introduction, *Singin' in the Rain* presents the history of entertainment as an entertainment. Thematically *Singin' in the Rain* is banal, but its self-reflective playfulness also makes it a complex aesthetic object.

The story is more than familiar. Escaping from fans after a Hollywood premiere, movie star Don Lockwood (Gene Kelly) meets actress Kathy Selden (Debbie Reynolds), who tells him that movies are only cheap entertainment, nothing to do with real art. It turns out, however, that she is performing in the chorus of the party Don goes to. Don pursues her, rousing the fury of his co-star Lina Lamont (Jean Hagen). Despite everything Don does to dissuade her, Lina believes the fan magazine stories about her offscreen romance with Don. Don's romance with Kathy begins to blossom, but the studio they work for, Monumental Pictures, is plunged into crisis by the coming of sound. Studio head R.F. Simpson (Millard Mitchell) decides to remake Don and Lina's current movie, *The Duelling Cavalier*, as a musical. The only snag is Lina's thick Brooklyn accent, but after Don's best friend Cosmo Brown (Donald O'Connor) invents dubbing, the solution is found: Kathy will speak and sing for Lina. The plan works, the movie triumphs, and Don, Cosmo, and Simpson foil Lina's scheme to force Kathy to go on singing and talking for her. Don and Kathy become the onscreen and offscreen lovers the fan magazine readers thought Don and Lina were, and we leave them embracing in front of a poster for their next movie, *Singin' in the Rain*.

The story is really constructed around the movie's 13 songs, which are used to express the characters' emotional states, explain the plot or interrupt it. In addition to the musical numbers, there is a 15-minute "Broadway Ballet" sequence, completely detached from the plot-line, showing the rise of a young dancer (Kelly) from burlesque to stardom. In the casino sequence of the "Broadway Ballet," Cyd Charisse appears in a white dress that echoes the wedding dress, the final costume in the earlier "Beautiful Girl" fashion number. From the casino the ballet dissolves into a fantasy sequence that makes obvious visual references to the paintings of Salvador Dali. It also repeats the motifs of wind and sky in Don's "You Were Meant for Me" number, where he revealed the devices of the sound stage in constructing a romantic fictional space in which he could declare his love for Kathy.

Through a number of different devices, the costuming and decor of this scene set up references to other levels of *Singin' in the Rain*'s fiction. Charisse's white dress evokes the fantasy of a wedding that doesn't come true, but that fantasy is replaced by the fantasy of dance which, like the dress, is repeated (restated, reborn, renewed) by the Kelly lookalike who revives Kelly's own spirits with the "Gotta Dance" call after Charisse has abandoned him in the ballet. All this, it should be added, goes on in a dream sequence that is a visualization of an offscreen verbal description of a scene to be shot in a movie to be put in a movie that is the subject of the movie we are watching. And yet, in *Singin' in the Rain*, these Chinese boxes of cross-reference and self-consciousness are discarded as a joke: when we leave the "Broadway Melody" number to return to Simpson's office, he announces, "I can't quite visualize it. I'll have to see it on film first," and

Cyd Charisse and Gene Kelly in the fantasy sequence of *Singin' in the Rain* (1952). MGM (courtesy Kobal)

Cosmo replies, "On film it'll be better yet." The same sense of a discarded or throwaway complexity is evident in the final image of the movie, where the screen dissolves from Don and Kathy's final duet to their images on a poster advertising their next Monumental Studios production: *Singin' in the Rain*, the movie we have just been watching, starring not Gene Kelly and Debbie Reynolds but Don Lockwood and Kathy Selden, the characters they play in the movie we have been watching.

The movie's own dismissal of any substance behind its complex levels of self-reflectivity makes it easy to both overlook and disregard the textual complexity of something so frivolous as *Singin' in the Rain*. As a backstage musical, it takes pleasure in exposing the technical workings of the activity of filmmaking that it represents. But at the same time as it demystifies the process of production, it also remystifies it. In one sequence, we see the mechanics of pre-recording a musical number, with Kathy singing "You Are My Lucky Star" with an orchestra while Don gazes adoringly on. The movie dissolves to Lina practicing lip-synchronization, then to the set where the number is being filmed. The device by which Lina is given

Don Lockwood and Kathy Selden advertise the movie Gene Kelly and Debbie Reynolds are starring in. MGM (courtesy Kobal)

Kathy's voice is revealed to us. But then we see a shot that begins as the studio camera's viewpoint on Lina and Don in costume. It tracks in to a closer shot of Lina, and changes from color to black-and-white. Then it pulls back along the same track and keeps going, to reveal that we are now in a projection room, watching rushes with Don, Cosmo, and Simpson. This transfer of location, and the move in and out of levels of the fiction signified by the color/black-and-white switch, is done without a cut, making its processes completely mysterious – for those members of the audience who notice it. For as important as this process of remystification of what has just been demystified is the invisibility of the whole procedure to the majority of the audience. Seduced by the perfect marriage of sound and image, most viewers simply fail to notice the absence of the cut, and remain unaware of the technical complexity of what they have been presented with.[74]

Throughout the movie, musical numbers are used as a means of entering and leaving a relatively flimsy and predictable plot that is itself concerned with the implausibility of the storylines on which Hollywood movies regularly rely. The story's familiarity, together with the movie's limited commitment to it (in the sense that it does not need very strongly

Cosmo (Donald O'Connor) conducts Kathy dubbing "You Are My Lucky Star." MGM (courtesy Kobal)

to tell this story, because we all already know it), minimizes the amount of attention the movie needs to devote to sustaining it or endowing it with any great conviction. *Singin' in the Rain* constantly discusses artifice, both overtly and in its own operation of artifice. We see performance conventions being undermined when Don and Lina insult each other while playing a love scene in the silent version. There is a dense pattern of references to the rest of "the world of entertainment": Donald O'Connor's invocation of the clown Pagliacci combined with an imitation of Chico Marx, or the references in Kelly's performance to silent movie star John Gilbert, for instance.[75] At the same time, the movie frequently dissolves between one level of fiction and another. In the opening scene, we are presented with two versions of Don's career, his own "highbrow" account contrasted with an image and music stream that describes a progression from pool hall to smalltime vaudeville. While we privilege the latter account, it is just as much a packaged fiction as Don's claim to artistry and "dignity, always dignity," and we also recognize that.

The movie's blatant willingness to crack open the shell of a coherent fictional world is at the center of its self-reflectivity. The end of the "Broadway Melody" sequence is transparent in its blatancy – transparent enough to raise a laugh at every screening of the movie – but its transparency hides the transfer in and out of levels of the fiction because it is so obvious. There is no attempt in *Singin' in the Rain* to propose that the movie's constant shifting between fictional levels demands perceptual skills beyond those of the ordinary spectator, because such a proposition would deter audiences. The movie explicitly underlines the arbitrariness and redundancy of plotting. Cosmo invents the plot of *The Dancing Cavalier*, the backstage musical version of *The Duelling Cavalier*, in a single speech, delivered very fast:

> The hero is a modern young hoofer in a Broadway show. Right? . . . Well, one night backstage, he's reading *The Tale of Two Cities* between numbers, see? A sandbag falls on his head, and he dreams he's back in the French Revolution! This way we get in modern dancing numbers – Charleston-Charleston – but in the dream part we can use all the costume stuff – right?

Simultaneously, Cosmo reprises the plot of *Dubarry was a Lady*, a Cole Porter musical filmed in 1943, and summarizes the way the storyline of *Singin' in the Rain* was itself devised to fit the predetermined ingredients of its songs, Kelly, and even O'Connor himself.[76]

Singin' in the Rain makes no more attempt to justify its own plot by integrating the musical numbers into a justifiable chain of events than *The Dancing Cavalier*. The "Moses Supposes" number, for instance, is performed without any evident plot motive, and also for no evident plot audience. At the same time as it naturalizes the exuberance of the characters' use of screen space and the apparent spontaneity with which they dance with whatever props and pieces of furniture they find to hand, much of it is staged as if directed out across a proscenium arch at the movie audience.[77] And the audience readily accommodates the multiple identities embodied in such performances. In the plot we watch Don Lockwood, but in the musical numbers we see Gene Kelly dance. These functions are unevenly distributed throughout the movie: Jean Hagen, for instance, is always in character as Lina, while Donald O'Connor seldom has any need to be Cosmo and spends most of his time in one or other performance piece. The nonsense lyrics of "Moses Supposes" verbalize a comparable contradiction:

> Moses supposes his toeses are roses,
> But Moses supposes erroneously.
> For Moses he knowses his toeses aren't roses
> As Moses supposes his toeses to be
>
> Hoopty-doopty-doodle!

Hoopty-doopty-doodle, indeed! The condition of erroneous supposition in the face of knowledge is as good a description of the audience's dual position, between star and character, performance and plot, convention and novelty, as the more usually invoked idea of a "suspension of disbelief." But more important than the terms of this description is the ease with which characters and audience move from one fictional level to another throughout the movie.

In the movie's final scene, the romance is brought alive to the audience in the preview theater by Don's asking them to stop Kathy from running away, and then singing a love duet with her. *The Dancing Cavalier* leaves the screen of the preview theater and is acted out in the space between the audience and the screen, in a literalized version of 3-D. *Singin' in the Rain* enacts the conventions that it parodies. It presents a love story between the two stars of a movie we don't see (the one in the hoarding at the end), who are also (as Kelly and Reynolds) contemporary stars. Thus their story parallels the love story for the fan magazines between Don and Lina, while inside the fiction those same fan magazines can write true love stories about the Lockwood–Selden romance. Although involved in an examination of its own mechanisms of self-reflectivity, *Singin' in the Rain* is also committed to an unchallenged and conventional notion of entertainment. What appears on one level to be banal and conventional – the love story between two stars – is, on another, intricately complex. Different levels of plausibility are established for different levels of immersion within the fiction, as the movie tells the same story, of the rise from obscurity to stardom, on three different occasions, in three separate modes.

Although *Singin' in the Rain* contains much spontaneity and celebratory behavior, invoking the condition of entertainment as Utopia, it also comprises a process of repeated deferral between levels of the fiction. Even the happy ending defers, opening up the possibility of another movie becoming or substituting for the movie we have ourselves just been watching. If we have gone this far down a critical path that interprets *Singin' in the Rain* against its entertainment function by taking its playfulness seriously, we will now be aware of the rehearsal and labor that has gone into making the prop dances appear so effortlessly spontaneous. At the same time, we can be convinced by the serendipitous nature of the movie's prop dances, and recognize the engineering skills that have gone into the production of such apparent serendipity. And if we are not, then *Singin' in the Rain* tells us that it takes "five hundred thousand kilowatts of stardust" to make *either* Debbie Reynolds *or* Kathy Selden *that* beautiful. The world of entertainment celebrates its ordinariness at the same time as it celebrates its illusion, and while it brings these elements together in its conclusion – the romantic couple are united at the moment of the show's success – it makes little attempt to sustain that moment beyond simply providing a point of rest that allows the audience to leave the cinema. As Jane Feuer puts it, "The Hollywood version of Utopia is entirely solipsistic. In its endless reflexivity the musical can only offer itself, only entertainment as its picture of Utopia."[78]

Notes

1 V.F. Perkins, *Film as Film: Understanding and Judging Movies* (Harmondsworth: Penguin, 1972), pp. 156–7.
2 Anonymous moviegoer (D.H.), quoted in Jackie Stacey, "Feminine Fascinations: Forms of Identification in Star–Audience Relations," in Christine Gledhill, ed., *Stardom: Industry of Desire* (London: Routledge, 1991), p. 141.
3 Reproduced in Russell C. Sweeney, *Coming Next Week: A Pictorial History of Film Advertising* (New York: Barnes, 1973), p. 17.
4 *Chambers Twentieth Century Dictionary* (Edinburgh: Chambers, 1977), p. 435. The *Oxford English Dictionary* offers "the act of occupying a person's attention agreeably; interesting employment; amusement . . . that which affords interest or amusement . . . a public performance or exhibition intended to interest or amuse" (Compact Edition, vol. 1 (1971), p. 871). *Webster's New World Dictionary* gives "something that entertains; interesting, diverting, or amusing thing; esp., a show or performance" (3rd College Edition (1988)).
5 Quoted in Joanna Coles, "Eastern Promise for Recession-hit Movies," *Guardian* (May 17, 1992). Of course, that is not how the process of cultural imperialism has been viewed from the other side. In 1948, for example, Maurice Thorez, general secretary of the French Communist Party, denounced the postwar American "invasion" of French cinema screens because they did "not merely deprive our artists, musicians, workers and technicians of their daily bread. They literally poison the souls of our children, young people, young girls, who are to be turned into the docile slaves of the American multi-millionaires, and not into French men and women attached to the moral and intellectual values which have been the grandeur and glory of our fatherland." Quoted in Jean-Pierre Jeancolas, "The Blum–Byrnes Agreement," paper given at the BFI–UCLA "European Challenge" seminar, London, 1993.
6 Richard Dyer, "Introduction," *Only Entertainment* (London: Routledge, 1992), p. 3.
7 Father Daniel A. Lord, SJ, Reporter's Transcript of a meeting of the Association of Motion Picture Producers, February 10, 1930, p. 11. 1930 Production Code File, Motion Picture Association of America, Inc., Archive, New York City (hereafter MPA).
8 In his celebration of the architecture of movie palaces, Ben Hall called John Eberson, the foremost architect of atmospheric theaters, "an archaeologist, weatherman, and landscape gardener rolled into one." He also reproduces a notice posted by the lighting switchboard of a small atmospheric theater in Faribault, Minnesota, written, Hall suggests, in language "worthy of a passage from Genesis": "Please do not turn off the clouds until the show starts. Be sure the stars are turned off when leaving." Ben M. Hall, *The Best Remaining Seats: The Golden Age of the Movie Palace* (New York: DaCapo, 1988), pp. 96, 102.
9 Jack Alicoate, "The Romance of the Roxy," reprinted in Hall, p. 82.
10 Although contemporary cinemas no longer show you movies in Persian rose gardens or Egyptian temples, they still claim to offer you "more of an experience," in terms of both their physical comfort and their capacity to transport you out of your humdrum existence to where "you've dreamed of going . . . Hollywood, home of the movies." Advertising campaign for UCI Multiplex cinemas running in Britain in September 1992.
11 Roy Armes, "Entendre, C'est Comprendre: In Defence of Sound Reproduction," *Screen* 29:2 (Spring 1988), p. 16.

12   Advertisement in the *Saturday Evening Post*, quoted in Robert S. Lynd and Helen Merrill Lynd, *Middletown: A Study in Modern American Culture* (New York: Harcourt, Brace, and World, 1929), p. 265.

13   Lary May, *Screening Out the Past: The Birth of Mass Culture and the Motion Picture Industry* (New York: Oxford University Press, 1980), p. 147.

14   Richard Dyer, "Entertainment and Utopia," *MOVIE* 24 (1977), pp. 2–13.

15   Although the Oscar year runs from January to December, Hollywood's production seasons traditionally began in September, because of the decline in attendance during the summer months before the widespread introduction of air-conditioning in cinemas in the 1930s.

16   Martha Wolfenstein and Nathan Leites, *Movies: A Psychological Study* (Glencoe, IL: Free Press, 1950), pp, 11–12.

17   Talking about his script for *Taxi Driver* (1976), Paul Schrader expressed a similar idea: "I saw the script as an attempt to take the European existential hero . . . and put him in an American context. In doing so, you find that he becomes more ignorant, ignorant of the nature of his problem. Travis's (Robert de Niro) problem is the same as the existentialist hero's, that is, should I exist? But Travis doesn't understand that this is his problem, so he focuses it elsewhere: and I think that it is a mark of the immaturity and the youngness of our country. We don't properly understand the nature of the problem, so the self-destructive impulse, instead of being inner-directed, as it is in Japan, Europe, any of the older cultures, becomes outer-directed. The man who feels the time has come to die will go out and kill other people rather than kill himself. There's a line in *Yakuza* (1975) which says, 'When a Japanese cracks up, he'll close the window and kill himself; when an American cracks up, he'll open the window and kill somebody else.' That's essentially how the existential hero changes when he becomes American. There is not enough intellectual tradition in this country, and not enough history; and Travis is just not smart enough to understand his problem. He should be killing himself instead of these other people. At the end, when he shoots himself in a playful way, that's what he's been trying to do all along." Richard Thompson, "Screenwriter: *Taxi Driver*'s Paul Schrader," *Film Comment* 12:2 (March–April 1976), pp. 10–11.

18   Wolfenstein and Leites, pp. 103, 193, 109, 87, 300, 24.

19   Wolfenstein and Leites, pp. 98, 178. Their sample group of 26 French films may have been somewhat less representative than the much larger sample of American movies.

20   Hortense Powdermaker, *Hollywood the Dream Factory: An Anthropologist Looks at the Movie-makers* (Boston: Little, Brown, 1950), pp. 71–2.

21   Mike Bygrave, "Jaglom and the Women," *Guardian* (December 12, 1991).

22   Theodor Adorno and Max Horkheimer, "Enlightenment as Mass Deception," in James Curran, Michael Gurevich, and Janet Woolacott, eds, *Mass Communication and Society* (London: Edward Arnold, 1977), pp. 361–2.

23   Clement Greenberg, "Avant-Garde and Kitsch," in Bernard Rosenberg and David Manning White, eds, *Mass Culture: The Popular Arts in America* (New York: Free Press, 1957), pp. 105–6.

24   Quoted in Robert Leedham, "Low, Low, Quick, Quick, Low," *Guardian* (October 3, 1991), p. 28.

25   F. Scott Fitzgerald, *The Last Tycoon* (Harmondsworth: Penguin, 1974), p. 5.

26   Robert Allen, *Speaking of Soap Opera* (Chapel Hill: University of North Carolina Press, 1985), p. 16.

27   Peter Wollen, *Signs and Meaning in the Cinema* (London: Secker and Warburg, 1972), p. 10.

28   David A. Cook, *A History of Narrative Film*, 2nd edn (New York: Norton, 1990), p. 653.

29   Ronald Lightbown, *Sandro Botticelli, Volume 1, Life and Work* (London: Paul Elek, 1978), p. 86.

30   The exact meaning of its Neo-Platonic allegory remains a matter of dispute among art historians, but their descriptions of the sensuousness of the representation of Venus recognize an erotic dimension to "the celebration of the body's beauty." It would vulgarize the subtleties of Neo-Platonism's identification between Venus and the Virgin Mary to describe the *Birth of Venus* as the fifteenth-century equivalent of a pinup, but perhaps the difference between a representation of the Neo-Platonic idea that "physical perfection is the mirror and emblem of a pure and noble spirit" and a pinup image of Betty Grable reminding American troops what they were fighting for in World War II is not all that great. Marina Warner, *Monuments and Maidens: The Allegory of the Female Form* (London: Pan, 1987), p. 331. Kenneth Clark, *The Nude: A Study of Ideal Art* (Harmondsworth: Pelican, 1960), p. 99. J.H. Plumb, *The Penguin Book of the Renaissance* (Harmondsworth: Penguin, 1964), p. 104.

31   In 1815, the *Birth of Venus* was moved from the grand-ducal wardrobe of the Medici villa at Castello to the Uffizi gallery. Gabriele Mandel, *The Complete Paintings of Botticelli* (London: Weidenfeld and Nicolson, 1970), p. 97.

32   Catherine Belsey, *Critical Practice* (London: Methuen, 1980), pp. 15–20.

33   Dwight MacDonald, "A Theory of Mass Culture," in Rosenberg and White, pp. 60, 62, 72.

34   Patrick Brantlinger, *Bread and Circuses: Theories of Mass Culture as Social Decay* (Ithaca, NY: Cornell University Press, 1983), p. 185.

35   Walter Benjamin, "The Work of Art in the Age of Mechanical Reproduction," in *Illuminations* (London: Cape, 1970), pp. 219–53.

36   Jan and Cora Gordon, *Stardust in Hollywood* (London: Harrap, 1930), pp. 79, 161.

37   Andrew Sarris, *The American Cinema: Directors and Directions, 1929–1968* (New York: Dutton, 1968), p. 31.

38   "What makes Hollywood so much better than anything else in the world is not only the quality of certain directors," suggested Bazin in a critique of the *politique des auteurs*, "but also the vitality and, in a certain sense, the excellence of a tradition. Hollywood's superiority is only incidentally technical; it lies much more in what we might call the American cinematic genius, something which should be analyzed, then defined, by a sociological approach to its production. The American cinema has been able, in an extraordinarily competent way, to show American society just as it wanted to see itself; but not at all passively, as a simple act of satisfaction and escape, but dynamically, i.e. by participating with the means at its disposal in the building of this society. . . . The American cinema is a classical art, but why not then admire in it what is most admirable, i.e. not only the talent of this or that filmmaker, but the genius of the system, the richness of its ever-vigorous tradition, and its fertility when it comes into contact with new elements." André Bazin, "La Politique des Auteurs," in Peter Graham, ed., *The New Wave* (London: Secker and Warburg, 1968), pp. 143–4, 154.

39   Quoted in Aljean Harmetz, *Round Up the Usual Suspects: The Making of Casablanca – Bogart, Bergman, and World War II* (New York: Hyperion, 1992), p. 64.

40   William R. Meyer, *Warner Brothers* [sic] *Directors: The Hard-Boiled, the Comic, and the Weepers* (New Rochelle, NY: Arlington House, 1978), p. 75.

41   Sarris, pp. 175–6.

42   Alfred Starr, "The 'Lost Audience' Is Still Lost," *Variety* (January 16, 1954), p. 61, quoted in Tino Balio, ed., *Hollywood in the Age of Television* (Boston: Unwin Hyman, 1990), p. 7.

43   The increasingly frequent video re-release of the "director's cut" represents perhaps

the clearest example to date of what Barbara Klinger has called "a commodified version of auteurism." Barbara Klinger, "Digressions at the Cinema: Reception and Mass Culture," *Cinema Journal* 28:4 (Summer 1989), p. 12.

44   Quoted in Kent, *Naked Hollywood*, p. 182.

45   Thomas Schatz, *The Genius of the System: Hollywood Filmmaking in the Studio Era* (New York: Pantheon, 1988), p. 5.

46   Robert Parrish, *Growing Up in Hollywood* (London: Bodley Head, 1976), p. 209.

47   Gore Vidal, *Screening History* (London: Abacus, 1993), p. 26.

48   Quoted in Richard Maltby, ed., *Dreams for Sale: Popular Culture in the Twentieth Century* (London: Harrap, 1989), p. 19.

49   Robin Baker, "Computer Technology and Special Effects in Contemporary Cinema," in Philip Hayward and Tana Wollen, eds, *Future Visions: New Technologies on the Screen* (London: British Film Institute, 1993), p. 38.

50   For an account of the development of these procedures, see Susan Ohmer, "Measuring Desire: George Gallup and Audience Research in Hollywood," *Journal of Film and Video* 43:1–2 (Summer 1991), pp. 3–28. A Reactograph chart for part of *Good News* (1947) is reproduced in Hugh Fordin, *The World of Entertainment: Hollywood's Greatest Musicals* (New York: Avon, 1975), pp. 220–1.

51   Thomas Elsaesser, "Why Hollywood?," *Monogram* 1 (1971), p. 7.

52   What is considered entertaining may nevertheless allow for some variation. Steven Bach described the end of *The Deer Hunter* (1978) as "a 'talk-about' ending that would encourage controversy and word of mouth, and if it hinted at character depths or thematic profundities that were on the murky side or if it stroked emotions that were confused or facile, so what? The poignance seemed no less genuine for its awkwardness. Or perhaps that was the point. Maybe the (anything but pat) ending hoped to invoke a feeling of loss that was inarticulated because it was finally unutterable, except as an ardently sentimental hymn. . . . We didn't know what it meant to Cimino – politically or otherwise – but we knew what it felt like was, well . . . poetry." Bach, *Final Cut: Dreams and Disaster in the Making of Heaven's Gate* (London: Faber, 1986), p. 101. In 1992, a "director's cut" of *Blade Runner* was released, with the "original" ending, a particularly ironic fate for a movie so preoccupied with demonstrating the disintegration of the aura of authenticity. The question of what constitutes an "original version" of a movie is discussed in relation to *Pat Garrett and Billy the Kid* in chapter 3.

53   Michael Hague, *Writing Screenplays that Sell* (London: Elm Tree Books, 1989), p. 3.

54   Quoted in Douglas Gomery, *Shared Pleasures: A History of Movie Presentation in the United States* (Madison: University of Wisconsin Press, 1992), p. 58.

55   Ronald Haver, *David O. Selznick's Hollywood* (New York: Knopf, 1980), p. 309; Stephen Rebello, *Alfred Hitchcock and the Making of Psycho* (New York: Dembner Books, 1990), p. 149.

56   David Bordwell, Janet Staiger, and Kristin Thompson, *The Classical Hollywood Cinema: Film Style and Mode of Production to 1960* (London: Routledge and Kegan Paul, 1985), p. 15.

57   Herbert Blumer, *Movies and Conduct* (New York: Macmillan, 1933), pp. 48, 115.

58   Kenneth Roberts, *Leisure* (London: Longman, 1970), p. 6. See also Chris Rojek, *Capitalism and Leisure Theory* (London: Tavistock, 1985).

59   We shall discuss the operation of generic convention in chapter 3.

60   Although Gore Vidal, recalling his experience of viewing *The Mummy* in 1932, notes that "since we knew that we would have only the one encounter, we learned how to concentrate totally." Vidal, p. 18.

61 Robert Warshow, "Movie Chronicle: The Westerner," in Gerald Mast and Marshall Cohen, eds, *Film Theory and Criticism*, 3rd edn (New York: Oxford University Press, 1985), p. 444.

62 Steve Neale, "Questions of Genre," *Screen* 31:1 (Spring 1990), p. 64.

63 *Mutual Film Corp.* v. *Ohio Industrial Commission*, 236 US, 230 US Supreme Court, 1915, reprinted in Gerald Mast, ed., *The Movies in Our Midst: Documents in the Cultural History of Film in America* (Chicago: University of Chicago Press, 1982), p. 142. See also Garth Jowett, "'A Capacity for Evil': The 1915 Supreme Court *Mutual* Decision," *Historical Journal of Film, Radio and Television* 9:1 (1989), pp. 59–78.

64 Will Hays, draft of 1932 Annual Report of the MPPDA, Will H. Hays Archive, Department of Special Collections, Indiana State Library, Indianapolis.

65 "The Reasons Supporting Preamble of Code," in Raymond Moley, *The Hays Office* (Indianapolis: Bobbs-Merrill, 1946), p. 244.

66 Will H. Hays, "Motion Pictures and the Public," An Address Before the Women's City Club of Philadelphia, April 20, 1925 (New York: MPPDA, 1925), p. 3.

67 "General Principles to Govern the Preparation of a Revised Code of Ethics for Talking Pictures," Reporter's Transcript, board meeting, Association of Motion Picture Producers (AMPP), February 10, 1930, Motion Picture Association of America Archive, New York, 1930 AMPP Code file, pp. 138–9.

68 Ruth Vasey, *Diplomatic Representations: The World According to Hollywood, 1919–1939* (Madison: University of Wisconsin Press, forthcoming).

69 Joy to James Wingate, February 5, 1931. Production Code Administration Case file, *Little Caesar*, Department of Special Collections, Margaret Herrick Library of the Academy of Motion Picture Arts and Sciences, Los Angeles.

70 Part of the terror and pleasure of Hollywood has to do with the play around emotional and behavioral reality. Nobody outside the movies behaves like Sharon Stone in *Basic Instinct*, but we equally recognize our own capacity to pick up and imitate behavioral mannerisms from the movies. One of the great official dreads about Hollywood has been that others – the socially or emotionally vulnerable – will go beyond mannerisms to adopt ideas or behavior – that, in particular, girls will become promiscuous and boys will become violent. Or alternatively, that Norman Bates and Hannibal Lecter are not representations of serial killers, but inspirations.

71 "American ways of fusing goodness and badness in women start with a good woman and spice her up. . . . An alternative procedure is to take a girl who appears too good and make her more sexy." Wolfenstein and Leites, pp. 27, 39. These two descriptions might equally apply to other American representations of female sexuality, for instance *Playboy*.

72 Wolfenstein and Leites, p. 189.

73 Wolfenstein and Leites, pp. 250, 301.

74 Most viewers will also miss a further level of ironic self-reflectivity in this sequence. The speaking voice actually used when Kathy speaks as Lina is not Debbie Reynolds' but Jean Hagen's own voice: Hagen is dubbing Reynolds playing Kathy dubbing Lina. (When Reynolds sings as Lina, the voice is that of Betty Royce.) Fordin, p. 358. See also Rick Altman, *The American Film Musical* (Bloomington: Indiana University Press, 1987), pp. 257–8.

75 For the true connoisseur of self-referentiality, the furniture in Don's mansion came from the set of the John Gilbert–Greta Garbo movie *Flesh and the Devil* (1927), while Kathy's car used to belong to Andy Hardy. In the "Broadway Ballet," Cyd Charisse's appearance is modeled on a combination of silent stars Pola Negri and Louise Brooks, Kelly's on Broadway star Harry Richman, and the gangster on George Raft in *Scarface*

(1932). References to other Hollywood musicals abound. Fordin, p. 355; Rudy Behlmer, *Behind the Scenes* (New York: Samuel French, 1982), p. 266.

76   Peter Wollen, *Singin' in the Rain* (London: British Film Institute, 1992), p. 42.
77   Jane Feuer, *The Hollywood Musical* (London: British Film Institute, 1982), p. 4.
78   Feuer, p. 84.

2 Industry

The modern industrial enterprise – the archetype of today's giant corporation – resulted from the integration of the processes of mass production with those of mass distribution within a single business firm. The first "big businesses" in American history were those that united the types of distributing organization created by the mass marketer with the types of factory organization developed to manage the new processes of mass production. They were the first enterprises to combine the economies of high volume throughput with the advantages of high stock-turn and generous cash flow. . . . The visible hand of managerial direction had replaced the invisible hand of market forces in coordinating the flow of goods from the suppliers of raw and semifinished materials to the retailer and ultimate consumer. The internalizing of these activities and the transactions between them reduced transaction and information costs. More important, a firm was able to coordinate supply more closely with demand, to use its working force and capital equipment more intensively, and thus to lower its unit costs. Finally, the resulting high volume throughput and high stock-turn generated a cash flow that reduced the costs of both working and fixed capital.

Alfred D. Chandler, Jr[1]

I gotta have a lot of money; I gotta have a lot of money to juice the guys I gotta juice, so I can get a lot of money, so I can juice the guys I gotta juice.
Marty Augustine (Mark Rydell) in *The Long Goodbye* (1973)

Hollywood's commercial aesthetic recognizes that to make money, you have to spend money, and that the reputation of a movie is enhanced by the conspicuous display of its production budget. Recent movies often advertise their budgets and even their box-office receipts as part of their general appeal, but the spectacle of "putting money on the screen" has always preoccupied Hollywood producers. Despite the industry's often apparently cavalier attitude to spending, it is in fact as constrained as any other business by the need to save time and money, to reduce unnecessary excess and risk, and to stabilize and regulate the flow of production. From the 1920s to the 1950s, the studio system was a way of organizing production to suit these economic preconditions, and the stability which it provided produced the familiar style, the immediately recognizable patterns of camera movement, editing, narrative, and genre that identify a Hollywood movie. As a description of the American film industry's organization, the "studio system" is, however, something of a misnomer, in that it overemphasizes the centrality of production to the economics of the industry as a whole. What characterized the functioning of the motion picture industry during the period of the studio system was not the existence of the studios as production centers, but the dominance of the major companies as distributor-exhibitors.

Distribution and Exhibition

In "Hollywood's greatest year," 1939, 33,687 people were employed in movie production. But the industry as a whole employed 177,420 people. For every actor, writer, electrician, or carpenter working in Los Angeles, there were five distribution company salesmen, theater managers, projectionists, ushers, and box-office clerks staffing the 15,000 cinemas in the United States.[2] The industry often claimed to be the fourth largest in America, a claim based on the total amount of capital invested in it. In 1940 this investment exceeded $2 billion, more than was invested in automobile production or the chemical industry. But 94 percent of this investment was in the real estate of movie theaters, and only 5 percent in the plant and facilities used in production. The industry's major concern was the successful commercial management of this real estate, turning a better profit than could be produced by putting the buildings to some other commercial use. During the 1930s, when on average Americans went to the movies once every two weeks, movie theaters took in two thirds of all the money spent in places of entertainment. By other measures of economic size, however, the industry was nowhere near so prominent as it claimed; smaller, in terms of its total sales, than hotels, restaurants, or the liquor or tobacco industries. As Douglas Gomery has suggested, "despite all the glamour and hype, the movie industry could never be considered more than a moderately successful industry, one affected by the usual booms and busts of twentieth-century US capitalism."[3] Even this cautious assessment may actually overrate its success: at the end of the silent period the average return for capital invested in the industry was estimated to be as low as 2 percent.[4] Technical advances like sound, or the absence of alternative choices for expenditure during World War II, produced short-term windfall profits, but the cost of the industry's real estate kept its overall long-term profitability quite low.

On the other hand, the value of its real estate holdings provided the industry with a good deal of economic stability, and attached it closely to the banking system. When the major companies expanded in the 1920s, building new studios and picture palaces, these developments were financed on Wall Street, where brokers and bankers looked to reap what one company called "the Golden Harvest of the Silver Screen."[5] The major companies' enormous purchases of real estate made them both attractive and secure investments in the boom market of the late 1920s. When the

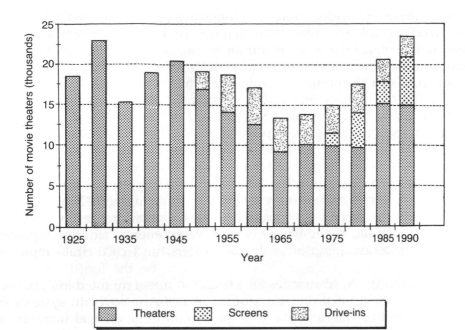

Movie theaters in the United States
After rising to a peak of over 23,000 in 1929, the number of theaters fell
sharply during the Depression, but recovered during the World War II
boom in attendance. The steady closure of "four-wall" theaters in the
postwar years was compensated by the spread of drive-in theaters catering
to the teenage and young adult audience. In the 1970s, increasing numbers of theaters housed multiple screens, showing two or more movies to
different (and smaller) audiences in the same building, which was most
likely to be in a shopping mall.

Source: adapted from Joel W. Finler, *The Hollywood Story*, London, Octopus
Books, 1988

Depression demonstrated that the industry had expanded too far too
quickly, the Wall Street firms that had financed this expansion recalled
their loans and effectively secured control over the major companies. This
change in ultimate ownership, however, produced no dramatic shift in
industry policy or behavior, and this fact in itself suggests that, however
much Hollywood's publicity claimed that no business was like the "show
business," in practice the American film industry was an industry much
like others, developing similar organizational structures for similar aims.

Before the American motion picture industry had established its production center in Hollywood, the most powerful interests within the industry sought to combine together to monopolize it and determine its
profitability. The first attempt at such a combination was the Motion Picture Patents Company, established in 1908. It failed because it tried to
dominate the industry by controlling the production of movies but, as was
already clear by 1915, the other two branches of the industry, distribution

and exhibition, provided more effective ways of dominating the industry as a whole. Until 1903, film manufacturers sold prints outright to exhibitors, which meant that each exhibitor owned a small collection of prints that he might use until they were physically worn out. While this arrangement worked well enough for traveling exhibitors putting on tent shows or playing the vaudeville circuits, permanent movie theaters needed a more elaborate system of film distribution. The creation of film exchanges, where an exhibitor could rent pictures rather than buy them, made possible the development of dedicated motion picture theaters: at first the "nickel-Odeons," often no more than converted stores or saloons charging five cents to enter – hence the name. By 1910, however, exhibitors had begun to construct increasingly grandiose, purpose-built theaters to accommodate the demands of middle-class audiences for better facilities, and from then on, in the words of one entrepreneur, "theaters replaced shooting galleries, temples replaced theaters, and cathedrals replaced temples."[6]

During the 1910s, companies also began to integrate the mass production of movies in purpose-built studios in Los Angeles with systems of mass distribution, the first stage in the evolution of **vertical integration** within the industry. A vertically integrated company is involved in all three branches of its business: manufacture, wholesaling, and retailing. A

A typical neighborhood theater in 1915 advertising a contest in which the prize is a chance to play in the movies. Courtesy BFI

vertically integrated food company, for instance, owns the plantations where its crops are grown, the canning factories where they are processed, the trucks that deliver the cans, and the grocery stores in which they are sold. The involvement in all branches of an industry obviously gives the vertically integrated company a much greater degree of control over its terms of trade than a company involved in only one branch of the business can exercise. A small number of vertically integrated companies, all pursuing the same business strategies, can between them dominate an industry. The history of American business in the twentieth century has been predominantly a history of the growth of vertically integrated corporations, and with it the growth of **oligopoly** control (monopoly power exercised by a small group) of individual companies.

This pattern emerged in the motion picture industry in the years immediately after World War I, when the largest producer-distributor, Adolph Zukor's Famous Players-Lasky, developed a theater chain. In retaliation First National Pictures, the largest exhibition consortium, began producing movies. During the 1920s a series of mergers produced three, then four, vertically integrated companies which dominated the industry: Paramount, which included Famous Players; Warner Bros., which expanded greatly in the late 1920s and took over First National; Loews, Inc., the parent company of MGM; Fox, which became Twentieth Century-Fox in 1935. By the late 1920s the scale of investment required meant that only the largest of concerns could contemplate setting up a vertically integrated company to compete with these four. RCA, the dominant presence in the radio industry, succeeded in doing so in 1928 when RKO was created out of the amalgamation of a number of smaller distribution and exhibition organizations, but even so, RKO was always the smallest and least profitable of the majors, and the only one to go permanently out of business, when Howard Hughes stripped its assets in the early 1950s. Although all the other four companies have been taken over or merged with other concerns since, they have remained dominant forces within the industry. From the late 1920s to the mid-1950s, however, the "Big Five," as they were known, dominated the industry not through their control of production but through their ownership of the most desirable and profitable movie theaters. Between them they owned no more than 15 percent of the theaters in the United States, but that included almost all the large metropolitan theaters, which charged the highest admission prices and took in almost 70 percent of the total American box-office income.

The picture palaces of the 1920s were perhaps the movie industry's most conspicuous occasions of excess, where the display in the auditorium rivaled the display on the screen. The pastiche ornamental styles of these theaters were accumulated from a jumble of earlier cultures, but their opulence had its own economic rationale and they were highly profitable business operations. Hollywood's extravagance was as democratic as it was vulgar: the inventive grandeur of the picture palaces proclaimed their availability to anyone who had the price of admission. Run according to

Interior of a picture palace. Courtesy BFI

the same commercial strategies as the rapidly expanding chain store business, they offered the clerks and shopgirls of American cities luxury at
prices they could afford. But though William Fox declared the motion
picture to be "a distinctly American institution" because "movies breathe
the spirit in which the country was founded, freedom and equality," one
group of Americans was excluded. The rich might rub elbows with the
poor in a theater, but African-Americans were at best seated in a segregated section, usually the balcony. In many Southern states the theaters
themselves were legally segregated as late as the 1960s, and throughout
the country, black audiences were largely restricted to their own neighborhood theaters.[7] Only in the largest American cities did the Big Five directly
compete with each other for theater audiences; elsewhere, because they
owned theaters in different parts of the country from each other, their
theaters normally exhibited movies made by other companies as well as
their own. MGM's parent company Loew's, Inc., made money in its
theaters by showing the best product of Paramount, Warner Bros., and
RKO as well as MGM, and thus benefited from the success of its off-
spring's rivals. Whichever studio actually produced a hit movie, it would
be profitable for all the vertically integrated companies.[8]

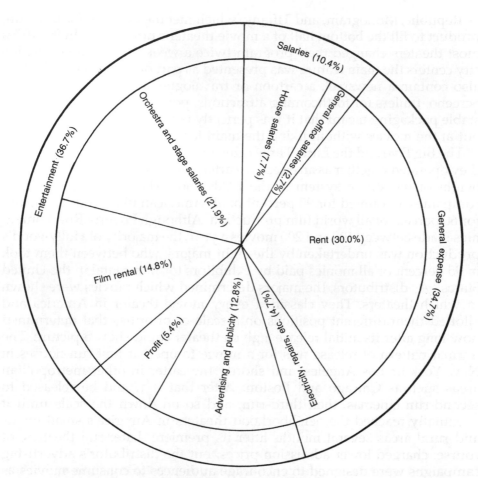

The costs of running a movie theater, 1927
The California Theater was a large, second-run neighborhood theater, seating around 800 patrons, and changing its program at least twice a week. The high cost of theater orchestras was one of the principal incentives behind the introduction of sound.

Source: adapted from Harold B. Franklin, *Motion Picture Theater Management*, New York, Doran, 1927

The Big Five's economic power came from their theaters; a movie denied access to these theaters was unlikely to make a profit. Three other companies – Columbia, Universal, and United Artists, known as the "Little Three" – owned no theaters, but were involved in production and distribution on a slightly smaller scale than that of the Big Five. As Harry Cohn explained in chapter 1, the majority of the movies produced by Columbia and Universal were mid- or low-budget features. United Artists was formed in 1919 by Douglas Fairbanks, Charlie Chaplin, D.W. Griffith, and Mary Pickford to distribute their own movies and later those of other independent producers such as Samuel Goldwyn. Most independent production, however, was undertaken by the "Poverty Row" companies such as Republic, Monogram, and Tiffany, which met the demand for B-feature product to fill the bottom half of a movie theater's double bill. In the 1930s most theaters changed their program twice a week or more, and outside city centers the main feature was presented as part of a package that might also contain a newsreel, a cartoon or travelogue, a B-feature, a game of Screeno, trailers for forthcoming attractions, popcorn, and ice cream. This stable packaging meant that it was perfectly possible to have a good night out at the movies without liking the main feature.

The Big Five and the Little Three came to be known as the "majors," and they operated together as an effective cartel controlling the industry. At the height of the studio system in the 1930s and 1940s, Los Angeles-based companies accounted for 90 percent of all American film production, and for 60 percent of all world film production. Although Poverty Row companies made between 100 and 200 movies a year, the majority of Hollywood's production was undertaken by the eight majors, who between them took in 95 percent of all monies paid by exhibitors for film rental in the United States.[9] As distributors, the majors determined which movies were shown in which theaters. They classified every movie theater in America and allotted them different positions on a scale of priorities that determined how long after its initial release a given theater could show a picture. The normal pattern of release was for a movie to open at first-run houses in New York or Los Angeles, and shortly thereafter in other metropolitan areas such as Chicago and Boston. After that it would be released to second-run cinemas, then third-run, and so on down the scale until it eventually reached the neighborhood theaters in America's small towns and rural areas several months after its premiere. Later-run theaters, of course, charged lower admission prices, but the distributor's advertising campaigns were designed to encourage audiences to consume movies as soon after their initial release as possible, while they were still "new." This maximized the distribution company's income by encouraging patrons to pay the highest prices to see a movie at a first-run house, which was in any case most likely to be owned by one of the Big Five.

In addition to this system of **clearance**, as it was known, the majors also imposed a practice known as **block-booking** on smaller exhibitors. Under this arrangement, theaters were not permitted to hire individual movies, but had to accept them in blocks, sometimes as large as fifty, but more commonly in packages of five or six. A block of this size might attach several lower-budget movies with less well-known stars to an expensive production. The system worked in the distributor's interest, by ensuring a wider distribution for lower-budget movies and preventing independent exhibitors from buying only the most successful product. Distributors argued that block-booking also benefited exhibitors by minimizing sales costs, so that it was still sufficiently profitable for the distributor to bother doing business with the smallest exhibitors.

As the domineering behavior of the distributors indicated, the central structuring tension within the industry was in the competition not between the major companies, but between the powerful, vertically integrated corporations and the large number of small, independent, or "unaffiliated" exhibitors, the 10,000 "Mom and Pop" theaters seating under 500 patrons and changing their programs three times a week or more. Although these outlets were of relatively minor economic importance to the majors, renting movies for as little as $7 a booking and totalling under 20 percent of the majors' distribution income, they were centrally important to the industry's presentation of the motion picture as a universal mass entertainment. Because almost every American lived within easy traveling distance of at least one movie theater, the industry felt able to justify its claim that movies were not a luxury item for their consumers but "a great social necessity, an integral part of human life in the whole civilized world."[10] During World War II the government acknowledged this argument by granting movies the status of an "essential industry," facilitating access to rationed goods and exemptions from military service for industry personnel. At other times, the industry used the same argument in resisting attempts to impose additional taxes on it.

Although it is best known for its administration of self-censorship, the industry's trade association, the Motion Picture Producers and Distributors of America, Inc. (MPPDA), was established in 1922 to prevent government interference in the operations of the major companies, and the most important part of its work involved safeguarding their political interests by countering attempts to impose a strict application of the US anti-trust

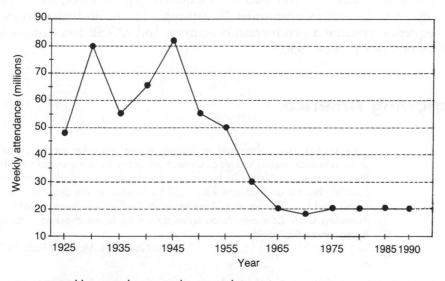

Weekly attendance in the United States
Recovering to pre-Depression levels during World War II, attendance fell steadily in the postwar period until 1965, when it stabilized at about a quarter of its wartime peak.

Source: adapted from Joel W. Finler, *The Hollywood Story*, London, Octopus Books, 1988

laws to the industry. According to its by-laws, the association was created "to foster the common interests of those engaged in the motion picture industry in the United States."[11] In practice, its restricted membership was dominated by the major companies, and it operated as an instrument of cartelization, by which the majors' non-competitive pricing and distribution policies were justified as "business self-regulation." However, although the majors often operated in collusion, their relationship during the studio era has been aptly described by Douglas Gomery as being "like a chronically quarrelsome but closely knit family."[12] Will Hays, president of the MPPDA from 1922 to 1945, often arbitrated these disputes and, as importantly, acted to ameliorate the majors' worst excesses in dictating terms to independent exhibitors.

Like the small exhibitors, few of Hollywood's workers were likely to have felt part of a family. Labor relations in the production industry were notoriously poor, the result of the studios' reliance on a casual workforce in a city infamous for its hostility to trade unions. The Academy of Motion Picture Arts and Sciences had its origins in an attempt to establish company unions in the late 1920s. Studio managements put up a vigorous and often violent resistance to unionization in Hollywood in the 1930s and 1940s, exploiting jurisdictional disputes and accusations of Communist influence among unions. For a period in the late 1930s, several studio heads paid extortion money to the corrupt Hollywood leadership of the International Alliance of Theatrical and Stage Employees (IATSE). In the late 1940s the IATSE's Hollywood representative, Roy Brewer, was a leading figure in the anti-Communist "cleansing" of the industry. Brewer subsequently became a production executive, and IATSE has dominated Hollywood labor since 1950.[13]

Exporting America

> If the United States abolished its diplomatic and consular services, kept its ships in harbor and its tourists at home, and retired from the world's markets, its citizens, its problems, its towns and countryside, its roads, motor cars, counting houses and saloons would still be familiar in the uttermost corners of the world . . . The film is to America what the flag was once to Britain. By its means Uncle Sam may hope some day, if he is not checked in time, to Americanize the world.
>
> *New York Morning Post*, 1923[14]

Hollywood was an international industry, not just an American one. It achieved its domination of the world's movie screens during World War I, and consolidated its hold during the 1920s with the aggressive marketing of a product that seemed to have universal appeal.[15] By the late 1920s, American movies occupied as much as 80 percent of the screen time in those countries that had not established quota legislation to protect their own film production industries. The foreign market brought the American film industry approximately 35 percent of its total income in the late 1920s and 1930s, of which nearly two thirds came from Europe.[16] The scale of the American domestic market, which had about half the world's cinemas, provided the major companies with a crucially important bedrock of economic security: they expected a movie to at least break even on its exhibition in the United States and Canada, and so they could look on foreign earnings as clear profit. As a result, American companies could sell their movies to exhibitors in Britain or Argentina at lower prices than domestic producers, to whom the American market was also effectively closed. For a German or French exhibitor, Hollywood's economic miracle was that it spent much more on the movies it made than domestic producers could, but sold them much cheaper, so that even in their own domestic market, European, Australian, or Latin American film producers did not compete on equal terms with Hollywood. This sales strategy was part of a deliberate American policy of weakening the international competition; a more visible aspect of the same policy was Hollywood's enthusiasm for luring European directors and stars to work in Los Angeles.

Hollywood's production values, encapsulated in the million-dollar movie you could watch for a few pennies or centavos or lei, projected a powerful image of American material abundance. Trade no longer followed the flag, argued Will Hays in the 1920s. Instead, "trade follows the film." Movies, declared one of his officials, were "demonstrably the greatest single factor in the Americanization of the world and as such fairly may be called the most important and significant of America's exported products."[17] An analyst at the State Department confirmed this sentiment when he commented in 1926 that "the peoples of many countries now consider America as the arbiter of manners, fashion, sports customs and standards of living."[18] The moviegoing habit was a familiar, domestic ritual around the world. American movies and their stars were a significant part of millions of non-American people's daily experience and personal identity. Hollywood's influence was literally domesticated in the 1930s, for example, when British working-class parents named their children Shirley, Marlene, Norma, or Gary.[19] European nationalists feared that the movies were bringing about what one British politician called "the annexation of this country by the United States of America."[20]

In the postwar period, the foreign market became an even more important source of income to Hollywood. By the early 1960s foreign sales generated about half of the majors' revenues, and, with minor fluctuations, the division between domestic and foreign income has remained roughly equal ever since.[21] With the foreign market so important a part of the industry's income, an "international" element in Hollywood's production became even more attractive than it had been before the war, but instead of bringing European stars to Hollywood, American production migrated abroad. The attractions of this policy included not only exotic locations and European co-stars, but also lower labor costs and subsidies from European

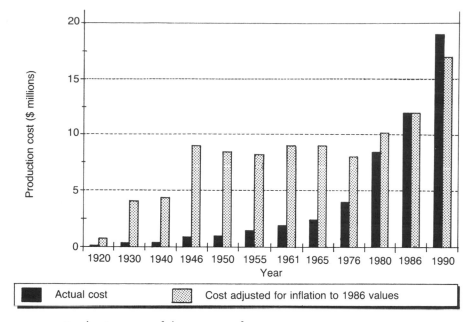

Production cost of the average feature
The costs of production have risen steadily, but when adjusted for inflation, they reveal a different picture. The largest jump in production costs occurred during World War II, and, as the graph opposite shows, it coincided with a sharp fall in the number of movies produced by the major companies. A similar amount of money was spent on production, but it was spent on the production of fewer movies. In the second half of the 1980s, the average Hollywood budget rose by 40 percent, reflecting the increase in the size of the overall world market brought about by the development of video as an additional system of release.

Source: adapted from Joel W. Finler, *The Hollywood Story*, London, Octopus Books, 1988

government legislation designed to protect domestic production industries from American competition. With the aid of the Motion Picture Export Association, as the Foreign Department of the MPPDA became in 1945, American companies became adept at maneuvering around this legislation by having their movies produced by subsidiary organizations classified as "British," "Italian," or "German." **Runaway production**, as this practice was known, reached its height during the late 1960s, when nearly half of the features made by American companies were produced abroad. Thereafter, rising foreign wage rates and the devaluation of the dollar reduced the attraction of overseas production, but the influence of the foreign exhibition market continued to be felt.[22] Since the 1930s, sales departments had told producers that action-oriented movies did better business abroad, particularly in non-English-speaking markets, than "walk and talk" pictures, as movies reliant on dialogue to develop their story were known.[23] For essentially unchanged reasons, the overseas mar-

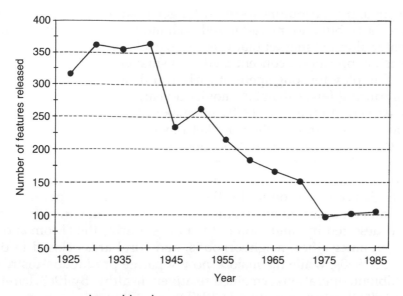

Features released by the majors

Source: adapted from Joel W. Finler, *The Hollywood Story*, London, Octopus Books, 1988

ket is particularly important to the profitability of the movies of Sylvester Stallone and Arnold Schwarzenegger. More than any other star Schwarzenegger personifies contemporary Hollywood's orientation toward a global market. Nicholas Kent calls him "a walking, talking brand-name" who, unlike Stallone, successfully diversified his appeal by making comedies as well as action-adventure movies.[24]

Divorcement

Although 1946 was Hollywood's most successful year at the box-office, the industry went into a precipitate decline over the next ten years. In 1953, only half as many people in the US were going to the movies as had gone seven years earlier. The primary cause of this industry recession was, perversely, the prosperity of the American economy that produced the migration to the suburbs and the baby boom. At the same time, the industry underwent drastic structural changes in its organization. In 1948, the US Supreme Court finally ruled that the majors' control of distribution and first-run exhibition constituted an illegal monopoly, and ordered the separation of exhibition from production-distribution. This decision (known as the **Paramount case** decision) signaled the end of the "studio system" of production, and with it the beginning of the end of the Classical Hollywood cinema. It was not, of course, the end of Hollywood, but the Supreme Court's decision undercut the economies of scale that provided the rationale for the system of production Harry Cohn described so vividly. **Divorcement**, as the separation of exhibition was known, meant that the producers and distributors were no longer guaranteed a market for all their products, but had instead to sell each movie on its individual merits. In an entertainment market that was also shrinking because of the growth of television, producers concentrated on a smaller number of productions designed to play for long spells at early-run theaters. By 1959 the majors were producing fewer than 200 movies a year, compared with over 350 a decade earlier.[25] In the early 1950s, the major companies reorganized their operations, concentrating their market power in their distribution activities. Although the smaller independent exhibitors had apparently won their case in the Supreme Court, the policy decisions taken by the majors ensured that they were, in fact, the principal victims of the Paramount decision. Starved of product by the majors' policies of phasing out B-features and medium-budget pictures, faced with competition from television and deserted by migration to the new suburbs, the "Mom and Pop" theaters in inner cities, neighborhoods, and rural areas closed in droves during the 1950s, while the majors' now separate production-distribution and exhibition operations remained relatively healthy. By 1963, barely half of the 18,000 theaters operating in 1947 were still open.

From the early 1950s on, the studios gradually produced fewer features, cut their permanent payrolls, and came to operate increasingly as providers of facilities for independent production companies constructed around an individual writer, director, or star. The enormous growth of television from the mid-1950s is often erroneously cited as the cause of the decline of the studio system. In fact, television in many respects perpetuated a studio system of production. Although the Paramount decision effectively prevented the majors moving into television broadcasting, by the mid-1950s the studios had entered television production and rapidly colonized it. They moved the center of television production from New York to Los Angeles, and established stock companies to produce television serials like *Father Knows Best* (1954–9) and *Gunsmoke* (1955–75). By 1963, 70 percent of American prime-time television programming was coming from Hollywood, and the major companies were earning 30 percent of their revenues from telefilm production.[26] The made-for-TV movie in the mid-1960s was a commercially logical development, but it began to confuse the boundaries between different kinds of Hollywood production, as watching movies on television had already begun to confuse boundaries around the consumption of Hollywood.

Changes in the industry since 1960 have largely continued the patterns established after the Paramount decision. The majors, concentrating their industrial power in their role as distributors, replaced the studio system of production with one in which they acted primarily as bankers, supplying finance and studio facilities to independent production companies. Production has become increasingly dependent on "packaging," by which a movie's basic "properties" – the script, one or two stars, and perhaps the director – are assembled by a producer or an agent, and sold as a package to a company. By the late 1960s, as much as two thirds of Hollywood's production output was "pre-packaged" in this way, and both the practice and the terminology of packaging stress what we have called the aggregated character of Hollywood's commercial aesthetic. Writer Joan Didion has argued that packaging the deal has itself become a Hollywood art form, described in aesthetic terms: " 'A very imaginative deal,' they say, or, 'He writes the most creative deals in the business.' . . . The action is everything . . . the picture itself is in many ways only the action's by-product."[27] More practically, perhaps, screenwriter Howard Rodman has observed that "When you are writing a screenplay, one of the things you are doing, in a sense, is writing a prospectus for a stock offering."[28] However, although packaging has altered the distribution of power within Hollywood production, greatly enhancing the influence and authority of talent agencies, it is not so very different in its procedures from the way that a studio head of production would assemble a team to produce a star vehicle in the studio system.

Hollywood after Divorce

In economic terms, it is perhaps necessary to think of the industry as being in two distinct parts. The $2 billion invested in the industry's real estate in 1939 was a largely fixed sum, quite separate from the $187 million spent on production in that year. The smaller figure can be thought of as the cost of the raw material required to make movies. The sale of the processed goods had to turn a sufficient profit not just to recoup its own costs, but to produce a worthwhile return on the $2 billion fixed capital investments. The stability of its fixed investments enabled the major companies to raise capital from Wall Street backers. Generating the resources for production by itself was, however, a different matter. This capital needed to be generated out of current resources; a movie had to pay for itself. The obvious economic facts of the industry complicated this simple equation, however. A movie had to be completed, and have all its costs paid for, before it could begin to earn money for anyone, and the money it earned reached the producer last. During the Classical period, a theater owner might keep between half and three quarters of the box-office receipts to cover overheads and profit. The remainder would go to the distributor as rental for the movie. The distributor would again keep at least half the rental to cover costs and profit, leaving as little as 15 percent of the box-office receipts to be passed back to the producer to cover the costs of production. Of the average 1930s seat price of 25 cents, a mere three or four cents would go to the producer, to pay off the costs of producing an item which might well have cost three quarters of a million dollars to produce.

Although the dollar sums involved have increased exponentially since then, with individual movies in the early 1990s occasionally budgeted at over $50 million, the split of the box-office dollar remains about the same.[29]

The size of the audience for the most successful movies has also, surprisingly, changed relatively little. In 1941, sixteen million people in the United States saw *Sergeant York*, the most successful movie of that year. In 1988, *Who Framed Roger Rabbit* drew an American audience of nineteen million, although it took nearly twenty times as much money at the box-office.[30] The great difference between the two periods has been that since 1970, attendance and profit have been concentrated on a relatively small number of **blockbuster** movies. In the studio period, far many more movies made profits, but on a relatively modest scale. The studio system allowed the production industry to spread the economic risks of production across several movies, with the intention of maintaining a constant level of income to finance its flow of product, with the income from one production financing the next. Distributors and exhibitors also needed a steady supply of product to keep audiences coming to the theater, and exhibitors worked hard to establish a sense of stability and continuity in supplying a standardized entertainment package to their audience. The exhibitor's concern was to promote the habit of moviegoing, and it was the maintenance of that habit, rather than the profitability of any individual movie, that was economically most important to the industry. Under these circumstances, it made little economic sense for any of the parties in production, distribution, or exhibition to buy or sell each movie as an individual item.

After divorcement, the logic of movie production changed, encouraging companies to concentrate on more lavish and spectacular features that would play for longer runs at higher ticket prices, and earn bigger grosses. The commercial success of CinemaScope pictures in the early 1950s confirmed the belief that big-budget movies were more profitable than smaller productions, particularly as far as distributors were concerned. Inevitably, this strategy led to profits being concentrated in fewer movies, as what became known as the "blockbuster phenomenon" developed. Before 1960, only 20 movies had grossed over $10 million in the domestic market; by 1970, more than 80 had.[31] For the successful, the profits were enormous, far greater than those made under the old studio system. In 1965, *The Sound of Music*, which was made for $8 million, earned $72 million in the US and Canada alone. Three quarters of the movies released, however, failed to recoup their costs at the box-office.

Attempts to repeat the phenomenon of *The Sound of Music* led to a number of very costly mistakes and a cycle of overproduction that nearly bankrupted several of the major companies. In the early 1960s Hollywood's feature film output had dropped to about 130 a year; in 1969, it rose to 225, and the major companies registered corporate losses of $200 million. Between 1969 and 1971 the industry was plunged into a financial crisis that suggested that it had lost the ability to predict what its audience wanted to see, but in fact had more to do with the industry simply spending too much money on production to make profits. By 1975, the level of production had fallen back to around 120 movies a year, but the successes of such movies as *The Godfather* (1972), *The Poseidon Adventure* (1972), and

Jaws (1975) confirmed the blockbuster principle by which the industry's profits were concentrated into a handful of enormously successful movies in each production season.[32] In 1977, for instance, the top six movies in the North American market earned one third of the total rental received by distributors. To an even greater extent than was the case in the studio system, figures such as these appear to make the movie business an immensely risky one. For production executives it is. In the 1980s, Twentieth Century-Fox and Columbia each had five different studio heads.

In the late 1960s many of the majors merged with, or were taken over by, large corporations with diverse interests. This was only the first stage of a gradual reorientation in which film production and distribution companies have become components in multimedia conglomerates geared to the marketing of a product across a number of interlocking media. The blockbuster evolved into the **event movie**: *Star Wars*, for example, became the highest-grossing movie of all time in 1977, taking in over $500 million at the box-office, but the income from sales of ancillary goods – toys, games, books, clothing, bubblegum – far exceeded its box-office takings, as well as extending the life of the product and thus guaranteeing the success of its sequels. In the early 1980s, world-wide sales of *Star Wars* goods were estimated to be worth $1.5 billion a year, while *Batman* (1989) made $1 billion from merchandising, four times its box-office earnings. *Jurassic Park* (1993) went so far as to advertise its own merchandising within the movie: at one point, the camera tracks past the Jurassic Park gift shop, showing a line of T-shirts, lunch boxes, and other souvenirs identical to the ones available for purchase in the lobby of the theater.

As well as stimulating this cross-marketing, the event movie is a product designed to maximize audience attendance by drawing in not only the regular 14-to-25-year-old audience, but also that section of the audience who attend the cinema two or three times a year, often as a family, at Christmas and summer holidays. This sales strategy requires a different form of distribution. A Classical Hollywood movie was released in a slow manner, playing to each tier of the exhibition sector in sequence, so that it might take as long as two years to work through a complete exhibition cycle from first-run to the lowest neighborhood theater. Big-budget event movies have to offset their costs much faster than that, and their use of television advertising has also encouraged saturation-booking, in which a movie is simultaneously released to theaters all over the United States. When this strategy was first used for *Jaws* in 1975, the movie opened in 464 theaters.[33] By 1990, it was not uncommon for a movie to be saturation-booked in 2,000 theaters, a practice that of course necessitated 2,000 prints of the movie to be struck, perhaps ten times more than might have been made of a movie released in 1940. From the mid-1980s, the growth of additional markets in video sales and pay-TV added a new life to both old and new movies. The earnings from these additional "profit centers" affected the structure of production in two ways. They forced companies to diversify into other businesses, from publishing to bottling Coca-Cola, since the profits from "supergrossers" like *Close Encounters of the Third Kind* (1977) or *E.T.* (1982) were larger than could sensibly be invested in servicing the limited demand for movies. They also affected the nature of the movie product: how well a movie could service ancillary markets became an increasingly important question as budgets escalated during the 1980s. Sequels, which were even more effectively "pre-sold" than adaptations of successful stage plays or novels, accounted for 10 percent of Hollywood's output.

Although divorcement had forced the majors to cut their direct ties with theatrical exhibition, they continued to be heavily involved in these other ways of circulating their product, through video, cable television, and associated merchandising of an expanding range of "software," from books-of-the-film and soundtrack CDs to toys and computer games. In the early 1980s, saturation-booking notwithstanding, the economic logic that emerged from this diversification downplayed the importance of cinema exhibition as a whole. Rather, a conglomerate such as Warner Communications Inc. (WCI) saw its goal as being to "bring movies conveniently and economically into the home," so that it can "reach the enormous market that rarely, if ever, attends movie theaters."[34] Along with Gulf and Western (Paramount), Disney and MCA (Universal), WCI dominated production and distribution during the 1980s. All four companies were diversified operations with interests in related businesses in publishing and music, but they shed most of their operations that were less connected to software distribution. A second tier of companies, with fluctuating shares of the market, were similarly connected to ancillary markets: MGM/UA, Columbia (owned for most of the decade by Coca-Cola), and Twentieth Century-Fox. Although the ownership, management, and profitability of these seven companies changed quite frequently during the decade, their common underlying strategy of diversification combined with multimedia distribution of software was firmly established. On a tier down the production hierarchy were the mini-majors, companies such as Orion, Cannon, and Dino De Laurentis, financing movies by pre-selling their distribution rights before production began. These companies flourished in the mid-1980s, then overexpanded through diversification and an excess of product. Cannon collapsed in 1986, De Laurentis in 1988, and Orion in 1992. Servicing the low-budget sectors of the market were the descendants of Poverty Row companies, including American International Pictures, Crown International, and New Line.[35]

In the latter half of the decade, encouraged by the Reagan administration's relaxed attitude to business regulation, several of the majors returned to theatrical exhibition, buying up some of the larger national theater chains. Although first-run theatrical release continues to be the vital evidence of product quality that will attract the interest of later "distribution windows,"[36] the distributors' return to ownership in the exhibition sector was not an attempt to recreate the vertical integration of Classical Hollywood. Rather, they were simply securing an additional element in a new strategy of what Wall Street analyst Harold Vogel has called "entertainment industry consolidation."[37] By the end of the decade, theatrical release accounted for only 30 percent of the studios' total receipts, while ancillary markets made up the other 70 percent. *Batman*, released in 1989, earned $250 million in the first five months of its theatrical release. When Warners released it on video, it earned another $400 million.[38] Expanding exponentially in the late 1980s, the second-run video market also provided a financial cushion for movies that failed at the theatrical box-office: the science fiction adventure *Willow*, produced by George Lucas in 1988, cost $55 million and grossed only $28 million in American theaters. But it earned an additional $18 million in video sales, and $15 million in television sales. Combined with its foreign earnings of $42 million in theaters and $22 million in video and television sales, its earnings from ancillary markets ensured its profitability.[39] Such profits fueled the continuing increase in production costs and budgets. During the second half of the 1980s, and allowing for inflation, the average Hollywood budget rose by 40 percent. In 1990, a major movie might be budgeted at $25 million, with additional marketing and distribution costs of $20 million. With overheads and interest charges, the studio that financed it would have to recoup more than $50 million to break even. Such budgets reflected the doubling of the total world market between 1984 and 1989, an expansion primarily brought about by the development of video as an additional system of release. But these extravagant budgets were also part of a cyclical economic pattern that has affected the film industry since the early 1960s, in which a number of spectacular successes push production costs to new heights until overproduction results in a sharp downturn in profits. Because its effect is concentrated on so few products, what is in effect a stabilization of the market appears to be the catastrophic failure of one or two movies: *Cleopatra* in 1963 and *Heaven's Gate* in 1980 are perhaps the two most notable examples.

Although the economic changes following the Paramount decision had substantial effects on the kinds of movie produced in Hollywood as well as the circumstances of their production, the system's consistencies are to be found in more than just the familiar names of the companies. Re-establishing something not unlike the previous oligopoly, the industry has stabilized its production and distribution system in alliance with the producers of associated "software" and the "hardware" manufacturers such as Sony, which bought Columbia in 1989 in order to be able to market a software library alongside its own new equipment. The same year also saw the creation of the world's largest media conglomerate, Time Warner Inc., through a merger of Warner Communications with Time Inc., which owned Home Box Office, the largest pay cable television service in the United States. The *Wall Street Journal* predicted that the end of the century would see the industry dominated by a few giant concerns, each "controlling a vast empire of media and entertainment properties that amounts to a global distribution system for advertising and promotion dollars."[40]

Nevertheless, the identity of that future industry is likely to remain "Hollywood." As one executive observed in 1983, "When television started in the 1950s, there was a strong view that that was the end of Hollywood. When cable came, we thought that would kill our sales to the networks. None of these things happened. Every time the market expands, the combination is greater than before. After all, it should be immaterial to Hollywood how people see its product so long as they pay."[41]

The Studio System

God has always smiled on Southern California; a special halo has always encircled this island on the land. Consider, for example, the extraordinary good luck in having the motion-picture industry concentrated in Los Angeles. The leading industry in Los Angeles from 1920 to 1940, motion pictures were made to fit the economic requirements and physical limitations of the region like a glove. Here was one industry, perhaps the only one in America, that required no raw materials, for which discriminatory freight rates were meaningless, and which, at the same time, possessed an enormous payroll. Employing from thirty to forty thousand workers, the industry in 1939 spent about $190,000,000 in the manufacture of films and of this total $89,884,841 was spent in salaries, $41,096,226, wages, and only $31,118,277 was spent on such items as film, fuel and energy, and miscellaneous items. . . . Like the region itself, this key industry is premised upon improvisation, a matter of make-believe, a synthesis of air and wind and water. . . . What could be more desirable than a monopolistic non-seasonal industry with 50,000,000 customers, an industry without soot or grime, without blast furnaces or dynamos, an industry whose production shows peaks but few valleys?

Carey McWilliams[42]

In marked contrast to the central position that movie production is accorded in popular memory and critical studies alike, an economic analysis downgrades it to a subsidiary role in the American film industry. That analysis explains the way that production was organized into the studio system. For a major company, committed to the distribution of a full range of product, the studio system provided economically the most rational way to provide the regulated stability of production and the economies of scale required by any major manufacturing operation – the means by which Harry Cohn could spit a movie out onto Gower Street every week.[43] Despite this level of regulation, one of the motion picture industry's favorite myths about itself is that it is always in crisis. Leo Rosten observed in 1941 that:

There are few places in our economy where fluctuations in earnings and security can be as violent and unpredictable as they are in Hollywood. . . . "You're only as good as your last picture" is a by-word in the movie colony . . . This is scarcely a climate conducive to psychological serenity or efficient digestion. . . . The movie colony gets a curious satisfaction out of drumming these facts home – to itself.[44]

In part this melodramatic view of Hollywood production as a quixotic and unstable business resulted from thinking only about individual productions, individual careers, and the amount that needed to be invested in each movie without any guarantee that it would produce a commensurate return. Compared with other industries, the motion picture business turned out few products, even in the studio period. The individual Hollywood product was extremely expensive, and carried a much larger share of the company's financial well-being than, say, an individual automobile did for General Motors. Moreover, the success or failure of these products was firmly attached to the popularity of individual personalities. As the number of movies being made fell after 1960, the sense of risk attached to each production, and each production decision, increased.

This vision of the riskiness of film production is substantially mitigated if the concerns of the industry as a whole are taken into account. Under the studio system, Hollywood sustained a level of production sufficient to supply the level of demand in the existing market, but to some extent the executives who ran the major companies from New York regarded production as an inconvenient necessity, at best only marginally profitable. It was expected that nine Hollywood-produced movies out of ten would turn a profit, but only a small one, while the larger profits were gathered in distribution and first-run exhibition. Although primarily designed to maximize the profitability of the whole industry, the studio system ensured that production itself was a very high-cost activity, not simply because "money on the screen" was assumed to be a necessary part of the entertainment package, but also because high entry costs, together with the general impression of instability and crisis, deterred any potential competitors.[45]

An incidental advantage of the high cost of production was that it allowed a proportion of the profits to be diverted away from the investors and shareholders toward the individual talents responsible for production, through the high salaries paid to stars, production heads, and successful writers and directors. Twentieth Century-Fox argued that since Shirley Temple earned the company something over $20 million in the 1930s, it was not unreasonable to pay her $5,000 a week. In the 1930s and 1940s half the cost of film production was spent on salaries, setting standards of pay and conditions that potential competitors would find hard to match, and thus helping to preserve the monopoly of the major companies. The highest salaries, however, went not to stars but to studio executives. In 1938, at least 217 people in the movie business were paid an annual salary of more than $75,000, and of the nation's 25 highest salaries, 19 of them went to people employed in the film industry, including the highest, of $1.2 million, paid out to Louis B. Mayer, head of MGM. Only the cement manufacturing industry spent a higher percentage of its annual volume of business on executive salaries than the movie business.[46]

In 1932, *Fortune* magazine described the MGM studios in Culver City as presenting:

> the appearance less of a factory than of a demented university with a campus made out of beaverboard and canvas. It contains twenty-two sound stages, a park that can be photographed as anything from a football field to the gardens at Versailles, $2,000,000 worth of antique furniture, a greenhouse consecrated to the raising of ferns, twenty-two projection rooms, a commissary where $6,000-a-week actors can lunch on Long Island oysters for fifty cents, and a Polish immigrant who sometimes makes $500,000 a year and once spent the weekend with the Hoovers at the White House.[47]

In this environment, frequently described by visiting writers as somewhere between the chaotic and the surreal, MGM produced between 40 and 50 pictures a year, and the other studios did the same. Each studio was presided over by two executives, the head of the studio and the head of production. The exact distance between these two roles was never absolute, and no two studios were completely alike in their practice. At Twentieth Century-Fox, for instance, the two roles were combined in the single figure of Darryl Zanuck. Along with Zanuck, the most stable management teams were at MGM and Warner Bros., and these two companies are the most frequently cited models, if only because Louis B. Mayer and Jack Warner were the most notorious studio executives. It was these figures that Leo Rosten was referring to when he observed that

> each studio has a personality; each studio's product shows special emphases and values. And in the final analysis, the sum total of a studio's personality, the aggregate pattern of its choices and its tastes, may be traced to its producers. For it is the producers who establish the preferences, the prejudices, and the predispositions of the organization, and, therefore, of the movies which it turns out.[48]

There was a much greater consistency of studio style in the product of those studios that had single heads of production for long periods than is evident in the output of studios like RKO and Paramount, which regularly changed their studio heads after bouts of political infighting. Darryl Zanuck, who was head of production at Twentieth Century-Fox from 1935 until 1956, and the company's president from 1962 to 1971, was one of the most influential figures in the history of Hollywood production, but as yet little critical attention has been paid to him.

One reason why Hollywood has not been taken seriously has lain in the assumption that "the fourth largest industry in America" was run by buffoons. There has never been any shortage of anecdotes caricaturing the studio heads as philistines or philanderers. Mayer, it is said, looked on all

Louis B. Mayer, MGM studio head, 1925. Courtesy Kobal

his stars as his children, wanted them to bring their problems to him, and, notoriously, cried on cue if they ever became recalcitrant over the details of their contracts or the parts he chose for them. After a visit to Fascist Italy in the early 1930s, Harry Cohn, whose nicknames included "His Crudeness," had his office at Columbia redecorated to look like Benito Mussolini's. Sam Goldwyn's abuses of the language were renowned, even if most of them were invented by writers. There was an apparently endless supply of stories about producers. Leo Rosten recalled

the producer to whom a writer, in telling a story, used the word "frustrated." The producer requested an explanation, and the writer resorted to this analogy: "Take a book-keeper, a little man earning twenty-five bucks a week. He dreams of getting a big, beautiful boat and sailing to the South Seas. But he can't fulfill his dreams – so he's frustrated." To which the producer cried: "I like that! Put a boat in the picture."[49]

Lurking not far below the surface of such caricatures was both a class prejudice against the movie audience and a racism that drew exaggerated attention to the number of first- or second-generation Jewish immigrants involved in the industry. Although several convincing explanations have been offered as to why entertainment industries might have proved particularly attractive to Jewish immigrant entrepreneurs, the extent of Jewish "domination" of the motion picture industry has always been exaggerated through cults of personality, whether in a positive or a negative manner.[50] Zanuck, for instance, was born in Wahoo, Nebraska, the child of a Swiss Methodist and a third-generation American of English stock, but he was frequently identified as Jewish. The mythologizing of the Hollywood moguls, whether as vulgar alien immigrants unable to master the language or as creators of "an empire of their own," has consistently tended to obscure their abilities as entrepreneurs and businessmen.[51]

The movie "moguls" have been poorly treated by movie critics and historians in the past, and often dismissed by melodramatic criticism of a melodramatic industry as little more than bullying philistines. Epitomizing all that is wrong with Hollywood to a criticism that seeks to divorce art from economics, they have come to represent the most tangible proof of all that movies are not really worthy of critical attention. They were, however, the men who decided which movies did and did not get made, and made innumerable decisions about those that did. Against the caricatures we might cite Jesse Lasky's paean of self-praise as being no less accurate:

> The producer must be a prophet and a general, a diplomat and a peace-maker, a miser and a spendthrift. He must have vision tempered by hindsight, daring governed by caution, the patience of a saint and the iron of a Cromwell . . . his decisions must be sure, swift, and immediate, as well as subject to change, because conditions change continuously in the motion picture industry. . . . The producer's resources must be such that no contingency can stop him from finding [a] star, soothing the director like a super-Talleyrand, or, in all-night conferences in shirt sleeves and heavy cigar smoke, "doctoring the scripts by his own creative power." . . . In his hands lies the supervision of every element that goes to make up the finished product. These elements are both tangible and intangible, the control of human beings and real properties as well as the control of the artistic temperament, the shaping of creative forces and the knowledge of the public needs for entertainment.[52]

The division of responsibility between the studio head and the head of production varied: both Mayer and Jack Warner, for instance, were quite heavily involved in, respectively, Republican and Democratic party politics in California, and much less involved in day-to-day production decisions than Zanuck. The studio head was, however, the conduit for communication between the studio and the New York offices of the studio's parent distribution and exhibition company. It was in New York that the basic decisions about a studio's production were made: how many movies to produce in a season, and at what budget; what their release schedule was to be. The job of the studio head was then to ensure the delivery of movies according to that budget and schedule. He was likely to approve the initial idea for the project, assign writers and director, approve the approximate budget, and supervise casting and the hiring of other personnel. He might also approve the final version of the script and check the movie's progress through production by viewing **rushes** (the first printing from the day's exposed negative stock) and supervising the final stages of editing, although many of these tasks might be left to the head of production.

One of the best accounts of a head of production's activities is F. Scott Fitzgerald's description of Monroe Stahr's work in *The Last Tycoon*.[53] Fitzgerald clearly modeled Stahr on Irving Thalberg, head of production at MGM during the early 1930s, and saw the heads of production, the "half a dozen men" who were "able to keep the whole equation of pictures in their heads," as the real "stars" of Hollywood.[54] Less enthusiastically, director Frank Capra complained in 1939 that "about six producers today pass upon ninety percent of the scripts and cut and edit about ninety percent of the pictures."[55]

At the executive level below the head of production were line producers, who were almost as frequently disparaged as the moguls themselves. Several Hollywood adages emphasized the executives' nepotism in such observations as "the son-in-law also rises," and Ogden Nash's epithet that

> Carl Laemmle
> has a very big family.

Sons-in-law and "Uncle Carl's" relations were most likely to rise to the rank of producer, and hence attract the vitriol of writers and directors about "front-office interference." In 1938, the Screen Directors Guild, struggling both for union recognition by the studios and for the establishment of minimum working conditions, argued for a change in the existing system of production to eliminate "the involved, complicated, and expensive system of supervision which separates the director and writer from the responsible executive producers." Directors were not questioning the need for executive supervision, they declared, nor were they telling the producing companies how to run their businesses. They did not condemn all producers, only those who "have little respect for the medium, less respect for their audiences and excuse their lack of imagination by ridiculing it in others." These they described as "the army of the inept, who have been promoted to positions of authority for which they are unqualified, inexperienced, and utterly lacking in creative ability."[56] This perspective is the one most often echoed in critical arguments that assign creativity to individual talents and crass commercialism to "the system."

But however vociferously writers or directors complained, and whatever they subsequently told their interviewers or ghost-writers about the crass philistinism of their producers, it was the position to which many of them aspired, since the producer oversaw and controlled the whole production, integrating the contributions of other personnel and balancing creative and financial considerations.[57] What the directors and others who complained were objecting to was the adaptation to Hollywood of a

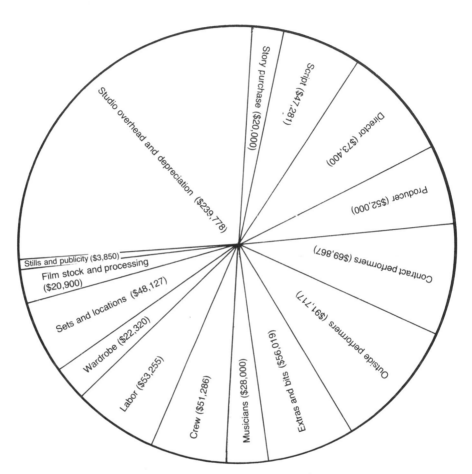

Casablanca's budget

At just under $900,000, *Casablanca*'s budget was typical for an A-feature in 1942, although it might have cost as much as $1,400,000 if it had been made at MGM instead of the notoriously frugal Warner Bros. *Casablanca*'s director, Michael Curtiz, was paid over twice as much as any of the movie's stars, and the studio spent more on outside talent hired at weekly rates just for the movie than it did on the salaries of its contract players. Salaries made up 85 percent of the movie's direct costs, with performers' salaries accounting for less than half of that. Much of the cost of set construction, props, costume, and the like were absorbed in the 35 percent charge attached to the budget for the overheads in running the studio.

Source: adapted from Rudy Behlmer, ed., *Inside Warner Bros (1935–1951)*, London, Weidenfeld and Nicolson, 1986

decentralized management system first introduced in American industry by General Motors in the 1920s, and itself evidence of the studios' assertion of their existence as industry rather than art form.[58] The head of production would assign a producer to each movie, and the producer then supervised the processes of writing, shooting, and editing. The major studios each had a staff of about ten "line producers," each responsible for six or eight productions a year. A producer would be working on three or four movies, in different stages of production, at a time. Since the producer was more closely involved in the production of a movie at all its stages, he or she (usually he – no more than a handful of women producers or directors worked in Hollywood studios) was in a position to exercise more control over the development of a movie's story, its script and editing than any other individual, although whether he or she either chose to exercise that control or was effective at doing so was another matter. The job involved balancing and integrating creative and financial considerations. Producers might or might not be good at what they did, and that consideration might or might not be related to how actively they were involved in productions.

Directors had a more circumscribed role in the studio system than critical theories of directorial authorship would imply. Frank Capra, then president of the Screen Directors Guild, observed in 1939 that "there are only half a dozen directors in Hollywood who are allowed to shoot as they please and who have any supervision over their editing." Within the studio system a director was not necessarily involved in either the writing or the editing of the movie, and it was quite normal practice for him or her to be given a script only a few days before he or she was due to start shooting. Since economic determinants in production included shooting out of sequence, it was perhaps not surprising that Capra went on to suggest "that 80 per cent of the directors today shoot scenes exactly as they are told to shoot them without any changes whatsoever, and that 90 per cent of them have no voice in the story or in the editing."[59] Although it was rare for a movie to have as many directors as the six or more who worked on *Gone with the Wind* (1939), it was common for action sequences to be shot by a second unit, and quite normal for additional scenes or retakes to be directed by other people. A director, however, might reasonably expect to have some influence over at least the final stages of writing and the early stages of editing. His or her main job was to translate the script into a movie, and he or she was in effective control of the project while it was shooting. A director, according to George Cukor, "should shoot the scene before the producer sees it." Producer David O. Selznick's insistence on dictating the spatial organization of each scene in *Gone with the Wind* was one of the factors that led Cukor to withdraw from the production.[60] The justification for claims of directorial authorship in Hollywood stem from the director's supervisory control of the movie's visual appearance and its performances. As we have suggested, however, many of Hollywood's industrial practices qualified the extent to which this control was exercised: producer–director and even producer–director–writer teams were quite common features of Hollywood's collaborative processes.

The influence of the writer on the final product was at least as circumscribed as that of the director. It was normal studio practice to employ several writers on a given movie, often working independently of each other at the same time. Writers were seen as technical staff, many of them employed for particular specialist skills. A writer's contribution to a script might, for instance, be limited to structuring a sub-plot or adding half a dozen gag lines. To an extent the studios traded in literary reputations, employing the likes of William Faulkner or Aldous Huxley for the cachet their names added to a movie as a production value rather than for their literary expertise. Many novelists found the experience of working in Hollywood intensely unsatisfying, in large part because of the industrial constraints of scriptwriting. Unlike a novel, a movie script is an incomplete form, merely an outline of dialogue and action. Given the multiplicity of hands through which it passes before production, it is seldom likely to be entirely the work of a single individual or the expression of a single personality – and as Joe Gillis (William Holden), the cynical scriptwriter in *Sunset Boulevard* (1950), observes, "people don't know that someone actually *writes* the picture. They think the actors make it up as they go along." The discipline of writing for the movies may have been as unattractive to many novelists as the banality of the work they were often required to produce.[61] Critics have often cited F. Scott Fitzgerald as the most prominent example of a major literary talent destroyed by Hollywood. But Fitzgerald's own accounts were much more sympathetic to the industrial system that employed him mainly to inject a few lines of classy dialogue into scripts on which his name never appeared.[62] Many of the most successful Hollywood screenwriters, including Ben Hecht, Charles MacArthur, and Jules Furthman, had been journalists, a profession in which their writing was also liable to be reworked by others.

More minor influential roles in production were occupied by figures whose work was limited to a particular aspect of the movie. The director of photography was responsible for lighting the set, and possibly camera placement if the director he or she was working with was primarily concerned with securing the actors' performances. Directors of photography were rarely engaged on a movie for any longer than the period of shooting. The art director was most involved at the pre-production stage, designing sets and supervising their construction.[63] Like other creative personnel, they were normally employed on long-term contracts, and this might give them the opportunity to exert an influence on the studio's house style. Editing was the only area of production other than writing in which there were more than a handful of women employed. The work of the editor was perhaps the most self-effacing in the studio system, because Hollywood's aesthetics chose not to draw attention to editing procedures, and movies were in the main edited according to a fairly inflexible set of conventions,

One of MGM's editing suites in the early 1930s. Editing was one of the few areas of production in which women were likely to be employed in the studio system. Courtesy BFI

which are discussed in more detail in chapter 5. Working largely independently of the other production personnel, the editor began assembling the movie from the daily rushes, producing an initial **rough cut** shortly after the shooting stopped. This rough cut was then refined under the supervision of the producer and sometimes the director, until a final version received the approval of the head of production. Music was usually added at a late stage in the editing, with the composer producing pieces of background music to timed sequences; the movie was seldom edited to fit musical scores that were already fully formed.

Apart from stars and supporting actors, production involved a much larger group of personnel in skilled labor. Camera, sound, and lighting "crews," electricians, carpenters, set decorators, makeup artists, hairdressers, wardrobe mistresses, continuity people, propmen, stand-ins, stunt men, and extras all exerted very little direct influence over the movie's finished form. Like the doctors, secretaries, dialogue coaches, caterers, transportation staff, and auditors, not to mention the staffs of the laboratories, these people all came under the general control of the production manager and the assistant directors who organized the logistics of production.

Crew on a sound stage. Courtesy Kobal

The Star System

Hollywood did not require its audience to possess a knowledge of its industrial processes in order to enjoy or understand its products. All its viewers, however, were familiar with the stars, whose public lives provided a glimpse into the melodramatic world of the dream factory. As well as being the most visible part of the industry, the star system was central to the standardization of movie product, and to its interrelations with other consumption industries and advertising. Under the studio system, stars had only a limited amount of power, in no way commensurate with their power to attract audiences at the box-office. Most stars were employed on long, fixed-term contracts with a single studio, and had relatively little control over the roles they were cast in or the movies they made. If they refused a part, their contract might be suspended without pay as punishment.[64] Once chosen for a part, however, they could exert some influence over their characterization, and hence over the whole structure of the movies in which they appeared. With the decline of the studio system, the power of the star was enhanced. Stars like Clint Eastwood and

Robert De Niro set up their own production companies (Malpaso, Tribecca), using their economic power to control the movies they appeared in, often producing and sometimes directing them themselves.

The real influence of the stars lay not with their employers, but with the paying public. Far more than the type of movie, stars were the commodities that most consistently drew audiences to the movies. A "star vehicle," a movie constructed around the appeal of one or more particular stars and sold on that basis, was bound to have a set of conventional ingredients, much like a genre. An Elvis Presley movie, for instance, offered its star several opportunities to sing, a number of girls for him to choose his romantic partner from, and a plot in which he would be misunderstood by older characters. The repetition of these standard ingredients created an audience expectation of these elements. Similarly, a star's repetition of performance elements over a number of movies would lead to the consolidation of that performance as a set of gestures and behavior patterns recognizable to the audience, who could then predict what the star was likely to do in any movie he or she appeared in. The studio system was committed to the deliberate manufacture of stars as a mechanism for selling movie tickets, and as a result generated publicity around the stars' offscreen lives designed to complement and play upon their screen images. The publicity machine at its height assumed almost the status of a peripheral industry in its own right. There were about 20 fan magazines in the United States in the late 1930s, with circulations between 200,000 and one million. *Photoplay, Modern Screen*, and *Shadowland* regularly reached the most devoted quarter of the weekly movie audience. "Gossip" was a requirement of the industry and seemed to circulate around it with an almost material force at times. Many stars and studio heads fervently believed that the main gossip columnists exercised very real power over public taste and opinion, and therefore had to be courted and feted at every possible opportunity.

The publicity surrounding the star system – which was a central part of its operation – worked to tell its audience that stars were basically like them. When the male star of *The Hurricane* (1937), Jon Hall, was sent on a publicity tour of the United States, his publicity agent made a point of telling his interviewers that Hall only owned one suit. He was presented as "just a typical American boy who happens to be working for his living in pictures instead of hardware."[65] As the boy next door, his persona imitated James Stewart's. Stewart's promotional publicity in the late 1930s featured remarks "overheard in the lobby," including: "He's a real American type, the kind I'd like to have around the house"; and "Reminds me of how my Frankie makes love, so modest like."[66] Margaret Thorp also noted of female stars that:

> If she is individual the admired star need not be extravagantly beautiful. The ranking box-office favorites must be good to look at certainly but they are not required to be creatures of classic perfection. In many ways it is an advantage

for a star not to be too beautiful. She stands then closer to the average and that is what the fans want, an ideal they can emulate, a creature not too bright and good, one whose heights they might actually scale themselves, given a little energy and a little luck. That is Janet Gaynor's great appeal: her home-town personality, the little blonde from the typewriter or the kitchen or the ribbon counter who has exchanged her imitation lapin coat for sables, her hall bedroom for a Beverly Hills villa, her Woolworth jewelry for real diamonds. The glamorous star today [1939] is as natural as possible. She does not pluck her eyebrows and paint in new ones; she develops the natural line. She does not tint her hair to exotic hues. She does not try to be a fairy-tale princess but an average American girl raised to the nth power. "Vivid" is the adjective she works for hardest.[67]

Thorp's idea of the average "raised to the nth power" was intricately interwoven with the "escapism" we have already discussed. At the height of its operation, the star system provided an ideal version of the self for every member of the audience, with sufficient variations among types for considerable nuance in the individual viewer's choice. Tyrone Power was like Robert Taylor, for instance – he was, in fact, Twentieth Century-Fox's version of MGM's Robert Taylor. The choice between Ronald Colman, Brian Aherne, and David Niven, or between Rock Hudson and John Gavin, was similarly a consumer choice among different but comparable branded goods. A superficially cynical, but perhaps more accurately a simple in-dustrial, description of the operation of studio publicity in this way was revealed by Leo Rosten, who charted all the romantic attachments of Tyrone Power during the production season 1937–8,[68] when the gossip columns and fan magazines solemnly reported him to be enamored of Loretta Young, Sonja Henie, Janet Gaynor, Simone Simon, and Arleen Whelan:

> Scarcely a week went by without hints of the infatuation existing between the versatile Mr Power and one or another of these charming maidens, each of whom, during this fecund period, was also reported to be profoundly jealous of at least two of the others. Wonderful to relate, it turns out that Mr Power and the Misses Young, Henie, Gaynor, Simon, and Whelan were all employees of the same ingenious studio, Twentieth Century-Fox!

Tracing the sentimental attachments of each of Power's paramours, Rosten further discovered that all of them had been romantically linked to Cesar Romero, four to Richard Green, and two to Michael Brooke, who were also all employees of the same studio. And a similar exercise conducted on Warner Bros. star George Brent produced the same result: his affections were shared among three of Warners' leading ladies, except for a brief involvement with Fox's Loretta Young while he was on loan to that studio for an appearance in *The Rains Came* (1939).

> The moral to be drawn from this whole quaint analysis is simple: the ro-mances, scandals, and inter-personal complications of Hollywood often in-

volve *the same individuals* week in and week out; and this leads to a somewhat lopsided impression of love and heartbreak in Hollywood. All is not true that appears in the gossip columns – to put it charitably.[69]

Nevertheless, it was important to the functioning of the star system that these archetypes were also connected to the audience's world. Fan magazines regularly ran articles such as "Who is Your Husband's Favorite Actress? And What Are You Going to Do About It?", which featured such advice as: "Many a quiet, stay-at-home man goes crazy over Harlow. If your husband comes out of the theater raving about Jean's radiant loveliness and bare shoulders, you should do something about it. And you had better not waste much time."[70] More pointedly, Margaret Thorp observed:

There is social and psychological significance in the fact that 70 per cent of Gary Cooper's fan mail comes from women who write that their husbands do not appreciate them. Their ideal is still the ideal husband of the Victorian era who told his wife at breakfast each morning how much she meant to him, but that husband is not a type which the post-war American man has any interest in emulating. He prefers to conceal his deeper emotions at breakfast, and during the rest of the day as well. His wife, consequently, has to spend her afternoons at the movies.[71]

Equally important, however, was the other half of the paradox, by which fans were discouraged from envying or emulating the stars. The fan magazines regularly ran pieces such as "So You'd Like to Be a Star" in which Myrna Loy told:

all of you little Marys and Sues and Sarahs who wish you could be movie stars, who see them through rainbow-colored glasses . . . that my work is nine parts drudgery and one part thrill and glamour. There is nothing I know of that is quite so exhausting . . . I'd give away two years of my life to be able to get together with girl friends and talk about my marriage and new house which are, naturally, the most thrilling topics in my life. If I could be the plain Myrna Williams I am at heart, instead of forever figuring out what Myrna Loy dare and dare not say, I'd talk about Arthur and our romance and marriage and new home.[72]

In the late 1930s fan magazines identified Loy as "the Movies' Model 'Mrs,'" declaring that offscreen and on, she had "established a reputation as the perfect wife" to Leslie Howard, William Powell, Clark Gable, and Warner Baxter in performance, and to producer Arthur Hornblow Jr in "real life." In one piece of studio publicity, she explained that she had acquired her philosophy for marital conduct from the roles she played: "mystery, Myrna insists, is the greatest weapon woman has in the love game. Men enjoy the chase. They are apt to weary when they have achieved their capture. The wise wife, therefore, does not allow romance to degenerate into familiarity."[73] In 1942, Loy featured in an article on "Why the Perfect Wife's Marriage Failed: These are things Myrna Loy might have told you about her breakup with Arthur Hornblow Jr. They are things that make you wonder if romance is, after all, the right basis for marriage."[74] Through this paradoxical representation of stars as characters to be envied and not envied, imitated and not imitated, the fan magazines sustained a discourse on romance, marriage, and sexuality, as well as a subsidiary industry of advertising through star endorsements. This discourse ran alongside the movies themselves.

The star system provided one of the principal means by which Hollywood offered audiences guarantees of predictability, while the plots within which the star persona was embedded offered a balancing experience of novelty. The audience's recognition of a star, in both the movie and its publicity, led viewers to expect a certain kind of performance, and as a result a certain kind of experience. Movie posters would typically create expectations about the kinds of performance that the star might offer, often literally foregrounding the star's image against a background of scenes from the movie. When an advert promised that in *Dark Victory* (1939), "Bette Davis brings you her Crowning Triumph," audiences could anticipate the known qualities of a Davis performance (one British fan described her as being "adept at mannerisms . . . clipped phrases and highly dramatic movements"), organized within the novelty of an unfamiliar story.[75] This kind of advertising established the star's performance as a separable element of the movie's aggregate package of potential pleasures, one that the audience could enjoy as a production value independently of the rest of the movie.

While audiences may have thought of individual stars as talented actors, idealized versions of the boy or girl next door, or creatures of fantasy, distribution executives saw commodities: the market would bear two or three vehicles for each major star every year, and exhibitors would often buy product in advance on the strength of no more information than the star's name. For instance, to Twentieth Century-Fox a "Betty Grable" was a musical starring the actress, who probably earned more money for her studio than any other female star in the Classical period. To the other companies, a "Betty Grable" was a product to be acquired or simulated – by Betty Hutton, Esther Williams, or Rita Hayworth. Frank McConnell suggests that the star vehicle existed to display "its leading players in as many of their famous postures as possible."[76] It provided its viewers with the familiarity of recognition when they were offered "Mr and Mrs Miniver . . . together again! Greer Garson and Walter Pidgeon give their best performance in their best picture, *Madame Curie*" (1943).[77]

Since stars were themselves examples of the principles of interchangeability, minor variation, and market placement that underlay the consumer industries of fashion and cosmetics, it was appropriate that their commercial function was not restricted simply to selling the movies in which they appeared. From very early on in its history, Hollywood recognized and accepted its role as a powerful sales agent for what advertising counselor Christine Frederick called "consumptionism."[78] In the late 1910s Cecil B.

DeMille responded to pressure from his company's sales department for "modern photoplays" like *Why Change Your Wife?*, displaying the latest styles in fashions and home decor. Stars became, as Irving Thalberg put it, "examples of style," conscious experimenters with roles, identities, and appearances, using their bodies as the sites of their experiments. They were to a large extent interchangeable: speaking in 1929, Thalberg commented that "it is no accident that Clara Bow with her representation of the flapper of today, is a star. If it hadn't been her, it would have been some other girl of exactly her type."[79] More fixed, perhaps, was the conception of the consumer at whom all these experiments were aimed:

> Out there, working as a clerk in a store and living in an apartment with a friend, was *one girl* – single, nineteen years old, Anglo-Saxon, somewhat favoring Janet Gaynor. The thousands of Hollywood-assisted designers, publicity men, sales heads, beauty consultants and merchandisers had internalized her so long ago that her psychic life had become their psychic life. They empathized with her shyness, her social awkwardness, her fear of offending. They understood her slight weight problem and her chagrin at being a trifle too tall. They could tell you what sort of man she hoped to marry and how she spent her leisure time.[80]

If trade followed the films, stars were its guides, coaching their fans in the use of new consumer products. Jean Harlow, for instance, advised readers of *Modern Screen* in 1933 to care for their stockings "the Hollywood way – with Lux! Never rub, never use ordinary soap or hot water. Stockings *do* look so much lovelier washed the Lux way."[81] By the 1930s Hollywood was so heavily embroiled in the promotion of fashions, furnishings, and cosmetics that it had become the biggest single influence on women's fashion throughout the world. Fans copied the dress and makeup styles of their favorite stars either from style photographs in women's magazines and Sunday supplements or from the movies themselves, where they could see "the dress in action," as one fan magazine put it. From the early 1930s, studios were also involved in publicity tie-ups with other manufacturers. MGM stars drank Coca-Cola between takes for "the pause that refreshes" in a tie-up worth $500,000 to the studio, while Warner Bros. movies featured the General Electric and General Motors products that their stars also advertised in magazines.[82] Product placement, as the practice of inserting brand-name goods into movies, has remained an established Hollywood practice: *2001* (1968) advertised a Pan Am space shuttle, *Back to the Future Part II* (1989) featured Toyotas, Texaco, Miller beer, and Nike shoes.[83]

A Star is Made

One of Hollywood's most telling characteristics is that, while appearing to draw attention to the mechanisms of its industrial processes, it masks one level of its operations by selectively highlighting another. Hollywood circulates accounts of its process of production, but these accounts obscure the profit motive that drives them by substituting a discourse on loss: "The Price They Pay for Fame," how "In Hollywood, Health, Friends, Beauty, even Life Itself, are Sacrificed on the Altar of Terrible Ambition."[84] Hollywood's most frequent version of this story is *A Star is Born*. First produced as *What Price Hollywood?* in 1932, the 1937 version was remade as a musical with Judy Garland in 1954, and again in 1976 with Barbra Streisand, when its setting was transferred to the rock music business. The 1937 version with Janet Gaynor, however, crystallizes Hollywood's self-representations, in which stardom is the central condition, the site at which ordinariness acquires charisma and acknowledges the cost of success. Its two central ingredients are the effortless chance discovery of the female star (the same thing happens in *Singin' in the Rain* (1952)) and "The Price They Pay for Fame," the dark side of this version of the American dream:

> Maybe after all it is enough – just a few short days, or years in the burning searchlight of motion picture fame. . . . Perhaps what comes after doesn't really matter. . . . Fame is the consolation prize which is given when everything else has been sacrificed. It is a killing pace, this winning and holding success on the silver screen. Not many of the glittering figures of filmland have withstood it for more than a few years. There have been far too many who have dropped by the wayside, health gone, beauty gone, money gone, youth gone before its time.[85]

The dream and the price of fame are staple features of Classical Hollywood's movies about itself, in which the function and meaning of Hollywood are mythologized as a complex relationship of desire and disavowal between the fan and her ideal. In its fictions, Hollywood peoples itself with heroes and heroines (handsome male leads, beautiful "rising" female stars), villains (tyrannical studio bosses, moneymen, jealous second-leads), and other malcontents (drunken screenwriters and aging starlets) all endlessly engaged in contests for power and celebrity, enacting the industry's myth of its constant crisis. Economic uncertainty drives the narrative, whether it tells of a young hopeful's struggles on the road to stardom or the attempted comeback of a once great director. Often the producer's last desperate gamble to prevent the imminent collapse of the whole studio gives a break to the kid who turns out to be just what the public have been waiting for. Although *Singin' in the Rain* represents a comic celebration of Hollywood, the industry's vision of itself is frequently as bleak as that of its most mordant critics. *The Big Knife* (1956) begins with a scene in which a vindictive gossip columnist threatens to destroy a star's career when he refuses to comment on the state of his marriage, and ends with the star's suicide after he refuses to be implicated in the murder of a bit player. In *Sunset Boulevard* (1950) a studio writer is murdered by a crazed silent movie goddess. *The Bad and the Beautiful* (1952) depicts the ruthless rise of an archetypal "boy genius" producer, and the refusal of those whose careers he has made to help him back to work after his precipitate fall.

While Hollywood's audiences negotiated the contradictions exposed by the fan magazines, Margaret Thorp illustrated an equally contradictory attitude within the industry toward "the Cinderella legend" of stardom. The studios, she said, published discouraging statistics about the number of people who came to Hollywood to break into the movies, and the difficulty of finding work even as a waitress.

> They explain how much difficult technique and hard training must be added to beauty and natural talent. They talk about the fearful cost. *But* – they keep on telling the Cinderella story over and over again, lovingly, in the biography of every other star. How Joan Crawford was once a shop girl; Janet Gaynor a clerk in a shoe store; James Cagney a thirteen-dollar-a-week elevator boy; Clark Gable not so many years ago an unnoticed extra; that the highest paid of scenario writers, Frances Marion, began as a twenty-five dollar-a-week stenographer. The moral is always that she stuck it out against odds; she would not be discouraged.[86]

The 1937 version of *A Star is Born* takes this contradiction to melodramatic extremes. The movie begins in a small backwoods town in North Dakota, where Esther Blodgett (Gaynor) spends her every spare moment in the movie theater, swooning over the stars and dreaming of joining them in Hollywood. Her particular favorite is Norman Maine. This fantasy life, nurtured by a constant reading of fan magazines, is ridiculed by the other members of her family. But Esther's dreams of stardom are encouraged by her grandmother (May Robson), who gives her money and puts her on the midnight train to California. Arriving in Hollywood, her first brush with stardom is far from propitious; she is silenced by a worse-for-drink Norman Maine (Frederic March) at a Hollywood Bowl concert. Later, taking a fill-in job as waitress at a party hosted by studio head Oliver Niles (Adolphe Menjou), Esther meets Maine in person. Attracted to her, Maine organizes a screen test ("she has the sincerity and honestness that makes great actresses") and she is soon contracted to Niles' studio. Scarcely has Libby (Lionel Stander) of the publicity department completed the studio "bio" that turns her into Vicki Lester, "Cinderella of the Rockies," than she gets a chance to play opposite Maine in his next picture. Hailed as an overnight success, she embarks upon a romance with her co-star. When Norman agrees to stop drinking, the couple are married and settle down in Beverly Hills. Esther's early dreams of "being somebody" seem completely fulfilled; the fantasy of consumption depicted by the fan magazines has become a reality.

An idyllic sequence set in the gardens of Esther's Beverly Hills mansion and reminiscent of fan magazine pictorial features on the homes of the stars is only the lull before a storm. As Vicki's career builds, Norman's goes into sharp decline. Left alone as his wife works on picture after picture, he begins drinking again. When Vicki's success is recognized with an Academy Award for Best Actress, he gets drunk and disrupts the presentation ceremony. Esther finally decides that he needs medical help to quit drinking. Following a spell in a sanitarium, Norman recovers, but is driven back to drink when he is humiliated in public by Libby. After a further binge and an appearance in night-court, he is remanded into Vicki's care. Now deeply concerned about his health, she tells Niles that she must give up her career to care for her husband. Already deep in depression, Norman overhears the conversation, and decides to commit suicide by drowning. Unable to cope with the trauma of Norman's funeral, Esther plans to abandon Hollywood forever. But just as she is leaving, her grandmother reappears and persuades her to stay. The movie ends with a scene depicting enthusiastic crowds gathered for the premiere of Esther's comeback picture.

A Star is Born is a melodrama, its characters subject to unseen forces apparently beyond their control in a world where whims of fashion and taste make careers and destroy lives. Hollywood is a community peopled by figures with a single character trait: the villainous Libby; the paternalistic Niles; the poor-but-honest assistant director McGuire (Andy Devine). Characters are prone to inflated gestures that declare their obvious significance, as when Norman and Vicki watch themselves kissing onscreen in huge close-up. As in any melodrama, coincidence plays a central role. When Esther arrives in Hollywood, a woman at the Central Casting Corporation where extras seek work explains to her, and to all the young hopefuls in the audience, that her chances of becoming a star are 100,000 to one. "But maybe," replies the thoughtful Esther, "I'm that one." And, because she is in the right place at the right time, she gets her break. At the same time as the movie announces that stardom is an impossible dream, it also asserts that any audience member with Esther's dedication can become a star. Significantly, questions of talent and training are obscured. Esther's talent is democratized as the imitative skill she displays in impersonating Greta Garbo, Katherine Hepburn, and Mae West, a skill shared by countless audience members. Although the movie repeatedly tells the audience of her hard work, we never really see Vicki performing, and we are given no opportunity to judge her abilities. From her screen test the movie cuts to her signing her contract; her appearance in *The Enchanted Hour* is reduced to a single screen kiss with Norman in which her face is entirely obscured; and we see nothing of her Oscar-winning performance as the "unforgettable Anna" in *Dream Without End*. Just as Esther's rise to stardom is extraordinarily rapid and unstoppable, a deliberation on American possibility itself, Norman's decline is equally inevitable, and the trajectories of their careers form a symmetry centered on the movie's intensely contradictory image of Hollywood, playing off the mythology of a "beckoning Eldorado" where dreams come true against the suffering of the stars for whom fame proves both artificial and ephemeral.

It is not simply the frequency with which *A Star is Born* has been produced that makes its particular mythology so central to understanding Hollywood's relationship with its audience. Its love affair between a rising and a falling star is also a recurrent story in the publicity surrounding Hollywood. For instance, it is reproduced in almost identical form in a fan magazine version of the story of Ruby Keeler and Al Jolson:

> Five years ago it was the great Al Jolson and "who was that little chorus girl he married? . . ." Even before talkies Al was the greatest entertainer in the world. He made more money than any of the then-great. Came talkies and he was the one great star . . . And just the other day he answered the 'phone and told me Ruby Keeler was out. Isn't it amazing that now this slip of a girl, not much over twenty . . . is now the star of the family and Al Jolson – the great Jolson – makes appointments for her and languishes away a California afternoon while she rehearses and has fittings at her studio?[87]

This eclipsing of the male head of the household had repercussions which extended beyond the lives of the one in 100,000 women who might be discovered by Hollywood, and the lesson was echoed repeatedly in the fan magazines in articles with titles like "Are Women Stars the Home Wreckers of Hollywood?"[88] If the stars were their audiences' surrogate explorers in a world of glamour and romance, the traveler's tales they brought back were often enough of conquest but seldom of settlement.

For a movie that represents Hollywood as a paradigm for the myth of success, the visual resonances of *A Star is Born* are anything but Utopian. Despite the resources of early Technicolor, the movie's somber images are marked by disturbing lighting patterns that leave playing spaces persistently shadowy and insecure. The primary colors of Hollywood are distinguished from the dark grays, browns, and cold blues of Esther's home-town, but the movie's foreboding visual style is deliberately at odds with what we see of *The Enchanted Hour* and the other products of Niles' studio. The story itself also works to qualify Esther's early fantasies. From the very outset, life in the movie colony is associated with artificiality and illusion. An early montage sequence shows an image of star lifestyles, figures at leisure around a swimming pool. As the camera pans we discover that it is only a movie set, and the sun-worshipers are revealed as playing for another camera. Stars are made, not born: we witness the fabrication of Esther's own star image in all its mechanistic detail, as she is processed into a marketable commodity. As her life-story is cynically reconstructed to play to the fantasies of her potential audience, the transformation of her identity is accompanied by a loss of personal control as she undergoes a gradual metamorphosis into a studio "property." Given a new face, a new walk, a new voice, and a new name, she is reconstructed as the spectacle of Vicki Lester.[89] In a telling irony, Niles tells her that she has been signed for her authenticity, because "tastes are going back to the natural."

Avuncular studio head Oliver Niles (Adolphe Menjou) gives his new star Vicki Lester (Janet Gaynor) the same advice her grandmother would have given her in *A Star is Born* (1937). United Artists (Aquarius Picture Library)

The movie's ambivalence toward Hollywood is suggested in its self-consciousness about its own fiction, beginning and ending with images of its own shooting script. It is also embodied in the opposed figures of Libby and Niles. The studio publicist is singled out as the architect of falsification. The movie is punctuated by inserts of front-page stories distorting the lives of the stars: "Night-court drama as star pleads for husband's freedom"; "Ex-star perishes in tragic accident." In search of "angles," Libby robs the stars of their private lives. Esther and Norman narrowly escape the ballyhoo with which Libby threatens to overwhelm their wedding, but their escape is only temporary, their marriage only a trigger for further column-inches of gossip: "Which famous male star has stopped gargling the grog and is now taking a non-alcoholic honeymoon?" At their Beverly Hills mansion, Norman tells Esther, "when we come through those gates we check the studio outside," only to be interrupted immediately by Libby and the studio photographer. Enjoying power without responsibility, Libby relishes and abuses his parasitical position, becoming more vicious as the movie progresses. His contempt for Norman lasts beyond his suicide, as he tells a barman, "first drink of water he had in 20 years, and he had to get it by accident. . . . How do you wire congratulations to the Pacific Ocean?"

Significantly, Libby works in a subsidiary industry, and his motives are contrasted with those of the industry proper. Set against his parasitical malevolence is the paternalist figure of Niles, head of the studio, whose only concern is the best interest of his stars. Louis B. Mayer, father-in-law to *A Star is Born*'s producer David O. Selznick, might well have recognized himself in Adolphe Menjou's performance, even if few of his stars would have agreed. Niles is presented as a paragon of virtue, his support the reward for Vicki's subjecting herself to the autocratic control of the star system. Prepared to take a loss at the box-office out of loyalty to Maine, he is also willing to offer him work as a way to build his confidence on leaving the sanitarium; he smothers Maine's disruption of the Oscar ceremony with a swift demand that Libby restart the music. This differing representation of the publicists and the studio heads reiterates the double image of Hollywood as both dream and nightmare that structures the remainder of the movie. Esther is certainly "reconstructed" out of the studio's economic self-interest, but also for some larger motive, in which her authentic self-realization is linked to a notion of public service. Esther's star quality lies in making "ordinariness" special, and according to the movie the manufacture of such a contradiction performs a vital role in American culture.

At the start of the movie, Esther's grandmother self-consciously links the idea of Hollywood to the foundation myths of American national identity, and her granddaughter's destiny to the archetypal American experience of the frontier:

> When I wanted something better I came across those plains in a prairie schooner with your grandfather. . . . we were going to make a new country, besides, we wanted to see our dreams come true. . . . There'll always be a new wilderness to conquer. . . . Maybe Hollywood's your wilderness now, from all I hear it sounds like it.

As the instruments and facilitators of a benign destiny, she and Niles share a rhetoric, revolving around the price "in heartbreak" that Esther may have to pay for her success. When, after Norman's death, Esther prepares to leave Hollywood her grandmother returns *ex machina* to remind her of her Faustian contract:

> It seems to me that you got more than you bargained for, more fame, more success, even more happiness . . . maybe more unhappiness . . . but you did make a bargain, and now you're whining over it . . . I don't think I'd feel so very proud of myself if I were you, Esther.

After she has enabled Esther to conquer her wilderness and fulfill her specifically American destiny, her grandmother extends her emancipatory power to the movie audience as a whole. She tells a world-wide radio audience on the occasion of Esther's comeback premiere:

> Maybe some of you people listening in dream about going to Hollywood, and maybe some of you get pretty discouraged – well, when you do, you just think about me. It took me seventy . . . sixty years to get here, but here I am and here I mean to stay.

Delivered in near direct-address outward from the screen, this message incorporates the movie's audience as part of Hollywood, with a role to play in the maintenance of its cultural power and with a lesson to learn from Esther's experience. The movie finally becomes a discussion of the mutual obligations of audiences and stars, and it offers two distinct representations of the audience as well as two versions of Hollywood stardom. As Niles explains, it is audiences who create stars and validate their images through the box-office, not studio promotion: the volume of Esther's fan mail provides the key evidence of her acceptability, and of Norman's fading stardom. Stars are representatives of the audience, as much their "property" as the studio's. Because the labor of acting is not shown in the representation of stardom, the ways in which stars are different from their audiences are concealed. Instead the audience is embodied in Esther/Vicki and celebrated as the industry's ultimate guarantor and harshest judge. Niles tells Norman that "every 25 cents they pay for a theater ticket buys them the right to be a critic."

But the audience's loyalty is not guaranteed. Crowds cheer outside premieres but they also riot outside churches where private funerals are taking place. Their desertion of Norman brings about his collapse and death. Their judgment can be fickle as well as harsh, and there is always the danger that their considerable power will be misguided by the publicists. "Don't worry dearie, he wasn't so much," cries one crowd member outside the funeral. The movie points various morals in making this opposition. Stars should keep in touch with audiences, and not abuse their positions of prestige and power; they should guard against excess and not succumb to the myths generated about them by their own studios' publicity machines. Fame can be fleeting and is never universal. On the other hand, perhaps the audience expects standards of behavior from the stars that they themselves could not meet; perhaps they should be more skeptical of studio "hype"; perhaps they should exercise their power at the box-office with more care. In such ways *A Star is Born* delivers a firm directive to the audience as to its function in the reproduction of Hollywood. The audience should no more consider deserting the stars in the hour of their greatest need than the stars should consider abandoning their audiences when the going gets tough.

Ronald Haver has suggested that *A Star is Born* is "the closest thing we have to an ideal of the movies: what they meant to the people who worked in them and to the people who went to see them."[90] Although our description of the movie suggests that the process is more complicated and less Utopian than that, it does make clear that Hollywood's mode of production has always been a tangible force on the way that its movies contain and produce meaning. The audience's knowledge of that mode of production and the industrial system behind it has also provided a source of pleasure to many of its consumers. The commercial incentives of product placement, and the ways in which stardom extends the boundaries of Hollywood into a range of interconnected media, may give some indication of why the economic factors that determine production cannot simply be dismissed as a "background" or prologue to critical analysis. The system of production that we have described presents problems for the development of a critical method that will encompass its multiple and often competing logics. This difficulty is exacerbated if the goal of such criticism is to establish and evaluate the "organic" or formal coherence of an individual "text." The conventions by which a viewer is guided through a movie presume an accumulated knowledge of what Hollywood is, a knowledge that extends beyond the boundaries of any individual movie fiction. The individual movie is, then, an incidental object within a longer-term act of consumption. The workings of the star system illustrate Hollywood's commercial commitment to acts of consumption. So does the subject of our next chapter, which examines Hollywood's stress on the generic.

Notes

1 Alfred D. Chandler, Jr, *The Visible Hand: The Managerial Revolution in American Business* (Cambridge, MA: Harvard University Press, 1977), p. 285.

2 Mae D. Huettig, *Economic Control of the Motion Picture Industry: A Study in Industrial Organization* (Philadelphia: University of Pennsylvania Press, 1944), p. 57.

3 Douglas Gomery, *The Hollywood Studio System* (London: Macmillan, 1986), pp. 7–8.

4 *The Film in National Life* (London: Allen and Unwin, 1932), p. 42.

5 *The Golden Harvest of the Silver Screen, Compiled from Reliable Sources as a Basis for Evaluating Motion Picture Securities* (Los Angeles: Hunter, Dulin & Co., 1927).

6 Adolph Zukor, quoted in Richard Maltby, ed., *Dreams for Sale: Popular Culture in the Twentieth Century* (London: Harrap, 1989), p. 86.

7 Few of these black neighborhood theaters were owned by African-Americans. A 1942 survey suggested that 90 percent of all-black theaters were owned by whites. Douglas Gomery, *Shared Pleasures: A History of Movie Presentation in the United States* (Madison: University of Wisconsin Press, 1992), p. 162.

8 Tino Balio, ed., *The American Film Industry*, revised edn (Madison: University of Wisconsin Press, 1985), p. 255.

9 The best sources of statistics on the industry are the annuals *Film Daily Yearbook* (New York: Jack Alicoate) and *Motion Picture Almanac*, later *International Motion Picture Almanac* (New York: Quigley Publications). Many useful industry statistics have been gathered together in Joel W. Finler, *The Hollywood Story: Everything You Always Wanted to Know about the American Movie Business but Didn't Know Where to Look* (London:

Octopus Books, 1988).

10 Will Hays, president of the MPPDA, quoted in Huettig, p. 55.

11 By-Laws of the MPPDA, quoted in Raymond Moley, *The Hays Office* (Indianapolis: Bobbs-Merrill, 1946), p. 227.

12 Gomery, *Hollywood Studio System*, p. 14.

13 Michael Nielsen, "Towards a Workers' History of the US Film Industry," in Manuel Alvarado and John O. Thompson, eds, *The Media Reader* (London: British Film Institute, 1990), pp. 166–80.

14 Quoted in Maltby, p. 11.

15 Kristin Thompson, *Exporting Entertainment: America in the World Film Market, 1907–1934* (London: British Film Institute, 1985), p. 50.

16 Ruth Vasey, *Diplomatic Representations: The World According to Hollywood, 1919–1939* (Madison: University of Wisconsin Press, forthcoming).

17 "Certain Factors and Considerations Affecting the European Market," internal MPPDA memo, October 25, 1928, Motion Picture Association of America Archive, New York (hereafter MPA).

18 James True, *Printer's Ink* (February 4, 1926), quoted in Charles Eckert, "The Carole Lombard in Macy's Window," *Quarterly Review of Film Studies* 3 (Winter 1978), pp. 4–5.

19 Jeffrey Richards, *The Age of the Dream Palace: Cinema and Society in Britain, 1930–1939* (London: Routledge and Kegan Paul, 1984), p. 27.

20 Quoted in Richards, p. 64.

21 That figure does, however, mask a number of shifts within the foreign market: for instance, the steady decline in the importance of the British market in the 1960s and 1970s, and the growth of the Japanese market until, in 1984, it became the largest single importer of American movies.

22 Thomas Guback, "Hollywood's International Market," in Balio, pp. 477–80.

23 Sam Morris to Jack Warner, November 12, 1937, JLW Correspondence, Box 59 Folder 8, Warner Bros. Archive, Department of Special Collections, University of Southern California.

24 Nicholas Kent, *Naked Hollywood: Money, Power and the Movies* (London: BBC Books, 1991), pp. 101, 108.

25 Finler, p. 280.

26 Tino Balio, "Introduction to Part I," in Tino Balio, ed., *Hollywood in the Age of Television* (Boston: Unwin Hyman, 1990), p. 37.

27 Joan Didion, *The White Album* (Harmondsworth: Penguin, 1981), p. 162.

28 Quoted in Kent, p. 121.

29 Motion picture economics has always presented opportunities for "creative accountancy." With the rise of independent production and ever-increasing advertising costs and merchandising opportunities, the opportunities have blossomed even more. This is Stanley Kubrick in 1980, discussing an imaginary budget similar to that of *The Shining*, released in 1980: "take a film that costs $10 million. Today it's not unusual to spend $8 million on USA advertising and $4 million on international advertising. On a big film, add $2 million for release prints. Say there is a 20% studio overhead on the budget: that's $2 million more. Interest on the $10 million production cost, currently at 20% a year, would add an additional $2 million a year, say, for two years – that's another $4 million. So a $10 million film already costs $30 million. Now you have to get it back. Let's say an actor takes 10% of the gross, and the distributor takes a world-wide average of a 35% distribution fee. To roughly calculate the break-even figure, you have to divide the $30 million by 55%, the percentage left after the actor's 10% and the 35%

distribution fee. That comes to $54 million of distributor's film rental. So a $10 million film may not break even, as far as the producer's share of the profits is concerned, until 5.4 times its negative cost." Michael Ciment, *Stanley Kubrick* (New York: Holt, Rinehart and Winston, 1984), p. 197.

30   Eddie Dorman Kay, *Box-Office Greats* (London: Tiger, 1990), p. 7.

31   Balio, "Introduction to Part I," in Balio, *Hollywood in the Age of Television*, p. 28.

32   Balio, "Introduction to Part II," in Balio, *Hollywood in the Age of Television*, p. 261.

33   Balio, "Introduction to Part I," in Balio, *Hollywood in the Age of Television*, p. 30.

34   Warner Communications Inc. 1981 Annual Report, p. 25. Quoted in Robert Gustavson, " 'What's Happening to Our Pix Biz?' From Warner Bros. to Warner Communications Inc.," in Balio, *Hollywood in the Age of Television*, p. 584.

35   Balio, "Introduction to Part II," in Balio, *Hollywood in the Age of Television*, pp. 277–82.

36   Bruce Austin, "Home Video: The Second-Run 'Theater' of the 1990s," in Balio, *Hollywood in the Age of Television*, p. 321.

37   Quoted in Balio, "Introduction to Part II," in Balio, *Hollywood in the Age of Television*, p. 245.

38   Kent, p. 59.

39   Kent, p. 60.

40   *Wall Street Journal* (March 7, 1989), p. B1. Quoted in Michelle Hilmes, "Pay Television: Breaking the Broadcast Bottleneck," in Balio, *Hollywood in the Age of Television*, p. 315.

41   *The Economist* (July 30, 1983), p. 73, quoted by Hilmes in Balio, *Hollywood in the Age of Television*, pp. 315–16.

42   Carey McWilliams, *Southern California: An Island on the Land*, 1st pub. 1946 (Santa Barbara: Peregrine Smith, Inc., 1973), pp. 339–40.

43   It could be argued that the studio system was, for most of its life, never truly economically efficient, since it encouraged overproduction, so that too many feature films were produced to earn to their maximum potential. Joel Finler argues that the major production companies never fully recovered from the effects of the Great Depression in the early 1930s, and that the decline in the movies' share of the entertainment dollar really began in the mid-1930s, not the late 1940s. Finler, pp. 33–4.

44   Leo Rosten, *Hollywood: The Movie Colony, the Movie Makers* (New York: Harcourt, Brace, 1941), pp. 41–2.

45   This tactic was, according to Alfred Chandler, an inherent feature of the "modern business enterprise": "The creation of distributing and marketing networks to provide . . . coordination, facilities, and services caused the mass producers to internalize several processes of production and distribution and the market transactions between them within a single enterprise. . . . Such administrative coordination in turn created formidable barriers to entry. High-volume throughput and stock-turn reduced unit costs. Advertising and the provision of service maintained customer loyalty. Rival firms were rarely able to compete until they had built comparable marketing organizations of their own." Chandler, p. 363.

46   Rosten, pp. 82–5.

47   "Metro-Goldwyn-Mayer," *Fortune* 6 (December 1932), p. 51. Reprinted in Balio, *The American Film Industry*, p. 311.

48   Rosten, pp. 242–3.

49   Quoted in Rosten, p. 240.

50   Lary May presents a version of this argument in *Screening Out the Past: The Birth of Mass Culture and the Motion Picture Industry* (New York: Oxford University Press, 1980), pp. 169–75. See also Lary L. May and Elaine Tyler May, "Why Jewish Movie Moguls: An Exploration in American Culture," *American Jewish History* 72 (September 1982),

pp. 6–25. An influential source for arguments about the particularly strong Jewish influence on movie production is Upton Sinclair, *Upton Sinclair Presents William Fox* (Los Angeles: Upton Sinclair, 1933).

51   In *An Empire of Their Own: How the Jews Invented Hollywood* (New York: Crown, 1988), Neal Gabler seeks to argue that the ideological landscape of Hollywood's fictions was the creation of a group hungry for assimilation into American society and culture. Gabler also labels Zanuck as having "been in Hollywood so long he might have been called a Jewish fellow traveler" (p. 349). His evidence, however, is almost exclusively a matter of biographical detail rather than of commercial practice. As Joseph Turow has observed, Gabler "marshals no real support for his argument . . . quotes no speeches, reveals no letters, exposes no other documents which reveal that the studio heads consciously tried to create 'an empire of their own.' " Joseph Turow, "Routes and Roots," *Journal of Communications* 39:4 (Autumn 1989), pp. 67–70.

52   Jesse Lasky, "The Producer Makes a Plan," in Nancy Naumberg, ed., *We Make the Movies* (New York: Norton, 1937), pp. 1–5. Quoted in Rosten, p. 239.

53   F. Scott Fitzgerald, *The Last Tycoon* (Harmondsworth: Penguin, 1974), pp. 36–76.

54   In his book about Warner Bros. in the 1930s, Roddick makes a similar argument for the studio's head of production, Hal Wallis, being its dominant creative presence. Nick Roddick, *A New Deal in Entertainment: Warner Brothers* [sic] *in the 1930s* (London: British Film Institute, 1983).

55   Frank Capra, letter to the *New York Times* (April 2, 1939). Quoted in Richard Glatzer and John Raeburn, eds, *Frank Capra: The Man and His Films* (Ann Arbor: University of Michigan Press, 1975), p. 15.

56   "An Analysis of the Motion Picture Industry by the Screen Directors Guild, Inc.," pp. 1–2, 4–5. Quoted in Rosten, p. 240.

57   There is an excellent description of the day-to-day activities of a producer in Rosten, pp. 231–8.

58   Chandler, pp. 460–3; Janet Staiger, "The Producer-unit System: Management by Specialization after 1931," in David Bordwell, Janet Staiger, and Kristin Thompson, *The Classical Hollywood Cinema: Film Style and Mode of Production to 1960* (London: Routledge and Kegan Paul, 1985), p. 322.

59   Capra, letter to the *New York Times* (April 2, 1939), quoted in Margaret F. Thorp, *America at the Movies* (London: Faber, 1946), p. 92.

60   Ronald Haver, *David O. Selznick's Hollywood* (New York: Knopf, 1980), p. 267.

61   "What you do," suggested Ernest Hemingway to Irwin Shaw after Shaw had complained about the changes made to his novel *The Young Lions*, "is sell your book to the movies, go to the bar, and take a drink. You don't think about the movie, you don't look at the movie, you know it's going to be a piece of shit. The idea of selling a book to the movies is to make money." Quoted in Richard Schickel, *Brando: A Life in Our Times* (London: Pavilion, 1991), p. 118.

62   Tom Dardis, *Some Time in the Sun* (London: André Deutsch, 1976), pp. 19–77; Richard Fine, *Hollywood and the Profession of Authorship* (Ann Arbor: University of Michigan Press, 1985).

63   Art directors in contemporary Hollywood are normally referred to by the more grandiose title of production designer.

64   Whitney Stine, *Mother Goddam* (New York: Hawthorne Books, 1974), p. 79.

65   Thorp, p. 49.

66   Thorp, p. 52.

67   Thorp, pp. 49, 52.

68   Before the introduction of air-conditioning, attendance was lowest in the summer months, and Hollywood's production seasons ran from September to September.
69   Rosten, pp. 112–14.
70   *Photoplay* (February 1935). Reprinted in Richard Griffith, ed., *The Talkies: Articles and Illustrations from a Great Fan Magazine, 1928–1940* (New York: Dover, 1971), p. 196.
71   Thorp, p. 17.
72   Quoted in Martin Levin, ed., *Hollywood and the Great Fan Magazines* (London: Ian Allen, 1970), pp. 142, 214.
73   "How to Hold Him When You've Hooked Him, by Myrna Loy," *Picturegoer Famous Films Supplement* for *Double Wedding* (February 12, 1938), p. 11.
74   *Photoplay*, quoted in Levin, p. 145.
75   J.P. Mayer, *British Cinemas and their Audiences: Sociological Studies* (London: Dobson, 1948), p. 104.
76   Frank D. McConnell, *The Spoken Seen: Film and the Romantic Imagination* (Baltimore: Johns Hopkins University Press, 1975), p. 171.
77   Malcolm Vance, *The Movie Ad Book* (Minneapolis: Control Data Publishing, 1981), p. 77.
78   Christine Frederick, *Selling Mrs Consumer* (New York: The Business Bourse, 1929), pp. 4–5.
79   Irving Thalberg, "The Modern Photoplay," Lecture at the University of Southern California, March 20, 1929, in John C. Tibbetts, ed., *Introduction to the Photoplay* (Shawnee Mission, KS: National Film Society, 1977), pp. 119–20.
80   Eckert, p. 10.
81   *Modern Screen* (September 1933), reprinted in Mark Bego, ed., *The Best of Modern Screen* (London: Columbus Books, 1986), p. 23.
82   Eckert, p. 3.
83   James Goldstone, "Deals on Reels," *Observer* (May 5, 1991), p. 32. Science fiction movies may appear less convincing predictions of the future if the products placed in them cease to exist: Pan Am, for instance, is shown running space flights in both *2001: A Space Odyssey* (1968) and *Blade Runner* (1982, set in 2019), but the airline filed for bankruptcy in 1991.
84   Marquis Busby, "The Price They Pay for Fame," quoted in Levin, p. 94.
85   Busby, quoted in Levin, p. 94.
86   Thorp, pp. 68–9.
87   Caroline Somers Holt, "It's Ruby's Turn Now . . . !," *Modern Screen*, reprinted in Levin, pp. 50–1.
88   Gladys Hall, "Are Women Stars the Home Wreckers of Hollywood?," *Motion Picture Magazine* (August 1932), pp. 44–5, 96. This piece argued that "We do NOT believe that any man can stand, for long, the ignominy of trotting about in the refracted aura of his wife. He simply cannot bear it, that's all. More than mere personal jealousy is aroused. The deep, sub-conscious antagonism of sex for sex is there. The pride of the male is hurt more than the heart. Men can bear to be all or they can bear to be nothing, but they cannot bear to be – *incidental*. . . . The danger lies in the wife's superseding the husband. If Joan Crawford, for instance, should rise to the unparalleled heights prophesied for her – if her consuming ambition and burning desire for preeminence should ride her too hard – she and young Doug [Fairbanks] may ride to a matrimonial split. . . . There seems to be only one way that is the safe way – the old, old way of the Missus being the Missus and the husband going into the arena to wrestle for the glory and the gold. When the wives are the stars, they wreck the homes

and the marriages. When the husbands are the stars, the homes are built upon a rock that endures."

89   The process is described in W. Robert La Vine, *In a Glamorous Fashion: The Fabulous Years of Hollywood Costume Design* (New York: Scribner's, 1980), p. 27.

90   Haver, p. 191.

3 Genre

These ambiguities, redundancies, and deficiencies recall those attributed by Dr Franz Kuhn to a certain Chinese encyclopedia entitled *Celestial Emporium of Benevolent Knowledge*. On those remote pages it is written that animals are divided into (a) those that belong to the Emperor, (b) embalmed ones, (c) those that are trained, (d) suckling pigs, (e) mermaids, (f) fabulous ones, (g) stray dogs, (h) those that are included in this classification, (i) those that tremble as if they were mad, (j) innumerable ones, (k) those drawn with a very fine camel's hair brush, (l) others, (m) those that have just broken a flower vase, (n) those that resemble flies from a distance.

Jorge Luis Borges[1]

I know Billy, and he ain't exactly predictable . . .

Pat Garrett (James Coburn) in *Pat Garrett and Billy the Kid* (1973)

Hollywood is a generic cinema, which is not quite the same as saying that it is a cinema of genres. Audiences, producers, and critics all discuss movies in generic terms, but what they each mean by those terms may be quite different. Critics place movies into generic categories as a way of dividing up the map of Hollywood cinema into smaller, more manageable, and relatively discrete areas. Their analyses often suggest a cartographer's concern with defining the exact location of the boundary between one genre and another. Audiences and producers use generic terms much more flexibly: for example, you might describe the movie you saw last night as a comedy, a thriller, or a science fiction movie. The local video store similarly labels its offerings by type: action, horror, musical movies. Such everyday distinctions are descriptive and, above all, functional. If you avoid horror movies, it is useful to know that *The Silence of the Lambs* (1991) falls into that category when choosing a video. This use of genre as a way of differentiating among movies assumes that there is a consensus about what constitutes a Western or a musical. As Andrew Tudor puts it, genre "is what we collectively believe it to be."[2] We know a thriller when we see one. Indeed, we know a thriller before we see one, and to some degree we also recognize that, beyond describing the obvious content of a movie, these generic categories have a broader cultural resonance. Tudor suggests that they are embedded features of our social lives, providing narrative structures and emotional landscapes that we can use to construct ourselves socially. The horror movie, for instance, allows us to experiment with the experience of fear, and gives us a vocabulary of images with which to describe and articulate the fearful.[3]

Generic categories such as these – the thriller, or the "weepie" – are identified by the emotional affect they produce in their audiences. Other descriptions, such as "Western" or "science fiction," concern themselves primarily with content.[4] These two methods of classification may be incompatible if the objective is to produce a single, coherent system of movie genres, but for everyday purposes, they indicate the ways in which categories intersect and overlap, confirming that the distinctions we make do not have to be either precise or mutually exclusive. Genres are flexible, subject to a constant process of change and adaptation. Because different audiences will use a genre in different ways at different times, its boundaries can never be rigidly defined, and at the same time it is susceptible to extensive subdivision. *Oklahoma!* (1955), for instance, is *both* a Western *and* a musical, and to suggest that it should be excluded from either category on the grounds that it belongs in the other would be to use generic classification in a very reductive fashion. At the same time, within the relatively small category of musical Westerns we might want to distinguish between *Oklahoma!* and *Rose Marie* (1936) on the grounds that they were both different types of musical (*Rose Marie* is an operetta) and different types of Western (*Rose Marie* is set in Canada).

Rather than occupying discrete categories, therefore, most movies use categorical elements in combination. We are familiar with generic hyphenates: musical-comedy, comedy-adventure, Western-romance. In 1979, the *Monthly Film Bulletin* described *Nocturna* as "the first soft-porn-vampire-disco-rock movie," while in 1991 *Arachnophobia* advertised itself as a "thrillomedy": generic mutants, perhaps, but these labels do give potential viewers quite a full description of what they might expect. Audiences, too, invent their own generic categories, both by making connections and by breaking genres down into ever smaller subsets. When the British sociologist J.P. Mayer asked readers of *Picturegoer* magazine to write about their film preferences in 1946, one 24-year-old female stenographer expressed her general enjoyment of "Love and Romance" movies, and then qualified this by adding: "Boy-meets-girl romances are always refreshing to me; triangles bore me; Bette Davis' acting I admire, but continual self-sacrifice irritates me; and the mask-like new faces with which we have recently been inundated, with the possible exceptions of Van Johnson and Lauren Bacall, bewilder me."[5] Stars and story-type distinguish preferences within the general category of romance. "Boy-meets-girl" and "triangle" stories might be regarded as sub-genres of romance; these classifications intersect with those expressed in preferences for particular stars or star types, and using this particular matrix of opinions, it would be possible to predict which 1947 romances would have been likely to appeal to this viewer. More analytically, a broad generic category such as the romance can be understood as a field containing a large collection of more or less familiar elements: stars, settings, plot events, motives, and so on. For both producers developing or promoting a movie and viewers determining their response to it, the individual genre movie achieves its uniqueness through the way that it combines those elements.

The specificity of a genre arises not from its possessing features exclusive to it so much as from its particular combination of features, each of which it may share with other genres. Steve Neale suggests that it is this overlap of elements between genres that makes the definition of any genre so difficult, since a genre is not simply a combination of repetition and difference, but a process of difference *in* repetition.[6] Genres may appear to be bound by systems of rules, but an individual genre movie inevitably transgresses those rules in differentiating itself from other movies in the same genre. The rules of a genre are thus not so much a body of textual conventions as a set of expectations shared by audiences and producers alike. Genre movies share family resemblances with each other, and audiences recognize and anticipate these familiar features. Generic consistency allows for the shorthand of convention and stereotype, but also for the interplay between confirmed expectation and novelty. The conventions of a genre exist alongside more general conventions of realism or verisimilitude (verisimilitude implies probability or plausibility, less a direct relation to the "real" than a suggestion of what is appropriate). Sometimes generic conventions transgress these broader regimes of social or **cultural verisimilitude**: when a character bursts into song while walking down a street, for instance.[7] Douglas Pye's account of genre as a context in which meaning is created suggests ways in which audience expectations and producers' commercial motivations form a common currency. The generic context is, he argues, "narrow enough for recognition of the genre to take place but wide enough to allow enormous individual variation." In any individual movie, "any one or more than one element can be brought to the foreground while others may all but disappear. Plot, character, theme, can each become central . . . characters can be fully individualized, given complex or conflicting motivation, or may be presented schematically as morality play figures, embodiments of abstract good or evil."[8]

The notion of a genre as a set of stable categories across which movies connect, or within which fluctuation occurs, is useful for both producers and critics. But it also presents critics and empirical audience researchers with the problem of how to sort the genres into mutually exclusive categories, despite the many constant features which they share, and the many ways in which categories dissolve into one another. A 1955 audience research study, for example, originally asked open-ended questions, somewhat like Mayer's, about preferences. This produced a "fuzziness . . . in the meaning of names given the program types by the respondents." Substituting a predetermined list of generic categories from which respondents had to select gave rise to another problem. "If we ask, 'What type of movie do you like best?' the answers depend upon the way the movie types are classified and upon the respondents' understanding of the terms we are using."[9]

When the motion picture industry has investigated its audience's generic preference it has usually done so by asking questions about "story-types." One 1942 survey by the Motion Picture Research Bureau enumerated eighteen types:

> Comedies: sophisticated comedies
>   slapstick comedies
>   family life comedies
>   musical comedies
>   "just" comedies
> War pictures
> Mystery, horror pictures
> Historicals, biographies
> Fantasies
> Western pictures
> Gangster and G-men pictures
> Serious dramas
> Love stories, romantic pictures
> Socially significant pictures
> Adventure, action pictures
> Musicals (serious)
> Child star pictures
> (Wild) animal pictures

The study's author, Leo Handel, remained dissatisfied with this classification because of "the overlapping of the different types. A war picture may also be a serious drama, a historical picture, and at the same time it may contain a love story. A socially significant picture may feature a child star." He also noted that "it has been found repeatedly that it is the particular story rather than the story type that determines the interest."[10]

The preferences his survey recorded, however, give some indication of why any individual movie was likely to contain a generic cocktail. Women expressed strong dislikes for mystery and horror pictures, gangster and G-men movies, war movies and Westerns. Their greatest enthusiasms were for love stories, which was the category most strongly disliked by men, whose strongest preference was for war movies. Hollywood's logic was to combine the two, a logic repeatedly expressed in movie advertisements that, for instance, summarized the Korean war movie *The Bridges at Toko-Ri* (1954) as "Tomorrow, the deadliest mission . . . tonight, the greatest love!" The advertising copy for *Twelve O'Clock High* (1949), about World War II pilots, promised "a story of twelve men as their women never knew them." It might have been addressing the reservations of women who felt that war pictures lacked "human interest" because they dwelt too extensively on their scenes of fighting at the expense of providing thorough characterizations. Even more blatantly, perhaps, the poster for *Destroyer* (1943) declared "Her only rival is his ship! . . . You feel toward a ship as you do toward a woman when you marry her . . . You take her for better or you take her for worse . . . and you don't leave her when the going gets tough!"

The production industry classified its product according to "story-type" from an early stage. In 1905 the Kleine Optical Company listed its offerings under the headings of comic, mysterious, scenic, personalities, and three types of story: historical, dramatic, and narrative.[11] In the mid-1940s, in the process of passing all Hollywood's feature movies through the Production Code, the industry's trade association classified them into a heterogeneous matrix that divided its six major categories into 57 subdivisions. The largest single category was melodrama, which accounted for between a quarter and a third of all production. Westerns, comedies (which included musical comedies), and drama each made up about 20 percent of annual production, with the rest falling into a small crime category and a larger miscellaneous group. The subdivisions within drama and melodrama overlapped considerably: each group had action, comedy, social problem, romantic, war, musical, psychological, and murder-mystery as sub-categories. But Hollywood never prioritized genre as such. Like that of other fashion industries, Hollywood production was cyclical, always seeking to replicate its recent commercial successes.[12] For instance, what the Production Code Administration classified as the "Farce-Murder-Mystery" was a one-season wonder: although eleven were made in 1944, only two were made in the following season, and none the year after. Some cycles might last for several seasons, and perhaps come to form subsets within a larger generic grouping: Biblical and Roman epics in the early 1950s, for instance. Barbara Klinger has called these subsets "local genres": categories that "functioned as a recognized and influential means of classifying films" for a historically specific period.[13]

On occasion, critics have elevated what the production industry understood as a cycle to the status of a genre. The "gangster film," for instance, was the product of a single season (1930–1) and, at least within the industry's operating definitions, comprised no more than 23 pictures; nonetheless, it has attracted critical attention as a genre, and most critical accounts have suggested that *Little Caesar* (1930), *The Public Enemy* (1931), and *Scarface* (1932) "forged a new generic tradition,"[14] in which they constituted "a point of classical development."[15] Tino Balio has argued that Hollywood production during the 1930s is more accurately described as following a number of production trends rather than working within genres in making its Class A pictures. Ranked in order of their production costs, duration, and box-office performance, these production groupings were: prestige pictures; musicals; woman's films; comedies; social problem pictures; and horror movies.[16] Some of these terms correspond to critically established genres while others, including the most important category of the prestige picture, fall across or outside academically recognized genre boundaries. In much the same way, the contemporary industry divides movies aimed at the family market into "drop-off" and "non-drop-off" movies, depending on whether they expect parents to watch the movie with their children or simply leave them at the theater.

For producers, then, generic distinction offers a layered system of classification, which they use in an opportunistic way that does not assume that one generic classification excludes others. These systems of classification are being constantly revised, so that there is always more than one system in operation at any one time, and inevitably contradictions in classification arise. Nevertheless, the advantages to producers of the principle of classifying movies by type are clear. Firstly, they offer a financial guarantee: generic movies are in a sense always pre-sold to their audiences because viewers possess an image and an experience of the genre before they actually engage any particular instance of it. Some genres, moreover, have predictably higher earning capacities than others. Until the 1960s, science fiction movies were expected to perform noticeably less well at the box-office than other movies with comparable stars and spectacle. An analysis of theatrical receipts during the 1970s suggested that had changed, and that science fiction now carried a generic premium higher than horror or comedy.[17] Secondly, genre movies promise that their fictional events will unfold with a measure of certainty for the audience and that expected satisfactions will be provided. By offering this foreknowledge, a generic cinema encourages that sense of pleasurable mastery and control that we have associated with entertainment. Andrew Britton describes his experience of watching *Hell Night* (1981) with an audience of teenage horror movie aficionados:

> It became obvious at a very early stage that every spectator knew exactly what the film was going to do at every point, even down to the order in which it would dispose of its various characters, and the screening was accompanied by something in the nature of a running commentary in which each dramatic move was excitedly broadcast some minutes before it was actually made. The film's total predictability did not create boredom or disappointment. On the contrary, the predictability was clearly the main source of pleasure, and the only occasion for disappointment would have been a modulation of the formula, not a repetition of it.[18]

This audience demand for predictability meshes harmoniously with the economic advantages to the industry that come with the standardization of production. In this context, genre serves as a central component of Hollywood's aesthetic regime of regulated difference, and also regulates the act of consumption. Every teenager in the audience for *Hell Night* was consuming a known quantity, and Britton describes the ritualized aspects of the viewing experience as well as of the movie itself.[19] Low-budget production emphasizes the formulaic and predictable, as an oft-told story about Bryan Foy illustrates. Foy ran B-feature production at Warner Bros. in the late 1930s and was known as the "keeper of the Bs." He is supposed to have kept a pile of about 20 scripts on his desk. Each time his unit completed a movie, its script would go to the bottom of the pile. Over a period of about a year, it would gradually work its way back up to the top. Then it would be dusted off and given to the scriptwriter to rewrite: a crime story would become a Western, the sex of the leading characters would be changed, the location moved.[20] In due course, the new script would return to the bottom of the pile to be recycled in the same way. Whether or not the story is apocryphal (and Foy did once boast that he had made the same movie 11 times), it illustrates the cost-effectiveness of Hollywood's system of constructing familiar fictions that fulfilled their audiences' requirement that movies be "just like . . . but completely different" from each other. The more recent tendency to produce sequels (*Friday the 13th* reached part 8) is an even less disguised practice, since in many cases the sequels could more accurately be described as remakes. *Halloween's* director, John Carpenter, has acknowledged that "basically, sequels mean the same film." People, he claims "want to see the same movie again."[21]

Foy's activities were, however, as much concerned with providing novelty as predictability, balancing recognizable features with elements of difference and variation. In addition to being like other movies which have in the past satisfied the audience, a movie also needs to have certain features that set it apart from those movies, "angles" or "edges" around which to promote and distinguish the movie as something new. The higher the budget, the more likely that its recognizable elements will be provided by its stars, and the novelty by its plot and setting; lower-budget movies may rely more heavily on conventions of plot and genre, but the same principle of regulated difference applies.

Hollywood's mode of promotion is similarly organized around the play between likeness and novelty. One way of summarizing a movie, used by writers "pitching" a story idea to a producer as well as by reviewers, is to describe it as a hybrid of two other pictures. A juxtaposition such as *"Pretty Woman* meets *Out of Africa"* (proposed by a character in *The Player,* 1992) conjures up a field of reference recognizable in the moment, but probably not over a longer period of time. Generic conventions offer more durable frames of reference, but they also accommodate change: the variations in plot, characterization, or setting in each imitation inflect the audience's generic expectations by introducing new elements or transgressing old ones. Each new genre movie thus adds to the body of the genre, extending the repertoire of conventions understood by producers, exhibitors, and ticket-buyers at any given historical point. This means that, as Steve Neale puts it, "the elements and conventions of a genre are always *in* play rather than being, simply, *re*-played; and any generic corpus is always being expanded."[22]

The boundaries of a genre dissolve not only to admit new movies, but also to incorporate the surrounding discourses of advertising, marketing, publicity, press and other media reviewing, reporting and gossip, and the "word-of-mouth" opinions of other viewers. These all contribute to the expectations and knowledge of the audience prior to the commercially crucial moment when they purchase their tickets at the box-office. Including these discourses magnifies the problems in studying the movies, certainly, but an attention to the generic fluidity of Hollywood is vital if we are to progress from a concern with the individual text as an autonomous object toward the emphasis that a consumerist criticism must place on the relationships among movies as elements in a system of production and consumption.

Genre Criticism

Criticism has understood genre in Hollywood quite differently from the industry itself, ignoring most of the industry's own categories and introducing alternatives of its own. In much the same way that auteur criticism found itself drawn to "rebel" directors such as Orson Welles, an ideologically oriented genre criticism has found itself involved in what Barbara Klinger has called "the critical identification of a series of 'rebel' texts within the Hollywood empire," distinguishing certain categories of movies such as film noir, fifties melodrama, and seventies horror movies as "progressive" or "subversive."[23] But as Klinger argues, to pursue "radical" or "progressive" categories of Hollywood production is to hunt for a chimera, since the politics of a genre are by no means immutably fixed. Some Westerns, for instance, are more racist than others, but few avoid the subject of racism altogether, any more than they avoid at least some gunplay.

Genre criticism also shares with auteurism a concern to delineate Hollywood cinema by defining sub-sets within the whole, but the map of Hollywood that it seeks to draw is concerned less with identifying individual creativity than with examining the kind of world in which the horror movie or the Western or the musical could make sense.[24] James Twitchell has suggested that genre criticism's concern with broader cultural and historical meanings requires an approach more akin to ethnology, one in which stories are analyzed "as if no one individual telling really mattered," since the search is for what is stable and repeated in them. In such an analysis, considerations of authorship or originality are, he maintains, "quite beside the point," since the critic's main concern is with trying to understand why some images and narratives "have been crucial enough to pass along."[25] In practice, however, many critics have used genre as a starting point for a discussion of authorship in Hollywood: perhaps the most frequent instances are critical essays examining John Ford's contribution to the Western.[26]

Twitchell's comments describe an underlying tendency in genre criticism to see the persistence of some genres as evidence that they represent a modern equivalent of folklore or mythology, stories in which contemporary social conflicts and contradictions can be explored. Writing about horror movies, Carol Clover has suggested that the swapping of themes and motifs between movies, their use of archetypal characters and situations in sequels, remakes, and imitations, are like oral narrative. In both there is "no original, no real or right text, but only variants; a world in which, therefore, the meaning of the individual example lies outside itself."[27] Robert Warshow makes a similar point about the therapeutic function of the Western's ritualized forms, which "preserve for us the pleasures of a complete and self-contained drama . . . in a time when other, more consciously serious art forms are increasingly complex, uncertain, and ill-defined."[28] These perceptions explain why genre criticism has drawn so heavily on what we can broadly term "structuralist" methods of analysis, and has argued that the recurrent structures of a genre distill social rather than individual meanings. In *Sixguns and Society*, for instance, Will Wright identifies the common plot patterns in a group of Westerns, and then suggests that each of the variant plots has a "mythical" significance, encapsulating a set of "concepts and attitudes implicit in the structure of American institutions." Like other structuralist approaches, Wright's analytical scheme borrows from the analysis of myth in "primitive" cultures by the French anthropologist Claude Lévi-Strauss, and in part from the formalist analysis of a group of Russian fairy tales.[29]

Generic distinction is of most value when it can be used to distinguish between types of object that share fundamental similarities. We do not, for instance, need a system of generic distinctions to establish the difference between a refrigerator and a camel.[30] The means to distinguish between types of object become more important as the objects concerned become more like each other – a camel and a dromedary, perhaps. Douglas Pye notes that the use of genre terms like "Western" or "thriller" focuses attention on the first part of what is in fact "a double-barrelled name, with the second term suppressed." That second term, "film" or "movie," identifies a larger generic category, the Hollywood movie, of which they are variations. Pye's point is that notwithstanding the differences between these genres, they share larger similarities, which is precisely why we need the tools of generic analysis to distinguish between them.[31] This gives rise to the recurring paradox of generic analysis: the attention that is paid to defining the boundaries of a genre, despite the fact that generic classification of essentially similar objects can seldom be exclusive. Not only do genres contain sub-genres, but the mechanism of generic criticism supplies different sets of criteria for making distinctions, and these sets tend to be overlapping rather than mutually exclusive. But in looking for the consistencies by which to establish stable and discrete systems of classification, genre criticism seeks to establish patterns of repetition between movies, and regards these as of more importance than differences of surface detail. Thomas Sobchack, for instance, argues that just because "the various genres have changed or gone through cycles of popularity does not alter the fact that the basic underlying coordinates of a genre are maintained time after time. . . . Any particular film of any definable group is only recognizable as part of that group if it is, in fact, an imitation of that which came before."[32] This critical definition of genre also distinguishes between movies that fall into specific genres and "non-genre films,"[33] in contrast to the industry's view that all of its output fell within one category or another.

Genre criticism usually identifies up to eight genres in Hollywood feature film production. The Western, the comedy, the musical, and the war movie are four uncontested categories. Different critics will then argue the relative independent merits of at least one of the thriller, the crime or gangster movie, and list the horror movie and science fiction as either one or two additional genres. Each of these genres is usually seen as stable enough to possess a history of its own, existing outside the flow of industry history. The history of a genre is commonly described as an evolution from growth to maturity to decay, or a development from the experimental to the classical to the elaborated to the self-referential, "from straightforward storytelling to self-conscious formalism."[34] As both Alan Williams and Tag Gallagher have suggested in relation to the Western, which is the genre that is usually accorded the greatest stability and the most longevity, such critically imposed accounts lack an awareness of the historical specificity of the genres they describe, and do not take suffi- ciently into account either the range of variation within any given group- ing at a particular moment, or the sensitivity of contemporary audiences to generic nuance.[35]

These generic histories, however, do not so much provide an accurate chronological account as delineate a body of work, a canon of texts, to be compared with each other, and when it does that genre criticism practices a form of discrimination similar to that we associated with auteurism in chapter 1. The imposition of an internal historical structure in which movies as texts influence each other actually eliminates the need to con- sider external questions of industry, economics, and audience in favor of a search for recurrent textual structures, whether narrative, thematic, or visual. Perhaps the clearest instance of strain between critical and industrial notions of genre concerns the group of movies produced in the decade after World War II which are usually called film noir. The term was first used by French film critics to identify "a new mood of cynicism, pessimism and darkness that had crept into American cinema"[36] in the postwar period. Film noir was entirely a critical classification, rather than an industry or an audience definition, something which does not invali- date it as a category, but clearly does privilege the critical recognition of common textual features (such as lighting or the characterization of the female lead) over other contexts and assumptions. The movies now usu- ally identified as film noir probably occupied more than a dozen different categories in the Production Code Administration's classification of 57 types.

Genre Recognition

Even where a critically established genre boundary more or less coincides with industrial parameters, as is the case with the Western, genre criticism reconstructs a slightly different history from that generated by other modes of research. Most accounts of the Western regard Edwin S. Porter's *The Great Train Robbery* in 1903 as constituting its birth. Recent historical research, however, suggests that such an identification came only several years later, and that contemporary audiences recognized *The Great Train Robbery* as a melodramatic example of one or more of the "chase film," the "railway genre," and the "crime film." The Western had emerged by 1910, its great appeal to American producers lying in its being an identifiably American product that could not be successfully imitated by their European competitors. This both strengthened their hold on their home market and improved their sales abroad. Not until the Italian film industry began producing "spaghetti Westerns" in the 1960s were European audiences, let alone American ones, prepared to accept foreign substitutes for the real American product.[37]

Discussions of genre recognition are commonly conducted around the Western, because the Western provides a clearer or more convincing demonstration of the case than most others. Almost every frame of a Western movie identifies it as such by the objects within it, whether these generic signifiers be setting, characters, costumes, or accoutrements. The image shown on p. 118, for instance, is dense with the Western's **iconography** or system of recurring visual motifs. These provide a shorthand system enabling a knowledgeable viewer to glean a great deal of information about the characters and the situation simply from the way the characters are dressed, the kind of clothes they wear, and so on, and this level of meaning provides such viewers with another means of gaining pleasure from the movie. An iconographic approach to genre allows us to establish quite precisely what we might expect to find in a Western. Along with the recognition of recurrent plot situations, the presence of familiar objects repeatedly confirms what kind of movie we are watching, and reinforces our expectations of how the story will develop.[38] This system of visual recognition works very well for the Western, which is atypically easy to identify. As part of the attempt to come to terms with visual discourse in cinema, early genre criticism concentrated on genres marked by their iconographic richness.

Along with their iconography, Westerns are equally easily identified by the actors who appear regularly in them (not just John Wayne or Henry Fonda, but also character actors in smaller roles, such as Slim Pickens, Andy Devine, or Jack Elam), and by their recurrent situations: gunfights, saloon brawls, the final scene in which the hero bids farewell to the woman he is leaving behind. While the representational conventions of these familiar icons and situations have changed over time, so that a silent Western

John Wayne asserts his authority in *Red River* (1948). The audience's knowledge of Western iconography tells us a great deal about what is happening in scenes like this. United Artists (courtesy Kobal)

such as *The Iron Horse* (1924) looks very different from *Pat Garrett and Billy the Kid* (1973), the situations, iconography, and characterizations recur with sufficient consistency to override historical distinctions and establish the Western as a consistent, transhistorical phenomenon.

The Western is not, of course, the only genre to possess such features. In looking at the crime film, for instance, we could identify an iconography and produce a list of recurring situations. We might, however, find more ambiguities at the visual level. For example, we can be sure that the image opposite, of Edward G. Robinson and Humphrey Bogart about to shoot it out, must come from the climax of the movie, in which the hero confronts the principal villain. But we are unlikely to know, simply from the iconography, which of them is the hero and which the villain. Such ambiguities are an inherent part of both the recurrent plots and thematics of the crime film: this image comes from a 1936 Warner Bros. movie, *Bullets or Ballots*, in which Robinson plays a cop masquerading as a racketeer. The movie's advertising made use of Robinson's persona as a gangster, while its thematic concern, like those of many crime films, examined the relationship between law, justice, and morality.

Edward G. Robinson confronts Humphrey Bogart in *Bullets or Ballots* (1936). The lighting tells us that this is the city at night, but which of the two actors is the villain? Aquarius Picture Library

It would be more difficult to come up with a consistent iconographic scheme for the horror movie or for the musical. On the other hand, just as the lighting in the image from *Bullets or Ballots* informs us that this is a crime movie because its play with shadow and strong areas of black and white tells us that this is an image of the city at night, so we recognize the image on p. 120 as unmistakably coming from a musical because only in a musical could all these people have any convincing reason for adopting the same pose at the same time. We can recognize gestures, and speak of there being gestural codes, although it is more difficult to attach precise meanings to them than to the iconographic elements we have discussed in relation to the Western. But in Westerns, too, we find hierarchies of gestural coding: the gunfighter's narrowed eyes, the hero's purposeful stride, or the familiar choreography of the saloon brawl feature in different movies to broadly the same effect, while other gestures, such as John Wayne's walk out of frame at the end of *The Searchers* (1956), are filled with meaning by the movie, and are specific to the movie rather than being implicit within the genre. To compound the problem, not all genres have systems of gestural coding that are exclusive to them, any more than they necessarily have specific lighting or iconographic codes.

West Side Story (1961). Only in a musical could all these people gesture in the same way at the same time. Mirisch-7/United Artists (courtesy Kobal)

Nonetheless, most genre critics argue that movies within a genre will share recurrent situations and consistent narrative patterns. For example, in a recent study of "the stalker film," a late-1970s sub-genre of the horror movie, Vera Dika outlines a specific sequence of plot functions that identifies them as a group. Their plots have "a two-part temporal structure," the first part of which presents a past event, structured as follows:

The members of a young community are guilty of a wrongful action.
The killer sees an injury, fault, or death.
The killer experiences a loss.
The killer kills the guilty members of the young community.

The second section of the movie, set in the present, also comprises a sequence of narrative events, ordered according to a strict pattern:

An event commemorates the past action.
The killer's destructive impulse is reactivated.
A seer warns the young community.
The young community takes no heed.
The killer stalks the young community.
The killer kills members of the young community.
The heroine sees the murders.
The heroine sees the killer.
The heroine does battle with the killer.
The heroine subdues the killer.
The heroine survives but is not free.[39]

Audiences recognize genres through plot structures like these, as well as through advertising, iconography, and gestural codes. Often such indicators overlap; in the practice of a genre-based criticism this is almost bound to be the case.

Rick Altman has distinguished between what he calls the "semantic" approach to genre – a cataloguing of common traits, characters, attitudes, locations, sets, or shots – and a "syntactic" approach that defines a genre in terms of the structural relationships between those elements that carry its thematic or social meaning.[40] Just as the semantic approach has been most often applied to the iconography of the Western, the structure of the Western has frequently been the subject of syntactic analysis. In John Cawelti's analysis, for instance, the Western takes place on the frontier between savagery and civilization, where the hero confronts his uncivilized double.[41] Another instance of the fruitful application of a structural approach to what Altman calls "the genre's fundamental syntax" is Jim Kitses' highly suggestive tabulation of "the shifting ideological play" between what he identifies as the genre's central opposition between civilization and the wilderness.

The wilderness	Civilization
The individual	**The community**
freedom	restriction
honor	institutions
self-knowledge	illusion
integrity	compromise
self-interest	social responsibility
solipsism	democracy
nature	**culture**
purity	corruption
experience	knowledge
empiricism	legalism
pragmatism	idealism
brutalization	refinement
savagery	humanity

The west	The east
America	Europe
the frontier	America
equality	class
agrarianism	industrialism
tradition	change
the past	the future[42]

Westerns contrast the west with the east, nature with culture, the individual with the community, but in describing these oppositions, the positive term in each of Kitses' pairings is sometimes in the wilderness and sometimes in civilization. This tabulation indicates that comparable situations and characters – semantic units, in Altman's terms – can be inflected with a wide variety of thematic significances, depending upon which of these oppositions is given most weight. Kitses' table clearly and concisely illustrates the potential thematic and ideological richness of a genre form.

A criticism that combines the various semantic and syntactic approaches to genre study that we have discussed can also look for the persistence of particular features in a genre, making it possible to trace fluctuations in their occurrence over time. This provides a means by which genre movies can be interpreted as rich sources of historical evidence. Film noir, for instance, could be examined as a fluctuation in the more persistent genre of the crime film, and its specific characteristics could be related to the historical circumstances of the period 1945–55. Similarly, an account of the Western might look at the ways in which the revisions of its conventions address the changing historical needs of its audience. Taking American history as its subject matter, the Western provides an opportunity to trace the changing construction of that history by the present. In its discussion of men taming a wilderness and transforming it into a garden, the Western has taken to itself a central aspect of American mythology: the civilizing spirit of American individualism. It has also become an arena in which Americans examine the relationship between individuals and society, and the tension between individual and community priorities. Along with iconographic conventions, the emphases within that ideological tension have shifted over time. Brian Henderson, for instance, has suggested that

> The emotional impact of *The Searchers* can hardly come from the issue of the kinship status and marriageability of an Indian in white society in 1956. . . . It becomes explicable only if we substitute black for red and read a film about red–white relations in 1868–1873 as a film about black–white relations in 1956.[43]

Henderson's is a common critical strategy, in part designed to elevate the text's status by way of demonstrating its cultural significance. By such a process critics can legitimize their own activity, finding ways to demonstrate that the texts they study are, when viewed from the "right" perspective, far more important than the familiar and predictable objects they might on the surface appear.

Genres, then, can be thought of as fields inhabited by thematic, iconographic, narrative, and political propensities, as instances and instruments of Hollywood's system of regulated difference. Their emphasis shifts over time, and from individual movie to movie. They are also subject to a range of industrial, aesthetic, cultural, and technical factors. At any time, an individual movie may be seen as crystallizing the forms and meanings of the genre as a whole – *My Darling Clementine* (1946), for instance, is sometimes cast in this role for the Western – but historical shifts in ideological and stylistic fashion make it difficult to speak for long about any single movie as definitive of its genre. One way of appreciating Hollywood's complex reflection of, and influence on, American culture is by looking at how such everyday phenomena as the family, romance, heroism, femininity, or childhood have been represented in different genres at different times. Generic features make it possible for us to account for the connections we make between one movie and another, not so much in terms of their similarities, or their resemblance to the imaginary composite which "typifies" a particular category, but in terms of the differences between them, and the extent to which they play with existing conventions.

The Empire of Genres: *Pat Garrett and Billy the Kid*

> The Westerner could not fulfill himself if the moment did not finally come when he can shoot his enemy down. But because that moment is so thoroughly the expression of his being, it must be kept pure. . . . The Westerner is the last gentleman, and the movies which over and over again tell his story are probably the last art form in which the concept of honor retains its strength. . . . Really, it is not violence at all which is the "point" of the Western movie, but a certain image of man, a style, which expresses itself most clearly in violence. Watch a child with his toy guns and you will see: what most interests him is not (as we so much fear) the fantasy of hurting others, but to work out how a man might look when he shoots or is shot. A hero is one who looks like a hero.
>
> Robert Warshow[44]

> Much that has been written about the Western film has been written . . . by men who cherish the fantasies embodied in these films and who, therefore, resent any effort at dispelling those fantasies.
>
> Jon Tuska[45]

The Western exhibits a number of different kinds of what Andrew Tudor has called "genre imperialism." One recent survey of the genre suggests that between 1926 and 1967, Westerns comprised a quarter of all

Hollywood's output, and on the basis of that statistic claims that it is not only the largest but also the most significant of Hollywood's genres.[46] Critic Robert Ray has argued that the genre is in a sense even larger than that, because "many of Classic Hollywood's genre movies" are best understood as "thinly camouflaged Westerns," concerned with the conflict between individualism and community. For Ray, the ability to reconcile this irreconcilable opposition makes the Western the thematic paradigm for Hollywood's commitment to "the avoidance of choice."[47] Douglas Pye argues for the centrality of the Western to genre analysis in similar terms. He suggests that its thematic richness comes from "the peculiar impurity of its inheritance," by which the archetypal imagery of romantic narrative could be blended with American history.[48] The genre imperialism exhibited here is similar to that of critics such as Will Wright, who see the persistence of genre, and of the Western in particular, as evidence that its formulae operate as particularly effective agencies for the circulation of cultural as well as purely cinematic meaning.

Central to the operation of any genre movie, including the Western, is the cumulative expectation and knowledge of the audience. Over time, this frame of reference grows ever more dense and extensive, although we should bear in mind that viewers forget as well as remember, and that the whole field of generic knowledge is unlikely to be available to any given audience, even of aficionados.[49] Loss of knowledge is particularly important in this case as Hollywood's production of Westerns declined precipitously after 1970, with barely a handful being made during the 1980s. Hollywood's apparent abandonment of what had been its most common genre raised questions about the critical arguments that claimed that the Western was central to the expression of an American mythology. Had the mythology changed, so that the Western was no longer relevant? Or had the mythology migrated elsewhere, to other genres, and if so, had it changed its meaning in the process? Or had Hollywood somehow stopped articulating American mythology? Whatever set of circumstances had brought about the change, it shows that even so self-generating and transhistorical a genre as the Western is subject to historical forces.

Pat Garrett and Billy the Kid is a Western made at the end of the line of continuous production in 1973, directed by one of the genre's last celebrated auteurs, Sam Peckinpah. As a retelling of one of the genre's most oft-told tales, it is a particularly good example of the ways in which a generic movie can set in play a complex dynamic of confirmation and revision of audience expectations. Its own case is given an added complexity by the fact that two quite distinct versions of the movie exist: one initially released by MGM in 1973 and a somewhat longer version, released for the first time in 1989, which was claimed to be much closer to the director's preferred final cut. Although auteurist criticism would certainly regard the latter as more "original," the existence of multiple versions can instead be taken as evidence of conflicting intentions among producers. In any case, multiple variants of movies have always been part of

Hollywood's production logic and the idea of an "original" is in significant contradiction to the norms of American film industry practice.[50]

The case of *Pat Garrett and Billy the Kid* is, therefore, only unusual in the amount of attention paid to the variations, a situation that came about because of the claims made for Peckinpah as an author whose "work" had been vandalized by the studio.[51] One critic went so far as to suggest that the "arbitrary and piecemeal" recut was ordered because the head of the studio, James T. Aubrey, "hated Peckinpah, and was bent on sabotaging his work."[52] A more probable motivation is that the studio executives thought Peckinpah's cut too long and uncommercial; their one addition was to elongate the scene of Sheriff Baker's (Slim Pickens) death, so that Bob Dylan's "Knockin' on Heaven's Door" could be played over it. Although this scene has been described as being "as moving as anything in Peckinpah's work,"[53] its presence in the movie owes more to the commercial considerations of emphasizing Dylan's contribution to the movie as an additional appeal to the audience. Because Peckinpah's argument with MGM was conducted so publicly, at least part of the audience at the time of the movie's release was aware of the major differences between the version they saw and Peckinpah's "original." The most important of these differences was the omission, in the MGM version, of a framing device, set in 1909, in which Garrett is murdered by the same people who employed him as sheriff to hunt down Billy. The presence or absence of this frame, which establishes the events of the movie as a flashback, clearly does affect how the movie is interpreted. But how it affects the interpretation of the release version for a viewer who knew that such a sequence was "originally" part of the movie is a different matter. This is an entirely cinematic equivalent of the more frequent situation when a viewer watches a Hollywood adaptation of a novel shorn of its more explicit elements to meet censorship requirements.

Like most Westerns, *Pat Garrett and Billy the Kid* is easily identifiable in terms of its setting and subject-matter. With what could hardly be a less oblique title, it establishes itself as a retelling of a familiar episode from Western history, the pursuit and killing of William Bonney by Pat Garrett. Expectations raised by the title are confirmed in the image track: a moving camera rapidly establishes the familiar Western iconography of landscape, architecture, costumes, and props, giving us some sense of certainty as to how the story will unfold. At the same time, we are alerted to stylistic emphases that give new inflections to these familiar forms. The most forceful of these are the shots of the live chickens being used by Billy and his fellow outlaws for target practice. We see their destruction in extreme close-up, and this encounter with a "realism" in the presentation of violence is likely to influence our attitudes to the rest of the movie. As the audience of "Sam Peckinpah's *Pat Garrett and Billy the Kid*" (as the movie was advertised), we may be aware of the director's reputation for the explicit representation of violence, often justified as a revision of Western conventions in the name of an enhanced realism. The use of setting and

costume, too, indicates that the movie is making claims to historical verisimilitude: this is, it implies, the "true" story of Billy the Kid. The title, "Old
Fort Sumner, New Mexico, 1881," locates the story with a geographical and
period precision that is typical of its revisionism.[54] Both the expansiveness
and timelessness of the "mythic" West will be replaced with an increasing
sense of "historical" claustrophobia; here both time and space are running
out. Mythical struggles give way to crudely political and economic ones. In
his first encounter with Billy, Garrett announces in very simple terms the
motivation of the action that will follow: "the electorate want you gone,
Billy." Their subsequent exchange summarizes the shifting values that
they represent and that will be contested through the story. "How does it
feel," asks Billy, to have "sold out" to the Santa Fe Ring? "It feels like times
have changed," Garrett replies. "Times maybe, but not me," is Billy's
response.

The central dramatic tension in the movie, established here and encapsulated in its very title, recapitulates what is perhaps the Western's key
structuring opposition, between the individualist values embodied by the
outlaw and those represented by the lawman on behalf of the community.
So enduring is this opposition that some critics have suggested that it
explains the persistence of the genre itself, because it answers a specifically
American cultural anxiety about the need to preserve both sets of ideals,
and stages the dramatic conflict between them at the historical moment
when America was formed as a modern nation. In Classical Westerns like
Stagecoach (1939) and *My Darling Clementine*, the official hero and the
outlaw hero overcome their differences in a larger battle to protect civilization from a greater savagery.[55] In revisionist Westerns that greater savage
threat no longer exists, and the value systems of sheriff and outlaw are
placed in what seems to the characters as an inevitable opposition in which
one must give way to the other. So in *Stagecoach*, the sheriff (George
Bancroft) acquiesces in the outlaw's escape from "the blessings of civilization"; outlaw hero Doc Holliday (Victor Mature) is redeemed by his death
at the end of *My Darling Clementine*. By contrast, in a revisionist Western
such as *The Man Who Shot Liberty Valance* (1962, and, like *Stagecoach* and *My
Darling Clementine*, directed by John Ford) the death of the individualist
hero (John Wayne) is greeted with melancholy regret and a strongly nostalgic awareness of the price paid for the democratic populism (perfectly
embodied by James Stewart) that replaces him. In *Pat Garrett and Billy the
Kid*, the values of the West will be replaced only by something more
meager, as civilization is associated not with community, but with the
corruption and corporate self-interest of the Santa Fe Ring who hire
Garrett. We should, however, be wary of suggesting too firmly that the
generic evolution of the Western has seen "the blessings of civilization"
subjected to increasingly hostile scrutiny. Tag Gallagher has pointed out
how tenuous and selective such evolutionary arguments tend to be, and in
counterpoint has suggested that because of changes in the conventions of
representation across American culture as a whole, "the films of the sixties

had to work harder, had to be more strident and dissonant, in order to try to express the same notions as earlier films." In support of his argument that Western heroes changed less in the 1960s than other critics have suggested, he offers an unconventional interpretation of Henry Fonda's performance as Wyatt Earp in *My Darling Clementine* that might also describe James Coburn's performance as Garrett:

> charm hides a self-righteous prig, and a marshal's badge and noble sentiments hide a "near-psychotic lust for violent revenge" even from Earp himself, but this upstanding Wyatt is all the more ambivalently complex a character for the sublimation of his hypocrisy and violence. . . . Wyatt clearly loves lording it over people without using his gun . . . there is no recognition in the film of Wyatt as "hero of the community": Ford cuts directly from the battle's last death to Wyatt's solitary farewell to Clementine outside of town. Nor is there any "reward" of a wedding.[56]

How convincing Gallagher's analysis would have been if the later movies did not exist to demonstrate the possibility of such interpretations is a moot point. For the moment, we might simply settle on the recognition that critics and audiences as well as filmmakers are capable of revisionist interpretations of the Classical.

For André Bazin, the Western had dramatized an epic and very public battle between "the forces of evil" and the "knights of the true cause." He saw the genre addressing basic human realities through the mythologization of a particular phase of American history.[57] The Western is an epic that works determinedly toward its final chapter; its antagonists will eventually meet to dramatize this trial of strength through the spectacle of a shootout in the main street. The morality play character of the shootout exemplifies perhaps best of all what Robert Warshow saw as the moral "openness" of the Western, "giving to the figure of the Westerner an apparent moral clarity which corresponds to the clarity of his physical image against his bare landscape."[58] But with moral terms more relative and positions more compromised, the Western universe depicted in Peckinpah's movie operates on an altogether cloudier and more domestic level; the bulk of the movie is presented as a private drama between former friends. Garrett is obsessively unwilling even to discuss the rights and wrongs of his actions, let alone to seek their ratification through their display in the public spectacle of the shootout. As the shared value-system of a Western "code" disintegrates, the traditional roles of sheriff and outlaw become confused and compromised.

Garrett is no longer the archetypal independent hero described by Warshow, reluctantly acting on behalf of the community to preserve its fragile civilization from the forces seeking to destroy it. He is rather the paid employee of a corporate interest group, hired for a dangerous job and expendable. From the outside he retains something of the character attributed to the Westerner as "last gentleman" by Warshow, and certainly displays the moral ambiguity which darkens his image and saves him from absurdity," but is no longer able to "defend the purity of his own image." He is a long way from the godlike figures wielding near-magical powers inherited by the Classical Western from American folklore and romantic narrative. Garrett no longer possesses the conviction of earlier lawmen, for all his maintenance of their physical decorum. Nor does he enjoy the support of the community itself. His silences, so long a trait of the Western sheriff, now bespeak not a moral status so much as the impossibility of his claiming any authority for what he does. As he arrives at a fuller understanding of the contradictions in which he is caught, stranded between a past he has rejected and a future he can be no part of, Garrett becomes increasingly introspective. These contradictions are not resolved with the death of Billy. When Garrett rides out of Fort Sumner, a small child runs into the frame to throw stones at him. The action ironically echoes the ending of *Shane* (1953), in which Joey (Brandon de Wilde) runs after the hero he idolizes (Alan Ladd), calling for him to come back.

Billy (Kris Kristofferson) is also a revised character, no longer embodying the primitivism and savagery that must be overcome by the force of law. Instead, the outlaw now represents the positive values that "lawful" society is itself destroying. It is the landowner Chisum's men who kill and torture for pleasure, and the character whose behavior comes closest to the psychopathic is not any of the outlaws but rather Ollinger (R.G.

Billy (Kris Kristofferson) and Garrett (James Coburn) play poker, watched by Ollinger (R.G. Armstrong), in *Pat Garrett and Billy the Kid* (1973). Aquarius Picture Library

Armstrong), the fundamentalist sheriff given custody of Billy in Lincoln. However, the movie avoids any sentimentalization of the outlaw as a doomed figure. Billy may be an anachronism, but he is scarcely a victim. He demonstrates a reluctance in the use of violence that certainly matches that of the traditional Western hero, but he can also act violently, and outside the "code," when circumstances require it, shooting Alamoosa Bill (Jack Elam) before the count in their duel is complete. A number of formal aspects of the movie echo these shifts in value and characterization. Barbed wire fences cut suggestively across a number of Classical Western compositions. The land is presented less as a symbolic scene for the realization of heroic potential than as a property value from which Billy, like everyone else, is to be excluded. As the land is closed, the protagonists are forced more than is usual into domestic spaces, where detail is emphasized at the expense of physical action. Outlaws wear spectacles, trading posts stock "fine quality tomatoes" in "airtights," colors are muted. Spaces are deprived of their mythic functions: any space can now become the scene of the violence once confined to the prairie and the main street. Tracked not to the summit of a mountain, but to a domestic interior, Billy is finally shot dead in the kitchen of an aging cowboy.

If the movie dissents from the Western's tendency to endorse the role of capitalism in the settlement of the West, its revision of the genre's conventional representation of women appears much less radical. Traditionally, the genre gives women little significant presence or responsibility. Where they do figure in the Western it is usually to signify value-systems that the hero is to endorse or ultimately refuse (the school marm, the saloon girl). As director Budd Boetticher notoriously observed: "What counts is what the heroine provokes, or rather what she represents. She is the one, or rather the love or fear she inspires in the hero, or else the concern he feels for her, who makes him act the way he does. In herself the woman has not the slightest importance."[59] Western men can be redeemed by eastern women, but western women are seldom offered the same opportunity. Doc Holliday's (Victor Mature) descent in *My Darling Clementine* is evidenced by his involvement with Chihuahua (Linda Darnell), whose quasi-Mexican name and overt profession as a saloon entertainer ensure that their relationship is doomed, and that she, like him, will meet her conventionally inevitable end. Traces of those roles are evident in *Pat Garrett*. In stark contrast to "baroque" 1950s Westerns such as *Johnny Guitar* (1954), which have been reappropriated by feminist criticism because they place women in narratively decisive roles, none of the central characters in *Pat Garrett* is a woman, or does anything for women or because of women. Sheriff Baker's wife (Katy Jurado) briefly occupies a traditional male role, taking part in a gun battle, but even as objects of display the movie's female characters are peripheral. The movie's credits include a reference to Aurora Clavell in the role of Garrett's wife, but she makes no appearance in the movie.[60] The spectacle of the brothel scene is considerably elaborated in "Peckinpah's" version, with Garrett attended to by five women. The scene's one plot point, however, in which Garrett beats up one of the prostitutes to find out where Billy is, is missing from this version. That information is provided by Poe (John Beck), the agent of the Ring who attaches himself to Garrett, and who kills him 28 years later.[61]

The movie's representation of masculinity perhaps suggests a more determined reconstruction of the genre, and there are rewards for a criticism sensitive to the ways in which homoerotic elements inform the movie. Relationships between men occupy the center of a story that revolves, as Terence Butler has put it, around "the enforcement of law versus the fraternal loyalty of male friendship." It is the male rather than the female body that is displayed and celebrated. Billy luxuriates in his already mythical status, and his body is repeatedly frozen in static postures in the image. Garrett, by contrast, is consistently framed in motion. Depicted from the outset as a fastidious dresser, he grows increasingly obsessed with his own image, aware that he will enter myth as Billy's executioner. Their shared narcissism revises Robert Warshow's observation that it is not violence which is the "point" of the Western so much as "a certain image of man, a style, which expresses itself most clearly in violence." Warshow's Westerner lives in a world of restrained violence: "There is little cruelty in Western movies and little sentimentality; our eyes are not focussed on the sufferings of the defeated but on the deportment of the hero."[62] Here violence is both less restrained and less orderly in its occurrence. The tidy rituals of the shootout are replaced by a series of haphazard ambushes, the outcomes of which are resolved not by skill but by sheer firepower. Lawmen and outlaws carry rifles or shotguns, not sixshooters. With the significant exception of the killing of Billy himself, most deaths are bloody. Peckinpah shows bodies cut to pieces in hails of rifle shot, or peppered by shotguns loaded with coins. Only the final gunplay reiterates the traditional stylization of the Western death, but the movie concludes not with a gunfight but with an execution, or, as some commentators have seen it, with the "crucifixion" that resolves the majority of Peckinpah's Westerns. The brutalization of the body that accompanies the death of male characters throughout much of Peckinpah's work is conspicuously absent in the treatment of the death of Billy, something for which Terence Butler offers a final (and controversial) explanation: "The sexual imagery of Billy's killing underlines his female dependence on Garrett in his friendship towards him. . . . Garrett seeks to hide from himself the manner in which an oppressive patriarchy has defiled him. Billy, on the other hand, finally openly assumes a female role and thus acknowledges the working of that tyranny."[63]

Pat Garrett and Billy the Kid is a complex object, both commercially and aesthetically. Our perception of its complexities depends on our awareness of the conventions that are being displaced or revised. As a revisionist Western, the movie is particularly self-conscious about the self-referentiality that is an implicit part of genre cinema, and therefore of Hollywood. This self-consciousness is most noticeable in the performances of Coburn and Kristofferson. Their dialogue, their delivery, and even the way they move convey a foreknowledge both of what will happen in the plot, and of the narrative tradition that has predestined those events. Pat, Billy, and the audience all understand the inevitability of Billy's death; little in the way of suspense is therefore sought or achieved. The wider structures of the movie also incline toward such self-consciousness. Garrett rather than Billy stands at the center of the story, concentrating our interest on the figure who will make Billy a myth by finally destroying him as a man. Peckinpah's movie thus emerges not simply as an attempt to demythologize the genre or move it toward a greater realism, but also as an attempt to revise mythology in the light of contemporary circumstances. As such it offers a particularly bleak account of American experience in the 1970s.

As the quotations from Robert Warshow suggest, the genre's conventional narrative is essentially one of ideological self-confidence. Defeat in Vietnam, the erosion of faith in domestic politics after Watergate, the oil crisis of the mid-1970s, and the long-term decline of the American economy all questioned the self-confidence at the core of the expansionist ideology represented in the Classical Western. The revisionism of *Pat Garrett and Billy the Kid* is an instance of the questioning of that self-confidence, but its self-consciousness also indicates the extent to which it, and other similar movies made in the same period, exposed the conventions by which the genre had operated. This excessive self-consciousness also contributed to the subsequent decline of the Western, as it became impossible to conceal the genre's conventions or render them transparent again. Criticism may well have played a part here, too. A writer, director, or producer working in the 1980s would have had to be extraordinarily cine-illiterate not to know that the Western is where Hollywood discusses American history and stages conflicts between alternative versions of heroism. The few Westerns made between the mid-1970s and the late 1980s all displayed an extreme generic self-consciousness, an awareness of their status within a generic tradition that some critics and some of its practitioners have chosen to elevate to the status of art.

At the same time, with so few Westerns made, audiences have lost a familiarity with their generic conventions. Movies can make fewer assumptions about their viewers' competence in the genre, and thus find themselves handicapped both by their self-consciousness and by the need to elaborate the genre's first principles for a new audience. It is perhaps hardly surprising that the few Westerns made in the 1980s were all very long movies – *Heaven's Gate* (1980) ran for 219 minutes in its original version. It is also an indication of the extent to which the Western has ceased to function fluently as a vehicle for American culture to tell itself the stories it needs to hear. Instead, the genre has acquired sufficient cultural respectability for Clint Eastwood's *Unforgiven* (1992) to become the first Western to win the Oscar for Best Picture since *Cimarron* in 1931. Contemporary Westerns are one-sided, serious affairs. Their heroes are outlaws on their way to defeat at the hands of a villainous corporate power. Instead of mythologizing individualism as a civilizing force through images of white men transforming a wilderness into a garden, in *Dances with Wolves* (1990) and *The Last of the Mohicans* (1991) civilization's malaise is registered through a celebration of the "natural" nobility of its savage opposite, the Indian. The play (in both senses) has gone out of the genre, and migrated, in the main, to science fiction and horror movies. But the argument that *The Hills Have Eyes* (1977) and *Aliens* (1986) are disguised Westerns is perhaps rooted too much in nostalgia for the apparently lost certainties of the Western's particular account of melodramatic male action. More importantly, representing the central opposition in the Western's narrative between civilization and savagery in traditional generic terms has become near-impossible given contemporary evaluations of the relation between nature and culture: the Indian as murdering, raping, ignoble savage is no longer a marketable commodity. Thus the Western's conventional thematics are severely restricted. Narratives dealing with civilization's conflict with the savage Other have migrated to other generic fields, where women can be given more to do, and where, since the alien Other is purely a creature of the imagination, no one will complain about cultural distortion, or argue that aliens are peaceful hunter-gatherers, leading a sustainable existence in a stable eco-system. In space, no one can hear you scream about misrepresentation.[64]

Genre and Gender

> Although mass media can scarcely be characterized as in any sense less self-conscious or analytic than criticism and theory about them, the fact that the discourse *within* horror cinema and the discourse *about* it diverge on some crucial points would seem to suggest that the folks who make horror movies and the folks who write about them are, if not hearing different drummers, then reading different passages of Freud.
>
> Carol J. Clover[65]

Given that the Hollywood genre about which most criticism has been written has little place for women, it is not surprising that genre criticism can hardly be described as gender neutral. Looking at the list of critically recognized genres reveals an extreme gender imbalance that perhaps reflects the simple fact that most genre critics have been men. Implicit in the preferences of much genre criticism is a valorization of patriarchal and masculine concerns, by which certain genres have been accorded an increased cultural status through a recognition of their larger thematic concerns, while the status of other genres in this critical hierarchy is demonstrated by their hardly being named or described.

In the generic mapping of Hollywood, the quantitatively overwhelming omission is that of romance, which features as the principal or secondary plot in 90 percent of Hollywood's output. Meanwhile, missing from our list on p. 116 is that category often identified as "melodrama," which in contemporary critical discourse usually refers to stories of family trauma, pathos, and heightened emotionalism. From the mid-1970s the term was often used as an alternative generic label for "the woman's film." The designation of a category of Hollywood movies for women was a more or less deliberate attempt to redress the gender imbalance within the genre categories then receiving critical attention. The two terms have since become fixed in their meaning. Melodrama has become synonymous with a group of movies preoccupied with the domestic, the sentimental, and heightened emotions: women's films, "weepies," soap operas, family and maternal melodramas. In much the same way as early genre criticism of the Western identified John Ford's *Stagecoach* as "the ideal example of the maturity of a style brought to classic perfection,"[66] the "ideal type" of melodrama was represented by a group of movies directed by Douglas Sirk in the 1950s, such as *All That Heaven Allows* (1955), in which wealthy widow Cary Scott (Jane Wyman) scandalizes the New England town of Stoningham by having an affair with her gardener, Ron Kirby (Rock Hudson). Along with this linkage has gone a critical assumption that the group of movies identified were regarded as "Hollywood's lowliest form, the woman's weepie."[67]

However, as Christine Gledhill has pointed out, this dismissive and pejorative use both of melodrama and of the "woman's film" reflected the preferences of a predominantly male group of critics, rather than the practices of the industry. Jackie Byars suggests that in a way very similar to the creation of film noir as a category, "a genre was born . . . the theoretical genre of 'melodrama' was now formed in the mold of a group of Hollywood family melodramas produced by a few talented directors obsessed with stylistic manipulation."[68] Byars goes on to observe that constructing melodrama in these terms "obscured the existence of other melodramatic genres, the melodramatic aspects of other genres like the Western, the historical variations within individual melodramatic genres, and the relationships between kinds of melodramatic genres." As she suggests, "melodrama" would more helpfully describe one of Hollywood's fundamental aesthetic strategies, the defining features of which would include a presentation of sensational events, a moral didacticism, and a determined attempt to provoke a sequence of emotional responses in the audience.

Melodrama was a term of product classification used within the industry, and its trade meaning seems to have been almost diametrically opposite to that to which criticism has put it. "Ask the next person you meet casually how he defines a melodramatic story," wrote a critic in 1906, "and he will probably tell you that it is a hodge-podge of extravagant adventures, full of blood and thunder, clashing swords and hair's-breadth escapes."[69] From then until at least 1960, the trade's understanding of "melodrama" continued to embrace this generic sense, deriving from the tradition of spectacular stage melodrama, full of "trap doors, bridges to be blown up, walls to be scaled, instruments of torture for the persecuted heroines," and the like.[70] The trade press, for instance, described *White Heat* (1950), *Body and Soul* (1947), and *Psycho* (1960), as melodramas, not *Stella Dallas* (1937), *Back Street* (1931 and 1941), or *Imitation of Life* (1934 and 1959). As far as the industry was concerned, James Cagney, not Joan Crawford, made melodramas, and directors of action movies and thrillers such as Alfred Hitchcock, Fritz Lang, Raoul Walsh, and Samuel Fuller were identified in the trade press as masters of melodrama.[71] In the 1940s the industry labeled about a third of its product as melodrama, and it clearly expected these pictures to appeal predominantly to the men in the audience.[72]

Within the trade's usage, "melodrama" was certainly not an elevated term. The "woman's film," on the other hand, had a relatively prestigious status in Classical Hollywood. Most woman's films, which would be identified as "melodramas" by the conventions of recent criticism, were placed by the industry in its other general category, of "drama." As an industry term, "woman's film" embraced a range of sub-groupings that included romantic dramas, "fallen women" films, Cinderella romances, and working-girl movies.[73] Given that Classical Hollywood assumed that the majority of its audience was female, it is hardly surprising that these "dramas" were generally of higher budget and status than the "melodramas" designed with a more masculine appeal.[74] Far from being a despised or denigrated production category, the "woman's film" was one of Hollywood's "quality" products.

This discrepancy between the language of the trade and that used by critics demonstrates with particular poignancy the difficulties in establishing an appropriate generic terminology. Although it would be possible to argue that much genre criticism, like much auteur criticism, has avoided Hollywood's history rather than explained it, that criticism has nevertheless provided many important insights into Hollywood as a cultural institution. The critical classification of melodrama also provides a useful example of the way in which, since the 1960s, critical assumptions have had a bearing on how post-Classical Hollywood has understood itself. The term has largely dropped out of currency within the trade, which has come to accept the derogatory overtones that critics incorrectly argued that it always possessed. When "melodrama" is used now to describe a movie like *The Prince of Tides* (1991), it implies something similar to its now established critical meaning, equating it with the woman's film.[75]

That point is at the center of our second reason for considering the case of melodrama. Because criticism has constructed histories for Hollywood – generic and authorial histories, for instance – that are in important respects different from Hollywood's economic history, it is at times necessary to consider these histories in tandem. It is not a simple matter of saying that one is right and the other wrong; histories are seldom that absolute. Feminist criticism of the 1970s and 1980s not surprisingly recognized

Classical Hollywood cinema's endorsement of patriarchal values. But one of the strategies it developed to both analyze and resist that endorsement, the creation of the "woman's film" as a genre, addressed the endorsement of patriarchal values in existing criticism at least as much as it addressed that endorsement in the practices of Hollywood itself. It both contributed to and hindered the analysis of Hollywood's representation of women. The valuable work done as part of that strategy cannot be ignored, but the discrepancies between the history produced by that strategy and other histories of Hollywood must be noted. In his essay, "Mass Culture as Woman: Modernism's Other," Andreas Huyssen explores the extent to which popular culture has been accorded pejorative feminine character-istics as a means of discrediting it from critical attention. From the turn of the century, Huyssen argues, political, psychological, and aesthetic discourses have "consistently and obsessively" gendered "mass culture and the masses as feminine, while high culture, whether traditional or modern, clearly remains the privileged realm of male activities." The gen-der imbalance of genre analysis represents an attempt on the part of critics, almost exclusively white and male, to identify some aspects of popular culture as part of that "real, authentic culture" which the aesthetics of Modernism have seen as "the prerogative of men."[76] In this respect, critical practice has differed significantly from Hollywood's own bluntly commer-cial project. For however it may have represented women, Hollywood did not exclude them either from its movies or from the audience it sought to attract.

Recognizing these historical circumstances may allow criticism to ex-plore the contradictions of Hollywood genres and its generic hybrids, rather than attempt to resolve those contradictions in the defence of an individual movie's internal coherence. When, in the early 1970s, critics first made the case for studying the domestic melodramas directed by Douglas Sirk, their arguments emphasized Sirk's subversive purposes in offering "a devastating indictment of the entire society's world view."[77] For once, a Hollywood director responded positively to the needs of critics to find ideologically acceptable hidden meanings. The posters for *Written on the Wind* (1956) had described it as the story of a Texas oil family's "ugly secret that thrust their private lives into public view!", but Sirk called it "a piece of social criticism, of the rich and the spoiled and of the American family." Declaring that "irony doesn't go down well with the American public,"[78] he compared the ironic happy endings of his movies to the Athenian plays of Euripides:

> There, in Athens, you feel an audience that is just as happy-go-lucky as the American audience, an audience that doesn't want to know that they could fail. There's always an exit. So you have to paste on a happy end. . . . This is what I call the Euripidean manner. And at the end there is no solution of the antitheses, just the *deus ex machina*, which today is called the "happy end."[79]

Sirk's comments gave support to critical arguments that saw his movies as Brechtian critiques of both the society they depict and their own generic conventions. As Christine Gledhill has pointed out, however, these arguments required their proponents to patronize the movies' original audiences: "Irony and parody operate between two secure points: the position which we who perceive the irony occupy and that which, held at a distance, it critiques. The 'radical reading' of the 70s belonged to the critics, made at the expense of the naïve involvement of American 'popular' audiences in the 1950s."[80] These "readings" proposed that the distance between the movie's sentimental plot and its ironic style had not been visible to the original audience. In Paul Willemen's analysis, irony was a property of the movie as a text, and the problem of the audience was dealt with by suggesting that "there appears to be a discrepancy between the audience Sirk is aiming at and the audience which he knows will come to see his films."[81] The implications for a politics of gender in critical references to Sirk's "mastery" of the "woman's film" were even more bluntly revealed in Jean-Loup Bourget's assertion that, "by systematically using the cliché-image he [Sirk] creates a distance not between the film and the audience (women ply their handkerchiefs at Sirk's films), but between the film and the director."[82]

Such criticism distinguished Sirk the subversive auteur from the genre he was working in by assuming the gullibility of the public, adopting a position that came dangerously close to the contempt for the mass audience that Huyssen drew attention to. But movies such as *All That Heaven Allows* or *Written on the Wind* provoke a multiplicity of interpretations, often in contradiction to each other, and most movies can provoke complex interpretations for reasons other than their own internal complexity. A movie may articulate contradictions powerfully without resolving them: in *All That Heaven Allows*, Cary's emotional and sexual liberation is achieved only when she subordinates her own desires to Ron's; the movie ends with the couple reunited, but only after Ron has been badly injured so that Cary becomes his nursemaid, not his lover.[83] A movie may simply be powerfully inarticulate, expressing the dramatic or ideological conflict at its center not through dialogue but in the form of spectacle, through decor, color, gesture, and composition, and through its ability to provoke an intense emotional response on the part of its audience. Or else a movie may derive its complexity from the number of contradictory viewpoints that it asks its audience to hold at the same time, something that generic hybrids do very frequently. Laura Mulvey has pointed out that ideological contradiction is "not a hidden, unconscious thread" in domestic melodrama, detectable only by special critical processes. Instead, contradiction is melodrama's "overt mainspring . . . the 1950s melodrama works by touching on sensitive areas of sexual repression and frustration," re-presenting contradictions in an aesthetic form.[84] The women Jean-Loup Bourget disparages may have gone to "weepies" like *All That Heaven Allows* not only to escape from reality but also to lament it.[85]

Situating a movie within the historical framework of its original reception can change the critic's perception of its relation to genre. Barbara Klinger has suggested that *Written on the Wind* and other domestic melodramas of the 1950s can be seen as part of a general industry trend toward more "adult" entertainment, "defined by a combination of sensationalistic and serious social subject matters."[86] In 1956 *Variety* suggested that along with blockbusters, "unusual, off-beat films with adult themes that television could not handle" allowed the industry to retain one section of its audience. The production of such "adult" movies was facilitated by revisions in the Production Code in the same year, permitting the treatment of drug addiction, abortion, and prostitution. Studios adopted novels and plays that already had "adult" profiles, and the cultural kudos of their original authors gave the movies prestige as well as notoriety. The "adult" movie category, which involved a combination of sensationalism, "adult" subject-matter, and a style emphasizing excess and psychodrama, cut across conventional generic boundaries: Klinger suggests that in the mid-1950s it included not only adaptations of Tennessee Williams' plays like *Baby Doll* (1956), Nelson Algren's novel about drug addiction *The Man with the Golden Arm* (1956), or Grace Metalious' *Peyton Place* (1957), but also *The Searchers*, more conventionally seen as a pillar of the Western, but "adult" in its sensationalist treatment of the theme of miscegenation. Certainly *Written on the Wind* fits into this cycle very well. Studio pre-release publicity described the movie as "a searing adult drama that at one time might have been considered too explosive to handle. Today, however, it takes its place among important Hollywood products that have dared to treat unconventional themes in a sensitive, realistic fashion."[87] While contemporary reviewers disagreed as to its relative sensitivity or sensationalism, many of its press reviews concurred with the opinion that "This adult drama, a penetrating exploration of morals and Freudianism of four people tossed into an emotional whirlpool by cross-relationships, a drama of vast dimension and delicacy, is further proof that Hollywood has really grown up."[88]

Genre criticism has provided an important counter-position to auteurism, and its intertextual approach provides one of the most useful points of access to Hollywood's commercial aesthetic. But genre criticism has often itself made ahistorical assumptions about its object of study. Looking at the ways in which a movie like *Written on the Wind* was situated for its potential audience complicates an analysis that requires that audience to be no more than "women plying their handkerchiefs," victimized by a text subverting generic conventions too cleverly for them to recognize. Instead, *WOW*, as it was often referred to in its publicity, can be placed within a matrix of alternative definitions, allowing its audiences and critics to interpret its complexities in a variety of generic contexts. The movie's visual appearance, the focus of many later critical claims for its subversiveness, was promoted as part of its spectacle on its first release. Articles publicizing the movie drew female spectators' attention to its decor as a source of inspiration for their own home decoration.[89] Barbara Klinger's historical examination of *Written on the Wind* helps to explain the way that generic conventions negotiate with and contradict each other across a single Hollywood movie. Such analysis may fragment a critically constructed genre such as "melodrama" into something much closer to the production industry's cycles, but it also extends our understanding of Hollywood as a generic cinema.

Notes

1 Jorge Luis Borges, "The Analytical Language of John Wilkins," in *Other Inquisitions 1937–1952* (London: Souvenir Press, 1973), p. 103. Michel Foucault cites this passage, and "the wonderment of this taxonomy," as the starting point for his work, *The Order of Things: An Archaeology of the Human Sciences* (London: Tavistock, 1974).

2 Andrew Tudor, "Genre," in Barry Keith Grant, ed., *Film Genre Reader* (Austin: University of Texas Press, 1986), p. 7.

3 Andrew Tudor, *Monsters and Mad Scientists: A Cultural History of the Horror Movie* (Oxford: Blackwell, 1989), pp. 5, 213.

4 It may be no coincidence that most of the genres delineated primarily by their content are action movies likely to appeal to a predominantly male audience.

5 J.P. Mayer, *British Cinemas and their Audiences: Sociological Studies* (London: Dobson, 1948), p. 217.

6 Steve Neale, *Genre* (London: British Film Institute, 1980), pp. 22–3.

7 Steve Neale, "Questions of Genre," *Screen* 31:1 (Spring 1990), pp. 46–7.

8 Douglas Pye, "Genre and Movies," *MOVIE* 20 (Spring 1975), p. 32.

9 Dallas W. Smythe, John R. Gregory, Alvin Ostrin, Oliver P. Colvin, and William Moroney, "Portrait of a First-Run Audience," *Quarterly Review of Film, Radio and Television* 9 (Summer 1955), p. 398; Paul F. Lazarsfeld, "Audience Research in the Movie Field," *Annals of the American Academy of Political and Social Science* 254 (November 1947), p. 166; both quoted in Bruce Austin, *Immediate Seating: A Look at Movie Audiences* (Belmont, CA: Wadsworth, 1989), p. 75.

10 Leo A. Handel, *Hollywood Looks at its Audience: A Report of Film Audience Research* (Urbana: University of Illinois Press, 1950), pp. 119–20.

11 Kleine Optical Company *Complete Illustrated Catalog* (1905), quoted in Neale, "Questions of Genre," p. 55.

12 In his "Cultural History of the Horror Movie," Andrew Tudor provides several different overlapping chronologies which correspond to cycles within the overall group. The main agency of development, he suggests, is a commercial version of the survival of the fittest: "financially successful films encourage further variations on their proven themes, thus generating a broadly cyclical pattern of successes which then decline into variously unsuccessful repetitions of the initial formula." Other, less immediately obvious patterns of commercial, cultural, and social factors overlay this crude commercial Darwinianism. Tudor, *Monsters and Mad Scientists*, p. 23.

13 Barbara Klinger, " 'Local' Genres: The Hollywood Adult Film in the 1950s," paper presented at the BFI Melodrama Conference, London, July 1992.

14 David A. Cook, *A History of Narrative Film*, 2nd edn (New York: Norton, 1990), p. 293.

15 Colin MacArthur, *Underworld USA* (London: Secker and Warburg, 1972), p. 34. For an

extended discussion of this case, see Richard Maltby, " 'Grief in the Limelight': Al Capone, Howard Hughes, the Hays Office and the Politics of the Unstable Text," in James Combs, ed., *Movies and Politics: The Dynamic Relationship* (New York: Garland, 1993), pp. 133–82.

16   Tino Balio, *Grand Design: Hollywood as a Modern Business Enterprise 1930–1939* (New York: Scribner's, 1993), p. 179.

17   Barry R. Litman, "Decision-Making in the Film Industry: The Influence of the TV Market," *Journal of Communication* 32:3 (Summer 1982), pp. 44–5, quoted in John Izod, *Hollywood and the Box Office 1895–1986* (London: Macmillan, 1988), p. 183.

18   Andrew Britton, "Blissing Out: The Politics of Reaganite Entertainment," *MOVIE* 31/32 (Winter 1986), pp. 2–3. The tendency of horror-movie audiences to engage with the movie in this fashion has often brought down the moral or political disapproval Britton exhibits here. Rather than indicating a vicarious and sadistic participation in the acts of mayhem, it may indicate, as Carol Clover and Marco Starr have suggested, a more complex act of self-defence by viewers identifying not with the killer but with his victims. It is also worth noting that vocal audience engagement was a normal feature of theatrical audience behavior until fairly late in the nineteenth century, and remained an element in moviegoing until the introduction of sound. Marco Starr, "J. Hills is Alive: A Defence of *I Spit on Your Grave*," in Martin Barker, ed., *The Video Nasties: Freedom and Censorship in the Media* (London: Pluto, 1984), p. 54. Carol J. Clover, *Men, Women and Chainsaws: Gender in the Modern Horror Film* (London: British Film Institute, 1992), pp. 118–19. Bruce A. McConachie, "Pacifying American Theatrical Audiences, 1820–1900," in Richard Butsch, ed., *For Fun and Profit: The Transformation of Leisure into Consumption* (Philadelphia: Temple University Press, 1990). Lawrence W. Levine, *Highbrow/Lowbrow: The Emergence of Cultural Hierarchy in America* (Cambridge, MA: Harvard University Press, 1988).

19   Carol Clover comes up with an alternative formulation, in which the movie's exhibition becomes "a cat-and-mouse" game in which the movie tries to catch the audience by surprise. She also understands the vocal responses of audiences in these terms. Clover, p. 202.

20   Ring Lardner Jr tells a version of this story in Aljean Harmetz, *Round Up the Usual Suspects: The Making of Casablanca – Bogart, Bergman, and World War II* (New York: Hyperion, 1992), p. 107.

21   Quoted in Clover, p. 10.

22   Neale, "Questions of Genre," p. 56.

23   Klinger's analysis of the "progressive/subversive" genre as an object manufactured by a particular critical practice (much like two of her instances, film noir and melodrama) is acute, as is her critique of that criticism's practice of "textual isolationism." Rather than attribute an immutable politics to a text by its possession of this or that narrative, thematic, or stylistic feature, Klinger sees generic variation as a form of regulated difference and an essential functioning element of the overall Hollywood system. Barbara Klinger, " 'Cinema/Ideology/Criticism' Revisited: The Progressive Genre," in Grant, pp. 74–5, 88–9.

24   Tudor, *Monsters and Mad Scientists*, p. 211.

25   James Twitchell, *Dreadful Pleasures: An Anatomy of Modern Horror* (New York: Oxford University Press, 1985), p. 84.

26   This move from genre to auteur is built into the organization of several of the important early works on individual genres, such as Colin MacArthur's *Underworld USA* and Jim Kitses', *Horizons West: Anthony Mann, Budd Boetticher, Sam Peckinpah: Studies of Authorship within the Western* (London: Thames and Hudson, 1969).

27 Clover, p. 11.
28 Robert Warshow, "Movie Chronicle: The Westerner," in Gerald Mast and Marshall Cohen, eds, *Film Theory and Criticism*, 3rd edn (New York: Oxford University Press, 1985), pp. 449–50.
29 Will Wright, *Sixguns and Society: A Structural Study of the Western* (Berkeley, CA: University of California Press, 1975), p. 15. Claude Lévi-Strauss, "The Structural Study of Myth," *Journal of American Folklore* 68:270 (1955), pp. 428–44; Vladimir Propp, *Morphology of the Folktale*, trans. Laurence Scott (Austin: University of Texas Press, 1968). Vera Dika's analysis of the "stalker film," discussed later in this chapter, provides an example of the structuralist approach to movie narrative.
30 Although we could, if we were distinguishing among devices that could be used for storing liquids. The quotation from Jorge Luis Borges at the beginning of this chapter is both funny and provocative, because its system of generic classification is nonsensical, but it might make us wonder if our own systems are any more coherent or appropriate.
31 Pye, p. 31.
32 Thomas Sobchack, "Genre Film: A Classical Experience," in Grant, p. 103.
33 For example, Barry Keith Grant, who identifies *Casablanca* (1942) as a "nongenre film." Barry Keith Grant, "Experience and Meaning in Genre Films," in Grant, p. 117.
34 Thomas Schatz, *Hollywood Genres: Formulas, Filmmaking, and the Studio System* (New York: Random House, 1981), p. 38.
35 Alan Williams, "Is a Radical Genre Criticism Possible?," *Quarterly Review of Film Studies* 9:2 (Spring 1984), pp. 123–4; Tag Gallagher, "Shoot-Out at the Genre Corral: Problems in the 'Evolution' of the Western," in Grant, pp. 202–16.
36 Paul Schrader, "Notes on Film Noir," in Grant, p. 169.
37 Charles Musser, "The Travel Genre in 1903–04: Moving Toward Fictional Narratives," *Iris* 2:1 (1984), p. 57; Neale, p. 54.
38 Thomas Elsaesser refers to this as a "phatic" process, by which the movie is greeting the audience, and letting them know what kind of experience they may expect. Thomas Elsaesser, "Narrative Cinema and Audience-oriented Aesthetics," in Tony Bennett, Susan Boyd-Bowman, Colin Mercer, and Janet Woollacott, eds, *Popular Television and Film* (London: British Film Institute, 1981), p. 271.
39 Vera Dika, "The Stalker Film, 1978–81," in Gregory A. Waller, ed., *American Horrors: Essays on the Modern American Horror Film* (Urbana: University of Illinois Press, 1987), pp. 93–4.
40 Rick Altman, "A Semantic/Syntactic Approach to Film Genre," in Grant, p. 30.
41 John Cawelti, *The Six-Gun Mystique* (Bowling Green: Bowling Green Popular University Press, 1970).
42 Kitses, p. 11.
43 Brian Henderson, "*The Searchers*: An American Dilemma," in Bill Nichols, ed., *Movies and Methods Vol. II* (Berkeley, CA: University of California Press, 1985), p. 444.
44 Warshow, pp. 438, 439, 449.
45 Jon Tuska, *The American West in Film: Critical Approaches to the Western* (Westport, CT: Greenwood, 1985), p. 263.
46 Edward Buscombe, ed., *The BFI Companion to the Western* (London: André Deutsch, 1988), p. 35.
47 Robert Ray, *A Certain Tendency of the Hollywood Cinema, 1930–1980* (Princeton, NJ: Princeton University Press, 1985), pp. 75, 84, 69.
48 Pye, pp. 34, 36.
49 We once witnessed a critical exchange in which one speaker's insistence that the

cutting between shots of the feet of the protagonists during the build-up to the climax of a spaghetti Western deliberately confused their identities was greeted with the contemptuous assertion by one listener that if the speaker could not tell a Mexican boot from an American one, he had no business expressing an opinion about Westerns. In *Pat Garrett and Billy the Kid* Billy also tells a story in which a mistake in etiquette over a pair of boots leads to a fatal gunfight.

50 Silent film was a highly malleable form: intertitles could be changed or movies short-ened by individual exhibitors as well as by distribution companies and censors. Al-though sound introduced a greater degree of material fixity, complete standardization was never achieved, and when the recycling of movies on television became acknow-ledged in the production process, the practice of making "protection shots" to preserve narrative continuity while using less explicit material once again became as common practice as it had been in the 1930s. *Close Encounters of the Third Kind* had a second theatrical release in a "special edition" three years after its initial appearance in 1977. As happens occasionally with more recent movies, the second video release of *Aliens* (1986) promoted itself by advertising that it contained "seventeen minutes of extra footage restored to the original film by its director James Cameron," who referred to it as "a dance mix." Peter Dean and Mark Kermode observe that "it is no longer enough to have *seen* a movie; the true cinéaste must *own* a favorite film (in its many different formats) and have ruthlessly dissected the work in an attempt to divine (and perhaps control) its indefinable power." Peter Dean and Mark Kermode, "WindUp," *Sight and Sound* 3:3 (new series, March 1993), p. 62. The newest technology thus promises to return to the idea that movies exist in multiple versions, reminding us of how question-able is the idea of an "original" version of a Hollywood movie.

51 Producer Darryl Zanuck removed thirty minutes from John Ford's director's cut of *My Darling Clementine*, "deleting some humor and 'sentimentality,'" and allegedly strengthening "the storyline and pace." To Ford's chagrin but on the basis of preview reactions, Ford's preferred ending was changed so that instead of shaking hands with Clementine before he rides off, Wyatt kisses her. Tag Gallagher, *John Ford: The Man and his Films* (Berkeley, CA: University of California Press, 1986), p. 233.

52 Philip French, in his introduction to a BBC television screening of the version released in 1989. The acrimony surrounding the movie's production and editing is detailed in Paul Seydor, *Peckinpah: The Western Films* (Urbana, IL: University of Chicago Press, 1980), pp. 183–211; Garner Simmons, *Peckinpah: A Portrait in Montage* (Austin, TX: University of Texas Press, 1976), pp. 169–88; and Marshall Fine, *Bloody Sam: The Life and Films of Sam Peckinpah* (New York: Primus, 1991), pp. 240–60. Michael Bliss dis-cusses the differences between the two versions, and suggests that the 1989 release version was an early, unfinished cut, in *Justified Lives: Morality and Narrative in the Films of Sam Peckinpah* (Carbondale, IL: Southern Illinois University Press, 1993), pp. 217–18, 327–8.

53 Buscombe, p. 289.

54 The title has a more obvious explanatory function in "Peckinpah's" version, where it distinguishes between the flashback and the framing scenes.

55 The opposition between "official" and "outlaw" heroes is explored in Ray, pp. 59–66.

56 Gallagher, in Grant, pp. 209–10.

57 André Bazin, "The Western: Or the American Film Par Excellence," in *What is Cinema? Vol. 2*, trans. Hugh Gray (Berkeley, CA: University of California Press, 1971), p. 147.

58 Warshow, p. 438.

59 Budd Boetticher, quoted in Laura Mulvey, "Visual Pleasure and Narrative Cinema," in *Visual and Other Pleasures* (Bloomington: Indiana University Press, 1989), p. 19.

Although Mulvey, whose use of the quotation has made it notorious, does not record the fact, Boetticher was referring specifically to the role of women in Westerns rather than movies in general.

60   Garrett's Mexican wife appears in one scene in the script, when Garrett returns to Lincoln after Billy's escape. She denounces his pursuit of Billy, and they argue. The scene was cut for the MGM release version, and is also missing from the version released in 1989. Seydor, p. 201; Doug McKinney, *Sam Peckinpah* (Boston: Twayne, 1979), p. 166; Terence Butler, *Crucified Heroes: The Films of Sam Peckinpah* (London: Gordon Fraser, 1979), p. 123.

61   As a result, Garrett's reluctance to pursue Billy, and the ambivalent attitude they share to the law, is more explicitly enacted in this version than in the "original" release.

62   Warshow, p. 449.

63   Butler, pp. 90–1.

64   Carol Clover produces a brilliantly perverse account of the generic migration of the "settler-versus-Indian" story to rape-revenge movies such as *I Spit on Your Grave* (1977): "by making the representative of urban interests (what would normally be taken as the white male elite) a woman, and the representatives of the country (what would in the western have been Native Americans) white males, these movies exactly reverse the usual system of victim sympathies. That is, with a member of the gender underclass (a woman) representing the economic overclass (the urban rich) and members of the gender overclass (males) representing the economic underclass (the rural poor), a feminist politics of rape has been deployed in the service of class and racial guilt. Raped and battered, the haves can rise to annihilate the have-nots – all in the name of feminism." Clover, p. 163.

65   Clover, p. 168.

66   Bazin, "The Evolution of the Western," in *What is Cinema? Vol. 2*, p. 149.

67   Christine Gledhill, "The Melodramatic Field: An Investigation," in Christine Gledhill, ed., *Home Is Where the Heart Is: Studies in Melodrama and the Woman's Film* (London: British Film Institute, 1987), p. 11.

68   Jackie Byars, *All That Hollywood Allows: Re-reading Gender in 1950s Melodrama* (Chapel Hill: University of North Carolina, 1991), p. 14.

69   Frederic Taber Cooper, "The Taint of Melodrama and Some Recent Books," *Bookman* (February 1906), pp. 630–5, quoted in Ben Singer, "Female Power in the Serial-queen Melodrama: The Etiology of an Anomaly," *Camera Obscura* 22 (January 1990), p. 95.

70   Montrose J. Moses, "Concerning Melodrama," *The Book News Monthly* (July 1908), p. 846, quoted in Singer, p. 95.

71   Steve Neale, "Melo Talk: On the Meaning and Use of the Term 'Melodrama' in the American Trade Press," *The Velvet Light Trap* 22 (Fall 1993), pp. 70, 75.

72   Neale, "Melo Talk," p. 72.

73   Balio, p. 235.

74   Carol J. Clover notes that video stores are more likely to classify a plot as "horror" when it is low-budget and "drama" or "suspense" when it is high-budget. Clover, p. 5.

75   *Halliwell's Film Guide* describes *The Prince of Tides* as "a lushly romantic melodrama." *Halliwell's Film Guide*, 8th edn (London: Grafton, 1992), p. 896.

76   Andreas Huyssen, "Mass Culture as Woman: Modernism's Other," in Tania Modleski, ed., *Studies in Entertainment: Critical Approaches to Mass Culture* (Bloomington, Indiana University Press, 1987), p. 191. Tania Modleski and Dana Polan also engage these issues in their essays in this book.

77   Roger D. McNiven, "The Middle-class American Home of the Fifties: The Use of Architecture in Nicholas Ray's *Bigger Than Life* and Douglas Sirk's *All That Heaven*

Allows," Cinema Journal 22:2 (Summer 1983), p. 55. A number of influential essays first appeared in a special issue of *Screen* 12:2 (Summer 1971).

78   "Irony doesn't go down well with the American public. This is not meant as a reproach, but merely that in general this public is too simple and too naïve – in the best sense of these terms – to be susceptible to irony. It requires clearly delineated positions, for and against." Sirk, quoted in Paul Willemen, "Distanciation and Douglas Sirk," in Laura Mulvey and John Halliday, eds, *Douglas Sirk* (Edinburgh: Edinburgh Film Festival, 1972), p. 26.

79   John Halliday, *Sirk on Sirk* (London: Secker and Warburg, 1971), pp. 116, 119.

80   Gledhill, p. 11.

81   Willemen, p. 26.

82   Jean-Loup Bourget, "Sirk and the Critics," *Bright Lights* 6 (Winter 1977–8), p. 8.

83   Brandon French, *On the Verge of Revolt: Women in American Films of the Fifties* (New York: Ungar, 1978), p. 102.

84   Laura Mulvey, "Notes on Sirk and Melodrama," *MOVIE* 25 (Winter 1977–8), pp. 53–6.

85   Rainer Werner Fassbinder suggested that the audience weeps during *Imitation of Life* (1959) because it understands why the movie's characters must be in conflict, and how that conflict is inevitably produced by social forces: "The cruelty is that we can understand them both [Annie and Sarah Jane], both are right and no one will be able to help them. Unless we change the world. At this point all of us in the cinema cried. Because changing the world is so difficult." Rainer Werner Fassbinder, "Six Films by Douglas Sirk," in Mulvey and Halliday, p. 106.

86   Barbara Klinger, "Much Ado About Excess: Genre, Mise-en-scène and the Woman in *Written on the Wind*," *Wide Angle* 11:4 (1989), p. 11.

87   Quoted in Klinger, " 'Local' Genres," p. 10.

88   Quoted in Klinger, "Much Ado," p. 12.

89   Klinger, "Much Ado," p. 15.

4 Technology

No-one ever bought a ticket to watch technology.

Syd Silverman[1]

Quaid: How real does it seem?
Bob McLean: As real as any memory in your head. I'm telling you, Doug, your brain will not know the difference. And that's guaranteed or your money back.

The salesman for Recall Inc., selling "the memory of your ideal vacation, cheaper, safer and better than the real thing," in *Total Recall* (1990)

Many of the scientific discoveries and inventions that gave rise to the cinema as we know it were designed for other purposes. To make photographs that moved required, among other things, the invention of a material that could be impregnated with chemicals sensitive to light, but was thin and flexible enough to be wound through a camera and then a projector at a constant speed. That material was celluloid, first used as a substitute for ivory in the manufacture of billiard balls and false teeth, and later to make detachable collars for men's shirts. Rather than being a technological innovator, the movie industry has routinely adapted the inventions of others, deploying technology – like genre – in the service of its system of regulated difference. In intermittently offering a "new and improved" product, Hollywood has used technology to renovate and on occasion to reinvent itself in what Philip Hayward and Tana Wollen have called "a continuing dynamic, a drive towards product upgrading in order to retain and revive audiences."[2] Novelty has been provided sometimes through technical innovations such as sound or widescreen. More consistently but less obtrusively, technology has supplied an element of predictability through standardization.

Technology has influenced what movies look and sound like in their small details as well as in the major changes occasioned by the introduction of color or electronic recording. Each studio's distinctive visual style in the late 1930s, for instance, was as much composed of myriad "background" decisions about film stocks and lighting systems as it was designated by the studio's contract roster of stars or writers.[3] Alongside production factors lay Hollywood's relationship with exhibition technology. From air-conditioning to laser discs or the "total sensory involvement" of recent large-format projection systems, technical developments have periodically revised the viewing experience. Sound, for instance, radically changed the interior architecture of movie theaters. Picture palaces were designed to sound like concert halls or churches, the appropriate acoustical settings for the large orchestras that accompanied silent movies. The talkies needed more intimate spaces with much less echo, and the Moderne theatres of the 1930s were engineered to minimize sound reverberation and maximize the intelligibility of dialogue.[4]

Because the determining effect of technological change on Hollywood is a subject of some controversy among cinema historians and critics, we must look not only at the various technologies, large and small, but also at the different ways in which the history of cinema technology has been understood. Most histories of cinema begin with a technical history, an account of the movies' invention in the 1890s. This reminds us that although the cinema became a form of expression and mass communication in the twentieth century, the sources of its technology lie in the scientific exploration and the thought of an earlier period. With their cogs, sprocket teeth, and gearing systems designed to produce the interrupted motion that holds a single frame of film still in front of the lens for a fraction of a second, and then moves on to the next frame, film cameras and projectors are complex mechanical objects not unlike spring-powered clocks or machine guns. They depend on a mechanical technology, and as such these "machines of the visible" are, as William K. Dickson, principal inventor of the Kinetoscope, put it, "the crown and flower of nineteenth-century magic" rather than pieces of twentieth-century technology.[5] Although cinema uses electricity, it is a mistake to think of it as an electrical medium. In its earliest forms it made no use of electrical power; it was hand-driven or "cranked" rather than powered by an electric motor, and illuminated by gas, not electric light. Even by the late 1920s, when the sound cinema of the picture palaces incorporated all the major features of cinema technology which we enjoy today, it was essentially synthesizing nineteenth-century inventions: mechanical sound recording (pioneered by Thomas Edison during the 1870s), an efficient film transport mechanism (produced by Edison and others in the 1890s), the electric light (also generally agreed to have been invented by Edison around 1878), and the electric motor (demonstrated by Michael Faraday in 1821 and perfected by Zenobe Theophise in Vienna in 1873).[6]

Although few histories of the cinema pay much attention to the development of sound technology, the cinematic apparatus is a machine of the audible as well as the visible, and more fundamental changes have taken place in the technology of electrical sound recording and transmission than in the optics and chemistry of image processing.[7] Many of cinema's technical pioneers were involved in the development of both sound and image reproduction. Thomas Edison developed the Kinetoscope with the intention of adding images to his phonograph sound recording system. Charles Pathé, who pioneered the phonograph in Europe, industrialized cinema

"The crown and flower of nineteenth-century magic," the early motion picture camera (this illustration dates from 1915) was a complex, but hand-driven, mechanical device. Unexposed film was stored on a reel in the box on the upper left, and passed through the shutter gate by a system of sprocket wheels, to be rewound in the lower box. The crank handle, with which the operator wound the film through the camera, can be seen on the lower right. Only when sound movies demanded an exact consistency in the rate at which the films passed through the camera did an electric motor replace "hand cranking."

Source: Bernard E. Jones, *The Cinematograph Book*, London, Cassell, 1915

and provided the model for its successful commercial exploitation. Between 1908 and 1911 the Cameraphone system, recording the sound of a vaudeville performance on a phonograph disc synchronized with a film image, enjoyed a brief commercial success. More recent developments out of sound recording have given us television and video-recording, and the shifting relation between image and sound technology continues to play a significant role in endlessly redefining Hollywood's commercial aesthetic.

André Bazin's *Total Recall*

Despite Hollywood's history of technological opportunism, determined in the last instance by economic motives, the counter-argument embedded in many critical accounts implies that the invention of the cinematic apparatus in the late nineteenth century came as a response to a pre-existing aesthetic and cultural need: to achieve the objective, unmediated reproduction of reality. Further, it is often argued that this has remained the motive force behind the technological development of the cinema ever since. The most influential expression of this position has been that of the French critic, André Bazin. In a 1946 article, "The Myth of Total Cinema," he suggested that:

> the guiding myth . . . inspiring the invention of the cinema, is the accomplishment of that which dominated in a more or less vague fashion all the mechanical reproduction of reality in the nineteenth century, namely an integral realism, a recreation of the world in its own image, an image unburdened by the freedom of interpretation of the artist or the irreversibility of time.[8]

Bazin gave technological innovation as such a secondary role in the development of cinema, seeing "basic technical discoveries" as "fortunate accidents" brought about by the "preconceived ideas of the inventors." In his account, ideas preceded inventions, and often had to wait for technology to "catch up" before they could be realized. Inventors were "prophets" not technicians, who as long ago as the 1880s visualized a "total cinema" that could produce a "total and complete representation of reality, . . . the reconstruction of a perfect illusion of the outside world in sound, color, and relief."[9] In emphasizing that vision over material forces, Bazin's explanation was idealist. It was also teleological: he thought the goal of "total cinema" was as predetermined as if it were "a fetus in its inventors' imaginations." "The basis of cinema since its origins . . . is a quest for realism of the image. A realism, one could say, implied by the automatic generation of the image, and which aims to confer upon this image as many common properties of natural perception as possible."[10] Bazin's history, like all history, was written retrospectively, looking for causes in the past to explain the present. He emphasized those events that best supported his evolutionary argument, and constructed them into a continuous narrative that recounted cinema's technological development as a far more direct and linear process than it would have appeared to any of its innovators or "prophets."

Bazin did not claim that cinema would eventually achieve an undetectable simulation of reality, but rather that the drive behind successive technical developments such as synchronized sound and deep-focus cinematography was to give the viewer "as perfect an illusion of reality as possible within the limits of the logical demands of cinematographic narrative and of the current limits of technique."[11] In taking this position, he was arguing against other theorists of cinema who saw sound and color photography as impediments to the cinema's development as an art that derived its power from its unreality. Bazin suggested that the particular aesthetic of the cinema lay in the contradiction between its goal and the inevitable failure of its achievement. "Perception," he held, "is a synthesis whose elements react against each other," and he illustrated his case by pointing out that stereoscopic filming in 3-D created an effective impression of objects in space – things seemed to be projected out of the screen toward the audience – but that these objects were "in the form of intangible phantoms" the audience could see but not touch. "The internal contradiction of this depth which one cannot touch gives an impression of irreality that is even more perceptible than that of flat cinema in black and white."[12] However, if the aesthetic possibilities of cinema were to evolve through such contradictions, it would be "absurd to resist every new technical development aiming to add to the realism of cinema, namely sound, color, and stereoscopy."[13]

What did Bazin mean by **realism**? It is a term with a multiplicity of meanings and a complex history of its own, on which an enormous amount of critical energy has been expended. It has a particularly troublesome relation to the study of cinema, and we shall return to its use in different critical contexts at several points in this book. Much of what Bazin proposes about realism in the cinema is a sophisticated version of commonly held assumptions about why the movies should be regarded as somehow inherently more "realist" than other, less mimetic media. For that reason, as well as because his propositions form the starting point for almost every discussion of the subject, Bazin represents an obvious place to begin our consideration of this thorny territory.

Bazin's complex interweaving of ideas about perception and ideas about space may also indicate that, whether they are fully articulated or not, our commonplace ideas about realism are more complex than we might at first imagine. In our everyday use of the term "realistic," we invoke realism to evaluate the extent to which a representation or a narrative is like some previously established reality – or, in a commonly used critical phrase, the extent of its "adequacy to the real." When, for instance, we describe a plot coincidence in a movie as unrealistic, we mean that coincidences like that don't happen in real life. Importantly, however, we need to know already what the "reality" or "real life" we are referring to is, before we can assess the "realism" of a representation in this sense.

This is in large part why definitions of realism seem so circular. Literary critic Raymond Williams has suggested that the purpose of realism in art is "to show things as they really are."[14] John Ellis maintains that "'Realism' denotes the expectation that a particular representation should present a 'realistic portrayal' of character and event," and then points out that beneath this tautology lie several other tautologies dealing with different ways in which "realism" can be "realistic": "[it] should have a surface accuracy; it should conform to notions of what we expect to happen; it should explain itself adequately to us as audience; it should conform to particular notions of psychology and character motivation."[15] But no account of realism progresses very far before it recognizes that realism, like all other approaches to art, relies on a system of conventions of representation. Terry Lovell explains that "Because the work of art is constructed out of different materials from the world it represents, the extent to which that representation is 'like' the thing represented must be strictly limited."[16] A photograph of a table is a photograph, not a table. To look at a photograph and see a table is to look through the system of representation, and choose to ignore its presence. But unless we are only talking about *trompe l'oeil* or special effects, we are not fooled about what we see: we do not believe the photograph to be a table. When we choose to ignore the representation we choose, in effect, to accept a representational convention as if it were transparent.[17] But as Lovell argues, it is not necessary to the success of realism in art that viewers should mistake the art object for what it represents. Viewers are "much more aware than conventionalist critics suppose, or than they themselves can articulate, of the rules which govern this type of representation. The critics' or the viewers' naïve complaint that such and such is 'not realistic' frequently masks a complaint that the rules have been broken."[18]

To an even greater extent than the photographic image, recorded sound is ordinarily assumed to be mimetic, mechanically neutral in its reproduction of the external world. Even critics who insist on the conventional nature of photographic representation regard sound as much less mediated: "Auditory aspects, provided that the recording is well done, undergo no appreciable loss in relation to the corresponding sound in the real world: in principle, nothing distinguishes a gunshot heard in a film from a gunshot heard in the street."[19] But as James Lastra observes, "anyone who has ever attempted to post-sync a gunshot for a film can tell you that there are dozens of acceptable substitutes – many of them more acceptable than an actual gunshot."[20] What matters is the viewer/auditor's ability to identify the source of the sound, and for this to happen, synchronization of sound and image is far more important than the fidelity of the recording: "Decades of tin-sheet thunder and coconut shell hooves . . . prove that fidelity to source is not a *property* of film sound, but an *effect* of synchronization. A gun firing on the screen accompanied by any brief, sudden, explosive sound *produces* the effect of source, it doesn't require it as a precondition."[21]

Sound recording, then, just as much as the photographic image, is better understood as sound *representation* rather than sound *reproduction*. The observable phenomenon that any brief, explosive sound can stand in for a gunshot is a reminder of the distance between representation and external reality, and of the extent of an audience's enthusiastic cooperation in bridging that distance. Amy Lawrence argues that the audience's awareness of the cinematic apparatus and its "ability to deceive" is fundamental to its appeal:

> When a phonograph listener of 1898 gazed at a flat wax disc and murmured to himself, "That's Caruso," he was participating in a sophisticated form of make-believe. This type of "play" openly demonstrates the listener/viewer's facility at a skill essential to subjectivity: the ability to construct "reality" or realism out of the most brazen artifice.[22]

But at the same time as we can recognize that what we invoke in the name of "realism" is a system of convention whose construction we cooperate in – it is what in the previous chapter we called cultural verisimilitude – we must also recognize the power of the term. The goal of realism is an illusion. Art cannot "show things as they really are," because the "real" in realism is defined as being that which is unmediated by representation. Since it is outside representation, it cannot be represented: representations can be only more or less inadequate imitations or substitutions for it. But precisely because it remains an absolute, untarnished by the compromises of representation, the "real" retains a tremendous power as a point of reference to be invoked in the rhetoric of criticism. And for theorists like André Bazin, the fact that a "total and complete representation of reality" was unattainable did not prevent its inventors and creators pursuing the quest for realism.

Bazin understood cinema to be fundamentally a photographic process, one that objectively recorded and revealed the concrete empirical reality of objects in space. In Bazin's sense, the object of realism was not to fool the eye but "to give significant expression to the world both concretely and in its essence." The significance of cinema in this general aesthetic project was not that it did this more accurately than other means – that would be part of what he called the pseudo-realism of deception – but that it worked by mechanical reproduction. The fact of mechanical reproduction gave photography its credibility, and made it "objective" in a way that painting could never be. In French, *"objectif"* not only means "objective," but also is the word for "lens." Bazin called cinema "objectivity in time."[23] He identified a fundamental distinction between those filmmakers "who put their faith in the image, and those who put their faith in reality." By "the image," he explained, he meant "everything that the representation on the screen adds to the object there represented." Against this tendency to embellish, he championed the aesthetic in which "the image is evaluated not according to what it adds to reality but what it reveals of it."[24]

What realism crucially revealed was the continuity of space and time and what Bazin called "the ambiguity of reality."[25] For Bazin, ambiguity was inherent in human perception: viewing an object or an event, we recognize that our perception of it is only partial, and that it remains available for perceptions and interpretations different from our own. "If perceptual space and time are rendered with honesty, a narrative will lie obscured within the ambiguities of recalcitrant sense data. If, on the other hand, narrative space and time are the object of a film, perceptual space and time will have to be systematically fragmented and manipulated."[26] Bazin understood cinematic realism as ultimately a matter of the cinema's fidelity to the psychology of human perception, rather than involving a physical imitation of the way we see objects. To achieve that fidelity, however, required a constant technical improvement in the imitation of our perception of space and time. Some examples may help. In 1898, a traveling exhibitor commented that in a film of the Spanish-American War he showed "the pictures of the battleships in action were so real that every time a shot was fired the women would duck their heads to let the thirteen-inch shells pass over."[27] Later, more sophisticated audiences would have had no difficulty in recognizing that particular cinematic illusion, but they would in turn experience a similar moment of vertigo when their perception of cinematic space and time became uncertain in other ways.

The plot of *Total Recall* (1990) revolves around a Bazinian sense of perceptual realism, for both its central character and the audience. In 2084 Douglas Quaid (Arnold Schwarzenegger) is a construction worker who buys himself "the memory of a lifetime," a fantasy vacation trip to Mars in which he will play the role of a secret agent. When the memory implantation procedure goes wrong, he discovers that he is really an agent called Hauser who is being hunted by an interplanetary conspiracy, and he escapes to Mars to avoid assassination. In the middle of his adventure a doctor appears, claiming that none of it is actually happening, and that Quaid is still really in the vacation parlor. "What you're experiencing," he explains, "is a free-form delusion based on our memory tapes, but you're inventing it as you go along . . . and we can't snap you out of it." What Quaid (and the audience) have experienced so far is "a paranoid episode triggered by acute neurochemical trauma," he says. Quaid within the fiction, and the audience as witnesses to it, are faced with an existential crisis about the ontological status of what they are perceiving: what cues could we use to tell delusion apart from reality? The only certainty for the audience is that we know we cannot distinguish between the reality of Earth in 2084 and Quaid's paranoid fantasy about Mars. The two *look* completely interchangeable, as perceptually real as each other. Quaid's decision to remain inside the fantasy, and the audience's compliance with that decision, make it impossible for either him or us to tell the difference between real perceptions and imagined ones – just as the salesman promised when he promoted the holiday: "By the time the trip is over, you get the girl, kill the bad guys and save the entire planet."[28]

The technology involved in manufacturing *Total Recall*'s perceptual illusions is vastly more complex than that involved in the 1898 film (and the technology the movie imagines is more complex still), but the blurring of perceptual categories is comparable. Technological innovators have most often invoked the rhetoric of greater realism to sell their product. Early filmmakers described their images as "life-like," Vitaphone insisted that sound made characters in movies "act and talk like living people." Cinerama proclaimed that it "creates all the illusion of reality . . . you see things the way you do in real life."[29] A producer of 3-D movies declared that he planned to exploit the three-dimensional effect by throwing things at the audience "until they start throwing them back," while in 1953, Twentieth Century-Fox claimed that CinemaScope "simulates [the] third-dimension to the extent that objects and things appear to be part of the audience."[30] More technical explanations of CinemaScope suggested that it activated the viewer's peripheral vision and required lateral eye movement. Together these ocular effects replaced the feeling of watching a framed picture with the sensation of viewing an actual space: "Scope places the spectator in an environment and creates a feeling of participation."[31] Along with more exotic systems such as Smell-o-Vision, used in the 1960 movie *Scent of Mystery*, or Sensurround, which used low frequency sound to simulate the sensations of an earthquake tremor in *Earthquake* (1974), all these devices were designed to provide not so much a greater realism as a greater illusion of audience involvement with the spectacle of the screen, requiring an ever-greater elaboration of that illusionist spectacle. John Belton observes that:

> the advent of sound, color, and widescreen was identified not only with realism but with spectacle. The attention of the audience was drawn to the novelty of the apparatus itself. The "greater realism" produced by the new technology was understood, it would seem, as a kind of excess, which was in turn packaged as spectacle.[32]

This habit of packaging spectacle had little appeal for Bazin, whose insistence on the ambiguity of reality meant that he preferred some outcomes of technological change to others. The special effects technology so abundant in *Total Recall*, for example, would count very much as an enhancement of "the image," not in any sense a revelation of reality.[33] But the technology of "morphing" used in *Terminator 2: Judgment Day* (1991), in which the image is altered through computer manipulation so that one object can be transformed into another in a continuous shot, questions Bazin's basic assumption that "the objective nature of photography confers on it a quality of credibility absent from all other picture making."[34] The computerized revision of the image – literally a re-vision – makes the distinction between reality and the image ever more difficult to maintain.[35]

The major events in Bazin's account of cinema's technological development included the arrival of sound and deep-focus photography, which he saw as coming about not as a solution to a "technical problem," but out of "a search for a style." Bazin celebrated Orson Welles, among others, for taking cinema closer and closer toward this complete illusion of reality, by using deep-focus to create dramatic effects "for which we had formerly relied on montage." What Bazin saw as important about deep-focus photography was that it allowed the viewer a continuous gaze over a continuous space, rather than fragmenting the viewer's perception of that space through editing. His objection to narrative editing was that it presupposed that a piece of reality or an event has only one sense at any given moment, and that by specifying the meaning of the raw material, editing conflicted with our normal, ambiguous relationship to empirical reality. There was, he maintained, "a deeper psychological reality, which must be preserved in realistic cinema: the freedom of the spectator to choose his own interpretation of the object or event."[36] In this way deep-focus had "reintroduced ambiguity into the structure of the image."[37] The idea of the ambiguity of reality is central to Bazin's thought: a movie ought to imitate this, and provide audiences with the opportunity for multiple, even conflicting, acts of interpretation. As Dudley Andrew suggests, this is almost a moral argument: "the spectator *should* be forced to wrestle with the meanings of a filmed event because he *should* wrestle with the meanings of events in empirical reality in his daily life. Reality and realism both insist on the human mind wrestling with facts that are at once concrete and ambiguous."[38]

Widescreen

Bazin's attitude to deep-focus, his theory of technological progress, and his preference for an observational cinema all encouraged him to view the arrival of widescreen cinema in the early 1950s as an important advance in the cinema's potential for realism, although his enthusiasm was somewhat tempered by his viewing of the first CinemaScope movie, a Biblical epic called *The Robe* (1953). Bazin recognized that widescreen had been innovated because of the economic crisis in the industry, but his sense of technological progression led him to conclude, nevertheless, that "this industrial art, prey to economic accident, has only known, fundamentally, technical advances which moved in the same direction as its aesthetic advances."[39]

The introduction of widescreen systems is a useful instance of the interrelationship between technological and economic forces in determining the appearance and the realism of Hollywood movies. The screen did not change shape in the early 1950s because producers were pursuing a more impressive simulation of reality for its own sake, but because of the catastrophic decline of movie audiences, from 90 million a week in 1948 to 51 million in 1952. For large parts of the audience, newly moved to the suburbs with their young families, moviegoing stopped being a regular weekly or twice-weekly experience. With profits falling even more drastically, the production industry had to repackage its product very rapidly, and sell it on a different basis. A movie had to become much more of a special event to draw its audience.

From 1952 onward the industry experimented with a number of enhancements to a movie's sound and image to lure the audience back, by giving them, literally, a bigger picture. The first widescreen process, Cinerama, involved a very extensive (and expensive) conversion for existing cinemas, building new booths for each of the three projectors it used, installing a much bigger screen, and reducing the number of seats. A handful of picture palaces in major cities converted, and played the few movies made in Cinerama in extended runs of as long as two years. The most successful Cinerama movies were travelogues, reminiscent of early cinema's initial production of "scenics" and "topicals" rather than dramatic stories. Reviewers compared the behavior of audiences leaning sideways in their seats or ducking to avoid passing spray to the responses of the earliest cinema viewers, but they also remarked that "the very size and sweep of the Cinerama screen would seem to render it impractical for story-telling techniques now employed in film."[40] Although Cinerama was profitable in the few locations in which it was installed, installation cost far too much for it to become an industry standard. By contrast, 3-D systems were much cheaper for exhibitors to install, but were technically far from perfect. Moreover, audiences disliked the glasses they had to wear to see the 3-D effect, and tired rapidly of the gimmick of having things thrown at them in a series of low-budget adventure and horror movies. Twentieth Century-Fox devised CinemaScope as a system that would also augment a movie's sound and image, but in a way that would enhance the kinds of fictional movie Hollywood made, attract the lost audience back on a regular basis, and prove economically acceptable to the great majority of exhibitors.

Widescreen was the most drastic shift in what the screen *looked* like in the history of cinema. It required alterations in the internal architecture of movie theaters almost as large as those required by sound. Widescreen processes literally changed the shape of the image, nearly doubling its width from the previous standard **aspect ratio** (image height : image width) of 1:1.33 to 1:2.6 in Cinerama or 1:2.35 in CinemaScope.[41] But the basic optical technology behind the widescreen processes of the early 1950s was not new. The CinemaScope anamorphic lens system, which compressed an image horizontally in photographing it, and "stretched" it out again in projection, had been invented in the 1920s, but unlike the technology of sound reproduction, no large corporate interests

Aspect ratios: the changing shape of the Hollywood movie
In 1932, the Academy of Motion Picture Arts and Sciences established a norm for the shape of Hollywood's screen. The Academy ratio (a), like the normal screen shape for silent cinema, was 1:1.33 (aspect ratios are expressed as image height:image width). This shape was revised in the 1950s. Cinerama (1:2.6) was the most extreme widescreen system (b), its curved screen filling the viewer's vision. During the 1950s, directors were encouraged to compose for the whole width of the CinemaScope frame (initially 1:2.55, but later reduced to 1:2.35, (c)), so that viewers would scan the frame horizontally as they watched. But as sales to television became more important to movie finances, less extreme widescreen systems replaced CinemaScope. Panavision, the most common widescreen process since the 1960s, has an aspect ratio of 1:2.25 (d). In 1960, the Society of Motion Picture Engineers (SMPE) adopted a revised standard aspect ratio of 1:1.85 (e). Because of the importance of sales to television, movie images are now normally composed to accommodate television screenings, with the important visual information being contained within the "safe action area" of television's aspect ratio (e), which is close to the original Academy ratio.

underwrote its development. CinemaScope was not, however, a piece of 1920s technology that had sat on the shelf for 25 years, waiting for a suitable set of economic circumstances. It relied on postwar technological developments in film stock, sound recording, computer lens design, and the materials used in making cinema screens, assembled together by TCF's Research and Development Department.[42] To persuade exhibitors to accept CinemaScope, TCF had to guarantee a supply of pictures in the format, and that involved persuading other major companies to adopt it. They also had to cut down the package they had initially developed. CinemaScope, like Cinerama, was designed for stereophonic sound, but the costs of installing this, and fitting the new metallic screens, deterred small independent exhibitors, and these requirements were eventually dropped to ensure the widespread adoption of the system.

CinemaScope was sold to exhibitors and audiences alike on its scale, its technological novelty, and its added realism. Studios were concentrating production resources on fewer, more expensive movies because of the decline in audiences, and CinemaScope allowed them to represent this in terms of the grandeur of the projects they were producing: a trade paper advert in December 1953 declared that "CinemaScope demands a bigger story, more action." As a result, Darryl Zanuck had adapted not one but "two great Broadway stage plays" to produce *How to Marry a Millionaire* (1953). "Exhibitors know that the public wants to see only great pictures, and since CinemaScope requires bigger and better pictures, this system represents to the theatre man the answer to the box office drop."[43] The system's association with scale, and most importantly the immediate success of its first releases, established CinemaScope as a drawing power in its own right; as Belton has argued, CinemaScope had to be "marketable as a *process*, to become a star."[44] In 1954, TCF announced a switch in their production strategy, from stars to "subject matter," movies that would emphasize the advantages of CinemaScope.

The way in which CinemaScope was marketed as an intensified experience was sharply at odds with Bazin's preference for technological developments that encouraged an observational cinema. If no one was exactly going to the movies to see technology, they were at least going because of the scale that technology implied. The experience that CinemaScope offered was often expressed in terms of a greater feeling of audience participation: "You're the same as in the front row of a legitimate theatre."[45] The industry's promotional connection between the movies and "the legitimate theatre" relocated some of the cultural assumptions attached to the moviegoing experience, as well as strengthening the major exhibition chains by differentiating their product from the conventional format movies shown in the neighborhood subsequent-run theaters. CinemaScope's success, however, meant that this commercial advantage was relatively short-lived: by 1956, only three years after its launch, 80 percent of American theaters were equipped to show widescreen movies.[46] The added realism that CinemaScope provided lay not so much in its simulation of reality as in the enhancement of fiction in terms of Hollywood's already established narrative and spectacular logic. Cinerama presented the reality of a rollercoaster ride or a flight through the Grand Canyon, but CinemaScope "reaffirmed a vision of the cinema as dramatic fiction, a form of illusion that was apparent as such to the spectator. . . . CinemaScope could provide a more realistic presentation of a fiction, and in so doing increase the power of the fiction."[47]

Color

In the same way as "silent" movies always had sound accompaniment of some kind, from very early on a number of pictures had been in color. In the 1920s, as many as 80–90 percent of silent movies had been printed on tinted film, associating color with mood rather than with naturalism.[48] The introduction of sound largely put an end to this process, initially because the dyes used in tinting the film reduced the quality of sound reproduction. Although this problem could, technically, have been overcome, the aesthetic regime of sound movies discouraged the symbolic use of color tints. This change can be seen as a move toward a greater realism, but it can also be seen as an uncertainty in how to use color in relation to sound. Color, like widescreen, might have been developed in the early 1930s, but the uncertain fortunes of the major companies during the Depression deterred them from adopting it except for specific, spectacular effect. For the best part of two decades until well into the 1950s, color was promoted as a spectacular production value in its own right, and no more than one movie in ten was made in color until the late 1940s.

The production of color film was initially the preserve of one company, Technicolor, which had a virtual monopoly over the color system used by the major studios until 1948, largely because of its agreements with Eastman Kodak. Technicolor's three-strip system recorded separate red, blue, and green images on different negatives, and required the use of a special camera, which the studios could only lease, not buy. Technicolor also controlled the supply and processing of film stock and the number of color films in production, rationing them out among the major companies and even demanding approval of subject-matter. The studios had to hire Technicolor cameramen and color consultants to work with the studios' art directors and set designers. As a result, Technicolor exercised a good deal of control over the aesthetic uses to which color was put. The bulky beam-splitter Technicolor camera restricted movement; the Technicolor stock's need for comparatively even lighting schemes deterred other kinds of visual experimentation.

Here, as with widescreen, we can observe Hollywood's attitude to the creation of the illusion of reality. Technicolor's color consultants keyed color reproduction to skin tones and forcibly discouraged the use of filters or unconventional effects. Above all, a movie's color was coordinated around the visual presentation of its female star, who "must be given undisputed priority as to the color of make-up, hair and costume which will best complement her complexion and her figure. If her complexion limits the colors she can wear successfully, this in turn restricts the background colors which will complement her complexion and her costumes to best advantage."[49] Technicolor exposed the "unnaturalness" of styles of makeup devised for black-and-white photography. It required a different technique: as Max Factor, who devised a new range of makeup for Technicolor, explained, "We are no longer striving for a purely artificial contrast but seeking to imitate and enhance the subject's natural coloring."[50] The making-over of Janet Gaynor in *A Star is Born* (1937) illustrates the considerable technology of cosmetic artifice directed toward the rendering of Hollywood's female stars as sites of "natural beauty." As Steve Neale puts it:

> Since women within patriarchal ideology already occupy the contradictory spaces both of nature and culture (since they therefore evoke both the natural and the artificial) and since also they are marked as socially sanctioned objects of erotic looking, it is no wonder that . . . they function both as a source of the spectacle of color in practice and as a reference point for the use and promotion of color in theory.[51]

Hollywood's female stars were both natural and glamorous, and the technology that produced them, like the others we have discussed, was meant to be both present and invisible. It fulfilled this contradiction by claiming to add art to reality: Technicolor advertised itself as "natural color" that had nevertheless "painted" a new world for movie fans.[52] Technicolor's chief consultant, Natalie Kalmus, explained in 1938 that color photography had brought an "enhanced realism" into being, which:

> enables us to portray life and nature as it really is, and in this respect we have made definite strides forward. A motion picture, however, will be merely an accurate record of certain events unless we guide this realism into the realms of art. To accomplish this it becomes necessary to augment the mechanical processes with the inspirational work of the artist. It is not enough that we put a perfect record on the screen. That record must be molded according to the basic principles of art.[53]

This meant planning and controlling the use of color to fit the mood of each scene and augment its dramatic value – a more elaborate version of the symbolic use of color in tinting silent movies. "Color should be used like music," wrote Lansing C. Holden, color designer on *A Star is Born*, "to heighten the emotional impact of a scene."[54] The realism invoked here was contradictory. "Natural" color was a spectacle, and as such at least potentially distracting from a movie's narrative and from its other spectacles. Color was organized into an aesthetic regime, the choice of color being motivated by some other element in any scene, and ultimately subordinated not to story-telling but to enhancing the pleasures of looking at the female star. When Technicolor introduced a more sensitive film stock in 1939, cinematographer Ernest Haller declared that it would allow a cameraman to use the same "little tricks of precision lighting he has used in monochrome to glamorize his stars"; the result would be "that color is going to be more flattering than ever to the women!"[55]

However, while color remained the exception rather than the rule, and therefore a spectacle in itself, it inevitably clashed to some extent with other conventions of Hollywood's particular understanding of realism, or what we have called cultural verisimilitude. One solution to the problem of motivating color was to reserve its use for fantasy movies: *The Wizard of Oz* (1939), in which dreary black-and-white Kansas gives way to the phantasmagoric colors of Oz, is a very clear-cut example of this.[56] In the 1940s, a color movie was most likely to be a musical; Hollywood represented itself in color, while the rest of the world was in black-and-white.

Color only lost these connotations when it became the norm, which was not until the mid-1960s. The number of color movies produced rose slowly but steadily during the 1940s, and much faster in the 1950s when Eastman Kodak introduced Eastmancolor, a single-film (or "monopak") color process that did not need a special camera.[57] Color, like widescreen, differentiated movies from television, but at the end of the 1950s only half of Hollywood's output was in color. It was only when television converted to color in the 1960s that Hollywood abandoned black-and-white. Since then, although the aesthetic regime of coordinated color used for symbolic purposes that Natalie Kalmus described remains in place, color has also been naturalized by audience expectation.

Sound

The introduction of sound from 1927 provides one of the clearest examples of the complex ways in which technological changes contribute to a reformulation of the Hollywood cinema. Sound had important aesthetic consequences for Hollywood, and a considerable impact on the cultural experience of filmgoing in the late 1920s and 1930s. *Sunny Side Up*, which set new box-office records for the Fox company on its release in 1929, shows both a certain hesitancy on the part of Hollywood filmmakers about how best to take advantage of the new technology, and a sense of relish about the possibilities created by the "sound-on-film" system that literally fused sound and picture on the same film strip, and guaranteed the synchronization of recorded speech with projected image.[58] The movie, which was also shot in the Grandeur large-screen process and boasted sequences in color, demonstrates that the sound "revolution" proposed no simple break with the cinema of the past.[59] Rather, the industry looked in the first instance for sound equivalents of the devices of silent cinema in order to preserve the basic strategies of the existing film style. With the expressive techniques of late silent cinema intersecting with those of the early "talkie" throughout the movie, *Sunny Side Up* suggests that sound renewed as well as revised the dominant aesthetics of Hollywood movies.

It is often suggested that the "talkies" provoked aesthetic conservatism in other aspects of cinematic form. The cumbersome recording equipment and the microphones' sensitivity to camera noise are alleged to have imprisoned the camera in fixed soundproof booths, bringing the increasingly mobile camera of the late 1920s to a standstill. Such accounts scarcely prepare us for this movie's opening, which uses camera movement not only to set the scene for the introduction of its central characters, but also as a way of displaying the elaborate setting and staging of action as a spectacle in its own right. The soundtrack augments a camera movement as fluent as those achieved by the most mature of the late silents, showing just how quickly Hollywood had found ways of recovering the visual flexibility that the technical requirements of sound had threatened to inhibit.[60]

A superimposed title sets the time and place ("New York, July the Fourth, with the Four Million"), and fades to reveal the opening image. We see a close-up of a water hydrant around which children are laughing and playing – the camera **cranes** up, and **tracks** forward to frame a game of street baseball – crane up and **pan** right to examine the occupants of a street-side tenement building through open windows: in one room a child cries as its hair is cut beneath a pudding bowl, while another practices the violin – crane up and pan right to show an old man being scolded by his wife – pan right again, to a young woman washing her hair in a bowl on her balcony, as a grandmother washes a child next door – crane down and pan left to frame a circle of dancing children – crane up and left to a young man taking refuge beneath a bed from his furious wife – crane down and right to follow a courting couple as they pass down the street, abandoning them to frame a family planning worker attempting to sell copies of the *Birth Control Review* to an Irish woman seated on a doorstep surrounded by children – track forward to a shop, introducing the first of the movie's central characters. After two minutes and twenty-five seconds the movie cuts for the first time (to allow an insert of the *Birth Control Review*) and after two minutes and forty seconds we cut to a new camera set-up.

The movie as a whole does not sustain the bravura display of its opening sequence, but it does routinely use camera movement: short lateral tracks to reframe action, and pans to cover character movement. There are occasions when camera movement is used as it would have been in silent cinema to aid narrative exposition. Near the beginning we move from one party scene to another, via a pair of matched camera movements either side of an intertitle ("Southampton, Long Island, with the 400"). A track-in on a bottle of home-made beer ends one scene, a track-out from a bottle of champagne begins the next. The movie efficiently contrasts the two

Early advertisements for Vitaphone pictures emphasized how "real" and "life-like" this new technology was. Courtesy BFI

An early sound stage, with the camera temporarily enclosed in a sound-proof booth. Courtesy BFI

lifestyles through the formal symmetry of its camera movements. Far more noticeable than any loss of camera mobility is the reduced range of optical effects (**dissolves**, **wipes**, and **fades**) and the much slower cutting rate of the movie in comparison to both late silent and subsequent sound movies. Nevertheless, retaining the fluidity of point-of-view and the sense of variable duration achieved by silent cinema remained a key goal for transitional movies such as *Sunny Side Up*. The techniques evolving in the exploitation of early sound could encourage camera movements as well as temporally longer shots.

Aiming to package the excess of its sound effects as production values, the movie seeks quite self-consciously to explain and demonstrate the new pleasures available to its spectator-auditors. In one sequence Jack (Charles Farrell), the romantic male lead, gazes at a framed photograph of Molly (Janet Gaynor), the object of his affections, and begins to sing "If I Had a Talking Picture of You." As he does so, Molly's picture comes to life and sings back to him. Sound has made the picture "speak," adding a new dimension to a familiar experience. But for the picture to talk, it must also move, and in providing "talking pictures" for its audience, *Sunny Side Up* defines the new sound/image relationship as one of complementarity, unity, and synchronization. Throughout the opening sequence, a continuous "mix" of significant sound recorded by several strategically placed microphones accompanies the mobile camera, with each "framing" of activity in the street or the tenement accompanied by an equivalent concentration on the soundtrack: we hear the children's songs and the boy playing the violin as the camera reaches them. Even before we reach the central characters, the possibilities of synchronized speech and other special effects are being relished. The soundtrack registers the cultural diversity of the street, playing accent off against accent (Irish, Swedish, and Italian voices are clearly discernible) and skillfully blending appropriate ambient sound (barrel organ music, the foghorns of ships in the nearby Hudson river, traffic noise) with the play of voices.

Once the physical problems of synchronization had been solved, perhaps the greatest technical difficulty facing early sound cinema was working out how to match visual and auditory perspective, so that sound was synchronized with its apparent source not only temporally but also spatially. If it was to conform to Hollywood's "invisible" style, dialogue had to sound as if it was being produced from an appropriate point within the image. Volume and the degree of reverberation could be "mixed" to suggest the apparent distance of the speaker from the auditory equivalent of the camera's viewpoint. Close-ups needed louder sound with less reverberation, longer shots needed fainter sound and greater reverberation to suggest the remoteness of the sound source from the point of the camera's observation. But standards emerged quite slowly.

Sound engineers debated whether the perspective fidelity of a recording made with a single microphone placed near the camera's line of sight was preferable to the greater intelligibility that might result from using multiple microphones. One technician argued against mixing because "the resultant blend of sound may not be said to represent any given point of audition, but is the sound which would be heard by a man with five or six very long ears, said ears extending in various directions."[61] On the whole, however, the matching of sound perspective to the image in each shot was subordinated to a combination of maximizing the intelligibility of the dialogue and keeping the volume level of the soundtrack constant.[62] If variations in aural timbre became too marked, they would draw attention to the shift in camera position between cuts. To accommodate the need for a consistency in sound levels, the image lost some of its priority. If the transitions between aural perspectives fell within the tolerable limits for the audience, sound perspective could follow the image. If they threatened to draw attention to themselves, the spatial synchronization of sound and image was sacrificed in the interests of narrative clarity. At the first Southampton party in *Sunny Side Up*, we hear the central characters conversing in the crowded room shown "over" the speech of guests who are actually closer to the camera. On other occasions, sound claims priority, resulting in simpler stagings and a more restricted range of camera setups. Dialogue scenes in *Sunny Side Up* show a marked reluctance to cut "in" from **establishing shots** to close-ups. Even the most minimal of

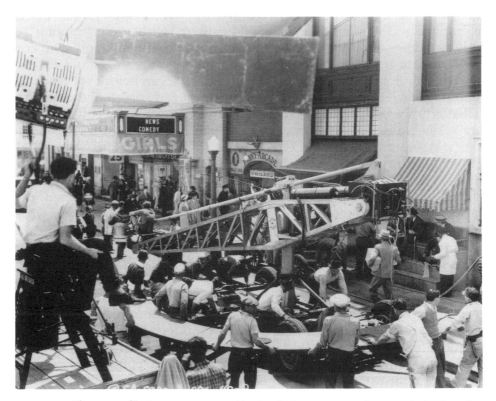

The crew filming a scene in *Mr Smith Goes to Washington* (1939) with a camera crane. In the center of the picture, the boom microphone records the principal characters' dialogue. Courtesy BFI

separations between sound and image are avoided: there are very few cut-aways to non-speaking figures in dialogue scenes, for instance. The movie prefers simply to present speakers speaking before the camera, demonstrating the visible synchronization of lip movement and vocal sound, and turning the speech act into the movie's principal spectacle of technology. This very formal staging slows the narrative's tempo drastically.

Those studios that used sound-on-disc recording systems until 1930 experimented with a technique of multiple-camera shooting similar to that subsequently used in television studios.[63] Each scene was played straight through, giving a continuous soundtrack. Shots from the various cameras, arranged round the edge of the set, could then be intercut without losing sound continuity. Since sound discs could not be edited, the soundtrack determined the length of a scene, and the image track was edited to fit it. The inflexibility of this method, combined with its restrictions on camera placement and movement, ensured that the industry would fairly rapidly find a more workable compromise between its preferred style and the requirements of the new technology. Far from being incompatible with sound technology, the mobile camera, used in combination with multiple microphones as in the opening shot of *Sunny Side Up*, was in fact one solution to the problem of matching sound and visual perspectives. *Sunny Side Up* does make some use of background sound to establish offscreen space and create a sense of the surrounding environment. In one scene, while the couple converse in a tenement room we hear distant band music slowly growing louder. We infer that an Independence Day parade is approaching, and in due course the scene cuts outside to show the parade. Two simultaneous events in discontinuous space have been represented without using any of silent cinema's visually intrusive devices such as **cross-cutting**. On the whole, however, other sources of sound are deliberately restricted, partly because of the limitations of the technology available for mixing soundtracks during editing, but also because of early uncertainty about the audience's ability to "read" sound confidently.

In order to avoid ambiguity about sound sources by anchoring sound to the image, almost everything audible, including the music in numbers, is **diegetic**: it appears to originate from within the fictional world described on the screen. There is very little **non-diegetic** sound, that is, sound not explained in terms of any perceived source, such as mood music, although some of the songs do have minimal orchestral support from an offscreen source.[64] The preference for identifiable sounds helps explain the movie's curious storyline, in which characters burst into song accompanied by conveniently located orchestras or else happen to find themselves pulled into stage shows that provide an opportunity for song-and-dance routines. The movie manages to introduce 12 musical numbers, and no opportunity is lost to motivate an impromptu song: Molly is established early on as a character given to expressing her innermost feelings lyrically, with the songs used to chart the ups and downs of her romance with Jack. The love story that provides the movie with its central narrative focus works its way toward its climax via a series of musical interludes: songs first trigger romance, then express its apparent impossibility, and eventually produce its inevitable conclusion, as well as contributing to the movie's production values.

Sound also enhances the movie's comic dimensions. Although there are plenty of sight-gags, the movie takes pleasure in the new possibilities of verbal comedy, with the script providing endless opportunities for the rapid-fire dialogue and virtuoso vocal display often associated with the "zany" comedy of the Marx Brothers and other ex-vaudeville teams. Eddie (Frank Richardson) and Bee (Marjorie White) provide a constant flow of comic repartee that balances the more melancholic sequences. Their low-life dialogue is contrasted with the upper-class diction of the Southampton colony inhabited by Jack, his family, and friends. As the figure who mediates between her surrounding company of poor-but-honest eccentrics and the less spontaneous world of Southampton, Molly is capable of improvising performances across a range of linguistic registers, allowing Janet Gaynor's skills of impersonation and mimicry free rein. The effect that

Jack (Charles Farrell) and Molly (Janet Gaynor) in *Sunny Side Up* (1929). Fox (courtesy Kobal)

sound had on performance styles is evident in the way that she uses her voice rather than her body to express herself.

Some historians have argued that sound's influence was not confined to strictly textual effects, but also changed the cultural role of American movies. Robert Ray and others have suggested that "talking pictures" made Hollywood more culturally specific than it had been when silent cinema met no language barrier in addressing its global audience: "Overnight, merely by the addition of voices, Hollywood movies became more American. The movies crackled with the localized inflections that drew an aural map of the United States: Cagney's New Yorkese complementing Cooper's Western laconicism, Hepburn's high-toned Connecticut broad ah's matching Jean Arthur's Texas drawl."[65] Ray also suggests that sound threw Hollywood back upon more specifically American mythologies as a basis for its story-telling. These movies preached an American "exceptionalism" that guaranteed success and fulfillment in a land of opportunity as a reward for integrity, hard work, and optimism. Thanks to the resources of the American environment and the abundance available to all in an egalitarian society based on infinitely expanding resources, there was no reason why every American's narrative should not have a happy ending – or so the mythology argued. There are certainly traces of this mythology in *Sunny Side Up*, and the movie's opening set, more naturalist acting styles, and vernacular speech all mark a renewed attention to the specifically local and American. But the movie does not resolve the conflict between "the 400" and the "Four Million" in its cross-class love story until after it has offered a more critical representation of society than was common in late silent cinema.

Ray's argument also oversimplifies the industry's relations with its foreign market, and with the domestic political forces that regulated the content of motion pictures. Silent movies were a universally available form, not because, as the industry sometimes claimed, they were in any sense an "international language" capable of communicating ideas and values across national and linguistic boundaries, but because they were so easily altered to the circumstances of their exhibition by censors, distributors, or even individual exhibitors. Through the use of intertitles Hollywood characters could speak any language or dialect; in Lithuania they spoke three languages at once, since historical and political circumstances required the intertitles to be rendered in German and Russian as well as the local language.

Sound greatly restricted this malleability, fixing dialogue and eliminating much of the ambiguity of silent movies. The duration of a sound movie was much less flexible: no longer could exhibitors project movies at faster speeds than they had been photographed at in order to shorten their running time, as had been common in the late silent period. Nor could local censor boards cut parts of scenes without the movie losing synchronization. Part of the reason that the industry agreed to adopt the Production Code in 1930 was because it recognized that the inflexibility of sound meant that they could be held much more accountable for the detailed meanings of their movies than had been the case with silent film. Their product had to be less ambiguously acceptable to its broad, undifferentiated audience, and also to the political and cultural elites who might not go to the movies but whose involvement in civic life gave them power over what it was acceptable to exhibit.[66]

When Hollywood's American identity became audible, European elites expressed alarm every time they encountered a shopworker affecting an American accent. In a British Parliamentary debate in 1937, a Conservative MP suggested that the movies were achieving "the annexation of this country by the United States of America.... Personally I have very little opportunity of visiting the pictures, and, if I do get an opportunity, I do not use it, because I dread having to spend an hour or two suffering from a mixture of glucose, chewing gum, leaden bullets and nasal noises."[67] But for those who did visit the pictures, the Utopianism of Hollywood was intensified by the distance between foreign audiences and the particulars of American social organization that movies depicted. James Cagney's accent lost its specific class coding and became generalized as American, not to be distinguished from, say, William Powell's.[68] George Orwell shrewdly suggested that American English "gained a footing in England . . . most of all, because one can adopt an American word without crossing a class barrier."[69] The movies offered European working-class audiences an escape into an imagined Utopian society in which the inflexibility of class distinction either did not exist or was not recognizable. By contrast, in every European production the coming of sound brought accents into play as unavoidable signifiers of social class. After 1929, Hollywood seemed to address its audience more clearly as a single, unified entity and to produce that same unity in its fictions. In America, sound made Hollywood more overtly an "official" cultural form, enhancing its potential for unification by more completely standardizing the movie experience for its many different domestic audiences. In the rest of the world, however, the American culture that Hollywood offered was an alternative to national culture, and could be adopted as a gesture of local resistance to "official" culture.

Standardizing the Experience

We must not destroy all truth in the theatre by too frequent use of conventions; but neither must we destroy the theatrical illusion by too great fidelity to fact. And by theatrical illusion I mean the pleasure in search of which people go to the theatre – that theatrical pleasure, partly composed indeed of the illusion that they are seeing a reality, but mingled with a feeling of personal safety and a sincere conviction that they are assisting only at an illusion. That sense of security must never be destroyed. If by dint of realism or artifice you succeed in making your spectator forget absolutely that he is witnessing a mere spectacle, he ceases to be amused; he becomes an actor instead of a spectator, and what is worse, a well-gulled actor, for he is the only sincere one. . . . Therefore, try to produce an apparent truth; but let it be true only in seeming.

Constant Coquelin, 1880[70]

Although the histories of sound, Technicolor, and CinemaScope are usually presented as accounts of innovation, they also indicate the tendency of cinema technology to move toward standardization. In order to gain audience acceptance, a new technology has to offer its novel appeal within the existing, predictable framework of Hollywood's formal conventions. Equally, technical innovations have needed to be compatible with existing equipment. Seen from this perspective, the history of film technology follows a pattern less of accumulated progress toward a predetermined goal than of assimilation into an existing aesthetic and institutional system. If a given technology could not be assimilated to the cinema system as a whole (that is, as a technological, industrial, and aesthetic system), it would either be abandoned or further modified to contain its difference. Technicolor, for example, went into rapid decline in the face of widescreen, which was incompatible with the three-strip Technicolor cameras. Meanwhile, Kodak developed the "monopak" EastmanColor system, which rapidly became the industry standard color film, simultaneously endorsing the possibilities of CinemaScope, and the extent to which these two technological innovations of the early 1950s sustained each other helps to explain the eagerness with which they were adopted by the industry.

The notion of technological assimilation also suggests the way that innovations are "overhauled" as circumstances change; few innovations have been truly permanent, as the history of widescreen formats since 1950 demonstrates. By the late 1960s CinemaScope had all but disappeared in favor of the less extreme widescreen system, Panavision, which had an aspect ratio of 1:2.25, while in 1960 the Society of Motion Picture Engineers adopted a new standard aspect ratio of 1:1.85. As subsequent sales to television became an increasingly recognized and important element of film budgeting, movies shot in widescreen formats were also composed with the television screen in mind. Camera manufacturers were producing viewfinders that marked the television frame inside the widescreen frame, allowing cinematographers to ensure that the essential object in each shot fell inside what was called the **safe action area** of the composition.[71] In 1992, distribution companies reversed the trend, and began reissuing some videos in widescreen format; naturally, they charged their purchasers more for this more complete version that actually only occupied half the picture on their television screens.[72]

Behind the standardization of audience expectation lies an economic motive common to all systems of mass production or distribution: the benefits in efficiency of economies of scale. This is most obviously seen in the standardization of such basic mechanical elements as the width or **gauge** of film itself (normally 35 mm), the speed at which the film travels through the camera and projector (24 frames per second for sound film), and the way in which sound is recorded onto film stock.[73] Such mechanical, chemical, and optical standardization ensures the consistency of the audience's movie experience at a fundamental level only likely to be disrupted by avant-garde filmmakers. However, if we recognize the similarities between these technological forms of standardization and those produced by genre or the star system, we can consider other ways in which technology operates to standardize our experience of "going to the movies." The area of our movie experience where this applies most is the most pervasive and also probably the most transparently invisible to the casual viewer: the standardization of optical representation and perspective relations within the image stream of Hollywood cinema. Hollywood's use of camera lenses makes going to the cinema a fairly predictable optical experience, and plays a key role in controlling our perception of movie fictions and thus the meanings they may be taken to produce. It is also clear that in this area Bazin's ideal goal of a "total" cinema capable of identically reproducing the perceived and sensed world is not within the capacity of optical technology.

The human eye is a far more complex optical instrument than a camera lens. Our stereoscopic vision, the brain's ability to combine the two distinct images from each of our eyes into a single picture, allows us to see in perspective and judge the shape, size, and distance of an object from the way it is located in the space around us. Flat surfaces such as cinema screens or painting canvases cannot reproduce stereoscopic images: super-imposing two images taken from different points on top of each other produces only a blur. One of the enduring legacies of Renaissance painting was the establishment of a perspective system that imitated the effect of stereoscopic vision. Before the Renaissance, European artists commonly represented the size of people and objects not according to how far away they were supposed to be from the painter at the time of painting the picture, but according to their relative importance. More consequential personages were literally represented as being of greater stature. Renaissance painting, however, perfected a system of representation that repli-cated the perspective relations between objects when viewed from a single point, as if looking at a landscape through a window. This system is known as **monocular perspective**: the perspective produced when viewing the world through a single lens. Seventeenth-century Dutch painters such as Vermeer painted with the aid of a camera obscura, a box with a lens in one side that projected an image in monocular perspective. This mode of representing the world dominated the central tradition of western Euro-pean art from the Renaissance until the early twentieth century.

Although monocular perspective is only a convention of representation (Japanese painting, for example, employs a principle of multiple perspec-tives, in which different objects in a single painting are seen from different viewpoints), the nineteenth-century inventors of photography worked within its tradition. A camera is simply a camera obscura with a film or plate on which the image is permanently recorded. It was in large part the ease and efficiency with which cameras could represent views in mono-cular perspective that led to expectations of its realist aesthetic, since photography's mechanical reproduction was far more densely detailed than could be achieved by drawing or painting. "From today," it was famously declared, "painting is dead,"[74] and photography is often indi-rectly credited with encouraging the early twentieth-century formal ex-perimentations in styles of painting that rejected monocular perspective, made by the Cubists. Photography fixed the conventions of monocular perspective as a set of optical principles and mathematical formulae for the design of camera lenses. Early cinema lenses relied on the optical systems devised for still photography, and so reproduced depth relationships between objects according to the conventions of monocular perspective. These conventions have become so firmly fixed by the development of photographic technology that their conventional nature is almost always invisible to us. We expect images to conform to the perspective relations we regard as normal, and we find them more difficult to comprehend if they do not. Unless its perspective relations are ostentatiously distorted, we tend to regard the photographed image as a transparent representation of the space it contains. Steve Neale has argued that photography constituted "an enormous social investment in perspective and its image of the world," an investment "in the centrality of the eye, in the category and identity of the individual . . . and in an ideology of the *visibility* of the world." Photography, he suggests, made perspective reality, and put reality, or reality as something we could see, into perspective.[75]

One of the attractions of widescreen is that it resembles the shape of the human field of vision more closely than the Academy ratio does. Cinerama was advertised as virtually filling the cone of human vision, which is about 165 degrees horizontally and 60 degrees vertically. However, no optical technology can duplicate all the properties of the human eye. In particular, our eyes have an intricate mechanism for differential focusing that no camera lens can reproduce. Although we have a very wide cone of vision, we keep only a very small proportion – as little as 2 degrees – in exact focus at any given moment, while the rest of our vision becomes increasingly blurred as we get nearer to the periphery of what we can see. We compensate for this limited field of exact vision by almost constantly moving our eyes about. The much simpler optics of a camera lens cannot reproduce this behavior. Instead, the lens keeps all objects in the same plane – that is, the same distance from the camera – in focus at the same time. How deep that plane is depends on how wide the lens's angle of view is, and how large the aperture of the lens is. The smaller the aperture, the greater the depth of the plane in focus, or **depth of field**. Since the aperture also controls the amount of light passing through the lens, the smaller the aperture, the more light is needed to expose the film.

The camera lenses that most closely approximate to our perception of depth and spatial relations have an angle of view of about 37.5 degrees vertically and, in the Academy ratio, about 50 degrees horizontally.[76] These are known as "standard" or "normal" lenses. Other lenses, with wider or narrower angles of view, produce apparent distortions in our perception of spatial relations. Wide-angle or "short" lenses (so called because they have a short focal length) on the one hand, and telephoto or "long" lenses on the other, change our sense of depth and perspective and alter the apparent depth relationships between objects within the space. Using these different kinds of lens a camera can, without physically moving, produce quite different representations of spatial and object relations.

The simplest way of demonstrating how different lenses represent spatial relations is by comparing three images in which one object – in this case a human figure – is kept the same size, moving the camera closer to the figure for the wide-angle lens, and further away for the telephoto. The differences in the way each lens represents space are then quite apparent: the wide-angle lens reveals a great deal of the background, with almost all of it in focus, while the telephoto lens, with its much more concentrated angle of view, shows much less of the background, and its much narrower depth of field concentrates the viewer's attention on the figure. While the

Depth of field is the term used to describe the amount of an image that is in sharp focus. It is controlled by the aperture of the camera lens: the smaller the aperture, the greater the depth of field, but also the more light is needed to illuminate the scene.

wide-angle shot draws us into the space of the image and emphasizes movement within it, particularly toward and away from the camera, the long shot tends to distance us from the subjects in the shot, and minimizes the significance of movement toward and away from the camera.

Optical technology can give us only an approximation of the way we see things in space, not an imitation of our vision. This approximation is also a way of ordering and representing space, and the significantly different ways in which different lenses present space can be used for dramatic and expressive purposes. Hollywood's conventions, however, ensure that in the vast majority of movies, audiences remain as little aware of the choice of lens as they are of cutting rates. A movie such as *El Dorado* (1966) relies heavily on the use of standard lenses to provide a consistent and easily comprehensible space in which we have no great difficulty perceiving the relationships between objects. In this space the audience can feel a comfortable sense of engagement with the characters. The system is not absolutely dependent on a technical choice, however. The audience's sense of spatial representation will tolerate some variation without undue attention being drawn to the mechanics of the image's production. Normal Hollywood practice, for instance, uses slightly wider-angle lenses on establishing shots, standard lenses for medium shots, and longer lenses for close-ups, to separate the character's face from the background, and concentrate

Cole Thornton (John Wayne) and J.P. Harrah (Robert Mitchum) in the normal space of *El Dorado* (1966). Aquarius Picture Library

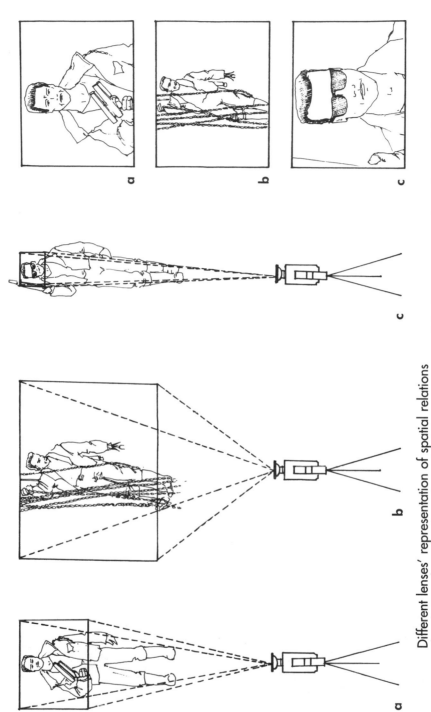

Different lenses' representation of spatial relations

The choice of camera lens determines the appearance of the image in a number of ways. If the camera stays at the same distance from the subject, a wide-angle lens will show more of the figure than a standard lens, while a telephoto lens will provide a close-up.

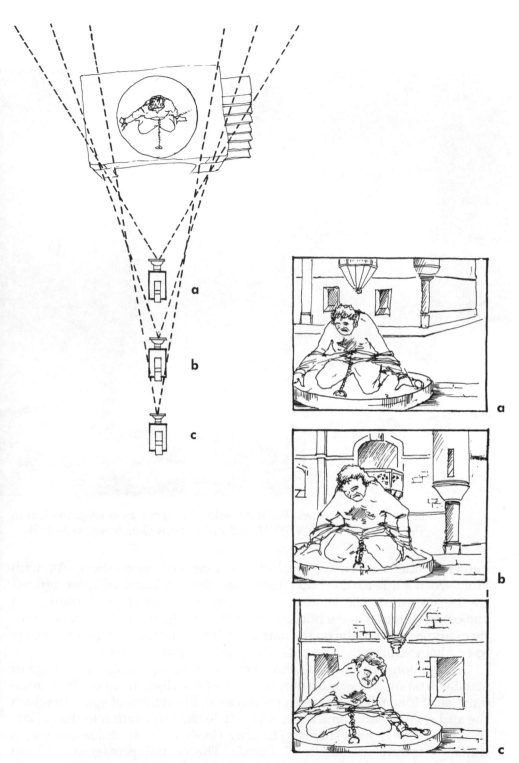

If the camera is moved so that the figure is kept the same size in the frame, the differences in the way that each lens represents space are revealed. The wide-angle lens (b) places the figure as part of the space around him, while the telephoto lens (c) isolates him from the background, concentrating the viewer's attention on him.

Eileen Wade (Nina van Pallandt) isolated in space by a telephoto lens in *The Long Goodbye* (1973). United Artists/Lions Gate (courtesy Kobal)

audience attention on his or her reactions and motivation. As with Hollywood's other conventional systems, the continuity of space offered by the use of standard lenses is provisional rather than absolute, and subject to variation in the interest of preserving the more abstract continuity of audience attention on the narration. It is, in fact, very rare for a movie to be shot exclusively with a standard lens, as *Psycho* (1960) was.[77]

On occasion, however, the choice of a lens falling outside the range of standardization draws attention to itself as a stylistic device. The consistent use of long telephoto lenses produces an impression of space in which the audience may feel much less securely located in relation to the fiction. In some 1970s movies such as *The Long Goodbye* (1973), space assumes a different texture to that in *El Dorado*. The central protagonist, Philip Marlowe (Elliott Gould), enjoys a much less secure purchase on the spaces in which he finds himself, and is often lost among other people in the general confusion of the movie's images. Likewise, the audience is less able to judge where people are in relation to each other, and as a result less able

Police chief Hank Quinlan (Orson Welles) interrogates Uncle Joe Grandi (Akim Tamiroff) in the threatening, distorted space of *Touch of Evil* (1958). Universal (courtesy Kobal)

to assess how they may behave or what will happen next. Telephoto shots represent a more discontinuous space than standard lenses, and because their images are more difficult to "match" against another, the audience is also likely to be more aware of the abruptness of cuts between shots.

The consistent use of wide-angle lenses produces an even more confusing and discontinuous sense of screen space. In *Touch of Evil* (1958), for instance, we are confronted with a sense of menace and threat in almost every image, partly as a result of the spatial distortion that the wide-angle lens produces. Perspective relations between objects are exaggerated to the extent that it sometimes becomes impossible to judge distance with any certainty. Characters move with threatening rapidity through the image space, and we are confronted quite literally with the distorted logic of the world they inhabit, a nightmare world of exaggerated and twisted space which is plainly organized according to rules quite different from our own. Director Orson Welles places figures against each other in individual frames and guides our attention not so much through the use of editing, but through performances and placement of objects in the frame. The wide-angle lens is therefore crucial in determining our understanding of substantial portions of the movie.

Both *The Long Goodbye* and *Touch of Evil* exhibit visual styles outside the norms of Hollywood's standardized representation of spatial relations, and conventional criticism recognizes these stylistic traits as markers of the work of an auteur director. Our own brief comments on *Touch of Evil* connect visual style both to the decision making of the director, and to thematic consistency. A similar argument might be made in the case of *The Long Goodbye* for director Robert Altman's use of the telephoto lens to demolish coherent screen space and direct our attention to his actors, if necessary at the expense of the narrative. Comparable stylistic choices are of course much less noticeable in movies that remain within the broad conventions of spatial and perspectival representation. Just as Welles makes use of high- and low-angle shots in *Touch of Evil* to intensify the distorting effects of the wide-angle lens, so director Howard Hawks maximizes the normative representation of space in *El Dorado* by shooting as consistently as possible from an eye-level camera position.

Technology and Power

Although André Bazin recognized the place of economics in cinema's technological development, hc gave the main roles in his history to individuals: either to the inventors of cinema or to the individual artists (usually directors) who put it to good aesthetic use. Any historical account that focuses on invention is likely to emphasize the ingeniousness and creativity of individuals – the "geniuses" of the nineteenth century who invented cinema's basic technology. Rather less is usually made of subsequent "geniuses," mostly because the major shifts in the appearance of cinema, such as widescreen, have come about through an accumulation of relatively minor technological developments, most of which have been produced almost anonymously in corporate research laboratories. A more consciously economic account of technical change distinguishes between the three stages by which a technological change is introduced. **Invention** requires only a limited financial commitment to fund experimentation and the development of a prototype. In the second stage, **innovation**, the invention is adapted to meet the requirements of a market, and involves much greater expenditure in developing the market. The final stage, **diffusion**, occurs when the product is adopted as an industry standard, so that the whole industry invests in its exploitation.[78] As the case of widescreen makes clear, the innovation and diffusion of a new technology are far more significant to both the economics and the aesthetics of cinema than the invention itself.

Recognizing the institutional place of technology allows us to see its history not as a matter of a single, intrinsic determination encouraging a steady progress toward some ideal mode of representation, but as a series of more erratic shifts, hesitations, and reversals, more in keeping with the multiple logics that shape Hollywood production. Any given technological innovation, whether major or minor, is likely to have contradictory aesthetic effects: innovations in one area may well produce setbacks in others, so that the history of technology is most properly seen as dialectical, constructed out of the clashes between contradictory forces.

In an overview of the history of cinema technology, Peter Wollen suggests that these contradictions are usually simplified into an account organized around a number of "great moments" or "breakthroughs." Even accounts that otherwise diverge radically, he argues, share the teleological assumption that these breakthroughs have led logically to the present, whether they see that present as one of greater realism or the improved illusions of special effects.[79] Wollen observes that the "breakthroughs" around which these histories are organized emphasize the technological shifts that reinvigorated the commercial viability of Hollywood and reinforced the existing power-relations of the film industry. As an experimental and independent filmmaker, Wollen suspects that the very construction of technological histories has important political consequences in this regard. History-writing as a mode of explanation can, and in histories of Hollywood often does, conceal the operations of economic power by presuming that the existing mode of operation is natural. By these means, the cinema is made to seem remote, inaccessible, and mythological: "the innovations that restricted access to filmmaking, that demanded enormous capital investment and caused real set-backs, have attracted attention, while the steady development of stock – chemical rather than optical or electronic – has never been comprehensively chronicled."[80] In suggesting the outline of alternative technological histories, Wollen draws attention to some technical innovations and developments considered too minor to feature in the grand teleological accounts. He concentrates on the consistent improvement of the recording media themselves. Changes in film stock and magnetic tape produce the most subtle (often even unnoticeable) rather than the most spectacular effects.

During the 1930s, the accumulation of a series of relatively minor changes in film stock and processing, and in lighting and lens technology, made possible the apparent "breakthrough" of deep-focus cinematography in *Citizen Kane* in 1941. In a valuable account of both these technical changes and the aesthetic impulses behind the development of deep-focus, Patrick J. Ogle traces the gradual development of the style in the late 1930s as well as its full-blown emergence in the combined work of Welles and his cinematographer Gregg Toland.[81] Rather than regarding deep-focus as the result of a commitment to realism and attributing the style to Welles' innovations, Ogle provides an impressive catalog of technological developments which allowed an aesthetic initiative to take advantage of them. He places what is usually thought of as a personal film style within a more appropriate technological and institutional context.

Ogle's analysis demonstrates the ways in which an examination of apparently minor or peripheral technical changes may revise the established dicta of Hollywood's history. Peter Wollen's argument is, however, more directly concerned with the political ramifications of technological change. In his account, new technology often generates resistance on aesthetic grounds, as filmmakers struggle against the new technology in order to master it and make it serviceable for the Hollywood style. While the effect of major technological changes has been to exclude people who did not have substantial financial backing from an involvement in film production, Wollen follows Walter Benjamin (discussed in chapter 1) in suggesting that the cumulative effect of the smaller and more gradual developments in optical and chemical technology has been toward the democratization of film production, by making possible first 16-mm, then 8-mm filming, and, most recently, low-cost video and the camcorder.[82]

Video has drastically revised Hollywood's relations with its viewers, a technological change that has in some ways done more than merely increase choice.[83] The habits of domestic viewing are more casual and intermittent than those of the cinema audience; attention is less firmly maintained, distraction and commentary arc a more important and constant part of the viewing experience. Occasional middle-aged cinemagoers

Walter Parks Thatcher (George Coulouris) confronts Mr Bernstein (Everett Sloane) and Charles Foster Kane (Orson Welles) in the deep-focus space of *Citizen Kane* (1941). RKO (courtesy Kobal)

note with displeasure the extent to which these viewing habits have been taken into the shopping-mall multiplex by the majority teenage audience, and fondly recall the passivity of the "better behaved" audiences they remember themselves to have been. An alternative analysis might see this more interactive behavior as a form of "making your own entertainment" out of the movie on offer, and later in the book we shall argue that this is, in fact, the dominant mode of consumption of the Hollywood text, and the one for which it was designed. New technologies will continue to carry the viewer's capacity to make his or her own entertainment further. In its promotion of "special collector's editions" and "director's cuts," the video distribution industry has adopted the music industry's concept of the "dance mix," which provides different versions of a product for different formats and different users. Beyond this, laser disc technology and full motion video on CD-i will make possible "interactive viewer re-editing." According to the head of research for Philips, "forget the director's cut of *Blade Runner*, CD-i will give you the punter's cut."[84]

Video represented the most substantial collision of interests between the cinema industry and another major media industry since the development of broadcast radio and the creation of sound movies in the 1920s. At first, the movie industry resisted the VCR with the vehemence with which they were often thought to have resisted televison. Jack Valenti, head of the Motion Picture Association of America, declared that it was a parasite likely to kill moviegoing, and Universal and Disney brought a lawsuit against Sony in 1976, claiming that the machine encouraged infringement of copyright and arguing that its manufacture should be prohibited. By the time the Supreme Court ruled in Sony's favor that home recording constituted "fair use," the production industry had reached something much closer to an accommodation with the makers of the hardware, recognizing the profits to be made by developing video as a subsequent release market.[85] The accommodation was further cemented when the Japanese hardware manufacturers bought production companies as suppliers of "software." This history in many ways repeats the industry's reaction to radio and to television, but video has also expanded audience choice over both what movies it consumes and how it consumes them, in ways that neither of the movies' other "rivals" did.

In its attitudes to technological development, the production industry perhaps most clearly reveals the extent to which it should be seen as a service industry. All the major technological developments we have discussed, as well as the great majority of the minor ones, were introduced to the industry from outside. The studios themselves undertook very little technological research, leaving the development of optical and chemical technology to others. Production departments were not geared or equipped for any but the most directly relevant and applied kinds of research and development. Studio personnel innovated in techniques such as Gregg Toland's use of improved technology to develop deep-focus, or the specialized equipment needed for more mobile camera styles such as the crab dolly in the mid-1940s and the Steadicam in the late 1970s.

These relatively minor studio-produced innovations did not create the spectacular disturbances to Hollywood's aesthetics that came with Technicolor or widescreen, and it is perhaps not surprising that little attention is paid to them in most histories of film technology. But some small developments, such as labor-saving editing devices, have had discreet but profound effects on the appearance and experience of cinema. Comparing, say, *Dracula*, made in 1930, with *G-Men*, made five years later, it is very noticeable that the latter cuts much more frequently. The average number of shots in a typical Hollywood movie nearly doubled in those five years, from around 400 in 1930 to around 700 in 1935.[86] Editing sound introduced a number of technical problems not encountered by editors of the silent image track alone. The most persistent of these was the need to keep sound and image in synchronization. This discouraged the kinds of cutting frequency that had been normal in late silent movies until several minor technical developments, including numbering the edges of film stock to more easily keep track of it and the appearance of the sound Moviola editing machine, made editing sound and keeping synchronization significantly easier.

If this was an instance of a breakthrough (sound) producing a setback eventually modified by minor technical adjustments to return to an aesthetic norm, then the other noticeable change in the frequency with which movies were cut involved the application of an external technology. Cutting rates increased in the 1960s, in part because using a magnetic soundtrack the same physical size as the film made sound editing much quicker and simpler, and in part because clear adhesive tape came into use as an alternative means of joining two pieces of edited film together. Previously, the editor would have to go through the laborious process of physically sticking the join with film cement. This was not only time-consuming, but also meant the loss of two frames every time a cut was adjusted. Using adhesive tape meant that the editor could stick the pieces of film together much faster and more easily, making it economical on studio personnel's time to cut more often and to experiment more with editing.

The industry itself seldom draws attention to changes such as these, however significant their cumulative effects on Hollywood's image system might be. The much more visible 'breakthroughs" represent only the tip of the iceberg that is Hollywood's technological history. But whether introducing large or small changes, technological innovation has been motivated less by the desire for progress toward an ever more perfect reproduction of reality than by a practical impulse to put technology to work within the larger economic and signifying systems of the American cinema, in the service of maintaining novelty within predictability, variation within a stable mode of production, and a hierarchy of industrial organization.

Notes

1   Syd Silverman, "Entertainment in the Satellite Era," *Variety* (October 26, 1983), p. 13.
2   Philip Hayward and Tana Wollen, "Introduction: Surpassing the Real," in Philip Hayward and Tana Wollen, eds, *Future Visions: New Technologies of the Screen* (London: British Film Institute, 1993), p. 3.
3   The rich, pearly-gray tones in which MGM's stars were photographed came from the studio's decision about how it exposed and processed its film, and the higher contrasts and starker blacks and whites of Warner pictures came from different decisions about the same technical questions. Barry Salt, *Film Style and Technology: History and Analysis* (London: Starword, 1983), pp. 257, 288.
4   Rick Altman, "The Material Heterogeneity of Recorded Sound," in Rick Altman, ed., *Sound Theory, Sound Practice* (New York: Routledge, 1992), pp. 27–8.
5   Jean-Louis Comolli, "Machines of the Visible," in Teresa de Lauretis and Stephen Heath, eds, *The Cinematic Apparatus* (London: Macmillan, 1980), pp. 121–42. Dickson, quoted in Richard Maltby, ed., *Dreams for Sale: Popular Culture in the 20th Century* (London: Harrap, 1989), p. 36.
6   We can take a film projector to pieces, and with practice and thought comprehend the arrangement of its mechanical parts, and see what relationship each part has to the working of the whole. This is seldom possible with twentieth-century technology; the interior of a television set or camera offers us little explanation of its operation in mechanical (which is to say, spatial) terms. To understand how television works we need a good deal of specialist knowledge of electromagnetism and physics.
7   Roy Armes, "Entendre, C'est Comprendre: In Defence of Sound Reproduction," *Screen* 29:2 (Spring 1988), p. 11.
8   André Bazin, "The Myth of Total Cinema," in *What is Cinema? Vol. 1*, trans. Hugh Gray (Berkeley, CA: University of California Press, 1967), p. 21.
9   Bazin, p. 20.
10 André Bazin, "Will CinemaScope Save the Cinema?," trans. Catherine Jones and Richard Neupert, *The Velvet Light Trap* 21 (Summer 1985), p. 13.
11 André Bazin, "An Aesthetic of Reality," in *What is Cinema? Vol. 2*, trans. Hugh Gray (Berkeley, CA: University of California Press, 1971), p. 26.
12 Bazin, "Will CinemaScope Save the Cinema?," p. 13.
13 Bazin, "An Aesthetic of Reality," p. 26.
14 This is by no means the simple statement that it may first appear, and Williams places this summary definition by observing that "it does not end, but only begins a controversy in art and literature when it is said that the purpose is 'to show things as they really are.'" A realism "of the surface," he says, "can miss important realities." Raymond Williams, *Keywords* (London: Fontana, 1976), pp. 218–19.
15 John Ellis, *Visible Fictions* (London: Routledge and Kegan Paul, 1982), pp. 6–7.
16 Terry Lovell, *Pictures of Reality* (London: British Film Institute, 1980), p. 79.
17 Imagine two photographs taken by the same camera in the same setting with the same lighting. One photograph is of an antique table, the other is of a reproduction antique table – that is, a close copy of the original. In all likelihood, we could not tell the representation of the reproduction apart from the representation of the original; only a close inspection of the objects themselves would allow us to do that. The point here is not to do with chairs or even photographs, but with linguistic conventions. To talk of photographic reproduction is to use a conventional shorthand that chooses to ignore the conventions of photographic representation, to look through the photograph and

see the object represented in it – just as talking about how realistic a representation is employs a similar shorthand.

18   Lovell, pp. 79–80.
19   Christian Metz, "Aural Objects," quoted in James Lastra, "Reading, Writing, and Representing Sound," in Altman, p. 65.
20   Lastra, p. 68.
21   Lastra, p. 81.
22   Amy Lawrence, *Echo and Narcissus: Women's Voices in Classical Hollywood Cinema* (Berkeley, CA: University of California Press, 1991), pp. 21–2.
23   Bazin, "The Ontology of the Photographic Image," in *What is Cinema? Vol. 1*, pp. 12, 14.
24   Bazin, "The Evolution of the Language of Cinema," in *What is Cinema? Vol. 1*, pp. 24, 28.
25   Bazin, "Evolution," p. 37.
26   J. Dudley Andrew, *The Major Film Theories: An Introduction* (New York: Oxford University Press, 1976), p. 163.
27   Quoted in Edward Lowery, "Edwin J. Hadley: Travelling Film Exhibitor," *Journal of the University Film Association* 28:3 (Summer 1976), p. 6.
28   Fred Glass notes that discussions of the movie among teenagers "mostly revolved around the question of whether or not the entire movie was a dream," and considers the extent to which the movie's raising the possibility that it was a dream permits it to avoid resolving the thematic and ideological conflicts it raises. Fred Glass, "Totally Recalling Arnold: Sex and Violence in the New Bad Future," *Film Quarterly* 44:1 (Fall 1990), pp. 2–13.
29   Quoted in John Belton, "1950s Magnetic Sound: The Frozen Revolution," in Altman, p. 159.
30   Quoted in John Belton, "CinemaScope and Historical Methodology," *Cinema Journal* 28:1 (Fall 1988), pp. 33–4.
31   Richard Kohler and Walter Lassally, "The Big Screens," *Sight and Sound* 24:3 (January–March 1955), p. 120.
32   John Belton, *Widescreen Cinema* (Cambridge, MA: Harvard University Press, 1992), p. 202.
33   Philip Hayward has referred to this use of new technology to produce novel image effects as "impact aesthetics." Philip Hayward, "Industrial Light and Magic: Style, Technology and Special Effects in the Music Video and Music Television," in Philip Hayward, ed., *Culture, Technology and Creativity* (London: John Libbey, 1990).
34   Bazin, "The Ontology of the Photographic Image," in *What is Cinema? Vol. 1*, p. 13.
35   Since the early 1980s, according to Robin Baker, many people working in computer graphics have been attempting to create "imaginary people." "Underlying this project is an ambition: if reality could be conquered (and what is more real than a person?) the supremacy of the synthetic over the real would be established." Baker's argument here strangely echoes aspects of Bazin's realist teleology, and even more eerily combines that with the cultural preoccupations of movies such as *Blade Runner* (1982), set in a future society in which only the most sophisticated combination of technological and psychoanalytical investigation can tell an android apart from a person. Robin Baker, "Computer Technology and Special Effects in Contemporary Cinema," in Hayward and Wollen, p. 42.
36   Andrew, p. 162.
37   Bazin, "Evolution," p. 40.
38   Andrew, p. 163.
39   Bazin, "Will CinemaScope Save the Cinema?," p. 12.

40   Bosley Crowther, *New York Times* (October 5, 1952), quoted in Belton, *Widescreen Cinema*, p. 94.

41   The standard aspect ratio of 1:1.33 of Classical Hollywood was known as the Academy ratio. This was the height-to-width ratio of silent film, but when sound was introduced, the optical soundtrack running down one side of the frame produced a squarer picture. This posed problems in projection, and in 1932 the Academy of Motion Picture Arts and Sciences established a standard image size which gave a 1:1.33 ratio but also left room for the optical soundtrack. CinemaScope's original aspect ratio was 1:2.55, but this was reduced to 1:2.35 by the addition of a stereophonic soundtrack.

42   Belton, "CinemaScope and Historical Methodology," pp. 28–30.

43   *Motion Picture Herald* (December 19, 1953), p. 14, quoted in Richard Hincha, "Selling CinemaScope: 1953–1956," *The Velvet Light Trap* 21 (Summer 1985), p. 46.

44   John Belton, "CinemaScope: The Economics of Technology," *The Velvet Light Trap* 21 (Summer 1985), p. 35.

45   *Hollywood Reporter* (June 28, 1954), quoted in James Spellerberg, "CinemaScope and Ideology," *The Velvet Light Trap* 21 (Summer 1985), p. 30.

46   Tana Wollen, "The Bigger the Better: From CinemaScope to IMAX," in Hayward and Wollen, p. 13.

47   Spellerberg, pp. 30–1.

48   R.T. Ryan, *A History of Motion Picture Colour Photography* (London: Focal Press, 1977), p. 77. In *Practical Motion Picture Photography*, Russell Campbell quotes surveys of American audiences that have suggested particular associations between colors and moods: blue is tender, cyan leisurely, green playful, yellow gay, red exciting or vigorous, magenta sad or solemn. He suggests that these associations "may perhaps explain why the American public appears to prefer prints with an overall reddish balance; in India, on the other hand, a greenish bias finds favor." Although Campbell is skeptical that these associations can be established by any form of systematic analysis, he concludes that "a cold (bluish) print has a distancing effect, while a warm (yellowish or reddish) balance tends towards audience involvement." Russell Campbell, *Practical Motion Picture Photography* (London: Zwemmer, 1970), p. 89. Perhaps the absence of system explains why Eastman Kodak's tinted film stocks bore such descriptive names as Firelight, Sunshine, Nocturne, and Aqua Green.

49   *Elements of Color in Professional Motion Pictures* (1957), quoted in Edward Buscombe, "Sound and Color," *Jump Cut* 17 (1978), p. 24.

50   Quoted in Fred E. Basten, *Glorious Technicolor* (London: Barnes, 1980), p. 71.

51   Steve Neale, *Cinema and Technology: Image, Sound, Colour* (London: Macmillan, 1985), p. 152.

52   Quoted in Neale, p. 147.

53   Natalie Kalmus, "Colour," in Stephen Watts, ed., *Behind the Screen* (London: Arthur Barker, 1938), p. 116, quoted in Neale, p. 150.

54   Quoted in Ronald Haver, *David O. Selznick's Hollywood* (New York: Knopf, 1980), p. 196.

55   "Faster Color Film Cuts Light in Half," *American Cinematographer* (August 1939), p. 356, quoted in Edward Braningan, "Color and Cinema: Problems in the Writing of History," in Paul Kerr, ed., *The Hollywood Film Industry* (London: Routledge and Kegan Paul, 1986), p. 139.

56   *The Wizard of Oz* was one of several movies to motivate a transition to color in the movement from reality to fantasy. In *The Blue Bird* (1940), a poor woodcutter (Nigel Bruce) tells fairy stories in black-and-white, while the stories themselves are in color. In *The Secret Garden* (1949), Margaret O'Brien discovers a magical, Technicolor garden in

an otherwise black-and-white Victorian Yorkshire.

57   Eastman Kodak had cooperated in Technicolor's maintenance of its monopoly, but government anti-trust action against Technicolor as part of the Paramount suit encouraged it to develop an alternative, a spin-off from its development of color film for the domestic market.

58   The movie set a new company record for Fox's domestic rentals, bringing in $3.5 million. Aubrey Solomon, *Twentieth Century-Fox: A Corporate and Financial History* (Metuchen, NJ: Scarecrow, 1988), p. 10.

59   Grandeur was a 70-mm wide-film process innovated by William Fox in the late 1920s. Although it offered the possibility of projecting a much larger image than the picture palaces' surprisingly small screens, none of the other major companies displayed much enthusiasm for absorbing the costs of conversion, and Grandeur became a victim of the collapse of Fox's business empire in late 1929. According to Upton Sinclair, *Sunny Side Up* was filmed in Grandeur, but it may well have been released before any theaters were equipped to show it in its 70-mm version. Sequences of the movie were filmed in Multicolor, a two-color bipack process. Belton, *Widescreen Cinema*, pp. 36, 48, 56; Upton Sinclair, *Upton Sinclair Presents William Fox* (Los Angeles: Upton Sinclair, 1933), p. 66; James L. Limbacher, *Four Aspects of the Film: A History of the Development of Color, Sound, 3-D and Widescreen Films and their Contribution to the Art of the Motion Picture* (New York: Brussel & Brussel, 1968), pp. 41, 270.

60   The first real camera crane was used on the Universal musical *Broadway* in 1929. Salt, p. 228.

61   John L. Cass, "The Illusion of Sound and Picture," *Journal of the Society of Motion Picture Engineers* 14 (March 1930), p. 325, quoted in Rick Altman, "Sound Space," in Altman, p. 49.

62   Rick Altman traces the development of these practices through the 1930s in "Sound Space," in Altman, pp. 49–62; and in more technical detail in "The Technology of the Voice," *Iris* 3:1 (1985), pp. 3–20.

63   The sound-on-disc system played the soundtrack back on a separate gramophone that was kept synchronized to the projector. The system was always liable to mechanical failure, and was rapidly abandoned in favor of the sound-on-film system, in which the soundtrack was imprinted on the film as a series of light pulses.

64   By 1933 recording equipment had improved sufficiently to allow the mixing of a separate music track with the dialogue without a loss of sound quality. This development allowed the return of **extradiegetic** background music, which had, of course, always accompanied silent movies, setting the mood of each scene in a similar way to the use of color tints in the image. Salt, p. 281.

65   Robert Ray, *A Certain Tendency of the American Cinema, 1930–1980* (Princeton, NJ: Princeton University Press, 1985), p. 29.

66   As one Motion Picture Producers and Distributors of America official put it in October 1929 when he reviewed Paramount's backstage melodrama *Applause*, "the folks who represent the intelligentsia in the country towns and small cities are not yet prepared to view with approval a long series of scenes including close-ups which show the heroine clad only in breechclout and brassiere." *Sunny Side Up*'s final spectacular routine, "Turn on the Heat," was also censored as too risqué in some places. Carl Milliken to Hays, October 9, 1929, PCA *Applause* file.

67   Quoted in Jeffrey Richards, *The Age of the Dream Palace: Cinema and Society in Britain, 1930–1939* (London: Routledge and Kegan Paul, 1984), pp. 63–4.

68   For many European audiences, neither spoke with his own voice, but with the dubbed voice of another actor.

69   George Orwell, *The English People* (London: Collins, 1947), p. 36.

70   Constant Coquelin, "Art and the Actor" (1st pub. in French, 1880, trans. Abby Langdon Alger, 1881), in Brander Matthews, ed., *Papers on Acting* (New York: Hill and Wang, 1958), p. 31.

71   Widescreen movies were initially prepared for television screening by a system known as "pan and scan," which allowed the technician preparing the television print to reframe a shot or cut from one side of the widescreen frame to the other. The end result often produced unbalanced compositions. Alternatively, the top and bottom of an Academy frame picture can be masked out for widescreen projection, and the whole image used for the television version. All these variations add to doubts that we have already raised about the idea of an "original" version of a Hollywood movie. Belton, *Widescreen Cinema*, pp. 216–25.

72   The first "letterbox" video, *Manhattan*, was released in 1985 because director Woody Allen's contract with United Artists gave him control over the video versions of his work. Belton, *Widescreen Cinema*, p. 226.

73   The industry's early standardization on a film width of 35-mm gauge and an aspect ratio of 4:3 (1.33:1) had less to do with either engineering or aesthetics than it did with the exploitation of patents in pursuit of monopoly by the Edison and Eastman Kodak companies. Belton, *Widescreen Cinema*, pp. 22–8.

74   By the historical painter, Paul Delaroche.

75   Neale, pp. 21–2.

76   With widescreen the horizontal angle of view is greater, although perspective relations remain constant.

77   According to *Psycho*'s script supervisor Marshal Schlom, director Alfred Hitchcock "wanted the camera, being the eyes of the audience all the time, to let them [view the action] as if they were seeing it with their own eyes." Quoted in Stephen Rebello, *Alfred Hitchcock and the Making of Psycho* (New York: Dembner Books, 1990), p. 93.

78   This model of the economics of technological change was adapted from business histories by Douglas Gomery in his work on the introduction of sound. J. Douglas Gomery, "The Coming of the Talkies: Invention, Innovation, and Diffusion," in Tino Balio, ed., *The American Film Industry*, 1st edn (Madison: University of Wisconsin Press, 1976), p. 211. See also Belton, *Widescreen Cinema*, p. 239.

79   Peter Wollen, "Cinema and Technology: A Historical Overview," in *Readings and Writings: Semiotic Counter-strategies* (London: Verso, 1982), p. 171.

80   Wollen, p. 171.

81   Patrick J. Ogle, "Technological and Aesthetic Influences upon the Development of Deep Focus Cinematography in the United States," in John Ellis, ed., *Screen Reader 1: Cinema/Ideology/Politics* (London: Society for Education in Film and Television, 1977), pp. 81–108.

82   Patricia Zimmermann has pointed out, however, that the hardware of "amateur" film has always registered its difference from Hollywood and "encouraged the idolatry of technical wizardry" to which only Hollywood or television "professionals" have access. It is hardly accidental that the role broadcast television has found for amateur video is in the recording of domestic accidents in a comedy of domestic cruelty; the moments that are edited out of professional production are the only ones left in the shows of amateurs. Patricia R. Zimmermann, "Trading Down: Amateur Film Technology in Fifties America," *Screen* 29:2 (Spring 1988), p. 42.

83   These changes are discussed more fully in chapter 7.

84   Simon Turner, quoted in Peter Dean and Mark Kermode, "Windup," *Sight and Sound* 3:3 (NS, March 1993), p. 63.

85   James Lardner, *Fast Forward: Hollywood, the Japanese and the VCR Wars* (New York: Norton, 1987).

86   Barry Salt uses the average shot length (ASL) of a movie as a means of comparing the frequency of cuts. This involves counting the number of separate shots in a movie, and dividing that by its running time. Salt suggests that ASLs fell steadily during the silent period to as low as 5 seconds, and then more than doubled with the coming of sound. After dropping to about 8 seconds in the mid-1930s, ASLs rose slightly through the 1940s and 1950s to about 11 seconds, and then fell during the 1960s to 7.5 seconds. There was, however, considerable variation between individual movies. Some studios and some filmmakers also cut faster than others. Salt, p. 282.

5 Space

The cinema exists in the space between the audience and the screen.
Jean-Luc Godard

In a place like Stoningham you can't ignore convention.
Cary Scott (Jane Wyman) in *All That Heaven Allows* (1955)

In the first four chapters of this book we have considered some of the ways in which the economic organization of the motion picture industry determines the aesthetic conventions of the movies it produces. It is now time to consider the more formal properties of Hollywood's commercial aesthetic. The flat image on the theater screen represents a three-dimensional space, which the audience can enter imaginatively, unimpeded by the two-dimensionality of the screen. The space that Hollywood provides for its characters and audiences is, however, highly conventionalized, and this chapter examines the conventions of representation through which Hollywood space is constructed. Just as generic convention requires the cooperative participation of the viewer, so Hollywood's spatial representations can only transform images into meaningful components of a spectacle or a story if audiences have the necessary experience to enter into the expected conventional relationship with the fiction. Although the specifics of these conventions have changed through history, their underlying goals have remained more or less consistent: "what we look *at* is guided by our assumptions and expectations about what to look for."[1] For the most part, movies in the 1990s still seek to direct us toward content – story and star performance – to the same extent that movies in the 1920s did, and despite a number of superficial differences, they do so according to a very similar set of principles.

Watching the movie from a comfortable seat in a darkened auditorium, we are gradually robbed of the sensory coordinates that we use to locate ourselves in the material world outside the theater. The movie theater constructs us as spectators, heightening our sense of vision and focusing our attention; in ideal viewing conditions our only sense that we ourselves occupy space comes from watching the screen.[2] Once the movie starts, it positions us physically and imaginatively as invisible spectators of the scenes we are shown. We are present to witness what happens, but unless one of the characters addresses the camera directly, we remain absent as far as they are concerned. Our usual relation to the characters is that of a participant observer, often literally looking over their shoulders, included within the pictorial space projected on the screen but not part of it, involved with the action but not impeding it, missing nothing. Hollywood's representation of space is usually organized to secure our attention to what is going on in that space. In return, it offers us the chance to oversee and overhear the action from a succession of ideal viewpoints. Hollywood space rewards us for looking at it by constantly addressing and satisfying our expectations in looking. We can take pleasure in looking simply because, in the benevolent space of a Hollywood movie, we repeatedly see what we want to look at.

A few months after Disneyland opened, the head gardener asked Walt Disney's permission to fence off one of the flower beds because visitors were walking on it to take photographs of the fairy castle. Instead of the fence, Disney ordered him to build a path with a sign saying, "This way for the best view of the castle." Hollywood's space is Utopian: in giving us the best view, it provides us with a pleasurable experience quite distinct from our more fragmented and less complete view of the world outside the movie. Hollywood's system of spatial construction, usually called the **continuity system**, constructs the space in which its action unfolds as a smooth and continuous flow across shots.[3] Within this system the camera remains relatively unobtrusive, seldom drawing attention to its mediating presence. Few shots are held long enough for the audience to consciously register the camera's position in the screen space, and each shot is presented as if "triggered" by the events unfolding in the fiction, as the camera reframes to accommodate figure movement, for instance.

The continuity system also discourages filmmakers from juxtaposing shots that will jar with each other or draw the viewer's attention to the cut. The graphic balancing of each shot with the one before and the one after makes it easier for the audience to understand the camera (or more exactly the movie's image stream) as an invisible presence in the screen space. Even at relatively conspicuous moments, when the camera draws the audience's attention to the microphone hidden in the flower vase by tracking in on it, we view the camera's movement and its act of looking as transparent. We look *through* the camera, and rather than pay attention to the camera's moving viewpoint, we attach a narrative significance to what we see. The **transparency** of the camera's look is often understood as contributing substantially to the particular kind of realism that Hollywood offers. In this chapter we shall suggest a slightly different emphasis and concentrate on the way that the continuity system provides a **safe space** for the development of a story, for the pleasure of spectacle, and most importantly of all for the secure placement of the audience in relation to the fictional world of the movie. Our sense of security within the continuity system is indicated by how little viewers normally notice editing, because cuts are placed where they will be as unobtrusive and as informative as possible. Because we expect the movie to explain itself to us, we assume that two juxtaposed shots show us a connected space, and each unemphatic cut confirms our ability to move freely around the space of a scene in search of the ideal viewpoint. For an audience in search of entertainment, Hollywood's conventions of spatial representation are benevolent because they offer us the best view. The rules that organize that space and make it as transparently comprehensible as possible also make it a safe place for the audience to be.

Making the Picture Speak: Representation and Expression

Midway through *Singin' in the Rain* (1952), Gene Kelly makes a piece of Hollywood space. The plot has reached the point where he must tell Debbie Reynolds that he loves her but he is, as he says, "such a ham" that he chooses to dramatize his desire in a song-and-dance routine. Playing a Hollywood star, Kelly can only declare his love in the proper setting. He ushers Reynolds onto an empty studio stage and literally constructs the romantic space he needs with the technological resources he finds there: lighting effects, a step ladder, a wind machine. As he explains when he sings "You Are My Lucky Star" with the aid of "five hundred thousand kilowatts of stardust, " the audience comes not only to witness, but also to share and experience the emotional intensity of their relationship.

The scene is a particularly revealing example of a process in which Hollywood is constantly engaged: alternating the viewer's relationship to the fiction between one based on watching and one based on imaginative or emotional participation. Often this alternation is achieved by transporting the audience from one kind of space into another. We move from a space we understand as representing the actual space in which the action of a scene takes place to a space that expresses something about what is happening or being said within it, and back again. Part of what the audience does while watching a movie is to recognize the movie's narration as a process of continual displacement between these two categories of represented and expressive cinematic space.

Represented space is the area that exists in front of the camera lens and is recorded by it. It is the recognizable space in which actors stand, in which props are placed and in which things happen. Unlike the writer's pen, the camera cannot simply conjure objects (or rather their representation) into existence. Whatever the camera records has to exist in material form; that existence involves its occupation of represented space.[4] Even imaginary creatures like the Wookies and robots of *Star Wars* (1977) had to be realized – constructed, costumed, and made to move in front of the camera – rather than simply being described as their literary equivalents might be.[5] At the beginning of the "You Are My Lucky Star" sequence, Kelly and Reynolds occupy represented space in a very obvious sense: we

Don Lockwood (Gene Kelly) constructs expressive space out of an empty sound stage in *Singin' in the Rain* (1952). Aquarius Picture Library

see them walking through the studio lot and into the sound stage, and we recognize these spaces as having a literal or material existence, which anyone could occupy.

As the sequence proceeds, however, Kelly gradually transforms this represented space into a more **expressive** one, endowed with meaning

Phyllis Dietrichson (Barbara Stanwyck) graphically positioned between lover and husband in *Double Indemnity* (1944)

In this image from *Imitation of Life* (1959), the audience knows that Sarah Jane (Susan Kohner) is embarking on an impossible relationship, because she is graphically separated from the man by the screen of the louvre door. Unaware of her place in the composition, Sarah Jane does not yet know the affair is doomed.

beyond the literal. We move from a space that signifies its own depth and continuity to a space that signifies the direct experience of "being in love." The empty sound stage has been transformed into a site for romance, and in this expressive space the intimacies of the courtship can safely be represented as a bravura display of song, dance, and special effects. In accepting this suspension of literal representation, we also accept the different texture and composition of space during the sequence, and Gene Kelly as the source of disruption. As soon as he finishes constructing his space, he can put what he wants to say into words. In the glow of the studio lights, he declares, "You sure look lovely in the moonlight, Kathy," and in the shot that follows, she does. Later in the sequence, when we see him draw in his breath, hear the musical accompaniment pause slightly, and spot the camera craning down onto him, we recognize the cue for a song. Subsequently, the screen is composed so as to offer the couple space to dance in. As they dance, the camera dances with them, demonstrating its acquiescence in Kelly's expressive world. The couple's ability to fill space harmoniously indicates that their courtship is complete, and the sequence as a whole illustrates how the audience of Hollywood cinema can be persuaded to abandon its secure perspective on a represented space, in order to build up an understanding of character, predict future movement in the storyline, or allow an expressive action to take place.

Although the disruption of represented space by a musical number is perhaps an extreme example, the displacement of the audience's perception between represented and expressive space occurs repeatedly in even the most run-of-the-mill movies. Represented space is three-dimensional; expressive space often combines the sculptural three-dimensionality of the space in the image with the graphic two-dimensionality of the image itself.

In a scene from *Double Indemnity* (1944), one shot positions Phyllis Dietrichson (Barbara Stanwyck) graphically between her lover (Fred MacMurray) and her husband (Tom Powers), whom they are plotting to kill. In the represented space she is sitting on the other side of the room, but the composition places her in an expressively more significant relation to the action. Her position creates a tension in the scene. Will the husband detect their plot against him? In other words, will he recognize the significance of the composition of which he is part? Significantly, the play between graphic composition and three-dimensional space is available only to the audience, not to the characters. Likewise, in the image from *Imitation of Life* (1959) on p. 193, the position from which the viewer looks is one of privileged knowledge: the two figures remain unaware that they are separated by the louvre door that splits the screen. In *All That Heaven Allows* (1955), there is a heavily ironic use of the graphic properties of expressive space in one confrontation between Cary (Jane Wyman) and her son Ned (William Reynolds), over her relationship with Ron (Rock Hudson). Ned has threatened to leave home unless Cary gives Ron up. About to leave the house, he is positioned in the frame so that a fire-screen divides him off from Cary and the camera. From the camera's viewpoint, When Ned declares, "Mother, we can't let this come between us," the screen has already separated them irreparably.

One distinction between the three-dimensional scene and the two-dimensional image is that the image is **framed**. The composition of an image takes place in relation first of all to its borders and its frame, something you can verify every time you put a still camera to your eye and then adjust your position to make a better composition. Many of the early aesthetic debates about the cinema posed the question of two- or three-dimensionality in terms of whether the cinema frame should be seen as a window opening onto a world which extended into the offscreen space beyond the limits of the frame, or as a border, much like a painting, in which composition was a crucial determinant of meaning.[6] In practice, Hollywood cinema uses the frame in both ways, encouraging us to accept a sense of the continuity of offscreen space, while simultaneously focusing our attention on specific points in the space actually represented onscreen. Hollywood's rules of composition for the single shot are borrowed from the conventions of painting and photography. The principle of the Golden Third, for instance, one of many geometrical principles of composition observed in western art since the Renaissance, suggests that compositions will be balanced if the main objects of attention are positioned on the lines that divide the image into thirds, horizontally or vertically. The idea of frontality is also derived from Renaissance painting, and indirectly from Greek and Roman theater. It assumes that characters will be grouped according to their compositional relation to the camera rather than their spatial relation to each other; figures tend to stand in lines or semi-circles, facing the camera rather than each other. David Bordwell has argued that Classical Hollywood cinema also uses:

Wyatt Earp (Henry Fonda) and Sam (J. Farrell McDonald) wait for the empty space at the bar to be filled by the Clanton gang in *My Darling Clementine* (1946).

George Rounby (Warren Beatty) argues with his girlfriend Jill (Goldie Hawn) in *Shampoo* (1975). The instability of their relationship is expressed in the awkward composition of the shot.

a privileged zone of screen space resembling a T: the upper one-third and central vertical third of the screen constitute the "center" of the shot. This center determines the composition of long shots, medium shots and close-ups, as well as the grouping of figures. . . . Classical filmmaking thus considers edge-framing taboo; frontally positioned figures or objects, however unimportant, are seldom sliced off by either vertical edge.[7]

The composition of an individual shot in a Hollywood movie is never as intricate as that of a Renaissance painting by Raphael or Piero della Francesca, however, in part because the composition of any one shot must be considered in combination with the other shots in the sequence, and in part because the composition of the moving image is itself dynamic. Frequently, a movie will make use of this by beginning a shot with an unbalanced composition that demands an action to fill the empty field. In the saloon scene from *My Darling Clementine* (1946) above, our gaze is drawn to the vacant space in the foreground by the diagonal line of the bar counter. We wait for the Clanton gang to walk into the frame. Composition anticipates the movie's action and creates audience expectation.

The composition of a shot often establishes meaningful tensions and anticipations within the frame that require the viewer to respond to the representation of space. However, this response is seldom consciously articulated. Instead, the audience's recognition of compositional stress is normally displaced into an insight about a character or the plot situation. A self-conscious disruption of the norms of composition can produce a space expressive of discomfort, as in the image above from *Shampoo* (1975). The awkward composition and uncomfortable postures in which the characters are caught express the unstable relationship between them. Their inability to fill the frame comfortably embodies their lack of equilibrium: the separation between them is made visible in the composition by the vertical lines between them. The image from *Written on the Wind* (1956) on p. 196 operates according to similar principles. Throughout the movie,

The spatially insecure Kyle Hadley (Robert Stack) in *Written on the Wind* (1956).

Kyle Hadley (Robert Stack) is in the way of other characters, his antisocial behavior making him a disconcerting and unwelcome liability to them. As an expression of this, he is constantly caught in uncomfortable compositions in which he either intrudes on the arrangement of other characters or is rendered spatially insecure by standing in awkward places – with a picture behind his head, or in front of a window, through which he seems likely to fall.

In these examples, framing produces meanings separate from those located in either dialogue or action. This capacity of the cinematic image to make the visible world express its deeper structures through composition has led some critics to see cinema as a language based on metaphor.[8] Characters in Hollywood movies have a pressing need to establish themselves spatially, to dominate the composition or to keep a secure hold on their place in it, in order to maintain their narrative centrality. Throughout *Shampoo*, George Rounby's (Warren Beatty) inability to make choices has been expressed in spatial terms as an inability to move purposefully in any given direction long enough to establish a course of action. Dialogue underlines the many images of George's restless but ineffectual motion: his girlfriend Jill (Goldie Hawn) tells him, "You never stop moving. You never go anywhere." Spatial indecision usually incurs a narrative penalty in Hollywood movies. George is finally abandoned in a featureless landscape after the last of his several lovers has left him for another man.

Deep Space: Three-dimensionality on a Flat Screen

> I think I'm in a frame . . . All I can see is the frame. I'm going in there to look at the picture.
> Jeff Markham (Robert Mitchum) in *Out of the Past* (1947)

The screen space of an individual shot is thus neither strictly three-dimensional nor two-dimensional, but constantly shifts between them, as our

The dark foreground in this still from *All That Heaven Allows* (1955) suggests that Cary Scott (Jane Wyman) will not easily escape from the trap of domestic respectability her children (William Reynolds and Gloria Talbot) want to keep her in. Later, Cary and her son Ned will find themselves separated by the screen behind Cary's left shoulder. Copyright © by Universal Pictures, a Division of Universal City Studios, Inc. Courtesy of MCA Publishing Rights, a Division of MCA Inc. (Courtesy The Ronald Grant Archive)

attention shifts between the graphic and the architectural or sculptural features of the image. The way a set is lit can emphasize its depth or draw attention to the existence of the frame by constructing another frame within it. Extreme lighting effects, such as those common in film noir, can present the frame predominantly as a graphic composition, in which the lines and shapes of the image are more communicative than the image's depth relations.[9] Color can serve similar functions. Through what the Society of Motion Picture Engineers called "color normalcy" it can contribute unobtrusively to the verisimilitude of the image. It can express a specific narrative meaning, for instance by drawing attention to a character's change in demeanor, as when Cary puts on a red dress in *All That Heaven Allows*, signalling a change in her sexual identity.[10] Or it can render the image unnatural, drawing attention to the image as image, or to tensions within the action that cannot be expressed through dialogue. *All*

That Heaven Allows contains a particularly vivid example of color used to excess, when Cary's daughter Kay (Gloria Talbott) confronts her mother over her relationship with Ron in a bedroom apparently lit through a multicolored glass window. The intensity of the color signals the unnatural intensity of the scene's emotional exchange.

When we look at the screen, our eyes are drawn to movement, and we are most likely to understand movement in the image as being movement through space. If we did not invest the screen with depth, we would find it very difficult to watch movies at all, particularly if we expected them to construct themselves as stories. Writing in 1923, French art critic Elie Faure registered his deliberate rejection of narration in favor of the purely graphic qualities of the cinematic image:

> The revelation of what the cinema of the future can be came to me one day: I retain an exact memory of it, of the sudden commotion I experienced when I observed, in a flash, the magnificence there was in the relationship of a piece of black clothing to the gray wall of an inn. From that moment on I paid no more attention to the martyrdom of the poor woman who was condemned, in order to save her husband from dishonor, to give herself to the lascivious banker who had previously murdered her mother and debauched her child.[11]

Faure's rejection of narration led him to stress the formal qualities of film as a mobile, two-dimensional image. His predictions of a future cinema that explored the play of light, color, and tone, approaching the condition of music at the expense of any discernible story content, were fulfilled by the work of avant-garde filmmakers such as Man Ray and Moholy-Nagy in the 1920s and 1930s and Jonas Mekas and Malcolm Le Grice in the 1960s and later.[12]

But against this High Modernist aesthetic of form we do not simply have to argue a populist preference for being told stories. There is no cinematic equivalent to the simple sentence, "A man walked down the street," because any cinematic image must add considerably to the bare statement, amplifying it by showing a particular man walking in a particular way down a particular street. An unwillingness to recognize the film image as a representation of a three-dimensional space is the equivalent of only recognizing the words on the pages of a literary text as shapes in black ink on a white background. But total belief in the three-dimensionality of the image is as unhelpful as total disbelief. If cinema ever achieved the perfect illusion of reality that Bazin envisioned for it in "The Myth of Total Cinema" it would disappear, at least in the form that we now recognize it. Story-telling – the highly artificial arrangement of information, including spatial information – would become impossible, and our attention would be arbitrarily distributed among central and insignificant details, much as it is in real life. Alternatively, our experience would be similar to that of the first cinema audiences, who reportedly ducked under their seats for fear they were about to be run over by an approaching locomotive.[13] As we mentioned in the last chapter, Cinerama sold itself successfully on a similar kind of audience participation in the screen space:

> You won't be gazing at a movie screen – you'll find yourself swept right into the picture, surrounded by sight and sound. . . . Everything that happens on the curved Cinerama screen is happening to you. And without moving from your seat, you share, personally, in the most remarkable new kind of emotional experience ever brought to the theater.[14]

The roller-coaster ride at the beginning of *This is Cinerama* (1952) often convinced viewers of its representation of three-dimensional reality strongly enough to make them sway, recoil, or even be sick.[15] But as critics observed at the time, so persuasively spectacular an illusion hindered the construction of a drama. A viewer worrying about motion sickness is hardly in the best frame of mind to catch the nuances of dialogue or the details of a plot. The space in a movie must provide the opportunity for spectacle *and* narrative, must be simultaneously two- and three-dimensional, graphic and architectural. What makes screen space a different kind of space from that which we normally see ourselves as inhabiting outside the theater is its representation of three-dimensionality by a two-dimensional image; its capacity to signify *and* to narrate originates in the play between the surface of the image and the depth it represents. Much of Hollywood's benevolence toward its audience (or, as some critics would put it, its exercise of control over their perception)[16] consists in the way that it reassures viewers that they have *comprehended* each image as both a three-dimensional space and the two-dimensional composition in which that space is always framed, as both represented and expressive space.

Mise-en-scène

In a movie designed for a single viewing, the representation of space must be both comprehensible and significant. It must provide the audience with a sense of the relation between characters, and between events unfolding in the fiction. Familiar elements in the organization of space may even help to make incoherent storylines accessible and acceptable. The image should not be so intricate as to disperse our interest away from the intended focus of action; in addition, it should create an expectation that leads smoothly from one shot to the next. This arrangement of screen space as a meaningful organization of elements is known as **mise-en-scène**: literally, the "putting into a scene" or staging of a fiction. It is through mise-en-scène that represented space becomes expressive. Classical Hollywood mise-en-scène balances and fills the frame, avoiding both distracting detail and empty spots in the composition, and using conventional compositional principles to focus attention on the main line of action.

In *The Searchers* (1956), the social isolation of Ethan Edwards (John Wayne) is expressed visually in shots that show him on the outside of a doorway, unable to cross its threshold.

We should think of mise-en-scène less as a list of devices or techniques, such as set design, lighting, or camera placement, than as a form of textual economy, comparable to the financial and generic economies we have already considered, and thus as another site at which the multiple logics of Hollywood cinema are met and resolved. Mise-en-scène makes the image, in Will Wright's phrase, "maximally meaningful."[17] An efficient mise-en-scène serves the needs of both the producers and the consumers of the fiction, maintaining the viewer's involvement in the action by allowing for understanding and interpretation without impeding its progress with intrusive explanation. Like generic convention, mise-en-scène is a system that requires recognition, but not necessarily articulation, on the part of its audience, since the meaning it produces is displaced to another area of the movie. Mise-en-scène fills out the meaning of otherwise neutral spaces in the interests of the audience's wider dramatic involvement. It also limits or closes down the potential meanings that even the simplest stream of images can suggest, by encouraging some meanings for its audience and discouraging others. When the system is functioning smoothly we have the sense of witnessing events unfolding in an extended three-dimensional space, in which we are nevertheless able to interpret specific details because of the way in which particular elements are highlighted for us. Hollywood space is thus something that we look both *at* and *into*.

In talking about the composition of the image we have already been discussing one major aspect of mise-en-scène, by which an action is framed to enhance the viewer's understanding of its significance. Sometimes the camera's viewpoint gives the audience knowledge the characters do not share, as in the example from *All That Heaven Allows*. In other instances, such as *Bigger Than Life* (1956), characters are as aware as the audience of the thematic significance of spatial arenas, and of the crucial importance of transitional spaces such as doors and staircases.[18] By drawing attention to everyday objects or architectural features, mise-en-scène can imbue them with narrative significance. In *The Searchers* (1956), a doorway becomes a powerful sign of Ethan Edwards' (John Wayne) exclusion from the community, when at the end of the movie he is framed by the doorway of a

The bar-room mirror frames Marylee Hadley's (Dorothy Malone) indiscretion in *Written on the Wind* (1956). Universal (courtesy Kobal)

homestead he cannot bring himself to enter. Throughout the movie he has been unable to pass through any doorway shot from inside looking out, a visual expression of his inability to enter the institutions of society. Elsewhere, doors can be much more ambiguous instruments of spatial organization: the closing of a door separates different arenas, while an open door provides the expectation of an entry or exit through it, rendering a room significantly less secure, and its occupants vulnerable to intruders.

Other architectural features that frame a space or produce a view, such as windows or corridors, are particularly useful expressive tools. In *Tea and Sympathy* (1956) a pattern of framing that emphasizes doors and windows transforms Laura Reynolds' (Deborah Kerr) house into a labyrinth of passages, disconnected and connected spaces. Familiar domestic sites become expressive of social and personal anxieties through the dramatic devices of eavesdropping and spying. Mirrors routinely encourage the two-dimensional nature of the screen to intrude into the three-dimensional space it represents: characters may be caught in moments of self-examination, or when they have to make a choice, and the audience is presented with spatial fields suggesting the divergent directions the story might take.

Whether through the use of these architectural features, graphic framing, or composition in depth, mise-en-scène determines the apparent shape and texture of screen space, signifies its representative or expressive status, and locates particular spaces in relation to the developing fiction. An examination of the way a Hollywood director stages and composes scenes is likely to provide the most convincing evidence of individual style: the examples we have used would set Nicholas Ray's architectural use of space in *Bigger Than Life* against Douglas Sirk's much greater emphasis on the graphic qualities of the image in *All That Heaven Allows*, *Written on the Wind*, and *Imitation of Life*. At the same time, mise-en-scène is the craft skill of a director, and a manual such as *Grammar of the Film Language* will teach the aspiring director what its author, Daniel Arijon, calls the "common set of rules . . . used to solve specific problems presented by the visual narration of a story." For instance: "A principle of editing is the alternation of two or more centres of interest. . . . Matched looks on the screen *are always opposed*. . . . In a group of *three*, one of them is the arbiter of attention. . . . All movement must be motivated, or must be made to appear so." What Arijon describes as the rules, laws, and formulae of the continuity system apply to staging, composition, and editing. Despite his book's title, Arijon does not explore how the metaphors of grammar or language apply to cinema. When he presents "Twenty Basic Rules for Camera Movement," he is describing the conventions of continuity technique which, he says, should be considered as: "one of the filmmaker's most precious assets. It serves us constantly to sustain our work even when the most essential element, imagination, fails us. If we rely on technique and dispense with imagination, we become mechanical. If we rely on imagination alone and ignore technique, our work will become chaotic."[19]

Like Arijon, Classical Hollywood preferred the mechanical to the chaotic. In 1933 the German director G.W. Pabst went to Hollywood to work for Warner Bros. Used to a considerable degree of directorial control over his projects, Pabst was quickly informed by Warners' head of production Hal B. Wallis not only that he could make no changes in the script, but also that he had to accommodate himself to the studio's shooting style. "I have asked you for close-ups repeatedly," wrote Wallis, "You will have to get used to our way of shooting pictures and the way we want them shot." One of the reasons for this was to give the editors, under Wallis' supervision, more control. "Overlap your action a little more when you change angles, " Wallis told him, "so that you don't finish one angle on a line and then pick up your next angle with the people picking up exactly in the same shot so that the stuff has to be cut that way . . . overlap a line now and then so that we have a little something to play with, so that the stuff will be smoother." The movie, *A Modern Hero* (1934), was Pabst's only American production, and Jan-Christopher Horak suggests that Pabst was probably fired "for not buckling under to the system."[20] At its most mechanical, that system would encourage a director to provide **coverage** of a scene by photographing the whole action in a master shot including all the characters, then rephotographing it several times with closer shots of each character to provide the editor with enough material to construct the scene as he, or the producer, saw fit. For some directors, including John Ford, the practice of "cutting in the camera" that Hal Wallis was objecting to was a means of maintaining authorial control over the mise-en-scène. Other directors, most famously Alfred Hitchcock, planned their movies shot by shot on storyboards, deliberately making the process of shooting itself as mechanical an act of recording a predetermined set of images as possible.

Whether it is seen as directorial style or a list of techniques and devices, mise-en-scène is obviously inseparable from the process of editing individual shots into a flow of images. Although editing is often regarded as a separate element in the production process, it is appropriate that we consider it here as a part of our discussion of mise-en-scène and Hollywood's presentation of space.

Editing

Hollywood's commercial aesthetics rely on editing. As well as the obvious appeal of frequent changes in the image, there are sound economic reasons for its practice of comparatively frequent cuts and short takes. Long takes with a mobile camera, such as the opening shot of *Sunny Side Up* (1929), are technically the most difficult shots to coordinate; breaking the action into small segments makes it easier to produce footage at a predictable rate. Directors in the dream factory of the 1930s were expected to shoot between 12 and 20 **set-ups** per day, producing two-and-a-half minutes of film that would end up in the rough cut of the movie.[21] As Hal Wallis' complaint to G.W. Pabst makes clear, a cinema constructed by editing also ensured that control over the appearance of the final product remained with producers. Wallis normally oversaw the final editing of major Warner Bros. productions, dictating the changes he required to a stenographer while watching the rough cut of the movie. His detailed cutting notes on *Angels with Dirty Faces* (1938), for instance, run to eight pages. Contracts providing the director with rights over the "final cut" have always been the rarest accolade of a company's confidence in him or her.

In combination with the framing and composition we have discussed, editing works to make space representative and expressive, informative of the present and predictive of the future, modulating audience interest from the general to the particular, and selecting significant details from other merely present information. Hollywood's editing codes have been among the most consistent of its practices over time, relatively little affected by changes in technology. Some writers would argue that audiences have gradually become visually more sophisticated, so that they need rather less guidance through the geography of a scene than their parents or grandparents. A contemporary Hollywood movie is more likely to cut from a long shot to a close-up, or to use a cut instead of a dissolve to indicate a temporal ellipsis. Whether these changes are enough to mark the end of Hollywood's Classical style, or merely its adaptation, is a subject of some debate, which we shall engage in first by outlining some of the conventional practices of Classical Hollywood, and then by examining the space in a more recent movie in some detail.

First we need to establish some terms for describing the different scales of shot, or **shot scale**, which we can discuss in terms of the most commonly represented object, the human body. An extreme long shot presents a landscape in which figures are barely visible: a horseman on a distant horizon, perhaps. In a **long shot (LS)**, people fill half or three quarters of the height of the screen, but the shot will emphasize the setting the figures are in. Such a shot will often be used at the beginning of a scene, to show the space in which the scene will take place. Then it is known as an **establishing shot**. In a **full shot**, the height of the frame is filled with the human figure, while a **medium long shot** covers the body from mid-calf or knees up. In the Academy frame, this shot balances the figure against its surroundings, presenting characters as the principal focus of attention, but giving them space to move and interact within the shot. French critics have called this shot (especially a two-shot, featuring two characters) the **plan Americain**, because of the frequency of its use in Hollywood; in English it is occasionally called a "Hollywood shot." A **medium shot (MS)**, cutting characters off at about the waist, offers similar possibilities for character interaction. A **close shot** takes in the character from the chest up, focusing attention on his or her face and expression when he or she is delivering or reacting to dialogue. The range from the long shot to the close shot encompasses the vast majority of shots used in Classical Hollywood cinema. **Close-ups (CU)** were comparatively rare, used mainly as an emphatic device.

The initials "LS ," "MS," or "CU" on a shooting script provide only a rule-of-thumb guide to the way a scene is to be shot. They are never absolute designations, merely points on a sliding scale, descriptive of relative distances between the subject of the shot and the viewer. Beginning with an establishing long shot that sets up the arena in which the scene will be played out and the relative positions of the characters, a typical scene will cut to medium shots to play out the characters' interactions in space. Dialogue scenes usually progress to closer shots of each of the characters, normally taken from over the other character's shoulder. The procedure operates unobtrusively, to encourage an equivalent focusing of audience interest upon the action, not upon the editing. We are gradually drawn into a space made safe and familiar to us because of the familiarity of the way it is presented to us. The smoothness of this progress is emphasized: a Classical Hollywood movie will almost never cut directly from long shot to close-up because of the jarring effect it would produce. Inside this safe space, we can direct our attention to engaging emotionally with the characters, confident that the movie's image stream

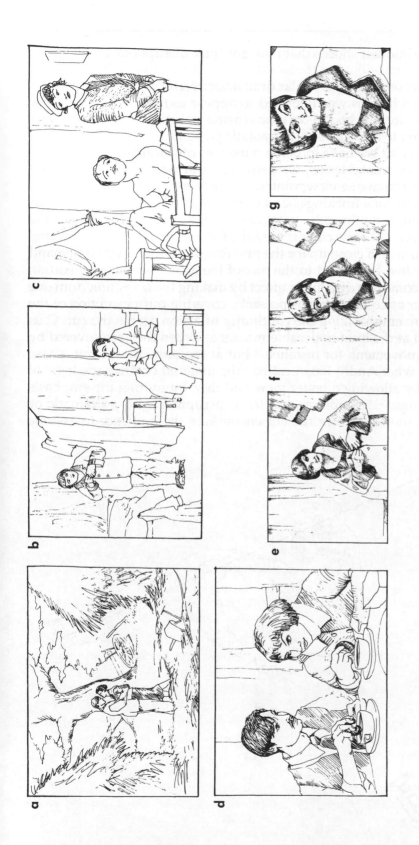

Framing heights for the human figure
This exterior long shot (a) from *It Happened One Night* (1934) places Ellie Andrews (Claudette Colbert) and Peter Warne (Clark Gable) in their setting. An interior long shot (b) is often an establishing shot, showing the space in which the scene will take place. From there the scene can cut to a medium two-shot (c) of both characters, a close medium two-shot (d), or a medium shot (e), close shot (f), or close-up of either player (g).

will avoid any sudden shocks that may abruptly disrupt our involvement in the action.

Unless it was seeking a particular dramatic effect, Classical Hollywood's cutting between images was intended to appear as fluid as possible. The obvious reason for this had to do with cinema's capacity to alter its viewpoint, compared to our own relatively static positioning. When we want to vary our viewpoint we have to move ourselves physically from one place to another. In cinematic terms, we perform a **tracking shot**, and without the ability to cut from one viewpoint to another we might describe waking experience as one long tracking shot. Because editing is so unnatural to our own perception, it ought to be particularly discomforting to us; and the anecdotal histories of early cinema are full of stories of producers worrying that, presented with a close-up for the first time, audiences would demand to know what had happened to the rest of the actor.[22] Continuity editing works to overcome this disruptive effect by making the transition from one shot to another as comfortable as possible, covering our perception of the shot change by emphasizing the continuity of action across the cut. Cuts are positioned at the least noticeable moment – when they are covered by a character's movement, for instance – but at the same time, a cut is also motivated by what André Bazin called "the material or dramatic logic of the scene . . . by allowing a better view and then by putting the emphasis where it belongs."[23] Combining the least disruption with a dramatic or psychological motivation for the cut encourages the audience to assume

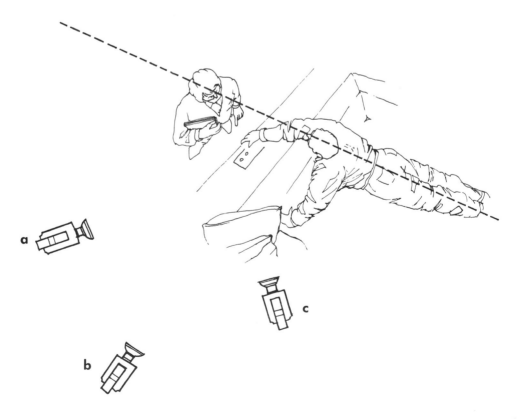

a

b

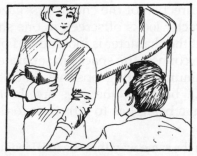

c

d

e

The center line; eyeline matching; shot/reverse shot
Jan Morrow (Doris Day) and Brad Allen (Rock Hudson) illustrate spatial
conventions in *Pillow Talk* (1959). The "180-degree rule" draws a line
between the two characters. So long as the camera stays on one side of the
line (as in a, b and c), Day will remain on the left side of the frame looking
to the right, and Hudson will stay on the right side of the frame, looking to
his left. If their eyelines remain matched, viewers can connect the spaces in
separate shots. Conversation scenes such as this are most often presented
in a sequence of shot/reverse shot, with the camera looking over the
shoulder of each character in turn (d and e).

that the space represented on the screen at any given moment is the most important segment of a larger space, into which we can be drawn. Reframing the shot by panning, tilting, or tracking the camera to accommodate figure movement has the same reassuring effect: the movie will show us what we need to see.

Another convention of camera placement and editing provides a particularly clear example of how the presentation of space has to conform to a conventional system in order that the audience can overlook it and concentrate on something else. In filming a scene between two characters, we can draw an imaginary line that connects them. So long as the camera stays on one side of this **center line** or **line of action**, the characters will stay in the same relation to each other in the screen space. In our example on pp. 206–7, so long as the camera stays below the line, in any image it takes the woman will appear on the left of the frame and the man on the right. If they are kept in these relative positions by the camera's placement, the movie can cut between any two images taken from below the line without disturbing the audience. It can, for example, cut to a close-up of either character without making the audience wonder where the other character is. If, however, the camera were to cross the line so that the woman appeared on the left of the screen, facing in the other direction, the audience would lose their secure sense of spatial position, and this might distract them from following the conversation. The center-line or **180-degree rule** maintains audience comprehension of figures' relative situations in represented space by granting the spectator a relatively stable point of view on the action. It applies with equal force but greater complexity in scenes involving three or more characters, but as with many of Hollywood's conventions, we only really notice the operation of this "rule" when it is broken.[24]

Audience comprehension is further aided by a convention governing the direction of the characters' gaze, known as **eyeline matching**. When a character looks offscreen in one shot, we expect the next shot to show us what the character is looking at. Following characters' eyelines thus allows us to connect the spaces in separate shots together across a cut. Manuals of continuity editing observe that "the most natural cut is the cut on the look," because "the eyes are the most powerful direction pointer that a human being has to attract or to direct interest":[25]

> In the same way that the focal length of the lens and the angle of the camera can place the viewer in a definite relationship with the subjects on the screen, the eyeline of a subject clearly determines spatial relations in the scene space. Viewers are particularly sensitive to incongruities in the sight lines between subjects who are looking at each other and in most situations can easily detect when the eye match is slightly off.[26]

Eyeline matching provides a means of cueing the cuts between a succession of shots, which we understand as the "looks" of characters in the fiction. Since what we see in each shot adds to our construction of the character whose gaze we share, this convention provides us with subjective information about the character, without robbing us of our sense of physical placement. The matching of imaginary lines between gazes helps to guide us between quite disparate spaces and to generate a sense of the story's action taking place in a three-dimensional, continuous dramatic space. The **blocking** or physical placement of characters in a scene can be constantly reframed around shifting ideal viewpoints without disturbing the audience's sense of spatial continuity.

These conventions, recognized but not consciously attended to by audiences, steer us through Hollywood's representation of space in the majority of its scenes. We describe these conventions as benevolent, because they make our perception of the movie's images more comfortable – more safe – and therefore allow us to concentrate on what is being presented. Nevertheless, the conventions can be breached for practical reasons or expressive effect. They have also changed over time, as a result of technological change affecting the possibilities of spatial expression. The more widespread use of telephoto and zoom lenses from the mid-1960s, for example, revised many conventions of spatial presentation. The more abrupt editing strategies of contemporary Hollywood still require a set of spatial conventions to maintain the audience's attention on what is being represented in the screen space, rather than on the manner of its representation.

The Three "Looks" of Cinema

"Participant observation" serves as a shorthand for a continuous tacking between the "inside" and "outside" of events: on the one hand grasping the sense of specific occurrences and gestures empathetically, on the other stepping back to situate these meanings in wider contexts. . . . Understood literally, participant observation is a paradoxical, misleading formula, but it may be taken seriously if reformulated in hermeneutic terms as a dialectic of experience and interpretation.

James Clifford[27]

In 1930, one of the authors of the Production Code, Father Daniel Lord, argued that the industry had special responsibilities toward its audience because "people go to the theatres; sit there passively – ACCEPT and RECEIVE; with the result that they go out from that entertainment either very much improved or very much deteriorated; and that depends almost entirely upon the character of the entertainment which is presented."[28] Ideas of the spectator's passivity have persisted into contemporary criticism: an influential strain of psychoanalytic criticism (which we consider in more detail in chapter 10) proposes "the spectator" as an abstract and empty figure "constituted" by the movie-as-text. Both these positions effectively construct the spectator as a victim or an "effect" of the movie, with the spectator's reflexive response simply mirroring the strategies of the text. But casual observation of audiences suggests that viewers retain a considerable range of options in engaging with a Hollywood movie; how often have you listened to the conversation of fellow audience members on leaving the cinema and felt that you had been watching a different movie from the one they were discussing? By looking more closely at our taken-for-granted notion of simply "watching a movie," we can begin to uncover an account of cinema spectatorship that implies a much more active collaboration with the cinema, one much closer to James Clifford's description of participant observation as the "dialectic of experience and interpretation" provided by the "continuous tacking between the 'inside' and 'outside' of events." This model of viewer engagement allows us to describe a more subtle and complex series of interactions between audiences and the movies they watch than one permitted by theories of the passive spectator.

In a more precise sense than we usually employ, it is never true to suggest that we simply look at cinema. Our attention to the image only intermittently stops, as Faure's did, at the surface of the screen. Rather, we alternately invest the image with depth and volume to make sense of figure movement, the continuity of action, and the acoustic "perspectives" cued by the soundtrack, and recognize the screen as a flat plane which allows graphic relations between elements to be readable. The curious status of cinematic space as neither strictly two-dimensional nor three-dimensional ensures that our attention to the screen is rather given as a play of looks *at*, *into*, and *through* the screen space; it fluctuates in its intensity, direction, and point of resolution, in much the same way as a reader's attention fluctuates between paragraphs in the course of reading a book. In cinema our viewing position is characteristically mobile, and Hollywood uses this mobility to hold the viewer's attention. The camera's shifting gaze lets us examine different perspectives within the frame, allowing us not only to explore space, but also to understand its meanings through identifications of and with characters. In this way, Hollywood encourages in us the sense that we can enter space and participate along with characters in the action played out within it.

Three different kinds of looking are in play in this mobile viewing: the audience's look at the screen; the camera's look at characters or action; and the characters' looks at each other.[29] The audience's look is the least frequently used by the movie itself, although voice-over narrations sometimes draw attention to our act of looking: "the picture you are about to see . . ." In addition, the audience's look at the screen can resist the camera's suggestions or the subjective looks of the characters, and can explore the screen according to its own interests, particularly if the scene is composed in deep-focus. But for most of the time our attention is directed insistently toward the action within the playing space; the camera's look is motivated as covering the action, allowing us to lose a sense of looking at the screen and participate imaginatively in the action. The environments the characters occupy seem appropriate and meaningful to the actions going on in them, and their contribution to the significance and legibility of the scene is almost unnoticed. The legibility of meaning with which we are rewarded for the surrender of our look to the camera generates some of the screen's transparency.

Some analysts have argued that Hollywood's use of the camera is governed by the justification of the camera's look, and therefore the audience's look, as apparently originating within the playing space. This argument derives from an analysis of one of Hollywood's most frequent formal figures, the **shot/reverse shot**, in which two consecutive shots depict complementary spaces. The most common instance of this figure occurs in dialogue scenes presented in over-the-shoulder close medium shots, where the looks of the characters at each other and the graphic similarity between the shots help the viewer infer that the spaces in the two shots are contiguous. French critic Daniel Dayan has argued that this figure is crucial to Hollywood's rhetoric of "realism" in that it constantly offers an explanation for the source of each shot as emanating from the shot that preceded it. Dayan suggests that editing constantly fragments the audience's look, abruptly shifting us from place to place, and thus "regularly and systematically raises the question . . . 'who is watching this?'"[30] Dayan's answer is that in the shot/reverse shot figure, the question of whose look is shown in the first shot is answered by the second, reverse shot, and its look is, in turn, explained by cutting back to the first shot. Dayan describes this operation as a process of **suturing**, by which the viewer perceives gaps in the space represented, only to have these gaps filled. The succession of views represented by the image stream is explained as having its own source. Camera looks are apparently motivated internally by the movie itself rather than externally by some agency of production, and Dayan argues that through this suture Hollywood cinema masks both its formal and ideological operations: "the code effectively disappears and the ideological effect of the film is thereby secured. . . . Unable to see the workings of the code, the spectator is at its mercy."[31]

Such an interpretation goes some way to explain how the audience can situate its own look as originating within the fiction, but it both overemphasizes the centrality and oversimplifies the operation of the shot/reverse shot figure in Hollywood's practice. Not every shot in Hollywood cinema can be understood as the subjective look of a character, and viewing a Hollywood movie involves a play between the three looks of character, camera, and audience.[32] They may function together, as Dayan suggests, with audience and camera looks disguised as character looks, but they can also be driven apart to emphasize the camera's mediating function, the subjective looks of characters at each other, or the audience's role as spectator. In long takes, such as the opening shot of *Touch of Evil* (1958) (discussed in more detail in the next chapter), the audience becomes uncomfortably aware of the duration of the shot and the movie's refusal to cut.

Meaning in Hollywood movies is often a matter of where events are viewed from, and how we are positioned to interpret them. Much film theory has maintained that the key function of point of view is to produce **identifications**, arguing that our primary identification with the camera (we have to look where the camera looks; the camera is the eye/I) is displaced in Classical Hollywood cinema, so that the look of the spectator is passed through the camera onto character, encouraging us to make a range of secondary identifications within the fiction.[33] The equation of looks is understood as an equation of knowledge and experience: we feel as though we are experiencing the events of the story at first hand, because we are shown them from the same point of view as a character. The very notion of point of view seems to imply a kind of sharing of position, a mutuality of vision. But at this point discussion of point of view is often confused by the way that the camera produces *literal* viewpoints, and if we are to avoid equating the camera's literal perspective with the fictional perspectives of either a movie's narration or its characters, and collapsing narration into camerawork, it is important to make a clear distinction between what we mean by viewpoint and point of view. The **viewpoint** of a shot is a matter of its position in space: its angle, level, height, and distance from its subject. **Point of view**, on the other hand, is a position of knowledge in relation to the fiction, a matter of its relative subjectivity or omniscience. Characters in a scene therefore have both viewpoints and points of view. They occupy literal positions in the playing space and direct their glances toward objects or characters within it, and they also possess degrees of knowledge, attitudes, prejudices relevant to their situations in the fiction. Shots from particular viewpoints may encourage the construction of a character's point of view, but differences between the optics of lenses and the human eye mean that it cannot literally show their viewpoints, even by taking up their exact position in the represented space.[34] Character vision and character knowledge can never be made entirely identical.

Hollywood cinema prefers to keep camera viewpoint and character viewpoint separate, principally to preserve its own narrational role. Camera viewpoint typically sides with a character in the playing space in order to signal a sharing of our fictive point of view with that of the character, but it seldom literally takes the place of that character. In a dialogue scene between two people, if the camera were to usurp the literal position of each character, both characters would address the viewer head-on. Such an arrangement restricts the viewer's ability to identify or empathize with either character. The shots quite forcibly remind us of the limitations of either viewpoint. Instead, the continuity system's over-the-shoulder shot/ reverse shot figure provides us with a more intricate sense of character subjectivity. By adopting viewpoints adjacent to those of the characters, we can witness their subjectivities, as they express their points of view through speech, reaction, or gesture, and we can move among these subjectivities to establish our own, more omniscient point of view. As

David Bordwell has suggested, the omnipresence of the camera's look suggests the omniscience of the narration.[35] For example, there is a scene about twenty minutes after the start of *Stagecoach* (1939) in which the passengers halt at Dry Fork for a meal (see p. 214). The scene explores the social divisions among the passengers, and in particular between the cavalry officer's wife, Mrs Mallory (Louise Platt) and the prostitute Dallas (Claire Trevor), who has been run out of the town of Tonto by the Ladies' Law and Order League. Mrs Mallory sits at the head of the table, and the gauche outlaw Ringo (John Wayne) invites Dallas to sit next to her. The crucial act in the scene is an exchange of looks between the two women. In a shot from down the table we see Mrs Mallory looking at Dallas, and then cut to a viewpoint adjacent to hers, showing Dallas, who recognizes her social inferiority and looks down, not meeting Mrs Mallory's gaze. We understand the significance of this moment (Dallas concurs in Mrs Mallory's judgment of her), but in approximating Mrs Mallory's viewpoint (necessary in order to see the gaze not met), we do not concur in her point of view. And as the story unfolds, Dallas' actions confirm our hypothesis that she is worthy of more respect than Mrs Mallory's superficial dismissal suggests.[36]

Although Classical Hollywood occasionally restricted the audience's viewpoint, it seldom sustained this position for long, and usually did it in order to produce a specific effect by withholding information from the audience. Hollywood's most sustained attempt to restrict the audience's viewpoint to that of a character was *The Lady in the Lake* (1946), an adaptation of a detective novel by Raymond Chandler. The movie attempted to imitate the novel's first-person narration by having the camera occupy the viewpoint of its detective hero Philip Marlowe. For most of the movie Robert Montgomery, the actor playing Marlowe, only appeared when Marlowe stood in front of a mirror, and the movie aimed to offer its audience the pleasure of investigating the series of crimes at first hand. Neither audiences or critics deemed it a satisfying experiment, primarily because it so heavily restricted the expressive use of space offered by editing. As David Bordwell argues, cinematic attempts to fabricate the first-person narration possible in the novel are doomed to failure so long as they seek to identify camera viewpoint with either literal viewpoint or fictive point of view, and Hollywood's predominant common practice is to use "the omnipresence of classical narration to move fluidly from one character to another."[37]

These experiments and variations from the norm point to the extent to which the continuity system's construction of screen space creates hierarchies of knowledge among characters, and between characters and the audience. These hierarchies resemble that "hierarchy of discourses" which some literary critics have suggested is one of the defining features of the "classic realist novel." In written forms, that hierarchy can be identified by the presence of inverted commas marking what each character says. These character discourses are, however, framed within the commentary of "a

1

6

2

7

3

4

Viewpoint and point of view in *Stagecoach* (1939)

Shot 1 establishes the scene, and puts Mrs Mallory (Louise Platt) at its visual center, so that the camera's views will pivot around her viewpoint. Shot 2 is taken from a position close to where she is sitting, and shots 3 and 5 show her looking with disapproval at Dallas (Claire Trevor). But though we share her viewpoint in shots 4 and 6, we do not share her point of view about Dallas, and as the story unfolds, our judgment about Dallas' worth is proved correct.

5

privileged, historic narration which is the source of coherence of the story as a whole."[38] Comparisons between literary and cinematic narratives are highly problematic, and perhaps nowhere more so than when considering the thorny question of realism, but both do organize their viewer's or reader's position through a hierarchy of knowledge of character. In their analysis of Hollywood movies in 1946, Martha Wolfenstein and Nathan Leites stressed the frequency with which plots turned on false appearances, and drew attention to the importance of "the character who sees things mistakenly," a character they identified as "the comic onlooker," "who habitually sees illicit implications in the innocent behavior of hero and heroine." In crime movies a comparable role may fall to the police, falsely accusing the hero of a crime. In either case, the role of mistaken interpreter is crucially important to the audience's activity in the theater, since his or her misinterpretation "conjures up a pleasurable aura of illicit possibilities around harmless acts." This character is engaged in the same activity as the audience: interpreting the action, and forming hypotheses about what it means and what will happen next. The misinterpretation provides a guarantee of the reliability of our interpretation:

> The comic onlooker makes us feel effortlessly omniscient. We in the audience know the true state of affairs; we know that what we see is all there is. ... The comic onlooker mistakenly believes that what he sees is only a fragment of a larger whole, the rest of which he attempts to reconstruct. We are able to laugh at his superfluous mental exertions. Without making any such effort we know everything since the film obligingly shows us everything there is. ... The significant events which he imagines are happening just out of sight exist only in his imagination.[39]

The subjectivity of a character is almost always nested within a more omniscient view, and within the continuity system a subjective viewpoint is established not by one shot, but by at least two and usually three. Shot 1 shows a character looking; shot 2 reveals what the character is looking at from a position close to but not identical with his or her viewpoint; shot 3, which usually reiterates shot 1, confirms that shot 2 was subjective but that we are now back with the omniscient view of the narration. Even in its most diagrammatic instances, such as its use by Alfred Hitchcock, shot 2 rarely originates exactly from the place described by shot 1, in case another character should return the gaze and look directly into the camera.[40] Instead, it originates from a position close enough to the viewpoint of shot 1 to signal its fictive status as standing in for that viewpoint. Such shots are often called "point of view shots," but that term elides the distinction between literal and fictional views that we have been making. A shot intended to represent a character's viewpoint must be marked by some convention. At the beginning of *Dirty Harry* (1971), for instance, a black mask in the shape of a target sight is superimposed over the image of a woman swimming in a rooftop pool, to represent the view of an assassin through the sight of his rifle, although the camera is placed at a

The target-shaped mask in this image from *Dirty Harry* (1971) stands in for the viewpoint of the assassin.

considerable distance from him. In such a case, the "point of view" shot is simply motivating a closer look in order to reveal a detail less obtrusively than an unmotivated camera movement might do.

If viewers are to interpret character subjectivity, they also need paired shots of what the character sees and the character's reaction to it. This structure is particularly important when it is used to reveal the look of one character at another. This is one of Hollywood's most consistent ways of establishing characters' desires, with the eroticized look of male characters at female characters (and, less frequently, vice versa) being the most recognizable example.

In an early scene in *All That Heaven Allows*, Cary (Jane Wyman) must decide whether or not she can put social etiquette aside and pay a visit with Ron (Rock Hudson) to his tree nursery. The majority of the scene is played out in unemphatic medium shots, but as soon as Wyman makes the decision to go, the camera cuts discreetly to a new view of Hudson. Instead of seeing him from the comfortable perspective of the third person observer interested in but detached from events, we suddenly glimpse Hudson from a new position that we recognize as Wyman's point of view: a low-angle shot, into which he looms slightly menacingly. We understand from this that she sees him as something exciting but also threatening. This shot offers us information about a new plot development, disrupting the space established by the previous two or three shots. We may have some difficulty in articulating this change, since its effect is almost more physical than intellectual, inducing a mild sense of disruption and loss of place. Yet that is the level at which spatial presentation operates in Hollywood; the mild sense of displacement produced by the change of view is itself displaced into an act of interpretation at the level of character, action, or story.

With all these mechanisms in place and understood, Hollywood is thus able in any movie to guide us through an extensive and apparently continuous spatial network, giving us a sense of actually occupying the movie alongside the characters. The resulting experience, of fluctuating between spectatorship and apparent participation, and between the points of view of different characters, is a marker of our engagement with Hollywood. It is a far less passive condition than the common-sense impression of moviegoing has implied. We can, for instance, detect some of the power relations being structured through a movie by looking at the distribution of viewpoints among the characters, and the balance between what is attributed to characters and what is retained by the movie's omniscient narration.

Spatial presentation is rarely stressed in Hollywood, making it difficult for us to appreciate its significance, but in the communication between a visual entertainment medium and its audiences its role is a crucial one. If we need further evidence, we have only to look at its centrality in the marketing of virtual reality technology, for despite its relatively crude representation, the spatial component of virtual reality confirms that the entertainment industries are now appealing directly to their audiences' interest in interacting spatially, precisely in order to generate their own narrative action.[41] What this undoubtedly suggests is that a richer understanding of a Hollywood movie can be obtained by examining its visual discourse than by presuming that its meaning is located solely in plot and dialogue.

Safe and Unsafe Space: *Ordinary People*

> The workings of patriarchy, and the mould of feminine unconscious it produces, have left women largely without a voice, gagged and deprived of outlets (of a kind supplied, for instance, either by male art or popular culture) in spite of the crucial social and ideological functions women are called on to perform. In the absence of any coherent culture of oppression, a simple fact of recognition has aesthetic and political importance. There is a dizzy satisfaction in witnessing the way that sexual difference under patriarchy is fraught, explosive, and erupts dramatically into violence within its own private stamping ground, the family. . . . Hollywood films made with a female audience in mind tell a story of contradiction, not of reconciliation.
>
> Laura Mulvey[42]

Much of what we have suggested about the way that Hollywood cinema creates a safe and stable space for the audience to experience the movie would apply equally well to any period of Hollywood's history. All the fundamental principles of the continuity system were established by 1920, and while Bordwell, Staiger, and Thompson's monumental account of *The Classical Hollywood Cinema* concludes its account of film style in 1960, its authors argue quite firmly that "most American commercial cinema has continued the classical tradition . . . the classical premises of time and space remain powerfully in force."[43] Like technological developments, changes in Hollywood's techniques of spatial representation can be considered as merely the exchange of "functional equivalents" or "minor instrumental changes" within a stylistic system in which the "enduring principles" remain constant.[44] Nevertheless, Hollywood space has a history. Part of that history has been discussed in our consideration of technology in chapter 4: in, for instance, the problems involved in constructing stories to fit the space of Cinerama. If selling movies to television brought the idea of the "safe action area" into being, it also implied that the represented space outside that area was redundant. Beyond television's frame within the Panavision frame was a new waste space, industrially disabled from making as complete a contribution to Hollywood's expressive space as the space within the smaller frame. The expressive qualities of Hollywood's space were diminished by the more restricted graphic potential of the new waste space.[45]

A critical history of Hollywood space might also correlate changes in spatial representation with shifts in subject matter, star images, or economic conditions, or with periods of thematic experimentation or ideological uncertainty. The "restless and unstable" space of film noir, for instance, with its unconventional lighting plots and composition, provides an appropriately unsettling environment for those movies' interrogation of some of Hollywood's more benign conventions: "no character can speak authoritatively from a space that is being continually cut into ribbons of light."[46] If we were to be arbitrary, however, it would be possible to argue, in support of the date at which *The Classical Hollywood Cinema* ends, that in or about June 1960, Hollywood space changed. Thirty-five minutes into the projection of *Psycho*, its central character, Marion Crane (played by the movie's most prominent star, Janet Leigh), is savagely, meaninglessly murdered by an unidentifiable figure with a butcher knife. Horror has escaped from its Gothic castle; *Psycho* brings it home to small-town California, to the intimate spaces of the family and the bathroom. *Psycho*'s shower scene destroys Hollywood's conventions of safe space with unique brutality and abruptness. The image itself is dismembered: the murder scene lasts under a minute, but contains 78 separate shots.[47] The soundtrack's shrieking violins stab repeatedly at the viewer's eardrums. Until it happens, the audience has been so engrossed in Marion's story and so secure in her potential salvation that, as Robin Wood puts it, "we can scarcely believe it is happening; when it is over, and she is dead, we are left shocked, with nothing to cling to, the apparent centre of the film entirely dissolved."[48] Our sense of the screen as a safe space to look at is destroyed with Marion's life on the first occasion we watch *Psycho*. From then on, not just in this movie but in every movie, we look on the screen more warily, in the knowledge that our comforting ability to predict what will happen in a space or a story can be arbitrarily violated.

It is, of course, an exaggeration to date the creation of **unsafe space** in Hollywood so precisely around the release of *Psycho*, but the movie did carry the destabilization of space practiced by film noir and by 1950s thrillers to new heights of malevolence, an impression that was widely recorded by critics at the time. One described the atmosphere surrounding its screening as "deeply charged with apprehension." The audience was constantly aware that something awful was about to happen, "indeed, it had the solidarity of a convention assembled on the common understanding of some unspoken *entente terrible*."[49] Against the benign character of Hollywood's safe space, in which the devices of invisible editing, eyeline matches, and shot/reverse shot patterns secure the viewer's mapping of a movie's spatial and narrative topography, the unsafe space of post-*Psycho* "nightmare movies"[50] is actively malign, victimizing its audience. *Psycho*'s director, Alfred Hitchcock, enthusiastically explained his apparently personal delight in manipulating the audience: when asked by critic Penelope Houston what "the deepest logic of your films" was, Hitchcock replied "to put the audience through it." *Psycho*, he said, was like taking the audience "through the haunted house at the fairground or the roller-coaster." In another interview in which he justified his policy of insisting on audiences not being allowed into screenings of *Psycho* after the start of each performance, he declared that the game he played with the public was "trying to outwit them."[51] Even more tellingly, perhaps, he told screenwriter Ernest Lehman that he thought of the audience as being "like a giant organ that you and I are playing. At one moment we play *this* note on them and get *this* reaction, and then we play *that* chord and they react *that* way."[52]

In this context, however, we are less concerned with exploring the psychology of the auteur or with a psychoanalytic interpretation of the movie-as-text than with the relationships that the new, unsafe space posited between the audience and the screen. Where a shot/reverse shot figure in safe space secures a character's viewpoint, in unsafe space the same device tells us that the character cannot see what she is looking for, and that we cannot, either. The climax of *Cop* (1988), for example, takes place in a school gymnasium, where Lloyd Hopkins (James Woods) is hunting serial killer Bobby Franco (Steven Lambert). For several minutes the sequence is constructed of alternate shots of Hopkins moving around the gym, looking and listening, and views of what he sees: the empty gym, with Franco nowhere in sight but always liable to intrude into the space of each shot. Typically, unsafe space empowers malign characters, capable of moving through screen space in a manner incomprehensible or invisible to the audience, and threatening both sympathetic characters and viewers with their sudden, unpredictable appearance. The "stalker" or "slasher" movies of the 1970s analyzed by Vera Dika (discussed in chapter 3) make extensive use of this device: a spatial convention of the genre is that the frame can be violently penetrated by a murderous implement, at any moment and from any angle. The movies' sadistic game is to catch their audience unawares, to stab screen space when they least expect it. In these scenarios, the audience is associated with the fictional victims, even when the camera's viewpoint is that of the monster as it attacks. Restricting the camera's viewpoint in this way, as many movies have done in imitation of *Jaws* (1975) and *Halloween* (1978), refuses the audience a sight of the monster itself and forces them to imagine the appearance of the threat.

Unsafe space disorients the viewer, emphasizing the power of a movie's image track to control the viewer's look. As well as depriving the viewer of the power of sight by not showing things, it can also make the audience look at whatever is presented to them. Movies may assault their audiences physically, stabbing them in the eye with flashes of light, rapid, disjointed cutting, or sudden movement.[53] Many 1980s horror movies delighted in the special effects technology of rubber prosthetics controlled by servo-motors to produce ever more excessive distortions of the human body, ever more liable to violate their audience's sensibilities. In one sequence in *The Thing* (1982), an alien being capable of assuming the physical shape of any creature it takes over erupts into a grotesquely distorted amalgam of its victims that few viewers are unsqueamish enough to watch without flinching. The shape-changer demonstrates that even the space occupied by a recognizably human or animal body is no longer safe to look at. Movies such as *The Thing* offer their audiences an experience in the exaggeration of anxiety, threatening them with a malign organization of space and rendering the act of looking itself dangerous and liable to punishment. The logical conclusion of what we might call this cinema of the unwatchable spectacle occurs at the climax of *Raiders of the Lost Ark* (1981), when Indiana Jones (Harrison Ford) tells Marion Ravenswood (Karen Allen) that the only way to survive the scene in which the ark is opened is not to look.

Audiences, however, have devised alternative defensive strategies for coping with their victimization in unsafe space, most prominent among them the anticipatory laughter Andrew Britton found so distasteful when watching *Hell Night* (1981).[54] Carol Clover argues that such screenings take the form of a game, substantially detached from the consumption of a movie's plot, in which the movie aims to catch the audience by surprise or "gross it out."[55] But the pleasure of viewing unsafe space is perverse in that it involves taking pleasure in associating with the victim, and audience behavior suggests that the most conventional form of this pleasure involves converting the masochistic pleasure of identifying with the victim into the sadistic pleasures of anticipating and enjoying the victim's experience. Conventionally, our culture genders sadism as a masculine pleasure, and when unsafe space is concentrated into generic form in the horror movie, empirical evidence confirms that its majority audience appeal is to young males.[56] As Tania Modleski remarks of *Psycho*, in the plots of slasher movies, "men's fears become women's fate."[57] But Carol Clover has argued persuasively that "sadistic voyeurism" is far too simple a notion to adequately describe the complex processes of identification going on be-tween the female victim and the male viewer of contemporary horror, pointing out that male audiences "cheer the killer on as he assaults his victims, then reverse their sympathies to cheer the survivor on as she assaults the killer," who is usually "a male in gender distress."[58] The male audience in these movies, she argues, identifies with the heroic self-rescuer whose body is female. The primary aim of horror cinema, the principal location of unsafe space, is in Clover's view, "to play to masochistic fears and desires in its audiences – fears and desires that are repeatedly figured as 'feminine.' It may play on other fears and desires, too, but dealing out pain is its defining characteristic; sadism, by definition, plays at best a supporting role."[59]

Whatever interpretation is placed on the way that male audiences iden-tify with female protagonists, it is also important to register that these overtly masochistic identifications take place more intensely in unsafe space than they do in the safe space of Classical Hollywood. It seems hardly coincidental that the diffusion of unsafe space into Hollywood movies occurred at a time when the industry was reorienting its strategies of appeal toward its audience, abandoning its earlier attachment to an audience it had always assumed was feminine, and developing the mar-keting strategies discussed in the introduction as the "Peter Pan Syn-drome."[60] Even such exactly formal devices as the destabilized shot/reverse shot structure can be related to the economic core of Hollywood's commercial aesthetic.

If Classical Hollywood projected a safe space for its audience's fantasies, we might very well argue that unsafe space is post-Classical. Certainly it has become a common feature of Hollywood movies since 1960. The stylis-tic experimentations of the Hollywood renaissance at the end of the 1960s were a response to the industry's loss of a clear sense of its audience as well as to the ideological uncertainties of the period. Some of the most promi-nent movies of that period presented a destabilization of Hollywood space, through the use of a wider range of lenses and a more discontinuous editing style. But if the early 1970s saw many of the certainties of Classical Hollywood re-examined, a good number of them were re-established in the latter part of the decade, and it seems more appropriate to describe a movie such as *Ordinary People* (1980) as a piece of late Classical Hollywood filmmaking rather than the product of a post-Classical sensibility. The movie's attachment to conventions of the horror genre, however, gave it an ideological inheritance from the 1970s as well as a stylistic one. Using *Ordinary People* as an occasion to examine Hollywood's changing historical representations of space affords us unexpectedly privileged access to the politics not only of this movie, but of the genres to which it alludes.

Ordinary People was felt to be a pivotal movie at the time of its release, and attracted considerable critical analysis. Marking the directorial debut of Robert Redford, the movie was a focus of attention even before it was produced. Industry commentary constructed it as a cultural signpost marking Hollywood's renewed commitment to a more socially conscious mode for the new decade, an opinion confirmed by its four Academy Awards. In a wealthy Chicago suburb, Calvin Jarrett (Donald Sutherland), his wife Beth (Mary Tyler Moore), and younger son Conrad (Timothy Hutton) attempt to come to terms with the accidental death by drowning of elder son Buck (Scott Doebler). Conrad, recently released from hospital after a suicide attempt, reluctantly agrees to counseling with psychiatrist Dr Berger (Judd Hirsch). Intent on not being reminded of what has happened, Beth refuses to show Conrad the love she had bestowed on his brother. Calvin attempts contact with both Beth and Conrad, but his efforts prove ineffectual. Meanwhile, Conrad forms a friendship with Jeanine (Elizabeth McGovern), but their first date is ruined by a group of boisterous schoolfellows. Disappointed by his friends and elders, and in turn disappointing to them, Conrad becomes increasingly lonely and introspective, until the taunts of a schoolfriend goad him into a furious physical assault. Immediately after this he learns that his friend Karen (Dinah Manoff), a former patient from the hospital, has killed herself. In desperation he turns to Dr Berger, and in a moment of catharsis purges himself of his feelings of guilt at his brother's death. He achieves a new point of stability, and is reunited with Jeanine, but as Conrad finds himself, his parents experience further crisis. Beth is unable to surrender to her own confused emotions, and insists on her right not to be disturbed by any sense of her own implication in the family's tragedy. Calvin is unable to hold the family together. As the movie ends, Beth leaves while father and son try to find some comfort together.

Ordinary People was one of several movies in the early 1980s that returned the attention of American audiences to their immediate domestic surroundings and to the fate of the middle-class family after the cultural upheavals of the previous decade. Its thematic focus on the affluent but troubled was a marked change from Hollywood's representation of more working-class milieus in the 1970s, and its tightly constructed plot also signaled a shift away from the more expansive structures of that decade's road and odyssey pictures. With their evident concerns with the home, family, and community, domestic melodramas became as prominent a feature of the Hollywood landscape in the first half of the 1980s as they had been in the 1950s. They were also endorsed by the industry via the Academy Awards: *Kramer vs Kramer* (1979) won five Oscars, *On Golden Pond* (1981) received three, *Tender Mercies* (1982) two, and *Terms of Endearment* (1983) five. Against the more militaristic strain of much of the most commercially successful product of the period (*An Officer and a Gentleman*, 1982; *Rambo*, 1985), these movies represented Hollywood's appeal to both an older audience and an established tradition of social commentary. In interviews, Robert Redford described *Ordinary People* as a polemic on behalf of understanding and as having the serious, necessary and difficult purpose of articulating the trauma of middle Americans after almost 20 years of neglect by movies and political culture alike:

The middle-class is tremendously neglected . . . in order for something to be dramatic, it has to be about the very, very poor or the very, very rich, as Scott Fitzgerald said. I have always been more interested in that part of America that really makes it go . . . The idea that there is something wrong with the middle-class has never hit the middle-class fully, so that the neuroses that exist are something that have never been attended to. It's now starting.[61]

A much less sympathetic version of that argument has been offered by historians Michael Ryan and Douglas Kellner, who argue that although these new melodramas indicated an audience need for representations of emotional and familial security in a time of economic and social instability, they were also a symptom of "the increasing self-concern of an ascendant white upper middle class that no longer wants to be bothered with questions of poverty or inequality."[62]

Critical responses to the movie were also less inclined to endorse its therapeutic function. By 1980, critical orthodoxy had come to understand that giving the heroine of *All That Heaven Allows* a voice had worked against the dominant social discourses about patriarchy in 1955. But a contemporary movie that deprived the central female protagonist of a voice offended critical understandings of how patriarchy should be represented. Andrew Britton saw the movie as belonging to a cycle of family melodramas centered on father–son relationships, whose "Reaganite" function was to refurbish ideas about patriarchy in light of feminist critiques. Describing the movie as being, "like the vast majority of contemporary Hollywood films . . . an unabashed apology for patriarchy," Britton jointly summarized the plot of *Kramer vs Kramer* and *Ordinary People*:

> the patriarchal family is threatened with dissolution by the mother's dereliction of duty . . . the films move towards the formation of an all-male family from which she is expelled. . . . the woman, the value of whose independence has already been undermined, is denied as well even her traditional sphere of competence, and is left, as the endings of both films make very clear, with absolutely nowhere to go.[63]

Britton's interpretation was echoed by Robin Wood, who saw the movie as a paradigm for Hollywood's understanding of gender relations in the 1980s, so that *Body Heat* (1981) became "merely the *Ordinary People* of film noir," and *Return of the Jedi* (1983) "the *Ordinary People* of outer space, with Darth Vader as Donald Sutherland and Obi One and Yoda in tandem as the psychiatrist":

> If the woman can't accept her subordination, she must be expelled from the narrative altogether, like Mary Tyler Moore in *Ordinary People* . . . leaving the father to develop his relationship with his beautiful offspring untrammeled by female complications. *Ordinary People* makes particularly clear the brutality to the woman of the Oedipal trajectory our culture continues to construct: from the moment in the narrative when our young hero takes the decisive

step of identification with the father/acquisition of his own woman, the mother becomes superfluous to Oedipal/patriarchal concerns, a mere burdensome redundancy.[64]

These ideological interpretations of the movie concerned themselves exclusively with plot and character, viewing its expressive use of space as sufficiently transparent to require no comment. But what is in some respects most striking about *Ordinary People* is its determined break with the stylistic impulses of much Hollywood cinema of the 1970s, and its insistent reconstruction of a Classical style that ensures the audience a secure sense of placement in the fiction, no matter how dislocated its characters may become. In *Ordinary People* doubt, anxiety, and ambiguity are the prerogative of Conrad and Calvin, and these experiences are shared by the audience insofar as they come to identify with these characters. But in contrast to their dislocation and panic, the movie's mise-en-scène remains calm and utilitarian, offering its viewers a firmly focused overview of plot events and their meanings.[65] Dialogue scenes are presented in graphically matched shots taken from complementary set-ups, with the editing balanced according to Bazin's "material or dramatic logic of the scene." The movie adheres firmly to conventions of eyeline matching, the 180-degree rule, and the connective possibilities of diegetic and non-diegetic sound, in a mise-en-scène that firmly asserts the benevolence of a Hollywood space given over to elaborating character psychology.

These emphases are manifest from the opening sequence, a textbook instance of Hollywood's preferred construction of screen space. A series of shots of progressively shorter scale locates the environment in which the plot will unfold, and leads us to the movie's central character. An empty image of blue sky gives way to a string of picturesquely composed images of a peaceful and affluent Chicago suburb, gradually taking us closer to the source of the soundtrack's choral music, a school choir in rehearsal. The camera's panning movements across the choir are resolved on a pale-faced youth whom we identify as likely to be the movie's protagonist – at which point a sudden cut to the same youth jarred awake from a nightmare confirms his status. This cut is an example of the way in which a device used with increasing arbitrariness in movies of the 1970s, the **"impact" edit**, is given a contained narrational function. The impact edit in *Ordinary People* still produces the violent disruption of spatial continuity that it did in *Easy Rider* (1969), but that disruption is now attributed to the character as an indicator of Conrad's sudden shifts in mood and stability. It thus comes to signify subjectivity rather than the disjunction of Classical narration or the director's sense of style. Even this degree of disruption is reduced as the plot progresses. As Conrad regains his stability, the flashbacks to his brother's drowning become less and less disruptive of continuity. Scenes of the boating accident become memories, not dreams that come upon him unawares, and rather than being disjointed individual shots they gain a continuity of their own. By the same means they cease to

Conrad Jarrett (Timothy Hutton) and Dr Berger (Judd Hirsch) in *Ordinary People* (1980). Paramount (courtesy Kobal)

unsettle the audience, and instead provide us with a means of understanding Conrad. The disjunctive effect of cuts between scenes also diminishes as the movie progresses, because the graphic matching of the two shots is progressively more balanced, and because many of the early scenes emphasize the abruptness of the cut by beginning with a percussive sound effect, while later scenes often carry the sound of one scene across the cut to smooth the transition between spaces.

Ordinary People's mise-en-scène echoes this gradual shift, drawing out the expressive possibilities of represented space in an understated way, so that the meaning produced by spatial representation is displaced onto character and event. Spaces become contexts for different stages of the plot and acquire connotations. As the movie unwinds and characters start to move across the initially empty spaces of the opening sequence, we come to recognize that those peaceful and ordered two-dimensional framings mask a more turbulent three-dimensional scene, in which action and event extend beyond the frame's attempts to lend them a balanced composition. The movie sacrifices the clarity, symmetry, and harmony represented by the opening images for a series of more ambiguous and unbalanced but also more expressive framings that admit movement and history and provide the story with the possibility of resolution.

This change is indicated most clearly in the interview sequences between Conrad and Berger. As they establish a relationship and Conrad learns to lose "control" and absolve himself of guilt for his brother's death, the unemphatic lighting in Berger's office becomes darker and more expressive. The architectural mise-en-scène of the movie's early scenes in the Jarrett home gives way to a more expressive image stream that provides an arena for the movie's psychological climax. When Conrad makes the verbal slip that leads him to realize his problem is forgiving himself, he stands up and walks to the window of Berger's office, where he is bathed in alternating red and green light from a neon sign outside. Although the sign and the nighttime setting offer a realistic motivation for the darkness of the final interview, this use of excessive color constructs expressive space in a way that closely echoes the spatial practices of 1950s domestic melodrama.

Ordinary People also gradually constructs a hierarchy of points of view that establishes the viewer in a privileged position, sharing the insights of characters but often knowing more than those characters do: we follow Beth and Calvin on their golf holiday in Houston and know about their arguments before Conrad does; we know that Conrad has quit his swim team long before his parents do. In keeping with our privileged knowledge, the camera's look at the action is motivated by an engagement with the action, and transitions into subjective points of view are cued in advance. Perhaps most importantly for an understanding of the ideological issues raised by Britton and Wood, *Ordinary People* restricts its proliferation of points of view, and gradually underlines not so much those with which we should concur as those through which we should organize our interpretation of character and ideology. In this respect, the movie's politics are impeccably patriarchal: Jeanine never acquires enough status to be given a point of view, but more importantly, Beth is persistently denied the right to subjectivity throughout the movie. When Cary shatters a Wedgwood jug in *All That Heaven Allows*, she, Ron, and the audience all share the same recognition that the jug has become a symbol of her relationship with Ron. When Beth breaks a plate in *Ordinary People*, the significance of the action is clearly signaled to the audience, but we do not know if Beth shares our understanding of its meaning.

Only Calvin and Conrad can motivate the flashbacks that provide the audience with some access to their thought processes, just as only Calvin and Conrad experience the talking cure of psychoanalysis. Beth is given no chance to gain viewer sympathy via access to her memory. She has only one scene to herself, when she enters the room of her dead son and is surprised out of her reverie by Conrad's sudden appearance behind her. This scene explicitly invokes the conventions of the "stalker" movie, with Beth presented as victim and Conrad as monster.[66] Beth is alone, and images of her isolation are intercut with shots of Conrad entering the house and climbing the stairs. The scene of Beth's reverie is silent, presented as a series of cuts between close shots of her blank, haunted expression and panning shots from nearly her viewpoint of the trophies and photographs on the walls: the emotional significance of the scene is provided entirely by what significance the viewer can place on the cutting between the two shots. Conrad's appearance abruptly curtails Beth's reverie before we have learnt its significance, but our prior sight of Conrad's arrival – and our knowledge that despite invoking the spatial conventions of horror, Conrad is the movie's hero – ensures that we are startled more by the vehemence of Beth's reaction to his intrusion than by his interruption.

From almost the start of the movie, Beth is regularly isolated in space, constantly trying to escape every two-shot in which she is caught with Conrad. This becomes explicit in a scene in which Calvin takes a family photograph. He tries to frame his wife and son in the same image, but fails because his ineptitude with the camera prevents him getting the "really good picture of the two of you" that he wants. Calvin's failure only repeats what the movie has been persistently pursuing as a strategy. In an early scene over dinner, Calvin and Conrad talk to each other in the dining room across alternating close-ups taken close to the center line. The matched shots emphasize their alliance, while Beth is photographed from behind both of them, distanced from them and trapped in the kitchen, framed in a composition that graphically boxes her in through the doorway. Beth is frequently vulnerable to such graphic boxes: another occurs when Calvin returns from his meeting with Dr Berger and insists on questioning her about her behavior at Buck's funeral. The composition of the full shot over Calvin's shoulder cuts her off at the knees and traps her in the narrow space of the garage doorway, where she is forced against her will to listen to Calvin's account of the funeral. While she is trapped in this way, Calvin is privileged with a medium close shot matching his over-the-shoulder shot. In the scene around the family Christmas tree, Calvin ends up forcibly holding Beth so she cannot escape from the medium two-shot that represents another composed image of family harmony that Calvin wants to cling to. But when Calvin offers his analysis of her ("You are beautiful, and you are unpredictable, but you're so cautious. You're determined, Beth, but you know something, you're not strong, and I don't know if you're really giving"), she is framed immobile in the doorway, denied entry into his space. As the movie drives toward reconciliation and conclusion, Beth is excluded and our attention concentrated on Calvin and Conrad.

An analysis of mise-en-scène, point of view, and spatial representation in *Ordinary People* does not afford the movie an inherently different politics from those suggested by Britton and Wood, but it can explain how those politics operate in the movie, rather than simply asserting their presence. The political significance of the movie's formal organization may well lie in its attempt to restage the domestic melodrama of female oppression in a classical space. Against a straightforwardly didactic reading of the plot as patriarchal, an interpretation of *Ordinary People* that pays attention to its construction of domestic space registers Beth as the movie's persistent victim, deprived of the representational rights accorded to the rest of her family. That interpretation equates her with Cary in *All That Heaven Allows*, boxed in by the TV set her children give her for Christmas and by the lover reduced to the status of a child at the end of the movie. Like Cary, Beth seeks her own space, in which she may speak with her own voice. Like Cary, and like the central female protagonists in most films noirs, she is consistently denied that space, and hence offered no opportunity to speak, in a movie that places the greatest of value on the curative power of the act of speech.

Notes

1   David Bordwell and Kristin Thompson, *Film Art: An Introduction*, 3rd edn (New York: McGraw-Hill, 1990), p. 141.
2   The increasingly common experience of watching movies in familiar domestic sur-roundings, where the video or television is in competition with a range of other activities and interruptions, has certainly breached this relationship of rapt attention. We remain fully aware of our occupation of real space, and in some cases consciously use this awareness in self-protection against certain extreme forms of affectivity with which Hollywood threatens us, for example in the horror movie. However, the disjunc-tion between the two viewing conditions may not be as radical as is often claimed: the theatre audience in practice remains conscious of its surroundings, while the home audience commonly recreates theater conditions in miniature, assembling a group, turning off the lights, and so on.
3   The continuity system is not unique to Hollywood; it is the dominant system of spatial representation in mainstream western cinema and television. Equally, since it evolved across several national cinemas in the period before World War I, Hollywood cannot really be credited with its creation. But Hollywood was and is its greatest exemplar and exponent, and has taken what we are calling the benevolence of spatial representation in the continuity system farther than other national cinemas. A discussion of alter-native modes of spatial representation can be found in Bordwell and Thompson, pp. 231–9.
4   The physical material of the scene prior to the act of filming is sometimes referred to as pro-filmic space. "The pro-filmic concerns the elements placed in front of the camera to be filmed: actors, lighting, set design, etc." Robert Stam, Robert Burgoyne, and Sandy Flitterman-Lewis, *New Vocabularies in Film Semiotics* (London: Routledge, 1992), p. 112.
5   As special effects work comes to make increasing use of computer-generated images, the need to construct cinematic illusions physically is diminishing. Not all the dino-saurs in *Jurassic Park* (1993), for instance, were "real."
6   This debate is often presented as being staged between André Bazin and Jean Mitry. André Bazin, "Theatre and Cinema: Part 2," in *What is Cinema? Vol. 1*, trans. Hugh Gray (Berkeley, CA: University of California Press, 1967), pp. 95–124; Jean Mitry, *Esthétique et Psychologie du Cinéma*, 2 vols (Paris: Editions Universitaires, 1963, 1965).
7   David Bordwell, Janet Staiger, and Kristin Thompson, *The Classical Hollywood Cinema: Film Style and Mode of Production to 1960* (London: Routledge and Kegan Paul, 1985), p. 51.
8   This idea is discussed in Stephen Heath, "Language, Sight and Sound," in *Questions of Cinema* (London: Macmillan, 1981), p. 215.
9   J.A. Place and L.S. Peterson, "Some Visual Motifs of *Film Noir*," in Bill Nichols, ed., *Movies and Methods* (Berkeley, CA: University of California Press, 1976), pp. 325–38.

10 "The red dress is marked by the characters as evidence of a change in Cary's identity as a sexual being. . . . the red costumes comment on the ideologies that constrain woman's identity. They are indicative of the role a woman's sexual identity plays in her life and in the life of her family." Mary Beth Haralovich, *"All That Heaven Allows*: Color, Narrative Space, and Melodrama," in Peter Lehman, ed., *Close Viewings: An Anthology of New Film Criticism* (Tallahassee: Florida State University Press, 1990), p. 67. This article contains an excellent discussion of the function of color in the movie.

11 Elie Faure, "The Art of Cineplastics," in Daniel Talbot, ed., *Film: An Anthology* (Berkeley, CA: University of California Press, 1969), p. 6.

12 Occasionally a comparable aesthetic argument still appears in criticism of Hollywood. Barry Salt, for instance, has argued that, in the movies directed by Josef von Sternberg starring Marlene Dietrich, there is a "kinetic use of light and dark" that has no significant expressive function in the movies' narratives. Barry Salt, "Sternberg's Heart Beats in Black and White," in Peter Baxter, ed., *Sternberg* (London: British Film Institute, 1980), pp. 103–18.

13 This story is often told about the first screening of the Lumière brothers' "actuality" film, *L'Arrivée d'un Train en Gare de la Ciotat* (1895), which showed a train pulling in at a railway platform and passengers descending from its carriages. See, for example, Eric Rhode, *A History of the Cinema from its Origins to 1970* (Harmondsworth: Penguin, 1978), pp. 19–20. The story may well be apocryphal, as Tom Gunning suggests in "Primitive Cinema: A Frame-Up? Or the Trick's on Us," in Thomas Elsaesser, ed., *Early Cinema: Space, Frame, Narrative* (London: British Film Institute, 1990), pp. 95–103. As early as 1901, it was being parodied in movies such as *The Countryman and the Cinematograph*, a British picture showing a country bumpkin watching a film of a train pulling into a station, and running away in terror. The significances of the story are considered in Dai Vaughn, "Let There be Lumière," in Elsaesser, pp. 63–7.

14 Cinerama publicity, quoted in John Belton, *Widescreen Cinema* (Cambridge, MA: Harvard University Press, 1992), pp. 188–9.

15 "Drugstores near the Cinerama theatre in New York did a landoffice business during intermission, selling dramamine to spectators who either became airsick in the first half or wanted to prepare themselves for the film's finale." Belton, p. 93.

16 André Bazin's critique of analytical montage, which only requires the viewer "to follow his guide, to let his attention follow along smoothly with that of the director who will choose what he should see," is one example of such criticism ("The Evolution of the Language of Cinema," in Bazin, p. 36). On a superficially more sophisticated level, so is the idea that Hollywood cinema **sutures** the place of the spectator, advanced by Jean-Pierre Oudart and by Daniel Dayan in "The Tutor-Code of Classical Cinema," in Nichols, pp. 438–51.

17 Will Wright, *Sixguns and Society: A Structural Study of the Western* (Berkeley, CA: University of California Press, 1975), p. 193.

18 Roger D. McNiven, "The Middle-class American Home of the Fifties: The Use of Architecture in Nicholas Ray's *Bigger Than Life* and Douglas Sirk's *All That Heaven Allows*," *Cinema Journal* 22:2 (Summer 1983), p. 38.

19 Daniel Arijon, *Grammar of the Film Language* (Los Angeles: Silman-James Press, 1976), pp. 4, 6, 20, 22, 528.

20 Jan-Christopher Horak, "G.W. Pabst in Hollywood or Every Modern Hero Deserves a Mother," *Film History* 1:1 (1987), p. 57. Quotations from memos from Wallis to Pabst, December 5 and 20, 1933, Warner Bros. production file, Warner Bros. Archive, University of Southern California.

21 A set-up is one positioning of the camera and accompanying lighting arrangement. One set-up may yield more than one shot in the final picture: the close-ups of one player in a scene may well all be photographed from the same set-up, for instance. In practice, the output of individual directors varied considerably, as did the demands of production executives at each studio. Warner Bros., famous for its economic production style, was a more natural home for a Mervyn LeRoy, a director capable of shooting as much as six minutes of finished film in one day, than for William Wyler, whose predilection for intricate camera movements invariably slowed down output. Thomas Schatz, *The Genius of the System: Hollywood Filmmaking in the Studio Era* (New York: Pantheon, 1988), pp. 140–5, 225–6.

22 The best of these anecdotal histories, and a book that has much to tell its reader about early American cinema, is Terry Ramsaye, *A Million and One Nights: A History of the Motion Picture through 1925* (New York: Simon and Schuster, 1926).

23 Bazin, "The Evolution of the Language of Cinema," pp. 24, 32.

24 David Bordwell reports that in the 100 movies he, Staiger, and Thompson subjected to shot-by-shot analysis, "less than 2 per cent of the shot-changes violated spatial continuity [the 180-degree rule], and one-fifth of the movies contained not a single violation. No wonder," he adds, "that, of all Hollywood stylistic practices, continuity editing has been considered a set of firm rules." A related editing convention, although one less firmly adhered to, is that if the camera angle changes between shots, it should change at least 30 degrees, or else it will appear to "jump." This convention is, however, much less strictly applied. Bordwell, Staiger, and Thompson, p. 57.

25 Steven D. Katz, *Film Directing Shot by Shot: Visualizing from Concept to Screen* (Los Angeles: Michael Wiese Productions, 1991), p. 123; Arijon, p. 32.

26 Katz, p. 123.

27 James Clifford, *The Predicament of Culture* (Cambridge, MA: Harvard University Press, 1988), p. 34.

28 Reporter's transcript of the Proceedings at Conference held at the Offices of the Association of Motion Picture Producers, Los Angeles, February 10, 1930, p. 14. 1930 AMPP Code file, Motion Picture of America Archive, New York.

29 Laura Mulvey's article, "Visual Pleasure and Narrative Cinema," identifies the three looks of audience, camera, and character, but develops her argument in a quite different direction to that followed here. Mulvey's article, first published in *Screen* 16:3 (Autumn 1975), had great influence on subsequent feminist and psychoanalytic film criticism, and has been widely anthologized, including in her own collection of essays, *Visual and Other Pleasures* (Bloomington: Indiana University Press, 1989).

30 Dayan, pp. 445–6.

31 Dayan, pp. 448–9.

32 William Rothman, "Against 'the System of the Suture,'" in Nichols, pp. 451–9.

33 This theory of identification is most fully elaborated in Christian Metz, *The Imaginary Signifier: Psychoanalysis and the Cinema*, trans. Celia Britton, Annwyl Williams, Ben Brewster, and Alfred Guzzetti (Bloomington: Indiana University Press, 1982), pp. 49–52. It has, however, been disputed, notably by Noel Carroll, who argues: "If I truly identified with the camera, I suppose that I would experience the entire visual array of the projection as coextensive with my visual field. Yet, when I look at a film image, I only focus on part of it, usually upon what is represented in the foreground . . . often the camera's field of view is broader than mine; my field of vision is not coextensive with its field of vision." Noel Carroll, *Mystifying Movies: Fads and Fallacies in Contemporary Film Theory* (New York: Columbia University Press, 1988), p. 40.

34   Other critics have borrowed the term "focalization" from Gerard Genette's analysis of literary narrative to describe what we are calling point of view. Edward Branigan takes another term from Genette in discussing the "filmic voice" that "speaks" the points of view of characters in much the same way as a narrator establishes subsidiary points of view in a novel. We prefer to retain the spatial metaphor for a process that works through the representation of space. Gerard Genette, *Narrative Discourse: An Essay in Method*, trans. Jane E. Lewin (Ithaca, NY: Cornell University Press, 1980), pp. 189–210; Edward Branigan, "The Point of View Shot," in Bill Nichols, ed., *Movies and Methods Vol. II* (Berkeley, CA: University of California Press, 1985), pp. 672–91, and in *Point of View in the Cinema: A Theory of Narration and Subjectivity in Classical Film* (New York: Mouton, 1984).

35   David Bordwell, *Narration in the Fiction Film* (London: Methuen, 1985), p. 161.

36   This scene is analyzed in detail in Nick Browne, "The Spectator-in-the-Text: The Rhetoric of *Stagecoach*," in Philip Rosen, ed., *Narrative, Apparatus, Ideology: A Film Theory Reader* (New York: Columbia University Press, 1986), pp. 102–19. Browne's argument is elaborated further in *The Rhetoric of Filmic Narration* (Ann Arbor: University of Michigan Press, 1982).

37   Bordwell, p. 31.

38   Catherine Belsey, *Critical Practice* (London: Methuen, 1980), pp. 71–2. This argument is made at greater length in Colin MacCabe, "Realism and the Cinema: Notes on some Brechtian Theses," *Screen* 15:2 (Summer 1974), pp. 7–27.

39   Martha Wolfenstein and Nathan Leites, *Movies: A Psychological Study* (Glencoe, IL: Free Press, 1950), pp. 248, 250.

40   One instance in which this does happen is in Hitchcock's *Rear Window* (1954), at the moment when murderer Lars Thorwald (Raymond Burr) realizes that L.B. Jeffries (James Stewart) has been spying on him and knows his secret. Thorwald stares across the courtyard directly into the camera, and his return of our look both implicates the audience in Jeffries' voyeurism and terrifies us with the realization that this movie character is staring not at another character in the same movie, but directly at us as we sit in the theater. A more benign version of this fantasy is enacted in *The Purple Rose of Cairo* (1984), when a movie's leading man comes through the screen into the theater to pursue a romance with one of his fans.

41   Philip Hayward, "Situating Cyberspace: The Popularisation of Virtual Reality," in Philip Hayward and Tana Wollen, eds, *Future Visions: New Technologies of the Screen* (London: British Film Institute, 1993), pp. 180–204.

42   Laura Mulvey, "Notes on Sirk and Melodrama," *MOVIE* 25 (Winter 1977–8), pp. 53–6.

43   Bordwell, Staiger, and Thompson, pp. 372, 375.

44   Bordwell, Staiger, and Thompson, pp. 9, 375. Bordwell explains that the model of film style he and his colleagues advance assumes that "the most distinct changes take place at the level of stylistic devices," while the historical continuity of the classical Hollywood style is established at a more general level: "If I say that a scene can begin by drawing back from a significant figure or object, that suggests that an iris, a cut, and a camera movement are all paradigmatic alternatives. But in 1917, the most probable choice would have been the iris; in 1925, the cut; in 1935, the camera movement. In discussing the general principles of classical style, I shall often project the historically variable devices on to the same plane to show their functional equivalence." Bordwell, Staiger, and Thompson, p. 9.

45   Richard Maltby, *Harmless Entertainment: Hollywood and the Ideology of Consensus* (Metuchen, NJ: Scarecrow, 1983), pp. 329–39.

46 Paul Schrader, "Notes on Film Noir," *Film Comment* 8:1 (January 1974). Reprinted in Barry Keith Grant, ed., *Film Genre Reader* (Austin: University of Texas Press, 1986), p. 175.

47 Hitchcock added a note to the description of the murder in the screenplay that read, "The slashing. An impression of a knife slashing, as if tearing at the very screen, ripping the film." Quoted in Donald Spoto, *The Life of Alfred Hitchcock: The Dark Side of Genius* (London: Collins, 1983), p. 419.

48 Robin Wood, *Hitchcock's Films Revisited* (New York: Columbia University Press, 1989), p. 146.

49 William Pechter, *Twenty-Four Times a Second* (New York: Harper and Row, 1971), quoted in Stephen Rebello, *Alfred Hitchcock and the Making of Psycho* (New York: Dembner Books, 1990), p. 162. Subsequent criticism has also established a firm orthodoxy about the pivotal significance of *Psycho* for the horror movie, and for larger cultural concerns. It is well summarized by Robin Wood: "*Psycho* is clearly a seminal work, definitively establishing two concepts crucial to the genre's subsequent development: the monster as human psychotic/schizophrenic and the revelation of horror as existing at the heart of the family. . . . Since *Psycho*, and especially in the '70s, the definition of normality has become increasingly uncertain, questionable, open to attack; accordingly, the monster becomes increasingly complex." Robin Wood, *Hollywood from Vietnam to Reagan* (New York: Columbia University Press, 1986), pp. 150–1.

50 The phrase is Kim Newman's: *Nightmare Movies: A Critical Guide to Contemporary Horror Films* (New York: Harmony Books, 1988).

51 Hitchcock also insisted on 30 seconds of darkness in the theater after the end-titles, so that the effect of the movie's ending would be "indelibly engraved in the mind of the audience, later to be discussed among gaping friends and relations. You will then bring up house lights of a greenish hue, and shine spotlights of this ominous hue across the faces of your departing patrons." Quoted in Rebello, pp. 174, 169, 150–1.

52 Quoted in Spoto, p. 406.

53 "Much of the art of horror lies in catching the spectatorial eye unawares – penetrating it before it has a chance to close its lid." Carol J. Clover, *Men, Women and Chainsaws: Gender in the Modern Horror Film* (London: British Film Institute, 1992), p. 203.

54 Andrew Britton, "Blissing Out: The Politics of Reaganite Entertainment," *MOVIE* 31/ 32 (Winter 1986), pp. 2–3.

55 Clover, p. 202.

56 Clover, pp. 6–7.

57 Tania Modleski, *The Women Who Knew Too Much: Hitchcock and Feminist Theory* (London: Methuen, 1988), p. 107.

58 Clover, pp. 23, 27. Clover also points out that the female survivor, whom she calls the Final Girl, is a boyish figure with an androgynous name (Stevie, Terry, Joey) whose "smartness, competence in mechanical and other practical matters, and sexual reluctance set her apart from the other girls and ally her, ironically, with the very boys she fears or rejects, not to speak of the killer himself." Ironically disposing of simple applications of gendered sadistic voyeurism to these movies, Clover declares, "woe to the viewer of *Friday the Thirteenth I* who identifies with the male killer only to discover that he is a middle-aged woman." Clover, pp. 43, 44.

59 Clover, p. 229.

60 Jo Seton has also argued that the shift in recreational practice that marked the disintegration of the idea of the undifferentiated audience, from the habit of "going to *the* movies" to the much more differentiated activity of "going to see *a* movie," may have contributed to the economic viability of unsafe space, because "the risk of alienating

the spectator from a single movie is economically considerably less than the risk of alienating him/her from the movies per se." *Psycho* itself had this effect, attracting a high proportion of teenagers and young adults for whom it became, according to Robert Karpis, "a major social event not to be missed," but alienating many of Hitchcock's older fans, particularly women. Jo Seton, "Hitchcock and Safe Space," unpublished seminar paper, University of Exeter, November 1990, p. 7; Robert E. Karpis, *Hitchcock: The Making of a Reputation* (Chicago: University of Chicago Press, 1992), pp. 60–1.

61   Redford, in interview on *The South Bank Show: Melvyn Bragg Talks to Robert Redford about Ordinary People* (London Weekend Television, 1981).

62   Michael Ryan and Douglas Kellner, *Camera Politica: The Politics and Ideology of the Contemporary Hollywood Film* (Bloomington: Indiana University Press, 1988), p. 160.

63   Britton, p. 24.

64   Wood, *Hollywood from Vietnam to Reagan*, pp. 173–4.

65   Significantly, Alvin Sargent's screenplay informs us about Buck's death much more quickly than the novel by Judith Guest from which it is derived.

66   *Ordinary People* invokes the horror movie earlier, when a group of children come to the Jarretts' house trick-or-treating on Halloween.

6 Performance

Perhaps Hollywood movies give us pleasure and a sense of identification simply because they enable us to recognize and adapt to the "acted" quality of everyday life: they place us safely outside dramatic events, a position from which we can observe people lying, concealing emotions, or staging performances for one another.

James Naremore[1]

We set an actor in front of us, asked him to imagine a dramatic situation that did not involve any physical movement, then we all tried to understand what state he was in. Of course, this was impossible, which was the point of the exercise.

Peter Brook[2]

In the early 1920s, one of the founders of Soviet cinema, Lev Kuleshov, may have edited together a sequence of shots that has since become probably the most discussed piece of lost film in cinema history. According to Kuleshov's pupil, Vsevolod Pudovkin, Kuleshov cut together a close-up of the actor Ivan Mosjoukine's face with three other shots: a bowl of soup, a child playing with a toy bear, and a woman lying in a coffin. The shot of Mosjoukine's expressionless face was the same in all three sequences, but when they were shown to audiences, "the public raved about the acting of the artist. They pointed out the heavy pensiveness of his mood over the forgotten soup . . . the deep sorrow with which he looked on the dead woman . . . the light, happy smile with which he surveyed the girl at play. But we knew that in all three cases the face was exactly the same."[3] The footage of the Kuleshov experiment, as it has become known, has long disappeared, but the claims based on its results were fundamental to the montage-based theories of Soviet cinema in the 1920s, and to much subsequent theorizing about how cinema – and cinema acting in particular – constructs meaning.

Pudovkin's argument was that "the film is not *shot*, but *built*, built up from the separate strips of celluloid that are its raw material."[4] He maintained that the juxtaposition of the close-up of Mosjoukine and each of the other shots generated a precise and predictable meaning in the mind of the spectator that was present in neither shot by itself. Spectators, however, understood the meaning to be the result of the actor's performance: a performance apparently created entirely by editing. The resulting theory of the production of cinematic meaning corresponded to both the ideological and aesthetic preferences of early Soviet society. Editing constructed meaning dialectically: the juxtaposition of two shots – thesis and antithesis – produced the synthesis of the spectator's recognition of sorrow or happiness. Pudovkin's theory of montage emphasized the power of the cinematic machine, under the control of the director and editor, to create meaning with the reliability of a factory assembly line. Much of the cinema's appeal as an instrument of ideological education and persuasion lay in this mechanical predictability: the correct assembly of a sequence would invariably result in the correct interpretation of the sequence by every spectator, since "the camera compels the spectator to see as the director wishes." Kuleshov and Pudovkin did not regard the spectator as entirely passive: cinema, Pudovkin argued, required from its viewers "an exceptional concentration of attention." But it was the task of the director, the creative intelligence guiding the construction of the image stream, to direct the spectator's attention.[5] "With correct montage, even if one takes the performance of an actor directed at something quite different, it will still reach the viewer in the way intended by the editor, because the viewer himself will complete the sequence and see that which is suggested to him by the montage."[6]

We rely on Kuleshov and Pudovkin themselves for the accounts we have of the Kuleshov experiments, and several critics have noted the imprecisions in their descriptions.[7] Attempts to duplicate the experiment have failed to reproduce the claimed results.[8] But whether or not the "Kuleshov effect" ever existed as it was described, it has had a substantial influence on subsequent theorizing about both the passivity of the spectator and the power of editing to create performative meaning. The readiness with which this account of the relationship between spectator and text has for so long been accepted contrasts noticeably with Peter Brook's description, at the beginning of this chapter, of a much less successful theatrical experiment in communicating meaning without movement: "Of course, this was impossible, which was the point of the exercise." Kuleshov's faith in the mechanical effectiveness of the cinema represents one extreme position in what Frank McConnell has described as "the warfare between personality and mechanism" which is "the prime datum of our experience of film narrative."[9] McConnell's assertion that "any performance by an actor in a film is a warfare between personality and mechanism" provides an alternative framework for looking at the Kuleshov experiment.[10] McConnell's concern is with what he sees as the "existential paradox" of film, "the real presence of human figures and faces who, although they are never really there as we watch the screen, are nevertheless the best and only reason anyone has for looking at the screen at all."[11] From McConnell's perspective, the spectator's ability to register and respond to an emotion speaks not to the power of the machine, but to "a crucial, archetypal aspect of all film personality: that struggle of the human to show itself *within* the mechanical, which we have described as film's deepest romanticism."[12]

Movie criticism has found it difficult to discuss the role of the actor. Almost every analysis of acting in the cinema begins by commenting on the paucity of the vocabulary available for the critical examination of performance. The explanation for this paucity is surprisingly simple: acting is difficult to analyze because it is not understood as a systematic or standardized practice. Acting is usually understood in more discrete terms, as the particular practice of particular actors. Most writers either give an impressionistic account of what it felt like to witness the performance ("a tight, brittle, monstrously subdued performance")[13] or else list in detail the gestures and intonations the performer uses (John Wayne expresses amusement "by the following performance: his eyes look slightly left, slightly heavenward, there is a faint smile on his face, he moves his right leg and upper body just a little, keeping his arms behind his back").[14] However detailed such notations become, they fail to catch the nuance of performance because acting is **analogical**, a mode of communication that works in terms of proportion, gradation, and inflection rather than the clear-cut distinctions and differences of **digital** sign systems.[15] The constant, subtle changes of expression and intonation that comprise a performance are easily comprehended within the context of a movie, but are notoriously difficult either to describe or to analyze in words. So description and analysis both fall back on what James Naremore, in his book *Acting in the Cinema*, calls "fuzzy adjectival language."[16] The great bulk of writing about film acting is evaluative, concerned almost exclusively with declaring how good or bad a particular performance was, although the criteria by which these judgments are made are usually very vague. As this chapter proceeds, we shall try to provide some terms by which movie acting can be described and different types of performance distinguished from each other. But this chapter is only partially about acting, and there are a number of senses of the term "performance" that are important to our discussion.

However unreliable they might be, accounts of the Kuleshov experiment suggest the extent to which a cinematic performance is never constructed by an actor alone. Cinematic acting differs most obviously from theatrical acting in the way that a cinematic performance is discontinuous, fragmented into the individual shots which are the movie's constituent parts before being reassembled in the editing room. In writing of his work with non-professional actors, Pudovkin emphasized the extent to which he constructed the performances of his untutored players in this way. But while that might be an extreme instance, Pudovkin was right to stress how far a movie performance is built, not shot. For an actor to "build" a performance is, however, more difficult in the material circumstances of movie production, where the recording of that performance will likely be out of order, than it is in the theater, where it occurs complete. In *Film Acting*, Pudovkin argued that:

The discontinuity of the actor's work must never be ignored, but always treated as a difficulty to be overcome. . . . The understanding and feel of the possibilities of the shooting of shots from various angles must be organically included in the process of the actor's own work on the external shaping of his role. . . . this concept, analogous to that of the stage image, demands from the film actor firstly a knowledge of how consciously to exploit the possibilities of vari-angled shooting for the purposes of his work on the external shaping of his role, and, secondly, clear consideration of its creative place in the edited composition of the whole film, in order that he may understand and bring out the most comprehensive and profound bases of his acting.[17]

But the constructed nature of a movie emphasizes the extent to which a movie performance is not only the work of the actor. Several different bodies may be used to construct a single performance: voices are dubbed, stunt artists are used for dangerous action sequences, and sometimes hand models and body doubles provide body parts to substitute for the actors. As an extreme example, in *Psycho* (1960), the performance of Mrs Bates is constructed from the bodies of three actors and the voices of three more.[18] A movie performance is also constructed out of the performance of the camera, the editing, and the mise-en-scène.

A movie is a performance and not a text. If movies were texts, we could write about them with much more critical confidence than we do. But all attempts to reduce movies to texts, whether through analogies between film and language, shots and words, or through formal analysis, ultimately fail to resolve the interpretive complexities of performance signs and thus to resolve the dialectic of cinema's warfare between personality and mechanism, and Frank McConnell's paradox of film presence, "the presence of absence, a 'reality' which is not there."[19]

Cinema criticism has borrowed its discourses of performance from theater. Some of those discourses have referred to acting, some to the star system, and others to the vocabulary of performance itself. In a commercial sense, a movie "performs" at the box-office, where the quality of its performance is strictly related to its profitability. A screening is also called a performance of the movie; perhaps this is the most mechanical sense of a movie's performance, since apart from the audience, the only thing performing during a movie's performance is the projector – suggesting that other aspect of mechanical performance, of the speed and efficiency of a well-engineered machine evoked in the language of Soviet filmmaker Dziga Vertov's "Kino Eye," the mechanical eye "more perfect than the human eye for examining the chaos of visual phenomena that resemble space."[20]

The Spectacle of Movement

The spectacle of movement was the cinema's first "production value." For the first time the world was revealed in motion, and the impression of lifelike movement amazed and excited its earliest viewers. An advertisement for the first exhibition of Edison's Vitascope in New York in 1896 promised that the audience would see the "Perfect Reproduction of Noted Feminine Figures and Their Every Movement."[21] Early "actuality" films were often primarily demonstrations of cinema's ability to record movement, in single shots of waves breaking on a shore, processions, or horse races. Reviewing the Vitascope exhibition, the *New York Herald* critic was most impressed by R.W. Paul's film of *Rough Sea at Dover*.

> Far out in the dim perspective one could see a diminutive roller start. It came down the stage, apparently, increasing in volume, and throwing up little jets of snow-white foam, rolling faster and faster, and hugging the old sea wall, until it burst and flung in shredded masses far into the air. The thing was altogether so realistic and the reproduction so absolutely accurate that it fairly astounded the beholder. It was the closest copy of nature any work of man has ever yet achieved.[22]

Film historian Tom Gunning has argued that these early films were organized "less as a way of telling stories than as a way of presenting a series of views to an audience, fascinating because of their illusory power . . . and exoticism."[23] Gunning calls this conception the "cinema of attractions," and suggests that while an alternative set of spectator relations came to predominate in narrative-oriented cinema after 1906, the cinema of attractions remained "a component of narrative films, more evident in some genres (e.g. the musical) than in others."[24] The word "cinema" itself is derived from the Greek word for motion, *kinema*, but the extent to which movement is emphasized in the terminology of different filmmaking practices varies considerably. Hollywood gives movement a much higher status than European cinema, calling its products movies or motion pictures rather than films, the term generally used by European institutions. Likewise, the most characteristic forms of Hollywood cinema display a remarkable consistency in their commitment to the moving image.

American fiction movies have stressed movement from the outset, with early chase films providing the first synthesis of narrative and the attractions of spectacular movement. Slapstick comedy incorporated frenetic chases, stage melodramas were "opened out" with climactic races against time, and Westerns developed a new rhetoric of dramatic exposition with their extended action sequences across expansive outdoor spaces. Hollywood cinema has never lost this initial excitement in, and celebration of, the spectacular attraction of sheer movement, quite separate from the construction of the movie's story. *Grand Prix* (1966) has several extended action sequences of Formula 1 cars driving around race tracks, in which the sequences are far more concerned with the spectacle of speed than they are with the narrative activity of telling us who is winning the race. Sports movies in general follow a convention of showing the highlights of their action in slow motion, presenting the cinematic performance of motion as spectacle in as pure a manner as *Rough Sea at Dover*, and giving us the chance to dwell on our delight in the representation of movement for its own sake. *Jurassic Park* (1993) spent millions of dollars on fabricating the lifelike movement of long-extinct animals.

In addition to early cinema's reliance on the movement of objects within a fixed frame, however, we can identify two further kinds of movement in Hollywood movies: that of the camera itself, and the movement which is produced in the editing process. These three kinds of movement usually work in combination. The car chase in *Bullitt* (1968), for example, suspends narrative development for 10 minutes while Steve McQueen pursues a pair of assassins through the streets of San Francisco in a spectacular high-speed car chase. The sequence makes effective use of a shot that has a similar effect on the audience to that of the roller-coaster ride in *This is Cinerama* (1952). The camera shoots through the windshield of McQueen's car as it hurtles down the steep inclines of San Francisco's streets, bouncing furiously every time he crosses an intersection. Audiences, too, bounce up and down energetically in their seats, their sympathetic motion an exaggerated, physical form of their willingness to cooperate with the movie in anticipating, perceiving, and reacting to movement within the image. These viewpoint shots, showing us forward movement seen through the fixed frame of the camera and of the car windshield, provide an analogue for the viewer's position in cinema, sitting in a fixed seat looking at a static screen, on which images move without him or her having to move to see them. They are intercut with two other representations of movement: panning shots from static camera positions of the two cars speeding by, and shots taken from vehicles moving at the same speed as the cars, in which the cars themselves remain fairly stable in the frame, while the background speeds by. The full effect of the spectacle comes from the intercutting of these viewpoints, as the audience's position alternates between being inside and outside the action, while the sequence as a whole emphasizes the general impression of speed for its own sake, rather than developing the narrational possibilities of the scene.

Hollywood's delight in movement for its own sake ensures that nearly every movie has at least one sequence which displays action or physical expertise as a production value, interrupting narrative and challenging its dominance. In the terms used by formalist criticism (and discussed in more detail in chapter 8), in these scenes an aesthetic motivation exceeds the motivation provided by narrative causality.[25] Again, musical sequences provide some of the clearest examples of this shifting between motivations. Midway through *Singin' in the Rain* (1952), Donald O'Connor gives an exuberant performance in a number called "Make 'Em Laugh," a demonstration of the art of laughter-making and a polemic on its behalf, reveling in bodily movement. Like most musical performances, it follows a cue for a song and features a lively, up-tempo lyric that escalates into a dance routine and a series of comic pratfalls. These devices mark it as taking place outside the narrative constraints of the movie. The obvious theatricality of its staging on a movie studio set provides O'Connor with a safe

Cosmo (Donald O'Connor) and Don (Gene Kelly) improvise an energetic dance routine in *Singin' in the Rain* (1952). Aquarius Picture Library

space in which the normal rules of physical mobility have been suspended, so that he can move in any way he chooses, completely controlling his environment and the props within it. Safe spaces for performance, where the human body is the center of the spectacle, are often marked by theatrical devices.[26] In this scene the back wall of the set is painted as a corridor receding in perspective, but O'Connor exposes it as illusion by running up the wall to perform a back-flip. The first couple of times he walks into solid objects we may worry about his being injured, but we soon recognize that in this performance space he cannot be hurt. By the end of the performance we watch him leap through a brick wall and still find it funny. The comedy of this final moment lies in O'Connor's unexpected re-entry into a cinematic space outside the confines of the proscenium arch stage he has constructed, but the routine guarantees our security by ending with a track-in on a smiling O'Connor, showing that he has survived his own energetic outburst undamaged.

As the sequence snowballs, O'Connor's movements become increasingly assertive and energetic: eccentric dance-steps, tumbles, and back-flips. Camera movement and editing are kept to a minimum: both simply recompose space to support O'Connor's performance. The camera keeps a fairly constant distance from the performance, positioning O'Connor clearly and centrally, showing the whole of his body and allowing him room to move, but concealing the physical effort involved in sustaining the routine. As important as shot scale is minimal cutting: a single **long take** covers most of the routine, with panning movements reframing the space to cover O'Connor's actions.[27] Musical sequences and comedy routines are often constructed like this, with the duration of the shots emphasizing the complexities of a sustained performance. In this case, shot duration intensifies our attention to O'Connor's antics and our sense of his skill.

This sequence suspends some of the causal logics that usually structure a Hollywood movie. O'Connor's routine is an autonomous spectacle, composed of movement for its own sake. To compensate for interrupting the plot, it celebrates its own surplus energy and promotes the idea of performance transcending narrative that underpins the movie as a whole. Our appreciation of the performer's skill concentrates our attention on O'Connor, and the expertise with which he performs his gymnastic feats, while his character, Cosmo, effectively disappears from the scene. The effect of movement in a performance routine contrasts markedly with the restrictions placed upon characters trapped within more solidly narrative spaces. Characters caught up in a particular narrative situation may be entirely deprived of the assertive power of movement. As *High Noon* (1952) approaches its climax, the townspeople who have refused to help Marshall Kane (Gary Cooper) are caught in static poses as they wait uneasily for the events that they cannot control to unfold. Their immobility is emphasized by the movie's cutting pointedly between them and the image of a clock in Kane's office, where the only movement visible in the sequence is the mechanical swinging of the clock's pendulum. Assertive movement, on the other hand, can not only suspend narrative but temporarily impose an alternative time-scale on events. In the opening scene of *On the Town* (1949) Frank Sinatra, Gene Kelly, and Jules Munshin tour New York City while singing "New York, New York." Subtitles tell us that the events covered during the number take over three hours, but by the energy of their movements and the way in which they are combined together into a single assertive performance, they not only turn the whole city into a safe space for their routine, they also subordinate the narrative time to a time-scheme

Marshall Will Kane (Gary Cooper) and retired lawman Martin Howe (Lon Chaney Jr) trapped by time in *High Noon* (1952). Stanley Kramer/United Artists (courtesy Kobal)

that better suits the needs of the audience. We get a three-hour guided tour of New York in two-and-a-half minutes, with the added bonus of the song.

The Movement of Narrative

> Nearly all editing points in narrative film are devised to set up a framework of expectations in a series of shots. The result is narrative motion.
> Steven D. Katz[28]

As well as offering spectacular interludes, physical movement within the frame is a principal source of story information and the basis of many of our perceptions about characters. Likewise, camera movement is usually used to emphasize the narrative significance of an action rather than the spectacular pleasures of its representation. The camera moves to accommodate the movement of characters across represented space, panning to follow a character as he or she walks across a room, for instance. Narrative motion is rarely produced through camera movement alone, however, but

On the Town (1949): a two-and-a-half-minute guided tour of New York, sung by Frank Sinatra, Jules Munshin, and Gene Kelly. Aquarius Picture Library

is completed in the editing process, so that cuts cover significant transitions and combine viewpoints. If the character goes through a doorway, the movie will cut to a new angle from the adjoining room. Expressive camera movement can also operate in a conventional fashion. At the death of Sheriff Baker (Slim Pickens) in *Pat Garrett and Billy the Kid* (1973), the camera draws back to a long shot, both to frame Baker and his wife (Katy Jurado) in the landscape and, crucially, to draw a veil over the precise moment of death. The movement accords Baker the closest thing to heroic dignity available in the movie.

One of Hollywood's conventional modes of reframing is what Edward Branigan has called "frame cutting":[29] just as a figure is moving out of the frame, the screen image cuts to the adjacent space, giving the audience the sense that the space represented on the screen at any given moment is the most important segment of a larger environment. Frame cutting also makes the cut smooth and speeds up the flow of the action. The continuity system encourages cutting on action, as the flow of the movement from one shot to the other diverts the viewer's attention away from the change in camera angle. Minimizing the viewer's attention to the presence of the

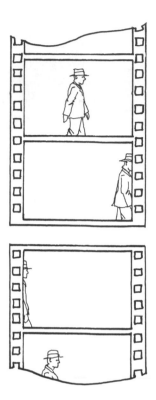

Frame cutting
As James Cagney moves out of the frame in shot 1, the image cuts to shot 2 just as he is entering the other side of that frame. The flow of movement from one shot to the next distracts the viewer's attention from the cut itself.

camera is also achieved by camera movements that reframe the action. Such movements imitate our human tendency to move our eyes and head to keep the object of interest in the center of vision, and seem less distracting than a static camera in which figure movement in the fixed frame unbalances the composition.[30]

Like editing, camera movement generally follows what André Bazin called "the material or dramatic logic of the scene,"[31] but that apparently transparent logic is highly mediated, even though camera movement, along with lens choice, editing, and other elements of mise-en-scène, directs audience attention without, for the most part, drawing attention to itself. Classical editing technique does not, for instance, cut when the camera is moving. Even when following a character walking from one room to another, the image will pause briefly at the end of one panning movement, cut to the other side of the doorway, and only after the cut from static frame to static frame will the camera pick up the movement again. A movie like *Nashville* (1975), in which this convention of not cutting on camera movement is systematically breached, produces a strong sense of disorientation and unease in most audiences.

When camera movement is not motivated by character movement the change of viewpoint may give the audience a new point of view on the action in the scene. The combination of points of view, or the move from one to the other, can offer the audience knowledge that characters do not share. Alfred Hitchcock's movies, always on the point of playfully exposing Hollywood's conventions, often dwell on the relationship between viewpoint and point of view, and occasionally do so through the use of elaborate camera movement. In one scene in *Notorious* (1946), Alicia (Ingrid Bergman) is trying to steal a key from her husband, Alexander Sebastian (Claude Rains). Almost caught in the act, she hides the key in her clenched fist. The camera's repeated movements in on their hands keep the audience's attention concentrated on where the key is, while Sebastian remains oblivious to what the scene is really "about." In the ballroom scene that follows, the same point is made in a more extreme fashion. It begins with a high-angle long shot from the top of a staircase, surveying the room in which Alicia and Sebastian are greeting their guests. In an elaborate crane movement, the camera descends the stairs and continues insistently to track in on Alicia, coming to rest on a tight close-up of the key being turned in her hand. At one level the function of this ostentatious visual gesture is to provide a kind of narrative focusing such as we discussed in relation to editing. But in drawing attention to itself, camera movement unmotivated by character can produce other effects on the audience's perception of the movie's performance. It may, for example, become the sign of a stylistic excess identifying the presence of a movie's auteur – in this case a kind of mischievousness on Hitchcock's part, as he insistently draws attention to the very thing that Alicia is trying to hide.

The opening sequence in *Touch of Evil* (1958) is staged as a long mobile shot involving several complex tracking and craning movements. Lasting for over three minutes, it covers all of the initiating action of the movie. The shot's very complexity draws attention to the presence of the camera. Viewers who notice the absence of cuts are likely to register the camera's bravura display and wonder at how difficult the shot must have been to stage. Even viewers who do not consciously register that the sequence is presented in a single shot become oppressively aware of the passage of time as the shot continues. Like the two scenes in *Notorious*, the shot produces a hierarchy of knowledge: the audience knows that a bomb has been planted in the car we intermittently follow, but its occupants and the couple walking beside it (Charlton Heston and Janet Leigh) do not. The longer the take goes on, therefore, the more uncomfortable the audience becomes, both dreading and longing for the explosion that will allow the movie to cut away from the oppressive viewpoint of the single camera position.

Long takes make the audience aware that they have no control over the passing of time. Much of the opening shot in *Touch of Evil* takes the form of a backward tracking movement, producing an effect rather like riding backwards on a train: you can't see where you're going or what's in front of you. Despite the expansiveness of its movement, it provides the audience with a single viewpoint and as a result a very restricted amount of story information. The shot forces us to wait, watch, and grow more nervous as the movie deliberately refuses us the luxury of escaping back into a more comfortable, edited narrative time or a safer vantage point. But the long take's effect is determined by its context. While a musical's use of the long take may allow the audience to celebrate the performers' skill, suspense movies are usually much less benign, turning the audience themselves into victims of the movie's manipulations.

Visual style is not usually so conspicuous an element in a movie's performance. In *Touch of Evil* we notice the emphasis on the camera as an active agent in the manipulation of the audience precisely because we are used to the more anonymous and self-effacing strategies associated with Hollywood camerawork. Long takes or extravagant camera gestures stress the existence of an instrumental, manipulative presence possessing more knowledge (of where the camera is going in both literal and metaphorical terms) than the viewer. It is, therefore, not surprising that the examples we have discussed are often cited as the directorial signatures of two of Hollywood's pre-eminent auteurs. The distinctive visual styles of both Hitchcock and Welles typically deploy a mobile camera to declare a controlling narrating presence.[32] In the performance of the movies he directed as well as in his public persona, Hitchcock – "the Master of Suspense" – turned his audiences into victims by emphasizing their powerlessness to influence the action on the screen. Auteurist criticism has often recognized visual style as a sign of the presence of an intending narrator – here "Hitchcock" or "Welles" – and has described this manipulation of the audience's position in terms of individual artistry. However, the claustrophobic effect of the opening shot of *Touch of Evil* is mitigated by the fact that the credits are superimposed over it. Auteurist critics have denounced this decision, made by the movie's producers against Welles' objections, as philistine. Our observations may suggest a somewhat more sympathetic account of their action. By providing a distraction from the intensity of the long take, the credits make it more comfortable to watch, offering a kind of cutting within the image. We may not applaud this motive, but we should recognize it as purposeful, not merely insensitive, an instance of the lengths to which Hollywood's commercial aesthetic will go to keep its customers satisfied. It also suggests the practical restrictions on an auteurist reading of even the most self-consciously authored movie.

Acting as Impersonation

I don't understand this Method stuff. I remember Laurence Olivier asking Dustin Hoffman why he stayed up all night. Dustin, looking really beat, really bad, said it was to get into the scene being filmed that day, in which he was supposed to have been up all night. Olivier said, "My boy, if you'd learn to act you wouldn't have to stay up all night."

Robert Mitchum[33]

Actors with only one dimension do not often become stars. Actors who create surprise, embody contradiction, impel the spectator to hold two conflicting ideas in the head at the same time, stand a better chance.

Robert Sklar[34]

Hollywood appropriates performance styles from a variety of theatrical traditions: from vaudeville, from circus and pantomime as in the "Make 'Em Laugh" number from *Singin' in the Rain*, and elsewhere from burlesque, radio, and television. In part this simply follows its industrial practice of exploiting talent already trained in other theatrical disciplines; in part, it suggests that different performance styles are necessary in different generic contexts. The presentation of performance as autonomous spectacle is not confined to musicals, of course. Comedies have gag-sequences, war movies have action sequences, thrillers their final chase. Alongside the notion of performance as action, however, Hollywood also draws on the different definition of performance associated with the concept of acting, a practice that enjoys a higher cultural status than the performance tradition represented by O'Connor's routine. The relative cultural status of Hollywood movies is in large part governed by the kind of performance they sponsor: some of Hollywood's most respectable movies, from *Cavalcade* (1933) to *Who's Afraid of Virginia Woolf?* (1966), have been versions of critically acclaimed stage plays, while few physical comedies, musicals, or action adventures have won Academy Awards for Best Picture or Best Performance. The higher status of acting is in part derived from the superior cultural prestige of **legitimate theater** by comparison to vaudeville, and in part from its aspirations to "truth" or verisimilitude in the imitation of character.[35]

Although acting performance can draw attention to itself and function as a separate spectacle, it more routinely aspires toward transparency, in the same way that codes of editing and camerawork seek to render themselves invisible. This "invisible" style of acting tries to imitate the expressions and emotions of the everyday world, since its aim is to create a sense of character for the audience without making them consciously aware of how that sense is created. Criticism often judges the quality of these performances in the rather vague terms of assessing their "sincerity" or their "truth." Acting manuals invoke an idea of "truth" in performance almost as often as they invoke the rhetoric of realism, although they seldom explain exactly what they mean by suggesting that "your job as an actor is to convince the audience of the truth of what is happening to you," or "the aim of acting in a picture is to be as real as the rock you sit on or the tree you lean against."[36] A more precise definition of what acting – movie acting as much as theatrical acting – attempts to achieve was offered by dramatic critic Bronson Howard in 1900: "The art of acting is the art of seeming to move, speak, and appear on the stage as the character assumed moves, speaks, and appears in real life, under the circumstances indicated in the play. In that word 'seeming' lie nearly all the difficulties, the intricacies, the technicalities of acting."[37] Even in a movie in which unpredictable or implausible events occur – a screwball comedy, for instance – characters need convincing motives for their actions, and these are most readily supplied by patterns of behavior and psychology that we recognize from the everyday world. In Frank McConnell's terms, acting is the site of the human in the machine of cinema. McConnell sees movie acting as being radically different from stage acting, not in its technical skills but in the actor's relation to space and the audience. While the craft of the stage actor is to assimilate himself or herself to a predetermined role that becomes realized in his or her physical presence on the stage, the movie performer never shares a common space with the audience, and thus the dynamics of their relationship are different. The stage actor has to persuade the audience to "see through" his or her presence to the character. The movie actor has first of all to assert his or her own coherent physical presence against the artifice and mechanisms of cinema's capacity to fragment and deconstruct time, space, and the body.[38]

From the audience's point of view, the work of the actor matters less than its consequences. Taking the romanticism out of McConnell's argument, we can say that acting is the site where we witness an *effect* of the human in the cinematic machine. Acting is the principal means by which audiences can attribute traits to characters and elaborate their individual psychologies, but Hollywood movies exploit the actor's performance at another level. The audience experiences the presence of the performer as well as – in the same body as – the presence of the character. The bodily presence of the performer is at the same time a distraction from the fiction and one of the principal means by which viewers invest in the existence of characters as if they were real people. Watching the sex scenes in *Basic Instinct* (1992), the audience wonders how close Michael Douglas and Sharon Stone came to intercourse during the filming at the same time as we make deductions about the story from our knowledge that Nick Curran and Catherine Tramell (the characters Douglas and Stone play) now have a passionate sexual relationship. In less spectacular or less prurient moments, a movie's storyline minimizes the discrepancy between what the body of the actor and the body of the character do, so that our recognition of the real body of Charlton Heston allows us to grant credence to the fictional existence of Michelangelo in *The Agony and the Ecstasy* (1965), or Ben-Hur in the movie of that name (1959), or Moses in *The Ten Commandments* (1956).[39] In a manner similar to the way a viewer's perception shifts easily between represented and expressive space, our impressions of an actor's presence and his or her "disappearance" into character readily alternate with each other.

In a cinema as goal-oriented as Hollywood, where the hero's desire – for money, love, power, adventure – drives the dramatic action, character serves as the principal means of plot motivation as well as the chief source of plausibility. Thrillers and comedies both work by putting convincing characters in improbable situations and watching how they behave. We can describe these acting performances, in which characters are bound up in the plot's progression, as being **integrated** into the narration, and contrast them with the more **autonomous performances** of routines like Donald O'Connor's. This distinction between autonomous and integrated performances will help us to distinguish the characteristics of Hollywood's various performance styles. In his book, *Acting in the Cinema*, James Naremore makes a related distinction between presentational and representational modes of acting. Presentational styles acknowledge the co-presence of performer and audience, usually through a conventionalized form of direct address such as a Shakespearean aside. Representational styles, on the other hand, offer the audience the illusion that they – or the cinematic apparatus that records the action – are invisible to the performers. As Naremore notes, "the impenetrable barrier of the screen favors representational playing styles," but in our description of star performance there is a substantial element of the presentational in the constant by-play between performance and role.[40]

Frank McConnell has suggested a similar opposition, more concerned with a typology of performers than with a typology of performance. On the one hand he identifies performers such as Charlie Chaplin and Humphrey Bogart who appear bound by the same laws as other characters, tied into the process of the narration with no opportunity to cease being characters. On the other hand there are those performers whom McConnell aptly describes as being in a "state of grace," living independently of other characters and by different rules. As instances he cites Buster Keaton and James Cagney, to whom we might add Donald O'Connor in *Singin' in the Rain*. Keaton moves through a world of threatening objects sublimely unaware of the danger they represent or even of the presence of other characters for most of the time. Cagney's "state of grace," however, is more akin to O'Connor's safe space, generated by his intense nervous energy, which allows him to dominate the spaces he is in by his unrivaled ability to move around in them.[41] McConnell's analysis is useful because it describes performance in terms of complementary and contrasting functions, rather than seeking to identify a definitive mode of screen performance as typical of Hollywood cinema.

One definition of good acting – the one articulated by Laurence Olivier in the quotation that heads this section – assumes that acting skill should be measured by the distance between the actor's characteristics and those of the character he or she is impersonating. This argument is frequently accompanied by the claim that since the technical resources of cinema appear to do the actors' work for them, a movie performance can hardly be compared to "real" acting in the "legitimate" theater. It is often suggested that the studio system restricted star performers by typecasting them into set roles, restricting the range of their acting and leading to charges that many stars – John Wayne is frequently mentioned – could not "act," since they always "played themselves." But many of these arguments are simply expressions of the perceived low cultural status of the movies, and they also ignore the fact that an actor's versatility has never been held in such high esteem in the American theatrical tradition as it has in Europe. All American acting, argues Vineberg, "assumes what would be sacrilege to a classically trained English or French actor: that the actor and not the text is the most important element in a play or movie."[42] Star acting simultaneously provides audiences with autonomous and integrated performances. The star is present as a production value and as a known bundle of personality traits, and therefore performs his or her star persona in a movie autonomously. At the same time the star is an actor "disappearing" into his or her role.

There is, however, a paradoxical element in the idea of the actor's disappearance. In every performance, two identities – actor and character – inhabit the same body, and in the **naturalist** style of acting we have so far been calling "invisible," the technical skill of the actor consists in eliding the difference between the two identities, in disembodying himself or herself to embody the role. But if the actor disappears, the performance becomes invisible; as Steve Vineberg puts it, "you don't see the process at all."[43] In this description, acting resembles makeup: "successful make-up is invisible to the audience; only its effect is noticeable."[44] This "invisible" technical skill is, paradoxically, most apparently exhibited when the character is physically different from the actor: Dustin Hoffman's performances as Dorothy Michaels in *Tootsie* (1982) and the autistic Raymond in *Rain Man* (1988) are examples; so are Lon Chaney's performances as Blizzard, the legless ruler of San Francisco's underworld, in *The Penalty* (1920), or the knife-throwing circus star Alonzo the Armless in *The Unknown* (1927).[45] But as Foster Hirsch has noted, part of what the audience does during such performances is to see "if we can detect the actor himself peering through his character's facade."[46] Hollywood's acting manuals were much concerned with this question of how visible the performer should be. In 1922, Inez and Helen Klumph suggested that the actor should "obliterate himself, as much as he possibly can."

> The audience must be kept from thinking, "How pretty Pauline Frederick looks there," or "How good looking Elliott Dexter is." If they think of the actor, they cannot be carried along by the story, or be caught up by the suspense that helps to build up the climax. They aren't going to be afraid the heroine won't be saved; they're going to sit comfortably back in their seats and know that of course Gloria Swanson won't be killed![47]

Lilian Albertson, on the other hand, argued in 1947 that the audience's synthesis of the competing presences of actor and character was more complex:

But live the part? . . . Do you think Robert Montgomery felt any pressing desire to cut off Rosalind Russell's charming head in *Night Must Fall* – or even Dame May Whitty's? But he gave you the creeps just the same, didn't he? . . . an audience is never quite that emotionally involved. Even in the presence of the greatest acting they always retain a little objectivity. The very presence of an audience is bound to impinge on the consciousness and keep them from forgetting entirely that it is, after all, *acting*.[48]

Albertson's observations touch on a long debate within performance theory about the relationship between the two identities of actor and character. Constant Coquelin, the French *comédien* for whom Edmond Rostand wrote the play *Cyrano de Bergerac* in 1897, argued that the actor must have a double personality.

He has his first self, which is the player, and his second self, which is the instrument. The first self conceives the person to be created, or rather – for the conception belongs to the author – he sees him such as he was formed by the author . . . and the being that he sees is represented by his second self . . . the first self works upon the second self till it is transformed, and thence an ideal personage is evolved – in short, until from himself he has made his work of art . . . in the actor the first self should be the master of the second; . . . the part of us which *sees* should rule as absolutely as possible the part of us which *executes*. Though this is always true, it is specially true of the moment of representation.[49]

Coquelin's own concern, along with that of most writers on acting, was with how the actor negotiated what he called the "paradox of dual consciousness," the co-presence of two identities in one body. But at the moment of representation, this negotiation is as complex for the audience as it is for the performer. However successfully the actor manages to create the illusion of character, the audience is not prevented from recognizing the illusion for what it is.[50] Actors work inside a set of performance conventions that viewers recognize as representing an absence of performance and producing a transparent effect of "the real." But as with the other conventional systems of transparency, the viewer must recognize the performance convention and at the same time see through it to register the effect. Otherwise, we could not tell acting apart from being, or identify a "sincere" performance. A movie's plot will often require the viewer to judge whether a character is being sincere or not: whether Bridget O'Shaughnessy (Mary Astor) is lying to Sam Spade (Humphrey Bogart) in *The Maltese Falcon* (1941), for instance.[51] As competent viewers, we must distinguish between two simultaneous performances: that of the character and that of the actress, and we end up complimenting Astor on her sincere performance of the character's insincerity. The audience enjoys the actress's performance as well as the role, while she exhibits not only the role, but also her technical prowess: that is, she exhibits herself.

Star Performance

A star has two things an actor doesn't have: charisma and the ability to sell tickets. Eddie Murphy will sell tickets around the world to a movie that is not a very good movie. That is a movie star.

Ned Tanen[52]

The emphasis on the person of the actor that we have been discussing is most explicit in star performances. The commercial imperatives of the star system require that stars are always visible through their characters: in *The Eiger Sanction* (1974), it is not just the fictional Jonathan Hemlock hanging over an Alpine precipice, it is also Clint Eastwood cutting the rope that stops him (both of them) from dropping hundreds of feet to certain death. The star is always himself or herself, only thinly disguised as a character: as the adverts announce, "Clint Eastwood IS *Dirty Harry*." As James Naremore notes, "a substantial body of intelligent critical writing has described the performances of the classic stars as if they were little more than fictional extensions of the actor's true personalities," and the instance he cites, Edward Wagenknecht's description of Lilian Gish in *True Heart Susie* (1919), is typical: "The part and the actress are one. In a very deep and very true sense, she is the profoundest kind of actress: that is to say she does not 'act' at all; she *is*."[53] "Being" is often offered as an almost technical description of Classical Hollywood's predominant acting style, and in these terms, a star's performance can resolve the tension of two identities in one body in a more complete manner than any "actorly" performance could reasonably hope to achieve.[54] An established star is, literally, a body of expectations, and these bodies function as very economical narrative devices. A great deal of information is conveyed about characters simply because they are played by Cary Grant or Bette Davis. Audiences know in advance what Charlotte Vale will sound like in *Now Voyager* (1942), how she will walk across a room or stub out a cigarette, and thus we can predict not only how Davis will act – that is, perform – but also how Charlotte is likely to act – that is, behave – in any likely dramatic situation.

Classical Hollywood's star system engineered a correspondence between star and role that was archetypally embodied in Clark Gable's casting as Rhett Butler in *Gone with the Wind* (1939). At the time of the movie's production, and ever since, it has seemed impossible to imagine the part being played by anyone else.[55] The common recognition that a role "might have been written" for a particular actor did no more than acknowledge the actualities of Hollywood industrial practice, by which scripts were written specifically to exhibit the already established traits and mannerisms of their stars. The fact that a star's persona circulated in the media as part of the promotion of specific movies allowed for a considerable interaction between the star's performance and offscreen persona, and in many respects substituted for variation in the roles a star undertook.

Clark Gable *is* Rhett Butler in *Gone with the Wind* (1939). Selznick/MGM
(courtesy Kobal)

Offscreen and onscreen, Dean Martin enacted the persona of an amiable
heavy drinker. In *Rio Bravo* (1958), Martin plays a drunken ex-gunfighter.
In one scene he resolves to stop drinking, and pours a shot of whisky back
into its bottle. His offscreen persona adds a resonance to the gesture that

extends beyond its significance in the story. Here we understand character less as a function of the fiction than as evidence of the performer's presence.

Many star careers have been constructed around the play of variation centered on a star's public persona. In Marilyn Monroe's case the play lay in the combination of an innocence expressed by her voice and gestures and a sexual promise expressed by her body, making her sexually alluring and vulnerable at the same time, and allowing for a constant play between aspects of her fictional character and her offscreen persona. In *Gentlemen Prefer Blondes* (1953) she plays a manipulative golddigger, but one too dumb to succeed in exploiting her millionaire fiancé. While she spends much of the movie berating Jane Russell for always falling in love with men without money ("I keep telling her, it's just as easy to fall in love with a rich man as a poor man"), she doesn't know what a letter of credit is when her fiancé gives her one. When he explains that it is "like money," she tells him, "Be sure and write me every day. I'll be so lonesome." If her performance is an attempt to provide a credible impersonation of the fictional character, it is completely unconvincing, but the playing with type is not intended to convince so much as amuse. Monroe and Russell's competition for the audience's attention turns their performances into a contest on an industrial level between the two stars as stars, but this has very little to do with the characters they are playing.

In the production of a star vehicle, the character is adapted to fit the star. A frequently used mechanism, in the story of the "reluctant hero," for instance, centers the plot on a character who eventually displays the skills that the audience already knows the performer possesses. A convincing performance is thus one in which the character becomes the star persona as the movie progresses: Gary Cooper in *Meet John Doe* (1941), Janet Gaynor in *A Star is Born* (1937), Bette Davis in *The Letter* (1940), or "the heroines of all Jane Fonda movies [who] begin as apolitical airheads, undergo sartorial and intellectual transformation, and end up as Jane Fonda."[56]

Cathy Klaprat has traced Bette Davis's early career as a sequence of experiments by her studio to develop a star persona for her. Using fan mail, sneak previews, exhibitor preferences, and box-office grosses as guides, Warner Bros. built her persona around the performances that produced the most favorable audience reaction. Davis's success in *Of Human Bondage* (made on a loan-out to RKO in 1934) established "the correct match between narrative role and actor," and led to repetitions of the role of "deadly seductress" in her next two movies, *Bordertown* (1935) and *Dangerous* (1935), as well as a representation of Davis "herself" as being "fiery, independent . . . definitely not domesticated . . . hard-boiled and ruthless, determined to get what she wants" in the fan magazines.[57]

Once Davis's persona had been sufficiently firmly fixed in the public imagination, however, it opened up opportunities for "offcasting" in roles opposite from those of her established image: as the good woman in *The Great Lie* (1941), for example, which advertised itself by announcing that *"contrary* to the former Davis pattern Bette Davis' new film does not find her killing anyone or acting nasty." The marketing logic of offcasting was simple. Davis was contracted to appear in three movies a year. Audiences might well tire of seeing three similar performances, but with offcasting the studio could invoke audience expectations while offering something different at the same time. Movie adverts repeatedly offered audiences the chance to see a star "as you've never seen her before." Offcasting was one way of extending a star's box-office potential through a form of product variation. It also enhanced the star's image as a great performer.

> Portraying only one type of character made the star vulnerable to charges that she wasn't acting but "just being herself." . . . However, once the studio offcast the star it could claim, "There are as many Bette Davises as there are Bette Davis-starring pictures! That's part of Miss Davis' greatness: the ability to make each character she plays stand by itself, a distinct and memorable triumph of screen acting."[58]

Negotiations such as these involving Monroe and Davis are the common currency in which the star system conveys information through convention and audience expectation, rather than a more realist-inspired characterization. The frequency with which this happens suggests the extent to which a mythological knowledge of Hollywood, derived from fan magazines or gossip columns, is assumed by the film industry. There could be no more graphic demonstration of the way that Hollywood addresses its audience as competent viewers of the fiction and as socialized subjects; that is, as consumers. Criticisms of typecasting misunderstand the industrial function of a star performance, where the audience must first recognize Clark Gable as Clark Gable, and then transform their engagement with Gable's presence into an investment in the character he plays and the story being told. This normal audience activity complicates any discussion of the psychological realism of any particular performance. As we have suggested, psychological plausibility is often offered as the explanation of plot development, but in a cinema so firmly framed by generic convention and star performance the plausibility of a performance may turn out to be at odds with the generically determined development of the plot. We can, for instance, take pleasure in the likable psychopaths Claude Akins plays in *Rio Bravo* and *Comanche Station* (1960) because we know that the Hollywood Western will restore order and moral certainty by its conclusion. The audience, suggests Robert Sklar, "can like a bad man who it knows is doomed."[59]

If performance can play against narrative inevitability in this way, in a different sense it can also determine the outcome of a plot. Questions raised at the level of the plot can be resolved at the level of performance, as the audience's attention is displaced away from the issues at stake in the fiction toward how the stars exhibit themselves under the pressure of those issues. On occasion this has proved to be useful to a cinema wishing to exploit political subject matter without abandoning its commitment to entertainment. In *All the President's Men* (1976), two junior reporters on a Washington newspaper uncover a story of political corruption that will eventually bring down a president. Although Robert Redford, who produced the movie, wanted to cast two unknowns in the central roles, he was unable to raise finance for the project unless the parts were played by stars; in the event, by Dustin Hoffman and himself. The movie is much preoccupied with the documentary accuracy of its representation: a good deal of it is played out on a set that precisely copies the *Washington Post* office, even down to transporting the contents of the actual office's wastepaper bins. Ultimately, however, the movie succumbs to the industrial logic of the star system, abandoning its documentary aesthetic. In a key scene toward the end of the movie, the investigation is about to stall unless Redford's character can extract some information from his contact in the White House, Deep Throat (Hal Holbrook). Deep Throat begins by refusing to do more than confirm information gleaned from other sources, as he has throughout the movie. But this is not enough, because the movie is already two hours long and must achieve a resolution. Redford, producer and star, exerts his industrial muscle. "Cut out the chickenshit and tell me what I need to know," he demands. For no convincing fictional reason, Deep Throat concedes, and reveals all Redford needs to know to expose the president. He succumbs not so much to the moral rectitude of the character Redford plays as to Redford's charismatic force as a star. The resolution, along with the audience's attention, is displaced from the movie's fiction to its status as a commodity.

To summarize: any individual performative act in a Hollywood movie can be seen as operating somewhere between the poles of autonomy and integration. Taking these as base terms, we can construct a table of oppositions that provides a structuring frame onto which individual performances can be mapped:

Autonomous performance	*Integrated performance*
Action	Acting
Presentational	Representational
Visibility	Invisibility
Display	Disguise
Spectacle	Narrative
Excessive	Motivated
Technical skill	Character psychology
Low status	High status

Few Hollywood performances would be so schematic as to fall entirely into one category, however. Different tendencies are emphasized at particular moments, or else are characteristic of particular performers, and most Hollywood movies are organized to accommodate both kinds of performance, and to produce tension between them. Sometimes the functions are split between performers in a single movie, as in the straight and crazy pairing of numerous screen comedy teams (Dean Martin and Jerry Lewis, for instance). Hollywood's most common strategy, however, is to synthesize them, simultaneously generating the pleasures of spectacular display and those of a more realist characterization. Even the most integrated performance contains an element of display; even the most autonomous routine contributes something to our understanding of a character's motivation.

Allowing for some variation in the relative authority given to the performances of stars and character actors, movies generally establish a broadly uniform acting style, by such simple means as having characters adopt convincingly similar accents.[60] The requirements of narrative economy, however, commonly mean that the smaller the part, the more its performance will resort to conventional signs of character type, broad gesture, and caricature. In *Acting in the Cinema*, James Naremore uses the term "ostensiveness" to designate the degree to which a performance is marked out as a performance for its audience, aligning it with the quality actor Sam Waterston has called "visibility."[61] To maintain the plausibility, performances within a movie must operate with roughly equal degrees of ostensiveness. While this uniformity may make performance conventions invisible to a contemporary audience, these conventions change over time to renew the effect of the real in performance. As historians of screen acting have often demonstrated, acting styles once read as natural subsequently often seem contrived, highly coded, and artificial. Equally, with the passage of time and the completion of a career, a star's presence tends to overwhelm the presence of character in his or her performances: in *The Shootist* (1976) we witness not so much the death from cancer of J.B. Books, famous fictional lawman, as that of John Wayne, whose last performance this was.

A History of Hollywood Acting: The Method

> In America, there is an opinion prevalent among actors, managers and the public at large to the effect that all work done on the stage should be the result of temperament rather than study; that if any study is given, it should be entirely personal, and should come from the actor's observation of his *own* emotions. More than this, they declare, is injurious, and will make one mechanical and elocutionary.
>
> Genevieve Stebbins[62]

> Acting is the expression of a neurotic impulse.
>
> Marlon Brando[63]

Although they took place less than a year apart, it is hard to imagine a style of screen performance more distant from Donald O'Connor's routine in

Singin' in the Rain than Marlon Brando's performance as Stanley Kowalski in *A Streetcar Named Desire* (1951). The performance style known as Method acting took shape during the 1930s in the work of New York's Group Theater, where Lee Strasberg taught his version of the theories of Russian director Constantin Stanislavski. Although others disputed Strasberg's interpretation,[64] the "Stanislavski system" emerged as a dominant force on the American stage immediately after World War II, when it was principally associated with a group of performers attached to the Actors' Studio in New York.[65] Although many of its practitioners were hostile to what they saw as Hollywood's crass commercialism, an increasing number of Method-trained actors – Montgomery Clift, Lee J. Cobb, Karl Malden – began working in movies in the early 1950s. In 1955 the Method achieved ascendancy in Hollywood when *On the Waterfront* won seven Academy Awards, including Brando's for Best Actor, and it subsequently came to represent in the public imagination an explanation of how a serious American acting performance was constructed. By the 1960s, the Method had been absorbed into mainstream acting practice to such an extent that audiences watching *The Godfather Part II* (1974) were offered no visible stylistic grounds for distinguishing between the performance of Actors' Studio devotee Al Pacino and that of Robert Duvall, who had distanced himself from the particular techniques of Strasberg's Method. In becoming the dominant account of how actors create naturalist performances, the Method had also become invisible.

In the 1940s and 1950s, however, when the Method's style of performance visibly challenged the protocols of Hollywood acting, its advocates argued that it constituted a radical break with previous theories of acting. The work of Stanislavski and his American interpreters was held up as offering a theoretical base for the profession of acting. More than just a set of techniques for achieving psychological realism in characterization, the Method proposed "a codifiable discipline, a teachable tradition, for acting."[66] It emphasized improvisation, ensemble playing, and emotional expressiveness, and it identified "the actor's own personality not merely as a model for the creation of character, but as the mine from which all psychological truth must be dug."[67]

Method acting is in one sense highly visible: we are usually intensely aware of the effort involved in the creation of a Method performance. On the other hand, the Method seeks to abolish the distinction between the actor and the role, and with it the artificialities and histrionics of other acting techniques it sees as insincere. The idea that the actor has "got inside" the character's psyche marks the performance as more "authentic" than other styles, creating a pure presence of character unadulterated by any sense of the performer's separate identity. But the Method's emphasis on the presence of the performer provided new opportunities for star exploitation, and before long its mannerisms of authenticity became codified into a stylistic resource to be drawn upon by generations of subsequent actors. The Method's quest for emotional truth in the unconscious of the actor rather than in the dramatic text also lent weight to the movies' emphasis on personality. However often its most enthusiastic advocates denounced the industry's vulgar commercialism, the physical organization of movie production – the short time between rehearsal and performance, which encourages improvisation, the camera's inevitable attention to detail, Hollywood's concern with character psychology as a motivating force in the plot – made the Method the performance style most able to deliver an effect of human "presence" in the machine of the movies.

Method acting is not, however, a technique so much as an approach to the creation of performance, an approach marked by its obsession with the "self" of the actor. Strasberg observed that "the actor need not imitate a human being. The actor is himself a human being and can create out of himself." The creation from the self was understood as an expressly psychological procedure, akin to therapy. An actor: "can possess technical ability to do certain things and yet may have difficulty expressing them because of his emotional life. The approach to this actor's problem must therefore deal first with whatever difficulties are inherent in himself that negate his freedom of expression and block the capacities he possesses."[68] Most contentiously, the Method's psycho-theatrical exercises encouraged the development of "affective memory" in its actors, by which they learned to manipulate their own psychological histories to identify with the character in creating the performance.[69] By understanding his or her own deepest motivations, anxieties, and drives, the actor could produce the appropriate surface behavior to convince the audience of the character's existence as a psychologically complex individual. In his sessions in the Actors' Studio, Strasberg encouraged actors to relive or imagine an experience for themselves alone, and many of the descriptions of the Method place the acting teacher (usually Strasberg) in the role of psychoanalyst. Acting was presented as a form of therapy, and the actor as the hero of a psychological adventure, probing his or her own psyche in order to comprehend that of his or her character's.

In comparison to the Classical Hollywood style, the Method was relatively representational: while Classical performance sought to fulfill the requirements of the plot with a minimum of psychological embellishment, the Method incorporated into its understanding of realism a sense of character as more complex and less subservient to the plot function he or she bore. At the same time, its commitment to authenticity ensured that the characters created by Method-inspired performances remained immersed within the warp and weave of the narration. While Classical Hollywood constructed characters to fit an already existing star persona, the Method's relation to character was more complex. Part of its claim to realism lay in the adaptability of its performers to an already established text, again registering a degree of cultural prestige in the literary and theatrical forms. But although in one sense Method actors seemed constantly to work on the edge of disappearance into their roles, the mannerisms of the Method were as visible as those of the comedian-comic. Where Donald O'Connor was admired for escaping from his role into a routine, Brando and James Dean were lauded for their skill in confining themselves to an expressive range plausible in terms of their character's psychology. Generally this involved distinctive patterns of body movement and vocal delivery, featuring a highly indirect and equivocal mode of addressing the audience, in contrast to the near-direct address of the comedian-comic. Brando's performances, in particular, were distinctively paced, slowed down by hesitations, measured pauses, and contemplative offscreen gazes. No movie with Brando, suggests Foster Hirsch, could be "action-packed."[70]

Brando's performance in *A Streetcar Named Desire* employs the conventions of Method acting in their most extreme forms and in a way that underlines their dissent from the rhetoric of what was then the dominant version of naturalist acting style. But the movie also suggests how the Method's representational emphasis allowed its techniques to be absorbed by the Classical Hollywood cinema, renovating rather than overturning mainstream style. The movie's director, Elia Kazan, described the intended effect of the Method as being to provide "a surface realism and strong feelings underneath,"[71] and insisted that

> *Streetcar* is the first non-sentimental picture we have made over here. It's a landmark. Its issues are not oversimplified, and you're not in there "rooting for somebody" – all that old shit the motion picture industry is built upon. There is no hero, no heroine; the people are people, some dross, some gold, with faults and virtues – and for a while you are muddled about them, the way you would be in life.[72]

Brando had achieved theatrical stardom when he played the male lead, Stanley Kowalski, in the Broadway production of Tennessee Williams' play in 1947, and the movie followed the original as closely as the Production Code would allow.[73] The neurotic Blanche DuBois (Vivien Leigh) arrives in New Orleans to stay with her sister Stella (Kim Hunter), and is gradually destroyed by the brutal behavior of Stella's husband Stanley. From the outset, Brando's acting functions to register Stanley's complexity and contradictions. His machismo and latent aggression are set against his childishness, his assertiveness contrasts with his vulnerability, the conviction of his body language plays against the inarticulacy of his speech. A dense network of signs is orchestrated to communicate a spontaneity and authenticity defined by its disturbance of performance conventions. His speech is vernacular, heavily accented, and often mumbled. He is incessantly chewing gum, and his facial expressions change abruptly, breaking into sudden grins or puzzled stares. His posture appears comfortably at ease one moment, tense and intimidating the next, and he has a collection of apparently involuntary behavioral tics. The muscularity of his body signals the physical threat he poses to Blanche. He paces constantly and is prone to sudden explosive action, at one point hurling a radio set through a window. According to James Scott,

Stanley Kowalski (Marlon Brando) and Blanche DuBois (Vivien Leigh) in *A Streetcar Named Desire* (1951). Aquarius Picture Library

In *Streetcar* Brando evidently built his performance around his sense of Stanley Kowalski's animal aggressiveness. Sometimes this is innocently canine, as when his incessant scratching of back and belly remind us of a dog going after fleas. But the Kowalski character is also destructive, as we are told in Brando's use of the mouth: he chews fruit with loud crunching noises, munches up potato chips with the same relentless jaw muscles, washes beer around in his mouth and then swallows it with physically noticeable gulps.[74]

But for all its intermittent excessiveness, as in Stanley's increasingly hyperbolic exchange with Blanche immediately before her collapse, the combination of these signs allows the viewer to build up a sense of Stanley's character in all its inconsistency through an apparently seamless flow of completely "natural" behavior.

To a cinema peopled by recognizable types performing generically prescribed functions and by stars occupying roles tailored to their known personalities, the Method was very disruptive, reducing the security previously afforded the viewer by characterization and performance style. It ascribed multiple, even contradictory, traits to characters, and as a result the Method made the motivation for action less predictable and the direction in which a character would turn uncertain. The audience's vulnerability to the whim of the fiction intensifies their involvement, and with it the apparent power of the performance. In *A Streetcar Named Desire*, Brando's performance so details Stanley's character that the future direction of the plot is very much in doubt. Only a prior knowledge of the play-text can supply a reassuring counter to the uncertainty generated by Brando's performance.

Stylistic innovations in performance almost invariably lay claim to a greater degree of realism than the mainstream style they are challenging. The Method, with its emphasis on the psychological investigation of both character and actor, was certainly no exception to this rule. But invoking "realism" as a description of a performance style – as in actress Maureen Stapleton's description of the Method's aim as being "to be true, to be real, to be true to the part"[75] – is just as much a rhetorical gesture as the claims of color, widescreen, and other technological innovations to bring "greater realism." The Method's rhetoric appeared to make large moral and mystical claims for "the power of truth in acting,"[76] but its ascendancy in the postwar decade had much to do with the appropriateness of its performance style to both the dramas and the cultural concerns of the time. In many respects the "realism" of Method acting in the 1950s, like that of the widescreen technology it coincided with, can be thought of as a kind of excess, packaged as spectacle, and in *East of Eden* and *Rebel Without a Cause* (both 1955) the excesses of James Dean's performance style served to fill the excess space of the CinemaScope frame.

The Method also addressed postwar American culture's preoccupation with psychoanalysis. Its construction of character in psychoanalytic terms corresponded to the psychological themes of postwar American drama and, increasingly, Hollywood. According to Thomas Atkins, the most effective Method roles – which are almost invariably male – are "characters with a subtle anxiety within them but with little external power to cope with it . . . divided parts based on the unresolved tension between an outer social mask and an inner reality of frustration that usually has a sexual basis." Because of the pressure of this conflict, they appear constantly "on the verge of breaking down, falling to pieces, or becoming violent."[77] Steve Vineberg suggests that the Method's popularity in the 1950s was mainly a consequence of the fact that "the rebel without a cause was the exclusive turf of Method actors."[78] Certainly, its emphasis on emotional meaning over other aspects of character succeeded in investing male performance with a degree of emotional expressiveness not seen since silent melodrama, and emphatically reasserted the connection between the display of emotion and "good acting." Method performances in the 1950s thus combined psychoanalysis and melodrama, and concentrated audiences' attention on the male psyche of Brando, Dean, and the characters they enacted.[79]

Much more explicitly than the performance styles of Classical Hollywood's star vehicles, the Method registered the distinction between actor and character, and exposed a fundamental tension between two opposed impulses in acting performance: naturalism and expressionism. The Method's concern with psychological realism attached it to the dominant tradition of naturalism in American acting, but Method performances were very visibly performances, collections of expressive gestures and techniques. Writing in 1966 in a manual *On Method Acting*, Edward Dwight Easty advised actors learning the Method to:

> Always remember that for an actor to give the appearance of reality, he cannot pretend or make believe he is thinking. . . . His thoughts must be real thoughts in order to produce real and believable actions. Remember, too, the audience never knows the thoughts which go on in the actor's mind and any which produce real behavior can and should be utilized.[80]

Easty's terminology catches the ambivalences of performance: his actor must communicate the action of thinking, and thus he or she must really think and not just pretend. The audience, however, will not recognize thought, or even thinking, so much as a series of gestural signs which convey the impression of thinking: the head angled down, a hand to the forehead, eyes focused on vacant space. These gestures, of course, are conventional, already known by the audience, and are realistic to the extent that they are recognizable as gestures in the everyday world. For Easty, the Method's techniques inflect and individualize the shared body of conventional signs to give the appearance of reality, and to achieve this appearance, the actor must discover a psychologically convincing justification for each of the character's actions. All of an actor's "actions, behavior and 'business' must have a purpose . . . they must have *real* reasons, reasons that are real to the actor's instrument. . . . These reasons are the actor's motivations."[81] These motivations are not, however, visible to the audience: they must work for the actor, so that he or she can produce the performance signs that persuade the audience. Although the actor must be convinced of the psychological "truth" of his or her character's actions, he or she must himself or herself become a spectacle of sign and gesture to communicate that psychological verisimilitude.

Easty's version of the Method occupies an extreme position in a long-established debate about acting. In *The Paradox of Acting*, written in 1773, the French philosopher Denis Diderot argued that the actor ought not to feel the character's emotion during a performance, but should instead concentrate on the technical devices by which he produces the effects of that emotion for the audience – on what Inez and Helen Klumph later called "the mechanics of emotion."[82] In his discussion of the actor's "dual consciousness," Constant Coquelin argued that "the true actor" was dispassionate:

> He commands us to laugh, to weep, to shiver with fear. He needs not wait until he experiences these emotions himself, or for grace to fall from above to enlighten him . . . the actor needs not to be actually moved. It is as unnecessary as it is for a pianist to be in the depths of despair to play the funeral march of Chopin or of Beethoven aright. He knows it; he opens his instrument, and your soul is harrowed.[83]

Diderot's approach encouraged a more rigidly conventionalized style of performance, in which the meaning of gestures could be codified with much the same precision as language possessed, and emotion could be objectified as a public gesture. During the nineteenth century a number of authors produced manuals of rhetorical gesture and "dramatic expression," in which actors could learn the appropriate pose to communicate pity, despondency, or pride.[84] Probably the most influential of these writers was a Parisian elocutionist, François Delsarte, whose analysis of what he called the "semeiotic" function of gesture was a major element in the training methods used in American theater schools at the end of the century, as well as in "recitation books" and courses in public speaking.[85] Both pantomime and melodrama employ the idea of a vocabulary of gesture, but the Delsartean proposition that the language of the body can be understood as a language was countered by a more naturalistic impulse, in part encouraged by the dramas of Ibsen, Chekhov, and Shaw.[86] These dramatists' concern with the inner psychological reality of their characters produced a quieter, more prosaic performance style, and made the semiotic conception of acting ("signal acting") appear overblown, flamboyant, and "melodramatic" in its most pejorative sense.[87] But Delsarte's system, which was far more nuanced than his later detractors suggested,[88] made it clear that acting is a semiotic activity: the audience comprehends emotions by recognizing their signs. Psychological theories of acting, of which the Method is the most famous, concentrate on the means by which an actor produces signs of emotion, but semiotic theories such as Delsarte's remind us that an audience does not intuit a character's emotion but recognizes it through a process of signification, and that as with any process of signification, there must be a consensus between actor and audience about the relationship between the emotion signified and the signifier the actor uses. Even the most internally motivated Method actor must use a range of gestures the audience will understand:

> The actor's art is to express in well-known symbols what an individual man may be supposed to feel; and we, as spectators, recognizing these expressions, are drawn into sympathy. In other words, we respond to the mental ideal of the actor, and so form a magnetic rapport with his artistic creation. But unless the actor follows nature sufficiently close to select symbols recognized as natural, he fails to touch us.[89]

EXTREME DESPAIR.   SURPRISE MIXED WITH FRIGHT.

COMPOUND MOVEMENT OF PAIN. VIOLENT MOVEMENT.

Late nineteenth-century acting manuals codified gestures and expressions, and described in detail how an actor could learn to arrange his or her face, hands and body to communicate the desired emotion to the audience. In *The Actor's Art: A Practical Treatise on Stage Declamation, Public Speaking and Deportment, for the Use of Artists, Students and Amateurs*, published in 1882, Gustave Garcia declared that acting "can be taught, like grammar, by means of a series of rules." The pictures reproduced here illustrate the "semeiotic" project of classifying "each movement of the face or action of the body according to the sentiments or passion that is to be expressed." In the expression of violent emotions, the features of the face "become disordered and take all sorts of directions, upwards, downwards, and lateral." Garcia's codification of gesture allowed him to prescribe the "attitudes and actions" an actor should perform to communicate a particular emotion to the audience. While later and more naturalistic performance styles would question the prescriptive quality of Garcia's project, his basic proposition that the actions of an actor communicate the thoughts of the character he or she is playing to the audience through a recognizable set of gestures, remains central to the audience's understanding of performance in Hollywood movies.

Source: Gustave Garcia, *The Actor's Art*, London, Pettitt, 1882

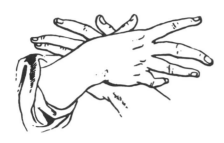

Grace.

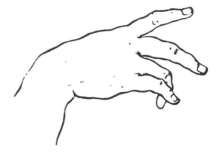

Elevated mind, taste and dexterity.

Energy, capable of great under-
takings.

Imploring.

Codified gestures (above and opposite)
Garcia suggested that "we express our sentiments by the direction we give
to the palm of the hand. If the sentiment we wish to indicate is favorable,
the hand will take an upward direction, and the reverse where the sentiment is unfavorable." To convey a sense of disgust, fear, contempt or anger
an actor was advised to arrange his or her face, hands and body into the
attitudes shown opposite.

Source: Gustave Garcia, *The Actor's Art*, London, Pettitt, 1882

Much of the debate within dramatic theory about the actor's expression of emotion took very little notice of the audience's reception of those emotions, and remained a largely internal debate among actors and their teachers about how acting performance should be constructed. Stanislavski, the most influential exponent of the new naturalist style of the late nineteenth century, has been the central figure in these debates in this century. Stanislavski's name appears on three textbooks on performance, but only the first of them, *An Actor Prepares*, was published during his lifetime. *An Actor Prepares* stressed the importance of spontaneity, improvisation, and introspection in the training of actors and the construction of performances. Published in America in 1936, *An Actor Prepares* provided the inspiration and the theoretical basis for the Method as formulated by Strasberg in the Group Theater and the Actors' Studio, but Stanislavski's later books, published after his death in 1938, contradicted much of Strasberg's practice by placing much less emphasis on psychological preparation and much more on the external elements of performance.[90] Stanislavski's various interpreters have argued that "the Stanislavski system" constitutes the most fully developed theoretical basis for acting and its teaching, although few of them agree on what that basis is. But whether it derived its principles from Stanislavski or not, a naturalistic performance style – one that emphasized emotional verisimilitude and the actor's use of his or her own personality in constructing a role – dominated American drama on stage and in cinema throughout the century. Strasberg acknowledged as much in his observation that "The simplest examples of Stanislavski's ideas are actors such as Gary Cooper, John Wayne and Spencer Tracy. They try not to act but to be themselves, to respond or react.

They refuse to do or say anything they feel not to be consonant with their own characters."[91] We could add a great many other names to Strasberg's list, but rather than claim Barbara Stanwyck, for example, as an "untrained Method actor," it would be more accurate to see the Method as a variant on the mainstream naturalist tradition rather than a revolutionary change in American acting techniques.

Valentino

> A Heart Breaker! A Record Breaker! . . . An eye feast of virile action, colorful settings and glowing climaxes.
> Advertisement for *The Son of the Sheik* (1926)[92]

As well as providing the main motive force for a movie's narration through the elaboration of character, Hollywood's performance styles have offered their audiences idealized versions of human behavior, and in particular of what it is to be masculine or feminine in American culture. At times – Brando's combination of sexual aggression and neurotic vulnerability in his early 1950s roles, for instance – these ideal types have confronted cultural norms, and moral conservatives have consistently found more to object to in Hollywood's performances than in its stories. Rudolph Valentino, with whom Brando has sometimes been compared, provided one of the movies' earliest and most significant questionings of the dominant representation of gender in the wider American culture.

Acting has always been a disreputable profession. In puritanical cultures, "playing" is what children do, not a job of work, while to pretend to be someone you are not is, outside the theater, most often the behavior of a criminal.[93] If the act of performance is inevitably associated with deception and dissimulation, the spectacle of performance has also been understood to carry moral dangers. At best it is identified as a site of voyeurism: in the safe space of the theater, the audience vicariously experiences the actors' passionate exhibition. At worst, it is held responsible for stimulating desire and leading to imitation.[94] As early as 1908, newspaper reports and advocates of censorship argued that the movies produced a cycle of addiction and crime: children watched movies in which criminal acts were committed, and then imitated the crimes to steal the money to attend the movies. More often, however, the moralists' concern has been with sexual rather than criminal behavior, and the theater has long been seen in European and American culture as a site of sexual license, its performers viewed with a mixture of envy and disapproval.[95] In their well-publicized "private" lives, actors have provided their audiences with another form of voyeuristic satisfaction. Audiences could vicariously violate cultural taboos by consuming accounts of the players' unconventional behavior, and enjoy imagining what the liberation from social restrictions would feel like, without themselves having to suffer the consequences.[96]

The actor's position in society began to change in the last quarter of the nineteenth century, as players' organizations made self-conscious attempts to improve their social status and new popular magazines developed a culture of celebrity. The movies inherited the star system, as well as some stars, from the stage: Valentino's predecessors included America's first "matinee idol," Henry Montague, a theatrical star of the 1870s whose sudden death at the height of his popularity was, like Valentino's, the occasion for a frenzy of public mourning on the part of his female fans. Matinees were afternoon performances, overwhelmingly attended by women, who used them as opportunities for an emotional expression otherwise denied them by social convention: "at the matinee, surrounded by other women, she could give vent to her desire to shout, blow kisses, even swoon at the sight of her idol making love to the lucky woman on the stage."[97] By 1912 the movies of Maurice Costello and Francis X. Bushman, America's "Most Handsome Man," were providing their audiences with similar opportunities for emotional satisfaction.

A star system began to take shape in the movies after 1907, as movies with actors came to be differentiated from other types, and individual actors were identified as "picture personalities" whose movie characters were created from the performer's own personality: Mary Pickford's "Little Mary," for example.[98] By 1914 the personality had evolved into the star. More attention was paid to the players' existence outside their movie appearances, and their private lives became increasingly a matter of public knowledge. During the 1910s, industry-controlled publicity emphasized the stars' health and moral virtue, implicitly contrasting the movies with the more questionable behavior of theater people. But a series of heavily publicized scandals in the early 1920s – Mary Pickford's divorce and remarriage to Douglas Fairbanks, the star Wallace Reid's death from heroin addiction, the unsolved murder of director William Desmond Taylor, and, most notoriously, the trial of comedian Fatty Arbuckle for the manslaughter of "starlet" Virginia Rappe – gave the tabloid press all the opportunities they needed to assert that behind the images constructed by Hollywood's publicists lay a secret world of social unconventionality and moral turpitude.

More blatantly than any previous male star, Valentino was presented in his movies as an object of desire, an erotic body to be exhibited and gazed at. In most of his movies Valentino's beautiful body was undressed, and in many of them, including *The Son of the Sheik*, it was beaten or whipped, perhaps to punish its beauty. The oscillation between sadism and masochism – Valentino often threatens the women in the movie who desire him with sexual violence – is only one of several ambivalences in his presentation as a figure of both power and weakness, alternatively (sometimes simultaneously) master and victim of the desiring gaze. This ambivalence about Valentino's sexual role extended, inevitably, to his star persona: he

The Son of the Sheik (1926): Rudolph Valentino's desiring gaze at Yasmin (Vilma Banky). United Artists (courtesy Kobal)

was rumored to be homosexual, impotent, dependent on domineering women, a "tango pirate" and gigolo who had lived off women, and at the same time a bigamist whose second wife, Natasha Rambova, gave him a platinum "slave bracelet" but kept their marriage unconsummated because of her lesbian relationship with Alla Nazinova.[99] But the enigma of Valentino's sexuality lay at least as much in the desiring audience as in the object of desire, and none of Valentino's own attempts to demonstrate his virility through publicity of him boxing or fencing had any effect in countering the assertion that he was a "Pink Powder Puff."[100]

Valentino's image needs to be placed in its historical setting. In the 1920s women's sexual desire became, for the first time in American culture, a subject of public discussion as a "new feminism" concerned with women's personal expression and satisfaction substituted for the overtly political feminism that had achieved women's suffrage in 1920. The language and preoccupations of modern psychology began to appear in social commentary, where the emancipation of female desire was most often seen as a threat to family, civilization, and American masculinity. "If it is true that man once shaped woman to be the creature of his desires and needs," wrote Lurine Pruette in 1927, "then it is true that woman is now remodeling man."[101] The movies, which sociologist E.A. Ross believed were making the young more "sex-wise, sex-excited, and sex-absorbed" than any previous generation,[102] were identified as a prime site of this cultural revolution, and the anxieties it provoked were focused most intensely on the body of Valentino, who seemed to personify the extent to which the "woman-made man" differed from the established ideals of American masculinity. Even more disturbing than his androgynous dancer's body was his "exoticism." Valentino, the "Latin Lover," invoked a set of racist stereotypes about the excessive, predatory sexuality of the ethnic or racial Other at precisely the historical moment when the United States was restricting immigration in a climate of xenophobia and nativism. Valentino threatened the norms of "100 percent American" masculinity because despite "his small eyes, his flat nose and his large mouth," and his failure "to measure up to the standards of male beauty usually accepted in this country,"[103] women, both on the screen and in the "Valentino traps" of the movies, desired to look at him. And male commentators who feared that female desire would lead to a "mongrelization" of the Anglo-Saxon race were unappeased by – or more likely simply did not hear – the comments of female fans that their relationship with the screen was more complex, that, as one put it, "we are speaking of actors and their acting and not of intermarriage with them." It was true, wrote another,

> that our feminine hearts go pit-a-pat when we see Valentino up on the screen. . . . But when the lights go up on every day life once more, how perfectly splendid it is for American women to have one hundred percent, plain, American husbands, who treat them as pals and equals and love them for saving pennies for the children's future, instead of spending them on sunken marble baths.[104]

Issues of race are part of the fabric of Valentino's movies, most evidently in his most famous role as *The Sheik* (1921), where the movie's plot both exploits aspects of his star image and tries to defuse hostility to that image by qualifying it. The exotic figure of sexual aggression ("When an Arab sees a woman he wants, he takes her," announced the movie's advertising), turns out in the plot to be the son of English and Spanish nobility, and once his secret is known, his behavior becomes much more restrained. His subsequent movies often provided him with some version of a doubled characterization, in which he would have to renounce "Valentino" to win the love of a deserving woman.[105] These movies thus negotiated the contradictions of his persona within their stories, but since those contradictions embodied cultural concerns much larger than Valentino or even the movies, a plot-line could hardly resolve them. Although it repeated this narrative pattern, Valentino's last movie, *The Son of the Sheik*, took a more ironic attitude to his star persona. Since the movie was released immediately after his sudden death in August 1926, the ironies of this interpretation were overridden in the "notorious necrophilic excesses" of his public mourning.[106]

The Son of the Sheik is one of silent Hollywood's last movies. Within a few months of its release, "talkies" would begin to alter Hollywood's performance styles and its organization of camera movement. Without the resource of synchronized dialogue, silent film depended on movement as a source of signification and meaning for audiences. Characterization and story relied on gesture and action, and audience attention was sustained by a mobile image, in which camera movement and editing played as important a performative role as the actors. But as we suggested in our discussion of *Sunny Side Up* (1929), the arrival of sound confirmed stylistic changes that were already under way, and although *The Son of the Sheik* frequently revels in the rhetoric and expressive techniques of much earlier cinema, some of its performance strategies anticipate the arrival of the talkies.

As a typical star vehicle, *The Son of the Sheik* organizes its mise-en-scène to emphasize the performances of its leading players. Valentino plays two roles, the eponymous hero "young" Ahmed, and his father from the earlier movie, Ahmed Ben Hassan. The movie showcases Valentino's personal repertoire of gestures – what James Naremore has called the star's "idiolect"[107] – and it adds a further fascination with performance in those scenes in which, through processing work and doubling, Ahmed and his father apparently play together. Agnes Ayres, who had portrayed the heroine in *The Sheik*, reappears as Ahmed's mother, Diana, while the new heroine, Yasmin, is played by MGM's new Hungarian "discovery," Vilma Banky. Pre-release publicity drew attention to this casting and the movie plays with cultural memories of *The Sheik*, using footage from it in one flashback sequence.

The movie's storyline could scarcely be more diagrammatic: Ahmed, a desert sheik, encounters and falls in love with a dancing girl, Yasmin. At the first of their rendezvous, Ahmed is taken prisoner and held to ransom by Yasmin's scheming father, André (George Fawcett), and his henchmen, led by the villainous Ghabah (Montague Love). After being tortured, Ahmed is rescued by his servant, Ramadan (Karl Dane), and returned to a friend's house. Believing that Yasmin had been a party to his kidnap, Ahmed determines on revenge and abducts Yasmin to his desert encampment, where he threatens her with physical and sexual violence. Across the desert, his father returns to his villa, and angered by his son's disappearance, leaves to bring him home. Meanwhile, relations between Ahmed and Yasmin are becoming more hostile by the minute ("I will hate you with my dying breath"), culminating in an attempt by Yasmin to kill her captor. When his father arrives, and the situation is explained, Ahmed is persuaded to release the girl. Ramadan escorts Yasmin to her camp, and learns of her innocence. He and Ahmed pursue her back to the town of Touggourt, where she is dancing in the casbah. Yasmin and Ahmed finally declare their love for each other, but at the last moment she is abducted by Ghabah. Ahmed is joined by his father, and after a lengthy fight sequence, he kills Ghabah and rescues Yasmin. They ride off together into the desert.

Devoid of sub- or parallel plots, the action is presented as a series of clearly motivated movements and counter-movements, captures and rescues, chases and escapes, allowing ample opportunity for autonomous set-piece displays of Valentino's idiolect: swashbuckling fight sequences, horseback races-to-the-rescue, torrid love scenes. Between such sequences, there are moments of more introspective performance, particularly in scenes between Ahmed and Yasmin, and between Ahmed and his father. The autonomous, presentational performance of separable action sequences is balanced against the more integrated, representational performances of scenes between major characters. Although these shifts are not as explicit as in a musical, a similar rhythm is established across the movie in the alternation of action with familial melodrama.

Although Hollywood seeks to balance performances in order to create an untroubling consistency, within these limits it also varies that uniformity to create further levels of pleasurable play and demarcate the relative status of particular characters. Acting style varies across the movie, from the understatement of Valentino at his most statuesque, gazing significantly offscreen, to the gestural excess of Ramadan's wide-eyed stares and face-pulling and Ghabah's endless grimacing and snarling. The performances of major characters, and those approved by the plot,

Ahmed (Valentino) stripped and beaten for his beauty by the villainous Ghabah (Montague Love) in *The Son of the Sheik*. Courtesy BFI

pull toward a greater naturalism, while second leads, villains, and minor characters are marked by a Delsartean declamatory excess. Yasmin's father is a compendium of actorly poses, grimaces, and inflated gestures; Ghabah's outlaw band frequently squabble and fight in accelerated motion. This variation of volume, intensity, and ostensiveness suggests the way in which Hollywood uses performance as an agency of narrative clarity. The moral authority granted Valentino by the story is reinforced by codes of supposedly greater authenticity at the level of performance.

Such strategies also have ideological implications. In *The Son of the Sheik* distinctions in terms of acting style are mapped onto the representation of race, in which the daughter of a Frenchman must be rescued from the lascivious Moor for Ahmed's legitimate desire. What makes the movie's racism so visible is the contrast in performance styles between Valentino's Ahmed ("English born, Sahara bred, undisputed ruler in this sea of sand," an intertitle informs us) and Montague Love's Ghabah ("The Moor, whose crimes outnumber the sands"). By this maneuver Valentino is cast on the heroic side of the racial divide, "playing the white man" through the transparent codes of naturalism, while Love is consigned to a near-animal excess of ostensiveness. The contrast is even stronger between Ahmed's family, with Agnes Ayres' performance as Diana the most understated in the movie, and the opposing "family" of Ghabar. They are a gaggle of grotesques, described by an intertitle as "a vagrant troupe, entertainers by profession, thieves by preference," and reduced from the outset to parody and stereotype. The racial distinction employed in the contrast between "sophisticated" and "primitive" performance styles is also registered visually by differences in makeup: Valentino's face is a white screen, while Ghabar and his crew have the exaggerated features of painted masks.

The Son of the Sheik was made during a period of transition, and to an extent the major players seem caught between the more declamatory modes of the silent cinema and the increasingly naturalist emphases that would find fuller fruition in the sound era. Vilma Banky's performance anticipates much of the mainstream style of later cinema, making use of expressive objects to reduce the burden placed on face and body. A ring, first given her by Ahmed and then thrown away, becomes the means by which she registers loss and regret simply by a close-up in which one hand touches the now ringless finger on her other hand. Such detail contrasts with the broad gestures of minor characters: Ramadan indicates the imminent arrival of Ahmed's father by outlining the shape of his beard on his own face. But at times all the performers fall back on the formalized sign languages of body movement and gesture. On arriving at his desert villa, Ahmed's father registers anger at his son's disappearance by clenching his fist determinedly. Yasmin poses balletically as Ahmed carries her around the interior of a desert tent.[108] Even Valentino can never entirely resist the summary posturing or face-pulling characteristic of the most exteriorized of expressive techniques. His contempt for Yasmin is signaled by the narrowing of his eyes when he spots her bartering for a necklace in a Touggourt casbah. He stands, feet apart, arms folded across his chest, refusing her gaze. This unequivocal delivery contrasts with an acting style that elsewhere displays a greater hesitancy and spontaneity, and has to be interpreted through the subtlest of facial gestures.

It has been argued that the development of pantomimic styles was part of an attempt to reduce the number of intertitles needed by silent Hollywood. In this respect, performance style fulfilled a realist goal, at the same time that it introduced new areas of artificiality in other ways. In a similar vein, many critics thought that, at least for a while, the advent of sound brought a return to the more artificial conventions and mannerism of stage acting. It may be that the persistence of exaggerated elements within acting styles even to the present day – think of any Arnold Schwarzenegger performance, or Sylvester Stallone's pantomimic version of the Method in *Cliffhanger* (1993) – is symptomatic of the requirements of film performance: a tradition of summary gestures, postures, and expressions fits comfortably into a production context where performances are constructed from fragments of action, shot out of sequence, and assembled for maximum narrative and character economy. Screen performance can never really be considered in isolation, however, but as a reciprocal orchestration of bodily and gestural codes with those of mise-en-scène, camera placement, editing, and soundtrack. In *The Son of the Sheik* figure placement at times emphasizes presentation, displaying a marked tendency toward stage-like frontality in the way that static figures turn outward toward the camera while their faces are twisted toward each other, producing an effect often referred to as "rubbernecking." The presentational effect of direct address is simulated by the occasional equation of camera viewpoint and character point of view, as when Ahmed advances threateningly on Yasmin in his tent, and the audience is offered a "head-on" track-in on her, until her eyes fill the screen in extreme close-up. The disproportionately long action sequences also show a continued commitment to the "cinema of attractions," rooted less in the traditions of psychological realism than in the presentational modes of more popular theatrical entertainment. In general, however, *The Son of the Sheik* uses camera movement prosaically, to help maintain an unimpeded view of action and aid the processes of characterization that were once the sole preserve of bodily designation.

Combining the work of actors, cameramen, and editors, Hollywood maintains a loose equation between shot scale and degree of ostensiveness: extravagant action sequences are filmed in long shot, but performances are scaled down in closer shots to pick up nuances of facial expression and build a greater intimacy between characters and audiences.[109] Conversations are regularly presented in shot/reverse shot structures that provide all the accessibility of the more primitive frontal style without its artificiality. The close-up helps to do this by eliminating the actors' bodies. Other scenes reduce body motion to an absolute minimum, as characters indicate crisis not by gesturing excitedly, but scarcely using their bodies at all, their presences animated by editing or by the sheer concentration afforded by the close-up. *The Son of the Sheik* exploits this most intensely in the erotic charge it develops between Ahmed and Yasmin, something achieved through a series of **reverse-angle** close-ups which do away with the need for more tangible signs of their passion.

Editing has often been seen as a limitation on the expressive importance of the actor, since shooting out of sequence breaks the expressive coherence of a performance. More constructively, it can shift the register of performance to new levels of designation. Eyeline matches reduce action and response to a matter of pupil-dilation and near microscopic variations in eyebrow lines. In return, the development of more naturalist performance styles demands a tighter adherence to continuity editing. When gestures are made on a large scale, their continuity is less vulnerable to shifts in camera position. In the confrontation between Ahmed and his father over Yasmin, the camera crosses the center line, gaze directions are scrambled, and the apparent continuity of space itself is disrupted without serious damage to the legibility of the scene, because of the level of the playing. Where the equivocation of the less declamatory naturalist style is more developed, a centered perspective becomes more important, as a compensating stability for the uncertainty on the level of gesture.

By generating a flexibility and fluidity of point of view, editing and camera movement also mediate performances through the perspectives of other characters. **Cut-aways** to characters listening or being watched can suggest a clandestine inspection of characters caught apparently simply "being themselves." Richard Dyer has pointed to the particular importance of such "private moments" in the audience's interpretation of characters in Classical cinema.[110] One of several such moments in *The Son of the Sheik* reveals Ahmed, lost in thought after his rescue from Ghabah. An intertitle interprets: "Like all youths, he loved a dancing girl. Like all dancing girls, she tricked him." Ahmed is framed simply sitting still, his inaction filled with significance by what the shot and the intertitle reveal of him. Editing also blurs the boundary between actorly performance and surrounding mise-en-scène, enhancing the naturalist effect by lending a particular expressive importance to props, such as Yasmin's ring. Even without the aid of synchronized sound, the late silent cinema had evolved strategies of staging and narration that enabled screen acting to pull toward a greater psychological realism. At the same time, Hollywood exploited the audience's pleasure in Valentino's performance as an autonomous attraction in their marketing of the movie. By reconciling action and acting, *The Son of the Sheik* offers a multiplicity of pleasures, allowing performance to provide another form of the play between repetition and difference that is Hollywood cinema's primary means of audience satisfaction.

Notes

1 James Naremore, *Acting in the Cinema* (Berkeley, CA: University of California Press, 1988), p. 70.
2 Peter Brook, *The Empty Space* (Harmondsworth: Pelican, 1972), p. 55.
3 Vsevolod Pudovkin, "On Film Technique," in *Film Technique and Film Acting: The Cinema Writings of V.I. Pudovkin*, trans. Ivor Montagu (New York: Bonanza, 1949), p. 140.
4 Pudovkin, p. xiv.
5 Pudovkin, p. 54.
6 Lev Kuleshov, "Art of the Cinema," in *Kuleshov on Film: Writings by Lev Kuleshov*, ed. and trans. Ronald Levaco (Berkeley, CA: University of California Press, 1974), p. 54.
7 V.F. Perkins, *Film as Film* (Harmondsworth: Penguin, 1972), p. 106.
8 Stephen Prince and Wayne E. Hensley, "The Kuleshov Effect: Recreating the Classic Experiment," *Cinema Journal* 31:2 (Winter 1992), pp. 59–75.
9 Frank D. McConnell, *The Spoken Seen: Film and the Romantic Imagination* (Baltimore: Johns Hopkins University Press, 1975), p. 174. It was a position from which Pudovkin himself withdrew in his later work on *Film Acting*, written under the Stalinist imperatives of Socialist Realism: an "incorrect attitude to the tasks of acting work . . . has given rise to the pseudo-theory of the *montage* (edited) image (a theory for which no single individual is responsible). This theory deduces, from the fact that an impression of acting can be created by sticking pieces together, the illegitimate assumption that separate pieces, not connected inwardly within the actor, will necessarily give an optimum result . . . [but] the concept of the edited image by no means implies (as some have sought to declare) a negation of the necessity for unified work by the actor on his role." V.I. Pudovkin, *Film Acting*, in Pudovkin, pp. 37, 55, 70.
10 McConnell, p. 182.
11 This existential paradox, he argues, "is a continual scandal to formalist theories of art, theories which attempt to discuss the artwork as if it were a proportioned, elegant object with only tangential connections to our own disorderly act of living. It may well be that the failure of film criticism to discuss adequately the role of the actor is a function of its failure ever adequately to come to terms with the truly radical, romantic antiformalism of the medium." This last argument might have been directed specifically at Kuleshov and Pudovkin, and the formalist assumptions of their theory. McConnell, pp. 174, 168.
12 McConnell, p. 177.
13 Foster Hirsch describing Bette Davis in *The Little Foxes* (1941): Foster Hirsch, *Acting Hollywood Style* (New York: Abrams, 1991), p. 47.
14 Richard Dyer, *Stars* (London: British Film Institute, 1979), p. 166.
15 "Analogic codification constitutes a series of symbols that in their proportions and relations are similar to the thing, idea or event for which they stand. . . . Such a form of communication deals with continuous functions, unlike digital communication which deals with discrete step intervals." Jurgen Ruesch and Weldon Kees, *Non-verbal Communication: Notes on the Visual Perception of Human Relations* (Berkeley, CA: University of California Press, 1956), p. 8. An analogue clock, for example, tells you that it is "almost a quarter past three," while a digital clock insists that it is either 15.13 or 15.14.
16 Naremore, p. 2.
17 Pudovkin, *Film Acting*, pp. 26, 67, 70.

18 Stephen Rebello, *Alfred Hitchcock and the Making of Psycho* (New York: Dembner Books, 1990), pp. 113, 123, 131–5. One of Kuleshov's other experiments demonstrated the cinema's Frankenstein-like power to construct a body from disparate parts: "I photographed a girl sitting before her mirror, making up her eyes and eye-lashes, rouging her lips, lacing her shoes. Solely by means of montage we showed a living girl, but one who did not actually exist, because we had filmed the lips of one woman, the legs of another, the back of a third, the eyes of a fourth. We cemented these shots, fixing a certain relationship among them, and we obtained an entirely new personage, using nothing but completely real material." Quoted in Jay Leyda, *Kino: A History of the Russian and Soviet Film*, 3rd edn (Princeton, NJ: Princeton University Press, 1983), p. 165. A feminist critique of this experiment would emphasize the way that it fragments and fetishizes the female body.

19 McConnell, p. 175.

20 Dziga Vertov, "The Cine-Eyes. A Revolution," *Lef* 3 (June–July 1923), trans. and reprinted in Richard Taylor and Ian Christie, eds, *The Film Factory: Russian and Soviet Cinema in Documents, 1896–1939* (London: Routledge and Kegan Paul, 1988), pp. 91–3.

21 *New York Journal* (April 4, 1896), p. 9, quoted in Charles Musser, *Before the Nickelodeon: Edwin S. Porter and the Edison Manufacturing Company* (Berkeley, CA: University of California Press, 1991), p. 60.

22 *New York Herald* (April 24, 1896), p. 11, quoted in Musser, p. 63. Musser adds that "patrons in the front rows were disconcerted and inclined to leave their seats as the wave crashed on the beach and seemed about to flood the theater," a similar account of the behavior of early cinema audiences to that often reproduced about the Lumières' *L'Arrivée d'un Train en Gare de la Ciotat* (1895).

23 Tom Gunning, "The Cinema of Attractions: Early Film, Its Spectators and the Avant-Garde," in Thomas Elsaesser, ed., *Early Cinema: Space, Frame, Narrative* (London: British Film Institute, 1990), p. 57. The largest chain of theaters exclusively showing films before 1906 was Hale's Tours, showing "Tours and Scenes of the World" at amusement parks across America. As one advertisement described the "panoramic effect" of this "ride," "The person wishing to make the tour enters what has every appearance of a regular [train] coach. A colored porter is at the door and the seats are arranged inside the same as in a regular tourist car. . . . By a splendid arrangement which is an elaboration on the moving picture scheme the passengers can without effort imagine that they are travelling on a train and viewing the scenery. There is a slight rocking to the car as it takes the curves, and in addition there is the shrill whistle of the locomotive and the ringing bell at intervals to carry out further the illusion." Charles Musser, *The Emergence of Cinema: The American Screen to 1907* (New York: Scribner's, 1990), p. 437. See also Raymond Fielding, "Hale's Tours: Ultrarealism in the pre-1910 Motion Picture," in John L. Fell, ed., *Film Before Griffith* (Berkeley, CA: University of California Press, 1983), pp. 116–30. Rides like Disneyland's Star Tours are contemporary versions of these attractions.

24 Gunning, p. 57. Gunning defines the cinema of attractions as directly soliciting "spectator attention, inciting visual curiosity, and supplying pleasure through an exciting spectacle – a unique event, whether fictional or documentary, that is of interest in itself. . . . Theatrical display dominates over narrative absorption, emphasizing the direct stimulation of shock or surprise at the expense of unfolding a story or creating a diegetic universe. The cinema of attractions expends little energy creating characters with psychological motivations or individual personality. Making use of both fictional and non-fictional attractions, its energy moves outward towards an acknow-

ledged spectator rather than inward towards the character-based situations essential to classical narrative." Gunning, pp. 58–9.

25   The best brief discussion of formalist ideas of motivation can be found in Kristin Thompson, "Neoformalist Film Analysis: One Approach, Many Methods," in *Breaking the Glass Armor: Neoformalist Film Analysis* (Princeton, NJ: Princeton University Press, 1988), pp. 16–21.

26   Ian Craven, "Alternatives to Narrative in the American Cinema: A Study of Comic Performance," PhD dissertation, University of Exeter, 1982, pp. 116–19.

27   A "take" is the term used to describe each version of any given shot; it is usual to film several takes of each shot so that the best combination of performances can be chosen during editing. A "long take," however, refers specifically to a single uninterrupted shot of unusual duration.

28   Steven D. Katz, *Film Directing Shot by Shot: Visualizing from Concept to Screen* (Los Angeles: Michael Wiese Productions, 1991), p. 147.

29   David Bordwell attributes the term to Branigan in David Bordwell, Janet Staiger, and Kristin Thompson, *The Classical Hollywood Cinema: Film Style and Mode of Production to 1960* (London: Routledge and Kegan Paul, 1985), p. 51.

30   Katz, p. 280.

31   André Bazin, "The Evolution of the Language of Cinema," in *What is Cinema? Vol. 1*, trans. Hugh Gray (Berkeley, CA: University of California Press, 1967), p. 24.

32   In 1948 Hitchcock directed *Rope*, a movie consisting of only a dozen shots, each lasting about ten minutes or the length of a reel of film. At the end of each shot the camera settles on a static scene, such as the lid of a trunk, so that the next shot can begin as if the whole movie were taken in a single shot. To compensate for the absence of editing, the camera has to keep moving to adjust composition.

33   Quoted in Doug McClelland, ed., *Starspeak: Hollywood on Everything* (London: Faber, 1987), pp. 9–10.

34   Robert Sklar, *City Boys: Cagney, Bogart, Garfield* (Princeton, NJ: Princeton University Press, 1992), p. 112.

35   "Legitimate" theater originally described plays with spoken dialogue, distinguishing them from melodramas in which the dialogue was accompanied by music. During the nineteenth century, the term gradually acquired overtones of identifying those plays deemed to have poetic quality or literary worth, and by the beginning of the twentieth century it distinguished drama from slapstick and acrobatics, which had by then become separate entertainment forms in vaudeville and burlesque. Lawrence W. Levine, *Highbrow/Lowbrow: The Emergence of Cultural Hierarchy in America* (Cambridge, MA: Harvard University Press, 1988), pp. 75–6.

36   Theodore Noose, *Hollywood Film Acting* (New York: Barnes, 1979), p. 11; Lilian Albertson, *Motion Picture Acting* (New York: Funk & Wagnalls, 1947), p. 10. With equal vagueness, one American acting school teaches that "to act is to do or to live truthfully under imaginary circumstances." Quoted in Steve Vineberg, *Method Actors: Three Generations of an American Acting Style* (New York: Macmillan, 1991), p. 109.

37   Bronson Howard, "Our Schools for the Stage," *The Century* (November 1900), quoted in Brander Matthews, ed., *Papers on Acting* (New York: Hill and Wang, 1958), p. 281.

38   McConnell, pp. 177–8.

39   Michel Mourlet famously described Charlton Heston as "an axiom of the cinema. . . . By himself alone he constitutes a tragedy, and his presence in any films whatsoever suffices to create beauty. The contained violence expressed by the sombre phosphorescence of his eyes, his eagle's profile, the haughty arch of his eyebrows, his prominent cheek-bones, the bitter and hard curve of his mouth, the fabulous power

of his torso; this is what he possesses and what not even the worst director can degrade." Quoted in Richard Dyer, *Stars* (London: British Film Institute, 1979), pp. 148–9. Heston exists independently of any of the characters he plays, but as Mourlet's enthusiastic prose suggests, the effect of Heston's presence on the screen is no less a function of the movie's formal organization than the characters are. Watching Heston play Moses, we are aware of the dual presence of both Heston and Moses; Hollywood's commercial aesthetic encourages performance styles that produce this dual presence, and allow the two halves of a performance to play against, or play with, each other.

40 Naremore notes that "different performing methods or styles of blocking can make acting seem more or less presentational, depending on the emotional tone of the players, their movements in relation to the camera, and the degree to which they mimic well-known forms of behaviour." Naremore, pp. 30, 36.

41 McConnell, pp. 79, 87.

42 Vineberg, p. 112. Benjamin McArthur cites nineteenth-century American actors such as Edwin Booth, Joseph Jefferson, and Minnie Maddern Fiske, and the Barrymores in the twentieth century, as examples of great players who "ruled the stage, dwarfing the roles they played." In 1907 theater critic Alan Dale complained that in New York "It is the personalities [on stage] we go to see, not the actors and sometimes not the play." Quoted in Benjamin McArthur, *Actors and American Culture, 1880–1920* (Philadelphia: Temple University Press, 1984), pp. x, 183.

43 Vineberg, p. 110.

44 Inez and Helen Klumph, *Screen Acting: Its Requirements and Rewards* (New York: Falk, 1922), p. 141.

45 "It is told of Lon Chaney that all his spare time is spent in obscure parts of cities, studying the people he finds there, and that when he wants to see whether or not his characterization is a true one, he gets into make-up and goes out among people. Because he has so often been called upon to portray underworld types, he has spent much time among them. It is told of him that when he was playing in Marshall Neilan's *Bits of Life* in San Francisco's Chinatown, the Chinese extras thought he was one of them." Klumph and Klumph, p. 137. Of his performance in *The Phantom of the Opera* (1925), Robert G. Anderson observes, "His disguise was so perfect that he was totally unidentifiable as Lon Chaney. The only clues to his identity were the unmistakable use of his expressive hands and the movements of his body." Robert G. Anderson, *Faces, Forms, Films: The Artistry of Lon Chaney* (New York: Castel Books, 1971), pp. 34, 70, 49.

46 Hirsch, p. 155.

47 Klumph and Klumph, p. 181.

48 Albertson, pp. 65, 75.

49 Constant Coquelin, "Actors and Acting," *Harper's Monthly* (May 1887), reprinted in Matthews, pp. 163, 173.

50 Naremore, p. 5.

51 This example is discussed more fully in Richard deCordova, "Genre and Performance: An Overview," in Barry Keith Grant, ed., *Film Genre Reader* (Austin: University of Texas Press, 1986), p. 135.

52 Quoted in Nicholas Kent, *Naked Hollywood: Money, Power and the Movies* (London: BBC Books, 1991), p. 79.

53 Naremore, pp. 18, 102. Edward Wagenknecht, *The Movies in the Age of Innocence* (Norman: University of Oklahoma Press, 1962), pp. 249–50.

54 "Acting on the screen is not acting, it is *being*. It is getting into a character, fitting it as

a hand fits into a glove, and then letting the public see what that character does under a given set of circumstances." Klumph and Klumph, p. 103.

55   For instance, early in the movie's production planning, *Photoplay* magazine declared that "to our mind there is but one Rhett – Clark Gable. . . . We like all the other handsome actors mentioned as Rhett – only we don't want them as Rhett." In the casting of Scarlett O'Hara, the magazine proposed, "the prime requisite" was that "Scarlett must be in Gable's arms." Gable himself, however, later claimed that he had not wanted the part: "Miss [Margaret] Mitchell had etched Rhett into the minds of millions of people . . . it would be impossible to satisfy them all. . . . The public interest in my playing Rhett puzzled me. . . . I was the only one, apparently, who didn't take it for granted that I was going to play the part." Ronald Haver, *David O. Selznick's Hollywood* (New York: Knopf, 1980), pp. 242, 251.

56   Philip French, "Faust Goes to Memphis," *Observer* (September 12, 1993), p. 48.

57   Cathy Klaprat, "The Star as Market Strategy: Bette Davis in Another Light," in Tino Balio, ed., *The American Film Industry*, revised edn (Madison: University of Wisconsin Press, 1985), p. 363. Robert Sklar takes a much less favorable view of Warner Bros.' handling of their stars, suggesting that typecasting stars in their personas had more to do with the pressures of the studio production schedule: "There were just too many stories to develop, too many pictures to cast, too many productions to watch over, too much product to move into theaters – and not enough good parts to go around. It was easier to pigeonhole or typecast performers, to slot them into familiar genre categories, to use them as often as possible in repetitive roles." Certainly the dispute that both Davis and James Cagney had with Warner Bros. had to do with the studio's insistence on restricting the range of roles they could play. Sklar, p. 76.

58   Klaprat, pp. 355, 363, 372, 375.

59   Sklar, p. 262.

60   In *Out of Africa* (1985), Meryl Streep's Danish accent stands out against the movie's other voices, not because it is Danish or because it is in itself unsuccessful, but because her adoption of an accent separates the register of her performance from that of her co-star, Redford, who just sounds like Robert Redford.

61   Naremore, p. 22.

62   Genevieve Stebbins, *Delsarte System of Expression* (New York: Edger S. Werner, 1902; reprinted New York: Dance Horizons, 1977), p. 76.

63   Quoted in Richard Schickel, *Brando: A Life in Our Times* (London: Pavilion, 1991), p. 126.

64   Most importantly Stella Adler, who disputed Strasberg's emphasis on the actor's own emotions and established her own acting school in New York, where she first taught Brando.

65   Strasberg argued that only Stanislavski – who had died in 1938 – was entitled to refer to his own practice as the "System." He chose the "Method" as a label for a practice that "emphasized elements that [Stanislavski] had not emphasized and disregarded elements which he might have considered of greater importance." Letter from Strasberg to Christine Edwards, April 1, 1960, quoted in Christine Edwards, *The Stanislavsky Heritage: Its Contribution to the Russian and American Theatre* (New York: New York University Press, 1965), p. 261.

66   Schickel, p. 15.

67   Vineberg, p. 6.

68   Toby Cole and Helen Kritch Chinoy, eds, *Actors on Acting* (New York: Crown, 1970), p. 623, quoted in Naremore, p. 18.

69   "Affective memory is the conscious creation of remembered emotions which have

occurred in the actor's *own* past life and then their application to the character being portrayed." Edward Dwight Easty, *On Method Acting*, 1st edn. New York: Allograph Press, 1966 (New York: Ballantine, 1989), p. 44.

70   Hirsch, p. 64.

71   Quoted in Michel Ciment, *Kazan on Kazan* (London: Secker and Warburg, 1973), p. 38.

72   Quoted in Bob Thomas, *Brando: Portrait of the Rebel as an Artist* (London: W.H. Allen, 1973), p. 74.

73   There is an account of *Streetcar*'s difficulties with the Production Code Administration and the Catholic Legion of Decency in Leonard J. Leff and Jerrold R. Simmons, *The Dame in the Kimono: Hollywood, Censorship, and the Production Code from the 1920s to the 1960s* (New York: Grove, Weidenfeld, 1990), pp. 172–7.

74   James F. Scott, *Film: The Medium and the Maker* (New York: Holt, Rinehart, and Winston, 1975), p. 249.

75   Maureen Stapleton, in Lewis Funke and John E. Booth, eds, *Actors Talk About Acting: Fourteen Interviews with Stars of the Theatre* (New York: Random House, 1961), pp. 170–1. Quoted in Vineberg, p. 223.

76   Vineberg, p. 7.

77   Thomas R. Atkins, "Troubled Sexuality in the Popular Hollywood Feature," in Thomas R. Atkins, ed., *Sexuality in the Movies* (Bloomington: Indiana University Press, 1975), p. 114.

78   Vineberg, p. 91.

79   Richard Dyer argues that: "Although in principle the Method could be used to express any psychological state, in practice it was used especially to express disturbance, repression, anguish, etc., partly in line with a belief that such feelings . . . are more 'authentic' than stability and open expression." Dyer also suggests that disturbance and anguish were the characteristics usually attributed to men, while repression was depicted as a female quality. Both Naremore and Frederic Jameson have added a further ideological dimension to the analysis of Method acting as particularly fitting a "middle-brow media usage" of existentialism as the posture of "the anti-hero of the sad sack, Saul Bellow-type, and a kind of self-pitying vision of alienation (also meant in its media rather than its technical sense), frustration, and above all – yesterday's all-American concept – the 'inability to communicate.'" Frederic Jameson, "Class and Allegory in Contemporary Mass Culture: *Dog Day Afternoon* as a Political Film," in Bill Nichols, ed., *Movies and Methods Vol. II* (Berkeley, CA: University of California Press, 1985), p. 722. Naremore adds, "Whether the character is a laborer, an upwardly mobile son of a wage-earning family, or an affluent teenager, he has the same problem: an uneasiness with official language and no words for his love or rage. At the same time, he brims over with sensitivity and feeling, the intensity of his emotion giving him a slightly neurotic aspect." Naremore, p. 201.

80   Easty, p. 67. This is Rod Steiger describing his own performance in *The Pawnbroker* (1965): "The last moment of *The Pawnbroker* when the boy is dead and I come out of the shop and I dipped my hand in the blood . . . I imagined it was my daughter. I was an emotional wreck before I started it. Then I remembered that Picasso picture of the bombing of Guernica, with the pointed tongues and the horses and the women shouting the loudest screams you have ever heard. Then I said to myself scream, but don't make a sound. That was one of my best moments." Stuart Jeffries, "A Method that No Longer Fits the Bill," *Guardian* (August 20, 1992), p. 21.

81   Easty, p. 116. Easty defines the actor's instrument as "his whole self . . . his body, his mind and being, complete with thoughts, emotions, sensitivity, imagination, honesty, and awareness. . . . try to imagine the actor's instrument in much the same way you

picture the musician and his violin, the artist and his canvas, paints, and brushes."
Although they have few other grounds of agreement, Easty's definition thus echoes
that of Coquelin. Easty, p. 15.

82   Klumph and Klumph, p. 125.

83   Constant Coquelin, "Art and the Actor," 1st pub. in French, 1880, trans. Abby
Langdon Alger, 1881, reprinted in Matthews, p. 26. In the late nineteenth century the
debate over whether the actor should experience the character's emotion in performance was characterized as being one between Coquelin and the British actor Henry
Irving. In 1888 William Archer gathered evidence scattered in theatrical biography
and dramatic criticism on the subject, and sent a questionnaire to British and American actors, the results being published in *Masks or Faces? A Study in the Psychology of
Acting* (London and New York: Longmans, 1888).

84   For instance, Gustave Garcia, *The Actor's Art: A Practical Treatise on Stage Declamation,
Public Speaking and Deportment, for the Use of Artists, Students and Amateurs* (London:
Pettitt, 1882), pp. 41, 62–3.

85   Delsarte defined "semeiotics" as "the science of signs, and so the science of gesture."
With semeiotics, he suggested, one could study the "organic form" of a gesture, and
infer the sentiment that produced it. His conception of semeiotics differed significantly from the later semiology of the Swiss linguist, Ferdinand de Saussure, whose
theories have a much wider currency in contemporary criticism. While Saussure
asserts that the relationship between signifier and signified (between a word and the
thing the word stands for) is arbitrary, Delsarte's semeiotics studied organic relationships, which he called correspondences. "Correspondence," he held, "is no arbitrary
relationship like metaphor or figure, but one founded alike on the inward and
outward nature of the things by which we are surrounded." Stebbins, pp. 135–42.

86   Following Raymond Williams, we can define naturalism as a style involving the close
observation and detailed reproduction of external appearances. Whether considered
as painting, literature, or drama, naturalism also assumes that this accurate external
representation can reveal individual or social truths. Raymond Williams, *Keywords:
A Vocabulary of Culture and Society* (London: Fontana, 1976), pp. 181–4. In addition
to the luminaries of high culture, a complete account of the growth of naturalism
would consider the plays of Steele MacKaye, Clyde Fitch, James A. Herne and other
American dramatists of the late nineteenth century whose work most often represented the American middle class in naturalistic plots.

87   American theatrical impresario David Belasco often claimed to have introduced the
"new, quiet acting" to the New York stage at the turn of the century, although
Belasco's naturalism was in practice more noticeable in the attention to detail he paid
in the construction of sets for his productions. During the 1910s, this sense of naturalistic detail became more closely coupled with a more "natural mode" of understated
acting that had been taking hold of the New York stage since 1875. Belasco wrote in
1913: "One day the heroine who used to shout her grief till the gallery shook found no
sympathy with her audiences . . . This sort of emotional display became too
unreal . . . so the ranting heroine of melodrama was banished from the stage." David
Belasco, "Stage Realism of the Future," *Theatre Magazine* (September 1913), p. 86,
quoted in Richard A. Blum, *American Film Acting: The Stanislavski Heritage* (Ann
Arbor, UMI Research Press, 1984), p. 9. Edwards, p. 195.

88   Providing an elaborate analysis of facial and bodily gesture, Delsarte's system was
designed to be combined with the study of character, observations from life, and
what Genevieve Stebbins called "*interior memory*, – that unconscious storehouse
where inherited tendencies, traits, and aptitudes are also found." Delsarte's foremost

American disciple was the actor, director, and theater manager Steele MacKaye, who opened his School of Expression in New York in 1877, where the aim of his course in "practical Pantomime, Stage Business, and Vocal Gymnastics" was to endow the actor with complete "spontaneity." These ideas place Delsarte's system in a much closer relation to Stanislavski than is usually suggested. Benjamin McArthur, however, points out that we should not "read back into this pre-Stanislavski era a psychological realism obsessed with sub-texts which did not yet exist. The early days of naturalistic acting merely involved a subduing of gesture and a less-cadenced speech." Nevertheless, by 1900 Broadway acting style had changed: "Freely expressed emotion and broad pantomime began giving way to restraint as actors conveyed emotions subtly. The pause became as important as the spoken word, and audiences had to scrutinize stage characters to discern the hidden motives of action." Stebbins, p. 142; McArthur, pp. 100, 182–3.

89   Stebbins, p. 429.

90   Of Stanislavski's three textbooks on performance, the first, *An Actor Prepares*, was published in Russia in 1926. *Building a Character* was not published in the US until 1949, 11 years after Stanislavski's death. The third, *Creating a Role*, was published in 1961, but neither of the later books, which contradicted many of the assumptions made from American readings of *An Actor Prepares*, was nearly as influential. Constantin Stanislavski, *An Actor Prepares, Building a Character*, and *Creating a Role*, all trans. Elizabeth Reynolds Hapgood (London: Methuen, 1988).

91   Quoted in Blum, p. 52.

92   Advertisement for *The Son of the Sheik*, reproduced in Russell C. Sweeney, *Coming Next Week: A Pictorial History of Film Advertising* (New York: Barnes, 1973), p. 95.

93   In 1642 the English Parliament decreed that "all Stage-Players, and Players of Enterludes, and common Players, are hereby declared to be, and are, and shall be taken to be Rogues, and punishable." Edmund K. Chambers, *The Elizabethan Stage*, vol. 4 (Oxford: Clarendon Press, 1923), p. 324.

94   In 1762, the New Hampshire House of Representatives banned an acting company on the grounds that the theater had a "peculiar influence on the minds of young people, and greatly endanger[s] their morals by giving them a taste for intriguing, amusement, and pleasure." Arthur Hornblow, *A History of the Theatre in America*, vol. 1 (New York: Benjamin Bloom, 1919), p. 24.

95   Mendel Kohansky, *The Disreputable Profession: The Actor in Society* (Westport, CT: Greenwood Press, 1984), p. 9.

96   McArthur, pp. 164–5.

97   Kohansky, p. 162.

98   Richard deCordova, *Picture Personalities: The Emergence of the Star System in America* (Urbana: University of Illinois Press, 1990), pp. 84–92.

99   Miriam Hansen, "Pleasure, Ambivalence, Identification: Valentino and Female Spectatorship," *Cinema Journal* 25:4 (Summer 1986), reprinted in Christine Gledhill, ed., *Stardom: Industry of Desire* (London: Routledge, 1991), p. 269.

100   Miriam Hansen, *Babel and Babylon: Spectatorship in American Silent Film* (Cambridge, MA: Harvard University Press, 1991), p. 262.

101   Lurine Pruette, "Should Men Be Protected?," *The Nation* 125 (August 31, 1927), p. 200, quoted in Gaylyn Studlar, "The Perils of Pleasure? Fan Magazine Discourse as Women's Commodified Culture in the 1920s," *Wide Angle* 13:1 (January 1991), p. 25.

102   E.A. Ross, "What the Films Are Doing to Young America," *World Drift* (New York: Century, 1928), quoted in Studlar, p. 16.

103   Adela Rogers St John, "What Kind of Men Attract Women Most?," *Photoplay* 21:5

(April 1924), p. 110, quoted in Hansen, *Babel and Babylon*, p. 257.

104   "Letters to the Editor," *Photoplay* 22 (July 1922), p. 115, and *Photoplay* 23 (September 1922), p. 113, both quoted in Studlar, p. 26.

105   Hirsch, p. 91.

106   Hansen, *Babel and Babylon*, p. 294. See also Studlar, pp. 6–34 and Studlar, "Discourses of Gender and Ethnicity: The Construction and De(con)struction of Rudolph Valentino as Other," *Film Criticism* 13:2 (1989), pp. 18–35.

107   Naremore, p. 4.

108   Gaylyn Studlar has argued that this scene appears as a "highly stylized balletic interpretation of rape," in which the "dance-like movement and repose" prevent it being understood as a realistic depiction of sexual assault. Gaylyn Studlar, "Valentino, 'Optic Intoxication,' and Dance Madness," in Steven Cohen and Ina Rae Hark, eds, *Screening the Male: Exploring Masculinities in Hollywood Cinema* (London: Routledge, 1993), p. 35.

109   Director Richard Fleischer tells an anecdote about working with actor Robert Mitchum, whose performances were famously underemphatic, on a Western called *Bandido* (1956). In one scene Fleischer needed a reaction shot of Mitchum. After the first take, he protested to Mitchum that Mitchum had not reacted. He had, Mitchum replied, it was just that Fleischer had not noticed the reaction. The shot was retaken, with Mitchum playing the scene as Fleischer wanted, although he insisted that Fleischer would end up using the first take. When he saw the scene in the editing room, Fleischer acknowledged that Mitchum had been right.

110   Dyer, pp. 133–5.

7 Time

Obviously, the photoplay has points of distinct superiority over the stage
drama. Its weakness, no less, is its transiency. Where nothing stands still,
nothing endures. . . . The circulation of a popular picture is immediate and
world-wide . . . but this vast diffusion is paid for by a corresponding brevity.
Joseph P. Kennedy[1]

As the song in *Casablanca* tells us, we must remember that one of the
fundamental things that applies in the cinema is that time goes by. The
projection of moving images in a temporal sequence is the most obvious
feature distinguishing cinema from earlier art forms. As we recognize
narrative motivation and dramatic effect largely through the representation of space, we experience cinema's representation of space by perceiving film's movement through time. In many ways, the function of space is
therefore actually to host the passing of time, although this relationship
is both so natural and so abstract as to be quite difficult to pin down.
Movies manipulate our experience of time with particular rigor, but audiences are skilled in recognizing the conventions by which these temporal
shifts are signaled. In the course of the most unremarkable movie, audiences may need to comprehend the significance of acceleration and delay,
parallel time-frames, and the mechanisms of temporal continuity and its
violation.

Time Out

Cinema is life, with the boring bits cut out.

Alfred Hitchcock

An interviewer once asked director Howard Hawks what his next movie
was about. "Well," he replied, "it's about two hours long." Apart from
demonstrating Hawks' notorious disdain for answering critical questions
about his work, this remark makes an obvious but important point
about the nature of movies: they take time, and they do so in a particular
way. Our perception of time and of the way we normally occupy it

fluctuates constantly. Our sense of history, too, is formed by the idea that some passages of time are more significant than others. Movies, on the other hand, occupy time with mechanical consistency. *Meet Me in St Louis* (1944) takes 113 minutes to screen, whenever and wherever it is shown. The price of admission to the movie theater is, effectively, the price of renting a seat for a couple of hours while you watch the movie. Cinema offers us nothing tangible, just the opportunity to spend time in a particular way, to take time "out" from the continuum of the rest of our lives.

The buying and selling of time is the central activity of the leisure industry in a capitalist economy. This process of commodification itself has a history. When the culture of consumption spread from the propertied classes down through the social system in the late nineteenth and early twentieth centuries, the form in which leisure activities occupied time became more mechanical. While books allowed readers to organize their own time and pace their own activity, records, radio, and movies all required their consumers to conform to the mechanical requirements of the medium. Theater advertisements told their patrons to see a movie "today, tomorrow and Thursday – then *Chang* will be gone forever."[2] Exhibition practice emphasized a transience that distinguished movies from more durable cultural commodities. When we buy a book or a picture we possess the physical object in addition to experiencing the act of consumption. Possessing the object allows us to repeat the experience, or use the book for any other purpose we choose: to prop up a table leg, or to fill up a bookshelf with titles chosen to impress our friends with our intellectual sophistication. The entertainment experience of cinema leaves us with no second, durable consumer commodity. We must return to the movie theater if we want to repeat the experience.

Although the appearance of video-tape seems at first glance to blur these distinctions, it can be used to clarify them. Since the mid-1980s it has been possible to come home from the local shopping mall or high street with a copy of a recent Hollywood movie – as easy as buying a paperback book or a CD. They each cost about the same, and the delay between theatrical and video release is comparable to that between hardback and paperback publication dates. This ought not to surprise us; the distribution and merchandising of these different forms of "software," all competing for a share of our leisure expenditure, have clearly learned from each other. Indeed, the marketing of video-tape took some time to settle into its present format, having initially set its retail prices at much higher levels and expected to do most business through low-cost rentals in a form of consumption that substituted a transient experience in the home for the visit to the movie theater.

As an incidental bonus to the industry's finding another way to sell its products, video has undoubtedly made the study of Hollywood a good deal easier. One of the pleasures of owning a movie is being able to view and repeat-view parts of it with almost the same ease that we read and re-

read a book. The difference between the cinematic experience and that of watching the same film on video-tape at home is not to be found in a purist notion of the superiority of celluloid, of image size or resolution, but in the transience and non-repeatability of the experience of consumption in the movie theater. It is possible, now, to walk into any video store and find a copy of *Singin' in the Rain* (1952) or *My Darling Clementine* (1946) or *The Public Enemy* (1931). At the time of their initial production and release, most moviegoers had one week, or even less, in which to see them, and then, like a restaurant meal, they were gone, with only traces in the audience's memories to mark their passing. That condition of consumption, more than any other, has marked their manufacture and the forms that they have taken.

As we discussed in chapter 1, critics of mass culture such as Theodor Adorno and Max Horkheimer stressed the extent to which the mechanical occupation of time by the leisure forms of capitalism approximated and imitated the work process. Movies sought to disguise this imitation, and one means by which they did so was through the superimposition of an alternative, narrative sense of time on the mechanical organization of time produced by the technology of film. A movie offers its audience a sense of temporal displacement, which viewers often register if, having gone into a cinema in daylight, they come out into darkness, and experience for a moment the shock of time having passed, in some sense, without them. In fact, one of the pleasures of cinema is the escape from historical time into the movies, where time passes according to its own internal logic, and where our pleasure comes in part from time passing in obedience to the continuity of the story.

This is, of course, no coincidence. Stories must be carefully plotted to fit into the block of time available for each screening. Contemporary screenwriting manuals declare emphatically that "proper structure occurs when the right events occur in the right sequence to elicit maximum emotional involvement in the . . . audience . . . good plot structure means that the right thing is happening at the right time."[3] To this end, they suggest that a movie screenplay should have three acts. Act 1, the **setup**, establishes the plot situation in the first quarter of the movie. Act 2, the **confrontation**, builds it during the next half. Act 3, the **resolution**, brings the story to its conclusion in the final quarter. Within this rigid structure, smaller rigidities exist. Declaring that "the standard screenplay is approximately 120 pages long," and that "one page of screenplay equals one minute of screen time," Syd Field argues that a script's first 10 pages must establish who the main character is, what the story is about (what its premise is), and what circumstances it takes place in (what the dramatic situation is). In *Chinatown* (1974), for instance, we encounter Jake Gittes (Jack Nicholson), a private detective specializing in divorce work in 1930s Los Angeles, and Mrs Mulwray (Diane Ladd), who wants to hire him to find out whether her husband is having an affair. At the end of Act 1, between pages 25 and 27, there is a **plot point**, an event or incident that "hooks into the story and spins it around into another direction."[4] In *Chinatown*, after Jake has discovered Mulwray in a "love nest" and the story has appeared in the newspapers, the plot point is the appearance of the *real* Mrs Mulwray (Faye Dunaway); Jake must spend Act 2 trying to find out who set him up, and why. Act 2 also has a plot point at its end, between pages 85 and 90, which again redirects the plot into the sequence of events that will lead to its conclusion. Field insists that "all good screenplays" fit this pattern, and encourages his viewers to watch movies with a stopwatch to identify the plot points that occur 25 and 85 minutes into the movie's running time.[5] The rigidity of these structures suggests the formulaic nature of Hollywood narration: Field unequivocally asserts that time in the movies is constrained by the need for linear continuity and the achievement of goals. He defines dramatic structure as "a linear arrangement of related incidents, episodes or events leading to a dramatic resolution," and insists on the importance of strong, conclusive, and preferably "up" endings: "There are better ways to end your screenplays than have your character shot, captured, die, or be murdered. In the '60s we had 'down' endings. The filmgoers of the '70s and '80s want 'up' endings. Just look at *Star Wars*. It has made more money than any other movie in history."[6] The assertion of Hollywood's commercial aesthetic could hardly be clearer. But though a screenplay's suitability for production may be evaluated according to a schema such as Field's, the commercial aesthetic also requires that it conceal its structure of acts and plot points behind the novelty of its plot events.[7] A convention of romantic comedies, for example, is that the lovers "meet cute": that is, they encounter each other in improbable circumstances. If the meeting is cute enough – on the back seat of a bus in *It Happened One Night* (1934) or, repeatedly, through a radio talk-show in *Sleepless in Seattle* (1993) – the audience's pleasure at the skillful variation of convention overrides any concern with the predictability of the event.

Even in Hollywood's rigid sense of temporal continuity, the play with conventions means that narrative progression can be interrupted by alternative forms of entertainment. There is always room for the incidental pleasures of spectacle and performance. Take the opening sequence of *Gentlemen Prefer Blondes* (1953, directed by Howard Hawks). Immediately after the Twentieth Century-Fox fanfare and before any credits appear, the image on the screen is revealed to be a set of curtains, which part far enough to allow Jane Russell and Marilyn Monroe, dressed in identical red floor-length dresses slit virtually to the waist in both directions, to step through. On a dark green staircase they sing "We're Just Two Little Girls From Little Rock." This minimal stage background sets their performance not only outside the diegetic world established by the movie's fiction, but also outside narrative time, before the credit sequence starts. The primary source of audience enjoyment in the scene is the pleasure we gain from watching Marilyn Monroe and Jane Russell perform for an offscreen audience; our reward is spectacular, rather than narrational.[8] The sequence draws its viewers out of their ordinary external relation to the passage of time, because the sequence itself has no identifiable temporal context: viewing it, we have no idea when or where it happens. As a result there are no visible constraints upon how long it may last. In fact, like the movie that is "about two hours long," it lasts for as long as its producers believe it can sustain the audience's interest. And at that point, almost at the end of the song, the movie cuts to a shot of a night-club audience, locating the sequence for the first time within a narrative framework.

As the excessive precision of Syd Field's rules of screenplay construction suggest, Hollywood movies structure time to meet the needs of their audiences, and, of course, define those needs in the process of meeting them. One often-repeated story about Harry Cohn, the acerbic head of production at Columbia, tells of his behavior at a preview of one of his studio's prestige productions. The production personnel gathered round him after the screening, eager for his good opinion. It was fine, he declared, except that it was exactly nineteen minutes too long. Their astonishment at the precision and speed of his analysis was immediately blunted by his declaration that "exactly nineteen minutes ago, my ass started to itch and right there I know the audience would feel the same."[9] The aesthetic assumption behind the story, so widely reproduced in anecdotal histories of Hollywood that it must be taken as a piece of industry lore, is that the requirements of narrative must be constrained within the limits of the audience's anticipated temporal tolerance. This principle applies not only to time out within the movies, such as the musical numbers, but crucially to the logics governing the typical duration of an entire movie, as time out from history.[10] Hollywood movies are not all "about two hours long," and the expected duration of a movie has varied significantly over Hollywood's history: few 1930s movies were longer than 100 minutes, few 1980s movies were under two hours long. But in any given period, the overwhelming majority of movies remain within a fairly predictable band in terms of running time, roughly corresponding to an ideal duration which most closely meets the needs of production efficiency, the economics of exhibition, and the comfortable limits of audience tolerance.

Film Time

> Any expressive form lives only in its own present – the one it itself creates.
> Clifford Geertz[11]

The distinction between film and movie that we made in the introduction and have used throughout this book should help to clarify Hollywood's articulation of different types of time. **Film time**, the amount of time a movie requires of its audience, is a matter of fixed duration, determined by the length of the film and the set speed at which it passes through the projector. *Once Upon a Time in America* (1984) runs for 3 hours and 48 minutes. **Movie time**, the time represented within the fiction, is much more flexible. The movie time of *Once Upon a Time in America* begins in 1922 and ends in 1968, and involves flashbacks and flashforwards, ellipses, parallel narratives, and sequences in slow motion.

In mechanical terms, a film camera moves a strip of film at a uniform rate past an aperture – a lens – through which light passes. Sprocket holes at the sides of the film engage with the teeth of the camera's sprocket wheels; the film is pulled forward, stops briefly in front of the lens to be exposed, and is then pulled on again, at a uniform rate, usually 24 times per second. If you then hold a strip of film up to the light you see the result of this process: a long string of almost identical still images. These images are then animated by being projected. Each frame is stopped in front of the projector gate and the projector light shows the image. Between the illumination of each frame, a baffle blocks out the light while the motor winds the film on to the next frame.

The illusion of continuous motion celebrated in a Hollywood movie is therefore actually based on the endlessly interrupted movement of the film through the projector. Significantly, the major mechanical complication involved in the development of the motion picture camera lay in inventing a reliable device for coordinating the interrupted motion of the film past the camera lens and projector gate. If the film did not stop exactly in the same place 24 times a second, while being exposed or projected, the movie would appear on the screen as an indecipherable blur. Moreover, the film must be projected at the same speed as it was shot to produce the conventional illusion of movement. Most silent movies were shot at a camera speed of about 18 frames per second, and if they are projected at the normal sound camera speed of 24 frames per second, the represented movement is speeded up by a third, making it appear quick and jerky. The effect disappears when the film is projected at the same speed as it was shot.[12] **Slow-motion** effects are produced by passing the film through the camera at a faster rate than normal, so that the film takes longer to project than the duration of the action it records.

Variations between camera speed and projector speed reveal the extent to which the cinema's illusion of movement is dependent firstly on the film's rigidly mechanical occupation of time. The illusion of movement depends secondly on a process of human perception, by which we recognize a sequence of rapidly viewed still images as being in continuous motion. Until recently, this perceptual quirk was explained by the theory of **persistence of vision**. This theory is at least as old as the classical Greeks, but it was formalized in 1824 by Peter Mark Roget (better known for his *Thesaurus*), who suggested that every time we look at something, a brief residual image is stored on the retina of the eye. You notice the effect if you stare at a bright light, and then close your eyes. A negative image of the light remains for a while, temporarily burned onto the retina. Roget's theory of persistence of vision suggested that this phenomenon occurs constantly, but over very short durations, so that in watching sequences of still images, each individual image is retained until the next one appears to replace it. More recent research into the psychology of perception, however, suggests that the process is much more complicated, and that seeing – and hearing – are positive mental activities, not involuntary physical processes. Rather than the illusion of movement being created by a deception of the eye, the brain constructs a continuous image from the sequence of stills, filling in the missing parts. It is the viewer, not the projector, who creates the illusion of movement; if you project a strip of film in an empty cinema, it is only a sequence of consecutive still pictures. Film needs an audience to become a movie, and the psychological explanation of the perception of motion is of considerable importance to our discussion of the interactive relationship between Hollywood and its audiences.[13]

At a number of levels, the basic apparatus of cinema insists on the ephemerality of film, graphically demonstrated at the end of *Two Lane Blacktop* (1972). In a sequence that will look all too familiar to amateur filmmakers, the movie appears to be being projected more and more slowly, at first giving the viewer time to register each separate image as a still picture. Eventually, a completely still frame seems to be held in the gate and overheated by the projector light until the celluloid melts and catches fire. We are given the impression that the film has, literally, brought the movie to an end. If a sense of this material evanescence has underpinned much critical dismissal of cinema, the fact that the base material itself moves may have also contributed to a sense that the movies were somehow never still enough long enough for critics to gain a purchase on them. For instance, the detailed analysis of spatial relations in a scene almost invariably requires the critic to look at individual still frames, studying them for much longer than is possible during projection. While this is comparable to the close textual analysis of a literary work, it involves a disruption of the movie's experiential form.

Hollywood's own commercial practices confirm that close criticism (which has often called itself "reading")[14] is a perverse activity based on the critical misconception of a movie as a fixed "text." The normal accountancy procedures of the major companies assumed that a movie would earn all its income within two years of its initial release, after which it would be taken off the company's books, and any further money it earned would be considered as windfall profits. Until television and then video demonstrated the commercial importance of a film company's library, the production industry made little effort to preserve what were regarded as last season's no longer fashionable goods. A movie might be remade – with added ingredients in the form of new stars, color, or widescreen – but it was unlikely to be re-released, at least into the first-run market.[15] It was, indeed, not uncommon for companies to destroy prints in order to recover the small amounts of silver in their emulsion. Hollywood movies thus offered themselves as doubly ephemeral, designed neither in content nor in material to persist as part of an artistic tradition, but to be consumed, exhausted, en route to further acts of consumption. In 1928 a San Francisco theater announced that, despite *The Way of All Flesh* being "the wonder engagement of all time . . . it cannot stay forever!," since Friday would see the arrival of *The Big Parade*.[16]

Even when a movie is preserved, abstracted from its original theatrical viewing conditions, and placed in a research archive, the notion that this represents the survival of a fixed, stable "text" corresponds poorly with the actual distribution and exhibition practices of the industry. In the silent period in particular, the movie was a highly malleable object: as well as the variable performance element provided by the musical accompaniment to silent movies, the prints themselves were regularly cut by distributors, local censor boards, and individual exhibitors for a variety of reasons.[17] Although the precise nature of this malleability changed with the introduction of sound, it is still the case that different versions of the same movie emerge as Hollywood tailors its products to different exhibition circumstances – for a television showing, for example, which requires a movie's running time (that is, what we are calling film time) to adapt to a predetermined time-slot in the schedule, to accommodate advertising time, and so on. In addition, just as "special editions" released to video include previously unavailable spatial material such as the extra portion of the screen in a widescreen version, these supposedly enhanced versions are also likely to be sold on the basis of extra footage previously excluded – literally, extra time.[18]

Perhaps more than any other factor, the movies' transient and unstable existence accounts for their relatively low cultural status. Artifacts that have "stood the test of time" are valued not simply for their material longevity, but also because they have claimed a place as part of a tradition or heritage, valued for its intrinsic and supposedly universal values. This process of cultural abstraction is celebrated in John Keats' "Ode on a Grecian Urn." The poem describes an object preserved in the British Museum, and discusses the way that cultural artifacts become museum pieces, preserved in a temporal limbo quite separate from the places and circumstances of their production. Keats celebrates the fact of the urn's survival through the uncertainties of history, to the point when, from the safety of the museum, its aesthetic certainties will continue to address viewers indefinitely:

> When old age shall this generation waste,
> Thou shalt remain, in midst of other woe
> Than ours, a friend to man, to whom thou say'st,
> "Beauty is truth, truth beauty", – that is all
> Ye know on earth, and all ye need to know.

This transcendent aesthetic value is connected to the form of the frieze on the urn. In describing the scenes on the frieze, the poet accords to the actions they depict a significance that transcends history precisely because they are frozen in time, and can never be completed:

> Bold lover, never, never can'st thou kiss,
> Though winning near the goal – yet do not grieve;
> She cannot fade, though thou hast not thy bliss,
> For ever wilt thou love, and she be fair!

Unprojected, a movie would be reduced to a sequence of still frames, static spectacles that would share many of the temporal properties Keats attributes to the urn. As with the urn, a viewer might decipher scenes and character types through the recognition of a conventional iconography of star and genre, but such iconographic recognitions cannot provide a precise narrative framework within which to locate the character of the exchanges taking place. Nor, crucially for the movie's organization of time, can the unprojected film strip provide any information about duration, pace, or performance.[19] The image requires the animation produced by its projection to restore its full dramatic and expressive activity.

Movie Time

> Time, though invisible and abstract, has many concrete ways of assisting or damaging the motion picture narration.
>
> Eugene Vale[20]

> It could mean that that point in time inherently contains some sort of cosmic significance, almost as if it were the temporal junction point for the entire space-time continuum. On the other hand it could just be an amazing coincidence.
>
> Doc (Christopher Lloyd) in *Back to the Future Part II* (1989)

Both film time and movie time are matters of duration, of different senses of how the passage of time is being measured. Film time is rigid and mechanical, while movie time – the time represented within the narrative – is much more flexible. Very early cinema engaged its audiences with a purely ahistorical occupation of time. The novelty and spectacle of cinema itself was enough to hold the audience's attention. Almost immediately, however, a complex of commercial, technical, and aesthetic motives led filmmakers to seek more complex systems of temporal representation. Dramatic fictions could be produced at a more predictable rate and cost than topical or actuality films, and the industry's wholesale switch to story-film production was instigated by the manufacturers rather than by audience demand. As well as allowing producers greater opportunities for stabilizing and controlling the market, they also offered ready opportunities for the development of forms that could sustain audience interest for longer durations. This in turn encouraged the development of technical apparatuses and discursive conventions that could make more complex stories comprehensible, and so the chain of development leading to the rhetoric of Classical Hollywood cinema proceeded.

Like the other formal properties of a Hollywood product, movie time operates according to established but permeable conventions. Movie time is usually longer and more complex than film time, involving time lapses or ellipses, where Alfred Hitchcock's "boring bits" have been cut out. Very occasionally movie narratives represent a continuous time: *Rope* (1948), for instance, tells a story that supposedly takes place in a period of just 80 minutes, exactly matching the film's projection time. At the other extreme, in *2001: A Space Odyssey* (1968) movie time covers several million years in the film's two-hour duration. In theory, movie time could also be shorter than film time. This happens most visibly in slow-motion sequences, where there is spectacular action – the final battle in *The Wild Bunch* (1969), the winning touchdown in *The Longest Yard* (1974) – and in a different sense it also happens during flashbacks that are presented as a character's act of memory; but no Hollywood movie has sustained this principle of organization for its entire length.

Within movie time (which you will often see referred to as narrative time), we must make a further distinction between the duration of the *story* and the duration of the *plot*. The duration of the story of *2001* is two million years, but the movie only dramatizes a few brief periods in this long span. Story duration encompasses the entire period covered by a narrative, including events merely referred to in dialogue or inferred by the viewer. Plot duration, on the other hand, includes only those periods of time directly presented on the screen, and across the entirety of a narrative will normally be much shorter than story duration. Within any one scene, however, plot and story durations will often appear to be the same.[21] In *Madigan* (1968), for example, film time is 101 minutes; plot duration is roughly 48 hours, from Friday morning to Sunday morning; story duration is considerably longer, going back several years, to previous encounters between characters.

Typically, film time dominates the temporal hierarchy. The rule that one page of screenplay equals one minute is a calculation in film time, and the iron laws of the three-act structure and plot-point positioning are devices by which movie time must be fitted to the commercial aesthetic of film time, which determines that a movie is "about two hours long." Hollywood cannot, therefore, tell stories that will be longer or shorter than about two hours in the telling. One of the perennial complaints about movie adaptations of novels is that the movie leaves so much of the original out – although the complainants seldom explain where they expect the missing parts to fit. In *The Technique of Screenplay Writing*, Eugene Vale suggests that a Hollywood movie has, on average, 30 scenes: that is, 30 discrete sections of its plot, each occurring in a separate place or time from the scene before.[22] Movies thus tell stories that shape themselves into about 30 separate events, each of which can show its section of the story in three or four minutes of film time. Thirty is, of course, only an average, and screenwriting manuals will dispute whether the scene or the sequence is the most important unit in screenplay construction. Syd Field defines a sequence as being a block of dramatic action unified by a single idea. A sequence may be a single scene, or even a single shot, but it may also be a series of scenes tied together by its unifying idea, and Field cites the wedding that opens *The Godfather* (1972) as one sequence, although it covers several hours of story time.[23] But whether a movie has 12 sequences (*Dog Day Afternoon*, 1975) or 31 scenes (*The Palm Beach Story*, 1942), there are limits to the range of variation. A movie cannot have 200 scenes or a single sequence without straining the conventional experience of its audience, and thus Hollywood cannot conventionally tell stories requiring those forms of organization.

Movies are always racing against time: "you've got thirty pages to set up your story, and . . . within the first ten pages, you must establish the *main character*, set up the dramatic *premise*, and establish the *situation*."[24] Field's imperatives sound like the deadlines so often imposed on movie characters. Just as the hero must rescue the heroine before the bomb explodes, the story must be over before film time runs out. Deadline-setting, digression, and coincidence help this commercial and industrial imperative to be disguised: movie time imposes fictional pressures on the characters' actions, so that the audience can overlook the external pressures of film time. You are not meant to be checking your watch for the plot point in the second act 85 minutes into the movie, because in the ideal Hollywood movie, the length of the film seems coincidentally to match the length of the story.

The promise of this coincidence – the audience's knowledge that the movie's story will resolve itself just when it is time for them to go home – allows for some play in the arrangement of an audience's temporal experience of a movie. The plot may, for instance, declare at the outset when it will end. *Madigan* opens with the simple title "Friday," when two detectives, Dan Madigan (Richard Widmark) and Rocco Bonaro (Harry Guardino), attempt to pick up a suspect, Barney Benesch (Steve Ihnat), for questioning. Instead, he escapes with their pistols and is later found to be wanted for murder. Police Commissioner Russell (Henry Fonda) gives the detectives 72 hours to bring Benesch in. The audience is immediately reminded that time will be a conscious preoccupation for the movie, and this is emphasized throughout by the mise-en-scène: calendars are frequently visible on office walls, and the plot's movement toward its climax is punctuated by titles announcing the arrival of "Saturday" and "Sunday." Setting a deadline makes it possible to read the relative temporal position of any given scene, and makes the movie's sense of pace meaningful. The urgency with which characters function becomes an index of how close the movie is to its closure. The detectives are constantly on the move, grabbing sleep where they can. With the pressure imposed on them by Russell's deadline, there is very little time for such luxury, and their attempts to withdraw from the action even briefly are usually interrupted by reminders that time is at a premium. "Can't you move this thing any faster?" Madigan asks Bonaro as they race to an appointment; elsewhere, after they have answered a false tip-off, he announces that he has "a lousy feeling that time is running out."

The race against time can also be lost if events move too quickly. Just as the movie must end before the last reel of film winds through the projector, it also must not end before then. Protagonists of suspense movies can never go to the police, for fear they may solve the mystery too quickly. But the plot, of course, must contrive some fictional reason to cover this implausibility. As a movie disguises its acceleration through deadline-setting, it will also introduce digressions to mask any delay or deceleration of its story. The most common strategy of delay involves the use of multiple plot lines. In *Madigan*, Benesch's escape establishes the main manhunt plot-line, but the detectives cannot simply recapture him as he

Detective Dan Madigan (Richard Widmark) races against time in *Madigan* (1968). Aquarius Picture Library

makes his break across the rooftops, or the movie would be concluded too quickly and with very little satisfaction. Instead, tension is generated around this main strand of action first by introducing subsidiary plots, and then by alternating between them. Sub-plots and minor characters have a number of functions in Hollywood dramaturgy: "they make excellent vehicles for comedy relief, crisis relief, and time-lapse cutaways. When the major story line becomes too tense, the action can always be cut away to the antics of the characters in the subplot."[25] As well as providing the audience with these incidental pleasures, this strategy places further pressure on the main characters by delaying the progress of the main plot and restricting the film time in which it must find resolution. The proliferation of sub-plots also covers over ellipses in the main plot, clarifying its advance.

Madigan develops four subsidiary plots, each with its own structure of deadlines and pressure:

1   The infidelity plot, in which Russell is having an affair with a married woman (Susan Clark), raising the question of whether she will stay with him or return home, and whether she will provoke a shift in his politics, principles, or sense of duty.

2   The brutality plot, in which a black clergyman, Dr Taylor (Raymond St Jacques), has made accusations about police brutality toward his arrested son, which Russell must investigate.

3   The corruption plot, in which Chief Inspector Charles Kane (James Whitmore) is discovered to be taking bribes from a local racketeer to protect his son, raising the question of how Commissioner Russell will decide to respond.

4   The domestic plot, in which Madigan's marriage comes under stress because of the demands made on his time by his work, raising the question of whether it will survive, or whether he will take up again with a former girlfriend, Jonesy (Sheree North).

The alternation between plot-lines hides the extent to which *Madigan* orders events in a firmly progressive sequence driven by its concentrated plot duration. The events that set the five plot-chains going are established early, but we join the stories relatively late on, at points where resolution already seems imminent. A clear causal sequence of action is made possible by beginning nearer to the end than the beginning, allowing viewers to concentrate on action likely to produce resolution rather than any further elaboration of causes.[26] Exposition is kept to a minimum. Dialogue is restricted to providing the necessary information, hooking scenes together, and performance is minimally distracting: Russell explains the corruption plot to his lover in a single toneless sentence, "Charlie Kane has done me in," and the movie cuts to the next scene. Despite its surface representation of the randomness of its milieu, causal coherence dominates in *Madigan*.[27]

Film time is distributed according to a temporal economy that concentrates the audience's attention on movie time. Events are given enough time for their staging and interpretation, but no more. Characters cooperate with this economy by anticipating outcomes, or creating future appointments that they then struggle to meet or avoid: Madigan must attend the captains' ball with his wife; Russell must investigate the accusations of brutality by Monday; another racketeer, Midget Castiglione (Michael Dunn), must produce information about Benesch's whereabouts before Benesch finds him. In this way, every scene advances at least one of the plots.

With duration thus dispersed among multiple plots, *Madigan* produces a sense of gradual acceleration both by the use of increasingly swift cutting rates, and by narrowing the focus of our interests as the subsidiary plots are successively resolved, with the main plot surviving longest.

1   In the infidelity plot, Russell's lover makes it clear that she will return to her husband and children when they return to New York.

2   In the brutality plot, Kane confirms to Russell that Dr Taylor's son was not assaulted by his arresting officers, implying that Russell will back his men and confront Taylor with his son's false accusations.

3   In the corruption plot, Russell confronts Kane with his corruption and Kane offers his resignation, but it is refused with a strong implication that he can be cleared.

4   In the domestic plot, despite a drunken spree that almost leads to her seduction, Julia reasserts her love for her husband.

5   In the manhunt plot, Madigan and Bonaro finally corner Benesch in an apartment, where both Benesch and Madigan are shot. Madigan dies on the way to hospital.

In all of these plots, the movie responds to the pressure to condense events with a heavy use of coincidence. Such coincidences are essential to Hollywood's temporal economy. They have become so thoroughly naturalized that they bypass our incredulous resistance to their likelihood, pushing the action on without needing elaborate explanation. However, characters in Hollywood movies frequently acknowledge the role of coincidence in their lives, and share a knowing complicity with the audience over this aspect of Hollywood's reconstruction of time. As Rick Blaine (Humphrey Bogart) says in *Casablanca*, "of all the gin joints in all the towns in all the world, she has to walk into mine." If she hadn't, there would be no story, in the sense that if the movie spent a credible amount of time waiting for its principals to reunite, there would be no time left for the rest of the tale.

The management of film time is a central function of a movie's narration. Detective movies employ a narrative of investigation, constructed around the timed release of plot information so that detective and audience explicitly share in the activities of hypothesis-forming and testing. In *The Big Sleep* (1946), for instance, the private detective Philip Marlowe (Humphrey Bogart) is in a sense employed by the audience to explain the plot, just as much as he is employed by General Sternwood (Charles Waldren) to protect his daughters from blackmail. Thrillers like *North by Northwest* (1959) have a "racetrack" narrative, bounded by deadlines and temporal pressure. But story-telling is not the only way that movies can manage the passage of film time. Physical comedy like that of Jerry Lewis or Steve Martin, or the team comedy of the Marx Brothers, breaks the plot up with gags and set-piece routines. Action movies such as *Lethal Weapon 2* (1989) devote more attention, and sometimes more time, to spectacle than to story, in much the same way as musicals use story premises as little more than an excuse for extended song-and-dance numbers which revel in their interruption of plot progression.

Alfred Hitchcock's remark that cinema is "life with the boring bits cut out" points to a fundamental principle of a movie's temporal organization: elision. In the movies, time lasts as long as necessary and no longer. This is why it seems much easier for characters in movies to get taxis than it does for the rest of us: we do not find it particularly entertaining to sit watching characters trying to hail a taxi for ten minutes when nothing else is happening. If a man in Chicago wants to go to Miami, and has the money, the time, and a good reason for his journey, there is very little entertainment value in our watching him go to the airport, buy his tickets, get on the plane, read the airline magazine, and so on. Eugene Vale advises screenplay writers that they can cut much of their exposition by losing it in the time lapses between scenes. The audience, he suggests, will assume that every intention ("I'm going to Miami on the next plane!") will be fulfilled unless an obstacle is placed in its path. The execution of an intention, he says, only becomes interesting if there is a possibility of its frustration ("We can't let him get to Miami alive!"). As our hyperbolic but all too typical example indicates, Vale's suggestion about temporal economy has a determining influence on what kinds of event can happen in a movie's plot: as he puts it, "in order to be permitted to show the execution of an intention, we must create an opposing difficulty." Movies thus, by an apparently iron law of construction, come to tell only those stories in which a sympathetic character overcomes a series of increasingly difficult obstacles to achieve a compelling desire:

> If a man and a woman with perfect affinity and no obvious difficulties meet each other, there is no doubt that they will attain their goal. The picture would have to show their marriage in the next shot, since we have no doubt of the fulfillment of their intention. All love scenes in between are without any interest. In order to show these love scenes, we must give the spectator a knowledge of some difficulties to prevent him from concluding to the goal.[28]

The process of constructing a coherent sequence without the boring bits relies on a series of conventions similar to those by which Hollywood constructs its spatial framework. Like mise-en-scène, these conventions are both obvious and virtually invisible to us – we recognize their operation, but find it hard to articulate them as such, instead displacing our awareness of them onto analysis of character motivation or narrative development. It therefore seems appropriate to label this parallel construction of movie time **mise-en-temps**.

Mise-en-temps

Movies take much longer to shoot than they do to project. On a good day in the Classical Hollywood production system, a film crew would hope to record four minutes of a movie's final footage in eight or ten hours' work, although two-and-a-half minutes was nearer the norm. In the compilation of a movie, each separately filmed shot is subsequently edited together into a narrative continuum, and in such a system of production there is no compelling logic for shooting a movie in plot order. In fact, Hollywood's commercial aesthetic generally militates against this. It is usually more economical to shoot all the scenes using one location, or one performer, at the same time, regardless of plot sequence. Thus the movie will finally be assembled out of radically discontinuous temporal fragments. In a literal sense, therefore, film makes time in the editing process, creating narrative time out of this process of assemblage, subsuming all other sorts of time to its needs.

In the same way as a system of spatial conventions converts potentially incoherent, partial views into a recognizable and expressive representation of space, the fragments of time recorded in each shot are assembled into a linear sequence to supply a comprehensible temporal experience. As audience members, we cannot alter this fixed sequential order in the way movies tell us stories. We can only keep our place in the story and understand the events unfolding before us by remembering the details we learned earlier on. If we watch a movie more than once, now knowing which clues to look out for, we may notice details that we ignored the first time around. Hollywood cannot, however, rely on its audience paying to see a movie twice, and it must therefore make sure that the most significant clues, relationships, or hidden character motivations announce themselves in some way.[29] The inflexibility of film time encourages movies to arrange themselves as a series of reiterated explanations – another aspect of the benign nature of Hollywood's conventions. A movie will state and restate character relationships, for example, "to sum up the situation for the benefit of those viewers who may have missed the beginning of the picture," or at least to ensure that the audience is not confused.[30] Significantly, these formal strategies, which evolved when Hollywood's audiences were watching movies exclusively in movie theaters, have become so natural to Hollywood's narrative aesthetic that they persist even in the age of video, whose domestic technology disrupts the normal relationship between film and movie time. Video enables the audience to fast forward, interrupt, or repeat film time in a way that might appear as perverse as the critical analysis of a single frame, but in fact conforms to the description of the audience's increasingly interactive relationship with Hollywood's output.

Hollywood's construction of time is more difficult to analyze than its construction of space, because temporal effects are less visible. We can see what a cut or dissolve does to space, but we must interpret its effect on the passage of time more indirectly. Perhaps the best way to identify Hollywood's elusive temporal strategies is to confront them at a moment when they are unusually exposed. Thrillers and action movies push Hollywood's temporal logic to extremes, and the generation of suspense involves a particularly assertive control over the audience's sense of time. In *North by Northwest*, the movie plays a temporal game with the audience to see just how much of this manipulation they will tolerate. Not only is the plot absurd, but there is often too much or too little time for the audience and the characters. The cropduster sequence in particular flouts our expectations of narrative time when the expected event – Roger Thornhill (Cary Grant) meeting a contact who will explain what is going on – does not happen, and the audience and Thornhill are left with time on their hands, loitering in an exceptionally bleak and featureless landscape in which there are no details with which we can occupy ourselves, and no visible hiding places for clues. For an uncomfortable length of time we seem to have life with the boring bits left in, while the movie withholds the next piece of action – the attack on Thornhill by the cropdusting plane which has been circling in the distance, but to which our attention has not been unduly alerted.

North by Northwest's malign treatment of the audience in this scene is revealing precisely because it is not typical. The movies of its director, Alfred Hitchcock, achieve their distinctiveness in large part because they work on the edges of Hollywood's conventions. As we discussed in chapter 5, Hitchcock's influence has revised those conventions of temporal and spatial representation in ways that encourage a more antagonistic relationship between movie and audience. But just as Classical Hollywood mise-en-scène seeks to avoid distracting visual information in the way it organizes an image, Classical Hollywood mise-en-temps works to avoid the very time in which that distraction might take place. This avoidance of "dead time" has the effect of concentrating our attention on the significant action. Journeys will often be presented as the juxtaposition of a point of departure with a point of arrival in a sequence that tells us not only that a character has gone from one place to another, but also that nothing consequential has happened en route. Events of less determinate status can be covered by narrative devices other than staging, by voice-over expositions, or by being reported by one character to another. Mise-en-temps is therefore another form of Hollywood's textual economy – excising the irrelevant and maximizing our attention to the relevant, showing us all we need to see and getting the most from what we do see. Hollywood cinema manages these multiple temporal obligations by evolving a narrational system that makes a virtue of the omissions and elisions it must practice for economic reasons, and that exploits film's ahistorical occupation of time to the hilt.

A second function of mise-en-temps is to preserve continuity within a scene assembled out of material shot weeks or months apart. If noticed by a viewer, errors in continuity – variations in the length of a character's cigarette, or changes in their clothing, for example – can be disastrous to the fiction, because they reveal so sharply the discontinuous fragments of external time from which the sequence is constructed. A system of conventions disguises this temporal discontinuity. The use of non-diegetic background music, for instance, smooths over the potential rupture between two discontinuous images. This bridging effect may be reinforced by elements of visual harmony in the two shots, such as matched compositions or camera movements. For instance, the camera might tilt up to the sky at the end of one scene, and begin the next scene with a tilt down from the sky, concealing a dissolve. Optical effects such as this have quite specific conventional meanings in their presentation of time. A dissolve from one image into another indicates a brief passage of time, shorter than that suggested by a fade to black and then a fade up to the next scene. A wipe, on the other hand, suggests less the passage of time than a spatial move from one location to another, in continuous time. More explicit devices occur in subtitles, or the intertitles of silent movies that declare "Two Years Later" or even "Meanwhile Back at the Ranch." The caption "meanwhile" effectively brings an event that has occurred (presumably while we were watching the parallel event) into the present.

Paradoxically, Hollywood may also establish continuity precisely by foregrounding temporal rupture in its mise-en-temps. In a **flashback** scene in *Casablanca*, Rick (Humphrey Bogart) and Ilsa (Ingrid Bergman) are shown driving down the Champs Elysées in a tight two-shot, with the Arc de Triomphe in the background behind them. Then the image in the background dissolves to a view of a country road, while the foreground image of Bogart and Bergman remains uncut. The shot is a conventional piece of studio-filmed back-projection, but the use of dissolves in back-projection is rare, because of the disturbing effect it has on the scene's temporal sense. Within the one image, two different kinds of time occur: more time goes by in the background than in the car. As we have come to expect, this semantic contradiction in the temporal organization of the material from which the scene is composed is properly resolved at the higher level of the fiction that viewers construct from that material, since what matters is what such literal discontinuities contribute to our understanding of character and situation. We interpret the romance between

Bogart and Bergman as being oblivious to the grand narrative of historical time, which passes behind them – although ultimately it will overtake them when their romance is interrupted by the German occupation of Paris.

Tense

For film to produce the illusion of movement, the projected image must be constantly and rapidly changed, with each image seen not in its singularity, but as part of a continuum that the viewer experiences as a constant present. At whatever point in a movie's story an event takes place, the audience always experiences it as being in the here and now of a **continuous present**. Movies are therefore characterized by a sense of immediacy that persists even during a second viewing, when the plot's future is already known. However, movies very rarely confine themselves to present action, with no reference to past motivations or future deadlines. In searching for the cinematic equivalent of the past tense, movies encounter a difficulty which is crucial for our understanding of Hollywood's organization of time. While a literary narrative is predominantly engaged in an act of telling, a cinematic narrative is an act of showing. As you can only tell something that has already happened, you can only show something that is happening as you show it. A movie audience has to "cook" its own story from the plot ingredients the movie offers, performing for itself the role that the narrator of a literary fiction undertakes. The sentence "The man walked down the street" is unfilmable not only because of its lack of spatial specificity, but also because film cannot visualize the past tense. Representing the future tense, rather than a future event staged in the continuous present, presents a further problem: the future can be discussed, or inferred ("We have fourteen days to save the Universe!"), but cannot be visualized without being translated into the present tense.

Hollywood must therefore find other ways to signal temporal change within the movie, and thus establish a chronology of events in the story. Such devices cannot function as subtly as changes of tense in spoken language, and are therefore likely to exist as highly visual markers: the changing date on a calendar, the changing time on a clock. In *Written on the Wind* (1956), the credit sequence stages the climax of the movie, ending with the camera tracking in to a tight close-up of a desk calendar. As the pages of the calendar start to blow backwards, the image dissolves to a similar shot of the same calendar, in a different setting. When the pages have stopped blowing, the camera tracks out to its new setting, and the movie's action, from then on organized in chronological sequence, begins. The effect of the shot is to take the audience back into the past so that it can experience that past as the present. In one sense it is a literal cinematic equivalent of the act of narration, but the effect of the shot does not reproduce the sense of temporal distance from the events described that the past tense provides in written or spoken language. During the sequence itself, film time moves forward as one present moment on the screen is replaced with another, while time in the movie's narration moves backward, frame by frame.

Hollywood often uses obvious narrational clues to establish temporal shifts, in particular with characters narrating **voice-overs** in the past (perfect) tense. At the start of *Double Indemnity* (1944) Walter Neff (Fred MacMurray) sets the plot in motion by confessing a crime into a recording machine. As he speaks into the microphone, the movie dissolves "back" to the events he is describing, and the voice-over runs on over images of his arrival at the house of the woman with whom he will commit murder. The viewer's comprehension of time in this sequence is complex and the tense involved contradictory. Just listening to the soundtrack reproduces the perfect (past) tense of a written narration: Neff, situated in the auditor's present, narrates events in the past tense. The images, however, all occur in the continuous present of film time. At one point in the sequence, this temporal contradiction is given spatial expression in a split between viewpoint and point of view. MacMurray is physically placed in the represented space of the scene, at the same time as he is describing his view of Barbara Stanwyck's legs in the narration. The shots we see of Stanwyck, however, are taken from a different position: they represent MacMurray's point of view, but not his viewpoint, since he is not in a position actually to see Stanwyck descend the staircase. The distinction between viewpoint and point of view is elided in the viewer's cooperative act of consumption in interpreting the convention of presentation. We recognize this sequence as being simultaneously a memory and an imaginative reconstruction of the scene, and displace the temporal contradiction into an elucidation of character psychology, much as we do with spatial conventions.

The voice-over points up differences in the knowledge available to the narrator and the audience: the narrator demonstrates her or his knowledge of the whole story, including the end, by setting it in the past, whereas the audience experiences the past tense as a present uncertainty while the story unfolds.[31] The device may be laid bare, in a formalist sense, by having the first-person narrator discovered in the act of narration at the end. In *Double Indemnity*, Neff discovers that Keyes (Edward G. Robinson), the man for whom he has been recording his confession, has actually been present to hear the last part of it. At the end of *The Postman Always Rings Twice* (1946, and, like *Double Indemnity*, based on a novel by James M. Cain), the narration is similarly brought into the present as the audience discovers that Frank Chambers (John Garfield) has been telling the story not to us, but to a priest in the condemned cell just before his execution. *Sunset Boulevard* (1950) goes one step beyond this, since its narrator, scriptwriter Joe Gillis (William Holden), is already dead at the start of the movie, which tells the story of the events leading up to his murder.

In his conversations with François Truffaut, Alfred Hitchcock suggested another example where the order in which information is revealed to the audience conditions their response to the scene:

> We are now having a very innocent little chat. Let us suppose that there is a bomb underneath this table between us. Nothing happens, and then all of a sudden, "Boom!" There is an explosion. The public is *surprised*, but prior to this surprise, it has seen an absolutely ordinary scene, of no special consequence. Now, let us take a *suspense* situation. The bomb is underneath the table and the public *knows* it, probably because they have seen the anarchist place it there. The public is *aware* that the bomb is going to explode at one o'clock and there is a clock in the decor. The public can see that it is a quarter to one. In these conditions the same innocuous conversation becomes fascinating because the public is participating in the scene. The audience is longing to warn the characters on the screen: "You shouldn't be talking about such trivial matters. There is a bomb beneath you and it's about to explode!"[32]

Hitchcock's hypothetical example demonstrates how suspense is generated by the mise-en-temps of a deadline. Even if the bomb is not visible, the memory of its earlier arrival governs the audience's response to the present scene. In Hollywood, bombs are not planted in order to be forgotten. The linear causality of Hollywood plotting ensures that, once a bomb is planted, a movie will progress inexorably toward either its discovery or its explosion. In the continuous present that we experience outside the cinema, the future is unknown. But in the continuous present of movie time, audiences recognize the conventions of causality and coincidence, which make it possible, in examples like Hitchcock's, for the movie itself (not just the camera) to be simultaneously innocent of and aware of its future.

The possibility of cinematic tenses closely resembling but existing outside positions on the continuum of historical time leads us back to the other significant temporal gesture made by *Double Indemnity* as Barbara Stanwyck comes downstairs. This lies in the offer made to the audience to pause in their decoding of the narrative to take pleasure in the spectacle of Barbara Stanwyck's legs. That the formal "time-out" qualities of a musical number, car chase, or saloon brawl can be encapsulated in this momentary diversion – no more than a double-take, barely calling attention to itself – is an important reminder that Hollywood's ability to interrupt itself is not restricted to exceptional situations, but is an absolutely routine part of its provision of spectacular pleasure. We can now describe "time out" as a cinematic tense operating outside the normal continuum of past–present–future. The splitting of audience attention between narrative and spectacle is diagrammatically represented in this example as a division between soundtrack and image, but it is entirely consistent with the subtle but rewarding tension generated by the spectacular performance of cinema itself as existing outside the audience's normal sense of historical time.

Some movies are explicitly preoccupied with the exploration of "time out" in the cinema. In *Groundhog Day* (1993), irascible television weatherman Phil Connors (Bill Murray) keeps waking up to discover that he is trapped on the same day of his life; while all the other characters experience February 2 for the first time on each occasion, he alone knows that he is stuck in a time loop, apparently doomed to repeat his actions indefinitely. For Connors, movie time mimics film time. It does not progress, but merely passes endlessly at the same rate. The movie creates an unusual anxiety in its audience, who are subjected to an apparently endless repetition of the same events – the radio alarm starts to play "I've Got You, Babe" at 6.00 a.m. on a dozen occasions. Powerless to prevent the repetition, we become increasingly desperate for Connors to learn how to behave properly in a sentimental story so that he can get the girl (Andie MacDowell), and all of us can escape back into the comfortable progressions of movie time. Only then can the movie come to an end, and the audience go home. In effect, the movie reminds us that the consequences of fast-forwarding or replaying linear time are potentially catastrophic, and should be restricted to the simulated version of the effect available to the viewer who watches a Hollywood movie twice.

Back to the Present

> It is sometimes very hard to stage things with historical accuracy ... For instance, in a picture we made about the life of Napoleon, he asked Josephine a certain question which she did not answer until four years later. When we made our picture, we took the liberty, for the sake of dramatic effect, of cutting out the four years ... If, in telling a story, we find it impossible to adhere to historical accuracy in order to get the necessary dramatic effect, we do change it and we feel that that is the right thing to do.
> Irving Thalberg[33]

> Footnotes cannot be filmed.
> David Herlihy[34]

Movies must bring the past and the future into the present in order to represent them. A number of 1980s Hollywood movies staged this process as a plot device. In *The Terminator* (1984) a cyborg soldier (Arnold Schwarzenegger) travels from the future to the present to kill the mother of the man who will become the leader of a resistance movement. The human warrior who pursues him, Reese (Michael Biehn), survives the movie long enough to become the father of his future leader, while the heroine, Sarah Connor (Linda Hamilton), tries not to "go crazy" thinking about the way Reese talks in the past tense "about things I haven't done yet," and about the Oedipal implications of *Terminator*'s scenario.[35] In *Back to the Future* (1985) and *Peggy Sue Got Married* (1986) the central characters find themselves propelled back into the 1950s, with their mid-1980s sensibilities intact. Peggy Sue (Kathleen Turner) has to decide whether to restage her romance with her husband Charlie (Nicholas Cage), despite her disappointment with her 25-year marriage. In *Back to the Future*, Marty McFly (Michael J. Fox) finds himself in an even more alarming predicament, since he has to persuade the woman who will become his mother, Lorraine (Lea Thompson), to abandon her crush on him and date his future father, George (Crispin Glover), the school nerd. Marty's own presence in the past is potentially so disruptive ("My mom has the hots for me!") that he rapidly realizes the need to return to his proper place in time. His extra knowledge of the future only proves burdensome, since his smallest gesture may change the course of history irreparably, even throwing his own existence into jeopardy. The only course of action open to him is to ensure that events turn out so that the fast-approaching future remains as it always was.

These two movies treat small-town 1950s America (*Peggy Sue* is set in 1960) as a Utopian landscape; Peggy Sue learns the same lesson that Dorothy (Judy Garland) learns in *The Wizard of Oz* (1939) and that George Bailey (James Stewart) learns in *It's a Wonderful Life* (1946), that there's no place like home. Marty, however, manages to improve his home. During his visit to the past he has taught George to be more assertive, and returns to the present to discover his father a much more successful businessman and more aggressively masculine than when he left.[36] In *Back to the Future*

Oedipal comedy – "My mom has the hots for me!" – Marty McFly (Michael J. Fox) and his future mother, Lorraine (Lea Thompson), in *Back to the Future* (1985). Amblin/Universal (courtesy Kobal)

Part II time travel becomes more explicitly an alternative to fantasy as the plot leans more heavily on *It's a Wonderful Life* for its organization. Where George Bailey is shown a fantastic dystopian vision of what his home-town of Bedford Falls would have been like without him, Marty experiences several alternative versions of the present, the future, and the past, including watching himself enact his previous temporal displacement in the climax of the original movie – as he remarks at this moment, "talk about *déjà vu*."

Back to the Future Part II's movements between past, present, and future become unspeakably complicated. At one point Doc (Christopher Lloyd) tells Marty that "Obviously, the time continuum has been disrupted, creating this new temporal event sequence, resulting in this alternate reality." When Marty demands an explanation in "English," Doc begins drawing diagrams of the movie's plot on a blackboard: "While we were in the future, Biff got the sports book, stole the time machine, went back in time and gave the book to himself at some point in the past . . . our only chance to repair the present is in the past, at the point where the time line skewed into this tangent." The movie's "temporal paradoxes" and its shifts from past to future to alternate present are, however, straightforward enough to follow, since the movie itself remains firmly, inevitably, in the present. However much the plot may disrupt the space-time continuum within its fiction (a time paradox, explains Doc, "could cause a chain reaction that would unravel the very fabric of the space-time continuum and destroy the entire universe"), the audience progresses through a narration staged in its own continuous present tense, moving from beginning to end according to its internal, tightly organized, dramatic logic.[37]

Although only a few Hollywood movies featured plots concerned with time travel before the 1980s (Mark Twain's *A Connecticut Yankee in King Arthur's Court*, for example, was filmed as a Will Rogers comedy in 1931 and a Bing Crosby musical in 1949), the movies' excursions into history are equally constrained by their position in the audience's present. In "bringing the past to life" or making the audience witnesses to past events, as Hollywood's historical movies have claimed to do, they have also transposed historical events into the cinema's continuous present. Historical events, of course, are not in any way inherently different from other screened events: watching Clark Gable pretending to be Fletcher Christian in *Mutiny on the Bounty* (1935) does not become a different experience from watching Clark Gable pretending to be Jake Thornton in *The Call of the Wild* (1935) because Fletcher Christian was an historical personage and Jake Thornton a fictional character. Placing historical events into a sequence, even in a history textbook, employs the conventions of fiction, and few historians would dispute that writing a history involves constructing a narrative that is of necessity a selective interpretation of the occurrences it describes.

Hollywood movies are, however, fictions before they are histories: *Mutiny on the Bounty* is shaped by a set of narrative and generic conventions

Clark Gable as Fletcher Christian and Charles Laughton as Captain Bligh in *Mutiny on the Bounty* (1935). Just as much as fictional characters, historical figures must conform to the personas of the stars playing them. MGM (courtesy Kobal)

little different from those that shape *The Call of the Wild*. In his account of Hollywood's biographical pictures (or **biopics**), George Custen notes that studio executives would frequently propose adopting a plot derived from a successful fictional movie. In devising *The Story of Alexander Graham Bell* (1939), Darryl Zanuck insisted that Bell's invention of the telephone had to be motivated by something more than "mechanical and scientific dreams." The scriptwriters must find ways of making Bell "so real, so human, so down to earth and such a regular guy" that the audience would "root for" him. The solution, which was borrowed from previous TCF hits such as *Drums Along the Mohawk* (1939) and *In Old Chicago* (1938), was to intertwine the invention with the movie's love story. As Custen argues, Bell and other protagonists of biopics are made like Frankenstein, "of bits of previous incarnations of already-lived lives . . . a hit life was constructed out of resurrected hit movies."[38] Every great biopic life resembled every other; as Lamar Trotti, one of the screenwriters for *The Story of Alexander Graham Bell*, declared: "In every great character story on the screen – Rothschild, Zola, Pasteur – the principal character, or characters, have battled against something great for something great."[39] Custen suggests that Hollywood's version of history, constructed around the story of "great characters" whom an audience is encouraged to "root for," has had a considerable influence on public perceptions of both history and fame. Hollywood's history can be criticized not merely because of its inaccuracies, but also because the biopic reduces the ambiguities of historical process to "a mechanical view of the universe," in which the past is compressed into a single, linear chain of cause and effect, with a single interpretation of events. "Such a narrative strategy," argues Robert Rosenstone, "denies historical alternatives, does away with complexities of motivation or causation, and banishes all subtlety from the world of history."[40] Historical causation is reduced to the deeds of the great, while the fact that movies set in different historical eras tell the same story encourages the idea that all historical periods have been the same.

Professional historians, certainly, have found little to commend in many of Hollywood's excursions into the past, and have sometimes expressed anxieties about the extent to which movies and television have become a prime source of most people's knowledge of history. Many have advanced arguments about the inevitably incomplete nature of a movie's representation of history.[41] But if we consider instead the uses to which Hollywood put history – history as a production value – we may be able to explore some of the ideological ramifications of representing the past in the present.

Immediately after *Mutiny on the Bounty* and *Call of the Wild*, Clark Gable made a third movie with an historical setting. *San Francisco* (1936) was set in 1906, and climaxes in the great earthquake and fire that destroyed much of the city. But the character Gable plays, saloon owner Blackie Norton, is an entirely fictional figure, and the story of his romance with singer Mary Blake (Jeanette MacDonald) is constructed according to the conventions of Hollywood's love stories, with the historical setting providing a background. *San Francisco*'s setting justifies its elaborate costume designs and sets, and anchors its spectacular restaging of the earthquake as historically correct. Although in every other respect fictional, the movie invokes historical accuracy as a form of verisimilitude. However, the earthquake is there less to persuade viewers of the movie's plausibility than to provide spectacle. The historical events in period films motivate and justify the elements of spectacle that exceed the requirements of the story, at the same time as they justify the movie's spectacle in terms of its historical truth: *San Francisco* could not, for instance, have climaxed with an earthquake if it had been set in Chicago in 1906. The known events of public history provide a relatively fixed background for the invented happenings of characters' private histories. Like Marty McFly in *Back to the Future*, *San Francisco* cannot change major historical events (in the movie the earthquake happens, as it did, on April 18, 1906), but the movie can devise whatever fate it sees fit for its fictional characters. Just as Marty's excursion into the past allows him to change the personal history of his father, but

History as spectacle: the 1906 earthquake in *San Francisco* (1936). MGM (courtesy Kobal)

not to prevent Ronald Reagan becoming president, so Hollywood's period movies take fictional liberties with the personal details of their characters, regardless of whether those characters had separate historical existences or not.

In 1946 Warner Bros. produced *Night and Day*, a biopic of composer Cole Porter. The studio's contract with Porter stipulated that in developing the story, the studio: "shall be free to dramatize, fictionalize, or emphasize any or all incidents in the life of Seller, or interpolate such incidents as Producers may deem necessary in order to obtain a treatment or continuity of commercial value."[42] The clause summarized Hollywood's relation to historical veracity and also to the exploitation of history. As George Custen points out, *Night and Day*'s version of Porter's biography bore little resemblance to the actual events of his life, suppressing any mention of his homosexuality behind a standardized representation of heterosexual romance. Hollywood's historical and period movies change the private histories of their characters, regardless of their fictional status. But there have been limits to the liberties Hollywood has been able to take with public history, even for motives of story-telling, because public history is the property of the audience. For this reason, Hollywood movies more often use historical events as spectacle passing in the background. *The Roaring Twenties* (1939), for instance, tells the story of the rise and fall of gangster Eddie Bartlett (James Cagney), intermittently tying his personal story to larger historical occurrences, such as World War I, the introduction of Prohibition, and the 1929 Wall Street Crash. Like the earthquake in *San Francisco*, these events appear in montage sequences, self-contained episodes of graphic display of angled shots dissolving into each other.[43] Although one function of these sequences in *The Roaring Twenties* is to present and explain the way that historical events affect the Cagney character, they also visualize history as a lavish spectacle, offering the same time out from narrative as a musical number. The Wall Street Crash, for example, is used as a transitional device to move from a scene in which we witness Cagney's loss of emotional equilibrium when his girlfriend leaves him for another man, so that he starts drinking, to a loss of his material security as a result of the Crash. History here functions as a separable production value, only partially integrated into the story.

To see history as a production value allows us to reconsider questions of historical realism, in much the same way as we have looked at realism in thinking about genre and technology. Hollywood publicity invokes the rhetoric of historical realism in terms very similar to the publicity attached to the spectacle of technology: "Here is blazing history written in the life blood of a great nation! Here is pomp, romance, struggle, glory, magnificently welded by Warner Bros. into stirring entertainment never approached by the screen before!"[44] Largely as a result of their investment in period movies, each of the major studios established a research department, principally concerned with authenticating the historical representations of the studio's movies. On occasion this involved copious research, which was frequently used as part of the advertising campaign for the resulting movie. Studio research was largely concerned with authenticating production details – of costume, sets, and props, for example – and to a large extent a movie's historical accuracy came to be defined as a matter of the authenticity of its detail. *The Charge of the Light Brigade* (1936), for example, received more public criticism in Britain for alleged inaccuracies in the details of its Lancers' uniforms and troop formations than it did for its total rewriting of the motivations and events of the Crimean War. In its reduction to questions of authenticity, historical realism resembles the "verisimilitude of surface" that Douglas Pye describes in his discussion of realism in the Western, where a "solidity of appearance" creates "an inhabitable world."[45] Westerns are, of course, period movies, and engage extensively in the interplay between historical facts and fictions.

The producers of *The Charge of the Light Brigade* did not, however, approach their distortions of history casually. During script development, Warner Bros.' head of production, Hal Wallis, commented to the movie's producer, Sam Bischoff, that he was concerned about its historical inaccuracies,

> particularly the total disregard for historical facts on the battle of Balaclava and "the Charge of the Light Brigade", the motivation therefor, the absence

of the "Kahn" from any historical date . . . I realize that we have a very highly fictionalized story and that it bears no relation to historical facts but, at the same time, if we are to save ourselves from a lot of grief and criticism in England, we must make our picture as historically accurate as possible, or at least surround our Battle of Balaclava and The Charge of the Light Brigade with historically correct incidents and details.[46]

Wallis compensated for the story's distortions of historical causality by investing in the period authenticity of the movie's mise-en-scène. His rationalization typifies Hollywood's understanding of its responsibility to history. *The Charge of the Light Brigade* was one of many historical and period pictures made in the late 1930s consciously aiming to appeal to educational groups. It was the subject of two study guides, designed to be used in high-school courses in film appreciation, "to afford both teacher and pupil the opportunity of utilizing the best in motion pictures for classroom discussion, and to help students learn all they can from the movies through a knowledge of their historical and literary background."[47] These study guides combined promotional material for the movie in question, including information on its stars that would not have been out of

On its release in 1936, high-school students were encouraged to consider whether *The Charge of the Light Brigade* was justified in distorting history for dramatic effect. Warner Bros. (courtesy Kobal)

place in fan magazines, with analysis of the movie and its sources, and exercises for the individual student and the class. Their declared intention, at least, was to better equip students "to measure the worth of the films you see and to praise or condemn them with authority." The Photoplay study guide to *The Charge of the Light Brigade* concentrated "on the way in which cinematographic conditions affect problems of history. . . . How far may screen authors go in dealing with history? Is there a cinematographic license that corresponds to the traditional poetic license?"[48] While non-scholastic audiences for the movie were provided with a love triangle, an oriental villain, and, in the charge itself, "a thrill seldom experienced in a motion picture theater,"[49] the hundreds of thousands of high-school students reading the guides encountered the movie in a context that exposed and explored its relationship to history in some complexity.

Hollywood movies projected history into the present in two other senses. It was not merely their stories that had to shape history into conformity with contemporary convention. Despite the claims to authenticity of detail, the same constraints applied to costume design, where, according to Edward Maeder, "authenticity rarely involved abandoning contemporary standards."[50] Thus, cave-dwellers' costumes would be cut to emphasize the 1940s silhouette, or antebellum dresses made with 1930s bias-cut fabrics. The stars' physical appearance, too, represented a compromise between historical accuracy and contemporary notions of glamor. Despite Alicia Annas' exquisite description of *Spartacus* (1960) as "quite simply a film about brown eyeshadow," makeup was seldom accommodated to the requirements of history; instead, period authenticity was adjusted to the leading players' star images. The same was true of hairstyles, for both men and women. *Some Like It Hot* (1959) is set in 1929, with Tony Curtis and Jack Lemmon spending most of the movie in drag, hiding from gangsters in an all-girl band whose lead singer is played by Marilyn Monroe:

> The two leading men wore female makeup disguises that combined rounded 1950s lips and thick 1950s brows angled like those of the 1920s. They also wore the heavy lashes and smudged eyeshadow of the 1920s. Their wigs were likewise a clever cross between periods. But Marilyn was pure Marilyn with 1950s formula makeup and hairstyle.

In *Spartacus*, Kirk Douglas "sported an ultra-fashionable, distinctly non-Roman, tough-guy flat top, almost identical to the one he wore earlier that year in the modern *Strangers When We Meet*."[51] Hollywood's commercial aesthetic could hardly be more clearly in evidence than in these preferences for the marketing of fashionable images over historical authenticity. In fact, historical movies provided more opportunities for experimentation in fashion than contemporary pictures did. Fashion reporter Lilian Churchill observed in 1940 that "clothes in period pictures do affect the modes of the moment. The dress in modern films may be of little importance, but costume pictures add notes, bars and passages to the symphony of dress."[52] Women's hats in costume movies were frequently fashion innovators, while *Bonnie and Clyde* (1967) was held "responsible for the midis and braless bosoms that are the trademark of the early seventies."[53]

If Hollywood has put history to work commercially in its promotion of fashion, it has also less systematically made history perform the work of ideology. In the second half of the 1930s, the major companies made prestige historical pictures as part of a calculated strategy designed to convince middle-class America of the bourgeois respectability of the cinema. As *Variety* put it, "the files of history" were thought less likely to offend the "busybody factions" that had been calling for stricter regulation of the movies. *The Charge of the Light Brigade* was part of this strategy, but more prominent in it were adaptations of literary classics and historical biographies. Warner Bros. produced a trilogy of biopics starring Paul Muni between 1936 and 1939 which showed an increasingly explicit concern with drawing lessons about present-day politics from past historical events. The first of these, *The Story of Louis Pasteur* (1936), preached a generalized, apolitical humanitarianism, but its sequel, *The Life of Emile Zola* (1937), included a more explicitly political issue in its plot, which centered on Zola's championing of Captain Alfred Dreyfus, a Jewish officer in the French army falsely found guilty of treason in 1894. The connection to contemporary events in Germany was obvious, and although *Zola* presented the issue of anti-semitism cautiously, many of those involved in the movie's production saw it as a politically significant act. Many of the German filmmakers who fled the Nazi regime in the 1930s came to work at Warners, among them the producer and director of the Muni biopics, Henry Blanke and William Dieterle, and they exercised a significant influence on the choice of material and its ideological attitude.

Partly because of events in Europe, and partly because of the lengthy campaign to unionize the production industry, there was widespread support for liberal and anti-Fascist causes in Hollywood in the late 1930s, encouraged by the attendant publicity that any event in the movie capital received. At Warners, it was echoed in some of the studio's output, including *Confessions of a Nazi Spy* (1939) and two movies dealing with racial prejudice made in 1937, *They Won't Forget* and *Black Legion*. This political concern also surfaced strongly in *Juárez* (1939), the third of the Muni biopics. The studio's original intention was to produce an adaptation of *The Phantom Crown*, Bertita Harding's romanticized history of Maximilian von Hapsburg and his wife Carlotta, inveigled by Emperor Napoleon III into accepting the crown of Mexico in 1864 as part of Napoleon's imperialist designs on Latin America. As the script developed, however, it became more concerned with Benito Juárez, president of the legally constituted Mexican government and a hero of Mexican political mythology. This was in part because the writers saw Juárez as a role for Paul Muni, but also because of the political possibilities available from this inflection of a lesson from history. These implications were explicitly stated by one of its writers, Wolfgang Reinhardt, in a memo on one of the early script treatments in which he suggested that a good writer, "with a sense of political correlations," could:

> point up in a dramatic and *entertaining* fashion the analogy between conditions prevalent then and happenings of today. The dialogue, as far as it is political and ideological, must consist of familiar phrases from today's newspapers; every child must be able to realize that Napoleon, in his Mexican intervention, is none other than Mussolini plus Hitler in their Spanish adventure.[54]

The script went through an extensive evolution that blunted its political sentiment in compromises with its generic status as historical romance and star vehicle. But its producer Henry Blanke maintained that the movie's representation of Juárez as a "Mexican Lincoln" explained "the ideology of a Democracy" to its audiences, and supported United States foreign policy doctrine in uniting the American continents against European totalitarianism. *Juárez*'s publicity campaign encouraged schools to stage debates about the meaning of democracy, and public-speaking contests about the parallels between the events in the movie and the aggressive foreign policies of the totalitarian states. The study guide to *Juárez* suggested that the movie reflected "a series of present day events," and that "the theme of the picture, *that democracy can make no condescensions to the most benevolent authoritarianism*, is significant to the present day world."[55] Within the movie itself, the contemporary relevance of its version of history was most overtly expressed in the speech Juárez makes to a group of European ambassadors when he refuses their pleas for him not to execute Maximilian:

> Your Excellencies make use of a jargon which was designed to conceal the principle that motivates your European civilization: a civilization which permits the oppression of the weak by the strong; wherein each great power in turn inflicts its will upon some weaker union. . . . By what right, senores, do the great powers of Europe invade the lands of simple people . . . kill all who do not make them welcome . . . destroy their fields . . . and take the fruit of their toil from those who survive . . .? Is it a crime against God, then, that the skin of some men is of a different color from others . . . that they do not wear shoes upon their feet . . . that they know nothing of factories and commerce . . . that there are neither bankers nor speculators in their land . . . ?[56]

In Hollywood as elsewhere, however, the lessons of history are always subject to revision in accordance with the needs of the present. *Juárez* was re-released in the very different political climate of 1954, when the formerly European villains had become Cold War allies. So the speech, and its motivation of the plot, were omitted, together with all other references to European imperialism. *Juárez's* revision of history, and its own subsequent revision, makes perhaps the overriding point about Hollywood and historical accuracy: whether at the level of costume or of ideology, it is most often the inaccuracies or reworkings of history in Hollywood movies that make the movies themselves such informative historical documents.

Notes

1 Joseph P. Kennedy, "Preface," in Joseph P. Kennedy, ed., *The Story of the Films* (Chicago: A.W. Shaw, 1927), p. vi.

2 Harold B. Franklin, *Motion Picture Theatre Management* (New York: Doran, 1927), p. 246.

3 Michael Hauge, *Writing Screenplays that Sell* (New York: McGraw-Hill, 1988), p. 82.

4 Syd Field, *Screenplay: The Foundations of Screenwriting* (New York: Dell, 1979), pp. 8–9. Field regards *Chinatown* as "the best American screenplay written during the 1970s." Field, p. 70.

5 Field, p. 116.

6 Field, p. 53.

7 In *The Player*, Michael Tolkin describes the reaction of his central character, studio executive Griffin Mill, to screenplays constructed according to such formulae: "Some [writers] tried to condense their ideas to twenty-five words, as they'd learned in some screenwriting class taught by someone who'd made a science out of yesterday's formula. They'd talk about the 'arc of the story.' They'd use little code words and phrases like *paradigm* and *first-act bump*. They were exact. 'At minute twenty-three she finds out . . .' What does she find out? That this movie won't get made." Four pages later, Mill is discussing "plot points." Michael Tolkin, *The Player* (London: Faber, 1988), pp. 13, 17.

8 Although there is obviously more narrative content in the South American pre-credit sequence of *Raiders of the Lost Ark* (1981), its function is also primarily spectacular, and it is equally self-contained, bearing no great relation to the main story that follows the credits.

9 The story is told, for instance, in Peter Bogdanovich, *Fritz Lang in America* (London: Studio Vista, 1969), p. 88; and in Philip French, *The Movie Moguls: An Informal History of the Hollywood Tycoons* (Harmondsworth: Penguin, 1969), p. 78. A slightly different version (there are doubtless many others) is in Jack Vizzard, *See No Evil: Life Inside a Hollywood Censor* (New York: Simon and Schuster, 1970), p. 74.

10 By comparison, television's sense of temporal organization is somewhat less demanding. Television's greater commitment to immediacy and the live event provides it with a much less intense obligation not to waste the time of the fiction.

11 Clifford Geertz, *The Interpretation of Cultures* (New York: Basic Books, 1973), p. 445.

12 Since silent movie cameras were hand-cranked, there were often signficant minor variations in the speed at which they were shot, and one of the skills required of silent cinema archivists is the ability to judge the correct projection speed. Silent movies were also often projected at speeds slightly faster than those at which they had been shot. More recently, some large-screen formats have used higher frame speeds than 24 frames a second to improve their image quality.

13 More detailed accounts of these mental processes can be found in David Bordwell, *Narration in the Fiction Film* (London: Methuen, 1985), pp. 30–3; and Susan J. Lederman

and Bill Nichols, "Flicker and Motion in Film," in Bill Nichols, *Ideology and the Image* (Bloomington: Indiana University Press, 1981), pp. 297–8.

14 See, for example, James Monaco, *How to Read a Film: The Art, Technology, Language, History and Theory of Film and Media* (New York: Oxford University Press, 1977). David Bordwell has argued cogently against the analogy implied by this usage; see in particular ch. 11, "Why Not to Read a Film," in *Making Meaning: Inference and Rhetoric in the Interpretation of Cinema* (Cambridge, MA: Harvard University Press, 1989), pp. 249–74.

15 During periods of product shortage, movies might be re-released several years after their initial exhibition, usually to make up the balance of double-feature programs. Before sales to television, however, this was a relatively unimportant and minor element in the major companies' finances.

16 Franklin, p. 246.

17 Discussing his work in reconstructing a print of *The Four Horsemen of the Apocalypse* (1921), Kevin Brownlow explains that the exported version of the movie was constructed from different shots to the American domestic release version. Because of the poor quality of duped (duplicated) negatives in the early 1920s, silent movies were normally shot on two cameras, to produce one negative for the domestic market, and one for export use. When a movie was photographed on a single camera and no spare export negative was made, sequences would be assembled from second takes of shots, or on occasion, if takes had not been repeated, from alternative set-ups. Kevin Brownlow, "Burning Memories," *Sight and Sound London Film Festival Supplement* (October 1992), p. 13.

18 On its video release in 1992, *Dances with Wolves* was almost immediately available in four versions: with and without an additional hour's footage, in widescreen and standard formats.

19 Both the freezing of the action on the urn, and the act of placing the urn in a museum, are actions that celebrate the interruption of the historical continuum to preserve an activity and an object in a fixed aesthetic attitude. Although this is not the place to dwell on the pervasive Eurocentric assumptions about "culture" and "universal values" expressed in the poem, or to discuss how and why the British Museum acquired the urn, we might note that the poem expresses no concern with what Greeks actually used urns for. Its original purpose has come to have no bearing on the use to which the urn is now put as a repository of transhistorical and crosscultural values, a use that it has only acquired through the process of its museumization.

20 Eugene Vale, *The Technique of Screenplay Writing*, 1st pub. 1944 (New York: Grosset and Dunlap, 1973), p. 63.

21 The distinction between plot and story duration is discussed by David Bordwell in ch. 6 of *Narration in the Fiction Film*, pp. 74–98. Bordwell's terminology differs somewhat from ours: as well as employing the formalist terms of *fabula* and *syuzhet* for story and plot, he also identifies what we are calling film time as "screen duration" or "projection time." The differences in terminology are, however, less important than the concurrence of ideas, although Bordwell might not accept our suggestion that the distinction between film time and movie time is of a different categorical order to that between plot and story duration.

22 "A scene in the motion picture is not determined by its content of action, nor by entrances and exits of actors, but by a change of place or a lapse of time." Vale, p. 56.

23 Field, p. 92. Critics and theorists of film from Pudovkin and Eisenstein on have also engaged in this debate, which touches on the idea of identifying the fundamental units of cinematic narrative. One of the most elaborate attempts was the "*grande syntagmatique*" of French theorist Christian Metz, which identified eight main types of

narrative segment. Metz's categorization, however, needed so many qualifications in its application that as an instrument of analysis it proved both unwieldy and restrictive. The more empirical categories deployed by Field, Vale, and other functional analysts of Hollywood structures turn out to be as useful as more elaborate structuralist models. Christian Metz, *Film Language: A Semiotics of the Cinema*, trans. Michael Taylor (New York: Oxford University Press, 1974), p. 146.

24   Field, p. 196.

25   Lewis Herman, *A Practical Manual of Screen Playwriting for Theater and Television Films* (New York: New English Library, 1952), p. 37.

26   Hollywood movies conventionally open "*in medias res*, " in the middle of the story, so that we are plunged "into an already moving chain of cause and effect." Action movies, however, tend to begin their plots closer to the end of their stories than other genres, so that they need to spend less time in the exposition of their cause-and-effect chain. David Bordwell, Janet Staiger, and Kristin Thompson, *The Classical Hollywood Cinema: Film Style and Mode of Production to 1960* (London: Routledge and Kegan Paul, 1985), p. 28.

27   Formalist criticism refers to this causal coherence as compositional motivation. Motivation (discussed in more detail in chapter 8) is the process by which a narrative justifies its story material; the elements of the story that must be present in order for it to proceed – as opposed to realistically or generically motivated factors – are its compositional elements. David Bordwell provides a formalist account of motivation in Bordwell, Staiger, and Thompson, *The Classical Hollywood Cinema*, pp. 19–21.

28   Vale, p. 154. The screenwriter of *Die Hard 2* (1990), Steve de Souza, identifies an "all-purpose formula [that] covers every Oscar-winning film or contender known to *Halliwell's Film Companion*" as being to "show a protagonist overcoming adversity against a background that exorcises the audience's guilt about an uncomfortable subject." Quoted in Clancy Sigal, "Cyberscribes," *Guardian* Weekend Section (March 19, 1994), p. 9.

29   A few Hollywood movies have always attracted repeat business, and television and video release have also provided a form of repeat viewing. Only in the 1980s did the blockbuster syndrome reach such proportions that the expectation of repeat attendances became part of a movie's financial planning and advertising. *Halliwell's Film Guide* review of *Raiders of the Lost Ark*, for instance, describes the pleasures and drawbacks of a repeat viewing: "Second time around, one can better enjoy the ingenious detail of the hero's exploits and ignore the insistence on unpleasantness; still, there are boring bits in between and the story doesn't make a lot of sense." Several weeks after its opening, *Jurassic Park* (1993) ran advertisements announcing that "If you've only seen it once, you haven't seen it all yet." *Halliwell's Film Guide*, 8th edn, ed. John Walker (London: Grafton, 1992), p. 917.

30   François Truffaut, *Hitchcock*, revised edn (London: Paladin, 1986), p. 381.

31   Novels and other published literary forms are inevitably structured like this. The book must already be produced as a material object before its consumption can begin, and the ending of the book is already present before a reader starts reading. Thus the writing of the book always appears to have taken place in the past of its reading, and it could be argued that the conventional use of the perfect tense in the narration of realist fiction is a response to this temporal order of events.

32   Truffaut, p. 91.

33   Irving Thalberg, "The Modern Photoplay," in John C. Tibbets, ed., *Introduction to the Photoplay* (Shawnee Mission, KS: National Film Society, 1977), p. 131.

34   David Herlihy, "Am I a Camera? Other Reflections on Films and History," *American*

Historical Review 93:5 (December 1988), p. 1188.

35 Critics have not resisted the latter desire as successfully as Sarah Connor. See, for example, Constance Penley, "Time Travel, Primal Scene and the Critical Dystopia," in Annette Kuhn, ed., *Alien Zone: Cultural Theory and Contemporary Science Fiction* (London: Verso, 1990), pp. 116–27.

36 Emanuel Levy sees *Back to the Future* as enacting "Children's ultimate fantasy to control the fate of their parents and supervise their own birth." Both movies could, certainly, be placed in a "local genre" in the mid-1980s in which characters occupy identities other than their own, a group that would include *Trading Places* (1983) and *Big* (1988), among others. Emanuel Levy, *Small-town America in Film: The Decline and Fall of Community* (New York: Continuum, 1991), p. 240.

37 It is, of course, not very difficult to find flaws in this logic, but the discovery and exploration of these flaws become part of the audience's entertainment at the movie.

38 George F. Custen, *Bio/Pics: How Hollywood Constructed Public Fiction* (New Brunswick, NJ: Rutgers University Press, 1992), pp. 111, 132.

39 Quoted in Custen, p. 136.

40 Custen, p. 165. Robert A. Rosenstone, "History in Images/History in Words: Reflections on the Possibility of Really Putting History onto Film," *American Historical Review* 93:5 (December 1988), p. 1174.

41 Herlihy, pp. 1186–92.

42 Quoted in Custen, p. 119.

43 Custen suggests that as many as four biopics out of five have montage sequences, most commonly used to present "the abbreviated evidence of the success that made the person famous. . . . Having established the greatness of an individual, the rapidity of the shots, often edited in dynamic combinations of overlapping dissolves, canted frames, altering scales of images, and the like, reinforce a sense of overwhelming certainty, of irresistible fate." Custen, p. 184.

44 Advertisement for *Juárez* (1939), reproduced in Russell C. Sweeney, *Coming Next Week: A Pictorial History of Film Advertising* (New York: Barnes, 1973), p. 288.

45 Douglas Pye, "Genre and Movies," *MOVIE* 20 (Spring 1975), p. 37.

46 Hal Wallis to Sam Bischoff, February 13, 1936, *Charge of the Light Brigade* Production File, Warner Bros. Special Collection, Department of Special Collections, University of Southern California.

47 Charles Swain Thomas, "Study Guide to *The Charge of the Light Brigade*," *Scholastic* (September 19, 1936), p. 29.

48 Max J. Herzberg, *Photoplay Study Guide to The Charge of the Light Brigade* (New York: Educational and Recreational Guides, Inc., 1936), p. 2.

49 Welford Beaton, review of *The Charge of the Light Brigade, Hollywood Spectator* (October 24, 1936).

50 Edward Maeder, "The Celluloid Image: Historical Dress in Film," in Edward Maeder, ed., *Hollywood and History: Costume Design in Film* (London: Thames and Hudson, 1987), p. 38.

51 Alicia Annas, "The Photogenic Formula: Hairstyles and Makeup in Historical Films," in Maeder, p. 63.

52 Lilian Churchill, "Modes à la Movies," *New York Times Magazine* (January 7, 1940), p. 8, quoted in Satch LaValley, "Hollywood and Fifth Avenue: The Impact of Period Films on Fashion," in Maeder, p. 78.

53 "Theadora Van Runkle's Sketch Book of the Thirties," *Show* 1 (July 23, 1970), pp. 16–17, quoted in LaValley, p. 95.

54 Wolfgang Reinhardt to John Huston, February 15 1938, *Juárez* Production File, Warner

Bros. Collection, USC.

55   Quoted in Nick Roddick, *A New Deal in Entertainment: Warner Brothers* [sic] *in the 1930s* (London: British Film Institute, 1983), p. 196.

56   *Juárez*, ed. Paul J. Vanderwood (Madison: University of Wisconsin Press, 1983), p. 241.

8 Narrative

Narrative is a perceptual activity that organizes data into a special pattern which represents and explains experience. More specifically, narrative is a way of organizing spatial and temporal data into a cause–effect chain of events with a beginning, middle, and end that embodies a judgement about the nature of the events as well as demonstrates how it is possible to know, and hence to narrate, the events.

Edward Branigan[1]

Narrative and Other Pleasures

Let's start from the beginning again, Jeff. Tell me everything you saw, and what you think it means.

Lisa (Grace Kelly) in *Rear Window* (1954)

Most critical writing on Hollywood assumes that the primary purpose of a movie is to tell a story. When we remember a movie, we normally recall it as a sequence of events rather than a sequence of camera angles. We do, in other words, what Lisa asks Jeff (James Stewart) to do in *Rear Window*: tell ourselves what we saw, and interpret it. The result is a story. Many everyday accounts of movies such as reviews treat a movie and its story as if they were interchangeable: we expect a movie adaptation to tell the same story as its source novel, for instance. More elaborate critical formulations also maintain that narrative has the dominant role in Hollywood. Jane Gaines has argued that a model of Classical Hollywood narrative cinema – "the protagonist-driven story film, valued for the way it achieves closure by neatly resolving all of the enigmas it raises as well as for the way it creates this perfect symmetry by means of ingenious aesthetic economies" – has dominated film studies since the 1970s.[2] David Bordwell suggests that: "In Hollywood cinema, a specific sort of narrative causality operates as the dominant, making temporal and spatial systems vehicles for it. These systems do not always rest quietly under the sway of narrative logic, but in general the causal dominant creates a marked hierarchy of systems in the classical film."[3] The common sense of everyday experience and the common wisdom of critical consensus would, then, expect to begin a discussion of Hollywood with an examination of its story-telling. Why have we left it until this late stage?

Put simply, our argument is that in a consumerist account of Hollywood, narrative functions as part of the provision of pleasure in cinema entertainment, not as the point of it. Story-telling helps ensure that the movie can be consumed as a coherent event, but it holds no privileged place among the pleasures a movie offers. At the most familiar level, we may enjoy the chase scenes in an action movie, the songs in a musical, or the performance of a favorite star, while remaining disengaged from the overly familiar or repetitive plot-line. It is every bit as hard to imagine a movie without spectacle or performance, without special effects or a star, as it is to imagine a movie without a story. This has important implications for critical practice. Rather than being a passive subject formed in the imagination of the movie-as-text, in this account the moviegoer actively constructs his or her own satisfaction by choosing to concentrate on some aspects of a movie and avoiding others.

Many theorists of narrative would agree with Edward Branigan that the construction of narrative is one of the strategies we use to make the world intelligible to us. As "a fundamental way of organizing data," narrative becomes a necessary feature of our consumption of movies as well as being fundamental to our consciousness of everyday events.[4] For some theorists, this position leads to the idea that as a principle of organization, narrative transcends the formal differences between the media through which it is expressed. **Narratology**, as the general study of narrative is called, assumes that narrative can be studied as a comparative phenomenon across different media. Seymour Chatman, for instance, defines narrative discourse as "a connected sequence of narrative statements, where 'statement' is quite independent of the particular expressive medium." He holds that the "transposability" of a story "is the strongest reason for arguing that narratives are indeed structures independent of any medium."[5]

Like critical arguments about realism, however, most arguments about narrative in cinema are derived from literary models, and there are sometimes problems in translation. The word "narrative" itself is both a noun and an adjective. It is often ambiguous in its meaning, describing both the activity of story-telling and the story that is told. It is commonly used interchangeably to refer to a process (a "narrative strategy") and to the object that results from that process (a "melodramatic narrative"), and in both everyday and critical usage its meaning floats between these various senses. This sense of play in the meaning of narrative makes it at the same time a useful and a difficult term. In order to understand the role of narrative in Hollywood, we must (not for the first time in this book) make some clear-cut distinctions between terms that are often seen as being interchangeable: plot, story, narration, narrative. First, however, we must consider how a movie narrates.

Show and Tell

> A character who acts, speaks, observes or has thoughts is not strictly telling or presenting anything to us for the reason that spectators, or readers, are not characters in the world. Characters may "tell" the story to us in a broad sense, but only through "living in" their world and speaking to other characters.
>
> Edward Branigan[6]

> In a movie you don't tell people things, you show people things.
>
> William Goldman[7]

What constitutes the story in a visual medium? A minimal definition of a story requires it to have a before and after, to register change over time. Contrary to popular wisdom, every picture does not tell a story. Rather, every picture, or at least every still photograph, *needs* a story to be constructed around it, to place it in a temporal context and provide it with a before and after, a story in which it is a significant moment. It could be argued that when a filmstrip is projected so that the sequence of pictures creates the illusion of movement, change over time becomes manifest and the minimal before-and-after definition of a story is met. But most analyses of narratives require something else, something that distinguishes narrative from the mere movement of the breaking waves in the "cinema of attractions" that entertained the movies' earliest audiences. For novelist E.M. Forster, the crucial distinction was between chronology and causality. The statement, "the king died and then the queen died," was not a narrative, but "the king died and then the queen died of grief" was.[8] The expression of causality requires a position of knowledge outside the events described: the speaker of the second sentence must know the relationship between the two events.[9] In stories that are literally told – in words – this position is a temporal one, articulated by the conventional use of the perfect tense or the "objective" third-person narration of historians. History books routinely describe events in ways that could not have been known by contemporary witnesses: for example the statement, "the Thirty Years War began in 1618," could not have been known to be true in 1618.[10] In the previous chapter, we argued that movies exist in the continuous present. So how might such a distinction operate in a movie?

In our discussion of *The Son of the Sheik* (1926) in chapter 6, we cited a title that is intercut with close-ups of Valentino apparently lost in thought: "Like all youths, he loved a dancing girl. Like all dancing girls, she tricked him." This sounds like the observation of a figure familiar from the analysis of the novel and history textbooks alike: the omniscient narrator, positioned outside the diegetic world of the movie's events and thus able to comment, generalize from, and interpret those events. A number of critics have argued that the written narratives of "classic realism" are composed of a hierarchy of different discourses. What each character says is enclosed within inverted commas and framed by the commentary of the omniscient narrator (" 'I am telling the truth,' he said, knowing that his lie would be believed"). This commentary is, according to Colin MacCabe, "privileged as the bearer of *the* truth, and therefore functions as a metalanguage by which to judge the truth or falsity of the other discourses."[11]

Hollywood's silent movies frequently feature the commentary of an omniscient narrator, and the function and formal conventions of a silent movie's intertitles echo those found in a realist novel. Dialogue is marked by inverted commas, while the narration uses either the perfect tense (as in *The Son of the Sheik*) or the historical present: in *The Conquering Power* (1921), a title informs us that "Woman has this in common with the angels – all suffering creatures are under her protection" – a remark comparable in its use of tense, as well as its ideological reverberations, with the opening of *Pride and Prejudice*: "It is a truth universally acknowledged, that a single man in possession of a good fortune, must be in want of a wife."[12] These generalized moral commentaries may alert us to the presence of a narrator, whom we may even identify: Sarah Kozloff suggests that in his silent films, D.W. Griffith "habitually took advantage of his titles to judge his characters, make personal asides, or draw parallels between the screen action and current events – in short, to open up a direct line of communication between himself and his audience and to suggest a personal tone of voice."[13] In a silent movie, the narrating intertitles are visibly located in a place of detachment outside the diegetic world. Our sight of them interrupts our viewing the action, and in watching a silent movie, a viewer constantly switches between the two discrete activities of viewing the images and reading the intertitles. The titles fix the meaning of the images, in much the same way as captions may fix the meaning of photographic images.[14] In *The Son of the Sheik*, the title tells us what Ahmed is thinking. This is perhaps the one situation in which it is accurate to speak of a viewer "reading" a movie.

With the coming of sound, Hollywood lost the mechanism of generalized moral commentary so readily provided by intertitles. The omniscient narrator ceased to be disembodied, and was obliged instead to speak with an individual voice: the voice of radio announcer Lou Marcelle in the opening narration of *Casablanca* (1942), for instance. *Casablanca* is typical of Hollywood sound movies in restricting overt acts of narration to the beginning of a movie, after which they give way to the movie's screen world. In the opening sequence of *The Pirate* (1948), the first shot we see is of the cover of a book called *The Pirate*. A voice we may recognize as Judy Garland's starts to recite its introduction, while hands turn the pages of brightly colored drawings. Gradually the camera pulls back to reveal Manuela (Garland) among a group of young women in a studio version of the eighteenth-century Caribbean, and they interrupt Manuela's recitation by mocking her romantic notions about piracy. As the movie slips into its dramatization we find ourselves no longer being told about the book *The Pirate*; we are in the screen world of the movie *The Pirate*. Its events have come to life in our present, and while the narration can move around freely within that world, it cannot enter and leave it with the ease that a literary form, like an intertitle, possesses.

The distinction here is one we introduced in our discussion of tense in the previous chapter, between modes of narrative that *tell* their audiences what happens, and modes of narrative that *show* them what happens. The distinction between showing and telling is as old as narrative theory itself. In the *Republic*, Plato distinguishes between "one kind of poetry and fable which entirely consists of imitation: this is tragedy and comedy," and "another kind consisting of the poet's own report."[15] While some forms such as epic poetry might contain both kinds, Plato's distinction between **mimesis**, in which the poet "makes a speech pretending to be someone else," and **diegesis**, in which "the poet speaks in his own person," was one between performance and report.[16] In the *Poetics*, Aristotle explains that a poet "may imitate by narration . . . or he may present all his characters as living and moving before us."[17] Some theorists of literary narrative have used this distinction between mimesis and diegesis to define narrative as a strictly verbal activity in which film cannot engage. Quoting a description of landscape from a short story, Slomith Rimmon-Kenan comments: "In a play or a film, all this would be shown directly. In narrative fiction, it has to be said in language." She continues:

> on stage there are characters (actors) who act, make gestures and speak, in a way analogous to people's behavior in reality. In narrative, on the other hand, all actions and gestures are rendered in words, and consequently . . . "an imitation of an action" becomes a more problematic concept. . . . no text of narrative fiction can show or imitate the action it conveys, since all such texts are made of language, and language signifies without imitating. All that a narrative can do is create an illusion, an effect, a semblance of *mimesis*, but it does so through *diegesis* (in the Platonic sense).[18]

Rimmon-Kenan is concerned to exclude drama and cinema from her analysis of linguistic narrative, but her use of the terms "narrative fiction" and "narrative" to refer exclusively to verbal forms leaves critics of the performing arts seriously short of terminology. Within Rimmon-Kenan's frame of reference, the crucial distinction is, she argues, "not between telling and showing, but between different degrees and kinds of telling." Equally, we shall argue, there are distinctions to be made within cinema not between showing and telling, but between different kinds of showing. That proposition, however, insists with Rimmon-Kenan that between written and cinematic forms of narration there is a crucial distinction: between telling – a verbal activity requiring temporal distance between its object (what is told) and its performance – and showing – a visual and therefore spatial activity requiring the temporal co-presence of the object shown and the performance of showing.

The theories of Plato and Aristotle have been repeatedly reinterpreted in the two millennia since their formulation, and both mimesis and diegesis have acquired broader meanings than the specific, Platonic sense. Because most narrative theories regard narrative as a way of organizing data, they frequently elide the Platonic distinction between mimesis and diegesis into something less fundamental. David Bordwell, for instance, employs the terms to distinguish between two bodies of narrative theory.

> *Diegetic* theories conceive of narration as consisting either literally or analogically of verbal activity: a telling. . . . *Mimetic* theories conceive of narration as the presentation of a spectacle: a showing . . . since the difference applies only to "mode" of imitation, either theory may be applied to any medium. You can hold a mimetic theory of the novel if you believe the narrational methods of fiction to resemble those of drama, and you can hold a diegetic theory of painting if you posit visual spectacle to be analogous to linguistic transmission.[19]

For Bordwell, the distinction between showing and telling becomes a way of distinguishing theories about narration, not a fundamental distinction between ways of narrating. In *Telling Stories*, Steven Cohan and Linda Shires initially acknowledge a distinction between narrative and drama, only to circumvent it:

> narrative resembles drama but with one important difference: a play presents an action – Hamlet's duel with Laertes, say – directly, and a narrative does so indirectly, through the words which recount or describe the action. That narrative recounts and drama enacts persuades some critics to propose a strict definition of narrative as a purely verbal medium. Other critics, ourselves included, believe that the term "narrative" applies to the visual medium of storytelling as well. In a film, for instance, the camera recounts – because it records – events no less than a novel does.[20]

Cohan and Shires' account hangs on a metaphor: in saying "the camera recounts," they describe the camera as performing a verbal activity. In Bordwell's terms, they offer a diegetic theory of film narrative, in which showing an action is subsumed within the dominant activity of telling a story. But movies are, in this sense, a "show" business. What they actually do is what the movie *The Pirate* does: an opening act of telling is subsumed within the dominant activity of showing the audience the action. This is not to suggest that a movie's images are any more "natural" or "objective" than words – far from it – but it is to argue that the conventions of cinematic narrative, and the way narrative information is conveyed in a movie, are radically different from those employed in verbal forms. If this seems to labor an obvious point, it is because the inheritance from literary criticism so often leads analysts of movies to make the metaphorical leap into treating a movie "as a sort of linguistic event, as the narrator's speech even when there is none."[21]

The verbal form allows its reader to contemplate the significance of an account's choice of words: what difference it makes, for instance, to describe the heroine's red hair as "russet tresses." A movie's showing is at once more concrete and less exactly interpretive: the choice is a matter not of what is described but of what is seen. The audience is most likely to be aware of the image's frame as a component of meaning when it is active – when, for instance, it pans away from the clandestine lovers' embrace to the villain who is watching them from behind the shrubbery. But framing is always selective, even when it is simply showing a fixed space, as in Donald O'Connor's "Make 'Em Laugh" routine (discussed in chapter 6), for example. Because it is always selective, it is always an active component of meaning. A movie's choice of camera angle, lens, lighting, shot scale, and editing pattern is analogous to a novel's choice of words in that these components of framing determine the way that the viewer is guided through the movie. But they are only analogous to word choice, not equivalent to it. The slippage occurs because we conventionally understand narrative to require language: "tell me what you saw," demands Lisa in *Rear Window*. The construction of a story seems inherently to involve a translation into the verbal, and the act of translation is so commonplace that we seldom notice it.

In the last chapter we discussed the temporal complexities of the opening of *Double Indemnity* (1944), which, like *The Pirate*, begins with an on-screen narrator and then dissolves into showing the events he began by describing. Although we return to Walter Neff's office to witness his continued narration several times in the course of the movie, our experience of being shown the events is evidently very different from having them recounted to us by Neff. Neff is a character in the scenes we witness, and except when we hear his voice-over narration, we have no more privileged insight into his motivation than we do that of any of the other characters. Neff only tells us those parts of the story that he literally recites. Perhaps most decisively, we must be shown Neff telling us: we see him enter his office at night, settle in a chair, put a wax cylinder in the dictaphone, light a cigarette, and begin. Movies *can* tell us things, and most movies do, in titles like "Old Fort Sumner, New Mexico, 1881," in *Pat Garrett and Billy the Kid* (1973), or "Most of what follows is true," in *Butch Cassidy and the Sundance Kid* (1969). But overwhelmingly, sound movies have abandoned the alternation between showing and telling provided by intertitles, and choose to show their audiences the actions and events that make up their narratives.

Diegetic theories of narrative have found the movies' practice of showing events to be particularly troublesome, and have frequently tried to escape the difficulties this creates by making a metaphorical equation between "the camera" and a literary narrator. Colin MacCabe's formulation of this metaphor has been a particularly influential one: he asserts that like the "metalanguage" of classic realist fiction, the camera "shows us what happens – it tells the truth against which we can measure the discourses [of the various characters]."[22] As an instance of his argument, MacCabe describes the final scene of *Klute* (1971), in which the image shows John Klute (Donald Sutherland) and Bree Daniels (Jane Fonda) packing to leave New York together, while on the soundtrack we hear Bree telling her psychiatrist that she doubts that the relationship will last. Although sound and image present discordant evidence, in MacCabe's interpretation, "the camera . . . tells the truth." *Klute*'s ending is "happy," not ambiguous, because "the reality of the image" "tells" him that what Bree "really wants to do is to settle down in the mid-West with John Klute."[23]

It is possible to argue with this interpretation on a number of levels,[24] but MacCabe's assertion is interesting because it involves a deliberate limitation of possible meanings which, according to Dudley Andrew, is an important function of cinematic narrative. In his book, *Concepts in Film Theory*, Andrew argues that because narrative is "above all . . . a logic for delimiting meaning," narrative is inevitable in cinema. In the cinema as much as in everyday life, our ability to construct, comprehend, and interpret stories is crucial to the way we organize the excess of information with which we are surrounded. Since cinema is, in Andrew's account, a medium in which there is an excess of signification, producing too many meanings, coherence is produced "by way of calculated or ideological limitation of this excess."[25] This is what MacCabe's interpretation does. Like any other interpretation, it actually depends on a number of choices made by the viewer about which evidence to privilege in constructing the story. Each choice, as Andrew suggests, fixes meaning in much the way as the intertitle in *The Son of the Sheik* fixes the meaning of Ahmed's expression.

If it is not true that "every picture tells a story," it is rather more true that "the camera never lies," because "seeing is believing." The audience trusts the images it sees, because the camera cannot show something that is not, in some sense, there. A movie's images cannot be unreliable in the ways that a verbal narrator can be. Bree and Klute do leave her apartment together. We have very little choice but to accept what we are shown, since we cannot choose to believe half of an image and not the other half. *Zelig* (1983) requires its viewers to overcome their knowledge that Woody Allen, playing "the human chameleon" Leonard Zelig, only appears in documentary footage with Adolf Hitler and Franklin Roosevelt through special effects. In a documentary about Hitler, these images would be fraudulent. But in a fictional movie about Leonard Zelig, if we do not accept them, we give ourselves no opportunity to enjoy the movie's parody of documentary style.

While the words we read or hear in a movie may be subsequently established as untruthful, the images we see may be partial but are almost never false. Sarah Kozloff cites the case of *Evil Under the Sun* (1982), a murder mystery in which the suspects each recount their alibis in a voice-over flashback. In their speeches, the two murderers lie, but when Hercule Poirot (Peter Ustinov) recounts what really happened, in another voice-over flashback at the climax, we see the same shots that were shown in the murderers' flashbacks – only now re-edited to include additional material. "The shots that the audience saw originally were *not* false, they were just partial and anchored by verbal lies."[26] Only once has a movie shown its audience a sequence in flashback that the plot later establishes did not happen. Perhaps not surprisingly, this one instance was in a movie directed by Alfred Hitchcock: *Stage Fright* (1950), in which Jonathan Cooper (Richard Todd) recounts a voice-over flashback in which "the scenic presentation colludes with the narrator's false account of events," convincing both the heroine and the audience of his innocence.[27] The "lying flashback" is not revealed as such until the end of the movie, and the device was widely condemned by critics outraged at being deceived and accusing Hitchcock of lying to them.[28]

The hostility to this practice gives some indication of the force of a conventional assumption about Hollywood's framing. A writer in *American Cinematographer* argued in 1935 that the camera's "omniscient eye . . . stimulates, through correct choice of subject matter and set-up, the sense within the percipient of 'being at the most vital part of the experience – at the most advantageous point of perception' throughout the movie."[29] David Bordwell reformulates the idea of the camera as an ideal, invisible observer as "the tendency of the classical film to render narrational omniscience as spatial *omnipresence*."[30] This formulation captures both the possibilities and the limitations of Hollywood's powers of narrative. Inside the screen world of *The Pirate* or any other movie, the narration can change its viewpoint at will, cutting freely between different camera positions within a scene and between scenes in different locations. But it has no spatial equivalent to the temporal distance of a literary narrator from the events he or she narrates. The closest a movie comes to that omniscience is in its musical accompaniment, the element in a movie most conspicuously located outside the diegetic world. Composer George Antheil neatly summarizes the narrative role of music: "The characters in a film drama never know what is going to happen to them, but the music always knows."[31]

Plot, Story, Narration

Just as we have suggested that "film" and "movie" can be seen as distinct terms, it is helpful to use the terms "plot," "story," and "narration" to refer to the different aspects of the process we are describing. In making a distinction between plot and story, we follow the practice adapted by Bordwell and Thompson from Russian Formalist criticism. The **plot** is the order in which events are represented in the movie, for which the Formalists used the word **syuzhet**: "the structured set of all causal events as we see and hear them presented."[32] The **story**, on the other hand, is the reconstruction of the events in their chronological order, through which we can establish the chain of causality which links them, designated the **fabula** by the Formalists. The Formalists' concern with the role of the author in literary production led them to argue that the author started with the fabula/story and out of it constructed the syuzhet/plot. Bordwell and Thompson's "neoformalist" film criticism, however, regards the story as being retrospectively constructed by the viewer as a means of explaining the causal relations between plot events. The viewer's position is analogous to that of the detective, who pieces together the original sequence of events from clues picked up in a different order, and rearranges them into a coherent sequence that links them and explains their meaning. Like the detective, whose account is often verified by the protagonists at the end of the investigation, a viewer may have to account for his or her understanding of the story when, for instance, discussing the movie on leaving the theater. Since the viewer constructs the story, an even more apt metaphor for the activity of the audience than the idea of detection is the work of an investigative reporter.

The distinction between plot and story also helps to define the term **narration**. Where plot and story can both be understood as objects – sequences of events – narration is a process: the process by which a plot is arranged to permit the telling of a story. One part of this process is undertaken by the movie's producers, when they arrange the sequence of events and actions within the plot, distribute cues encouraging viewers to form hypotheses about the connection between events, and position devices that either confirm those hypotheses or introduce ambiguities. The procedures of mise-en-scène and editing become the means by which viewers are guided through the plot. While the devices of narration are constructed on the sound stage and in the editing room, the process of narration is only completed in the movie theater, when viewers use their knowledge of convention and the plot information provided for them to construct the story in their own minds.

The ambiguous senses of the term **narrative** – which is often used as a synonym for all three of the other terms – only become useful if we understand the term as identifying the play between senses of plot, story, and narration in our experience of viewing a movie. The distinction between narrative and narration is of greater significance to movie criticism than to literary criticism. Because cinematic fictions unfold in the continuous present, they are often taken to be self-narrated. This is perhaps the most potent source of cinema's so-called "reality effect": the idea that a Hollywood movie promotes the illusion that its viewers are watching an unmediated reality. It is hard to know how literally critics expect us to take their statements about cinema's ability "to convince viewers that it is one and the same with the physical world."[33] Taken at their face value, such comments propose an idea of the viewer as extraordinarily naïve, apparently capable of forgetting his or her physical circumstances and surrendering his or her identity to the flow of images. Such an "ideal spectator" may be a critical convenience, but it does not have much to do with what real viewers actually do in movie theaters.

On the other hand, Hollywood's conventional systems of spatial and temporal representation encourage audiences to treat what they see *as if it were real*: to see space as three-dimensional, characters as having psychological motivations akin to our own, and so on. That is to say, Hollywood's conventions of representation assist the audience in bringing their conventional perceptions of the everyday world – from a perception of the hardness of a brick wall to the perception of a motivation for jealousy – to bear on the events they witness on the screen. In the idea that audiences see what they see in the movies as if it were real, the "as if" is crucial. This is a conditional state, conditional on a movie's performance not in imitating reality but in sustaining audience pleasure. Individual viewers or whole audiences can and often do withdraw their voluntary support for a movie's plausibility if an alternative source of pleasure – such as pondering the hydraulics of Becky's (Dana Wynter) strapless gingham dress in *Invasion of the Body Snatchers* (1956), for example – suggests itself.

In addition to its conventional systems of space and time, narration sustains a movie's plausible performance by arranging plot events according to a principle of cause and effect, with a minimum of redundancy and a maximum of coherence. The operation of causality enjoys a privileged place in most aesthetic accounts of Hollywood cinema. David Bordwell's analysis of the Hollywood style, for example, suggests that:

> psychological causality, presented through defined characters acting to achieve announced goals, gives the classical film its characteristic progression. . . . The conventions of the well-made play – strong opening exposition, battles of wits, thrusts and counter-thrusts, extreme reversals of fortunes, and rapid denouement – all reappear in Hollywood dramaturgy, and all are defined in relation to cause and effect. The film progresses like a staircase: "Each scene should make a definite impression, accomplish one thing, and advance the narrative a step nearer the climax." Action triggers reaction: each step has an effect which in turn becomes a new cause.[34]

In prioritizing the causality of the narrative system over what he sees as the possibly disruptive effects of the temporal and spatial systems, Bordwell's analysis emphasizes those conventions and devices that establish causality, linearity, and clarity. From this perspective, the typical Hollywood movie appears as a coherent, unified, story-telling whole:

> Coincidence and haphazardly linked events are believed to flaw the film's unity and disturb the spectator. Tight causality yields not only consequence but continuity, making the film progress "smoothly, easily, with no jars, no waits, no delays." . . . The ending becomes the culmination of the spectator's absorption, as all the causal gaps get filled. The fundamental plenitude and linearity of Hollywood narrative culminate in metaphors of knitting, linking, and filling.[35]

Screenwriting manuals also usually set out the aesthetic consequences of an adherence to causal logics, in terms that our own viewing experience may readily confirm. In *A Practical Manual of Screenplay Writing*, Lewis Herman, for example, argues that:

> story holes engender vague dissatisfaction in the audience with the story as a whole. A well planned, well plotted, holeless story leaves the audience with the feeling that they have witnessed a completely unified, satisfying tale of events that could have happened to anyone, even themselves.
>
> Everything in any story must be completely understandable to the audience, at least after the denouement. . . . Care must be taken that every hole is plugged; that every loose string is tied together; that every absence is fully explained; that every entrance and exit is fully motivated, and that they are not made for some obviously contrived reason; that every coincidence is sufficiently motivated to make it credible; that there is no conflict between what has gone on before, what is going on currently, and what will happen in the future; that there is complete consistency between present dialogue and past action – that no baffling question marks are left over at the end of the picture to detract from the audience's appreciation of it.[36]

Herman's rhetorical ambition to produce the perfectly closed text, however, is at odds with the norms of audience experience. While it explains some of Hollywood's most persistent traits, such as its emphasis on continuity, it is nonetheless the case that in any Hollywood movie we certainly find coincidences, inconsistencies, gaps, and delays. Moreover, so total a commitment to causal explanation of character-and-event-relations takes little account of the competing logics which also inform the commercial Hollywood movie. Describing the trailer he made for *Casablanca*, Arthur Silver explained, "We sold the adventure. We sold the action, the romance, and the stars," while the plot "was left vague."[37] What Barbara Klinger has called the "consumable identity" of a movie – the promotional values by which it is identified as a commodity – may distract the viewer into selecting some other aspect of the movie than its story to entertain us: performance, mise-en-scène, star biography, or the conspicuous display of budget and technical wizardry. From a consumerist perspective, these digressions are not so much evidence of a malfunction within the aesthetic system as the manifest signs of a commercial entity. Both during a viewing and afterward, movies provide frameworks for what Klinger calls "momentary guided exits from the text . . . set off by promotional narratives that address how a scene was done, the star's marital history or status as a romantic icon, what other films a director has made." Hollywood, she suggests, is less concerned with producing coherent interpretations of a movie than with promoting "multiple avenues of access" to it, so that it will "resonate as extensively as possible in the social sphere in order to maximize its audience."[38] A consumerist account of Hollywood would therefore modify Bordwell's position by arguing that the movie does not exist primarily as coherent narrative, nor is it necessarily dominated by narrative. Narrative operates alongside other spatial and temporal articulations, as part of the complex means whereby Hollywood fulfills its industrial obligation to entertain for profit.

Formalist criticism also ultimately withdraws from the suggestion that every hole can be plugged and every string tied together, choosing instead to suggest that stories do have **excess** material that escapes the unifying narrative structure, revealing the hidden psychic or ideological processes at work in the text. According to this account, narrative is the attempt to contain this excess, an attempt that is paradoxically bound to fail. In her analysis of an "ordinary film," *Terror by Night* (1946), Kristin Thompson suggests that while Classical Hollywood narrative lends the movie the *appearance* of single-minded linear progression, very little of the constant stream of information the audience is given actually leads them toward the conclusion of the movie's mystery story: "much of it, in fact, may be deflecting us into digressions."[39] This account, too, leaves open the possibility of incidental pleasures available to the audience outside the inexorable progression of the "completely unified, satisfying tale of events."

Clarity: Transparency and Motivation

> I am sure that you will agree that the very worst fault a picture can have is lack of clarity. If an audience doesn't know what is going on, and is worried by its own conclusion, inevitably dramatic values suffer greatly.
>
> David Selznick[40]

> Paradoxically, the more exactly we describe the narration, the more fragmented it becomes.
>
> Edward Branigan[41]

Hollywood's commitment to establishing causal relations between the elements of a movie ensures that the audience's experience of its story will usually be one of clarity. The spatial and temporal conventions that we have discussed in previous chapters work to efface themselves through their very familiarity, producing an apparently unimpeded access to the events of the plot and their meaning in the story. The Hollywood movie then seeks an effect of transparency in which devices like "invisible" editing draw no attention to themselves in contributing to the movie's narration. At the same time, the movie's obligation to the continuous present enhances senses of presence and immediacy, so that the movie becomes almost impossible to "see" as an assembly of rhetorical and descriptive strategies *producing* an effect of transparency.

In fact transparency is produced as much by the moviegoer as the moviemaker, and is as much an effect of watching and interpreting as it is of showing and telling. In the Hollywood movie, material is placed at our disposal by all manner of stylistic devices, but the movie assumes our competence in dealing with these materials through its reliance on conventions of spatial representation, temporal organization, genre, and star recognition. The audience must work within those conventions if it wishes to give priority to its attention to a movie's story. At any moment in any movie narrative, several of these conventional fields of information will be operating together: at the opening of *High Plains Drifter* (1973) we watch Clint Eastwood playing a character with no name ride into the town of Lago, as we listen to suspenseful music, knowing that we are watching a Western, directed by Clint Eastwood. Provided that we understand *why* a particular element or device is present in such a scene, and *how* a particular device is being deployed, it can contribute positively to our pleasure in the movie, as well as to our comprehension of it.

In making sense out of the assembly of devices active in any given scene or sequence of scenes, the audience seeks a sense of **motivation**, a logical justification for its inclusion. Formalism distinguishes between four kinds of motivation within the typical Hollywood movie: compositional, realistic, intertextual, and artistic. **Compositional motivation** explains the presence of a device in terms of its necessity for story comprehension: something happens because it causes something else to happen. **Realistic**

Clint Eastwood rides into Lago at the start of *High Plains Drifter* (1973). Universal (courtesy Kobal)

motivation justifies the presence because it enhances a movie's surface verisimilitude: an object is there because it makes the movie look more authentic, something happens because it helps the audience to accept a sequence of plot events as plausible, or because it provides a level of consistency for character. **Intertextual motivation** appeals directly to the audience's familiarity with convention: an event happens in this movie because events like that usually happen in movies of this kind. **Artistic motivation** offers a possible explanation of a particular feature by appealing to notions of "showmanship": something is present because it produces a particular affect, such as spectacle. Usually these kinds of motivation operate collaboratively. In *High Plains Drifter*, compositional motivation explains the character's arrival at the saloon; realistic motivation justifies his costuming; intertextual motivation helps the audience come to terms with the sudden, violent shootout which follows, and artistic motivation helps us to make sense of the self-conscious playing, framing, and editing of the scene in terms of our knowledge of its authorship as "a Clint Eastwood movie."

A more consumption-oriented account of Hollywood certainly recognizes the functioning of motivation, but needs to broaden its focus to acknowledge other types. From the audience's perspective, artistic motivation in particular needs to be subdivided to cover not only the explanation of a movie's features in terms of "artistic license," but more specifically in terms of legal, moral, technical, political, industrial, and cultural factors. Subdividing the category of artistic motivation produces a more diversified sense of the range of activities open to the audience as they watch even the most typical Hollywood movie.

The way in which Formalism suggests that motivations are organized encourages the viewer to use all available information to make *narrative* sense of the events depicted; even realism in this model tends to be understood as *narrative* realism. Formalism's privileging of compositional motivation in general, and of psychological causality in particular, also suggests that we take the coherence and credibility of behavior within a movie as an indication of its merits as a whole. At stake is the internal coherence of the movie as an object, and formalist accounts usually suggest a strong sense of hierarchy among the pleasures that a movie offers its audience. For example, the final blending of a character's behavior with the persona of the star playing the character could be seen as supporting a Formalist argument that other pleasures are ultimately subordinate to the story. But this takes no account of the agency of the viewer, who might choose to reject the consistency of the character in favor of the pleasurable activities of watching the star's performance, right up to the movie's conclusion. Movies often subordinate character consistency to other objectives, such as an obligation to display their highly paid stars in their most emblematic and desirable positions. For fans of a particular star, the continuity of the star's persona across individual performances matters more than subordinating the star to the dictates of character. Richard Dyer argues that if you like Gary Cooper or Doris Day, "precisely what you value about them is that they are always 'themselves' – no matter how different their roles, they bear witness to the continuousness of their own selves."[42] In recognizing and admiring the star's favorite mannerisms, fans achieve a transparency of access to the star's "real" personality rather than using transparency to support their belief in the narrative.

"Comedian" comedies built around a comic personality make the tension between star and character especially evident, and undermine the dominance of causal motivation. Comedians such as Bob Hope and Woody Allen first constructed their comic personas outside the cinema, in vaudeville or night-clubs, and brought to their movies a style of performance that involved a direct address to their audience. This mode of direct address makes it uncertain whether the character or the performer is speaking: is it Alvy Singer or Woody Allen who is telling us jokes at the beginning and end of *Annie Hall* (1977)? In *The Road to Bali* (1952), does Bob Hope or Harold Gridley tell us, "He's [Bing Crosby – or George Cochrane?] going to sing, folks. Now's the time to go out and get the popcorn"?[43]

A "screwball" comedy such as *Bringing Up Baby* (1938) is built around a comic loss of the coherence that Formalism argues is supplied to the Hollywood movie by compositional motivation. Professor David Huxley (Cary Grant) continually tries to escape from the chaotic and implausible succession of events in which he is caught up, and get back to the saner, more tranquil world of an altogether more ordinary narrative. But as Susan Vance (Katherine Hepburn) tells him, he has made too much of a spectacle of himself to be allowed back into any simple, believable story. *Bringing Up Baby* demonstrates very little by way of a credible plot logic. It proceeds at breakneck speed, fabricating not narrative progress but what Stanley Cavell calls "purposiveness without purpose" in which "the attempt at flight is forever transforming itself into a process of pursuit."[44] Its effect depends upon the very precise timing and overlapping of dialogue and the subjection of the audience to the pressure generated by this rapid-fire exchange. David's every attempt at the fabrication of a chain of causally related actions is sabotaged by the misunderstandings of other characters, utterly unbelievable coincidences, and an absolute refusal to recognize Cary Grant's industrial status as the movie's major star. The movie's sustained implausibility obliges David to make a spectacle of himself even as he tries to reassert a more orderly storyline. In a restaurant, he finds himself trying to conceal the fact that he has accidentally torn Susan's dress and exposed her underwear by hitting her on the bottom with his top hat. After losing his clothes he is forced to explain to Susan's Aunt Elizabeth (May Robson) that he is wearing Susan's negligee "because I just went gay all of a sudden." Despite his best attempts to preserve the agenda with which the movie has furnished him, David is doomed to succumb to the competing plot logic represented by Susan, even though their romance culminates in the destruction of his brontosaurus.[45]

David Huxley (Cary Grant), unable to escape from Susan Vance (Katherine Hepburn) and Baby into a more rational plot in *Bringing Up Baby* (1938). RKO (courtesy Kobal)

Hollywood regularly uses compositional motivation to serve the exhibition of its stars: in the Western, the reluctant hero is finally forced by narrative circumstance to accept that he must buckle on his gun and display his physical prowess; in the backstage musical the ingenue star eventually gets the lucky break that lets her sing and dance as the audience always knew she would. Hollywood narration must negotiate the pleasurable interruptions of performance or spectacle, before reasserting itself in order to bring them (and consumption) to an end. The two elements of story-telling and spectacle are held in an essential tension, and the movie exists as a series of minor victories of one logic over the other. Narration is therefore crucial to the organization of the audience's pleasure, but this is far from saying that story-telling in itself is the primary source of that pleasure, or the main instrument by which it is provided.

Ambiguity: Narrative and the Regulation of the Erotic

In addition to providing the opportunity for Hollywood to make a spectacle of itself, narrative also allows a movie to control the potential diversity of meanings accruing from a visual medium. We have already encountered something of this process of control in our discussion of mise-en-scène, which was understood as orchestrating visual meaning to facilitate the audience's comprehension of story-telling. Mise-en-scène can never entirely stabilize narrative meaning, however, and the Hollywood cinema involves many further levels of regulation. Principal among these is the regulation of the erotic, both in the specific sense of the representation of sexuality, and in the more generalized notion that the very act of looking at cinema depends on the **scopophilic** instinct: that is, the eroticized love of looking which spectacle plays upon and satisfies, very often through the display of the human body. We can understand Hollywood's mechanisms of regulation as a form of intertextual motivation: consistent modes of treatment arose from strategies developed to deal with the representation of "sensitive" or "dangerous" subjects.

Hollywood's need to regulate the erotic was most obviously articulated in the Motion Picture Production Code of 1930. The Code's stipulations explicitly state the ways in which narrative might be used to contain the sexually or ideologically disruptive power of the image. The three "General Principles" of the Production Code were,

1 No picture shall be produced which will lower the moral standards of those who see it. Hence the sympathy of the audience shall never be thrown to the side of crime, wrong-doing, evil or sin.
2 Correct standards of life, subject only to the requirements of drama and entertainment, shall be presented.
3 Law, natural or human, shall not be ridiculed, nor shall sympathy be created for its violation.[46]

The Code's authors were sensitive not only to the problem of difficult subject matter, but to the impact of moviegoing in general upon the industry's diverse audiences. As Father Daniel Lord, largely responsible for the drafting of the Production Code, put it in 1930, "In general, the mobility, popularity, accessibility, emotional appeal, vividness, straightforward presentation of fact in the film make for more intimate contact with a larger audience and for greater emotional appeal. Hence the larger moral responsibilities of the motion pictures."[47] This argument is characteristic of what might be called a "fear of entertainment," whereby cinema's potential for the production of pleasure through the projection and fulfillment of desire is thought to be innately threatening to the moral health of both the individual and the community. We might recognize the legacy of this argument (that entertainment as a process has inevitable negative consequences, regardless of its content) in contemporary anxieties about the effects of television, or the playing of video games.[48]

Although the Code was written under the influence of the assumption that spectators were only passive receivers of texts, the texts themselves were constructed to accommodate, rather than predetermine, the variety of their audiences' reactions. The economic logic for that construction came out of what Umberto Eco has called "the heavy industry of dreams in a capitalistic society."[49] Having chosen not to divide its audience by means of a rating system for its product, which would to a certain extent have segregated the "innocent" viewers from the "sophisticated," Hollywood was obliged to devise a system which would allow "sophisticated" viewers to read whatever they liked into a formally "innocent" movie, so long as the producers could use the mechanics of the Production Code to deny that the sophisticated interpretation had been put there in the first place. Much of the work of self-regulation in the 1930s and 1940s lay in the maintenance of this system of conventions, and so it operated, however perversely, as an enabling mechanism at the same time as it was a repressive one: essentially it was designed to find strategies by which socially sensitive subjects could be represented on the screen, rather than to "censor" such material out of existence.

Sexuality was the primary site of private pleasure to be simultaneously concealed and disclosed in public. Those charged with administering the Code worked in cooperation with the studios to devise complex strategies of ambiguity in order to address more than one audience at the same time. As Ruth Vasey has argued, the early sound period in which the Production Code was developed was of central importance to this process.[50] In a letter to Will Hays during the production of *The Smiling Lieutenant* (1931), a Code administrator detailed his successes in making changes to the script:

> The scenes in which Franzi, who wants to put off Niki, says, "First tea – then dinner – and then, maybe – maybe breakfast," and the succeeding action which fades in to show them having breakfast together, indicating that Niki persuaded her to spend the night with him, will be changed as follows: Franzi, after saying "First tea, etc.," will definitely *leave the apartment* and go away, breaking the sequence. The camera will then fade in on a tea set, indicating that they are having tea together at a later time, then on supper dishes, indicating that they are having a supper together, and then to the scene on the balcony where they are having breakfast. This will, of course, delicately indicate that Franzi is Niki's mistress, but the time element removes most of the worry and adds a delicacy of treatment in my opinion.
>
> The scenes in which Franzi is shown gathering her negligee, stockings and a handkerchief from under Niki's pillow, etc., which serve only to pound home the fact that she was his mistress, will be altered to show her gathering up her music, her violin, etc., things which first brought them together. This will remove the personal property, the body connection, of the scene, and be far less offensive. In fact it should leave them rather in doubt of their connection.[51]

On the one hand the Production Code strove to eliminate any moral ambiguity in a movie's narrative progression by imposing a rigidly deterministic plot-line that ascribed every character a position on a fixed moral spectrum. But at the same time, precisely the same forces obliged movies to construct strategies of ambiguity around the details of action which they were not permitted to present explicitly.[52] On September 18, 1931, Darryl Zanuck, then head of production at Warner Bros., wrote a memo to his scriptwriters dealing with the script treatment of an illegal operation in *Alias the Doctor*:

> We should stress the point that the operation is not an abortion, but at the same time the audience will guess that it is an abortion but in all dialogue and everything, it must be treated as merely an operation, and at the climax when Carl is found with the girl, he is not arrested for performing an abortion, but is arrested for illegally operating because of the fact that he is not yet a graduated doctor.[53]

Two months later, Colonel Jason Joy, head of the Studio Relations Committee, wrote to him pointing out that the inclusion of an abortion was prohibited by the Production Code and would make the movie "utterly unusable in censorship territories." Zanuck replied that he was "amazed and bewildered" at Joy's suggestion: "We make mention of an operation, but this has nothing whatsoever to do with an abortion." When Joy insisted that, "abortion . . . will be the inference which the audience and the censors will draw from the picture," and that "the mere insertion of a medical term for the operation to indicate that it was not an abortion will not be sufficient to escape the fact," Zanuck blustered defensively,

> If it is impossible for us to tell a story of a boy who has a love affair with a girl – gets tired of the girl – avoids her, and then in a drunken argument causes an accident to occur to her, then illegally operates to save her life and instead causes her death, we might just as well quit making motion pictures. . . . The trouble, if I may be permitted to say so in this case, is whoever has been handling this script with you is reading between the lines and reading in conditions which cannot possibly prove to be facts.[54]

The knowing double-entendre, whose greatest exponent was Mae West, "the finest woman who ever walked the streets," was a step toward a satisfactory economic solution to the problem of censoring sexuality. In providing pictures that, as the trade paper *Film Daily* put it, "won't embarrass Father when he takes the children to his local picture house," it accommodated both the sophisticated and the "innocent" viewer at the same time. Through the 1930s, Hollywood developed the double-entendre to the point reached by Zanuck in this argument, where the responsibility for the sophisticated interpretation could be displaced entirely onto the sophisticated viewer ("whoever has been handling this script with you is reading between the lines and reading in conditions which cannot possibly prove to be facts"). Late 1930s movies achieved a particular "innocence" by presenting a deadpan level of performance that acted as a foil to the secondary "sophisticated" narrative constructed within the imagination of the viewer. In screwball comedies and Fred Astaire and Ginger Rogers musicals, characters remained innocent of the suggestiveness that typically underpinned their social relations. The more the movie world diverged from what audiences knew went on in the real world, the more the movies took on a comic sophistication of their own. They gained a wit, a knowingness that audiences could take pleasure in, because it revealed and rewarded their own sophistication.

Screwball comedies such as *Bringing Up Baby* require that we disregard their considerable implausibility, and tease us into reading beneath their surfaces through innuendo and symbolization. But because the comic and erotic effects of these movies are so dependent on what each individual viewer recognizes as lying beyond the rapid-fire dialogue and the disintegration of plot logic, their meanings become impossible either to determine in any absolute sense, or to regulate. Stanley Cavell describes the position of the viewer who is encouraged to make an interpretation of *Bringing Up Baby* that the movie, at another level, denies:

> While an explicit discussion, anyway an open recognition, of the film's obsessive sexual references is indispensable to saying what I find the film to be about, I am persistently reluctant to make it very explicit. Apart from more or less interesting risks of embarrassment (for example, of seeming too perverse or being too obvious), there are causes for this reluctance having to do with what I understand the point of the sexual gaze to be. It is part of the force of this work that we shall not know how far to press its references.[55]

An audience willing to play a game of double-entendre could find hidden, "subversive," or "repressed" meanings in almost any movie by supplying "from its own imagination the specific acts of so-called misconduct which the Production Code has made unmentionable."[56] They might in the process supply more plausible motivations for the behavior of characters in scenes that had been designed, according to Elliott Paul, to "give full play to the vices of the audience, and still have a technical out" as far as the Production Code was concerned.[57] In the case of adaptations from novels, the repressed of the text might often be the original story, the "unsuitable" or "objectionable" elements of which had been removed in the process of adapting it to the screen.[58] Looked at in this way, regulatory motivation raises questions about the extent to which Hollywood movies were and are characteristically "transparent," and suggests that narration in Hollywood movies has had as much to do with promoting ambiguity as with maintaining clarity.

In the journey that a knowledgeable audience takes through a Hollywood narrative, they always know where they are going, and they never know the route. Imagining that it is "being made up as they go along" is the intertextually innocent response to this combination of a determinate outcome and an unpredictable progression. The "sophisticated" viewing of a movie, on the other hand, can be an act of fatalistic resistance to the inevitability of its moralistic ending. In the early days of the Production Code, reformers often castigated the industry for having "invented the perfect formula – five reels of transgression followed by one reel of retribution."[59] But as the implementation of the Code developed, it insisted on an ever-more coherent narrative, and audiences "viewing against the grain" found themselves also viewing against what David Bordwell has called the "stair-step" construction of narrative causation. "Sophisticated" or perverse viewing strategies survived within Hollywood cinema, because compositionally coherent story-telling was overlaid with, or even constructed from, plot implausibility, character inconsistency, melodramatic coincidence – all opportunities for audiences to escape from the conventional moral constraints of the movie-as-text, to allow the repressed of the text to return in some parallel imagined version, no less implausible than the one on the screen. But for the "sophisticated" audience, the "escape" from Hollywood convention is only temporary, a momentary optimism that the narrative will end somewhere other than where it always does, with transgression just for once triumphant.

Clarity and Ambiguity in *Casablanca*

> Whatever a spectator *first believes* may be enough to drive the story forward. Just as essential plot details are usually repeated several times to promote clarity, so a variety of motivations circulating in the text may be useful options in filling out, and making definite, causal sequences. . . . This allows the story to be made "unique" in many different ways to many spectators . . . it would be better to think of narration not as a single process, but as several processes moving on different levels, proposing and abolishing contradictions with varying degrees of explicitness and success.
>
> Edward Branigan[60]

> I've heard a lot of stories in my time. They went along with the sound of a tinny piano playing in the parlor downstairs. "Mister, I met a man once," they'd always begin.
>
> Rick Blaine (Humphrey Bogart) in *Casablanca*

Casablanca is regularly cited as exemplifying the ways in which the Hollywood movie constructs and explains its storylines. However, the movie's idiosyncrasies also indicate the flexibility of Hollywood's narrative conventions. The movie has, it seems, been all things to all critics: while much of the popular criticism of the movie has described it as perfectly blending "a turbulent love story and harrowing intrigue," Umberto Eco has, with equal affection, insisted that it is "a hodgepodge of sensational scenes strung together implausibly," its plot and its characters "psychologically incredible." It endures, he argues, because of its "glorious ricketiness."[61] In part because of its enduring popularity as "America's most beloved movie," in part because of the frequent claims for its typicality – Eco suggests that *Casablanca* "is not *one* movie. It is 'movies' " – *Casablanca* makes a particularly suitable case for the examination of the practice of Hollywood narrative.[62]

Normally, argues Edward Branigan, "the classical narrative does not give the appearance of ambiguity, nor does it encourage multiple interpretation, but rather, like the chameleon, it is adaptable, resilient and accommodating. It will try to be what the spectator believes it to be."[63] *Casablanca* is at least two movies at once, and in that respect it is quite typical of Hollywood's product, in which the heterosexual romance is counterpointed by an alternative plot. In *Casablanca* a romance and an adventure-war story coexist as separable commodities, and although it is possible to reconcile them into a unified whole, it is not necessary to do so. Different viewers can, as Branigan suggests, construct different stories from the variety of motivations the plot provides, and the accommodating "classical, chameleon narrative . . . will congratulate the spectator for his or her particular selection by intimating that that selection is uniquely correct."[64]

The plot of *Casablanca* is skeletal. An introductory voice-over describes the refugee trail from Europe to America, arriving at Casablanca, which is controlled by the Vichy French government. Then the movie announces what formalist criticism would identify as its "first cause," an initial act of villainy. Letters of transit allowing their bearers to leave Casablanca unhindered have been stolen from their German couriers.[65] Meanwhile, Gestapo Major Strasser (Conrad Veidt) arrives in Casablanca in pursuit of escaping Resistance leader Victor Laszlo (Paul Henreid). Ugarte (Peter Lorre) arrives at the Café Americain run by expatriate American Rick Blaine (Humphrey Bogart) and persuades him to conceal the letters of transit, which Ugarte intends to sell to Laszlo. Moments later, he is arrested by the local chief of police, Captain Renault (Claude Rains).

Renault introduces Rick to Strasser, but Blaine refuses to be drawn on his opinions or beliefs. "Your business is politics," he tells Strasser, "mine is running a saloon." Then Laszlo arrives at the café with Ilsa Lund (Ingrid Bergman). She and the café's piano-player Sam (Dooley Wilson) recognize each other, and despite his alarm at seeing her, he reluctantly agrees to play "As Time Goes By" "for old time's sake." The music brings Rick over for the first of a string of tense encounters with Ilsa, but the revelation of their past is delayed by Strasser's ordering Laszlo to meet him at Renault's office the next day. Later that night, Rick gets drunk remembering his love affair with Ilsa in Paris, interrupted by the German invasion. When Ilsa comes to the café to explain why she did not leave Paris with him, Rick cannot forgive her, and she leaves.

Next morning, Strasser and Renault tell Laszlo that he will never leave Casablanca. Meanwhile, Rick meets Ilsa in the market, and attempts an apology, but now she refuses him, telling him that she and Laszlo are married. Ferrari (Sydney Greenstreet), the "leader of all illegal activities in Casablanca," tells the Laszlos that even he cannot obtain exit visas for both of them, but suggests that they ask Rick about the letters of transit. That evening, all the protagonists assemble at the café. Rick's discarded lover Yvonne (Madeleine LeBeau) arrives in the company of a German, and he and a French officer start a fight. Rick stops it, telling them to "lay off politics, or get out." However, his neutrality is weakening: he rigs his own roulette table for a young Bulgarian couple to enable them to purchase exit visas from Renault. Laszlo offers to buy the letters of transit, but Rick refuses to sell, telling Laszlo to ask Ilsa for an explanation. When German officers in the café start singing the "Wacht am Rhein," Rick consents to Laszlo leading the band and other customers in a stirring rendition of the Marseillaise. Infuriated by this affront, Strasser orders Renault to close the café.

On their second night in Casablanca, the Laszlos go their separate ways; Victor to a meeting of the local resistance, Ilsa to see Rick in an attempt to obtain the letters of transit. Becoming desperate, she threatens him at gunpoint, but breaks down. They are reconciled, and she explains that she abandoned him in Paris because she had just discovered that Laszlo, her husband, was alive and on the run from the Germans. He accepts her explanation and she tells him, "I ran away from you once. I can't do it again. Oh, I don't know what is right any longer. You'll have to think for both of us, for all of us." Events now accelerate. Laszlo returns from the meeting to the café. Before he is arrested he asks Rick to take Ilsa to America. Rick persuades Renault to release Laszlo by promising to frame him with the letters of transit, but when Renault attempts to arrest Laszlo that night, Rick restrains Renault at gunpoint. At the airport Rick sends Ilsa away with Laszlo and shoots Strasser. He and Renault plan to leave Casablanca together, to continue the fight against Germany.

As this summary suggests, there is more talk than action in *Casablanca* and the movie repeatedly stresses the immobility of its central characters. Casablanca is a staging post that few can leave, and the movie rarely strays from the confines of Rick's café. Plot and story times are clearly explained, and events for the most part occur in their chronological order. The passage of time is registered by transitions from daytime to night-time sequences and the daily departure of the Lisbon plane. However, parallel and sub-plots abound in the movie, introducing areas of meaning that are far less integrated into the narrative than the summary suggests. Although the credit sequence in which Bogart, Bergman, and Henreid are given joint billing tells us that the Rick–Ilsa–Laszlo plot-line will be the emotional center of the movie, much of *Casablanca*'s early development remains incidental to this familiar "triangle" plot. Rick's appearance is delayed until contextual material has established the milieu, discussed the plight of refugees from occupied Europe, and set up the letters of transit as the trigger to the causal chain of events which motivates the majority of the action. Even when the movie's trio of stars has moved to the center of our attention, *Casablanca* suspends its storyline for autonomous performances such as the Marseillaise scene.

The usual suspects: Captain Renault (Claude Rains), Victor Laszlo (Paul Henreid), Rick Blaine (Humphrey Bogart), and Ilsa Lund (Ingrid Bergman) in *Casablanca* (1942). Warner Bros. (courtesy Kobal)

Setting the scene of the story also elaborates the psychology and ideological beliefs of the movie's central character, Rick: reluctant hero, noncombatant, and isolationist, insistently aloof from the dramatic crises around him, but unable to return to America for reasons that are never explained. His reluctance to act (he is first introduced playing chess against himself) initially displaces the responsibility for narrative progress onto a circle of subsidiary characters, all of whom seem intensely goal-oriented and desperate to change the story's initial situation. The movie's delays intensify our desire for Rick's eventual intervention as a fulfillment of his "true" character, hinted at by Renault when he points out that he had fought for the Loyalist cause during the Spanish Civil War, and implicit in Bogart's star image. Rick's cynicism and instinct for self-preservation provide far more resistance to his taking on narrative responsibility than any external obstacles. The delay that occurs while Rick struggles with his conscience creates a correspondingly greater level of satisfaction when he finally decides to act. *Casablanca* needs its hero: only when Rick commits himself to effecting a resolution can the central plot assert its priority and the movie pull toward closure. To put it another way, only when the production values of its credit sequence come into synchronization with the priorities of its storyline can the audience's act of consumption be concluded.

Casablanca is a remarkably "knowing" movie. Not only does it verbally acknowledge its dependence on coincidence ("of all the gin joints in all the towns in all the world, she has to walk into mine"), it also suspends plot chronology to justify that dependence by inserting supplementary information which will make it plausible. Placed at the precise moment when we require information about Rick and Ilsa's earlier relationship, the Paris flashback confirms the hypotheses we constructed from the worried looks between Sam and Ilsa and the interlocked gazes of Ilsa and Rick in the bar. When we return from the flashback in time for Ilsa's appearance, Rick's hostility seems justified on the basis of what has "just" occurred. It takes a further flashback of sorts, although not a visual one, to engineer Rick's conversion to the cause of both the Resistance and the progression of *Casablanca*'s narrative. This time the narration itself grants Ilsa the time to explain why she abandoned him, and as she tells her story the camera shows her to us, supplying the evidence by which we judge her truthfulness. But even with Rick convinced, motivated, and narratively engaged, the plot continues to withhold information from us about his plans. This concealment increases the moral force of his responsible action in asserting fidelity and self-sacrifice in the name of a greater cause at the movie's end: "Ilsa, I'm no good at being noble, but it doesn't take much to see that the problems of three little people don't amount to a hill of beans in this crazy world."

Casablanca is committed to clarity in the sense that its storyline articulates a propagandist message which seems utterly unambiguous to present-day audiences.[66] Its drama of personal relations is, however, much less clear, and causal connection much harder to establish. Very early on in *Casablanca* we come to understand that the movie will be centrally concerned with the relationship between Rick and Ilsa, without really knowing any details of that relationship. We must formulate hypotheses about, for example, the reactions of Rick and Ilsa to each other and Ilsa's reaction to Renault's enigmatic description of Rick: "He's the kind of man that, well, if I were a woman, and I were not around, I should be in love with Rick." Above all, the sustained close-ups of Bergman's expressionless face declare themselves to be pregnant with significance, without specifying exactly what is being signified: viewers are invited to supply their own interpretations, or else simply to contemplate her luminously photogenic features.

Casablanca's "chameleon narrative" is most evident in an ellipsis at the center of the movie's romance, when the lovers are reconciled in Rick's apartment. As they kiss, the image dissolves to a shot of the airport tower, and then back to the apartment, with him standing looking out of the window. He turns to Ilsa, sitting on a sofa, and asks, "And then?" She resumes her story of events in Paris as if there has been no interruption.[67]

The audience must guess the length of the ellipsis, and what, if anything, happened in it. Lacking any incontrovertible evidence in the scene itself, each viewer must decide whether their regenerative romance has been consummated or not on the basis of his or her interpretation of convention. Is the tower a phallic symbol, is that a post-coital cigarette Bogart is smoking? Or has Rick's decision to provide the young Bulgarian couple with money to pay for their exit visas so that Annina (Joy Page) will not have to do "a bad thing" with Renault established his commitment to marital fidelity? The movie provides equally persuasive evidence for either interpretation, and returns self-consciously to the ellipsis in an exchange between Rick and Laszlo in its final scene:

Rick: You said you knew about Ilsa and me?
Victor: Yes.
Rick: You didn't know she was at my place last night when you
           were . . . she came there for the letters of transit. Isn't that true,
           Ilsa?
Ilsa: Yes.
Rick: She tried everything to get them and nothing worked. She did
           her best to convince me that she was still in love with me. That
           was all over long ago; for your sake she pretended it wasn't and I
           let her pretend.
Victor: I understand.

What that means is anybody's guess, but like Stanley Cavell's embarrassed concern with the sexual references in *Bringing Up Baby*, the issue at stake in this instance is more substantial than a merely prurient concern with whether these two characters had sex or not.[68] In an important demonstration of Hollywood's contradictory refusal to enforce interpretive closure at the same time as it provides plot resolution, the movie neither confirms nor denies either interpretation. Indeed, it goes beyond this ambiguity to provide supporting evidence for both outcomes, while effectively refusing to take responsibility for the story some viewers may choose to construct. This is a particularly fruitful example of the principle of deniability in action. As Lea Jacobs has argued, under the Code "offensive ideas could survive at the price of an instability of meaning . . . there was constant negotiation about how explicit films could be and by what means (through the image, sound, language) offensive ideas could find representation."[69] At this later stage of the Code's operation, the groundrules of "delicate indication" had been tacitly established between producers and regulators, replacing the earlier, more overt discussions of the desirability of the double-entendre. Two letters PCA Director Joseph Breen wrote to Jack Warner over *Casablanca* illustrate this mutually cooperative understanding:

> With a view to removing the now offensive characterization of Renault as an
> immoral man who engages himself in seducing women to whom he grants

visas, it has been agreed with Mr Wallis [the producer] that the several references to this particular phase of the gentleman's character will be materially toned down, to-wit:

Page 5: the line in scene 15 "The girl will be released in the morning" will be changed to the expressed "will be released later." . . .

Page 75: The word "enjoy" in Renault's line is to be changed to the word "like." "You like war. I like women."

. . . [The scene in Rick's apartment] seems to contain a suggestion of a sexual affair, which would be unacceptable if it came through in the finished picture. We believe this could possibly be corrected by replacing the fade out . . . with a dissolve, and shooting the succeeding scene without any sign of a bed or couch, or anything whatever suggestive of a sex affair.[70]

To a large extent what is at issue here is the relationship between the boundaries of the text and the boundaries of interpretation. On several occasions *Casablanca* invokes offscreen space: in doing so, it invites its audiences to imagine narrative events not represented within its plot-chain. Some of these events also lie outside the permissible sphere of textual representation; as "offensive ideas" their presence can only be indicated by drawing our attention to their absence. We must, for example, decide what Annina means by her oblique reference to doing "a bad thing." Much of the work in the narration of any Hollywood movie involves offering the audience incentives to "read into" or activate these absences in a way that opens up an intertextual field of possible meanings that the movie-as-text does not itself articulate explicitly.

The intertextual field of a movie is part of its commodity existence, in which there is a constant interplay between innocence and sophistication in intra- and intertextual response. When Ilsa tells her version of events in Paris, for example, the camera's soft-focus close-ups on Bergman's face validate her testimony and suggest how much Rick has misjudged her. This is an indication of the extent to which the narration relies not only on the act of showing, but on the appearance of the star. As in every star vehicle, it is the conviction of the central performances, the extratextual information of star biographies, and our innate understanding of the commercial operation of stardom that furnish the plot and establish the trustworthiness of the characters, not simply the verifiability of their statements.

The audience may know nothing about Rick Blaine ("cannot return to America, the reason is a little unclear . . .") and Ilsa Lund ("we said no questions . . ."), but we know a good deal about Humphrey Bogart and Ingrid Bergman from other movies we have seen, and from fan magazine articles, newspaper stories, or biographies we have read. We would, therefore, be astonished if a movie starring Bogart and Bergman did not involve them having a love affair, although their previous histories in other movies do not necessarily lead us to assume that the affair will have a happy outcome. Our knowledge of how the plot will progress means that narrative energies that might otherwise be directed to the manufacture of the couple can be diverted into the movie's explicit ideological project, "the overcoming of its audience's latent anxiety about American intervention in World War II,"[71] to which *Casablanca* was as institutionally committed as it was to its observance of the Code. At one point Bogart asks rhetorically, "If it's December 1941 in Casablanca, what time is it in New York? I bet they're asleep in New York. I bet they're asleep all over America." This concern in fact determines its ending, whatever the production anecdotes about its script being written as it went along, with no one knowing the outcome of the romance, might suggest.[72]

No other ending is possible: in order to avoid the suggestion of an "illicit sex affair," Rick and Ilsa can only be united at the death of Laszlo, but to have the Nazi villain kill a Resistance leader who has "succeeded in impressing half the world" would clearly undermine the movie's ideological project. While it might succeed in satisfying the sophisticated viewers of the movie's entirely deniable sex scene, any outcome that united Rick and Ilsa would be at the expense of the movie's essential premise. It would represent, in other words, an insupportable change of heart. The charm and power of *Casablanca*'s production mythology lie in their suggestion that an alternative ending was possible: one that transgressed the rigid control of the Production Code, one that permitted the escape of repressed desire from the confining closure of a deterministic narrative, and one that did not remind its audience that Hollywood's products were inevitably trivially conventional. That ending could not exist on the screen; it could only exist in its audience's imagination.

Narrative Pressure

> What do we "consume" when we go the cinema? We consume a story, certainly, but not a story that could be recounted by a friend or summarized in prose to the same effect. Our experience of film is tied more to the specific telling of the story than to the abstract result of that telling, the story told. Our pleasure, in short, follows from our engagement in the film as process.
>
> Richard deCordova[73]

> I didn't allow any dull moments to develop in my films. I was always afraid that the audience might get ahead of me and say to themselves: "That guy is going to get killed in a minute." Therefore, I had to go faster than them.
>
> Raoul Walsh[74]

The broadly Formalist accounts of Hollywood story-telling that we have been discussing make up the dominant paradigm by which narrative in Hollywood cinema is discussed. The possibilities of a more consumerist account have been less fully explored, but a starting point is provided by an essay by Thomas Elsaesser entitled "Narrative Cinema and Audience-oriented Aesthetics."[75] Elsaesser examines the aesthetics of Hollywood not simply as a narrative cinema, but as a particular response to the temporal and sensory regime of the movie theater. The psychological terms of this discussion provide a more complete framework for considering what we have previously suggested about the Hollywood cinema's benevolence to its audiences. According to Elsaesser, the primary material of cinema is not celluloid but the viewing situation itself: "in the cinema we are subjected to a particularly intense organization of time, experienced within a formal structure which is closed, but in a sense also circular: we are 'captured' in order to be 'released,' willingly undergoing a fixed term of imprisonment."[76]

This almost physical explanation of Hollywood narrative sees the cinematic experience as potentially anxiety-provoking, as the viewer is rendered uncomfortable by the restrictions imposed by the viewing situation. Anyone who has had to sit through a movie he or she absolutely loathed will recognize the discomfort that can be imposed by the experience. (In an extreme example within a movie, in *A Clockwork Orange*, 1971, Alec [Malcolm McDowell] is forced to watch movies with his eyelids taped open and his head clamped facing the screen as part of an aversion therapy program.)[77] The pressure that the cinema's organization of experience places upon the viewer is an important element in the sensory experience we purchase when we enter the movie theater. Elsaesser argues that this pressure has "a strong psychic component" that demands "some form of manipulation and cathexis," meaning that it must be relieved by its transference to other subjects or agents. The viewer must sit still in a darkened space for a fixed period of time. With no opportunity for the expression of physical motor energies, he or she must rely on the screen to provide an outlet for psychic energy, through a process of transformation.

According to Elsaesser, transformation occurs at a variety of levels in the process of the interaction between the viewer and the events on the screen. The viewer's psychic energy is transformed into segments of action on the screen, which in turn provoke an emotional response from the viewer. He or she transforms that emotional response into a consistent interpretation of the screen events, providing the coherence that the screen events themselves lack, by filling in the gaps between events in a manner akin to the way he or she fills in the gaps between the movie's successive still images. The viewer then transforms events into plot, and plot into story:

> The fact that the spectator is pinned to his seat and has only the screen to look at, causes impulses to arise which demand to be compensated, transferred and managed, and it is on this level that style, ideational content, causality, narrative sequence, plot, themes, point of view, identification, emotional participation enter into the viewing situation: whatever else they are, they are also ways in which the film manipulates, controls and directs the defenses and impulses mobilized by motor-paralysis.[78]

At its most basic level, this provides an explanation of Hollywood's enthusiasm for action, as a vicarious substitute for the movement the viewer has been deprived of. As we have discussed, early cinema presented movement as a spectacle in itself, and the exhilaration of movement remains one of the pleasures of the Hollywood movie. But narrative also offered possibilities that the "cinema of attractions" could not by itself fulfill. As it developed from 1912 to 1917, the feature-length movie transformed the performance and spectacle of early cinema into a variety of goal-oriented activities. In an economic sense, the feature extended the act of purchase; by persuading the spectator to buy longer periods of time, exhibitors could charge higher entrance fees at the box-office. Narrative added another commodity, the story, that the movie could sell. The story also fitted the psychic requirements of the viewing situation. Unlike the cinema of attractions, a story has a clearly marked beginning and end that match the sense of closure and enclosure characterizing the cinematic experience.[79] In this account, narrative is the dominant form of cinema not because the movies acquired an established aesthetic from the realist novel, or for reasons to do with the aims and desires of filmmakers or questions of commercial competitiveness, but because it provided the most effective means of satisfying the inherent psychological needs established by the viewing situation itself.

This argument disposes of one of the most frequent critiques of Hollywood: that its stories are psychologically unrealistic, mechanically conventional, "melodramatic," implausible, excessively dependent on coincidence, or however the particular version of the charge is phrased.[80] An interviewer once complained to Alfred Hitchcock about the implausibility of one of his plots. Why, he asked, did the characters not simply go to the police? Because, replied Hitchcock, then the movie would be over. In that answer we can see not only the workings of an industrial logic that dictates the duration of a movie, but also the logic of a narrative system that functions less in terms of a psychological realism among the characters than in terms of the construction and release of a suitable amount of pressure exerted on both characters and audience.

The possibility of exerting this pressure allows the movies to construct stories in quite different ways to literature. Faced with a scriptwriter's complaint that he was making a character behave illogically, *Casablanca*'s director Michael Curtiz allegedly responded, "Don't worry what's logical. I make it so fast no one notices."[81] An action movie like *White Heat* (1950) is bound together not so much by characterization or causal explanation as simply by the pace at which it moves. Driven by the momentum of the image stream, the audience race to keep up with Cody Jarrett (James Cagney) as he places everyone around him under intense physical and psychological stress. We grow restless during the movie's longueurs when the FBI agents tell each other what is going on. Cody Jarrett is provided with a personality disorder, but only the most psychoanalytically committed of critics could take his Oedipus complex seriously.[82] Rather, *White Heat* is typical of action movies in which the central protagonist is defined dynamically as "the focus of perpetual agitation and motion," reflecting and catalyzing "the pressures and constraints which the psychic matrix mobilizes in the spectator."[83] Elsaesser points out the recurrence of "plots of pursuits, quests, treks and themes centered on the ambition to arrive, make it, get to the top, or avenge, control," which require characters to respond to pressure, struggle against deadlines, or solve a puzzle. Elsaesser's persuasive account of the persistence of these patterns is worth quoting at length:

> The narrative tradition developed by Hollywood is based on strongly pro-filed, "typical" plots: geometrical in shape (linear, though occasionally circular or tangential), consecutive, generated by an alternating rhythm of conflict, climax, resolution. . . . These dramatic configurations engineered through plot and protagonists are evidently important structural constants in the American cinema . . . precisely because of the high degree of schematization the plots provide a possible way of regulating psychic pressure. . . . This would help to account for the inordinate emphasis of the Hollywood tradition on action, violence, eroticism, the predominance of energy-intensive heroes, the graphs of maximum investment of vitality, phallic models of identity and self-assertion, instinctual drive-patterns, the accentuation of voyeuristic and fantasizing tendencies and projections, as well as the value placed on the spectacular, the exotic, the adventurous. Being quite possibly subliminal ways of charting a course of energy expenditure/management, these plots compensate very directly, and from a psychological point of view very efficiently, motor inhibitions and allow for massive discharges of anxiety feelings through the arousal of less primary but dramatically or intellectually validated tensions and "suspense" which is then managed by the plots and the action.[84]

Elsaesser's account provides a fuller articulation of the notion, nervously anticipated by the authors of the Production Code, that the peculiar physical characteristics of cinema produce effects that are inevitably erotic, scopophilic, and potentially transgressive, and that its careful management is a cultural necessity. In part, this management involves the use of narrative to control Hollywood's pleasures by restricting what can be said or shown to what can be delicately, ambiguously, and above all deniably indicated. If entertainment is to function smoothly within the general requirements of the organization of work and leisure under capitalism, it must open the Pandora's box of pleasure, but then reseal it by the end of the movie, confining the expression and satisfaction of desire to the safe space of licensed public fantasy. That is why narrative closure appears to be so heavily stressed in the Hollywood movie. At one level it asserts the determinist morality of the Production Code. At another, it licenses the movies as a site for the expression of desire, by emphasizing their artificiality and the extent to which they are governed by the external forces of the viewing situation, rather than being spontaneously generated by the logic of their own narratives.

Just as we construct a history around the still picture, a movie can only exist as a selected portion of a temporal continuum, and a specific location within potentially infinite offscreen surroundings. In this sense, narrative closure is less secure than it appears. *Casablanca*, for example, concludes with an opening rather than a closing statement: "Louis, I think this is the beginning of a beautiful friendship." The story is "to be continued" even though the plot is over.[85] This is characteristic of Hollywood's ambivalence toward closure: put the camera on the other side of the mesa toward which Henry Fonda rides at the end of *My Darling Clementine* (1946) and you have the opening shot of another Western. The residual feeling of a narrative process extending beyond the confines of the particular plot events in any movie is an important element in the economic patterns of movie consumption preferred by Hollywood cinema.[86] *Casablanca* typically presents a crisis in the lives of its characters, but it is important for the audience to accept that these characters have existences before and after this crisis in order for us to feel that the story is in any way significant. It is a means by which the cinema can both complete the individual narrative and at the same time renew the audience's enthusiasm for the repeat experience of narration as process. Narrative closure releases the viewer from the movie in full awareness that the story never really ends, and thus arouses, satisfies, and, crucially, reawakens the desire to be entertained.

Notes

1   Edward Branigan, *Narrative Comprehension and Film* (London: Routledge, 1992), p. 3.
2   Jane M. Gaines, "Introduction: The Family Melodrama of Classical Narrative Cinema," in Jane M. Gaines, ed., *Classical Hollywood Narrative: The Paradigm Wars* (Durham, NC: Duke University Press, 1992), p. 1.
3   David Bordwell, Janet Staiger, and Kristin Thompson, *The Classical Hollywood Cinema: Film Style and Mode of Production to 1960* (London: Routledge and Kegan Paul, 1985), p. 12.
4   Branigan, p. 1; Dudley Andrew, *Concepts in Film Theory* (New York: Oxford University Press, 1984), p. 76.
5   Seymour Chatman, *Story and Discourse: Narrative Structure in Fiction and Film* (Ithaca, NY: Cornell University Press, 1978), pp. 31, 20.
6   Branigan, p. 100.
7   William Goldman, *Adventures in the Screen Trade: A Personal View of Hollywood and Screenwriting* (New York: Warner Books, 1983), p. 37.
8   E.M. Forster, *Aspects of the Novel* (New York: Harcourt, Brace, 1927), p. 130.
9   Edward Branigan suggests that narrative requires knowledge to be unevenly distributed. In a universe in which all observers were all-knowing, "there can be no possibility of narration since all information is equally available and already possessed in the same ways." So "narration is the overall regulation and distribution of knowledge which determines *how* and when the spectator acquires knowledge, that is, how the spectator is able to know what he or she comes to know in a narrative." Branigan, p. 76.
10 Arthur C. Danto, *Narration and Knowledge* (New York: Columbia University Press, 1985), p. xii; Branigan, p. 168.
11 Colin MacCabe, "Realism and the Cinema: Notes on Some Brechtian Theses," *Screen*

15:2 (Summer 1974), p. 8. See also Robert Lapsley and Michael Westlake, *Film Theory: An Introduction* (Manchester: University of Manchester Press, 1988), p. 171.

12 Jane Austen, *Pride and Prejudice*, 1st pub. 1813 (Oxford: Oxford University Press, 1990), p. 1.

13 Sarah Kozloff, *Invisible Storytellers: Voice-over Narration in American Fiction Film* (Berkeley, CA: University of California Press, 1988), p. 25.

14 Roland Barthes, "The Rhetoric of the Image," in *Image Music Text* (London: Fontana, 1977), pp. 32–51.

15 Plato, *Republic*, in D.A. Russell and M. Winterbottom, eds, *Classical Literary Criticism* (Oxford: Oxford University Press, 1989), p. 31.

16 Russell and Winterbottom, p. 30.

17 Aristotle, *Poetics*, trans. Gerald F. Else (Ann Arbor: University of Michigan Press, 1967), p. 13.

18 Slomith Rimmon-Kenan, *Narrative Fiction: Contemporary Poetics* (London: Methuen, 1983), pp. 97, 107–8.

19 David Bordwell, *Narration in the Fiction Film* (London: Methuen, 1985), p. 3.

20 Steven Cohan and Linda M. Shires, *Telling Stories: A Theoretical Analysis of Narrative Fiction* (London: Routledge, 1988), pp. 2–3.

21 Eric Smoodin, "The Image and the Voice in the Film with Spoken Narration," *Quarterly Review of Film Studies* 8 (Fall 1983), p. 19.

22 MacCabe, pp. 8–9, 10.

23 MacCabe, p. 11.

24 For instance, the camera style used in Bree's scenes with her analyst marks them as more "documentary," and therefore more "truthful," than the fiction that surrounds them, while Jane Fonda's performance in the psychiatric encounter emphasizes the confessional verity of her statements by comparison to her dissembling in other scenes. The confident dismissal of the closing contradiction between sound and image assumes, rather than demonstrates, the hierarchy of image over sound. In the particular case of *Klute*, it could be argued that the soundtrack has received more support as the authoritative discourse in the movie. MacCabe, p. 11. Bordwell offers a sharp critique of MacCabe's analysis, p. 20.

25 Andrew, pp. 75–6.

26 Kozloff, p. 115.

27 Kozloff, p. 115.

28 Kristin Thompson discusses this case and several other instances of duplicity in "Duplicitous Narration and *Stage Fright*," in *Breaking the Glass Armor: Neoformalist Film Analysis* (Princeton, NJ: Princeton University Press, 1988), pp. 135–61.

29 A. Lindsley Lane, "The Camera's Omniscient Eye," *American Cinematographer* 16:3 (March 1935), p. 95; quoted in Bordwell, p. 161.

30 Bordwell, p. 161.

31 Quoted in Bordwell, Staiger, and Thompson, p. 34.

32 Thompson, p. 39. Thompson has argued for the retention of the terms "syuzhet" and "fabula" for the distinctions between plot and story being made here, pointing out that "the English terms also carry the burden of all the other senses in which non-Formalist critics have used them, while fabula and syuzhet relate only to the Russian Formalists' definitions" (p. 38). Our preference, here as elsewhere, is to aim for a greater precision in the use of a non-specialist, everyday critical vocabulary.

33 Gaines, p. 1.

34 Bordwell, Staiger, and Thompson, p. 17. Quotations from Francis Taylor Patterson, *Cinema Craftsmanship* (New York: Harcourt, Brace, and Howe, 1920). Michael Hauge's

insistence that every screenplay have three acts, discussed in chapter 7, is a case in point.

35   Bordwell, Staiger, and Thompson, p. 18. Quotation from Barrett C. Kiesling, *Talking Pictures* (Richmond, VA: Johnson Publishing Co., 1937), p. 2.

36   Lewis Herman, *A Practical Manual of Screen Playwriting for Theater and Television Films* (New York: New American Library, 1974), pp. 87–8. Bordwell quotes the latter part of this passage, p. 18.

37   Aljean Harmetz, *Round Up the Usual Suspects: The Making of Casablanca – Bogart, Bergman, and World War II* (New York: Hyperion, 1992), p. 267.

38   Barbara Klinger, "Digressions at the Cinema: Reception and Mass Culture," *Cinema Journal* 28:4 (Summer 1989), pp. 10, 14, 16.

39   Thompson, p. 70.

40   Quoted in Rudy Behlmer, ed., *Memo from: David O. Selznick* (New York: Avon, 1973; 1st pub. New York: Viking, 1972), p. 394.

41   Branigan, p. 190.

42   Richard Dyer, *Heavenly Bodies: Film Stars and Society* (London: Macmillan, 1987), p. 11.

43   Steve Seidman, *Comedian Comedy: A Tradition in Hollywood Film* (Ann Arbor: UMI Research Press, 1981), pp. 19–57; Steve Neale and Frank Krutnik, *Popular Film and Television Comedy* (London: Routledge, 1990), p. 104.

44   Stanley Cavell, *Pursuits of Happiness: The Hollywood Comedy of Remarriage* (Cambridge, MA: Harvard University Press, 1981), p. 113.

45   George Segal has exactly the same problem with Elliott Gould in *California Split* (1974).

46   "A Code to Govern the Making of Talking, Synchronized and Silent Motion Pictures," Motion Picture Producers and Distributors of America, Inc. (hereafter MPPDA), 1930, reprinted in Raymond Moley, *The Hays Office* (Indianapolis: Bobbs-Merrill, 1945), p. 241.

47   "The Reasons Supporting Preamble of Code," in Moley, p. 245.

48   Recent examples of these arguments are Neil Postman, *Amusing Ourselves to Death: Public Discourse in the Age of Show Business* (London: Heinemann, 1986), and Michael Medved, *Hollywood vs America: Popular Culture and the War on Traditional Values* (New York: HarperCollins, 1992).

49   Umberto Eco, *The Role of the Reader: Explorations in the Semiotics of Texts* (London: Hutchinson, 1979), p. 9.

50   Ruth Vasey, *Diplomatic Representations: The World According to Hollywood, 1919–1939* (Madison: University of Wisconsin Press, forthcoming).

51   Lamar Trotti to Hays, February 2, 1931. Production Code Administration Archive, Margaret Herrick Library, Academy of Motion Picture Arts and Sciences, Los Angeles (hereafter PCA), *The Smiling Lieutenant* file.

52   Little in these strategies changes. In March 1991 the British Board of Film Classification concluded 18 months of deliberation and gave Nagisa Oshima's *Empire of the Senses* (*Ai No Corrida*) an 18 certificate without asking the distributor (the British Film Institute) to make "a single cut." The scene that caused most difficulty in this decision was a "very, very brief" shot of the central female character touching a boy's penis. "The final solution was an ingenious optical distortion so that, as one BFI spokeswoman put it, 'We know everything happens . . . you see what she's doing but you don't fully see what she's doing.'" Farrah Anwar, "The Empire Strikes Back," *Guardian* (March 28, 1991).

53   "Mr Zanuck's Suggestions on Proposed Treatment of 'Environment,'" September 18, 1931. Warner Bros. *Alias the Doctor* Production File, University of Southern California.

54   Joy to Zanuck, November 23, 1931; Zanuck to Joy, November 24, 1931; Joy to Zanuck,

November 24, 1931; Zanuck to Joy, November 30, 1931. PCA *Alias the Doctor*.

55   Cavell, pp. 116–17.

56   Harold J. Salemson, *The Screen Writer* (April, 1946), quoted in Ruth Inglis, *Freedom of the Movies: A Report on Self-regulation from the Commission on Freedom of the Press* (Chicago: University of Chicago Press, 1947), pp. 183–4.

57   Elliott Paul and Luis Quintanilla, *With a Hays Nonny Nonny* (New York: Random House, 1942), pp. 63–4.

58   Richard Maltby, " 'To Prevent the Prevalent Type of Book': Censorship and Adaptation in Hollywood, 1924–1934," *American Quarterly* 44:4 (1992), pp. 554–83.

59   "Virtue in Cans," *The Nation* (April 16, 1930), p. 441.

60   Branigan, pp. 30–1.

61   Umberto Eco, "*Casablanca*: Cult Movies and Intertextual Collage," in *Travels in Hyperreality* (London: Picador, 1987), pp. 197–8.

62   Entry on *Casablanca*, in *Cinemania Interactive Movie Guide* (Microsoft, 1992); Eco, "*Casablanca*," p. 208.

63   Branigan, p. 98.

64   Branigan, p. 149.

65   *Casablanca*'s letters of transit are an archetypal instance of the "Maguffin" of a movie plot. Alfred Hitchcock defined the term as "the device, the gimmick, if you will, or the papers the spies are after. . . . the 'Maguffin' is the term we use to cover all that sort of thing: to steal plans or documents, or discover a secret, it doesn't matter what it is. And the logicians are wrong in trying to figure out the truth of a Maguffin, since it's beside the point. The only thing that really matters is that in the picture the plans, documents, or secrets must seem to be of vital importance to the characters. To me, the narrator, they're of no importance whatever." François Truffaut, *Hitchcock*, revised edn (London: Paladin, 1986), pp. 191–2. The whole of *Casablanca*'s plot hinges on the implausible presumption that the permission to leave Casablanca granted by the letters cannot be rescinded, even if they are in the hands of "an enemy of the Reich." It also relies on the Nazis' observance of the city's neutrality in their pursuit of Victor Laszlo, on no grounds other than those Laszlo himself offers Strasser, that "Any violation of neutrality would reflect on Captain Renault." *Casablanca*'s narrative, like that of many Hollywood movies, is dependent for its coherence on its own system of internal pressures, not on the accuracy of its external references. "Suspension of disbelief" somehow seems too mild a term to describe the audience's required relationship to such fictions.

66   Historian Richard Raskin, however, notes that at the time of the movie's release, American foreign policy was actually more hostile toward the Free French than is enacted in *Casablanca*: "men like Victor Laszlo were being arrested by the police of the administrators the U.S. supported in North Africa." Richard Raskin, "*Casablanca* and United States Foreign Policy," *Film History* 4:2 (1990), p. 161.

67   The published script, which does not describe its source, describes the action at this moment in the following terms: "Rick has taken Ilsa in his arms. He presses her tight to him and kisses her passionately. She is lost in his embrace. Sometime later, Rick watches the revolving beacon at the airport from his window. There is a bottle of champagne on the table and two half-filled glasses. Ilsa is talking. Rick is listening intently." Howard Koch, *Casablanca: Script and Legend* (Woodstock: Overlook Press, 1973), p. 156.

68   For the prurient, such instances abound, even in movies well worked over by critics. Lea Jacobs has pointed out another elliptical Bogartian indiscretion, in his encounter with Dorothy Malone in the antiquarian bookstore in *The Big Sleep* (1946).

69   Lea Jacobs, "Industry Self-regulation and the Problem of Textual Determination," *The*

Velvet Light Trap 23 (Spring 1989), p. 9; Jacobs' argument is enlarged in *The Wages of Sin: Censorship and the Fallen Woman Film, 1928–1942* (Madison: University of Wisconsin Press, 1991).

70 Breen to Wallis, June 5, 1942; Breen to Warner, June 18, 1942. Quoted in Gerald Gardiner, *The Censorship Papers: Movie Censorship Letter from the Hays Office 1934 to 1968* (New York: Dodd, Mead, 1987), p. 3.

71 Robert B. Ray, *A Certain Tendency of the Hollywood Cinema, 1930–1980* (Princeton, NJ: Princeton University Press, 1985), p. 90. See also Richard Maltby, *Harmless Entertainment: Hollywood and the Ideology of Consensus* (Metuchen, NJ: Scarecrow, 1983), pp. 193–210.

72 Several recent accounts of the production of *Casablanca* have established the inaccuracy of many of these anecdotes. The ending of the movie was never in doubt, in that no version of the script ever concluded with Ilsa staying with Rick. See Harmetz; Frank Miller, *As Time Goes By* (London: Virgin Books, 1993); Harlan Lebo, *Casablanca: Behind the Scenes* (New York: Simon and Schuster, 1992).

73 Richard deCordova, *Picture Personalities: The Emergence of the Star System in America* (Urbana: University of Illinois Press, 1990), p. 13.

74 Oliver Eyquen, Michael Henry, and Jacques Saada, "Interview with Raoul Walsh," in Phil Hardy, ed., *Raoul Walsh* (Edinburgh: Edinburgh Film Festival, 1974), p. 43.

75 Thomas Elsaesser, "Narrative Cinema and Audience-oriented Aesthetics," in Tony Bennett, Susan Boyd-Bowman, Colin Mercer, and Janet Woollacott, eds, *Popular Television and Film* (London: British Film Institute, 1981), pp. 270–82. This is an abridged version of a British Film Institute Occasional Paper, first published in 1969.

76 Elsaesser, p. 271.

77 Other movies, including *The Ipcress File* (1965), have also used the apparatus of cinema as an instrument of torture.

78 Elsaesser, p. 272.

79 Although this argument might appear to support Dudley Andrew's suggestion in Andrew, p. 76, that narrative is "natural" to the movies, in fact it confirms that narrative is a convention which aids in the industrial standardization of Hollywood entertainment, and not an aesthetic goal in itself. Significantly, a cinema of attractions persists not only in avant-garde cinema but also in many Hollywood-produced short subjects, while the production of pleasure by means of technological spectacle and performance persists within the general framework of the feature-length narrative movie.

80 It is worth noting, in passing, the extent to which such charges insist that Hollywood movies precisely do not fulfill the objectives outlined by Lewis Herman in the passage we quoted from his screenwriting manual.

81 Otto Friedrich, *City of Nets: A Portrait of Hollywood in the 1940s* (London: Headline, 1987), p. 137. A different version of the same anecdote appears in Harmetz, p. 185.

82 Lucy Fischer provides a valuable contextualization of the movie's psychology in "Mama's Boy: Male Hysteria in *White Heat*," in Steven Cohan and Ina Rae Hark, eds, *Screening the Male: Exploring Masculinities in Hollywood Cinema* (London: Routledge, 1993), pp. 70–84.

83 Elsaesser, pp. 275–6.

84 Elsaesser, pp. 274–5.

85 *Casablanca* has been the site of a multiplicity of alternative narratives, from the unproduced play on which it was based, *Everybody Goes to Rick's* ("revived" as *Rick's Bar, Casablanca* in London in 1991), to the unmade versions starring Ronald Reagan or George Raft or Ann Sheridan, to two television series in 1955 and 1983, to Woody

Allen's *Play It Again, Sam* (1972), which enacts the ritual relationship between cult spectator and movie when film critic Allen Feliz (Woody Allen) renounces his best friend's wife (Diane Keaton) at an airport by reciting Rick's "hill of beans" speech and adding, "That's from *Casablanca*. I've waited my whole life just to say it," to Robert Coover's "You Must Remember This," a piece of *Playboy* postmodernism that inserts four sex acts into the elided encounter between Rick and Ilsa. Robert Coover, "You Must Remember This," in *A Night at the Movies or, You Must Remember This* (London: Paladin, 1989), pp. 185–6. The story was originally published in *Playboy* (January 1985).

86   "In our common experience films move to the end that is their very closure as 'films,' achieved commercial units. At the same time, however, it has also to be seen that a film must never end, that it must exist – and even before it begins, before we enter the cinema – in a kind of englobingly extensive prolongation. The commerce of film depends on this, too . . . since the individual film counts for little in its particularity as opposed to the general circulation which guarantees the survival of the industry and in which it is an element, a unit, film is a constant doing over again, the film as an endless variation of the same." Stephen Heath, "Screen Images, Film Memory," *Edinburgh Magazine* 1 (1976), p. 34.

9 Politics

A conservative director may work with a liberal writer, or vice versa, and both, even if they are trying to impose their politics on their films (which often they're not), may be overruled by the producer who is only trying to make a buck and thus expresses ideology in a different way, not as a personal preference or artistic vision, but as mediated by mainstream institutions like banks and studios, which transmit ideology in the guise of market decisions: this idea will sell, that one won't. The very question "Will it play in Peoria?" masks a multitude of ideological sins. . . . Hollywood is a business, and movies avoid antagonizing significant blocs of viewers; they have no incentive to be politically clear.

Peter Biskind[1]

Hollywood is too deeply embedded in America's culture to be isolated from its politics.

Ronald Brownstein[2]

Despite its promise of "escape" from the everyday world, Hollywood remains a social institution, and its movies describe recognizable social situations in their plots and themes. But Hollywood's engagement with "the other America out there in reality" is most often indirect. In *America in the Movies*, Michael Wood notes the presence of two newspaper headlines in *For Me and My Gal* (1942), a Gene Kelly–Judy Garland musical set in World War I. At one point, Harry Palmer (Kelly) is holding a newspaper headlined "Germans Near Paris," but he is not reading the story. Later, he is asleep under a paper headlined "Lusitania Sunk." Wood sees in these unnoticed events a paradigm of the way entertainment works: "the world of death and war and menace and disaster is really there, gets a mention, but then is rendered irrelevant by the story or the star or the music." Movies, he argues, dramatize "our semi-secret concerns" in a story, allowing them a "brief, thinly disguised parade": "Entertainment is not, as we often think, a full-scale flight from our problems, not a means of forgetting them completely, but rather a rearrangement of our problems into shapes which tame them, which disperse them to the margins of our attention."[3]

Hollywood movies contain themes of social relevance not so much because their viewers need to have those issues dramatized as because that thematic material establishes a point of contact between the movies' Utopian sensibility and the surrounding social environment of its audience.

My Man Godfrey (1936) invited its middle-class audiences to imagine what the Depression would be like if it took place on a studio back-lot where events were played out according to the conventions of a screwball comedy. *West Side Story* (1961) and *Do the Right Thing* (1989) invited their audiences to imagine what racial conflict would look like if it happened according to the conventions of the musical or the teenpic. *Mississippi Burning* (1988), which we discuss in more detail below, invited its audience to imagine institutionalized racism as if it could be solved by the conventions of a detective story.

It would be wrong to conclude from this that Hollywood's politics are inevitably trivial, but they are always mediated by the systems of convention that we have been discussing throughout this book. As Danny Madigan (Austin O'Brien) discovers when his magic movie ticket takes him through the screen in *The Last Action Hero* (1993), Hollywood is not so much a distorted mirror of American society as a parallel universe, in which the conditions of existence are subtly – or not so subtly – different. This universe is, however, recognizably like our own, in that it shares many of the same social, cultural, and political conventions. Even in order to read cause and effect within a movie, we rely on our culturally acquired knowledge of human behavior, social organization, and moral principles. In the casual, everyday sense in which we identify one movie as more "realistic" than another, "realism" implies that the conventions operating in it more closely resemble those we pessimistically assume to operate in the world outside the cinema. Happy endings are as notoriously "unrealistic" as they are emotionally satisfying.

But if Hollywood's politics are always mediated and almost never, in that everyday sense, "realistic," that is not to say that they are irrelevant. If it is to sustain its appeal, Hollywood's parallel universe has to demonstrate its relevance to the lives of its viewers, to the very lives it allows them to escape from. The movies' relation to the preoccupations of ordinary life may be, as Michael Wood suggests, one of wish, echo, transposition, displacement, inversion, compensation, reinforcement, example, or warning. But they also affect the circulation of those preoccupations in ordinary life by providing us with structures of thought and feeling, "pictures of probability," and shapes that we can give to experiences outside the movie theater. These structures, shapes, and pictures explain why movies matter so much to us, even though we seldom give them a second thought.[4] They are the most ingrained aspect of Hollywood's politics.

The Politics of Regulation

Entertainment is the most political issue in America. . . .
It's very hard to grasp
what America understands as "political"
because this notion all too often

exists only in its negation,
as the absence of the political.

Wim Wenders[5]

Although our use of the term "political" certainly includes overt forms of party-political activity, it obviously extends some way beyond their boundaries. The politics of Hollywood's representations embrace its treatment of social organization in the broadest sense, taking in large issues such as race, class, nationality, and sexuality, refracting them in various different circumstances, and routinely repressing or emphasizing different aspects at different times, for different reasons. The industry's own representatives have, however, always routinely denied that Hollywood is a political entity. In 1938 Will Hays declared that:

> In a period in which propaganda has largely reduced the artistic and entertainment validity of the screen in many other countries, it is pleasant to report that American motion pictures continue to be free from any but the highest possible entertainment purpose. The industry has resisted and must continue to resist the lure of propaganda in that sinister sense persistently urged upon it by extremist groups. . . . The distinction between motion pictures with a message and self-serving propaganda is one determinable only through the process of common sense. . . . Entertainment is the commodity for which the public pays at the box-office. Propaganda disguised as entertainment would be neither honest salesmanship nor honest showmanship.[6]

Regardless of this attempt to declare that entertainment was free from propaganda, the industry was the subject of constant government and legislative attention. In any given year between 1925 and 1940, an average of more than 250 bills affecting the industry (almost invariably adversely) were presented in the state legislatures, while each session of the US Congress saw the introduction of bills intended to tax theater admissions, establish federal censorship, or prohibit industry trade practices such as block-booking. Between 1934 and 1941 there were five major investigations of the industry by committees of Congress, the last of which investigated charges "that the motion picture and the radio have been extensively used for propaganda purposes designed to influence the public mind in the direction of participation in the European war."[7]

In its foreign markets the industry also faced censorship and quota restrictions on the number of Hollywood movies that could be exhibited, as well as bearing the brunt of cultural complaints about the Americanization of other national cultures. As a major domestic and export enterprise, the motion picture industry had similar interests at stake in the country's political and economic policies to those of other large commercial concerns, and like other businesses, this "harmless" and "apolitical" industry maintained a substantial and expensive lobby in Washington, assiduously courting the State Department to gain its support in disputes with foreign countries over questions of tariffs and quotas. In this specific sense, Holly-wood cinema was very much a political institution, with an active engage-ment in state, federal, and international affairs. But the overwhelming majority of its political activity was defensive in nature, undertaken for the primary purpose of sustaining the profitability of the industry's enterprises.

In 1936, MGM decided to abandon a planned adaptation of *It Can't Happen Here*, a novel by Sinclair Lewis about a Fascist take-over of the United States. The company was accused of bowing to political pressure from the Republican party and the German and Italian governments. Lewis claimed that "an extremely important and critical question concern-ing free speech and free opinion in the United States" was at stake,[8] and the case has often been cited as one demonstration of the "almost contemptible timidity" of Hollywood's foreign policy in making concessions in order to continue doing business with European dictatorships.[9] There is certainly no question about the industry being run by conservatives, but insofar as it is possible to distinguish them, MGM's decision was motivated by economic considerations, not political ones. The movie was bound not to be profitable because its political content would exclude it from many foreign markets – not simply the German and Italian markets but also those over which they could exert diplomatic pressure, including Britain and France. This, then, was a matter of commercial aesthetics. In an edito-rial in *Motion Picture Herald*, Terry Ramsaye explained the distinction the industry made between one of Lewis's books and a movie:

> If a reader of his works, for instance, take violent exception to the content, that reader is merely annoyed with Mr Lewis. He is not outraged at Doubleday, Doran and Company, and at the whole art of the printed word. But the motion picture spectator, when he is annoyed, is annoyed with "the damned movies" and likely as not the theatre where he saw the annoying picture. . . . If his publishers were continuously on a battlefront defending the book business from attempts at punitive taxation, from measures of censorship, from measures addressed at nationalization of their industry, they would perhaps at times weigh the possible effect of product of political implication and influence.[10]

At the root of Hollywood's denial that its representations engaged in politics was a politically self-interested calculation about the industry's public image. Many people in the 1920s and 1930s believed that the movies had demonstrated their enormous potential as instruments of propaganda in inciting popular support for American entry into World War I, and much of the academic writing on cinema in this period was by social scientists concerned with the influence of movies on the conduct and beliefs of those who saw them. Particular movies added momentum to this debate. In 1915 D.W. Griffith's *The Birth of a Nation* provoked extensive and sometimes violent protests at its viciously racist representation of the South under Reconstruction. The movie's capacity to "grind and pound

Posters advertising the Ku Klux Klan as heroes of *The Birth of a Nation*
(1915). Epic (courtesy Kobal)

and pulverize your emotions," to stir its audiences to "a perfect frenzy,"[11]
greatly intensified liberal anxieties at what reformer Jane Addams called
its "pernicious caricature of the Negro race."[12]

The Birth of a Nation was directly influential on the rebirth of the Ku Klux
Klan; advertising and publicity stunts for the movie's openings stressed
the Klan's role as the movie's heroes. The number of lynchings of African-
Americans by white mobs increased dramatically in the few years after its
release. The outcry over the movie ensured among other things that the
industry was, from then on, far more circumspect in its representation of
African-Americans: with few exceptions, they were confined to the stereotypes of servitude.[13] This reticence, however, resulted from the industry's
excessive deference to the Southern box-office, expressed, for instance, in
the reservations Colonel Joy, head of the Studio Relations Committee, had
over the script for *I Am a Fugitive from a Chain Gang* (1932):

> While it may be true that the [chain gang] systems are wrong, I very much
> doubt if it is our business as an entertainment force to clear it up, and thereby
> possibly get into trouble with the Southern States who, as our Southern
> representative puts it, can stand any criticism so long as it isn't directed at
> themselves.

He wondered whether it was wise "from a business standpoint for our medium of entertainment . . . to incur the anger of any large section." Joy subsequently suggested minimizing the number of black prisoners shown on the chain gang, so as to make its setting less "unmistakably Southern," exemplifying Thomas Cripps' observation that "antebellum Hollywood's aversion to the racial contradictions in American life reduced African Americans to absent, alibied for, dependent victims of marketing strategies aimed at a profitable universality."[14]

Debates over the censorship of the movies, like those over the regulation of other forms of popular culture, were actually debates over the nature of social control. Although they focused on the content or structure of the entertainment form, their real concern was with its effects of consumers. This was most commonly expressed as an anxiety about the influence of entertainment on children, specifically on the criminal behavior of adolescent males and the sexual behavior of adolescent females. These concerns partially concealed deeper, class-based anxieties about the extent to which the viewing conditions in movie theaters provided opportunities for the mixing of classes. In addition, since the first motion picture censorship ordinance came into force in Chicago in 1907, public debate revolved around the question of whether a commercially motivated industry was morally fit to control the manufacture of social recreation. As we explained in chapter 1, it was in this context that the Supreme Court determined that movies were not to be granted freedom of speech under the First Amendment of the Constitution, because while they might be "vivid, useful, and entertaining," they were also "capable of evil, having power for it, the greater because of their attractiveness and manner of exhibition."[15] By categorizing the movies as potentially harmful entertainment, the 1915 Supreme Court ruling imposed an obligation on the industry to produce demonstrably harmless entertainment that needed no further, externally imposed censorship. Its decision established the legal status of the cinema until the court reconsidered the question in 1952 and granted movies First Amendment protection, but the effect of the 1915 ruling has persisted, encouraging the industry to avoid political controversy in its products.

When the major companies established the Motion Picture Producers and Distributors of America, Inc. (MPPDA), as its trade association in 1922, their principal purpose was to safeguard the political interests of the emerging oligopoly, and the association's central task was to counter the threat of legislation or court action that would impose a strict application of the anti-trust laws to the industry. The public means to achieve this was through a demonstration of the industry's respectability, and so the declared purpose of their organization was "to establish and maintain the highest possible moral and artistic standards of motion picture production."[16] As well as being the most respectable man their money could buy, the MPPDA's president, Will Hays, was one of the most able political organizers in the country. He had masterminded the Republican election campaign of 1920 that brought Warren Harding to the White House. His skills and influence were invaluable in securing government cooperation with the industry, and maintaining a network of political contacts throughout the country that protected the industry from the flood of hostile local legislation. Although the MPPDA was always careful to differentiate the "self-regulation" of its advisory activities from "political censorship," Hays recognized that the most effective means of containing the threat posed to the industry by external censorship was to render it unnecessary. This could be achieved by ensuring that the entertainment his member companies produced was "pure," comparable to the pure meat guaranteed by the Federal Food and Drug Administration, according to an analogy widely used at the time. Although the great majority of controversies over what was or was not harmful revolved around the representation of sex or violence, implicit in the definition of "pure entertainment" was the idea that it was "entertainment unadulterated, unsullied by any infiltration of 'propaganda.'"[17]

Under Hays' leadership, the industry therefore strove to maintain a neutrality in the representation of party politics. Newsreels, for instance, balanced the amount of coverage given to the two parties so carefully, according to the Motion Picture Herald, that "in the 1932 campaign a tally showed a difference of only six feet in the footage given to the Republicans and Democrats."[18] The Herald's publisher, Martin Quigley, was one of the godfathers of the Production Code in the early 1930s. Primarily out of a concern to preserve the political neutrality of the exhibition site, the movie theater, he insisted that entertainment ought to be entirely free of political or propagandist content. In 1938, during a public controversy over Blockade, a movie set in the Spanish Civil War and denounced as Communist propaganda by a number of Catholic groups, Quigley proposed an amendment to the Production Code, that: "No motion picture shall be produced which shall advocate or create sympathy for political theories alien to, and subversive of, American institutions, nor any picture which perverts or tends to pervert the theatre screen from its avowed purpose of entertainment to the function of political controversy."[19] The amendment was not added, because it was not felt necessary. The industry presumed that the producers, their audiences, and the civic groups that sought to exercise a parental concern over American public culture shared a common view about "what is right and what is wrong" – politically as well as morally.

The industry's insistence that its entertainment was apolitical was part and parcel of the way it displaced responsibility for the interpretation of a movie's content onto its audience. Despite the frequent use of the word "controversial" as a promotional value, producers chose overwhelmingly to avoid subjects of genuine political controversy.[20] In preparing The Public Enemy for production in 1931, Darryl Zanuck, then head of production at Warner Bros., concocted the movie's "environmentalist" explanation of the causes of crime as the product of poor social conditions in order to evade discussing the more urgent, substantial, and politically sensitive question of the repeal of Prohibition.[21] Even "social conscience" pictures like I Am a

Fugitive from a Chain Gang maintained a respectful distance from specific questions of political intervention. In defending *I Am a Fugitive* before state censor boards, the MPPDA argued that "it is not a preachment against the chain gang system in general, but a strongly individualized story of one man's personal experiences arising from one particular miscarriage of justice."[22] Jack Warner later claimed the movie as "the first sermon I had ever put on film," but the movie's commitment to social reform was more a matter of the studio publicity department's opportunism than principle.[23] Nick Roddick has argued that social conscience movies such as *I Am a Fugitive* contained the conflict they apparently staged between an individual and the law within "the context of a *fundamentally* just society which offered the individual, even under the most extreme circumstances, the chance to reestablish himself . . . through hard work."[24] Such movies therefore remained within the industry's consensual definition of entertainment, by which Hollywood could promote itself as offering an affirmative vision of national community, and affirm the movie theater in which that vision was experienced as being a safe and apolitical space. Beyond that, it was invariably argued that "political" movies were in any case "box-office poison." At the time of the 1941 Senate investigation, Leo Rosten noted that *Abe Lincoln in Illinois* (1940), *Our Town* (1940), *The Long Voyage Home* (1940), *Juárez* (1939), *Confessions of a Nazi Spy* (1939), *Escape* (1940), and *The Mortal Storm* (1940) had all "either lost money or made a disappointing profit. . . . In nineteen separate surveys made by Dr George Gallup, it was found that only New York audiences seem to want pictures with political content involving Hitler and the Nazis."[25]

Hollywood Goes to Washington

Given these circumstances, the fact that the industry ever turned to political subjects is evidence of the extent to which no single logic has entirely shaped production decisions in Hollywood. The quest for topicality has often drawn it to political subjects, albeit those capable of being represented without violating the industry's political neutrality. Sometimes this has been achieved by taking a period interest in past political crises still felt to affect the present (*Guilty by Suspicion*, 1990, *JFK*, 1992). On other occasions it has involved negotiating more immediate political realities in an attempt to "capture the *Zeitgeist*." Recent instances include *Falling Down* (1993) and *Grand Canyon* (1992), which both represent the American urban crisis of the 1990s. Such movies usually achieve neutrality by using their political subject matter as a background for a story that conforms to a familiar generic norm. The Russian Revolution of 1917 served as a backdrop for a love story between Douglas Fairbanks Jr and Nancy Carroll in *Scarlet Dawn* in 1932; in 1982 the same event served the same purpose for Warren Beatty and Diane Keaton in *Reds*. Plots develop against the logic of their political content in order to remain within the broader logic of their status as apolitical entertainment. *Grand Canyon* begins as if it is going to be a movie about the decay of America's inner cities, but it becomes a movie about individual and family regeneration.

This pragmatic response to the assumed preferences of the audience is not in itself sinister, but is simply evidence of the industry's expectation that political subject matter must be dramatized in some way to make it palatable for the audience. In his survey of American political movies, Terry Christensen suggests that movies have been hampered in their representation of politics by a reluctance to articulate any but the most general and consensual political ideas. To exclude ideological conflict as a source of political motivation, however, reduces all political motives to self-interest: "the bad guys act out of greed or ambition, and the good guys act to stop the bad guys." To avoid offending anyone's political beliefs, politics is trivialized, reduced to the "need for occasional individual action to regulate an essentially good, smoothly functioning process by pointing out flaws in the form of bad individuals and sometimes bad organizations like gangs, machines and corporations."[26] In such movies politics may be little more than the framework for a generically familiar plot, but as the reception of *Mr Smith Goes to Washington* (1939) makes clear, even these stories retain a power to offend in a political context.

James Stewart plays Jefferson Smith, a Boy-Scout leader from a small midwestern town who is appointed to the Senate by a group of corrupt politicians on the death of the incumbent senator. They assume that he is so naïve, and so in awe of Joseph Paine (Claude Rains), the senior senator from his state, that he will not realize that Paine and the party machine are using a senate bill to push through a crooked land deal. Throughout the movie Stewart's star image coincides with the political image of innocent idealism that the movie is endorsing. Smith's first action in Washington, for example, is to go on a tour of the Capitol buildings and to read, reverently, the inscriptions on the Lincoln memorial. As the plot progresses, however, Smith discovers that he has been duped and made a scapegoat. On the point of being expelled from the Senate, Smith delivers a long, filibustering speech about political principles, quoting extensively from the Declaration of Independence and the Constitution. This expression of American first principles provokes a magical transformation, in which Paine breaks down and confesses his part in the conspiracy, exonerating Smith and declaring his own unworthiness to serve the people.

The movie's production history reveals the way in which Hollywood's interest in representing party politics grew in part from its response to criticism that the Production Code was politically repressive. In January 1938 MGM and Paramount asked the Production Code Administration (PCA) for their opinion of a manuscript by Lewis Ransom Foster called "The Gentleman from Montana," a fictionalized account of the early career of Senator Burton K. Wheeler. PCA Director Joseph Breen discouraged them from pursuing the project because its "portrayal of the United States

Jefferson Smith (James Stewart) defending his American principles against corruption in the form of Senator Joseph Paine (Claude Rains), in a perfect reproduction of the Senate chamber in *Mr Smith Goes to Washington* (1939). Columbia (courtesy Kobal)

Senate as a body of politicians, who, if not deliberately crooked, are completely controlled by lobbyists with special interests" produced a "generally unflattering portrayal of our system of government, which might well lead to such a picture being considered, both here, and more particularly abroad, as a covert attack on the democratic form of government."[27]

Breen saw the PCA as "participants in the processes of production" along with producers, directors, and writers. Part of his role was to represent a national consensus on political issues as well as moral ones. He therefore saw nothing sinister in his rejecting material that characterized "a member of the United States Senate as a 'heavy'; or . . . in which police officials are shown to be dishonest; or . . . in which lawyers, or doctors, or bankers, *are indicted as a class*." He defended his rejection of a script that portrayed "the unfair treatment of the blacks by the whites . . . an alleged attack by a black man on a white woman, [and] an attempted lynching of a negro," because "it deals with such an inflammatory subject":

Surely the organized motion picture industry is performing a useful public service when spokesmen for the Association insist that screen material involving racial conflicts between whites and blacks be handled in such a way as to avoid fanning the flame of race prejudice. The film *Fury* proves conclusively that there is a way to handle satisfactorily and with tremendous dramatic power the heinous crime of lynching without including the racial angle.[28]

The studios, he claimed, expected him to give them "sound guidance on matters of political censorship."

By 1938, however, Breen's success in keeping controversy from the screen was itself becoming controversial in the face of allegations that "self-regulation . . . has degenerated into political censorship." With the industry facing an anti-trust suit, its chief Washington lobbyist argued that the rejection of a movie "on the ground that it was politically 'dangerous' " would provide exactly the kind of evidence of monopoly behavior that the Department of Justice might use against them.[29] So when producer-director Frank Capra revived "The Gentleman from Montana" as *Mr Smith Goes to Washington* in January 1939 and submitted a script to the PCA, Breen's attitude had changed:

> I think if we could emphasize the thought, which is now present in the script, that the Senate is made up of a group of fine, upstanding citizens, who labor long and tirelessly for the best interests of the nation, and that Fletcher and his two Congressmen are not typical of the character of the men of Congress, no serious offense will be taken from this particular story. . . . It is a grand yarn that will do a great deal of good for all those who see it and, in my judgment, it is particularly fortunate that this kind of story is to be made at this time.

Most analyses of the movie have followed a contemporary review in seeing in it a reflection of the shift in American social values in the late 1930s, from the concerns of the Depression to new wartime ideas of nationalism that invoked an idealized American political tradition – what Breen called "the rich and glorious heritage which is ours and which comes when you have a government 'of the people, by the people, and for the people.' "[30] At the time of its release, however, the movie was viewed very differently, at least by some of its audience. Capra meticulously reconstructed the Senate chamber on a Columbia sound stage and hired the ex-superintendent of the Senate as a technical advisor to ensure that the movie accurately represented Congressional procedure. But when it was premiered in Washington, the senators of the 78th Congress were grievously upset not by such details, but by its "cynical approach to the political scene," which many of them regarded as an "insult."[31] They were outraged at its apparent allegation that they themselves did not embody the fundamental American political principles the movie trumpeted, and at the suggestion that they needed to be reminded of those principles by a Boy-Scout leader or an equally upstart movie. Senators expressed strong opposition to the scenes on the Senate floor depicting senators "as smugly acquiescent in the perpetration of the fraud." The Washington press corps expressed their anger at being represented, once again, by "an amiable drunk."[32] Press coverage of the reaction widely recorded the rumor that senators would take their revenge by engineering the passage of a bill to prohibit block-booking. More threateningly, Burton Wheeler, the Montana senator who had been misrepresented by James Stewart, was the chairman of the Senate Committee on Interstate Commerce, responsible for the 1941 investigation into propaganda and monopoly in the movies. With such power at its disposal, the Congress of the United States was perhaps the most extreme among interest groups capable of exerting political pressure in ways that might prove damaging to the industry. Despite its commercial success, then, the case of *Mr Smith* may explain why the industry was so concerned that its representation be politic rather than political.

Washington Goes to Hollywood

> If you have something worthwhile to say, dress it in the glittering robes of entertainment and you will find a ready market . . . without entertainment no propaganda film is worth a dime.
>
> Darryl Zanuck, 1943[33]

> This is Humphrey Bogart. Is democracy so feeble that it can be subverted merely by a look or a line, an inflection, a gesture?
>
> Humphrey Bogart, 1947[34]

> It is time for us to be courageous, but we must also be sensible, and not too courageous with other people's money.
>
> Darryl Zanuck, 1950[35]

Most accounts of the politicization of Hollywood begin with the 1934 campaign for the governorship of California, in which the Democratic candidate was the socialist novelist Upton Sinclair. As part of his EPIC (End Poverty in California) campaign, Sinclair announced his intention of taxing the movie industry, provoking studio executives into threatening to migrate en masse to Florida. They also provided propaganda newsreels for the Republican campaign, and levied contributions from their employees to save California from "Russianization."[36] This conscription stirred a reaction among studio personnel, already involved in attempts to unionize several branches of the production industry, and the bitterness created by the moguls' actions consolidated the left in Hollywood. From 1890, Los Angeles had been "the last citadel of the open shop," its hostility to unionism being one of the features that had attracted the movie industry there in the first place. According to Carey McWilliams, the mass political movements that emerged in southern California in the mid-1930s were "the inevitable expression of political aspirations that had been maturing for a quarter of a century and which, during this period, had been brutally and systematically suppressed."[37] Sinclair's campaign, indeed, was itself evidence of the absence of an established Democratic political machine in the state. Compounded by the conditions of the Depression, that absence encouraged extremism in the politics of the film community.

Although studios discouraged actors from taking political positions to avoid alienating any of their fans, Hollywood became an important center of progressive political activity in the late 1930s. Three of the country's most important organizations in the alliance of liberals and radicals known as the Popular Front were based in Los Angeles: the Hollywood Anti-Nazi League, the Motion Picture Artists' Committee, and the Motion Picture Democratic Committee.[38] These organizations, together with many others, would be labeled Communist fronts in the late 1940s, and their members attacked as "fellow travelers." The Communist party was indeed the most active force in Hollywood's progressive politics until 1939, but Hollywood's Popular Front organizations were a conscious coalition of liberal and radical political opinions, broadly supportive of the New Deal and concerned particularly to draw attention to the threat of Fascism in Europe. Very little of this politics ever surfaced in the movies, however: *Mr Smith Goes to Washington*, for instance, bears few signs of having been written by a Communist party member.[39] Gore Vidal summarizes:

> It is true, of course, that some of the movie writers *were* Communists but, as they all agreed in later years, you couldn't get anything of a political nature into any film. . . . On the other hand, it is worth at least a doctoral thesis for some scholar to count how often in films of the thirties and forties a portrait of Franklin Roosevelt can be found, usually hanging on a post-office wall; and then try to discover who put it there: the writer, the director, the producer – the set designer?[40]

The threat of Fascism led some producers to a partial reassessment of Hollywood's social role. Harry Warner signed his name to a public statement arguing that, above and beyond their primary commercial obligation to the box-office, "the men and women who make a nation's entertainment have . . . an ever present duty to educate, to stimulate, and demonstrate the fundamentals of free government, free speech, religious tolerance, freedom of press, freedom of assembly, and the greatest possible happiness for the greatest possible number."[41] Warner's attitude was most visible in his own studio's movies, such as *Juárez* and *Confessions of a Nazi Spy*. As Hollywood's foreign markets contracted after the outbreak of war in Europe, the studios took an increasingly interventionist line, and were far more assertive in defending themselves against the isolationist senators investigating propaganda in 1941. Warner defended the company's right to "portray on the screen current happenings of our times," and argued that these films were similar to the "pictures on current affairs" that the studio had always made; that other media were paying much more attention to the war and "the Nazi menace"; and that Warners' representation was, therefore, consensual. It was true, he said,

that Warner Brothers has tried to cooperate with the national defense program. . . . It is true that we have made a series of shorts portraying the lives
of American heroes. To do this, we needed no urging from the government
and we would be ashamed if the government would have to make such
requests of us. We have produced these pictures voluntarily and
proudly. . . . You may correctly charge me with being anti-Nazi. But no-one
can charge me with being anti-American.[42]

He insisted that *Sergeant York* (1941) was "a factual portrayal of one of the
great heroes of the last war . . . If that is propaganda, we plead guilty."[43] "If
you charge us with being anti-Nazi you are right," declared Darryl
Zanuck, "and if you accuse us of producing films in the interest of pre-
paredness and national defense you are also right."[44]

The two major political parties had begun to recognize Hollywood's
potential as a source of funds and celebrity endorsements in the 1940
presidential election campaign, but Hollywood's political standing
changed fundamentally during World War II. In 1942 the government
established a Bureau of Motion Pictures in the Office of War Information
(OWI), staffed in the main by former journalists of liberal and progressive
opinions. The bureau issued a *Government Information Manual for the Motion
Picture Industry*, "the clearest possible statement of New Deal, liberal views
on how Hollywood should fight the war."[45] Among other questions, it
asked producers to consider:

> Will this picture help win the war?
> What war information problem does it seek to clarify, dramatize or inter-
> pret?
> If it is an "escape" picture, will it harm the war effort by creating a false
> picture of America, her allies, or the world we live in?
> Does it merely use the war as the basis for a profitable picture, contributing
> nothing of real significance to the war effort and possibly lessening the effect
> of other pictures of more importance?
> . . . Does the picture tell the truth or will the young people of today have
> reason to say they were misled by propaganda?[46]

The bureau never acquired an authority within the industry to match that
of the Production Code Administration, but it did give a degree of legitimacy to Hollywood's expression of political ideas. Some of those expressions – the endorsement of the USSR as America's ally in *Mission to Moscow*
(1943), for example – would return to haunt their makers in the early years
of the Cold War.

The OWI discouraged studios from dealing with domestic problems,
advocating that they "write out" difficult characters or situations. In the
same way as the Production Code prohibited movies from showing systematic corruption, the OWI only allowed the depiction of social problems
if the movie showed them being solved. The historians of the OWI's
involvement in Hollywood conclude that wartime movies showed social

problems to be individual, ephemeral, and easily solved, a treatment that contributed to "the impoverishment of dialogue about American society."[47] Some changes did, however, result from the OWI's support of what Thomas Cripps calls Hollywood's "conscience-liberalism,"[48] a broad commitment to racial and social equality unattached to any specific political program. The OWI's Director Elmer Davis proposed that "the easiest way to inject a propaganda idea into most people's minds is to let it go in through the medium of an entertainment picture when they do not realize that they are being propagandized": by, for instance, "casually and naturally" introducing propaganda messages into "ordinary dialogue, business and scenes,"[49] in the way that Gore Vidal suggests Roosevelt's portrait was exhibited. Casting women and black extras in uniform in crowd scenes emphasized both the pervasiveness of the war and a sense of equal participation. Cripps argues that the war was "a moment of high opportunity" for African-Americans, and if these "small deliberate acts" seem relatively inconsequential, they were also irreversible.[50] The surface verisimilitude of Hollywood's depiction of contemporary America changed during the war. African-Americans were no longer represented primarily by their absence.

Hollywood's occasional mild liberal advocacy continued after the war, encouraged by the commercial success of two 1947 movies about anti-semitism, *Crossfire* and *Gentleman's Agreement*. A liberal consensus was also evident in the widespread support in the film community for Henry Wallace's Progressive party in the 1948 election, despite the intrusion, the previous year, of the House Committee on Un-American Activities (HUAC) investigating "Communist Infiltration of the Motion Picture Industry." The committee included in its membership some of the most extreme right-wingers in the Congress, intent on discrediting the New Deal and wartime administration of President Roosevelt by alleging that its policy-makers were Communist sympathizers. The purpose of its investigation of Hollywood was to suggest that card-carrying members of the Communist party had written, produced, or directed "subversive" movies with the connivance of government officials. The committee held hearings in Washington in November 1947, where it rapidly became clear that there was no evidence to support these paranoid claims. Since HUAC's interest in Hollywood was primarily for its publicity value, however, the behavior of the ten 'unfriendly witnesses" who refused to testify to their political affiliations and denounced the committee in vitriolic terms served its purpose almost as well. Testimony like that of Jack Warner, that the "intellectual" writers were the most avid supporters of the Soviet Union, and that "some of these lines have innuendoes and double meanings, and things like that, and you have to take eight or ten Harvard law degrees to find out what they mean," also suited the committee's attempts to induce paranoia.[51] They could assert, without needing proof, that the Communists had done and were doing things to the movies, and they were so smart that Joe Public didn't even know he was being brainwashed.

The "Hollywood Ten" were cited for contempt of Congress and subsequently imprisoned. Although studio heads had argued against the committee's proposal to blacklist "subversive" writers on both moral and practical grounds, they fired the Ten because, they claimed, their "actions, attitude, public statements and general conduct" had brought them "into disrepute with large sections of the public, have offended the community, have prejudiced this corporation . . . and the motion picture industry in general."[52] The committee did not return to its investigations of the movies until 1951, by which time the political atmosphere had worsened. The Communist victory in the civil war in China, the outbreak of war in Korea, the successful testing of an atomic bomb by the Soviet Union, and the federal government's institution of a loyalty program had created a climate of fear and reaction, in which it was no longer necessary for HUAC to provide evidence that left-wing opinions were subversive.[53] Between 1951 and 1954 HUAC called several hundred witnesses from the industry, demanding that they testify to their past political allegiances and demonstrate their present rectitude by naming their former associates in the Communist party or "front" organizations. The 200 people who refused to cooperate were blacklisted from further work in the industry. A larger number, who failed to clear their names against unsubstantiated allegations about their political beliefs or activity, found themselves on a "graylist" for "fellow travelers." Careers were destroyed by little more than rumors, and many blacklisted personnel were forced to leave Hollywood or work under assumed names.

The history of "the Inquisition in Hollywood" has most often been told as a melodrama of villains and victims, with roles pivoting around the clear moral choice of whether to "name names" before HUAC.[54] The moral dilemmas of the informer appeared in a number of dramas in the mid-1950s, most notably, perhaps, in *On the Waterfront* (1954), a crime melodrama set and shot in the New Jersey dockyards, in which Terry Molloy (Marlon Brando) is eventually persuaded to testify to the Crime Commission investigating waterfront corruption. Scripted and directed by "friendly witnesses" who had "named names" to save their careers, the movie received the industry's accolade by winning eight Oscars in 1955.[55] Hollywood's acquiescence in the anti-Communist witchhunts undoubtedly reflected the industry's timidity as well as its consistent desire to avoid political controversy, but it was also in keeping with national sentiment. Movie producers behaved no worse (if also no better) than university administrators, business executives, or union leaders; it was merely that some of the Hollywood victims of the anti-Communist witchhunts were more prominent public figures.

Devastating as the experience of the blacklist was to the individuals it affected, it failed to destroy Hollywood's liberal consensus. In one sense the destruction of the Popular Front ultimately strengthened the influence of the left in Hollywood by steering it toward the political mainstream of the Democratic party, and also by branding the right with responsibility for the purge. The Inquisition was "a victory from which the conservatives never quite recovered."[56] Throughout the 1950s, the Democratic and Republican parties competed on roughly equal terms for the allegiance of Hollywood notables, but Hollywood's prominent Republicans were older, and the right's failure to secure support in the movie colony indicated that:

> for the generations that succeeded those maimed by the investigations, it was the inquisitors, not their victims, who bore the shame. As the 1960s progressed and the Vietnam War called into question the entire Cold War edifice, the blacklistees were resurrected in Hollywood as well-meaning progressives hounded for their prescience by the forces of ignorance, reaction and hysteria. Their ruined careers were raised like bloody shirts as monuments to the danger of reflexive anticommunism.[57]

In other aspects of Hollywood's politics it was also clear that even in the reactionary climate of the early Cold War the ground gained by liberals during World War II would not be surrendered. In its ruling on the Paramount anti-trust case in 1948 the Supreme Court declared that it now regarded movies as "included in the press whose freedom is guaranteed by the First Amendment," an opinion it confirmed in 1952 when it declared that it was unconstitutional for the New York censor board to ban the Italian movie *The Miracle* (1950) because they considered it "sacrilegious." The MPPDA – after 1945 the Motion Picture Association of America (MPAA) – joined forces with the National Association for the Advancement of Colored People to challenge the legitimacy of racist municipal censorship in the Southern states. Beginning in 1949, a cycle of movies applied the liberal formulas of *Crossfire* and *Gentleman's Agreement* to the issue of racial prejudice: *Home of the Brave, Lost Boundaries, Pinky, Intruder in the Dust* (all 1949), *No Way Out* (1950). The cycle, which continued throughout the next decade, preached an unmistakable message of integrationism. A lone African-American protagonist – archetypically Sidney Poitier – is set down in a small town or a hospital, where he teaches the white community tolerance by example. These movies betray the virtues and faults of Hollywood's political simplicity. The Poitier hero's excessive decency reduces the issue of prejudice to no more than a matter of skin pigmentation, but as Stanley Kramer, producer of *Home of the Brave, The Defiant Ones* (1958), and *Guess Who's Coming to Dinner* (1967) observed, it also obliges the viewer to regard race as the *only* reason for discrimination.[58] Thomas Cripps points out, too, that these movies' formula for discussing racism through the admission of a single, iconic African-American character into a white circle anticipated and perhaps even influenced the shape that racial integration would actually take, in confrontations over the admission of a lone African-American figure to a school, a university, or a lunch counter, and then in the pattern adopted by American businesses of engaging "token Negroes."[59]

The social commentary in Hollywood's movies was neither frequent nor radical, and it was no more free of the effects of the multiple logics of production than were other themes. Just as many of the movies of the 1930s had purported to criticize the vices of the 1920s while giving them generous screen-time, so a movie like *Blackboard Jungle* (1955) could defend its representation of juvenile delinquency in schools by claiming in its opening titles that "public awareness is a first step toward a remedy for any problem" – language that curiously echoed the self-justifications of friendly witnesses before HUAC. That did not prevent the movie from being denounced by moral conservatives, among them the American ambassador to Italy, who insisted that it be withdrawn from the Venice film festival. The publicity from that denunciation, in turn, helped the movie at the box-office. The political position of Hollywood's movies of social comment was, however, overtly and consistently conscience-liberal: no Hollywood movies in the 1950s actively endorsed segregation, for instance. This is not by any means to suggest that all Hollywood movies were liberal or free from racism, but rather to argue that when Hollywood movies overtly asserted a political position they declared to be political, that position belonged to the liberal center.[60]

The predominant support in Hollywood for a liberal agenda showed itself in the film community's overwhelming support for John F. Kennedy in 1960 and Lyndon Johnson in 1964, and in the conspicuous gathering of stars at Martin Luther King's March on Washington in 1963. Kennedy and his legacy attached "an entire generation of celebrities" to the Democratic party.[61] While the moguls had almost all been Republicans,[62] the later generation of studio executives – Lew Wasserman at MCA, Arthur Krim at United Artists – were prominent Democrats. Jack Valenti was one of Lyndon Johnson's senior advisors when he became the MPAA's third president in 1966. From the 1960s, industry figures were increasingly willing to lend their celebrity presence to political causes and campaigns, as fundraisers and spokespersons, feeding television's insatiable appetite for the famous. As Warren Beatty, campaign strategist for George McGovern in 1972 and Gary Hart in 1984 and 1988, has argued, television requires political debate to be conducted by "people who can express themselves clearly and dramatically to sway public opinion . . . Reagan was no accident."[63] But if the increasingly close relationship between Hollywood and Washington reached its apotheosis in 1980 with the election of an actor as president, it was not a sign of any substantial support for Ronald Reagan among his former colleagues, many of whom were eager to "expose" him.[64] His election reinvigorated the Hollywood left into a wave of organization-building after its quiescence during the Carter administration.[65] Nevertheless, the personal political beliefs of industry figures have not necessarily meshed either with the industry's need to do political business in Washington or with the ideological effects of their products. Any suggestion that Hollywood's political liberalism systematically informs the way it does business, or the kinds of movie it makes, is simply mistaken.[66] Hollywood's attitude to politics has consistently combined a pragmatic concern for political influence to secure its business interests with a desire

The party convention in *The Best Man* (1964) wants to elect Henry Fonda president. United Artists (courtesy Kobal)

not to damage the profitability of its product with undue controversy. Since 1960, however, its representation of politics has reinforced the disillusionment of its audiences with the political process.

Representing the Political Machine

The Best Man (1964) illustrates Hollywood's negotiations between content, spectacle, message, and neutrality. The movie concerns the competition between two contenders for the presidential nomination of one of the two main American political parties, but quite consciously avoids naming the party depicted. Its premise is that whichever candidate is nominated will win the election, although, again, the reasons for this are never made explicit. The central character, William Russell (Henry Fonda), is one of the two main contenders; the other is the McCarthyite anti-Communist demagogue Joe Cantwell (Cliff Robertson). Russell, played by Fonda as an archetypical image of East Coast liberal intellectualism, refuses to engage in a smear campaign against Cantwell because it would violate his political idealism even though it would also win him the nomination.[67] He keeps the nomination from Cantwell, but only by abandoning the race himself and throwing his support behind a previously unconsidered third candidate. In the process, he manages to recover the affection and trust of his estranged wife (Margaret Leighton) and, by the end of the movie, he finds a space outside the world it has depicted from which he can comment upon it. In this way *The Best Man* reveals its own central irony: that through the industrial mechanics of the audience's identification with its star, the movie itself relies on exactly the politics of image and personality that its central character denounces. Completely disregarding the fact that Henry Fonda is delivering the line, Russell declares that "Men without faces tend to get elected President, and power or personal responsibility tend to fill in the features." In effect, the movie finds a way to practice exactly what it rejects: it provides a representation of party politics exclusively in terms of images, without ever actually discussing issues or espousing a cause.[68]

In several subsequent movies, Hollywood has represented the political by repeating *The Best Man*'s concentration on the divide between image and issue as a strategy for avoiding issues of political substance. *The Candidate* (1972) follows the progress of Bill McKay (Robert Redford) from idealistic radical lawyer to newly elected senator, deploring the way his campaign managers maneuver him away from discussing the issues of the campaign. Like *The Best Man*, *The Candidate* employs the stylistic devices of documentary – and the presence of several professional politicians and television newsreaders – to assert the accuracy of its representation of the political process.[69] But the movie inevitably becomes caught in its own conundrum about the politics of image. Although apparently intended as a political instrument – Redford, director Michael Ritchie, and scriptwriter Jeremy Larner wanted it shown to delegates at the 1972 Democratic national convention – *The Candidate* itself remains trapped within the web of irony it constructs for its central character. Its description of the electoral process is caustic in its cynicism, but at the same time, the movie relishes its opportunities for glamorously backlit close-ups of its star, Redford. The movie asserts that politics has no place for sincerity, but it relies on the sincerity of Redford's performance to convey its theme. Thus it becomes primarily concerned not with the political attitudes of its characters, but with those of its producers.

In *Mr Smith Goes to Washington*, James Stewart's performance mannerisms, and in particular his hesitant vocal delivery, become signs of Jefferson Smith's sincerity, "his emotion at being called to embody the democratic ideal," while Senator Paine's eloquence signifies that he is false to the democracy he supposedly represents.[70] *Mr Smith* is a star vehicle, so that Stewart's star persona matches and reinforces his character as his character conforms to that persona. Stewart's idealistic sincerity is inseparable from that of Jefferson Smith or the movie. By contrast, *The Candidate*'s irony creates a distance between Robert Redford's performance and the character of Bill McKay. Throughout the movie questions are raised about McKay's honesty and integrity, and the extent to which he has been corrupted by a political machine. The political sincerity of Robert Redford, on the other hand, is not in doubt. It is indeed demonstrated by his willingness, as both star and producer of the movie, to put his own image on the screen as the image to be questioned. The sincerity of Redford's motives in criticizing the political process are established by the movie's questioning of his character, but the ironic distance which is created between performer and role leaves the movie itself without a platform for any alternative political position. A promotional stunt for the movie demonstrated its hollow representation of political vacuity: on a parodic whistle-stop tour through Florida, Redford told the crowds he assembled, "I have absolutely nothing to say."[71] The final layer of irony involved in the movie's sincere articulation of political insincerity is the revelation that it was *The Candidate* that allegedly inspired J. Danforth Quayle, vice-president to George Bush from 1988 to 1992, to enter politics. The same irony attaches itself to *Bob Roberts* (1992), which, according to its director, documents "how politics has exploded with an obsession on image rather than substance, and how the media is compliant with that," but also unavoidably participates in the process it deplores.[72]

Terry Christensen concludes his study of American political movies by arguing that above all, these movies "tell us that politics is corrupt." The most radical and pessimistic, those that present an image of politics as "evil and corrupting, best avoided by decent people," may reinforce the system they condemn by confirming the prejudices and entrenching the political alienation and apathy of their audiences. "After all, if it takes Warren Beatty, Jane Fonda or Robert Redford to beat the system, what chance do the rest of us have? And if even they can't beat it, how can we?"[73] There is, however, an element of blaming the messenger for the message in this account. Ronald Brownstein argues that it is not Hollywood but politicians, their consultants, the disengaged public, and the "inexorable demands of television for abbreviated debate" that have trivialized American politics by encouraging national politicians to become "actors playing a broadly scripted part – virile young hero (John F. Kennedy), ascetic moral leader (Jimmy Carter), benevolent father (Ronald Reagan), read-my-lips tough guy (George Bush)."

> At a time when public debate revolves around personalities who stand as political symbols, it is inevitable that causes will deploy as spokespeople stars who are themselves symbols – of intelligence, empathy, bravery, compassion, desire. . . . We have all lowered the level of discussion to a point where stars can more easily participate.[74]

This apparently symbiotic relationship between political and entertainment celebrity shapes the version of politics staged in *Dave* (1993), in which Kevin Kline plays Dave Kovic, the manager of an employment agency who is persuaded to impersonate President Bill Mitchell (also played by Kline), after Mitchell suffers a stroke. In many respects *Dave* is a self-conscious reconstruction of *Mr Smith Goes to Washington*: at one level it is concerned with what would happen if an ordinary person who just looked like the president became the president. But at the same time as *Dave*'s representation of politics replays the sentimental populism of *Mr Smith* (in place of Mitchell's program of cutting welfare, Dave proposes policies that will "help people"), the movie is far more self-referential in its treatment of political celebrity. *Dave* is populated with celebrities playing themselves: several senators and congressmen give simulated interviews on CNN, comedians and political pundits appear on TV talk shows; Oliver Stone, director of *JFK*, is seen on TV propounding a conspiracy theory about President Mitchell's stroke. These appearances, however, work not to guarantee *Dave*'s realism so much as to comment ironically on its fiction. The authenticity of Dave Kovic's performance as president is attested to by his public celebrity appearance with Arnold Schwarzenegger, who is playing Arnold Schwarzenegger the celebrity. But when Dave visits a Washington factory and is photographed using automated lifting arms like those in *Aliens* (1986), the movie makes a conscious reference to the celebrity presence in *Dave* of Sigourney Weaver, who is playing not Sigourney Weaver but Ellen Mitchell, the president's wife.

In its post-Classical playfulness, *Dave* assumes that a state of complete flux exists between the fictions of politics and the fictions of Hollywood, and on that premise, it might as well have a feel-good happy ending as not. Dave resolves the plot by confessing to all of President Mitchell's misdeeds, bringing down the villainous Chief of Staff Bob Armstrong (Frank Langella) with him, and then staging a second, apparently fatal stroke. Thus he succeeds in handing over power to the vice-president, whom we know to be an honorable politician, partly because the movie tells us so and partly because we recognize him as Mahatma Gandhi from *Gandhi* (Ben Kingsley, 1982). Dave, inspired by his experience as president, decides to run for election to his local council, and the movie ends with him in a romantic clinch with the president's widow. Unlike *The Candidate* or *The Best Man*, *Dave* makes no attempt to be coherent about the political issues it touches on. Its politics are purely a matter of images, and it is happily unconcerned about its own implication that these images have no political content.

Controversy with Class: The Social Problem Movie

"Let's give 'em controversy with class," said the boss, Spyros Skouras. "Shock America, Darryl."[75]

I suppose I see myself as a serious artist, and it felt right to do something of historical import. . . . It's really the story of how two guys from totally different backgrounds work out their relationship in the process of solving a problem

– in this instance the violation of civil rights, and murder. I suppose it's the difference between a right-wing Republican and a fairly liberal Democrat – though we never discussed politics.

Gene Hackman on *Mississippi Burning*[76]

To make a film about racism, Hollywood uses the buddy movie.

Gavin Smith[77]

Despite repeated assertions that entertainment should shun "the lure of propaganda" and be without political position or effect, Hollywood has persistently produced movies that blur distinctions between entertainment and politics. Social problem movies of the kind Will Hays termed "motion pictures with a message" have formed a recurrent category of Hollywood production, despite the controversies they have regularly triggered and their often unimpressive record at the box-office. They are part of Hollywood's claim to cultural integrity, and their numbers have increased since 1950. Once television became the primary provider of the affirmative cultural vision of America as a national community, Hollywood could engage controversial material on a more routine basis than the studios had attempted before. Only a few movies such as *The Candidate* and *Bob Roberts* have depicted the American political apparatus explicitly, but many more have discussed political questions and strategies more obliquely.

In part this simply reflects Hollywood's enduring concern for topicality, but it is also part of a refined political logic that has preserved Hollywood from outside interference. Although these movies have often drawn adverse government or interest group attention to the industry, Hollywood has generally viewed their production as a necessary element in its defensive political strategy for safeguarding its freedom of movement and the profitability of its enterprises. There are contradictory impulses behind the social problem movie, involving both the recognition and disavowal of Hollywood's power. By indicating its ability to deal responsibly with issues of political import to American audiences, Hollywood has sought to acknowledge the political influence attributed to its movies by social scientists and lobby groups, but also to show that such power is indeed safe in its own hands. As we have suggested elsewhere, the movie moguls recognized early that if handled appropriately, overtly "concerned" cinema could lend prestige to its producers, by demonstrating a serious-minded concern for a wide range of social problems.

Appropriate handling involved integrating a politically controversial theme with the forms of entertainment preferred inside the cinema. Where the industry itself has understood this fusion in terms of "dramatic potentials" and "angles," the metaphor most regularly employed by criticism to describe the process has been one of sugaring the didactic political pill by the more pleasurable dimensions of genre and star performances, and above all by individualizing the issue depicted. In adapting *Dust Be My Destiny*, Jerome Odlum's novel about vagrancy among young people in the Depression, Hal Wallis instructed his scriptwriters to take out all the "sociological references." The script outline declared itself to be "the story of two people – not a group. It is an individual problem – not a national one."[78]

By contrast to most of Hollywood's output, social problem movies represent their settings as dystopian rather than Utopian.[79] In particular, community is almost invariably absent from them, replaced by the worst excesses of individualistic behavior in a war of each against all: "Do it to him before he does it to you," as Terry Molloy explains to Edie Doyle (Eva Marie Saint) in *On the Waterfront*. One of the distinctive generic features of social problem movies, however, is a denial that the movie takes place in "America." When Father Barry (Karl Malden) tells the dockers that no other union in the country would stand for the conditions they work under, he is told "the waterfront's tougher, Father, like it ain't part of America." Characters make similar observations in *Bad Day at Black Rock* (1955) – "it just seems to me that there aren't many towns like this in America, but one town like it is enough" – and *Storm Warning* (1951), both movies dealing with a community's attempts to conceal a racist murder. *I Am a Fugitive from a Chain Gang* had all references to its setting in Georgia removed. A montage sequence in which James Allen (Paul Muni) travels across America looking for work includes a map marking his journey, but as he heads South it fades away, suggesting that he has now entered a space that cannot be found on an American map. When Hollywood was not romancing the South it frequently demonized it, casting it as America's geographical Other in movies as diverse as *The Long Hot Summer* (1957), *In the Heat of the Night* (1967), *Deliverance* (1972), and *Southern Comfort* (1981).

Mississippi Burning, a detective movie dealing with the murder of three civil rights activists during the voter-registration campaigns that preceded the 1964 presidential elections, reinstated this vision of the South against the "good old boy" version of the New South portrayed in *Smokey and the Bandit* (1977) and its sequels. Joe Breen's injunctions against Hollywood's raising the "racial angle" in *Fury* seem light years away from the focus of *Mississippi Burning*. The politics of racism are central to the movie, not a background to more familiar generic elements. The movie is a fictionalized account of the events following the murders of civil rights activists James Chaney, Andrew Goodman, and Michael Schwerner, which had focused national attention on the role of the Ku Klux Klan in Southern state politics. In the publicity surrounding the movie's release its director, Alan Parker, suggested that he was drawn to *Mississippi Burning* by its "potential for social and political comment."[80] *Mississippi Burning* constructs the South as a backwoods Other to the more liberal America that its protagonists, FBI agents Ward (Willem Dafoe) and Anderson (Gene Hackman), are presumed to share with the audience.[81] Mayor Tilman (Lee Ermey) tells Anderson, "the simple fact is . . . we've got two cultures down here, the white culture and the colored culture . . . the rest of America don't mean jack shit, you're in Mississippi now." The voices of racism therefore identify themselves as being un-American, while Ward expresses the movie's

Mississippi Burning (1988): only in Hollywood could FBI agents Anderson (Gene Hackman) and Ward (Willem Dafoe) be the heroes of a detective story about racism. Orion (courtesy Kobal)

moral after the suicide of Mayor Tilman: "anyone is guilty who watches this happen and pretends it's not."[82]

Parker's sense of the movie as a contribution to the struggle for civil rights indicates the extent to which Hollywood in the late 1980s faced as much pressure to display politicized images as to avoid them. Like its manufacture of other genres, Hollywood's production of social problem movies was cyclical, but this cycle has probably been more directly affected by external political conditions than any other, flourishing best in a liberal climate. Like the late 1950s, the late 1980s saw the emergence of such a climate in Hollywood, although its manifestations in more explicit political arenas were more delayed. If *Rambo: First Blood Part II* (1985) represented the apotheosis of what Andrew Britton called "the politics of Reaganite entertainment,"[83] its revision of the Vietnam war was answered within a year by *Platoon*'s account of Vietnam as a war in which Americans fought Americans, and both sides lost. In the terms suggested by Raymond Williams, we might suggest that there were by 1987 signs of an emergent liberal discourse reassessing the politics of the previous decade – *Wall Street*'s (1987) critique of Gordon Gecko's (Michael Douglas) philosophy of "greed is good," for instance.[84]

In this context, *Mississippi Burning* can be seen as a liberal revision of the nostalgia for the time before Vietnam, visited by so many 1980s movies. Its commemoration of the civil rights campaign of the early 1960s and the "Great Society" liberal reform program undertaken during the Kennedy and Johnson presidencies provided an alternative to conservative idealizations of the 1950s suburban white middle-class family. The movie also declared the relevance of the civil rights campaign to its contemporary audience. Parker argued that the movie "is not intended to be a history lesson. . . . It's not about racism 24 years ago, it's about racism now, the racism that is everywhere and in all of us."[85] In its depiction of race relations *Mississippi Burning* has a firm sense of "what is right and what is wrong," and wears its conscience-liberalism on its sleeve. Its protagonists disagree only at the level of tactics, and these disagreements are framed within a political attitude that the audience is presumed to share. Some critics saw the movie's modification of historical fact as an attempt "to create a better story for a racially-mixed audience," and to construct the liberal consensus it claimed to address. On its release, however, the movie proved as controversial as any of the earlier pictures mentioned in this chapter. It was condemned by several African-American civic leaders and denounced by *Time* magazine as "a cinematic lynching of the truth."[86] Negative criticism focused not only on its alleged inaccuracies of period detail and historical fact (a standard critique of the period picture as history) but also on its portrayal of African-Americans as passive objects of irrational white prejudice and violence.[87] As more than one critic observed, a movie about racism that has no central African-American character has at its center an absence, "a deafening silence."[88]

The producers' response to this criticism indicated that Hollywood's strategies of denial have changed relatively little. Parker defended the movie by insisting on its good intentions, at the same time as he drew attention to the inevitable commercial constraints imposed on it:

> Our film cannot be the definitive film of the black Civil Rights struggle. Our heroes are still white. And in truth, the film would probably never have been made if they weren't. This is a reflection of our society not the Film Industry. But with all of its possible flaws and shortcomings I hope our film can help to provoke thought and allow other films to be made because the struggle still continues.

In the movie's "Production Notes," Parker acknowledged the compromises necessary to construct it as a Hollywood product: it had to have attractive locations and omit scenes that slow the action; for legal reasons it could not name the murder victims. But he also argued that the movie's treatment of African-Americans as passive victims was historically accurate: "I did my homework on that and in Nashoba County in 1964 where the incident took place, there were no aggressive blacks."[89] This defense displays an opportunism that matches its good intentions: accused of historical inaccuracy, the movie defends itself as fiction; accused of failing to address contemporary requirements, it defends itself on grounds of historical accuracy. This position is caught exactly in the movie's final title:

"This film was inspired by actual events which took place in the South during the 1960s. The characters, however, are fictitious and do not depict real people either living or dead."[90]

But even within the consensus it addresses, a movie's politics must be understood not only by its overt political statements, but also by the concessions it makes to its commercial obligations. Like *All the President's Men* (1976) and *The Best Man*, *Mississippi Burning* is constrained by the dramatic conventions within which it operates. These conventions ensure that the very form of the movie works to reinforce our expectation that solutions exist to the problems it presents. Its first obligation to its audience is to entertain them. Institutionalized racism is not in itself entertaining, any more than is the movie's message that it can be overcome. *Mississippi Burning* must find other ways of entertaining its audience, less through its story than through the way the story is revealed: action, spectacle, subplots, character relations, music, and cinematography provide the audience's entertainment. The movie's generic conventions place the political and moral questions it raises within the familiar, overlapping contexts of the detective story and the Western. Along with these generic elements, the structure of retrospect that orders the fiction offers the audience an escape from the traumatic issues raised by the movie into the relative safety of familiar conventions. Set not in 1989 but in 1964, the movie implies that the disorders represented have been ameliorated if not entirely overcome in the present. Nevertheless, Jessup County, Mississippi, exists within Nick Roddick's "fundamentally just society,"[91] even if very little of that society has actually found representation in the movie and our knowledge of subsequent events might lead us to less optimistic conclusions outside the cinema. As a narrative movie, *Mississippi Burning* holds out the promise of resolution and closure, and with it the expectation that the audience will leave the theater with an optimistic sense that good has once again triumphed over evil.

The detective story structure dramatizes the relationship between racism, authority, and social order, as Anderson and Ward's federal authority is brought into conflict with the local forces of law and order. In this context, Anderson and Ward operate less as embodiments of political principle than as agents of closure. Our pleasure in the movie as entertainment assumes that they will solve the murders, convict the killers, and enable the plot to reach a point of resolution. Their political affiliations are subordinate to this formal responsibility to the entertainment audience. Somewhat less evidently, the movie evokes Western conventions: Anderson and Ward ride into a town on the edge of civilization at the beginning of the movie, establish order, and ride out at the end, with Anderson even bestowing on Mrs Pell (Frances McDormand) the Westerner's kiss to the woman he must leave behind. Echoes of the Western occur in individual scenes: Anderson greets the residents of Shiloh with a "Howdy," and two of his exchanges of violence with the Klan members take place in the barber's shop. In Western terms, Anderson is the self-confident, renegade outlaw hero to Ward's self-righteous, repressed official hero. When Ward warns Anderson, "Just don't lose sight of whose rights we're violating," their debate over the rule of law takes place in terms that Tom Doniphon (John Wayne) and Ransom Stoddard (James Stewart) would have recognized in *The Man Who Shot Liberty Valance* (1962).[92]

Tension between the two men fuels the drama, which is repeatedly diverted from the process of investigation to consider their differing motives and strategies. They disagree about personal methods and about the political nature of their investigation. Anderson sees the case as a simple missing-persons inquiry, while Ward ("a Kennedy boy") regards their inquiries as an active intervention into the political life of the South, part of a positive drive toward changing attitudes and reforming the culture. They pursue their hunt for clues in different ways. Ward employs marine reservists to drag a swamp for the bodies, and drafts in hundreds of FBI agents in an outright display of federal power and official political will. Anderson, himself a Mississippian, makes leisurely inquiries based on his local knowledge, then explodes into a violence that disturbingly echoes the behavior of the racists he is hunting. The political dilemma for the audience is posed in terms of personal behavior. What should our position as audience members be? Are Anderson's tactics justified by the situation they face? Do these tactics reproduce racist attitudes? Are Ward's liberal protestations and commitment to "procedure" impediments to an effective defeat of the Ku Klux Klan? These questions are posed for the audience not as abstract political or ethical problems, but through the more generic issue of finding the evidence to solve the murder, while the political friction between the two investigators is staged as a temperamental discord.

As the movie drives toward its conclusion, Anderson and Ward find themselves agreeing more and more, learning from each other, and defending each other against threats from outsiders. But their cooperation is not between equals. As in *All the President's Men*, the superior industrial status of one performer over another ensures that, despite Ward being Anderson's superior, Willem Dafoe concedes the investigative initiative to the bigger star, Gene Hackman. Anderson, not Ward, produces the hard evidence that convicts the Klan murderers and allows the movie to reach its resolution. After Mrs Pell is assaulted Ward agrees to "new rules – we nail them any way we can, even your way." From then on he moves to the sidelines of the action, and his principal function becomes the articulation of white guilt. Anderson solves the case by brute intimidation: one Klan member is subjected to a mock lynching, while Mayor Tilman is threatened with castration by a caricatured African-American man of violence (Badja Djola) specially imported by Anderson from Chicago. "As usual in Hollywood, vigilantism wins."[93] There is more than a little of the vigilante in Anderson, and the movie owes as much to what Robert Ray terms the "right cycles" of *Death Wish* (1974), *Dirty Harry* (1971), and even *The French Connection* (1971) as it does to earlier, more manifestly liberal depictions of the South, *In the Heat of the Night* and *The Chase* (1966).[94]

While *The Best Man* – made in the year in which *Mississippi Burning* is set – advocated the preservation of principles at all costs, the sacrifice of those principles in the accomplishment of political goals is here seen as acceptable. The movie's political ambivalence thus comes down, in the end, to the viewer's understanding of Anderson's motives, and therefore to her or his interpretation of the ambivalent qualities of Gene Hackman's central performance. Hackman's performance seems designed to raise questions about his character's sincerity, rather than to answer them. His relationship with Mrs Pell remains ambiguous: are his advances toward her a sign of romantic affection or is he simply using her to elicit the information that will help convict her husband?[95] His political attitudes are little clearer. At the beginning of the movie, he sings a Klan song with as much relish as he later brings to telling Mayor Tilman that he likes baseball because "it's the only game where a black man can wave a stick at a white man without starting a riot." But he has no confessional scene, in which he unequivocally states his motives, either to Ward or to the audience. The closest he comes is when Ward asks him where all this hatred comes from. Anderson tells a story about his father, a poor white farmer, poisoning an African-American neighbor's mule simply to keep him in comparative poverty. When Ward asks, "Where does that leave you?," Anderson answers, "With an old man so filled with hate, he didn't realize that it was being poor that was killing him." Parker argued that the scene was present to offer an economic explanation of racism, that a "black underclass had always been there as a pathetic comforter to the poor whites – there was always someone worse off than they were."[96] But if the speech airs the movie's conscience-liberalism, it does not clarify Anderson's own attitude. Hackman's performance may be a tour de force in conveying the divided loyalties and ambiguity of Anderson's position, but what makes it "great acting" is also what contributes to the ambivalence surrounding Anderson's motivation, and that motivation is finally left to the audience to evaluate.

Hollywood still routinely insists that committed movies such as *Mississippi Burning* are about characters caught up in political events rather than politicized statements in their own right. What political charge they may possess is thus an expression of the audience's political convictions, rather than those of the producers. Such movies, in other words, still see themselves as reflecting Irving Thalberg's popular "tastes and manners and views and morals."[97] The ambivalence centered on Hackman's performance affects other aspects of the movie's interplay between authenticity and commitment. The movie's use of documentary scenes and television-style interviews opens up a space for political commentary that is never directly engaged. Its most extravagant occasions of spectacle are the African-American churches, schools, and houses it burns at frequent intervals, with sufficient visual flair for the movie to win an Oscar for Best Cinematography.[98] Its ambivalence – its inability to resolve the issues it raises as readily as it can resolve its storyline – is evident in its final scenes. The optimistic graveside spirituals sung at the burial of the murdered African-American activist (Christopher White) are followed by a slow track across the cemetery to a desecrated tombstone, on which the only words legible are "1964, not forgotten." The image declares the continuing relevance of the movie's thematic concerns, which are still unresolved. But the morale-raising gospel music resumes over credits that last almost 10 minutes, so that as a commodity the movie ends on a point of elevation. Both by what it includes and by its exclusions, hesitations, and absences, the movie remains equivocal, not about the rights and wrongs of racism so much as about how a movie can make its discourse about racism entertaining, and what an entertainment movie can say about racism.

Ideology

I shall define an ideology as a possible relation between individual consciousness and its social ground. It is a largely coherent system of images, ideas, values, feelings, and actions by which, and through which, persons experience their societies at various times; for instance a "philosophy" or theology, although an ideology need not be formalized in this way.

Edward Branigan[99]

The more impossible and unthinkable wars become,
worldwide ones in particular,
the more evident worldwide entertainment will appear
as the "continuation of politics by other means."

Wim Wenders[100]

Several times in this book we have suggested that entertainment is Utopian. Movies offer their audiences a sense of escape or displacement from their immediate surroundings into a more nearly ideal environment. Paradoxically, however, the Utopian world is always partially familiar. Descriptions of Utopian space and social organization almost always involve a tension between elements we recognize from our present situation and elements that have been altered in some way. In the details of this tension, we can discover the central political concern of a particular Utopian point of view. Richard Dyer relates the compensations offered by entertainment to specific inadequacies in society: in response to scarcity, exhaustion, dreariness, manipulation, and fragmentation, the movies represent abundance, energy, intensity, transparency, and community. He points out, however, that although "we are talking about real needs created by real inadequacies . . . they are not the only needs and inadequacies of the society." Absent from the list of tensions or absences addressed by this Utopian sensibility is any mention of class, race, or patriarchy.

The ideals of entertainment imply wants that capitalism itself promises to meet. Thus abundance becomes consumerism, energy and intensity personal freedom and individualism, and transparency freedom of speech. . . . The categories of the sensibility point to gaps or inadequacies in capitalism, but only those gaps or inadequacies that capitalism proposes itself to deal with. At our worst sense of it, entertainment provides alternatives *to* capitalism which will be met *by* capitalism.[101]

The politics of Hollywood, then, like so much else of it we have discussed, lie as much in the gaps in its representation as in what it chooses to represent. To examine Hollywood as a political institution we must look beyond the ways in which it engages with the politics of Washington. We must examine the terms of its inclusions and exclusions, and at the frameworks within which those choices are made. We must look, that is, at ideology.

We have, in fact, been discussing ideology in Hollywood a good deal already, for example in our accounts of *Mr Smith Goes to Washington*, and of *Casablanca* (1942) in the previous chapter. Most of the criticism in this book, indeed, could properly be considered ideological criticism, in that it is concerned with understanding how movies function as forms of social expression. Although we have used the terms "ideology" and "ideological" freely in earlier chapters, we have not yet provided a formal definition of ideology. Like a number of the other terms we have discussed, "ideology" is imprinted with its own difficult history. Writing about "the exhaustion of political ideas" in 1960, American sociologist Daniel Bell declared that "the ideologies . . . which emerged from the nineteenth century . . . have lost their power to persuade" in the face of "such calamities as the Moscow Trials, the Nazi–Soviet pact, the concentration camps," and "such social changes as the modification of capitalism, [and] the rise of the Welfare State." Bell understood ideologies to be singular and distinct entities: the "Communist ideology," for instance. This account of ideology saw it as a dogmatic and inflexible system of beliefs, a secular form of political faith, adhered to by its followers independently of its empirical "truth." For Bell such beliefs were dangerous. "Ideology," he suggested, "makes it unnecessary for people to confront individual issues on their individual merits. One simply turns to the ideological vending machine, and out comes the prepared formula. And when these beliefs are suffused with sufficient fervor, ideas become weapons, and with dreadful results."[102]

Bell's account of ideology is close to the most common, commonsensical meaning of the word, in which ideology involves thinking by rote, according to a prescribed mode of thought. It is the opposite of common sense, the antithesis of empirical thinking. In this usage, there is always a pejorative overtone to the word: it refers to a coherent and unified set of political beliefs mistakenly held by people other than ourselves. This common-sense usage of ideology also defines it as being explicitly political: ideology politicizes experiences such as entertainment which common sense tells us are not political at all. Thus while *they* have an ideology, which is explicitly political, *we* have a way of life, in which we recognize that some things are political, and some things are not, and in which we can distinguish, for instance, between propaganda and entertainment. This account of ideology suggests that it is something to be avoided or over-thrown. In Bell's terms ideology ends when there is consensus, when "serious minds" agree, when "they" come to believe the same things "we" believe.

This version of ideology, in which the word is a term of abuse used by the victors, will be of little use to us. As critics of culture we must recognize that our consensus, our common sense, and our way of life are as ideologi-cal as anybody else's. As Catherine Belsey suggests, this is to understand that "ideology is not an optional extra, deliberately adopted by self-conscious individuals ('Conservative ideology,' for instance), but the very condition of our experience of the world, *un*conscious precisely in that it is unquestioned, taken for granted."[103] For any society, the maintenance of its people's belief in its political and economic system and in its cultural values is a matter of primary importance. This is the work that ideology performs, manufacturing and maintaining consent to the existing social formation. For the most part, this maintenance activity passes unnoticed, like the maintenance work of painting bridges. Because the bridge-paint-ing is continuous, and because the painters always paint the bridge the same color, the results of their work are never particularly noticeable. In the same way, ideology works to make a society's institutions, customs, practices, beliefs, vocabulary – the existing social formation – appear nor-mal, "natural," and immutable to us. This naturalizing function of ideol-ogy explains why it is so much easier to recognize other people's ideology than it is to identify our own.[104]

In this definition, ideology is not a separate entity, existing indepen-dently of culture or society. Rather, the terms "culture," "society," and "ideology" overlap each other. Ideology pervades culture; culture is both a site and an instrument of ideology. As a *system* of beliefs and practices, ideology has no material form, but it has material effects in the way that a society translates its beliefs into political or cultural practices. This is to understand ideology not as a specific *list* of beliefs or ideas, but as a *process* by which beliefs become conventions, norms, and standards, by which ideas and institutions become and continue to be seen as natural, normal, and conventional, to such an extent that they are not really seen at all. Like the conventional systems for representing space, time, and movement in Hollywood, ideology works by rendering complex structures transparent to viewers or users through familiarity. Ideology is not, therefore, simply a matter of the expressions of conscious intent. Ideology is also attitudes, habits, feelings, and assumptions, and, as the French Marxist theorist Louis Althusser suggested, it is experienced less as ideas than as images and most of all as structures: structures of thought, structures of storytelling, structures of experience. In Althusser's terms, ideology is a matter of "the *lived* relation" between people and their world: "Ideology is *inscribed in* discourse in the sense that it is literally written or spoken *in it*; it is not a separate element which exists independently in some free-floating realm of 'ideas' and is subsequently embodied in words, but a way of thinking, speaking, experiencing."[105] It is, indeed, a way of life, but a way of life perceived and analyzed through a political consciousness. Far from being completely outside ideology, in this definition entertainment becomes the ideal location for the process of ideology – the maintenance of consent – to take place.

Despite the fact that we are usually unconscious of it, our experience of ideology is always layered, operating at several levels at the same time. For example, our discussion of *Casablanca* in chapter 8 concentrated on its overt ideological project, but we could also identify a whole catalog of other ideological processes in the movie, in which existing cultural assumptions about race, ethnicity, gender roles, sexuality, the family, and heroism are expressed and enacted. For instance, we encounter monogamy not as an idea in the movie, but as a plot device. When Rick fixes the roulette game so that Annina does not have to risk losing her husband's trust, we attach the nobility of his gesture to his renunciation of Ilsa and then more generally to his rediscovery of principle and the need for sacrifice. An ideology of gender roles and sexual behavior structures the story, and in doing so reinforces a social convention. As we have seen, although neither Joe Breen nor Hal Wallis would have been likely to identify this plot element as ideological, the Production Code explicitly recognized its role in ensuring that Hollywood movies maintained cultural conventions.

This example may also indicate why it is often so difficult to pin down the effect of the work of ideology. Much of the sociological study of the media has been concerned with quantifying its effects, and it might have been possible in 1943 for the OWI to investigate how effective *Casablanca* was in its overt ideological project by surveying audience attitudes to American isolation before and after viewing the movie. A comparable question about the ideology of gender roles would be much more difficult to construct: "To what extent have you been dissuaded from committing adultery by watching *Casablanca*?" However preposterous this question sounds, most inquiries into the "effects" of violence in the media have asked questions of this type. Such simple questions, looking for single causes of single effects, fail completely to recognize the main work of ideology, which is not to change attitudes or behavior, but to confirm and reinforce them by reminding us of their familiarity.

Using the term "ideology" instead of "way of life" or "common sense" implies a critique of the social system under discussion, or at least a degree of critical distance from it. Louis Althusser has argued that ideology constantly addresses individuals with an ideal version of their way of life, leading them to "work by themselves" to "freely accept their subjection."[106] What we have called the maintenance activity of ideology is thus an act of perpetual partial deception, as Catherine Belsey argues:

> Ideology obscures the real conditions of existence by presenting partial truths. It is a set of omissions, gaps rather than lies, smoothing over contradictions, appearing to provide answers to questions which in reality it evades, and masquerading as coherence in the interests of the social relations generated by and necessary to the reproduction of the existing mode of production.[107]

Belsey points out, however, that ideology "is in no sense a set of deliberate distortions foisted upon a helpless working class by a corrupt and cynical bourgeoisie. If there are groups of sinister men in shirt-sleeves purveying illusions to the public these are not the real makers of ideology."[108] Ideology is not, in that sense, a conscious creation, and there is no position outside it from which it may be manipulated. "The study of ideology," Terry Eagleton suggests, "is among other things an inquiry into the way in which people may come to invest in their own unhappiness. It is because being oppressed sometimes brings with it some slim bonuses that we are occasionally prepared to put up with it."[109] Richard Dyer's set of relations between the categories of the Utopian sensibility and the inadequacies of society presents an instance of the way in which people may come to invest in their own unhappiness: entertainment is one of Eagleton's "slim bonuses." Ideological analysis of this entertainment therefore seeks to bring to consciousness the concealed politics of its operation.

Representations of the political in *Mr Smith Goes to Washington* or *The Best Man* conform very closely to Althusser's definition of ideology as "images," "concepts," and "structures": the images of James Stewart and Henry Fonda invoke the concepts of American political fundamentalism the movies endorse. The dominant critical interpretation of *Mr Smith* has concentrated on what Frank Nugent called a "celebration of the spirit, rather than the form, of American government";[110] in other words, not on those representations of political procedure to which the senators objected, but on the ideology of the movie's images, the way that they might be examined as "an index to the popular mind,"[111] and the way that they represented Joe Breen's "rich and glorious heritage . . . which comes when you have a government 'of the people, by the people, and for the people.'" From this perspective, the main ideological burden, both in terms of the movie and in supporting the wider institution of Hollywood as star system, is carried by the image of Stewart, rather than by any specific discourse on corruption within the American political machine.

Ideological analysis argues that Hollywood movies represent the political just as emphatically when they appear to be harmless and apolitical entertainment. An analysis of Hollywood's politics must consider their mode of representation, treating the movies themselves as instances of ideology rather than as imitations or simulations of the political from somewhere outside politics. This line of argument views the consumption of movies itself as a significant ideological activity, since the movies exem-

Conflicting ideologies in *The Best Man*: a clash of different images of politics. United Artists (courtesy Kobal)

plify what Althusser calls the "lived relations" between the viewer and his or her world. We can expect to find ideology, then, not so much in Hollywood's themes as in its processes, in the ways in which images and stories are produced and consumed. To find the politics of the cinema we must examine the interaction between the movie and the viewer, in the space between the audience and the screen.

Ideology, Realism, Gender

> I like writing pictures. I'm no realist.
>
> J.C. Benson (Pat O'Brien) in *Boy Meets Girl* (1938)

After describing the extensive and essentially unavoidable operation of ideology, and the ordinary subject's inability to spot it in action, Louis Althusser argues that there is, nevertheless, "a form of knowledge which is 'outside' ideology in the sense that it is subjectless, which knows ideology for what it is and knows the mechanisms of ideology."[112] How one qualifies for this selective ideological amnesty is not clearly explained, but it is a position that many of Althusser's followers have granted to criticism. The critic can establish a distance between the text and herself or himself, and with it a freedom to maneuver ideas and texts apparently outside the gravitational field of ideology. From this position the critic can expose the ideological workings of a text. This criticism is most commonly deployed to examine the "classic realist text," a category wide enough to embrace the novels of George Eliot and the movies of George Lucas, identified as carrying dominant ideological values inside an aesthetic ideology of realism. Its weakness, however, is that it has to presume the existence of a conventional reader, an imaginary but rather unimaginative figure under the sway of the text's ideology, whose gullibility demonstrates the relative superiority of the critical position: for example, the women who "ply their handkerchiefs at Sirk's films," invented by Jean-Loup Bourget and mentioned in chapter 3.[113]

An article that has had great influence on subsequent discussions of the relationship between cinema and politics provides a starting point from which to examine the complex vanishing trick by which criticism removes itself like an astronaut from ideology's orbit in order to look back and report on its true shape and significance. Appearing originally as an editorial in *Cahiers du Cinéma* in October 1969, "Cinema/Ideology/Criticism" by Jean-Louis Comolli and Jean Narboni was a call to film critics to undertake a politically oriented criticism in the wake of the student protest movements against the Vietnam war and the political uprisings in France in May 1968.[114] Comolli and Narboni argued for a criticism explicitly grounded in an Althusserian concept of ideology, one that recognized the ideological in cinema at every level from style to content to technology itself. In a famous passage, they argued that "the classic theory of the cinema that the camera is an impartial instrument which grasps, or is rather impregnated by, the world in its 'concrete reality' is eminently reactionary." As an alternative, they argued that "the tools and techniques of filmmaking are a part of 'reality' themselves, and furthermore 'reality' is nothing but an expression of the prevailing ideology. . . . What the camera in fact records is the vague, unformulated, untheorized, unthought-out world of the dominant ideology."[115] Cinema, they suggested, "is one of the languages through which the world communicates itself with itself," and as a result "the film is ideology presenting itself to itself." From this they concluded that as a sub-set of the ideology it endorses, cinema has its own ideology in "the cinema's so-called 'depiction of reality.'" The purpose of their article was to establish a system of categories by which critics could distinguish between movies that "allow the ideology a free, unhampered passage," and those that "attempt to make it turn back, intercept it and make it visible by revealing its mechanisms."[116] Their system of classification involved first a distinction between fiction and "live cinema" (documentary), and then within each of these a distinction between form and content. These well-established critical distinctions provided them with four categories of fiction film:

(a)   The vast majority of films, whose form and content both carry and endorse the dominant ideology unthinkingly.

(b)   A small number of films which attempt to subvert the dominant ideology through both their content and formal strategies that breach the conventions of "realist" cinema.

(c)   Movies whose content is not explicitly political, but whose formal radicalism renders them subversive.

(d)   The reverse of category (c): movies whose explicitly political content is contained within the realm of dominant ideology by their conventional form.

Comolli and Narboni expressed their aesthetic and political preferences when they declared that movies in categories (b) and (c) "constitute the essential in cinema," and should be the chief subject of critical work. This preference for formal experimentation in the name of ideological subversion was one that much of the criticism that called itself film theory pursued for the next decade and more. The canon of politically "progressive" work established by that criticism included little of Hollywood. However, the most innovative and influential part of Comolli and Narboni's argument entirely cut across the structure of the schema they advanced, and established at least some space for considering Hollywood. They created a fifth category that was logically incompatible with the other four. It comprised

(e)   films which seem at first sight to belong firmly within the ideology and to be completely under its sway, but which turn out to be so only in an ambiguous manner.... The films we are talking about throw up obstacles in the way of the ideology, causing it to swerve and get off course.

Movies in this category expressed the ambiguities and contradictions of the dominant ideology: "An internal criticism is taking place which cracks the film apart at the seams. If one reads the film obliquely, looking for symptoms; if one looks beyond its apparent formal coherence, one can see that it is riddled with cracks."[117]

As with Althusser's assertion of a position outside ideology, this category contradicted the framework the remainder of the article established, but was a necessary move in establishing some room for maneuver on the part of the critic. Its function was clearly established when they argued that what happened when the critic applied the right investigative methodology from the right perspective was the revelation that "The ideology ... becomes subordinate to the text. It no longer has an independent existence: it is *presented* by the film. This is the case in many Hollywood films for example, which while being completely integrated in the system and the ideology end up by partially dismantling the system from within."[118] In many respects the raison d'être for this category was a rationalization of pleasure, in that it provided the means for recuperating Hollywood movies of apparent ideological disrepute. The approach that Comolli and Narboni argued for was historically very important in opening up possibilities for ideological analyses of Hollywood, and was in many respects highly productive. Analyses of *Young Mr Lincoln* (1939) and *Morocco* (1930) by the editors of *Cahiers* provided a model that remained extremely influential for well over a decade, for instance on discussions of the melodramas of Douglas Sirk (see chapter 3).[119]

Comolli and Narboni's proposition that cinema possessed its own ideology of realism initially led film theory in a different direction, as Jean-Louis Baudry and others developed the claim that bourgeois ideology was built into the cinematic apparatus itself. The "apparatus theory" of Baudry and Christian Metz will be considered in more detail in the next chapter, but perhaps the most significant work to develop from this position was a body of feminist criticism that suggested that within mainstream cinema the gaze of the camera, and the position of the spectator, were inherently masculine. The most influential contribution to this argument was Laura Mulvey's 1975 article "Visual Pleasure and Narrative Cinema," in which she appropriated the psychoanalytic approach of apparatus theory "as a political weapon," to demonstrate "the way the unconscious of patriarchal society has structured film form."[120]

One important aspect of Hollywood's "magic," she argued, was its "skilled and satisfying manipulation of visual pleasure." Hollywood "coded the erotic into the language of the dominant patriarchal order," so that an active male spectator gazed at a passive female object. Mulvey proposed that the cinematic pleasure in looking was gendered: within the cinematic fiction, "woman is posited as image, man as bearer of the look." Although the spectacle of femininity appears at first to disrupt the narrative, "the split between spectacle and narrative supports the man's role as the active one forwarding the story, making things happen." In addition, a movie's male protagonist "emerges as the representative of power in a further sense: as the bearer of the look of the spectator," deploying it to neutralize and contain the disruptive spectacle represented by the woman. This containment takes the form either of a narrative sadism, in which the woman is investigated and either punished or saved (film noir, for example), or fetishism, in which the glamorized image of the woman (Marlene Dietrich in *Morocco*) is presented as a "perfect product," in "direct erotic rapport with the spectator."[121] By orchestrating the "three looks" of spectator, camera, and character, the cinematic apparatus naturalized a masculine gaze in the service of patriarchal ideology, leaving the female spectator without a gaze of her own.

Mulvey's analysis relied on a body of psychoanalytic speculation whose relevance to cinema was only asserted. It also depended on the claim that a link could be made by analogy between the look of some (but not all) characters in the fiction and the look of the spectator (all spectators) in the movie theater. This link allowed her to support an account of the spectator's subject position with evidence drawn from the plots of movies.

Despite these logical weaknesses, Mulvey's article provided the foundation for feminist film theory's discussion of both Hollywood's representation of gender, and alternatives to it.[122] The article itself called for the destruction of visual pleasure, "a total negation of the ease and plenitude of the narrative fiction film" and much energy was subsequently devoted to debates about how an alternative feminist film practice might represent the female body differently.[123] But feminist analysis also returned repeatedly to the principal site of ideological contestation, to reconsider the limitations on both female expression and the female viewer proposed by Mulvey's original formulation. If patriarchal ideology was structured into the apparatus of mainstream cinema so that the female spectator had no choice but "to identify either with Marilyn Monroe or with the man behind hitting the back of my seat with his knees," then a feminist analysis was bound to place all Hollywood movies in the unredeemable category (a).[124] Avenues of critical exploration that looked for signs of "female enunciation" in the work of the few women directors in Hollywood (particularly Dorothy Arzner, the only woman working regularly as a major studio director in the 1930s) were at odds with the theoretical claim that the apparatus of cinema constructed subject positions. But, as Mary Ann Doane argued, that theoretical position compounded the patriarchal repression of the feminine that it described, since it traced "another way in which the woman is inscribed as absent, lacking, a gap, both on the level of cinematic representation and on the level of its theorization."[125]

The solution to this theoretical impasse, for feminist criticism as well as for other politically committed ideological analyses of Hollywood, was a development out of the Comolli/Narboni category (e). "Reading against the grain" of a Classical Hollywood movie became a widely adopted and productive strategy for textual analysis. As with category (e), movies could be examined for their gaps and fissures, in which the workings of ideology were exposed. In this kind of interpretation, declared the editors of a 1984 collection of feminist essays, "the critic is less concerned with the truth or falsity of the image of woman than with gaining an understanding of the textual contradictions that are symptomatic of the repression of women in patriarchal culture."[126] The idea of "the contradictory text" proved enormously fruitful in developing the ideological analysis of Hollywood. Contemporary feminist analyses continue to acknowledge Mulvey's formulations for providing a significant insight into the inscription of femininity in Hollywood movies, but they also present a more nuanced, less monolithic case. Despite the structuring presence of patriarchy, women's discourses are seen to permeate such "contradictory" Hollywood texts as *Pretty Woman* (1990) and *The Little Mermaid* (1989), so that the real concerns of women are expressed in fragmented or "subtextual" ways. Susan White suggests that contemporary feminist criticism sees "most cultural products as a complex weave of oppression, rebellion, play with existing structure, recuperation, and transformation."[127]

The pattern of development charted by feminist film theory shared many features with other analyses of Hollywood's ideology. The idea that it was possible to "read" Hollywood movies for their ideological subtexts and structuring absences, to make them say "not only what this says but what it doesn't say because it doesn't want to say it,"[128] amounted to what David Bordwell has called a "search warrant" for the investigation of repressed meanings.[129] "Reading obliquely" or "against the grain" offered the possibility of discovering the textual fissures of a category (e) movie; the argument that such textual analysis revealed the movie's "unconscious" meant that the analysis neither expected nor required external corroboration from, for instance, the movie's producers. It also justified the psychoanalytic metaphors that usually structured this critical approach. In the article that served as a prototype for these investigations, the editors of *Cahiers du Cinéma* asserted that *Young Mr Lincoln* operated under a "double repression – politics and eroticism."[130] These two preoccupations have remained dominant in subsequent analyses of Hollywood. Where politically committed auteurist criticism had been under an obligation to discover the overtly radical in a director's work (an obligation it often found difficult to meet), the ideological criticism of category (e) movies could identify unconscious "rebel" texts within the Hollywood empire. For example, Charles Eckert's analysis of *Marked Woman* (1937), a gangster melodrama about prostitution in New York, contended persuasively that the movie is "rooted in class conflict." Its class oppositions are, however, displaced onto a number of surrogate conflicts: the characters' ethical dilemmas, and the regional oppositions of city and country. The "muddled logic" with which these are expressed reflects "a struggle between desires to articulate and to repress class conflicts. . . . There are, in addition, tonal overlays (toughness, sentimentality) which cover the film like a skin, masking the real and substitute conflicts alike, and enticing the audience into solipsism and false emotion."[131]

Analyses such as Eckert's demonstrated the extent to which ideological criticism could reassess a movie's cultural function. More often, however, textual analysis sought to identify "progressive" or "subversive" features in individual Hollywood movies or in genres, with the implicit intention of redeeming the text in question, at least as an object of study. Critics paid particular attention to groups of movies deemed to be in some sense marginal to Classical Hollywood – film noir, women's films, family melodrama, exploitation and B-movies – giving rise to what Barbara Klinger has identified as the "progressive genre." The distinguishing features of these movies, she suggests, are a pessimistic world view, a thematic demolition of the values attached to such social institutions as the law and the family, a narrative structure that exposes contradictions rather than represses them, and a tendency to stylistic self-consciousness and formal excess.[132] Claims for the existence of "progressive genres" made clear that the abiding legacy film criticism inherited from Comolli and Narboni was of the opposition between category (a) and category (e) movies. As Klinger argues, the critical investment in designating and elucidating progressive genres was "financed through a staunch conception of classic textuality." Ideological criticism required a fixed conception of classical narrative against which it could define progressive practice and identify "the inventions and departures of the progressive text."[133]

Most of these analyses emphasized the formal or stylistic differences of the progressive text, to the extent that specific formal features – "expressionist" lighting, a "refusal" of narrative closure – were understood as embodying the progressive position. This often led to what Klinger has called "a sort of 'textual isolationism,'" an intrinsic formalization of the cinema/ideology inquiry ... based on a rather rigid sense of both what 'makes' and 'breaks' the system" of Classical Hollywood.[134] From a consumerist perspective, the problem lies in the way these arguments attribute the properties that they claim to identify through "reading" strategies to the texts they examine. The distinction between movies that allow the dominant ideology free passage and movies in which the ideology is dismantled from within is solidified on the basis of a "reading" which is also, as the *Cahiers du Cinéma* editors asserted, a "rewriting."[135] This line of argument validates formal and stylistic subversion at the expense of overt ideological statement, and does so in part because the validation of subversion also validates the critic's skills in "reading" the text's repressed meanings, and in the process, the political relevance of the critic's activity.

Most ideological analysis of Hollywood, and indeed most academic film criticism (including our own), is written from a political position significantly to the left of the consensus Hollywood conventionally addresses. One of the anxieties frequently manifested by that criticism is that its attention to the forces of political repression, such as Hollywood, may become complicit with those forces. Strategies of subversive reading offer a way to resolve these anxieties positively, as a critical "rewriting" of the text. Henry Louis Gates Jr has observed that similar strategies in literary criticism have turned the analysis of literary texts:

> into a marionette theater of the political, to which we bring all the passions of our real world commitments. ... Academic critics write essays, "readings" of literature, where the bad guys (you know, racism or patriarchy) lose, where the forces of oppression are subverted by the boundless powers of irony and allegory that no prison can contain, and we glow with hard-won triumph. We pay homage to the marginalized and demonized, and it feels as if we've righted an actual injustice.[136]

If ideological analysis sometimes has to carry this much political cargo, it is hardly surprising that the movies that have fared worst from such analysis have been those that have dealt with explicit political subject matter within the conventions of Hollywood, movies that fall into Comolli and Narboni's category (d), where their politics are too close to the surface to need much decipherment. Where the repressed subtext of an overtly reactionary movie may turn out to be progressive, the repressed subtext of those movies Colin MacCabe damned with the sin of "progressive realism" invariably turns out to be reactionary.[137] Our own accounts of *The Best Man* and *The Candidate* exhibit this tendency, and *Mississippi Burning* offers plenty of fissures for a critical deconstruction of its liberal ideological presumptions. Along with every movie we have discussed in this book, it qualifies as a category (e) text in *Cahiers* terms. But the movie seems to acknowledge this property in the knowingness of its narration, which underlines its status as a site of conflicting logics and discourses. Rather than requiring us to "work against the grain" of the text and take it by surprise in our criticism, *Mississippi Burning* almost invites its audience to engage in a *Cahiers*-style critique. This knowingness, which is most visible in the wry humor of Hackman's performance, is a strategy for self-preservation, affording the movie some distance from the controversy it provokes. As a comedy, *Dave* can carry this strategy of self-referentiality and knowingness even further, exposing itself as a political fiction, declaring in its closing credits that any reference to actual persons or buildings is coincidental and unintended – despite most of the movie being set in the White House and the credits listing a string of roles as having been played by "Himself" and "Herself." *Dave* carries the clear implication that the only place in which an ordinary person could become the president is in a fictional movie, just as *Mississippi Burning* carries the implication that the only place the FBI can become the heroes of the civil rights struggle is in a fictional movie.

In these movies, the freedom of critical maneuver that Catherine Belsey claims for the critic-as-subject seems on offer to the audience in general. At times, the possibility of deconstructing the movies' ideology in the way we have done feels almost like a precalculated production value, as though this is the way that they are intended to be used. Use is very much the ultimate issue here, for it is at the level of satisfactory and satisfying use that the Hollywood movie seeks to unify its audience. What matters is continuing the consumption of the movie by as large an audience as possible, rather than a uniform political commitment to the value systems the movie expresses. The significance of a movie's themes is not to be ignored, but they are necessarily subordinate to its status as a commodity, which constantly overrides its existence as a fiction.

From a viewpoint outside the consensus that *Mississippi Burning* addresses, it can hardly appear as anything other than a white liberal equivocation. But without denying the Hollywood opportunism evident in Parker's defense of the movie, it is important to acknowledge that no movie could adequately respond to criticism from outside the ideological consensus it addresses. From such a position, the politics of any movie will always appear imperfect. For example, the critical enthusiasm that initially greeted the commercial success of black director Spike Lee's "guerrilla filmmaking"[138] has been tempered by suggestions that *Do the Right Thing* and *Jungle Fever* (1991) fail, as Hollywood movies do, to analyze the causes of the racism they depict.[139] Mark Reid criticizes Spike Lee's use of black idioms in *Do the Right Thing* for seducing its audience into "accepting a simulated form of blackness" as an adequate "filmic representation of urban black 'reality.'" According to Reid's analysis, the attention focused on Lee has meant that "the ongoing work of independent black filmmakers and video artists is ignored, and the variety of black voices is smothered by the masculinist and often homophobic black images that reign in major studio-produced black films." In a persuasive rebuttal of such arguments, Malcolm Turvey points out that

> an argument that insists that a black film-maker *should* adequately represent "the oppressed" or "the underclass," that he *should* include "the woman's point of view," that he *should* always and everywhere address homophobia . . . produces an image or fantasy of black film-makers that severely limits and above all controls *who* may be a "black film-maker" and what black film-makers may produce . . . the demand that [Lee] and others like him be the perfect, radical *real* black film-maker is an impossible and dangerous one.

Turvey's comments address what he calls "the burden of desire" placed not only on *Malcolm X* (1993, and also directed by Lee), but on any movie or producer identified as articulating a political position against the expectations of Hollywood entertainment cinema.[140]

The ideological analysis we have considered in the last two sections of this chapter has frequently exhibited a contradiction in its focus, one that we have located in the two main influences developing out of Comolli and Narboni's essay. On one side, it has understood dominant ideology as being structured into the cinematic apparatus and the subject position of the spectator. On the other, it has argued for the existence of texts and textual strategies that subvert or expose the dominant ideology or its "unconscious." The apparent contradiction between these two positions raises the question of whether the ideology of a movie can be located in its formal structures, its content, or its interpretation. In practice it is impossible to maintain the distinctions between categories (a) and (e) other than through the purely empirical criterion of the level of skill involved in the interpretation. In the two decades since Comolli and Narboni's original formulation, deconstructive criticism has demonstrated that any text is sufficiently fissured to expose its ideological operations if read closely enough. We suggest that a criticism that looks for ideology only in the text as an object to be adjudged progressive, reactionary, or contradictory sets itself a number of interrelated problems. The problem of how the critic explains his or her own apparent ability to either penetrate or evade ideological constitution is closely tied to the notion that the text is innately determining and authoritative in a way that everyone but the critic fails to perceive. Unlike most of the ideological analysis we have been considering, consumerist criticism makes no claim to be independent of the ideological system in which it sees Hollywood to be situated. Instead, it regards its own activity as another variety of consumption.

At several points in this discussion, we have returned the often hermetically sealed frame of ideological analysis to the brutely commercial context of Hollywood's industrial assumptions. In understanding why Hollywood's politics are so equivocal, we would argue that Hollywood's commercial interests are best satisfied by maximizing its audiences and allowing for the unpredictable satisfactions of specific audience members. In that sense any movie is an infinitely open text, a showcase of endless incidental pleasures encouraging, rather than repressing, consumer choice. The political process in the cinema is finally constructed by the audience's engagement, as consumers, with movie texts designed to accommodate their consumers' desires for meaning and likely to allow those meanings to be discovered wherever viewers (including critics) choose to look.

Notes

1   Peter Biskind, *Seeing is Believing: How Hollywood Taught Us to Stop Worrying and Love the Fifties* (London: Pluto Press, 1983), p. 5.
2   Ronald Brownstein, *The Power and the Glitter: The Hollywood–Washington Connection* (New York: Pantheon, 1990), p. 391.
3   Michael Wood, *America in the Movies; or, "Santa Maria, It Had Slipped My Mind!"* (New York: Basic Books, 1975), pp. 17–18.
4   Wood, pp. 15–16, 190–3.
5   Wim Wenders, "The American Dream," in *Emotion Pictures*, trans. Shaun Whiteside and Michael Hoffman (London: Faber, 1989), pp. 140–1.
6   Margaret Thorp, *America at the Movies* (London: Faber, 1946), p. 161.
7   *Hearings before a Subcommittee of the Committee on Interstate Commerce, United States Senate, 77th Congress, 1st Session, on S. Res. 152, A Resolution Authorizing an Investigation of War Propaganda Disseminated by the Motion Picture Industry and of any Monopoly in the Production, Distribution, or Exhibition of Motion Pictures* (Washington, DC: Government Printing Office, 1942), p. 1.
8   *Motion Picture Herald* (February 22, 1936), p. 16.
9   Ian Hamilton, *Writers in Hollywood* (London: Heinemann, 1990), p. 127; Leo Ribuffo, *Right, Center, Left: Essays in American History* (New Brunswick, NJ: Rutgers University Press, 1992), pp. 187–8.
10 "Whose Business is the Motion Picture," *Motion Picture Herald* (February 22, 1936), pp. 15–16.
11 Ned McIntosh, *Atlanta Constitution* (December 7, 1915), quoted in Fred Silva, ed., *Focus on The Birth of a Nation* (Englewood Cliffs, NJ: Prentice-Hall, 1971), pp. 34–5; Dorothy Dix, quoted in Richard Schickel, *D.W. Griffith and the Birth of Film* (London: Pavilion, 1984), pp. 278–9; Michael Rogin, *Ronald Reagan, the Movie and Other Episodes in Political Demonology* (Berkeley, CA: University of California Press, 1987), p. 217. Dix, a journalist and reformer, urged her readers to see the movie because "it will make a better American of you."
12 Quoted in Schickel, p. 283.
13 Among the first memos David O. Selznick sent writer Sidney Howard about the script of *Gone with the Wind* (1939) was one encouraging him to "cut out the Klan entirely. It would be difficult, if not impossible, to clarify for audiences the difference between

the old Klan and the Klan of our times. (A year ago I refused to consider remaking *The Birth of a Nation*, largely for this reason. . . . In our picture I think we have to be awfully careful that the Negroes come out decidedly on the right side of the ledger, which I do not think should be difficult.) . . . The revenge for the attempted attack can very easily be identical with what it is without their being members of the Klan. A group of men can go out to 'get' the perpetrators of an attempted rape without having long white sheets over them." Quoted in Rudy Behlmer, ed., *Memo from: David O. Selznick* (New York: Avon, 1973; 1st pub. New York: Viking, 1972), p. 188.

14   Jason Joy to Will Hays, February 26, 1932; Joy to Irving Thalberg and Darryl Zanuck, February 26, 1932; Joy to Zanuck, July 26, 1932. Production Code Administration (hereafter PCA) case file, *I Am a Fugitive from a Chain Gang*; Thomas Cripps, *Making Movies Black: The Hollywood Message Movie from World War II to the Civil Rights Era* (New York: Oxford University Press, 1993), p. 5.

15   *Mutual Film Corp.* v. *Industrial Commission of Ohio*, United States Supreme Court, quoted in Gerald Mast, ed., *The Movies in Our Midst: Documents in the Cultural History of Film in America* (Chicago: University of Chicago Press, 1982), p. 142.

16   "Certificate of Incorporation of Motion Picture Producers and Distributors of America, Inc.," March 10, 1922, quoted in Raymond Moley, *The Hays Office* (Indianapolis: Bobbs-Merrill, 1945), p. 226.

17   Thorp, p. 160.

18   *Motion Picture Herald* (February 15, 1936), p. 24.

19   Quigley to Hays, July 11, 1938, Motion Picture Association of America Archive, New York, 1939 Production Code file.

20   The promotional material for *It Happened in Springfield* (1946) even went so far as to praise its "neat story which . . . neatly sidesteps a controversial issue": racism. Cripps, p. 204.

21   In a letter to Jason Joy of the MPPDA, Zanuck argued that "PROHIBITION is not the cause of the present crime wave – mobs and gangs have existed for years and years BECAUSE of *environment* and the only thing that PROHIBITION has done is to bring these unlawful organizations more noticeably before the eye of the public. REPEAL of the Eighteenth Amendment could not possibly stop CRIME and WARFARE." Zanuck to Joy, January 6, 1931, PCA case file, *Public Enemy* (emphasis in original).

22   Joy, October 7, 1932, PCA case file, *I Am a Fugitive from a Chain Gang*.

23   Jack L. Warner, with Dean Jennings, *My First Hundred Years in Hollywood* (New York: Random House, 1964), p. 218.

24   Nick Roddick, *A New Deal in Entertainment: Warner Brothers* [sic] *in the 1930s* (London: British Film Institute, 1983), p. 126.

25   *Time* (July 21, 1941), p. 73, quoted in Leo Rosten, *Hollywood: the Movie Colony, the Movie Makers* (New York: Harcourt, Brace, 1941), p. 327.

26   Terry Christensen, *Reel Politics: American Political Movies from Birth of a Nation to Platoon* (New York: Blackwell, 1987), p. 212.

27   Breen, Letter to John Hammel at Paramount, and to Louis B. Mayer at MGM, January 19, 1938. PCA case file, *Mr Smith Goes to Washington*.

28   In *Fury* (1936), the victim of mob violence is Spencer Tracy, playing a man falsely accused of murder. Joseph Breen, letter to Will Hays, June 22, 1938. 1939 Production Code file, MPA.

29   Ray Norr to Francis Harmon, January 1, 1939. 1939 Production Code file, MPA.

30   Charles Wolfe, "*Mr Smith Goes to Washington*: Democratic Forums and Representational Forms," in Peter Lehman, ed., *Close Viewings: An Anthology of New Film Criticism* (Tallahassee: Florida State University Press, 1990), pp. 310–11.

31   *Los Angeles Times*, October 22, 1939.

32   Donald J. Stirling to Hays, December 5, 1939. PCA case file, *Mr Smith Goes to Washington*.

33   Darryl Zanuck, Address to the Writers' Congress in Los Angeles, October 1943, quoted in Roger Manvell, *Films and the Second World War* (New York: Dell, 1974), p. 203.

34   Humphrey Bogart, "Hollywood Strikes Back," radio broadcast by the Committee for the First Amendment, October 26, 1947, quoted in Robert Sklar, *City Boys: Cagney, Bogart, Garfield* (Princeton, NJ: Princeton University Press, 1992), p. 195.

35   On *No Way Out* (1950), quoted in Brian Neve, *Film and Politics in America: A Social Tradition* (London: Routledge, 1992), p. 104.

36   Larry Ceplair and Steven Englund, *The Inquisition in Hollywood: Politics in the Film Community, 1930–1960* (Berkeley, CA: University of California Press, 1983), p. 92.

37   Carey McWilliams, *Southern California: An Island on the Land*, 1st pub. 1946 (Santa Barbara: Peregrine Smith, Inc., 1973), pp. 274, 293.

38   Ceplair and Englund, pp. 98–100; Brownstein, p. 49.

39   Sidney Buchman, the writer of a number of screwball comedies who became a producer at Columbia in the early 1940s, testified to his own membership of the Communist party at a hearing of the House Committee on Un-American Activities in 1951, but refused to inform on others. He was found guilty of contempt of Congress, and blacklisted. He worked again in the 1960s as a screenwriter and producer.

40   Gore Vidal, *Screening History* (London: Abacus, 1993), p. 29.

41   Harry M. Warner, *Christian Science Monitor* (April 1939), quoted in Mark Crispin Miller, "Introduction: The Big Picture," in Mark Crispin Miller, ed., *Seeing Through Movies* (New York: Pantheon, 1990), pp. 3–4.

42   Quoted in Rudy Behlmer, *Behind the Scenes* (New York: Samuel French, 1982), p. 191.

43   US Senate, 77th Congress, 1st Sess., *Propaganda in Motion Pictures*, Hearing before a Subcommittee on Interstate Commerce, on S. Res. 152, September 9–26, 1941 (Washington, DC: Government Printing Office, 1941), pp. 19–20.

44   Darryl Zanuck, speech to the American Legion, September 1941, quoted in Mel Gussow, *Don't Say Yes Until I've Finished Talking* (New York: Doubleday, 1971), p. 105.

45   K.R.M. Short, "Note on *Government Information Manual for the Motion Picture Industry*," *Historical Journal of Film, Radio and Television* 3:2 (October 1983), p. 171.

46   *Government Information Manual for the Motion Picture Industry*, quoted in Clayton R. Koppes and Gregory D. Black, *Hollywood Goes to War: How Politics, Profits and Propaganda Shaped World War II Movies* (New York: Macmillan, 1987), pp. 66–7.

47   Koppes and Black, p. 184.

48   Cripps, p. ix.

49   Elmer Davis to Byron Price, January 27, 1943, quoted in Koppes and Black, p. 64.

50   Cripps, pp. 27, 65.

51   Jack L. Warner, testimony to HUAC, October 1947, quoted in Gordon Kahn, *Hollywood on Trial: The Story of the Ten who were Indicted* (New York: Boni and Gaer, 1948), p. 22.

52   RKO letter to Adrian Scott and Edward Dmytryk, November 26, 1947, quoted in Kahn, p. 191.

53   In 1947 President Truman had created a Federal Employee Loyalty Program, authorizing the security services to draw up a list of organizations deemed "subversive," and to examine the political affiliations of federal government employees. Any suspicion of "disloyalty" could provide grounds for dismissal. By the early 1950s, the program had spread, so that perhaps one out of every five working people – federal

and state employees, teachers, members of professional associations, and industrial workers – had to swear a loyalty oath or receive "clearance" as a condition of employment. William H. Chafe, *The Unfinished Journey: America Since World War II* (New York: Oxford University Press, 1986), p. 99; David Caute, *The Great Fear: The Anti-Communist Purge under Truman and Eisenhower* (London: Secker and Warburg, 1978), p. 270.

54 Victor Navasky, *Naming Names* (New York: Viking Press, 1980). For an examination of the role of melodrama in Hollywood's encounter with HUAC, see Richard Maltby, "Made for Each Other: The Melodrama of Hollywood and the House Committee on Un-American Activities, 1947," in Philip Davies and Brian Neve, eds, *Cinema, Politics and Society in America* (Manchester: Manchester University Press, 1981), pp. 76–96.

55 *On the Waterfront* had begun as a collaboration between its director, Elia Kazan, and playwright Arthur Miller. Kazan, who had directed Miller's plays *All My Sons* (1947) and *Death of a Salesman* (1949) on Broadway, was among the most notorious of those who named names because of the self-serving justification he produced for his actions – Victor Navasky calls him "the quintessential informer." Miller, who refused to cooperate with the Committee and broke with Kazan over his testimony, wrote two plays that directly addressed the politics of the period, *The Crucible* (1953) and *A View from the Bridge* (1955). A story is told that Miller sent Kazan a copy of *A View from the Bridge*, and Kazan replied saying he would be honored to direct it. "You don't understand," Miller told him. "I didn't send it to you because I wanted you to direct it. I sent it to you because I wanted you to know what I think about stool pigeons." Navasky, p. 199.

56 Brownstein, p. 119.

57 Brownstein, p. 176.

58 Quoted in Cripps, pp. 220–1.

59 Cripps, p. 250.

60 Peter Biskind provides an extended analysis of the consensus of corporate-liberal pluralism in Hollywood's movies of the 1950s, and its preoccupation with therapy and social control. He also argues that, in this period, "left- and right-wing films resembled each other like two peas in a pod. Radical films generally obscured the differences between right and left in order to create a broad-based coalition against the center. They portrayed themselves as above politics, neither right nor left but just 'moral,' and they did so for commercial as well as ideological reasons." Biskind, p. 48.

61 Brownstein, p. 174.

62 Harry and Jack Warner were the principal exceptions, being active supporters of Roosevelt during the 1930s. Jack Warner later became a Republican. In the main, however, the moguls' political affiliations were matters of business rather than principle, and "it would not be uncommon for a movie executive who hated everything about the New Deal to proudly display a signed photograph of Franklin Roosevelt in his office, or, like Mayer, nonetheless angle for invitations to the White House when he was in Washington." Brownstein p. 26.

63 Quoted in Brownstein, p. 274.

64 After his election as governor of California in 1966, liberal director William Wyler said ruefully to Charlton Heston, "You know, if we had given Reagan a couple of good parts, he'd never be in Sacramento now." Brownstein, p. 278.

65 Brownstein, p. 279.

66 This argument is, for example, made by Michael Medved in *Hollywood vs America: Popular Culture and the War on Traditional Values* (New York: HarperCollins, 1992), pp. 216–35. Medved's argument is a conspiracy theory: that Hollywood is run by an elite

coterie of "cynical sophisticates," whose "perverse" values are at odds with those of "Middle America," and whose "sense of mission . . . to defy the values of the public at large . . . leads to business decisions that often bear little connection to the pressures of the marketplace." Not surprisingly, Medved advocates that "the products of popular culture should become *less* propagandistic, not more so" (pp. 64, 235, 297, 309, 90).

67   Fonda had played a similar role two years previously, in *Advise and Consent*; Robertson had played the young John F. Kennedy in *PT 109* (1963).

68   The only issues raised in the movie itself are the bi-partisan questions of anti-Communism and civil rights, and the discussion of both of them is heavily conditioned by the caricatured images the movie presents of Cantwell and T.T. Claypool (John Henry Faulk).

69   James Monaco suggests that several of the movie's characters are recognizable caricatures of political campaign organizers. James Monaco, *American Film Now: The People, the Power, the Money, the Movies* (New York: New American Library, 1979), p. 361.

70   Charles Affron, *Cinema and Sentiment* (Chicago: University of Chicago Press, 1982), p. 119.

71   Brownstein, p. 267.

72   Tim Robbins, director and star of *Bob Roberts*, quoted in Martin Walker, "A Downhome Demagogue on the Stump," *Guardian* (July 29, 1992), p. 36.

73   Christensen, pp. 211–15.

74   Brownstein, pp. 136, 273, 391.

75   On *Pinky* (1950), quoted in Cripps, p. 232.

76   Quoted in Beverly Walker, "Hackman: The Last Honest Man in America," *Film Comment* 24:6 (December 1988), p. 23.

77   Gavin Smith, " 'Mississippi' Gambler," *Film Comment* 24:6 (November/December 1988), p. 30.

78   Quoted in Neve, p. 26.

79   The other frequent generic home for Hollywood dystopias is in science fiction movies: for instance, *Soylent Green* (1973), *Rollerball* (1975), *Outland* (1981), *Blade Runner* (1982). They, too, take place in a setting that "ain't America," yet.

80   Alan Parker, "Notes on the Making of the Film," *Mississippi Burning* "Production Notes," p. 1.

81   As a setting, the South fulfills this function in a number of exploitation horror movies such as *I Spit on Your Grave* (1977). In mainstream cinema, this version of a contemporary Gothic South, which *Mississippi Burning* evokes in its imagery of burning churches, occurs in *Deliverance* and *Southern Comfort*. Carol J. Clover, *Men, Women and Chainsaws: Gender in the Modern Horror Film* (London: British Film Institute, 1992), p. 163.

82   In the "Production Notes," Parker wrote: "I wrote a speech for Willem in his concluding scene as the Mayor hangs at the end of a short rope. I didn't include all of it in my final cut because we thought it to be too preachy and probably it articulated all that I'd said, or was trying to say, in the previous two hours of film. It was a hard cut to make, so I'll include it now.

Bird: Why did he do it? He wasn't in on it. He wasn't even Klan.
Ward: Oh, he's guilty. Anyone's guilty who watches this happen and pretends that it's not. All of them. Every governor or senator who allows the hate to fester to gather a few votes. Every college kid who ever laughed at a racist joke. Everyone who ever chewed their tongue when they should have spoken up.

> Mr Mayor was guilty all right. As guilty as the lunatics who pull the triggers. Maybe we all are.

83 Andrew Britton, "Blissing Out: The Politics of Reaganite Entertainment," *MOVIE* 31/32 (Winter 1986), pp. 1–42.

84 Williams suggests that what the cultural historian studies is "the social practice and social relations which produce not only 'a culture' or 'an ideology' but, more significantly, those dynamic actual states and works within which there are not only continuities and persistent determinations but also tensions, conflicts, resolutions and irresolutions, innovations and actual changes." This leads him to stress the interplay between what he terms residual, dominant, and emergent ideological discourses present within a culture at any given historical moment. Raymond Williams, *The Sociology of Culture* (New York: Schocken, 1982), p. 29.

85 Quoted in Joan Goodman, "Taking Flak for Fiction," *Guardian* (May 4, 1989).

86 Quoted in Goodman.

87 Robert Stam summarizes: "it turns the historical enemy in the 1960s – the racist FBI which devoted most of its energies to harassing and sabotaging the civil rights movement – into the heroes, while turning the historical heroes – the thousands of blacks who marched, suffered, and died – into passive victim-observers waiting for white official 'rescue.' " Robert Stam, "Bakhtin, Polyphony, and Ethnic/Racial Representation," in Lester Friedman, ed., *Unspeakable Images: Ethnicity and the American Cinema* (Urbana: University of Illinois Press, 1991), p. 253.

88 Smith, p. 29.

89 Quoted in Goodman.

90 Parker shunned any "based on a true story" credit because placing such a credit on *Midnight Express* (1978) "got me into far too much trouble." Quoted in Smith, p. 29.

91 Nick Roddick, *A New Deal in Entertainment: Wamer Brothers* [sic] *in the 1930s* (London: British Film Institute, 1983), p. 126.

92 This generic context was recognized by *Mississippi Burning*'s writer, Chris Gerolmo, whose initial premise was "say, Clint Eastwood and Bill Hurt in those roles . . . a working-through of a Western-type conflict like *The Man Who Shot Liberty Valance*, where the rule of law needs the rule of force." Quoted in Smith, p. 28.

93 Goodman.

94 Robert Ray, *A Certain Tendency of the Hollywood Cinema, 1930–1980* (Princeton, NJ: Princeton University Press, 1985), pp. 296–325.

95 In interview, Hackman commented, "I never quite resolved the conflict in my own head. I felt he did care for her a lot, and in the end made a decision to just let her be, not to complicate her life further." When asked how he plays such an unresolved scene, he responded, "You cannot play a lie. You must play some kind of truth, and if you make the right choice, the audience will read it right." *"You mean you count on the film's montage to give the right information?"* "Yes." Quoted in Walker, p. 24.

96 Parker, p. 5.

97 "General Principles to Govern the Preparation of a Revised Code of Ethics for Talking Pictures." Reporter's Transcript, board meeting, Association of Motion Picture Producers (AMPP), February 10, 1930, Motion Picture Association of America Archive, New York, 1930 AMPP Code file, pp. 138–9.

98 Parker's "Production Notes" remark, "March 10. Another church to be burned . . . March 14. Began a week of night church burnings and also the burning of Vertis Williams' farm." *Mississippi Burning* was nominated for five Academy Awards,

including Best Film, but won only one. Parker felt that the controversy surrounding the movie damaged its chances of winning others.

99   Edward Branigan, "Color and Cinema: Problems in the Writing of History," in Paul Kerr, ed., *The Hollywood Film Industry* (London: Routledge and Kegan Paul, 1986), p. 135.

100 Wenders, p. 139.

101 Richard Dyer, "Entertainment and Utopia," *MOVIE* 24 (1977), pp. 6–8.

102 Daniel Bell, *The End of Ideology* (New York: Collier Books, 1960), p. 373.

103 Catherine Belsey, *Critical Practice* (London: Methuen, 1980), p. 5.

104 It is also one reason why the most fully articulated theories of ideology have been developed by Marxist political theory in examining the tradition of western liberal democracy. The farther away from the consensus you are, the easier it is to recognize ideology at work.

105 Belsey, p. 5.

106 Louis Althusser, "Marxism and Humanism," in *For Marx* (London: NLB, 1977), p. 233; Louis Althusser, "Ideology and Ideological State Apparatuses: Notes towards an Investigation," in *Lenin and Philosophy and Other Essays* (London: NLB, 1971), p. 169.

107 Belsey, pp. 57–8.

108 Belsey, p. 58.

109 Terry Eagleton, *Ideology: An Introduction* (London: Verso, 1991), p. xiii.

110 Frank Nugent, *New York Times* (October 29, 1939), quoted in Wolfe, p. 311.

111 Richard Griffith, *New Movies* (November 1939), quoted in Wolfe, p. 301. Wolfe suggests that analyses of the movie that emphasize "the capacity of director Frank Capra to articulate a social vision for his audience" can be traced back to Griffith's review.

112 Belsey, p. 62.

113 Belsey, p. 69.

114 For a discussion of these events and their relation to film criticism, see Sylvia Harvey, *May '68 and Film Culture* (London: British Film Institute, 1978).

115 Jean-Louis Comolli and Jean Narboni, "Cinema/Ideology/Criticism (1)," trans. Susan Bennett, in John Ellis, ed., *Screen Reader 1* (London: Society for Education in Film and Television, 1977), p. 4. 1st pub. in *Cahiers du Cinéma* (October–November 1969); 1st pub. in English in *Screen* 12:1 (1971).

116 Comolli and Narboni, p. 3.

117 Comolli and Narboni, p. 7.

118 Comolli and Narboni, p. 7.

119 "John Ford's *Young Mr Lincoln*, a Collective Text by the Editors of *Cahiers du Cinéma*," originally pub. in *Cahiers du Cinéma* 223 (August 1970), trans. Helen Lackner and Diana Mathias, *Screen* 13:3 (Autumn 1972), pp. 5–44; "*Morocco*, a Collective Text," originally pub. in *Cahiers du Cinéma* 225 (November–December 1970), trans. Diana Mathias, in Peter Baxter, ed., *Sternberg* (London: British Film Institute, 1980), pp. 81–94.

120 Laura Mulvey, "Visual Pleasure and Narrative Cinema," 1st pub. *Screen* 16:3 (Autumn 1975), reprinted in Mulvey, *Visual and Other Pleasures* (Bloomington: Indiana University Press, 1989), p. 14.

121 Mulvey, pp. 19, 20, 22.

122 David Bordwell suggests that "the look" provided more concrete evidence of a play of power around sexual difference in Hollywood movies than the pursuit of sexual symbolism: "A cane or a cave is only an analogy, but a look is there, so to speak, for all to see. In addition, since in most films characters spend a lot of time looking, the critic is seldom at a loss for an occasion to disclose an ongoing power struggle." David

Bordwell, *Making Meaning: Inference and Rhetoric in the Interpretation of Cinema* (Cambridge, MA: Harvard University Press, 1989), p. 174.

123 See, for instance, Claire Johnston, "Towards a Feminist Film Practice: Some Theses," and B. Ruby Rich, "In the Name of Feminist Film Criticism," both anthologized in Bill Nichols, ed., *Movies and Methods Vol. II* (Berkeley, CA: University of California Press, 1985), pp. 315–27, 340–58.

124 B. Ruby Rich, in Michell Citron, Julia Lesage, Judith Mayne, B. Ruby Rich, and Anna Maria Taylor, "Women and Film: A Discussion of Feminist Aesthetics," *New German Critique* 13 (Winter 1978), p. 87.

125 Mary Ann Doane, "Misrecognition and Identity," *Cine-tracts* 11 (Fall 1980), p. 31.

126 Mary Ann Doane, Patricia Mellencamp, and Linda Williams, "Feminist Film Criticism: An Introduction," in Mary Ann Doane, Patricia Mellencamp, and Linda Williams, eds, *Re-Visions: Essays in Feminist Film Criticism* (Frederick, MD: University Publications of America, 1984), p. 8.

127 Susan White, "Split Skins: Female Agency and Bodily Mutilation in *The Little Mermaid*," in Jim Collins, Hilary Radner, and Ava Preacher Collins, eds, *Film Theory Goes to the Movies* (London: Routledge, 1993), pp. 182–3. In the same collection, see also Hilary Radner, "Pretty Is as Pretty Does: Free Enterprise and the Marriage Plot," p. 69.

128 J.A. Miller, quoted in *"Young Mr Lincoln*, a Collective Text," p. 9.

129 Bordwell, p. 84.

130 *"Young Mr Lincoln*, a Collective Text," p. 9.

131 Charles Eckert, "The Anatomy of a Proletarian Film: Warner's *Marked Woman*," *Film Quarterly* 27:2 (Winter 1973–4), reprinted in Nichols, pp. 424–5.

132 Barbara Klinger, " 'Cinema/Ideology/Criticism' Revisited: The Progressive Genre," in Barry Keith Grant, ed., *Film Genre Reader* (Austin: University of Texas Press, 1986), pp. 74–90.

133 Klinger, pp. 77, 87.

134 Klinger, pp. 87, 89.

135 *"Young Mr Lincoln*, a Collective Text," p. 9.

136 Henry Louis Gates Jr, "Whose Canon Is It Anyway?," *New York Times Book Review* (February 2, 1989), p. 44.

137 Colin MacCabe, "Realism and the Cinema: Notes on some Brechtian Theses," *Screen* 15:2 (Summer 1974), pp. 7–27.

138 See, for instance, the discussion of *School Daze* (1987) in Ella Shohat, "Ethnicities in Relation: Toward a Multicultural Reading of American Cinema," and in Robert Stam, "Bakhtin, Polyphony, and Ethnic/Racial Representation," both in Friedman, pp. 215–50, 251–76.

139 "The *how* of racism . . . makes good cinematic spectacle. But what is never explained is the much more political *why* of racism." Ed Guerrero, "Spike Lee and the Fever in the Racial Jungle," in Collins et al., p. 178.

140 Mark A. Reid, *Redefining Black Film* (Berkeley, CA: University of California Press, 1993), pp. 106–7; Malcolm Turvey, "Black Film-making in the USA: The Case of *Malcolm X*," *Wasafiri* 18 (Autumn 1983), pp. 54–6.

10 Criticism

Criticism is neither a science nor a fine art, but it resembles both. Like them, it depends upon cognitive skills; it requires imagination and taste; and it consists of institutionally-sanctioned problem-solving activities. Criticism is, I think, best considered a practical art, somewhat like quilting or furniture-making. Because its primary product is a piece of language, it is also a rhetorical art.

David Bordwell[1]

It is intriguing and useful to listen to the sacred rhetoric of the cinema groups and intellectual critics, but very little of it gets up on the screen in the next picture.

Jerry Lewis[2]

The critical discourses that surround Hollywood play an important role in defining our understanding of it. Criticism is not something detached from the movie industry. Instead, Hollywood requires criticism to help it fix its social and cultural identity. Even at the rarefied level of university courses, criticism is a necessary part of the sense-making apparatus that allows cinema to be meaningful in society. Pam Cook argues that cinema is "kept alive not just through systems of production, distribution and exhibition, but also through the circulation of debates which provide the cultural context in which it can flourish."[3] The circulation of debate has been an important sub-industry for Hollywood cinema, one in which its cultural status has been established and its significance contested. Some critical approaches to Hollywood, such as the idea of the director as auteur, have permeated the industry's understanding of its own processes, altering the history of movie production itself.

From Reviewing to Criticism

The vast majority of people are in need of guidance in the matter of photoplays. It is no longer a question of giving them what they want. It is a question of so directing their tastes that they will want what is best. And they can come to know what is best only through that organ of universal enlightenment, the public press.

Frances Taylor Patterson, 1920[4]

The species of movie criticism that we encounter most frequently is the review, a short account of a newly released movie in a newspaper or on the television program guide. Reviews outline the plot, identify the stars and perhaps the director, and offer an opinion about whether the movie is worth paying to see. Reduced to its minimal form, it is literally encapsulated in the one-liner reviews and star ratings of *Halliwell's Film Guide* and its imitators, in which *Desperately Seeking Susan* (1985), for instance, is awarded one star and assessed as a "mildly diverting romantic mystery which could have been both funnier and more thrilling."[5] The review is a form of consumer criticism, often taken by reviewers themselves, and sometimes other critics, to be the function of all criticism. Donald C. Willis, for instance, regards "the main concern of the critic" as being "to determine if and why a film is good or bad or partly good and partly bad."[6] More loquaciously, Michael Church, in a newspaper review of anthologies of the reviews of C.A. Lejeune and Dilys Powell, opined that 'true criticism is a rare substance, presupposing both knowledge and love, and requiring that head and heart speak with one voice. It has to entertain – otherwise it won't be read – but it must never lose sight of its primary function (Is this book/film/show worth the reader's time and money?)."[7]

The evaluative criticism being so extravagantly praised here is ultimately concerned with value for money, and is commonly delivered in the "entertaining" terms that it often disparages in the movies it assesses. This premise leads it, on the whole, to accept Hollywood on its own terms. Leslie Halliwell again provides a case in point. "Hollywood at its best," he suggests, "was the purveyor of an expensive and elegant craft which at times touched art, though seldom throughout a whole film." Even during its "golden age," however, "the worthwhile movies were the tip of the iceberg: probably eighty per cent of what was produced was ghastly rubbish." At points, review discourse is openly hostile to other kinds of criticism. In describing "the Decline and Fall of the Movie," Halliwell blames, among others, "verbose and pompous critics who were determined to turn it into serious art."

> Listen to a modern critic in the British Film Institute's *Monthly Film Bulletin*, once a terse and reliable guide to film trends, on *Alice Doesn't Live Here Any More*: "What Scorsese has done, however, is to rescue an American cliché from the bland, flat but much more portentous naturalism of such as *Harry and Tonto* and restore it to an emotional and intellectual complexity through his particular brand of baroque realism." . . . Spare us.[8]

Although we might often find ourselves in agreement with his account of Hollywood's procedures (his account of the "golden age," for instance, echoes the one we quoted from Harry Cohn in chapter 1), and more occasionally with his critical opinions, we recognize that the way we write about those procedures and opinions would be fundamentally unacceptable within his populist rhetoric. Halliwell represents Hollywood as the provider of a service, entertainment, which is in need of no further analysis. To that extent his critical judgments on a movie contribute to the endorsement of the production system, regardless of whether any individual judgment is positive or negative.

From our perspective, reviewing is a secondary, supplementary activity supporting the motion picture industry as a whole, a part of the machinery of publicity that the industry propagates. Aspects of journalistic reviewing attach themselves to the publicity operations served by fan and celebrity magazines such as *Premiere*, and television shows combining clips from new releases, celebrity interviews, and "inside news" from Hollywood. These forms of reviewing have evolved from the activities of gossip columnists such as the notorious and nationally syndicated Louella Parsons and Hedda Hopper during the Classical period. At the height of the studio system, press books supplied by studio publicity departments to exhibitors for each movie included complete reviews that could be printed by the local paper; not surprisingly, given their source, they were invariably unstinting in their praise, and unquestioning in their promulgation of entertainment as self-evidently valuable. Although often carried on with a more subtle gloss, the enthusiastic festival report or the deferential celebrity interview still present the industry's publicity on the industry's terms. More generally, most journalistic reviewing has made its judgments according to criteria established by the industry, rating movies for their "entertainment value" or on the strength of their central performances. At the other extreme of sophistication from the advertisement-as-review produced by studio publicity, some reviewers have elevated evaluative criticism to the status of a "practical art." For many years after the original publication in 1937 of an anthology of British and American reviewing, *Garbo and the Night Watchmen*, this kind of writing on the movies constituted the only major body of criticism of Hollywood cinema and the only critical material to be offered the longevity of publication in book form.[9]

Journalism and publicity provided the basis for several other discourses on cinema, including the star biographies that performed a similar function to fan magazines in circulating the persona of the star. Embryonic movie criticism with a more industrial, technical, and commercial emphasis developed from the 1930s around more professional trade publications. With the exception of *The Hollywood Reporter*, which for much of its history was as much a gossip sheet as it was a newspaper, the trade papers were aimed primarily at the exhibition sector, and their reporting of industry affairs is a salutary corrective to the emphasis on production in the body of anecdotal accounts that for so long passed as film history. Although *Variety* is the best known of the "trades," *Motion Picture Herald* has perhaps a greater claim to be regarded as the industry's journal of record, for the completeness of its account of the industry's economic and political affairs. Professional journals such as the *Journal of the Society of Motion Picture Engineers* and *American Cinematographer* circulated much less widely, mainly among members of the craft guilds that sponsored them. As well as information on guild or union matters they also included material on new technologies and new techniques being developed on the lots.[10] These journals played an important role in disseminating standards of practice among cinematographers and other technicians, and also sought to promote the prestige of particular crafts both inside and outside the industry. At a crucial point in its development, the emerging academic subject of film studies resisted the industrial discourses contained in both the trade papers and the professional journals in favor of discursive practices drawn from elsewhere in the Academy. Although we discuss this in more detail later, it is worth noting here that what was lost or postponed in that process was any sustained critical engagement with the industry's professional and trade journals, and with it, any emphasis on the historical investigation of the industry.

The kind of criticism we have examined so far is seldom informed by much theoretical consideration; the trade papers and professional journals were publications of the moment, concerned with the day-to-day practicalities of their industry. Reviews in *Variety* provided, as their primary function, an assessment of a new movie's box-office potential. The ideological assumptions underlying their assessments were seldom explicitly articulated, and when they were, the terms used were little different from those that Will Hays himself might have employed. In 1938 Martin Quigley, publisher of *Motion Picture Herald*, expressed his belief that "the sole, exclusive business of the motion picture theatre of entertainment is entertainment." On these grounds he warned the producers of *The Life of Emile Zola* (1937) against promoting the movie as if it were "a learned and scholarly inquiry into the life and times of Zola." As an evening's entertainment about an idealized character, he suggested, the movie was excellent; but to consider it serious biography or history was absurd.[11]

Reviewing as it is practiced today remains consciously impressionistic, guarding against excesses of seriousness and absurdity, with the reviewer and his or her readership gradually constructing a relationship by which readers come to trust the reviewer's opinion or else know the extent of their divergence from it. This involves a professional, even institutional investment in the maintenance of a personal basis for the formation of opinion on the part of the reviewer; that "head and heart speak with one voice," in Michael Church's phrase. Undoubtedly, such writings can provide us with valuable insights into movies, and critics such as Pauline Kael use consistent procedures and criteria in making their evaluations. However, a more general reluctance to employ a consciously adopted, systematic method in asking and answering questions about movies means that the use-value of this criticism may well come down to a matter of whether the critic's value-judgments accord with those of his or her readership. If criticism wishes to escape the limitations of unrestrained subjectivity and an obligation to evaluate, it needs to be informed by a consistent and systematic method which asks different questions from those of an impressionistic reviewer, and comes to different conclusions. In the attempt to elaborate such a criticism, many writers on cinema have appealed to a concept of **theory** as a way of defining and developing a less parasitical practice.

Early Theory and Criticism in America

The cinematic critic ought to take his mission in life seriously. He ought to learn all there is to be learned about his profession, cultivating a knowledge of all the other arts from which the photoplay borrows.

Frances Taylor Patterson, 1920[12]

The word "theory" has its origins in a Greek root, *thea*, meaning sight. It shares a common linguistic point of origin with "theater," and a common point of derivation with ideas of both spectacle and speculation. To formulate a theory is thus to articulate a point of view, which clearly cannot be innocent of the political, since a point of view by definition cannot be objective. An adequate history of film theory, giving even minimal space to the points of view of its most important figures, would require at least a full-length book.[13] Although the shelves of university libraries testify to the burgeoning "theory industry" of the 1970s and 1980s, a great deal of significant film theory was written during the cinema's first 60 years. The fact that it had comparatively little influence on either criticism or the practice of film production in America is no reason to ignore it, since much of early theory has come to be seen as important both in itself, and as a starting point for our contemporary discussions.

The earliest film theorists, such as the American poet Vachel Lindsay, were primarily concerned with staking out the artistic ground that film might occupy. They consciously sought to elevate movies to the level of Art, which would allow them to be evaluated according to traditional critical principles. Usually they did this by comparing motion pictures with the arts of music or theater, and in most cases their comparisons were metaphorical, lyrical, and lacking in much of the precision we would normally associate with more recent theory. An exception, and perhaps the most important of the early theorists, was the psychologist and philosopher Hugo Münsterberg, who undertook the first rigorous inquiry into the nature of film in his book *The Photoplay: A Psychological Study*, first published in 1916.[14] Münsterberg's theorizing was primarily concerned with the audience's reception of narrative cinema, and his account of the correlation between cinematic properties and the viewer's psychological processes bears comparison with Thomas Elsaesser's "audience-oriented aesthetics," discussed in chapter 8. Like his contemporaries, Münsterberg also addressed the question of whether cinema was an independent art, but unlike many of them he did so from within a broadly grounded, philosophically based aesthetics. He argued that cinema's claim to aesthetic validity lay in the fact that it transformed reality into an object of the viewer's imagination; a claim he justified through the argument that the "photoplay" only exists in the mind of the viewer, and is constituted in the act of its consumption.[15] Historically, however, his writing had much less impact than it deserved: the coincidence of his own death in 1917 and the anti-German propaganda of World War I obscured his reputation not only as a film theorist but also as a psychologist.

Similar considerations were also to limit the importance, in America at least, of the first important group of practitioner-theorists of film, the Russian Constructivist filmmakers, of whom the most famous and influential was Sergei Eisenstein. Eisenstein's importance as a filmmaker, and his stress on editing and montage as cinema's central creative act, have ensured the continued currency of his ideas. However, their origins in Soviet revolutionary cinema kept them in only limited circulation, particularly in the United States, where his influence was largely restricted to a handful of left-wing critics writing for magazines such as *New Theatre and Film* in the 1930s.[16] Elsewhere in the west, Eisenstein's movies were for a long time dismissed as propaganda, and his theories, insofar as they were considered at all, were dismissed as explanations of a propagandist activity. An indication of the extent of Hollywood's lack of attention to Eisenstein might well be the specific Hollywood meaning of the word "montage," the central term in Eisenstein's theory.[17] A Hollywood "montage sequence" was a highly stylized inserted sequence, such as that depicting the Wall Street Crash in *The Roaring Twenties* (1939), generally involving fast cutting and a variety of optical effects with the intention of rapidly conveying the impression of an event or the passage of time. Hollywood credited the principles of its montage not to Eisenstein, but to an emigré Serb, Slavko Vorkapich, whose "Principles Underlying Effective Cinematography" were, according to Richard Koszarski, "quite similar to Eisenstein's, although leaning more to a subjective analytical technique grounded in physiological rather than intellectual principles." During the 1930s Vorkapich was employed by a number of Hollywood studios as a specialist creating what were first known as "Vorkapich shots" and later "montage sequences," which was as close as Hollywood came to a stylistic imitation of Eisenstein.[18]

The one early film theorist whose work can be said to have had much influence on the criticism of his time was the German aesthetician Rudolph Arnheim, whose book *Film as Art* was published in 1932. The core of Arnheim's theoretical position was that film art lay in the tension between the medium's necessary representation of reality, and the equally inevitable inadequacies of that representation. Artistic expression took place because of and through the limitations of film's ability to reproduce reality perfectly. While this position was not unique to Arnheim, he used it to draw a particularly conservative set of conclusions. Writing at the moment of the introduction of sound, Arnheim argued that this amounted to a regression for film art, since by increasing the extent of film's representation of reality, it decreased the medium's possibilities for artistic expression. It was an argument he later repeated in relation to other technological innovations, such as color and 3-D. This was an influential argument in the early 1930s, because it maintained that the height of cinema's expressive powers had been reached in the final years of silent cinema, and that the musicals and adapted stage plays of the early sound years were inferior not simply because the new technology had not yet been fully mastered, but because the technology itself made them inherently inferior. In the conservative revision of cultural assumptions that accompanied the early Depression, Arnheim's argument provided many intellectuals who had flirted with the cinema as art during the 1920s with a convenient escape route from a medium then under strenuous attack as mercenary and mediocre.

Intellectual engagement with cinema on aesthetic terms declined noticeably from the mid-1930s in the United States. The acceptance of Arnheim's arguments was an important element in this, as was the absence of an available countervailing theory in defense of sound movies. This retarded the development of film criticism considerably, and until the 1960s no American filmmaker was accorded the degree of intellectual respect that Chaplin in particular had received in the 1920s. Curiously, the figure who came closest to that position, especially in the 1930s, was not John Ford or Irving Thalberg or even Orson Welles, but Walt Disney: this was in part perhaps because Disney's animated movies lay outside the world of photographic representation altogether, and in part because, in works such as *Fantasia* (1940), Disney displayed a manifest aspiration to something other than naturalist realism.

From the mid-1930s to the mid-1960s, the dominant aesthetic theory of film was broadly realist. Its most articulate advocate, André Bazin, incorporated Hollywood's general aesthetic intentions into the system of his own realist aesthetics (discussed in chapter 4). For example, he understood the adoption of deep-focus in Hollywood as a positive endorsement of realist aesthetic goals. There is little evidence, however, that such theoretically motivated explorations of cinema aesthetics had any significant effect on what actually happened in Hollywood studios.

At the same time, a good deal of academic energy in the United States was directed toward the investigation of a quite different set of concerns about the movies: their effect on society and on the attitudes of individual spectators. From the beginning of cinema this had been an area of immediate, practical concern, which manifested itself most obviously in censorship legislation.[19] With the rapid growth of sociology departments in American universities from the 1920s on, a large number of studies of mass communication began to appear. Early works in this field drew their inspiration from the general opinion that the propaganda produced by both sides in World War I, and particularly that produced by the Allies, had been extremely effective in influencing attitudes on the Home Front. Investigations into the propagandist effect of the mass media continued until well after World War II, influenced by an awareness of first Russian and then Nazi propaganda, and then by the need, during the war, for the allies themselves to produce effective propaganda.

This sociological approach asked very different questions about the movies from those posed by aesthetic film theory. Sociology offered itself as a scientific inquiry into social organization based quite consciously on investigative models drawn from the natural and physical sciences. Applied to the movies, this new discipline had little to do with ideas of cinema as art, and was hardly interested in asking questions about the forms and structures of the movies themselves. Instead, it was concerned with what institutions such as the cinema could reveal about the habits and the obsessions of the societies in which they existed. Much of this work was highly critical of what it saw as the damaging effect of Hollywood on American society, and particularly on its youth. The first large-scale sociological and psychological examination of the movies' effects, the Payne Fund Studies (1933), were widely interpreted as concluding that those effects were almost entirely pernicious, and that the movies therefore required very close scrutiny. Although they were later derided for the inadequacy of their research methods, at the time of their publication the Payne Fund Studies were generally accepted as scientifically valid, and had a considerable influence on debates about regulating the movies, and more generally on the drift of sound cinema into comparative intellectual disrepute.[20] The broad methodologies of empirical inquiry they undertook have also continued as the basis for most subsequent research into the effects of cinema and television.

Another aspect of this sociological approach was a body of work studying the sociology of moviegoing and Hollywood itself. Important works in this field were Margaret Thorp's *America at the Movies* and Leo Rosten's *Hollywood: The Movie Colony, the Movie Makers* (which remain two of the best accounts of Hollywood cinema during the studio period); and Hortense Powdermaker's *Hollywood the Dream Factory*.[21] For historians of American culture, it is unfortunate that with the partial exception of Thorp these works concentrated on the sociology of movie production rather than on their audiences; our lack of reliable information about movie audiences, particularly during the studio era, is one of the greatest gaps in our knowledge of the Hollywood cinema, and one that it is almost impossible to fill.[22]

During the 1940s, the sociological tradition of inquiry gradually absorbed influences from the study of psychology, especially in the period immediately after World War II. During the war the American military put substantial resources into psychological investigations of their troops, some of them concerned with the effectiveness of propaganda on individual soldiers. The publication of this research was partially responsible for the growth of a hybrid form of study into American (and other) culture, which was part sociology, part anthropology, and part psychology. Geoffrey Gorer's *The Americans* and David Riesman's *The Lonely Crowd* are important examples of what Gorer called "psychocultural studies," and both referred to movies as revealing and exemplifying the conscious and unconscious concerns of American society.[23]

At a time when Hollywood was itself preoccupied – especially in film noir – with the psychology and psychoanalysis of its characters, there was an immediate appropriateness to this type of inquiry into the movies' function in society. A number of books examining cinema from this perspective appeared in the late 1940s and early 1950s. Perhaps the most influential dealt not with Hollywood, but with German cinema in the 1920s: Siegfried Kracauer's *From Caligari to Hitler: A Psychological History of the German Film*. Kracauer also wrote about Hollywood, and one of his students, Barbara Deming, produced a work in the same vein: *Running Away From Myself: A Dream Portrait of America Drawn from the Films of the Forties* (written in 1950 although not published as a book until 1969). Another important work in this area was Martha Wolfenstein and Nathan Leites' *Movies: A Psychological Study*, which we discussed in chapter 1. Like Deming, Wolfenstein and Leites drew out the largely unconscious inferences of Hollywood's plot material. In a far more whimsical and witty way, so did Parker Tyler, for whom Hollywood was "the industrialization of the mechanical work's daylight dream." His two books, *The Hollywood Hallucination* and *Magic and Myth of the Movies*, delighted in exploring Hollywood's construction of popular mythology, as well as its "displacements" of sex, without the tone of concerned responsibility the academics brought to the task.[24]

The concerns of this cultural criticism anticipated the ideologically oriented analysis of the 1970s and 1980s, although it was based on the examination of content and little concerned with questions of form. It assumed, rather, that the academic value in studying movies lay in their significance as a phenomenon of mass culture rather than in any intrinsic aesthetic values they might have. Although after 1950 American audiences could see more foreign (mainly European) movies, which were often recognized as having legitimate artistic pretensions, Hollywood itself remained a primary target for the critiques of "mass culture" that appeared in the 1950s, whether they came from liberal humanists alarmed by what they saw as a decline in cultural values, or the disaffected Marxist social critics of the Frankfurt school, who saw the politically oppositional role of Art being destroyed by its absorption into a capitalist system of production and consumption.[25]

The movies' return to intellectual respectability began in the 1960s, and happened for a number of interrelated reasons. One was that they had been replaced as the aestheticians' *bête noir* by television. Another was that the substantial growth in universities on both sides of the Atlantic during this period made possible the introduction of new subjects, particularly in humanities departments. A third was the increasing visibility of the European art cinema, providing thematically dense, formally self-conscious material in the best traditions of European modernism, well suited for inclusion on university courses teaching critical skills. The increasing availability of English translations of theoretical works also offered a framework for a more rigorous kind of film criticism than had previously existed in America. Bazin was translated into English in 1967; Walter Benjamin's important essay "The Work of Art in the Age of Mechanical Reproduction," written in 1936, was first published in English in 1968; while major works in the Russian Formalist tradition had begun appearing in translation a few years earlier. The work of Roland Barthes was published in English from 1970 onwards.

From Criticism to Theory

> Sometimes the inadequate criticism of current plays is due to the more or less antagonistic attitude the critic adopts toward the motion picture. . . . Often his criticism is not analysis, but vituperation and abuse.
>
> Frances Taylor Patterson, 1920[26]

Early in this book, we looked at two important critical methodologies: auteurism and genre-based criticism. The first purpose of both these approaches is to organize the large, undifferentiated corpus of "the Hollywood cinema" into smaller, related, and comprehensible groups of movies. From there both identify common features within a group, and they may then go on either to draw some aesthetic or ideological judgment about the group as a whole, or to comment on one movie in relation to the group. Although these critical approaches "avoid the dangers of impressionistic connoisseurship which haunt the unsystematic critic," neither of them constitutes a theory as such. As Dudley Andrew argues, auteurism resembles other critical methods in relying on theoretical principles, but deploying them to evaluate particular movies and rank directors in a hierarchy of worth, rather than achieve a systematic understanding of cinema as a general phenomenon.[27] Andrew distinguishes between theory and criticism by suggesting that theory is concerned with the properties of cinema as a whole, or what he calls "the cinematic capability." Criticism, on the other hand, can put theory into practice, but its primary object of investigation is the individual movie, a group of movies, or the study of particular techniques. Despite its undoubted explanatory power, criticism alone could not establish the movies as a legitimate object of academic study. For the activity of criticism to gain acceptance as a discipline (that is, for movie criticism to become film studies and enter the academy within departments of film studies), it had to develop a set of theoretical concerns recognized by the academy's established institutional criteria. Only with these concerns in place could study of the movies proceed to the higher ground of the established humanities or social sciences.

The importation of European thought helped to give the emerging subject of film studies a degree of cultural and academic legitimacy that the movies themselves had not possessed. However, evaluative critical paradigms initially borrowed from Leavisite or New Critical methods of literary studies rapidly revealed the difficulties inherent in their application to cinema. In the wake of the political and intellectual turmoil caused by *"les événements"* of May 1968, the combination of radical politics and theoretical sophistication offered by the work of *Cahiers du Cinéma* (discussed in the previous chapter) proved a more attractive alternative.[28] It heavily influenced the London-based *Screen*, the dominant English-language journal of film theory in the 1970s, which in turn bore markedly on the academic study of cinema in the USA. Although the political persuasion of almost all the theoretical criticism produced in the 1970s was clearly on the left, concerned with championing the "progressive text" that denied the easy pleasures of Hollywood, many writers retained a residual attachment to Hollywood cinema that drew them back, repeatedly, to its critical assessment.[29]

No single term provides an exact description of the work produced around these journals, but we can group the wide range of theoretical discourses brought to bear on the Hollywood cinema in the 1960s and 1970s as broadly **structuralist** in orientation, because rather than attending to the apparent characteristics of a movie – usually in isolation – they sought to identify the wider structures within which a particular movie was produced and against which it was "read." Deriving from the **semiology** (literally, the study of signs) of Swiss linguist Ferdinand de Saussure, structuralism directed intellectual attention to the organizing principles and relationships underlying human behavior, institutions, or texts. As an intellectual movement, structuralism originated in the proposition, by anthropologist Claude Lévi-Strauss, that kinship relations and primitive myths were structured like language, and could be studied by using Saussure's principles of linguistic analysis.[30] Structuralism maintained that the elements within a structure did not possess meaning as independent units, but gained their meaning through their relations to other elements. Meaning is, for instance, often constructed through binary oppositions: "good" means something only in relation to "bad"; "raw" and "cooked" signify opposing states. Applications of the structuralist approach proliferated in European thought in the 1960s, and cultural theorists such as Roland Barthes and Umberto Eco argued that cultural events could be understood by examining the structure that underlay them as if it were a language. In another important instance, to which we shall return, French psychoanalyst Jacques Lacan claimed that the unconscious was "structured like a language." Applied to cinema, structuralism produced a variety of analytical methods. It might have been logical to expect the structuralist approach to provide a firmer theoretical framework for genre studies, which had obviously related concerns. But in the first instance, as Anglo-American criticism awaited the translation of the major texts of French structuralism, its approach was more influential in revising notions of authorship.[31]

An attempt to avoid the Romantic excesses of the auteur theory was developed by a number of critics in the late 1960s and early 1970s, and has come to bear the cumbersome name **auteur-structuralism**. This work recognized the advantages of the auteur approach as a way of classifying Hollywood cinema, but it resisted the idea of autonomous creativity as a supreme value. Combining a system of classification by director/author with a text-based inquiry into the structuring principles of any given work, it breathed new life into a set of debates about the status of (usually) the director that had otherwise reached a point of near-exhaustion by the early 1970s. What most clearly differentiated auteur-structuralism from auteurist studies was not its mode of analysis so much as its project of detaching the common structural features of a body of movies "signed" by the same name from the cult of personality encouraged by auteurism. Movies marked by the sign "Directed by Alfred Hitchcock," for example, could be shown to possess recurring structures, but auteur-structuralists relieved themselves of the burden of having to demonstrate that Alfred Hitchcock had intentionally placed them there. "Hitchcock" became a body of structuring principles that could be divined from a critical examination of films, and bore no necessary relation to the small, fat, male body of Alfred Hitchcock the person, which routinely appeared in each of these movies.

This proposition alleviated many of the problems created by the homages of auteurism, and established the critic's interpretive independence from the intentions of the director, but it produced as many contradictions of its own. Beginning with the assumption of individual creativity as the basis for its system of classification, it then leaned toward the other half of its hyphenate in denying any credit to that individual for the structural consistencies it identified, even when it accorded aesthetic value to them. Protesting rather too much, auteur-structuralism associated the structure it identified in a movie with its director, "not because he has played the role of artist, expressing himself or his vision in the film, but because it is through the force of his preoccupations that an unconscious, unintended meaning can be decoded in the film, usually to the surprise of the individual involved." Arguing that the movies it examined were "unconsciously structured," auteur-structuralism insisted on a categorical distinction between the person of a director and the critically deciphered structure that bore his or her name: "Fuller or Hawks or Hitchcock, the directors, are quite separate from 'Fuller' or 'Hawks' or 'Hitchcock,' the structures named after them, and should not be methodologically confused."[32]

In trying to avoid an approach based on a director's intentions, auteur-structuralism thus found itself propelled toward the uncertain waters of a psychoanalytic explanation of directorial consistency. Peter Wollen quoted Jean Renoir as having observed that a director spends his whole life making one film, and Wollen saw the critic's task as being to reconstruct this "one film" out of the whole body of a director's work.[33] In describing the movies of an auteur in terms much closer to genre criticism, auteur-structuralism proposed that the auteur's "one film" constituted a myth, in the precise sense in which structuralist anthropologist Claude Lévi-Strauss used the term.[34] The recurrent thematic consistencies or binary oppositions from which this myth could be distilled were usually attached both to the unconscious preoccupations of the director, and to those of the wider social group for which he or she was taken to speak. Where auteurism celebrated an individual's genius, auteur-structuralism seemed, at times, to come dangerously close to celebrating his or her unconscious as symptomatic of the equally unconscious preoccupations of the culture surrounding his or her work. Ultimately, the "one film" constructed by auteur-structuralists revealed social rather than individual meaning.[35].

More productively, another version of auteur-structuralism simply declared its lack of interest in explaining how any given set of structures had come into being, limiting its activity to observing those structures in a common body of texts. This approach demonstrated a more consistent and rigorous attitude to the activity of textual criticism, but in the process it abandoned any relationship between the text and history. It could explain neither how the texts themselves came into being as the result of a particular mode of production in Hollywood, nor what the wider relationship between those texts and the culture for which they were produced might have been. Instead, the system of production was seen simply as an obstacle to critical comprehension: "A great many features of films analyzed have to be dismissed as indecipherable because of 'noise' from the producer, the cameraman or even the actors."[36] In Wollen's account of the means whereby the critic could unscramble meaning from this background of noise, metaphors of psychoanalysis compete with metaphors of detection: what was proposed was a careful treatment of textual evidence leading to a correct induction.

Nevertheless, the structuralist approach provided the necessary theoretical support for criticism to distance itself from the insufficiently rigorous practices of journalistic writing, producing a form of textual analysis that would meet the criteria of the academy. As a method by which the detailed study of movies could be validated in terms borrowed from literary criticism, and as a pedagogic instrument by which the skills of "practical criticism" could be imparted on film studies courses according to the timetable convenience of one "movie-as-text" per week, structuralism displayed its institutional usefulness in establishing film studies as a discipline. It is, therefore, hardly surprising that in practice, auteurist criticism proved much more successful in dealing with thematic meaning, derived from verbal sources in the text, than with the significance, and the signifying practices, of Hollywood movies' image streams. Auteurism and auteur-structuralism have both produced important and valuable bodies of critical knowledge, but they cannot provide complete or satisfactory methods for understanding Hollywood cinema, primarily because their concern with the internal organization of a movie can supply only very partial answers to the historical and ideological questions of the cinema's relation to the culture within which it is produced and to which it is addressed.

Semiology offered a structuralist methodology that was at least potentially more able to take account of the cinema's visual nature than that offered by the thematic approach of auteur-structuralism. As a complex orchestration of verbal and non-verbal signals, cinema lends itself readily to a semiotic approach. Semiology began to formalize attention to the expressive systems of cinema that were scarcely amenable to other structural approaches, such as mise-en-scène, performance, and soundtrack. The rigorous study of sign systems as forms of non-verbal language had developed separately but simultaneously in Europe and America in the early years of the twentieth century. Saussure had described the new "science of signs" in his *Course in General Linguistics*:

> A science that studies the life of signs within society is conceivable; it would be a part of social psychology and consequently of general psychology; I shall call it *semiology* (from Greek *semeion* "sign"). Semiology would show what constitutes signs, what laws govern them. Since the science does not yet exist, no one can say what it would be; but it has a right to existence, a place staked out in advance. Linguistics is only a part of the general science of semiology; the laws discovered by semiology will be applicable to linguistics, and the latter will circumscribe a well-defined area within the mass of anthropological facts.[37]

The American philosopher Charles Sanders Peirce developed a "speculative grammar" of signs, which he called semiotics, at approximately the same time. In keeping with the European domination of theoretical work in the humanities, Saussure's work has proved far more influential than Peirce's, and is regularly cited as the foundation of structuralist criticism in general.[38] Saussure's *Course in General Linguistics* (published posthumously in 1915) was first translated into English in 1959, and the influence of semiology on film theory and criticism began to be strongly felt in the late 1960s, due mainly to the influence of the French writers Roland Barthes and Christian Metz. Together with Italian theorist Umberto Eco, Barthes played a leading role in the re-emergence and popularization of semiology as a method for analyzing the production of meaning in culture, communication, and behavior. Barthes' own work varied between comparatively playful analyses of advertisements, striptease, and "The World of Wrestling," and dense pieces of theoretical writing, such as his essay "Myth Today."[39] Although, like Eco, he did write about cinema, it was not a major preoccupation of his. Barthes' impact on film studies was more indirect, through his proposition of a theoretical method that looked for meaning in the underlying structures of a text, and the traces of these structures in the signs or symbols on its surface.

Unlike Barthes' and Eco's, Metz's writings have been almost exclusively concerned with cinema, and particularly with the cinema as a "specific signifying practice." Rather than simply invoking the commonly used metaphor of "the language of cinema," Metz set out to explore systematically the proposition that cinema operated like a language, with its own equivalent of syntactical rules and structures. His early work, presented in *Film Language*, proposed a typology of the different ways in which time and space could be organized through editing.[40] His "Grand Syntagmatique," with its eight principal categories and further subdivisions, encountered much detailed criticism and has since been largely discarded. Nevertheless, Metz has exercised a substantial influence over the direction that the critical study of cinema has subsequently taken. His idea that a movie should be understood as a "textual system," a matrix of codes and conventional structures, has provided the organizing principle for a great body of critical interpretations and textual analyses of movies.

As a discipline in itself, semiotics is exclusively concerned with the study of the visual and aural devices of film communication rather than with its technology, industrial organization, audience response, use of the star system, and so on. Inevitably, however, the critics and theorists who employ the terminology of semiotics (code, system, message, text, structure) have sought to connect the two fields. In the late 1960s, when the new theoretical insights derived from semiotics and the structuralist approach interacted with the energetic political radicalism of the New Left, a strong emphasis was placed on the ideological analysis of film texts and of the apparatus of cinema. That analysis combined an understanding of ideology derived from the work of Louis Althusser with a semiotics increasingly influenced by the linguistically informed psychoanalytic theories of Jacques Lacan. It understood cinema to be an ideological apparatus that constructed "the spectator" as the subject of its totalizing system.[41]

Psychoanalysis and Cinema

> The critic is responsible to a degree for articulating those voices dominated, displaced, or silenced by the textuality of texts . . . finding and exposing things that may otherwise be hidden beneath piety, heedlessness, or routine.
> Edward Said[42]

The construction of a psychoanalytically based paradigm for understanding the ideological functioning of Hollywood movies marked both the ultimate achievement of cine-structuralist approaches, and something of a theoretical watershed. Probably no other theoretical rethinking of Hollywood has proved more tenacious or more controversial, with the result that much of the subsequent history of movie theory and criticism has been preoccupied with contesting or revising the psychoanalytic inheritance. Providing film scholars with a common medium of discourse for most of the 1970s, psychoanalytic approaches fragmented and proliferated through the 1980s, in part as a consequence of the insights they themselves provided into the complex and multivalent character of movie–audience relations. General propositions about how the study of cinema appropriated psychoanalysis are difficult to formulate, as different theorists drew on the work of differing clinical authorities (Sigmund Freud, Carl Jung, Jacques Lacan, Melanie Klein) and gave attention to cinema at a variety of different levels. As its borrowings from Marxism and semiology meshed increasingly smoothly with its preoccupation with the workings of the unconscious mind, however, **cine-psychoanalysis** slowly coalesced around certain key principles and practices. Its concerns extended the agendas of semiotics, and it has often been identified as a "second semiology" or a "second-phase" semiotics. Its preoccupation with issues of gender and sexuality also created new questions and whole new critical sub-industries.[43] "Psychoanalytic film theory" and "contemporary film theory" have become more or less synonymous terms.

Psychoanalysis was understood primarily as a cultural theory, and at the heart of cine-psychoanalysis there remained an insistence that movie analysis should be a politically sensitive activity that could contribute to a transformation of wider social relations. Followers of French psychoanalyst Jacques Lacan argue that the usefulness of psychoanalysis as an explanation of culture stems from Lacan's emphasis on the mediations of language in the unconscious. However, the persistence of psychoanalytic interpretations of culture for much of the twentieth century suggests that its attraction may have more to do with what a psychoanalytic framework allows critics to do, rather than what it explains. The promotional publicity for a 1991 book on *Hitchcock and Homosexuality*, for example, claimed that it used "orthodox psychoanalysis" to offer insights to "anyone wanting to learn how to arrive at hidden meanings in films."[44] Freud's concept of the unconscious as a repository of deeper meaning concealed by the processes of repression has been perhaps the most powerful influence on artistic theory and practice in this century. The idea that dreams contain unconscious material susceptible to expression only in symbolic form constituted an immensely powerful new critical procedure when it was applied to artistic production. Not only could a text be interpreted as a symptom of its author's, its characters', or its culture's condition, but the concern of psychoanalysis with repressed meaning granted critics a license to examine texts as much for what they displaced, condensed, or censored as for what they said. Many of the earliest applications of psychoanalysis to critical study were hopelessly literal, often directed at the psychobiography of the author. Lacan's reformulation of Freud in linguistic terms provided the means by which critics could generalize the unconscious beyond the site of the individual. This led to the idea that analysis could reveal a text's unconscious, examining the repressed material that surfaced in the details of its narrative, form, or style.

The practitioners of cine-psychoanalysis admired the precision and rigor of early semiology, but they recognized it as largely descriptive rather than evaluative, and viewed its relation to political debates as some-what oblique. Those critics concerned with the wider "use-value" of their activity drew on psychoanalysis to renew the political momentum of cin-ema study, restoring a social dimension to the work of criticism. However, their appeal to psychoanalysis ensured that "the political" would be redefined in more personal terms. The ideological operation of a movie had to be examined not only at the level of *representation* (how does a given movie construct a version of the "real"?) but also at the level of *affect* (how does a particular movie engage our psychic lives, and whose interests does that engagement serve?). From Louis Althusser, critics such as Jean-Louis Commoli and Stephen Heath took the argument that "ideological state apparatuses," such as the church and the education system, addressed individuals as "subjects." Althusser's argument interwove the legal, gram-matical, and psychological meanings of the word "subject." The grammati-cal subject ("I") was free, "a centre of initiatives, author of and responsible for its actions." The legal subject, however, was "a subjected being, who submits to a higher authority, and is therefore stripped of all freedom except that of freely accepting his submission." The apparatuses of ideol-ogy, Althusser suggested, addressed legal subjects as if they were gram-matical subjects, leading them to misconstrue their subjection as freedom.[45] The "viewing subject" constituted by the cinematic apparatus was under-stood to be equally misinformed about his or her position.

The concern with the affective dimension of the movies led cine-psycho-analysis in search of analogies for the experience of moviegoing in dream, daydream, fantasy, and other kinds of intensely experienced psychic phe-nomenon. Cine-psychoanalysis sought to attach these analogies to a theory of ideology in order to explain how we experience ourselves as subjects in cinema. Stephen Heath hypothesized that "an important – determining – part of ideological systems in a capitalist mode of production is the achievement of a number of machines (institutions) which move, which *movie*, the individual as subject – shifting and placing desire, the energy of contradiction – in a perpetual retotalization of the imaginary."[46] Closely linked to questions of affectivity was an analysis of pleasure, a remarkably neglected area in the study of Hollywood given that its provision remains a central function of entertainment. In an essay on *Jaws* (1975) Heath summarized:

> films are industrial products, and they mean, and they sell not simply on the particular meaning but equally on the pleasure of the cinema, this yielding the return that allows the perpetuation of the industry (which is why part of the meaning of *Jaws* is to be the most profitable movie); a film is not reducible to its "ideology" but is also the working over of that ideology in cinema, with the industry dependent on the pleasure of that operation.[47]

With its concern for issues of desire, gratification, and sublimation, psychoanalysis offered one starting point for an understanding of pleasure in western culture. It could pose some very basic questions about why people go to the movies, and how that event is organized to maximize enjoyment. With its attention to gender relations, psychoanalysis could provide insights into the differing pleasures of masculine and feminine subjects. In the context of wider struggles around sexual liberation, feminism, and gay politics in the early 1970s, cine-psychoanalysts appropriated this body of theory to formulate understandings of the differing viewing pleasures of male and female moviegoers. As we discussed in the previous chapter, Laura Mulvey's influential 1975 article "Visual Pleasure and Narrative Cinema" triggered an avalanche of theoretical writing addressing questions of gendered spectatorship and the relations of patriarchal power "inscribed" in the movie text.

As well as opening out new fields, psychoanalytic theory reconsidered some traditional areas of concern for movie analysts, including the movie image itself. Work on the image had been relatively marginal to structuralism and semiotics while they attended to other levels of discourse: character function, editing, the directorial code. Psychoanalysis redirected attention toward questions of mise-en-scène and point of view, not only in relation to the questions of "classic realism" explored by Colin MacCabe (discussed in chapter 8), but also in terms of pleasurability and unconscious functioning. They were increasingly understood as "eroticized" elements, representing and playing upon their viewers' "scopophilic" desire, and triggering fantasies of gratifying engagement with the movie and its protagonists. In a much-quoted passage from his essay "The Imaginary Signifier," Christian Metz proposd that:

> the cinematic institution is not just the cinema industry (which works to fill cinemas, not to empty them), it is also the mental machinery – another industry – which spectators "accustomed to the cinema" have internalized historically and which has adapted them to the consumption of films. The institution is outside us and inside us, indistinctly collective and intimate, sociological and psychoanalytic.[48]

Cine-psychoanalysis promised to make an enduring contribution to the understandings of Hollywood's ideological operations by exploring the relationship between the "economies of desire" set in play by a movie and the capitalist economy that financed it. In practice, however, psychoanalytic criticism took little interest in the industrial conditions under which cinema was produced and consumed.

In stark contrast to auteurism and genre analysis, psychoanalytic criticism proceeded not by dividing its object of study into smaller units of inquiry (a director's oeuvre, a genre) but by addressing supposedly universal aspects of the medium itself. Work by Jean-Louis Baudry and others on the minimal "apparatus" of cinema (a network initially defined by relations between the screen, spectator, and projector and later expanded to incorporate the spectator's "metapsychology") sought to understand movie-watching as a state akin to what psychoanalysis understood dreaming to be. The analogy between dream and viewing was crucial to the application of psychoanalysis to cinema. On the strength of this analogy, the rhetorical power of psychoanalysis was appropriated by film study as if it had the authority of an established science. Baudry emphasized some of the same circumstances of viewing that Thomas Elsaesser raised in his discussion of cinematic narrative: the spectator's motor inhibition, for instance (see chapter 8). But unlike Elsaesser, Baudry related these conditions of viewing to those of the dream, and then extended the analogy to compare the movie screen to the "dream screen": the blank background on which, according to some psychoanalysts, dreams seem to be projected. Baudry suggested that cinema, like the dream, was an expression of a nostalgic desire to return to earlier stages of psychosexual development. He thus redefined popular understandings of the movies as "wish-fulfillment" as "regression":

> the dream screen is the dream's hallucinatory representation of the mother's breast on which the child used to fall asleep after nursing. In this way, it expresses a state of complete satisfaction while repeating the original condition of the oral phases in which the body did not have limits of its own, but extended undifferentiated from the breast.[49]

Apparatus theory also engaged and shifted debates about realism, since it credited the **cinematic apparatus** with delivering an impression of reality so charged as to be, like dreams, more than real, an effect Baudry described as the "fantasmatization of objective reality":[50]

> The cinema can achieve its greatest power of fascination over the viewer not simply because of its impression of reality, but more precisely because this impression of reality is intensified by the conditions of the dream. The cinema thus creates an impression of reality, but this is a total effect – engulfing and in a sense "creating" the spectator – which is much more than a simple replica of the real.[51]

The engulfing, "womblike" sensation of cinema's "reality-effect" restaged childlike experiences of unrestraint and libidinous expression, and the "real" that cinema's impression of reality addressed was seen to be defined by unconscious rather than conscious mental activity. Metaphors of "projection" favored by the discourse of psychoanalysis helped to secure the analogies involved, and a long history of popular association between cinema and dream lent work at this level considerable persuasive force.

It was a short step from work on the "apparatus" as dream-state to work on the movie as dreamlike, and writing soon emerged that examined the ways in which textual style or technique could be considered analogous to the processes of the "dream-work" (the dreamer's production of unconscious fantasy). Could movie form be comparable to the "secondary revisions" of the dream-work which impose coherence on the raw material of the dream? To cine-psychoanalysts, montage and editing seemed akin to Freud's description of the "dream-work" processes of displacement and condensation, through which unconscious desire is transformed into the manifest content of the dream. Some theorists went on to speculate that these devices of "invisible" narration could actually grant the movies the power of objectifying unconscious process itself. For Christian Metz the spectator's recognition of this "externalization" accounts for much of the joy of moviegoing: "The spectator, during the projection, puts himself into a state of lessened alertness (he is at a show; nothing can happen to him); in performing the social act of 'going to the cinema,' he is motivated in advance to lower his ego defenses a notch and not to reject what he would reject elsewhere."[52]

Less radically, the psychoanalytic approach could narrow its focus still further, to consider the contents of a movie. Storylines could be considered in terms of their Oedipal trajectories, or characters construed as "patients" driven by unconscious motivations and drives. In a final move, the supposed "author" of a movie could be redefined as a point of "enunciation," from which the process of cinematic fantasy and desire emanates. Just as psychoanalysis could disinter the latent structural content of a dream from the confusing manifest content of the dream's surface narrative content, cine-psychoanalysis could interpret recurrent plot motifs or stylistic traits as symptoms of deep-seated anxiety and neurosis made manifest unknowingly in the organization of movie aesthetics.[53]

The Spectator

> The psychoanalytic conception of the cinema spectator is the matrix from which all other descriptions in the field flow. But this is a very particular kind of viewer . . . psychoanalytic film theory discusses film spectatorship in terms of the circulation of desire. . . . [It] sees the viewer not as a person, a flesh-and-blood individual, but as an artificial construct, produced and activated by the cinematic apparatus.
>
> Sandy Flitterman-Lewis[54]

Without doubt the most enduring contribution of cine-psychoanalysis to movie criticism was its formulation of a theory of film spectatorship. Most prominent at this level was Christian Metz, who had moved on from his work in early semiotics to examine the relationship between cinematic signs and their users in the actual movie theater. Metz's later work concluded that audiences acquire the competences necessary for understanding movies not only from their exposure to convention over a period of time, but also by recognizing in the apparatus of cinema structures that which they already "know" from their own psychosexual pasts. Invoking the psychoanalysis of Jacques Lacan's "mirror stage," Metz theorized that cinema engages us by recalling decisive moments in our development as subjects. For Lacan, the mirror stage was a crucial element in childhood development, in which the child acquires its sense of autonomous identity when it encounters its own mirror image and identifies with its reflection. Like the mirror, the cinema screen confers a sense of perceptual mastery on its spectator, but according to Metz that sense of mastery is based on a misapprehension, as the spectator falsely identifies with the cinematic apparatus.[55]

The figure of the spectator is central to cine-psychoanalysis, but this spectator bears little resemblance to the audience studied by sociologists or market researchers, or to the viewer proposed by Formalist theory, who consciously constructs hypotheses about narrative development. The spectator of psychoanalytic film theory is not a person, but a conceptual "space." Like a seat in the movie theater, this subject position is "empty," in the sense that anyone can occupy it. And just as every seat in a well-designed movie theater will provide an interchangeable view of the screen, so the experience of each spectator is identical, since the subject position that is "the spectator" is constructed by the cinematic apparatus. Subjected to a movie, the empty space of the spectator becomes "productive" as the spectator identifies both with the act of looking and with the apparatus that stages the spectacle. Metz constructed an elaborate diagram of a movie's projection to propose that cinema constructs the spectator as an apparently unified subject:

> There are two cones in the auditorium: one ending on the screen and starting both in the projection box and in the spectator's vision insofar as it is projective, and one starting from the screen and "deposited" in the spectator's perception insofar as it is introjective (on the retina, a second screen). When I say that "I see" the film, I mean thereby a unique mixture of two contrary currents: the film is what I receive, and it is also what I release, since it does not pre-exist my entering the auditorium and I only need close my eyes to suppress it. Releasing it, I am the projector, receiving it, I am the screen; in both these figures together, I am the camera, which points and yet which records.[56]

Metz's spatial representation of spectator–movie relations as mutually productive suggested that the ideological importance of this structure lies in cinema's re-securing of our self-hood while mystifying its own role in the process. Hollywood's cinematic apparatus simultaneously proffers us attractive illusions of ourselves as unified and autonomous identities and positions us as its ideological subjects. By masking its own point of enunciation as the spectator's point of access to the fiction, the movie deludes us into imagining that its discourse is in fact our own. Metz therefore saw the viewer's "primary" identification in cinema as being not with the characters in a movie, but with "the (invisible) seeing agency which *puts forward* the story and shows it to us": that is, with the movie itself as a discourse. "Insofar as it abolishes all traces of the subject of enunciation, the traditional film succeeds in giving the spectator the impression that he is himself that subject, but in a state of emptiness and absence, of pure visual capacity."[57]

This may all seem very remote from our discussions of moviegoing, consumption, and the economic logics of the Hollywood movies. At least for non-believers, cine-psychoanalysis constructs a complex and highly indirect theoretical edifice on the basis of a suggestive but also questionable analogy between viewing and dreaming. Seldom does it attempt to justify its project: that is, to explain why we should psychoanalyze cinema. Its critics argue that its reasoning by analogy becomes hermetically self-fulfilling, in the sense that the cinema it constructs can be understood only in the terms proposed by its analogy to the dream.[58] Arguing that psychoanalytic theory was originally intended "to conceptualize irrational behavior," Noel Carroll questions why it should be deployed to explain behavior, like attending and understanding movies, that could equally be explained by "conscious or merely tacit intentions, beliefs, and reasonings."[59] But whatever else cine-psychoanalysis has achieved, it has helped to illustrate the profound difficulties involved in accounting for the taken-for-granted pleasures that are inherent in moviegoing in other than anecdotal terms. The enduring importance of psychoanalytic investigations into cinema lies not in their conclusions about its psychic "regime" (is movie-watching akin to voyeurism?) or the unconscious preoccupations of this or that practitioner (is Alfred Hitchcock a sadist or a misogynist?), but rather in the extreme example they offer of a "symptomatic" criticism making the assumption that surface meanings can only be understood as symptoms of deeper realities waiting to be uncovered by the discerning analyst.

The origins of cine-psychoanalysis within the New Left of the late 1960s ensured that the deeper reality it uncovered would be understood politically as the operation of a dominant ideology, in which mainstream cultural forms such as cinema were seen to operate in the service of ruling interests, to mystify its consumers and inhibit the consciousness-raising that could lead to liberation. To established theories of ideological subordination, psychoanalysis contributed an account of how this process might be made pleasurable, and how subjects might be relied upon to cooperate with their own containment. We may leave sociologists and political scientists to argue over why cultural criticism insisted on the primacy of ideological struggle. More crucial from our perspective is the obsessive desire to identify the operation of ideology at the most basic levels of cinema, and so reiterate the disempowerment of the moviegoer that this implies. Jean-Louis Baudry's account, for example, seems to leave little space for political contradiction within cinema, as it locates the operation of ideology in the very mechanics of film projection. Baudry reads the very illusion of movement produced by the camera/projector as symptomatic of a fundamental denial by the "apparatus" that the moving image has a material base. Therefore, he argues, it performs an act of ideological deception no filmmaker can escape. The concept of the spectator as predetermined by the ideological operations of the cinematic apparatus, and constituted at the level of unconscious fantasy, also proposes an extreme account of cinema as a manipulative practice.

Whatever else it signified, writing of this kind was indicative of a profound political paranoia, far in excess of any governing the protective politics of the Hollywood film industry. Albeit supported by a very much more sophisticated methodology, cine-psychoanalyis's account of what cinema did to its spectators resembled nothing so much as the conspiratorial fantasies of the HUAC investigators in 1947. Rather than the "eight or ten Harvard law degrees" that Jack Warner had suggested, you now needed years of theoretical study to find out what the "innuendoes and double meanings" meant. In part the very "unprovability" of the theses of cine-psychoanalysis (how could one test an assertion about the operation of the cinematic unconscious empirically?) could only serve to feed this paranoia. Despite, or perhaps because of, the depth of its paranoid assumptions, a psychoanalytically grounded model of cinema provided the dominant framework within which academic criticism approached Hollywood in the dozen years between the mid-1970s and the mid-1980s. Because these years saw the consolidation of film studies as an academic discipline, cine-psychoanalysis has been a determining influence on the priorities that the discipline has established for itself. Film studies has often led other humanities subjects in its adoption of theory, to the extent that in many academic settings, the study of cinema has been justified because of the theory that has underpinned it rather than through any claims about the intrinsic value of the movies themselves. At the same time, however, many of the fundamental assumptions of the attempts of "Grand Theory" to explain cinema as a total phenomenon have become subject to increasing question. More recent moves in the history of movie criticism suggest that cine-psychoanalysis may, in the long run, prove to have been important mostly for what it has provoked.

Theories after Poststructuralism

> What permits the endless variety of meanings to be generated from a film are in large part the critical practices themselves . . . The ambiguity sought by the New Critic, the polysemy praised by the structuralist, and the indeterminacy posited by the post-structuralist are largely the product of the institution's interpretive habits.
>
> David Bordwell[60]

Despite its aspirations to deal with questions of spectatorship, cine-psychoanalysis ultimately operated as a text-centered theory. Work on the "apparatus," film style, or subject positioning rarely left space for an account of the actual, socialized subject who might take up Daniel Dayan's "empty spot predefined" by the address of a movie. Nor did it consider the status of the spectator as part of a wider viewing collective such as an audience. Analogies between cinema and dream led Metz to define the cinema experience as "privatized," despite the evidence that many different forms of cinema event – cult cinema, for instance – involve a sharing of experience between audience members. Finally, cine-psychoanalysis seldom recognized any historical dimension to questions of spectatorship, and very few analysts were prepared to suggest how the psychic structures invoked by Baudry, Metz, and others might have changed over time. Rather, in an echo of André Bazin's formulation of movie history as a continuing struggle for an ever-fuller effect of the real, Metz saw movies as satisfying a transhistorical desire for contact and presence, with moving pictures as only one example of a far longer line of projection apparatuses that stretched back to ancient times.

Attempts to deal with the frustrating "unprovability" of cine-psycho-analysis became evident from the early 1980s. As structuralist models seemed to reach points of exhaustion, a host of new "poststructural" methods began to make inroads into the critical edifice of cine-psycho-analysis, most importantly through a rejection of the totalizing claim that the spectator was determined by the apparatus and the text. Feminist criticism led the way in arguing for a range of ideological positions from which a suitably equipped spectator could read against the grain to produce a "subversive reading." **Poststructuralism** can best be understood as a reaction to structuralism's attempts to establish broad, incorporative theoretical procedures. Rather than being a theory in itself, post-structuralism proposed a mode of inquiry concerned with what had been left out of, or repressed by, structuralism's totalizing systems. Instead, it argued for a "decentering" of the attention paid to the structures of a text, and a deconstruction of textual meaning. Although post-structuralism involved a rejection of the structuralist claim to scientific status, it also evolved out of structuralism's concerns and shared several of its fundamental assumptions. Cine-psychoanalysis was itself in part a poststructuralist theory. Jacques Lacan is usually considered a poststructuralist, and the concerns of cine-psychoanalysis with repressed meaning and with the fissures of a text were typically poststructuralist preoccupations. But the origins of cine-psychoanalysis in apparatus theory indicate its attachment to structuralist Grand Theory; cine-psychoanalysis demonstrates the difficulty of establishing categorical distinctions between structuralism and its successors.

Rejecting the claim to science allowed poststructuralist critics to abandon the requirement to prove theoretical precepts. Rather, they came to rely on different bodies of assumptions held within a number of distinct critical communities. In imitation of other established disciplines, distinct "schools" of critical thought, with increasingly diverse interests, emerged and consolidated. By the mid-1980s it was more appropriate to talk of film theories than Film Theory. At the same time, however, the various approaches came to share a canon of "texts" now generally acknowledged to be central to the field of film studies. Through the canon, different methodologies communicate about (rather than with) each other; and the role of the canon is to permit this common body of cross-reference. Yet the poststructuralist Balkanization of the empire of Grand Theory has produced a situation in which canonic texts proliferate interpretations and accommodate multiple meanings that, if not exactly mutually unintelligible, are under no obligation to speak to each other. As Deborah Linderman writes of her account of *Vertigo* (1958): "my remarks . . . resonate both with [Robin] Wood's and [Tania] Modleski's, but although I traverse some of the same features of the text as they do, my analysis is very differently elaborated."[61] The critical capacity to discover a limitless plurality of meanings within a movie is one important element in the movie's qualification for the canon. The more it can be read and re-read to fuel critical argument, and the more it can sustain multiple but not necessarily conflicting meanings, the better. But as David Bordwell's comment at the head of this section suggests, the source of these multiple meanings lies in the questions the critic asks and the methods by which she or he tries to answer them. In this environment the reader of criticism becomes another kind of consumer, exercising choice among a range of critical styles and conclusions.

Debates about authorship evaporated in the 1970s, more because poststructuralist criticism bypassed them than because the idea of directorial authorship was recognized as being an historically inaccurate account of Hollywood production. But criticism continues to need an authority for the text, a figure for the critic to engage with, argue with, and reassess, and if the auteur theory is surely dead, so are the debates over "the death of the author" initiated by Roland Barthes and Michel Foucault at the outset of poststructuralism.[62] Hardly any academic critic would now call himself or herself an auterist. Nevertheless, the great majority of academic criticism continues to be written as if the director could be named as the author of the text – for instance, in the normal critical practice of citing movies as "Sean Cunningham's *Friday the 13th*," or attaching the director's name in parentheses after the title: "*City Slickers* (Ron Underwood)."[63] The cinematic author may now be understood, in theory, as the name of a sign, a matrix of textual devices, or "merely a term in the process of reading and spectating," but critical practice continues to treat it as if it were a person.[64] In her book on "Hitchcock and Feminist Theory," for instance, Tania Modleski declares her intention of treating "Hitchcock's work as the expression of cultural authority and practices existing to some extent outside the artist's control."[65] But Hitchcock is an active presence in Modleski's text, placing the camera, arousing sympathy for characters in the spectator, offering opinions on the sanity or otherwise of "his" characters, and even imagining himself bisexual.[66]

In Modleski's book, as in most writing on Hitchcock, the term "Hitchcock" functions as a synonym for "Hitchcock's films" or the "Hitchcock text." The relationship between the term and the person of the director is seldom discussed in poststructuralist criticism, but as Virginia

Wright Wexman suggests, the canonic status of several "Hitchcock" texts from the 1950s and early 1960s attests to "the continuing vitality of the auteur theory."[67] Slavov Zizek, for instance, responds to reproaches that his analysis elevates Hitchcock into "a God-like demi-urge who masters even the smallest details of his work" by suggesting that this is merely a critical strategy, in which "Hitchcock functions as the 'subject supposed to know.' " For Zizek, the strategy is justified because it is theoretically productive.[68] But if "Hitchcock" here becomes no more than an element in a Lacanian theoretical procedure, the critic-analyst assumes the authority to speak in the name of the author. In doing so, the critic both claims the authority of the author for his or her interpretation, and simultaneously attributes responsibility for that interpretation to a textual source. In his essay on *Vertigo*, for example, William Rothman claims that although "the *Vertigo* that emerges . . . in this essay is not the film as viewers ordinarily experience it," his reading accounts for that ordinary experience, explaining it as "the experience that fails to acknowledge Hitchcock and hence misses *his* meaning" (italics added).[69] Although Modleski dismisses Rothman's claims for Hitchcock's "masterful" control over the spectator as a form of male masochism, and calls for feminist critics to resist being "absorbed by male authority and male texts . . . and withhold the authorial acknowledgment the texts exact," she nevertheless concludes her book by identifying herself as one of "Hitchcock's daughters," sharing a "monstrous father" with Patricia Hitchcock and other female viewers.[70]

Hitchcock is evidently an exceptional case, and one reason for the canonic status of so many of the movies he directed may well be the extent to which these movies bear the distinctive marks of an authorial, indeed a self-referential presence that encourages the terminological slippage between Hitchcock and "Hitchcock." The canonic status of Hitchcock the auteur-enunciator also depends on the aesthetic distance between these movies and Classical Hollywood narrative, and the extent to which "his films constantly denaturalize themselves, calling attention to the components of film production, in order to point up the 'enunciated', discursive, constructed quality of film story."[71] But the Hitchcock persona seems to alter with each critic. Ann West suggests a far more hesitant figure than William Rothman's "master": for her, Hitchcock "seems to have been gently calling attention to the idea of plot as contrivance."[72]

Poststructuralism's lack of interest in historical questions has allowed critics to largely ignore the extent to which the figure of "Hitchcock" was a deliberate commercial creation. Before Hitchcock the author there was Hitchcock the marketing strategy, promoting the visibly self-conscious presence of Alfred Hitchcock in the movies he directed.[73] This marketing strategy continued after Hitchcock's death, transmuted into critical accounts of self-reflexivity but more materially present in the commercial activity surrounding the re-release, in the early 1980s, of five previously unavailable Hitchcock movies, including *Rear Window* (1954) and *Vertigo*. For the Hitchcock estate, these movies quite literally constituted capital

Scottie Ferguson (James Stewart) questions Madeleine Elster (Kim Novak) in *Vertigo* (1958). Universal (courtesy The Ronald Grant Archive)

that accumulated both commercial and aesthetic value because they were withheld from circulation. In their scarcity they acquired something of the aura of art, contributing to the fetishization of Hitchcock "as a lost figure of high culture."[74] Their re-release capitalized on "Hitchcock's" critical reputation, and the volumes of criticism that followed represented an investment in Hitchcock's canonic status by both the exhibition industry and the critical industry of academic interpretation. However, if *Vertigo*'s second appearance has released a range of meanings unavailable to its audiences in 1958, it is equally the case, as Virginia Wright Wexman points out, that some elements of its appeal to its original audiences, including its function as a tour guide to San Francisco, have been ignored by later analysts.[75]

At the same time that this capitalization on Hitchcock's creative persona is typical of Hollywood's commercial opportunism, it also makes these movies exceptions to the norms of Hollywood, precisely because of the emphasis placed on the name of their author. Our analysis has suggested that part of the pleasure of movies lies in their apparent *lack* of an authorial voice, which makes it possible for their consumers to value them for whatever they care to take: for Grace Kelly's dresses in *Rear Window*, for the way Robert Mitchum drives one-handed around parking lots in *The Friends of Eddie Coyle* (1973), or for Susan Sarandon's T-shirt, jeans, and "unruly red hair" behind the wheel in *Thelma and Louise* (1991).[76] In that sense any movie is an infinitely open text, a showcase of endless incidental pleasures encouraging, rather than repressing, consumer choice. Poststructuralist criticism enacts this consumer choice, selecting aspects of the text for its ruminations, and justifying its choice by the psychoanalytic proposal that, as Slavov Zizek says of Hitchcock, *"everything has meaning* in his films, the seemingly simplest plot conceals unexpected philosophical delicacies."[77] Frederic Jameson, for example, finds a "peculiar and obsessive" pattern in the serrated grooves of the furrowed cornfield and Mount Rushmore carvings in *North by Northwest* (1959),[78] while Lucretia Knapp seeks to redirect attention to the "relatively unexplored" issue of lesbianism in Hitchcock. In exploring lesbian positions of spectatorship, and how a lesbian interpretation "may focus on other moments or gazes" within *Marnie* (1964), Knapp suggests that "A lesbian perspective opens up the possibility of reading the ambiguities in a film like *Marnie,* seeing what is in a film in a different way and therefore constructing a different text than the heterosexual eye might observe." At the same time, however, she asserts her critical position against what she takes to be a dominant one. The female space and female voices in *Marnie,* she suggests, "have been repressed or overlooked" by Raymond Bellour, "who sees in the film nothing but a male oedipal drama." In preferring her own analysis to Bellour's, Knapp cites authorial authority: "The explicitly Freudian text [Bellour uncovers] is almost too obvious, as if Bellour's discovery is no more than Hitchcock's trap."[79]

Poststructuralist criticism has therefore come to practice what we described in chapter 8 as the sophisticated viewer's fatalistic act of resistance to the inevitability of a movie's moralistic ending. It converts that viewer's momentary optimism that for once the narrative will end with transgression triumphant into a critical "re-reading" of the text. Interpretations of this kind have come to constitute what David Bordwell has called the current practice of "ordinary criticism," the equivalent in humanities disciplines of what Thomas Kuhn called "normal science": the application of established problem-solving routines to expand and fill out a realm of knowledge.[80] Paul Willemen has, however, noted the tendency of such criticism to reach "the familiar conclusion that the 'text' under analysis is full of contradictory tensions, requires active readers and produces a variety of pleasures."[81]

This re-reading is, however, all too often achieved at the expense of the audience. According to Slavov Zizek:

> If . . . the pleasure of the modernist interpretation consists in the effect of recognition which "gentrifies" the disquieting uncaniness of its object ("Aha, now I see the point of this apparent mess!"), the aim of the postmodernist treatment is to estrange its very initial homeliness: "You think what you see is a simple melodrama even your senile granny would have no difficulties in following? Yet without taking into account . . . /the difference between

symptom and *sinthom*; the structure of the Borromean knot; the fact that Woman is one of the Names-of-the-Father; etc., etc./ you've totally missed the point!"[82]

Although Zizek's poststructuralist criticism studies objects available for universal consumption, the practice by which their meanings are determined has become more elitist than ever. While the distinction between high and low culture has ceased to be tenable at the level of the aesthetic object under examination, much academic criticism has nevertheless sought to maintain a distinction at the level of reception. The Hitchcock who is Zizek's "subject supposed to know" is almost certainly unrecognizable to the moviegoer ignorant of the difference between symptom and *sinthom*. That, perhaps, measures the distance that criticism has traveled from Eric Rohmer's declaration in 1957 that the goal of *Cahiers du Cinéma* was to "enrich" its readers' reflections on the movies they saw.[83]

Neoformalism

> The neoformalist critic assumes that spectators are able to think for themselves, and that criticism is simply a tool for helping them to do it better in the area of the arts, by widening the range of their viewing abilities.
>
> Kristin Thompson[84]

In the mid-1980s, as poststructuralism questioned the grand edifice of Film Theory from within, it also came under siege from without. The obfuscations and jargon-laden language of semiotics and cine-psychoanalysis had often been attacked by journalist critics and historians, but these attacks seldom possessed any degree of theoretical sophistication and were easily dismissed. By 1985 this situation had changed, as an alternative theoretical paradigm challenged many of the fundamental assumptions of cine-psychoanalysis. The new paradigm, **neoformalism**, took its inspiration and many of its theoretical premises from the work of a group of Russian literary critics of the 1920s known as the **Formalists**. These premises were integrated with an understanding of viewing activity informed by the branches of psychology concerned with perception and cognition rather than with psychoanalysis. Like cine-psychoanalysis, neoformalism understood cinema as a system, but as an essentially rational rather than irrational one. "Contrary to psychoanalytic criticism," wrote Kristin Thompson, "I assume that film viewing is composed mostly of nonconscious, preconscious and conscious activities. Indeed we may define the viewer as a hypothetical entity who responds actively to cues within the film on the basis of automatic perceptual processes and on the basis of experience."[85]

The claims for neoformalism were argued in David Bordwell's 1985 book, *Narration in the Fiction Film*, and put into critical practice there and in

The Classical Hollywood Cinema, co-written by Bordwell, Janet Staiger, and Kristin Thompson and also published in 1985. The first part of Thompson's 1988 book, *Breaking the Glass Armor*, provides a concise and accessible account of neoformalism's premises, and its arguments with psychoanalytical approaches.[86] We have referred frequently to the work of these scholars throughout our account of Hollywood, and the principal tenets of neoformalism are outlined in chapter 8. Bordwell's critique of cine-psychoanalysis, amplified by that of Noel Carroll, has also informed our writing earlier in this chapter. Much of our account of Hollywood concurs with a neoformalist approach, differing mainly in emphasis. Some of these differences have already surfaced: where neoformalism understands Hollywood to be primarily concerned with narrating stories, we have seen narration as being one among a range of pleasures that a movie offers its audience, and not necessarily the most important.[87] Our account of the viewer as actively recognizing cues and constructing hypotheses from the movie accords with a neoformalist analysis, but our viewer is more often distracted from the narrative, or perhaps more independent of a movie's linear temporal progression. These are, however, differences in emphasis rather than incompatibilities. Our larger disagreements with neoformalism have to do with our pursuit of a different object of inquiry.

Neoformalism is an aesthetic theory, and as such it is concerned with the aesthetic processes of cinema, with film as an aesthetic system. Our object of inquiry is in some ways narrower and in others broader. In chapter 1 we distinguished Hollywood from other cinemas on grounds that were not primarily aesthetic, but rather industrial and economic, and we might reiterate now that our specific concern has been with Hollywood, not with film as a medium or cinema as a formal category. At the same time, our concern to understand Hollywood as a cultural phenomenon has frequently taken us outside the limits of purely aesthetic inquiry into questions of ideology and power. Neoformalism positions such questions as part of the "background" to its principal concern, which is to analyze the formal relationships within an artwork.

In *Making Meaning*, Bordwell suggests that one type of meaning that viewers construct from a movie is the *"repressed* or *symptomatic"* meaning that the movie divulges "involuntarily":

> Taken as individual expression, symptomatic meaning may be treated as the consequence of the artist's obsessions (for example, *Psycho* as a worked-over fantasy of Hitchcock's). Taken as part of a social dynamic, it may be traced to economic, political, or ideological processes (for example, *Psycho* as concealing the male fear of woman's sexuality).[88]

Bordwell's terminology invokes a psychoanalytic context for the interpretation of symptomatic meanings, as does his example. But in the same way that in chapter 8 we proposed an extension of the Formalist category of artistic motivation, here we would subdivide the broad category of symptomatic meaning to distinguish among different types of cultural signification – for instance, between the unstated ideological assumptions about the relation between idealism and political practice in *Mr Smith Goes to Washington* (1939) and its unstated assumptions about patriarchy. If our consumerist critical practice needs more categories here than neoformalism does, this largely reflects our greater emphasis on the cultural and ideological functions of entertainment cinema.

Neoformalism, and Bordwell's work in particular, has attracted much more vituperative criticism than this. Precisely because neoformalism provided itself with an alternative theoretical base from which to question cine-psychoanalysis, it was first of all seen as a challenge to "contemporary film theory." As cine-psychoanalysis fragmented, neoformalism was rapidly promoted into an orthodoxy less by its advocates than by some of its opponents, who preferred to see themselves dissenting from an orthodox doctrine rather than practicing one. Critiques of neoformalism have in the main focused on its self-declared limitations. In the conclusion to *Narration in the Fiction Film*, Bordwell suggests that his "partial theory of narrative in fictional cinema" makes no attempt to address "issues such as sexuality or fantasy" or to answer "broader cultural, economic, or ideological questions about the filmmaking institution."[89] Those who see neoformalism as a new orthodoxy, however, fear that its disinclination to consider such questions implies that the questions themselves are in danger of disappearing from the critical agenda. To them, neoformalism is insufficiently radical. Bill Nichols, for instance, sees in its appropriation of cognitive theory a claim to scientific accuracy and objectivity, but a claim made at the expense of any consideration of history or subjectivity in a system "that treats narrative as data or information for genderless, classless, stateless 'processors,' " rather than "gendered, historically situated subjects whose very being is at stake within the arena of history."[90] Critiques of Bordwell in *MOVIE* have similarly seen neoformalism as seeking to make criticism a scientific practice. V.F. Perkins argues forcibly that interpretation must not be understood as an attempted proof, but as "a description of aspects of the film with suggested understandings of some of the ways they are patterned." "The interesting meanings of films," he argues, are not discovered by a critical practice that extracts from them "statements which are hidden but otherwise resemble messages ... They consist rather in attitudes, assessments, viewpoints – balances of judgment on the facts and behavior portrayed."[91]

These arguments recapitulate the debates around structuralism's claim to science in the early 1970s, and also invoke more enduring debates about the provision of a scientific or theoretical basis for work in the humanities. The claim to science – a claim that, importantly, neoformalism does not make for itself – has primarily been a rhetorical one, defining the opposite pole to that of complete critical subjectivity. Critical theories are, however, best not understood as attempts at scientific theory, since they lack some of the essential features of such theory: they cannot, for instance, be subject to experimental disproof. However, a critical methodology may be judged by such criteria as clarity, rigor, consistency, its use of evidence, and a knowledge of its limitations. Neoformalism's project of "a historical poetics of cinema" is not an attempt to reformulate an all-inclusive Grand Theory, precisely because of the self-imposed limitations that its antagonists have understood as its weaknesses. As Thompson describes it, it is a "modest approach," seeking only to explain the realm of the aesthetic and its relation to the world.[92] In this less intimidating form, it can readily coexist with other approaches, particularly those seeking answers to questions concerning the cultural and ideological function of cinema. As Barbara Klinger suggests, textual analysis does not necessarily have to claim that the text determines or constitutes its spectator. It can restrict its activity to describing the textual features and forces that influence a viewer's act of reception.[93]

From Reception to History

In reaction to the often conscious ahistoricism of poststructuralism, a renewed interest in film history has recently given fresh attention to neglected questions of reception, audience, and movie exhibition.[94] Along with neoformalism, this work distanced itself from psychoanalysis by its interest in the *conscious* activities of both audience members and industry practitioners. Its dual authorities were cognitive psychology and the archival, historical record of the motion picture industry itself. Paralleling the development of New Historicism and reader-response criticism in literary studies in the 1980s, what became known as **reception studies** operated with a variety of scales of reference; from consideration of the individual reader or viewer to the group audience, defined either by particular traits of their subjectivity such as race or gender, or by a shared historical setting. Most of this work acknowledged a debt to neoformalism's confident break with psychoanalysis, and also made use of the insights of cognitive psychology.

In her account of the "return" of the reader to the agenda of literary criticism, Elizabeth Freund explains that aesthetic reception theory assumes that perception involves an act of interpretation, and that the idea of the "text-in-itself" is an empty one, because a poem or a movie cannot be understood in isolation from the act of its interpretation. Reader-response criticism had its foundations in the branch of philosophy called phenomenology, which "concerns itself with the relationship between the perceiving individual and the world of things, people, and actions that might be perceived." Phenomenology understands this relationship not as one between "two separate realms connected only by the passive sensory mechanisms of the individual," but rather as "inextricably linked aspects of the process by which we know anything."[95] Phenomenology describes that process as one of "intention," a concept which refers to the conscious direction of sense-making faculties toward the surrounding world. The subject exercises intention and makes sense of the world in perceiving, and is committed to "consistency building" and the fabrication of rational explanation. A study in the aesthetics of reception might therefore be a matter of studying the ways in which a movie stimulates and regulates an "intending" viewer.

These issues have been implicit in most of our discussions of individual movies in this book. In the Hollywood movie, "intention" is largely stimulated by the creation of quite deliberate lacks in the viewer's knowledge, opening gaps or "indeterminacies" for the viewer to fill by constructing hypotheses about the presence of latent relationships and meanings. Our account of controlled ambiguity in *Casablanca* (1942) would be an instance of this at work, and some reception theorists refer to the result of this process as a particular "concretization" of the text. Studies in the aesthetic reception of Hollywood seek to establish the systematic bases on which indeterminacy might be structured to produce viewer participation. In *The Role of the Reader*, Umberto Eco stresses that a reader's experience of conventions enables him or her to resolve indeterminacies with some confidence. As a result, the author "has to foresee a model of the possible reader (hereafter Model Reader) supposedly able to deal interpretively with the expressions in the same way as the author deals generatively with them."[96] Similarly, in deciding how a storyline should be plotted, a movie's producers can and do presume a level of competence on the part of their audience. This stress on the active participation of the conscious subject places aesthetic reception studies in stark contrast to psychoanalytically based models which see the "constitution" of the viewer as the basic effect of a text or the cinematic apparatus itself.

Identifying a pattern of indeterminacy is one thing, but not all viewers exhibit "model" characteristics or share the same levels of competence. Interpretations are, therefore, always acts of negotiation on the part of the viewer. When the possibility of generalizing "interpretive strategies" to cover shared response to literary texts began to be considered by Stanley Fish and others, it soon became clear that this work could be applied to the role of audiences in the overall system of Hollywood cinema.[97] Among others, Janet Staiger has used historical studies of reception to reconstruct a movie as an *event*, rather than to identify its meaning as an object.[98] This has allowed her to delineate the boundaries – or what Hans Robert Jauss terms the "horizons" – within which a movie has been interpreted.[99] At this level the basic questions being asked are those of relativity (what were the range of interpretations?); constraint (what governed the limits to interpretation?); and appropriateness (at what points did interpretation shade into something resembling a misreading?). Far from narrowing or distilling a movie's meaning, this critical activity recognizes its capacity to generate a spectrum of interpretations. It is, indeed, prepared to appropriate whatever methods of poststructuralist and ideological textual analysis best suit its immediate project, on the understanding that "the connections and difference among the frameworks and perspectives must be theorized."[100]

As an example, Staiger has charted the shifting reception of *The Birth of a Nation* (1915) across its always controversial re-exhibitions. Her account shows how its reception in the late 1930s contrasted sharply with the response to its initial release, and suggests reasons for that shift in interpretation. Controversy originally centered on its racist depiction of African-Americans, with charges of its potentially provocative effects being countered by its producers in terms of its technical expertise, historical accuracy, and balance. In the late 1930s, however, Communist party journalist David Platt argued that the movie was part of a Hollywood conspiracy to divide African-Americans and white Americans against their shared class interests. In its defense, liberal critic Seymour Stern invoked contemporary historical events to support an allegorical reading blind to the race issue. "By paralleling northern carpetbagger politics to fascist totalitarianism and, eventually, to Stalinism, Stern made *The Birth of a Nation* express liberal, democratic values."[101] Staiger traces the movie's subsequent critical history, in which it became a counter in aesthetic debates about whether subject-matter and narrational procedures could be separated, and political arguments about the desirability of limits to free speech. She concludes that the contexts of pre-war isolationism and post-war anti-Communism framed responses to *The Birth of a Nation* which remain as extratextual "encrustations" to be negotiated by present-day viewers of the movie. Rather than exhausting the meaning of the movie, this accumulation of response expands the boundaries of the textuality to which the critic must now respond:

> historicizing the reception of *The Birth of a Nation* transforms the text's polysemy, for the political foundation underlying some of the historical debates becomes more apparent. In the film's later reception, racial attitudes are not autonomous effects; they relate to the political agendas of the debaters, causing strange alliances in which a former progressive defends the film using much of the rhetoric and the arguments of 1915 radical conservatives.[102]

One of the paradoxes of reception studies is that despite their refocusing critical attention from the text to the viewer, they nevertheless operate with a model of the text as their generative point of reference. Most studies of reception turn around "case studies."[103] As Terry Eagleton comments: "For an interpretation to be an interpretation of *this* text and not of some other, it must in some sense be logically constrained by the text itself. The work, in other words, exercises a degree of determinacy over readers' responses to it, otherwise criticism would seem to fall into total anarchy."[104] But the sense of textuality at work in reception studies is a revised one. A movie is seen not as a set of structures (with or without psychoanalytic effects), but as a dense network of responsive incentives awaiting "activiation" by competent moviegoers, reading particular "cues" against "background" knowledges that provide the conditions for its intelligibility. The concern of historical reception studies may then be summarized as the desire to detail the probable sense-making practices of viewers confronted by the network of cues and triggers composing the movie in projection.

In their various guises, reception studies are largely differentiated by the degree of determinacy they are willing to recognize in the text, and indeed by their degree of willingness to accept some independent existence of the text beyond "concretizations" of it. Anxiety around the potentially infinitely "open" text has taken different forms since the mid-1980s. On the one hand neoformalist criticism has sought to identify the objective, irreducible features of the textual schemata, in an attempt to restore the solidity of the text in the face of reader-power. On the other hand, the new historiography has increasingly turned away from texts to a consideration of their discursive and material contexts.

The desire to account for the experience of movie audiences has increasingly drawn movie analysis away from the totalizing theories of Metz and Mulvey toward a plurality of methods with less grandiose ambitions. It has also led to work on smaller-scale and more local accounts of moviegoing. Robert Allen and Douglas Gomery begin their study of movie historiography with a refusal of "superhistory," an account that "could be written if only this or that 'correct' perspective were taken and all the 'facts' of film history uncovered . . . this is a futile task, since the domain of 'all the facts' is infinite."[105] Noel Carroll calls for a similar shift at the level of theory, calling for "theorizing that is 'piece-meal' and 'bottom up' . . . where contemporary film theory presents itself as The Theory of Film . . . I propose film theories . . . with no presumption that these small-scale theories will add up to one big picture."[106] Carroll's call to avoid the "extravagant ambiguity and vacuous abstraction" of semiotic and psychoanalytic theory is echoed in Robert Stam's suggestion that "semiotics has become diasporic, scattered and dispersed among a plurality of movements."[107] It is, however, a sustained commitment to the historical study of Hollywood cinema through its empirical traces that seems likely to provide the most effective restraint on the wilder excesses of poststructuralist invention. A glance through any recent historical account of Hollywood will quickly indicate a commitment to archival research, factual accuracy, and verifiable evidence that was utterly absent from the largely anecdotal and personal histories of earlier periods. As if in flagrant refutation of the "unprovability" of symptomatic criticism (the term used by Bordwell to describe the psychoanalytic critical tradition in which the movie-as-text is examined as a symptom of a cultural condition or an unconscious state), the accumulation of "hard evidence" usually now precedes even the most tentative assertion of historical interpretation. Instead of attempting to understand movies in terms of psychic/transhistorical dreams and wishes, the new historiography aims to chart Hollywood in relation to rather more material and contingent desires, finding form and expression in concrete institutional circumstances.

Criticism in Practice:
Only Angels Have Wings

> The only way to keep a work reasonably fresh upon many repeated viewings is to look for different things in it each time – more subtle and complex things, seen in new ways.
>
> Kristin Thompson[108]

> Not that you're trying to make every scene a great scene, but you try not to annoy the audience. If I can make about five good scenes and not annoy the audience, it's an awfully good picture.
>
> Howard Hawks[109]

One way to see how these different critical approaches have worked is to compare their responses to a single movie or group of movies. What follows is an account of criticism as it has been directed toward the work of one Hollywood director, Howard Hawks, and to just one of the movies directed by him, *Only Angels Have Wings* (1939). In a recent assessment Robert Sklar has suggested that Hawks was "the most successful independent director in Hollywood," working at every major studio, where he managed to flout budget restrictions, ignore production schedules, undermine studio rules, and subvert the established screen personas of the stars with whom he worked.[110] Hawks survived in Hollywood long enough to become the subject of a wide range of different critical approaches, although his reputation and those of his movies have seen considerable fluctuation. He directed his first movie, *The Road to Glory*, in 1927 and his last, *Rio Lobo*, in 1970. He died in 1977.

There is, however, another reason for selecting *Only Angels Have Wings*, one that returns us to the starting point of this book in asking the question, "How do we take Hollywood seriously?" In this context, the question is a sign of film studies' preoccupation with its self-justification and legitimation, constantly seeking to demonstrate its claims to "seriousness" against the surface of the material it studies. On its surface, which is by far the most important part of a Hollywood text, *Only Angels Have Wings* does not aid the critic determined to take it seriously. Set vaguely in the Latin American port of Barranca, recognizable only as the Columbia studio back-lot, it also features papier-mâché Andes mountains, a number of very obvious model planes, and, to the profound embarrassment of any earnest critic, Napoleon the donkey. To those already persuaded by Hollywood or Hawks, *Only Angels Have Wings* appears to be a deeply moving work; to those insufficiently persuaded, the movie, and the very idea of taking it seriously, are only absurd. We want, therefore, to discuss the ways in which critics have evaluated and valued *Only Angels Have Wings*, in order to examine the critical projects in which they were engaged. We shall also add some new consumerist perspectives of our own.

Hawks' well-established industrial reputation as a capable action director is indicated by the steady pattern of his output throughout his career. His early critical reputation, on the other hand, rested on the writings of the group of French film critics associated with *Cahiers du Cinéma* in the 1950s. Jacques Rivette, for instance, maintained that,

> Hawks epitomizes the highest qualities of the American cinema: he is the only American director who knows how to draw a *moral*. His marvelous blend of action and morality is probably the secret of his genius. . . . There seems to be a law behind Hawks' action and editing, but it is a *biological* law like that governing any living being: each shot has a functional beauty, like a neck or an ankle. The smooth orderly succession of shots has a rhythm like the pulsing of blood, and the whole film is like a beautiful body, kept alive by deep, resilient breathing . . . even if he is occasionally drawn to the ridiculous or the absurd, Hawks first of all concentrates on the smell and feel of reality, giving reality an unusual and indeed long hidden grandeur and nobility; how Hawks gives the modern sensibility a classical conscience. The father of *Red River* and *Only Angels Have Wings* is none other than Corneille.[111]

Hawks' reputation among Anglo-American reviewer critics was, however, rather more as a skilled craftsman than as a latter-day Corneille. Most were initially less enthusiastic. Peter John Dyer found *Only Angels Have Wings* "childish, banal, phony and enjoyable," its story "frankly terrible":

> Inside the big cliché are the small ones: the equation of maturity with an acceptance of sudden death; the heroine playing Liszt in the lounge at one a.m.; the stiff upper lip inventory of the dead pilot's belongings; the pseudo tough byplay accompanying the lighting of a cigarette or the flipping of a double headed coin; the probing for the bullet in the hero's shoulder; the nursemaid relationship between him and the old friend too blind to fly.[112]

Manny Farber, one of the best examples of the reviewer as critic, saw Hawks as "a bravado specialist who always makes pictures about a Group," and *Angels* as "a White Cargo melodrama that is often intricately silly." No artist, he suggested, "is less suited to a discussion of profound themes than Hawks, whose attraction to strutting braggarts, boyishly cynical dialogue, and melodramatic fiction always rests on his poetic sense of action."[113]

An altogether more conscious attempt to read Hawks' work as the sign of an authorial presence developed in the United States in the 1960s. In 1961 Andrew Sarris, beginning to shift the discourse of reviewing toward

Bonnie Lee (Jean Arthur) and Jeff Carter (Cary Grant) join the colorful Barrancans in a song of defiance against darkness and chaos in *Only Angels Have Wings* (1939). Columbia (courtesy Kobal)

a more systematic director-based criticism, wrote that in *Only Angels Have Wings*, "the themes of responsibility and expiation are applied to men striving to perform the impossible for purely gratuitous reasons." The movie was:

> the most romantic film of Hawks's career, and its pessimistic mood was the director's last gesture to the spirit of the Thirties reflected in the doomed cinema of Renoir and Carné. . . . In the violent world of Howard Hawks, one has to be good to survive honorably and at least on this level, Hawksian heroes follow the canons of Sophoclean tragedy enunciated by Aristotle more closely than do Blanche du Bois, Willy Loman, and the tormented protagonists of Eugene O'Neill.[114]

By 1968, when Sarris published what was to become perhaps the central statement of Anglo-American auteurism, *The American Cinema: Directors and Directions, 1929–1968*, Hawks' place in Sarris's pantheon was assured.

As if answering Sarris's call for a program of more detailed study of the major Hollywood directors, Robin Wood's book on Hawks, first published in 1967, provided the English-speaking world with its first full-length

study of his work, and a near-archetypal statement of traditional authorial
criticism. Wood's innovation was to examine the Hawksian "oeuvre" as a
whole rather than merely responding pragmatically to individual movies.
He developed his analysis by grouping the movies together not by genre
but by the thematic concerns they evidenced. For film studies the procedure was radical and productive, but in entirely erasing questions of
economics, industry, and technology, it represented only a small step
forward in understanding the movies as specifically "Hollywood" forms.
The book contained a number of strained parallels between the movies and
the novels of Joseph Conrad and others. According to Wood, *Only Angels
Have Wings* was one of the greatest works, because it was one of the most
unified: it was "a completely achieved masterpiece, and a remarkably
inclusive film, drawing together the main thematic threads of Hawks's
work in a single complex web."[115] What were seen as clichés by Dyer and
Farber became for Wood the building blocks of an original aesthetic statement: "That Hawks does not feel himself superior to material many may
find 'corny,' 'melodramatic' or 'banal' is not a sign of inferior intelligence
or sensibility. He responds, directly and spontaneously, to all that is valid
in the genre, assimilates it and transforms it into a means of personal
expression."[116]

For Wood the movie as artwork was a deeply emotional experience, in
which both the artist's and the characters' sensibilities were exposed to the
spectator:

> No one who has seen the film will forget Jeff's singing (with Bonnie's partici-
> pation) of the "Peanut Vendor," as the culmination of the sequence of
> Bonnie's initiation into, and acceptance of, the fliers' code. Joe has been dead
> perhaps an hour. We haven't forgotten, and we know that they haven't. But
> Joe's death has ceased to be the issue: the song becomes a shout of defiance
> in the face of the darkness surrounding human life and the chaos of the
> universe.[117]

In Wood's interpretation, artist and characters speak in a language that is
transparent and expressive, uncluttered by the uncertainties of communication and the instability of meaning so central to post-Saussurean
thought. At the same time, for all its dependence on the conventions and
practices of Hollywood studio cinema, Wood took the movie to be both
"realist" and intensely relevant to our contemporary experience:

> The directness – the vital, spontaneous frankness – with which the characters
> confront and attack each other is enormously affecting, because this urgency
> of contact derives from their constant (not necessarily conscious) sense of the
> imminence of death, of the surrounding darkness, a *physical* intuition that
> prompts them to live, *now*, to the maximum. It is partly this that makes
> Hawks's films, in fact, so modern: in the world of the hydrogen bomb, one
> doesn't have to be an Andes mailplane flier to feel that one may be dead
> tomorrow.[118]

Wood's arguments remain often fascinating and convincing, but within the study there are also signs of doubt about the validity of the basic critical activity. Although Wood values above all a "freshness" and "total lack of self consciousness" in Hawks, his own writing betrays a self-consciousness missing from the reviews and the early writing of Sarris. He apologizes for his tone, concerned that anyone reading his book, "with its talk of fugues, of stylistic and structural rigour, of moral seriousness, will be totally unprepared for the consistently relaxed, delightful, utterly unpretentious film that *Rio Bravo* is. In fact, when it first came out, almost nobody noticed that it was in any sense a serious work of art."[119] Writing of a scene in *Red Line 7000* (1965), he self-consciously identifies the limits of structural criticism: "the beauty of the scene . . . arises not from any content that can be intellectualized and removed from the images, but from the very precise timing of the acting and the editing, form, gesture, expression, intonation, exchanged glance. That is why (the reader had best be warned now) Hawks is ultimately unanalyzable."[120]

Hardly had the auteurist case been made before its methodology came under criticism. Peter Wollen's *Signs and Meaning in the Cinema*, published the same year as Wood's book, offered a sustained assault on traditional critical practices and included a re-reading of Hawks from a structuralist perspective. Instead of talking about Hawks as the author/producer of the movies bearing his name, Wollen regarded Hawks as the "sum of the attitudes manifest in the movies' recurrent structural oppositions." Drawing on the structuralist criticism of Claude Lévi-Strauss, he set about detaching the production of meaning in the movies from any individual's intention and saw it as a fundamentally social phenomenon, addressing the ideologies in which the movie was immersed, as they were represented by these sets of oppositions. The "objective stratum of meaning" Wollen found in Hawks' movies was ideologically rather than authorially determined, and as a result Hawks could only really be understood as a critical construct, an invisible narrational function guiding our response and playing with our subjectivity.[121] Along with this methodological critique went a catalogue of thematic objections: "Hawks sees the all-male community as an ultimate; obviously it is very retrograde. His Spartan heroes are, in fact, cruelly stunted."[122]

Wollen's re-reading of Hawks eventually produced a rejoinder from Wood, who took offense at Wollen's reading of the movies as implicitly, if not explicitly, patriarchal and misogynist. Wood found Wollen's account of supposedly "typical" Hawskian dialogue between men and women as a "destructive parody" of "the specific complexities and qualifications brought by context" to particular dialogues and male–female relationships.[123] Wood saw the attempt to reduce the movies to a single structural pattern as a reduction of the range of available meanings in the movies, and questioned the legitimacy of a structural method more intent on discovering deep-rooted core oppositions than examining the nuances of performance and mise-en-scène. This insistence on the reductionism of the structural approach was to become a keynote in many of the debates that followed; it remains, for instance, the essence of V.F. Perkins' critique of neoformalism.[124] This critical dispute opposed methods as well as evaluations: Wollen's structures against Wood's interpretations; Wollen's oppositions against Wood's unities; Wollen's examination of ideology against Wood's concern with the stature of Hawks as an artist.

Subsequent criticism took other directions. Ideological criticism brought a new concern for the structuring of gender relations in cinema, and when the schema set out by Comolli and Narboni in "Cinema/Ideology/Politics" (discussed in chapter 9) was considered in relation to patriarchy, few Hawks movies appeared to fit easily into category (a). Early feminist criticism of the "images of women" school found crucial ambiguities that troubled the movies' relation to dominant ideology. Molly Haskell saw Hawks as both a product and a critic of sexual puritanism and male supremacy: "In the group experience of filmmaking, he lives out the homo-erotic themes of American life, literature and his own films."[125] Although centered on male groups involved in traditionally "masculine" generic pursuits such as investigating crimes or big-game hunting, many of Hawks' movies also qualified their endorsement of patriarchy by exposing male fears of women and deconstructing masculinity. Haskell, however, did not regard this as a redeeming quality. For her, Hawks was "like the young boy who, recoiling from his mother's kiss, refuses to acknowledge his debt of birth to her and who simultaneously fears revealing his own feelings of love and dependency."[126] In this context *Only Angels Have Wings* was hardly Hawks' central achievement:

> In *Only Angels Have Wings*, Jean Arthur provides an alternative to the all male world of stoical camaraderie on the one hand, and to the destructive femininity represented by Rita Hayworth on the other, but what an alternative! A man dies trying to land a plane in a storm for a date with her, she breaks down in defiance of the prevailing stiff upper lip ethic, and thereafter she hangs around like a puppy dog waiting for Cary Grant to fall in love with her. For female Hawksians, this is the film most difficult to accept. . . . Still, technically, *Only Angels Have Wings* is a transition film. When Mitchell dies, Arthur takes his place, marking the progression of woman from second to first string.[127]

Broadening the terms of this discussion of individual character to encompass the movies' ideological function, Richard Dyer produced a rather different reading:

> What seems to me to be happening in the narrative of these films is that there is a contempt for female characteristics yet an obligation to have female characters. This problem is resolved in the person of the woman who becomes a man (almost) . . . "Femininity" is primarily a social construction and, moreover, a construction made by men. Yet it is a construction men often find it hard to cope with – it is the category into which they project

more fundamental fears about gender, which one can conceive psychoanalytically in terms of castration or socio-historically in terms of men's power over women and simultaneous dependence on them. Hawks' films like most films legitimate this fear. They say, in effect, that women, especially "feminine" women, really should be feared by men; in other words, they take what is a projection from men and claim that it really emanates from women.[128]

Haskell and Dyer reached different conclusions about Hawks' progressiveness by reading the movies at two different levels with two different critical practices. More generally, debates about the relative appropriateness of authorial criticism and "structuralist" approaches (semiotics, narratology, and psychoanalysis) continued behind and between the criticisms we have identified here in relation to one movie. Each new contribution to those ongoing debates drew upon earlier work, challenging or revising it, or introducing new critical methodologies. Traditional criticism persisted. John Belton's work, for example, focused principally on questions of visual style, mise-en-scène, and performance, finding evidence of directorial authority in the "intuitive and organic . . . coherence and integrity" of Hawks' work.[129] By the late 1970s, such traditional approaches could be sustained only with considerable effort under the impact of the new criticisms. Gerald Mast's study of Hawks as "storyteller" described a curious combination of Wood's author and Wollen's narrative function. Although a celebration of Hawks, Mast's book also drew on Wollen's work on the structuring oppositions of the movies, sometimes making for a revealing confrontation between logically opposed critical discourses:

> The stories expose several of our culture's familiar moral and psychological oppositions as either false or facile abstractions. It is perhaps in the nature of our language and our culture to organize meaning paradigmatically; a word or a value can be known only in contrast with its opposite: male and female, adult and child, human and animal, and so forth. Although such polarities may be both linguistically and culturally necessary, Hawks exposes their artificiality by collapsing these abstract dichotomies into specific human actions which reveal that the tidy verbal oppositions are neither so tidy nor so valid as the existence of the words suggests.[130]

Mast described the movies' representation of women as progressive in so far as they exposed the social construction of gender identities in ideology, but reactionary in so far as they suggested that a discourse (specifically that of Hawks the "storyteller") could escape that ideology. Such was the inheritance of the critical revolutions of the 1960s and 1970s for film criticism in the 1980s.

Mast's work was published in 1982, as was Leland Poague's book, *Howard Hawks*. These remain the most recent book-length contributions of any merit to the study of what was once almost unproblematically called Hawks' oeuvre.[131] That in itself is indicative of the relation of auteur studies to the dominant paradigm Noel Carroll identifies as contemporary film theory: the auteur position is far from abandoned, but it is certainly marginalized by debates that have centered on abstract questions of spectator position and ideologies of representation. Hawks' movies are more likely to have been recently assessed in terms of their representation of masculinity, for instance, than in terms of their visual style or thematic concerns. Unlike Hitchcock, Hawks has not been "canonized" or productively reconfigured as a space where discourses intersect. Poststructuralist criticism made few attempts to dissect or deconstruct the "beautiful body" that Jacques Rivette described – perhaps because the body too closely typified Classical Hollywood's lack of formal self-consciousness. However, as cinema criticism has moved away from its initial need to justify its own existence by finding artists in need of discovery, so it has become possible to recognize the existence of Hollywood as a mode of production. Bolstered by such (literally) weighty tomes as *The Classical Hollywood Cinema*, film studies departments can now confidently run courses in the study of Hollywood as a culture industry and system of representation without feeling obliged to defend its reputation as Art.

Yet *Only Angels Have Wings* continues to present the same critical problem: how to take it seriously? In 1975 Donald Willis argued that it was difficult for a critic to justify a claim that the movie's value lay more in the performances of Cary Grant and Jean Arthur than in the story or its themes: "It may seem condescending to say that a work that has been praised for its depth should instead be praised (and just as highly) for its surface excitement, but I don't think it is."[132] For an evaluative criticism of Hollywood, Willis's concerns remain: is it more condescending to assess a Hollywood movie "on its own terms" as no more than a success or failure of surface excitement, or to argue for the critically inventive project of discovering profundity? Whether or not *Only Angels Have Wings* is identified as "Hawksian," the question, symbolized perhaps by Napoleon the donkey, will not disappear.

As is clear from our review of critical responses to *Only Angels Have Wings*, while in one sense the movie has remained constant, any critical notion of it as an autonomous object is clearly a fiction; questions of its Conradian high moral sense, central to its initial recognition in the 1960s, can no longer be posed with much conviction. What, then, might be asked of *Only Angels Have Wings* from within the critical-historical paradigm being advocated in this book? Many of the issues raised by previous critical accounts retain their relevance: the representation of masculinity, femininity, and heroism, for instance, can benefit from a more specific historical contextualization than they have commonly been given. Less studied, but perhaps as important, are more precisely historical issues of representation and its relation to politics that arise from the portrait of Barranca and its inhabitants. Ruth Vasey has argued that *Only Angels Have Wings* presents a typical instance of Hollywood's solution to the problem of representing "the foreign" by the use of a mythical locale. The device of the "mythical kingdom" allowed the industry to deny that its invocation of cultural stereotypes was an offense to foreign countries, since no actual country was being represented. Nevertheless, these representations were often the subject of heated exchanges between foreign embassies, the Motion Picture Producers and Distributors of America, and the State Department. Barranca is such a mythical location constructed out of the most recognizable, and hence most offensive, of cultural stereotypes. It could not possibly have been identified as an actual place without provoking a diplomatic incident. For Vasey, Barranca is "a South American diplomat's nightmare, literally rendered as a banana republic," described in a title as a "port of call for the South American banana boats." As she describes it, the movie opens on

> a crowded wharf bustling with peasants, children, dogs, donkeys, ducks and loads of bananas. Bonnie Lee (Jean Arthur) descends from a boat to experience the local colour, and discovers the natives, who for some reason are holding an impromptu song and dance in the middle of an operating port, to be charming and musical. Nevertheless, she is outraged when approached by two young men (Allyn Joslyn and Noah Beery, Jr.), until she discovers that they are Americans. She exclaims, "Why, I thought you were a couple of – !" (Perhaps "Barrancans" would have sounded too ridiculous). "It sure sounds good to hear something that doesn't sound like pig-latin," she tells them. The party is nearly mown down by a quaint-looking vehicle mounted on rails, driven by hat-waving locals, blasting its horn and pursued by cheering children. Then her companions take her through more throngs of banana-toting natives to meet Dutchy, the "postmaster and leading banker of Barranca."[133]

The element of artifice and self-parody in this setting has not always been recognized, for instance in Robin Wood's claim that the movie's opening shots "vividly create . . . the South American town in which the film is set."[134] While being nowhere in particular and thus a Utopian setting for romance, Barranca is generically South American in a manner that proclaims the ethnic, cultural, and economic superiority of the United States. Although the plot displays no overt interest in questions of hemispheric power relations, it centers on the attempts of Jeff (Cary Grant) to secure contracts for South American airmail routes, the same strategy used by American carriers such as TWA in their contemporaneous corporate colonialism of South American commercial airspace. The movie's politics are on its surface, visible "on the level of performance and decor . . . in the easy sexuality of the local girls, and in the ubiquitous bananas."[135]

Vasey's analysis offers a recontextualization of both the movie and much of its criticism, attaching them to a substantive ideology by which *Only Angels Have Wings* is in several senses an imperial adventure. Perhaps this offers a way to re-engage Wood's parallels with Conrad, but rather than develop that theme, we would simply note one other area for exploration, in the repression and censorship within the movie. Critics who have commented on the relative emotional inarticulacy of the characters have described it variously as being anything from stoic to adolescent. Rather, we suggest, what might be involved in the movie's stunted emotional exchanges (on the whole quite typical of Hollywood) is a mechanism of transformation by repression, by which the audience is obliged to articulate the emotions not fully articulated by the characters. Through such a device, the movie offers its audience opportunities for the discovery of emotional resonances drawn from their own lives and concerns. What is, in one sense, being represented (at the same time as it is being manipulated) is the emotional state of the audience. The characters' emotional commonplaces are counterpointed by the exotic settings, but in its representation of masculinity and femininity the movie declares Hollywood's democracy of sentiment: film stars and exotic characters share the emotional characteristics of their audience. As a fan wrote in *Motion Picture* magazine in 1936, "these glamorous people are just simple human beings like ourselves."[136]

It would be wrong to conclude without recognizing the limitations of Hollywood's expressive range. In their several guises as ideological projects Hollywood movies represent and legitimize the already dominant power. Dismissing them, whether as entertainment, ideology, or art, does not make that cultural function disappear, and its persistence and power provide, for us, an important justification for analysis of the movies. The dominant ideology, however, is only dominant; it never succeeds in being totalizing. The critical procedures discussed in this book provide us with opportunities to identify the spaces in the texts we examine, the sites at which they reveal their mechanisms and the cultural forces behind them. By examining these sites we can come to comprehend the ideological and aesthetic work of Hollywood, and, as importantly, that of its audiences.

Academic criticism has often sought to establish the importance of its own activity in the claimed importance of its object; that is no less true of the claim that cinema is an agent of subject positioning or a symptom of ideological constitution than it is of the claim that *Only Angels Have Wings* is a work of high moral seriousness. Much of the discomfort experienced in critical attempts to find a respectable approach to Hollywood results from the hesitation in acknowledging that although the industries of culture are of central importance to the daily life of all western and most other societies, they are not important because of any inherent profundity they may possess. On the contrary, their lack of profundity is, on the whole, a condition of their status as entertainment. *Only Angels Have Wings* is "about" the response to death, heroic stoicism, imperialism, racism, and contempt for femininity, but it is not profoundly about those things. It is shallowly, sentimentally, and inarticulately about them. It is about the surfaces of these themes and commonplace attitudes and assumptions about them, and it is about them on its own surface. But this does not diminish Hollywood's importance. For if we are to study a culture, then its sentiments, its commonplace attitudes, its silences, and its hesitations are a vital part of that study. A criticism that takes Hollywood seriously can look less to the discovery of profound meanings or concealed purposes in its texts, and more to the equally difficult task of articulating the silences and equivocations, the plenitudes, excesses, and banalities of their surfaces. It is there, on the surface, that we may find answers to some of the American cinema's most mysterious and important questions: what can explain the success of Hollywood's cultural imperialism, and why do people like to cry at sad movies?

Notes

1 David Bordwell, *Making Meaning: Inference and Rhetoric in the Interpretation of Cinema* (Cambridge, MA: Harvard University Press, 1989), p. xii.

2 Jerry Lewis, *The Total Film-maker* (London: Vision Press, 1971), p. 157.

3 Pam Cook, ed., *The Cinema Book* (London: British Film Institute, 1985), p. v.

4 Frances Taylor Patterson, *Cinema Craftsmanship: A Book for Photoplaywrights* (New York: Harcourt, Brace, and Howe, 1920), p. 150.

5 Leslie Halliwell, *Halliwell's Film Guide*, 7th edn (London: Paladin, 1990), p. 267. In Halliwell's classification, "Four stars . . . indicate a film outstanding in many ways, a milestone in cinema history, remarkable for acting, direction, writing, photography or some other aspect of technique. Three stars indicate a very high standard of professional excellence or high historical interest: or, if you like, three strong reasons for admiring it. Two stars indicate a good level of competence and a generally entertaining film. One star draws attention to minor points of merit, usually in a film not very satisfactory as a whole; it could be a failed giant or a second feature with a few interesting ideas among the dross. No stars at all indicates a totally routine production or worse; such films may be watchable but they are at least equally missable" (p. xxxiv).

6 Donald C. Willis, *The Films of Howard Hawks* (Metuchen, NJ: Scarecrow, 1975), p. 178.

7 Michael Church, "Two Reel Women," *Observer* (December 8, 1991).

8 Halliwell, pp. 1161–7.

9 Alistair Cooke, ed., *Garbo and the Night Watchmen*, 1st pub. 1937 (London: Secker and Warburg, 1971). Another significant date would be the publication, in 1958, of James Agee's collected reviews as *Agee on Film* (New York: Beacon).

10 See, for instance, the technical discourse on deep-focus photography in *American Cinematographer*, published by the American Society of Cinematographers, between 1932 and 1947. Cited in Patrick L. Ogle, "Technological and Aesthetic Influences upon the Development of Deep Focus Cinematography in the United States," in John Ellis, ed., *Screen Reader 1* (London: Society for Education in Film and Television, 1977), pp. 81–108.

11 Martin Quigley, "Dr Dale and Martin Quigley Debate Screen and Education," *Motion Picture Herald* (April 2, 1938). Behind Quigley's argument in this particular case was a specific concern with the cultural reputation of Emile Zola. Several of Zola's novels, including *Nana*, were then on the Roman Catholic Index of Forbidden Books; hence the reference to Zola as a pornographer. Quigley, a prominent lay Catholic, was also therefore disapproving of Warner Bros.' idealization of the novelist.

12 Patterson, p. 150.

13   It is a book that is not yet written. Robert Lapsley and Michael Westlake, *Film Theory: An Introduction* (Manchester: Manchester University Press, 1988), is an intellectual history of semiotic and psychoanalytic theory that requires too much prior knowledge really to work well as an introductory guide. It also spends too much of its time charting the cul-de-sacs of that very variable body of work. Noel Carroll's *Mystifying Movies: Fads and Fallacies in Contemporary Film Theory* (New York: Columbia University Press, 1988), on the other hand, declares that "the purpose of this book is to oppose that which I take to be wrong in the area of contemporary film theory" (p. 7). Carroll explains the theory he dislikes with admirable clarity, but it would be charitable to suggest that Carroll's tone toward his opponents is uncharitable. Robert Stam, Robert Burgoyne, and Sandy Flitterman-Lewis, *New Vocabularies in Film Semiotics: Structuralism, Post-structuralism and Beyond* (London: Routledge, 1992), provides a more dispassionate treatment, but does not always overcome the intense user-unfriendliness of much film theoretical writing. Although they do not cover the most recent developments, two books by Dudley Andrew, *The Major Film Theories* (New York: Oxford University Press, 1976) and *Concepts in Film Theory* (New York: Oxford University Press, 1984), remain the best concise introduction to the area.

14   Hugo Münsterberg, *The Photoplay: A Psychological Study* (New York: Appleton, 1916; reprinted New York: Dover, 1970).

15   If you by now find this argument familiar, that is in large part because it is central to the theoretical assumptions underlying this book. To an extent that this paragraph insufficiently acknowledges, our analysis has been strongly influenced by Münsterberg's thinking.

16   The most important and perceptive of these critics was Harry Alan Potamkin, whose work has been collected in a volume entitled *The Compound Cinema*, ed. Lewis Jacobs (New York: Teachers College Press, 1977). See also Herbert Kline, ed., *New Theatre and Film, 1934–1937* (New York: Harcourt Brace Jovanovich, 1985).

17   The evolution of the term "montage" in Soviet cinema can be traced in Richard Taylor and Ian Christie, eds, *The Film Factory: Russian and Soviet Cinema in Documents, 1896–1939*, trans. Richard Taylor (London: Routledge and Kegan Paul, 1988).

18   Slavko Vorkapich, "Cinematics: Some Principles Underlying Effective Cinematography," in Hal Hall, ed., *Cinematic Annual, 1930*. Reprinted in Richard Koszarski, ed., *Hollywood Directors 1914–1940* (New York: Oxford University Press, 1976), pp. 253–9. Koszarski notes that Vorkapich himself did not use the word "montage" in his own writings.

19   See, for instance, Jane Addams, *The Spirit of Youth and the City Streets* (New York: Macmillan, 1909). Extracts of this and other early expressions of this concern are reprinted in Gerald Mast, ed., *The Movies in Our Midst: Documents in the Cultural History of Film in America* (Chicago: University of Chicago Press, 1982).

20   Denunciations of the studies were largely orchestrated by the Motion Picture Producers and Distributors of America (MPPDA), which sponsored the production of Raymond Moley's attack on them, *Are We Movie Made?*, in 1936, and the more considered philosophical dismissal by Mortimer Adler, *Art and Prudence: A Study in Practical Philosophy* (New York: Longmans, 1937). A more balanced account of the studies can be found in ch. 2 of Shearon Lowery and Melvin L. DeFleur, *Milestones in Mass Communication Research: Media Effects* (New York: Longman, 1983).

21   Margaret Thorp, *America at the Movies* (London: Faber, 1946); Leo Rosten, *Hollywood: The Movie Colony, the Movie Makers* (New York: Harcourt, Brace, 1941); Hortense Powdermaker, *Hollywood the Dream Factory* (Boston: Little Brown, 1950).

22 For summaries of audience research, see Leo A. Handel, *Hollywood Looks at Its Audience* (Urbana: University of Illinois Press, 1950), and Bruce A. Austin, *Immediate Seating: A Look at Movie Audiences* (Belmont, CA: Wadsworth, 1989).

23 Geoffrey Gorer, *The Americans: A Study in National Character* (London: Cresset, 1948); David Riesman, *The Lonely Crowd: A Study of the Changing American Character* (New Haven: Yale University Press, 1950). For a general discussion of the relationship of this literature to the movies, see Richard Maltby, "Film Noir: The Politics of the Maladjusted Text," *Journal of American Studies* 18:1 (1984), pp. 49–71.

24 Siegfried Kracauer, *From Caligari to Hitler: A Psychological History of the German Film* (Princeton, NJ: Princeton University Press, 1947); Barbara Deming, *Running Away from Myself: A Dream Portrait of America Drawn from the Films of the Forties* (New York: Grossman, 1969); Martha Wolfenstein and Nathan Leites, *Movies: A Psychological Study* (Glencoe, IL: Free Press, 1950); Parker Tyler, *The Hollywood Hallucination* (New York: Simon and Schuster, 1944), p. 237; Parker Tyler, *Magic and Myth of the Movies* (New York: Simon and Schuster, 1947).

25 Bernard Rosenberg and David Manning White, eds, *Mass Culture: The Popular Arts in America* (New York: Free Press, 1957); Theodor Adorno and Max Horkheimer, *Dialectic of Enlightenment* (New York: Herder and Herder, 1972).

26 Patterson, p. 150.

27 Andrew, *Major Film Theories*, pp. 4–5.

28 Sylvia Harvey, *May '68 and Film Culture* (London: British Film Institute, 1978), provides the best account of the relationship between radical politics and the developments in film criticism during this period.

29 For instance, Laura Mulvey's essays, "Visual Pleasure and Narrative Cinema" and "Afterthoughts on 'Visual Pleasure and Narrative Cinema' inspired by King Vidor's *Duel in the Sun*," in *Visual and Other Pleasures* (Bloomington: Indiana University Press, 1989), pp. 14–38; Colin MacCabe, "Realism and the Cinema: Notes on some Brechtian Theses," *Screen* 15:2 (Summer 1974), pp. 7–27.

30 Claude Lévi-Strauss, *Structural Anthropology*, trans. Claire Jacobson Brooke Grundfest Schoepf (Garden City, NY: Doubleday, 1967).

31 Two genre studies that show a clear structuralist influence are Jim Kitses, *Horizons West: Anthony Mann, Budd Boetticher, Sam Peckinpah: Studies of Authorship within the Western* (London: Thames and Hudson, 1969), and Will Wright, *Sixguns and Society: A Structural Study of the Western* (Berkeley, CA: University of California Press, 1975).

32 Peter Wollen, *Signs and Meaning in the Cinema* (London: Secker and Warburg, 1972: 1st pub. 1968), p. 168.

33 Wollen, p. 104.

34 Lévi-Strauss's idea of myth is discussed in chapter 3.

35 The convoluted conclusion to the *Cahiers du Cinéma* analysis of "John Ford's *Young Mr Lincoln*" would serve as an example. In Ellis, pp. 147–52.

36 Wollen, p. 104.

37 Ferdinand de Saussure, *Course in General Linguistics* (London: Fontana, 1974), p. 16.

38 However, as many critics have pointed out, Peirce's more complex account of iconic and indexical signs almost certainly offers a more fruitful basis for explaining visual sign systems than Saussure's linguistically derived assertion of the arbitrary nature of the sign. See, for instance, Wollen, pp. 120–5.

39 Roland Barthes, *Mythologies* (London: Paladin, 1973).

40 Christian Metz, *Film Language: A Semiotics of the Cinema*, trans. Michael Taylor (New York: Oxford University Press, 1974).

41 A summary and critique of this position can be found in James Spellerberg, "Technology and Ideology in the Cinema," in Mast and Cohen, pp. 761–75.

42 Edward Said, *The World, the Text, and the Critic* (Cambridge, MA: Harvard University Press, 1983), p. 53.

43 Noel Carroll also uses the term "psychosemiology" to refer to what we have called "cine-psychoanalysis." Christian Metz referred to it as the "semio-psychoanalysis of the cinema." Carroll, p. 9.

44 Theodore Price, *Hitchcock and Homosexuality: His 50-Year Obsession with Jack the Ripper and the Superbitch Prostitute* (Metuchen, NJ: Scarecrow, 1991).

45 Louis Althusser, "Ideology and Ideological State Apparatuses: Notes towards an Investigation," in *Lenin and Philosophy and Other Essays* (London: NLB, 1971), p. 169.

46 Stephen Heath, "On Screen, in Frame: Film and Ideology," in *Questions of Cinema* (London: Macmillan, 1981), p. 8.

47 Stephen Heath, "*Jaws*, Ideology and Film Theory," in Bill Nichols, ed., *Movies and Methods Vol. II* (Berkeley, CA: University of California Press, 1985), p. 514.

48 Christian Metz, *The Imaginary Signifier: Psychoanalysis and the Cinema*, trans. Celia Britton, Annwyl Williams, Ben Brewster, and Alfred Guzzetti (Bloomington: Indiana University Press, 1982), p. 8.

49 Jean-Louis Baudry, "The Apparatus," in Theresa Hak Kyung Cha, ed., *Apparatus* (New York: Tanam Press, 1981), p. 54.

50 Jean-Louis Baudry, "Ideological Effects of the Basic Cinematic Apparatus," in Nichols, p. 537.

51 Sandy Flitterman-Lewis, "Psychoanalysis," in Robert C. Allen, ed., *Channels of Discourse* (London: Methuen, 1987), p. 182.

52 Metz, *Imaginary Signifier*, pp. 125, 127–8.

53 See, for example, Raymond Bellour, "Hitchcock the Enunciator," *Camera Obscura* 2 (Fall 1977), pp. 66–91; Thierry Kuntzel, "The Film Work 2," *Camera Obscura* 5 (Spring 1980), pp. 6–69.

54 Sandy Flitterman-Lewis, "Psychoanalysis," in Stam, Burgoyne, and Flitterman-Lewis, pp. 146–7.

55 For Lacan, the child's primary identification in the mirror stage is also a misapprehension, since the image the child identifies with is not the child himself or herself, but an image.

56 Metz, *Imaginary Signifier*, p. 51.

57 Metz, *Imaginary Signifier*, p. 96.

58 Charles F. Altman, "Psychoanalysis and Cinema: The Imaginary Discourse," *Quarterly Review of Film Studies* 2:3 (August 1977), pp. 257–72; Barbara Klinger, "In Retrospect: Film Studies Today," *Yale Journal of Criticism* 2:1 (1988), pp. 133–4.

59 Carroll, p. 194.

60 Bordwell, p. 245.

61 Deborah Linderman, "The Mise-en-abîme in Hitchcock's *Vertigo*," *Cinema Journal* 30:4 (Summer 1991), p. 53.

62 James Naremore, "Authorship and the Cultural Politics of Film Criticism," *Film Quarterly* 44:1 (Fall 1990), p. 20.

63 Examples are from Jeffrey Sconce, "Spectacles of Death: Identification, Reflexivity, and Contemporary Horror," and Susan Jeffords, "The Big Switch: Hollywood Masculinity in the Nineties," both in Jim Collins, Hilary Radner, and Ava Preacher Collins, eds, *Film Theory Goes to the Movies* (London: Routledge, 1993), pp. 105, 197.

64 Stam, Burgoyne, and Flitterman-Lewis, p. 191.

65   Tania Modleski, *The Women Who Knew Too Much: Hitchcock and Feminist Theory* (London: Methuen, 1988), p. 3.

66   Modleski, pp. 97, 100.

67   Virginia Wright Wexman, "The Critic as Consumer: Film Study in the University, *Vertigo*, and the Film Canon," *Film Quarterly* 39:3 (Spring 1986), p. 33.

68   Slavov Zizek, "Introduction: Alfred Hitchcock, or, the Form and its Historical Mediation, in Slavov Zizek, ed., *Everything You Always Wanted to Know about Lacan (But Were Afraid to Ask Hitchcock)* (London: Verso, 1992), p. 10.

69   William Rothman, "*Vertigo*: The Unknown Woman in Hitchcock," in *The "I" of the Camera: Essays in Film Criticism, History and Aesthetics* (Cambridge: Cambridge University Press, 1988), p. 173.

70   Modleski, pp. 120–1. Janet Staiger remarks of canonic texts that, "As ideal fathers, these select films are given homage or rebelled against." Janet Staiger, "The Politics of Film Canons," *Cinema Journal* 24:2 (Spring 1985), p. 4.

71   Katie Trumpener, "Fragments of the Mirror: Self-Reference, Mise-en-abîme, *Vertigo*," in Walter Raubicheck and Walter Srebnick, eds, *Hitchcock's Rereleased Films: From Rope to Vertigo* (Detroit: Wayne State University Press, 1991), p. 175.

72   Ann West, "The Concept of the Fantastic in *Vertigo*," in Raubicheck and Srebnick, p. 171.

73   The conscious marketing of Hitchcock's persona is the subject of Robert E. Karpis, *Hitchcock: The Making of a Reputation* (Chicago: University of Chicago Press, 1992). Part of Alfred Hitchcock's legacy, indeed, has been the deployment of a commercialized variant of auteurism in Hollywood since 1970, which identifies *Mississippi Burning* (1988) as "An Alan Parker film" in its credits, and that has led to the self-conscious creation "Steven Spielberg" or "Martin Scorsese." Timothy Corrigan argues that this commercialization of a critical practice means that auteurism may "in fact be more alive now than at any other point in film history." Jim Hillier has suggested that the industry's adoption of the director as author may be related to the disappearance of any distinguishing studio or genre identity for a movie, leaving a vacuum that director identities have helped to fill. Timothy Corrigan, *A Cinema Without Walls: Movies and Culture after Vietnam* (New Brunswick, NJ: Rutgers University Press, 1991), p. 135; Jim Hillier, *The New Hollywood* (London: Studio Vista, 1992), p. 4.

74   Ann Cvetkovich, "Postmodern *Vertigo*: The Sexual Politics of Allusion in De Palma's *Body Double*," in Raubicheck and Srebnick, p. 149. See also Linderman, p. 51.

75   Wexman, p. 36.

76   Sharon Willis, "Hardware and Hardbodies, What Do Women Want?: A Reading of *Thelma and Louise*," in Collins et al., p. 126.

77   Zizek, p. 5.

78   Frederic Jameson, "Spatial Systems in *North by Northwest*," in Zizek, p. 64.

79   Lucretia Knapp, "The Queer Voice in *Marnie*," *Cinema Journal* 32:4 (Summer 1993), pp. 7, 11, 13.

80   Bordwell, p. 95. See also Barry Barnes, *T.S. Kuhn and Social Science* (New York: Columbia University Press, 1982), pp. 45–6.

81   Paul Willemen, "For Information: Cinéaction," *Framework* 32/3 (1986), p. 227.

82   Zizek, "Introduction," in Zizek, p. 2.

83   Eric Rohmer, quoted in Bordwell, p. 47.

84   Kristin Thompson, *Breaking the Glass Armor: Neoformalist Film Analysis* (Princeton, NJ: Princeton University Press, 1988), p. 33.

85   Thompson, p. 29.

86 Kristin Thompson, "Neoformalist Film Analysis: One Approach, Many Methods," in Thompson, pp. 3–47.

87 Bordwell suggests that narrative causality operates as "the dominant" in Classical Hollywood cinema. Formalist criticism defines the dominant as the focusing component of a work of art; the dominant guarantees the integrity of its structure. Rick Altman offers a critique of neoformalism's use of this concept in "Dickens, Griffith, and Film Theory Today," in Jane Gaines, ed., *Classical Hollywood Narrative: The Paradigm Wars* (Durham, NC: Duke University Press, 1992), pp. 9–47.

88 Bordwell, p. 9.

89 David Bordwell, *Narration in the Fiction Film* (London: Methuen, 1985), p. 335.

90 Bill Nichols, "Form Wars: The Political Unconscious of Formalist Theory," in Gaines, p. 75.

91 V.F. Perkins, "Must We Say What They Mean? Film Criticism and Interpretation," *MOVIE* 34/5 (Winter 1990), p. 5. See also Douglas Pye, "Bordwell and Hollywood," *MOVIE* 33 (Winter 1989), pp. 46–52.

92 Thompson, p. 9.

93 Klinger, p. 148.

94 In 1985, Robert C. Allen and Douglas Gomery's *Film History: Theory and Practice* (New York: Knopf, 1985) both summarized the then-current state of film historiography and outlined a range of potential developments.

95 Robert C. Allen, "Reader-oriented Criticism and Television," in *Channels of Discourse* (London: Methuen, 1987), p. 76.

96 Umberto Eco, *The Role of the Reader: Explorations in the Semiotics of Texts* (London: Hutchinson, 1979), p. 7.

97 Stanley Fish, *Is There a Text in this Class?: The Authority of Interpretive Communities* (Cambridge, MA: Harvard University Press, 1980).

98 The object of analysis "is an *event*, not a text: that is, it is a set of interpretations or affective experiences produced by individuals from an encounter with a text or set of texts within a social situation. It is not an analysis of the text except in so far as to consider what textually might be facilitating the reading." Janet Staiger, "Taboos and Totems: Cultural Meanings of *The Silence of the Lambs*," in Collins et al., p. 144.

99 Hans Robert Jauss, *Toward an Aesthetic of Reception*, trans. Timothy Bahti (Minneapolis: University of Minnesota Press, 1982).

100 Staiger, p. 144.

101 Janet Staiger, *Interpreting Films: Studies in the Historical Reception of American Cinema* (Princeton, NJ: Princeton University Press, 1992), p. 150.

102 Staiger, *Interpreting Films*, p. 152.

103 Tony Bennett, "Text and Social Process: The Case of James Bond," *Screen Education* 41 (Winter/Spring 1982), pp. 3–14.

104 Terry Eagleton, *Literary Theory: An Introduction* (Oxford: Blackwell, 1983), p. 85.

105 Allen and Gomery, p. iv.

106 Carroll, p. 8.

107 Stam, Burgoyne, and Flitterman-Lewis, p. 220.

108 Thompson, p. 34.

109 Howard Hawks, "A Discussion with the Audience of the 1970 Chicago Film Festival," in Joseph McBride, ed., *Focus on Howard Hawks* (Englewood Cliffs, NJ: Prentice-Hall, 1972), p. 18.

110 Robert Sklar, *City Boys: Cagney, Bogart, Garfield* (Princeton, NJ: Princeton University Press, 1992), p. 37.

111 Jacques Rivette, "The Genius of Howard Hawks," *Cahiers du Cinéma* (May 1953),

reprinted in McBride, pp. 73, 76.

112   Peter John Dyer, "Sling the Lamps Low," *Sight and Sound* (Summer 1962), reprinted in McBride, p. 85.

113   Manny Farber, "Howard Hawks," in *Negative Space* (London: Studio Vista, 1971), pp. 27, 30; 1st pub. in *Artforum* (April 1969).

114   Andrew Sarris, "The World of Howard Hawks," *New York Film Bulletin* (1961), reprinted in McBride, pp. 48, 52.

115   Robin Wood, *Howard Hawks* (London: Secker and Warburg, 1968), p. 17.

116   Wood, pp. 17–18.

117   Wood, p. 21.

118   Wood, p. 24.

119   Wood, p. 56.

120   Wood, p. 10.

121   Wollen, pp. 91–3.

122   Wollen, p. 90.

123   Robin Wood, "Hawks De-Wollenized," in *Personal Views: Explorations in Film* (London: Gordon Fraser, 1976), p. 201.

124   Perkins, p. 5.

125   Molly Haskell, *From Reverence to Rape: The Treatment of Women in the Movies* (Chicago: University of Chicago Press, 1973), p. 209.

126   Haskell, p. 209.

127   Haskell, p. 210.

128   Richard Dyer, *Stars* (London: British Film Institute, 1979), pp. 64, 178.

129   John Belton, "Hawks & Co.", *Cinema* (1971), reprinted in McBride, pp. 107–8.

130   Gerald Mast, *Howard Hawks, Storyteller* (New York: Oxford University Press, 1982), p. 68.

131   Leland Poague, *Howard Hawks* (Boston: Twayne, 1982), pp. 30–43.

132   Willis, p. 81.

133   Ruth Vasey, *Diplomatic Representations: The World According to Hollywood, 1919–1939* (Madison: University of Wisconsin Press, forthcoming).

134   Wood, *Howard Hawks*, p. 17. In a parallel instance, when sociologist Edgar Dale analyzed the content of motion pictures in 1935, he distinguished those pictures set in "foreign locales" from those set in "imaginary" settings. In the "foreign" category he included a "quite adequate presentation of Orambo, a little, hot, dreary town some place on the coast of South America." Edgar Dale, *The Content of Motion Pictures* (New York: Macmillan, 1935), p. 30.

135   Vasey, *Diplomatic Representations*.

136   The writer, Agnes Specht from Cleveland, Ohio, described the fan magazines as "the medium through which Hollywood phantoms become our next-door neighbors . . . Through them we learn that all these glamorous people are just simple human beings like ourselves and that they have ambitions, struggles, heartaches and hopes. And through this knowledge we understand them better and are apt to be less critical of them or envious of their success." *Motion Picture* (August 1936), quoted in Martin Levin, ed., *Hollywood and the Great Fan Magazines* (London: Ian Allen, 1970), p. 7.

Chronology

This chronology includes the release dates of movies discussed in the text, together with other movies that were either commercially successful or significant in the history of American cinema. Information on the box-office popularity of stars comes from polls among exhibitors.

1891 Thomas Edison files a patent application on a moving picture camera (Kinetograph) and film.

1892 Edison's patents rejected.

1893 Edison copyrights the first moving pictures ~ first public demonstration of the Kinetoscope.

1894 Edison Manufacturing Company established ~ the first Kinetoscope parlors open.

1895 William K. Dickson, principal inventor of the Kinetoscope, leaves Edison and helps found the American Mutoscope Company ~ the Latham's Eidoloscope in New York, Thomas Armat's Phantascope in Atlanta and the Lumières' Cinématographe in Paris show the first public projection of moving pictures.

1896 The first public performance of the Edison Vitascope pictures ~ J. Stuart Blackton founds the Vitagraph Company of America ~ William Selig forms the Selig Polyscope Company.
      Rough Sea at Dover.

1897 Edison is granted a patent for his camera and film, and begins legal actions for patent infringement against other companies ~ the Lubin Manufacturing Company is formed ~ the Eden-Musee in New York is the first exhibition venue devoted to the full-time exhibition of moving pictures.

1898 "Actualities" of the Spanish-American war are immensely popular as a pictorial news service, shown in "legitimate" and vaudeville theaters, in

amusement parks and by traveling exhibitors.
The Passion Play.

1899 American Mutoscope becomes the American Mutoscope and Biograph Company (Biograph).

1900 Biograph produces some of the first multiple-shot fiction pictures, including *The Downward Path* and *A Career in Crime*, but most pictures are actualities, re-enactments, or single-shot comedies.

1901 A strike of vaudeville performers encourages the use of moving pictures in vaudeville theaters ~ many install permanent projection equipment ~ Edison brings a patent suit against Biograph.

1902 Edison loses his patent case against Biograph ~ his patents are declared invalid, but then reissued ~ the Electric Theater, Los Angeles, is the first purpose-built cinema ~ the Biograph catalog offers 2,500 titles.

1903 Legal battles over patents leave the American industry disorganized and reliant on European product.
The Great Train Robbery ~ Life of an American Fireman.

1904 Story films begin to replace actualities as the dominant form of product ~ William Fox opens his first theater in New York ~ Adolph Zukor and Mitchell H. Mark form the Automatic Vaudeville Company.

1905 As the storefront theater becomes the dominant site of exhibition, the term "nickelodeon" is coined in Pittsburgh ~ the first "Hale's Tour" opens in Kansas City ~ *Variety* is first published ~ the first film exchanges appear in Chicago.

1906 Vitagraph becomes the leading American producer, but imports from French companies Pathé and Gaumont continue to provide a large share of the American market ~ Kinemacolor is the first color photography system ~ *Humorous Phases of Funny Faces* is the first cartoon.

1907 Edison and Biograph's patents are deemed valid, and Edison initiates new lawsuits against rivals ~ the Kalem Film Company and the Essanay Film Manufacturing Company are formed, and the industry's first trade association, the United Film Protective Service Association, is established ~ Chicago enacts the first motion picture censorship ordinance ~ *Moving Picture World* begins publication ~ in response to the nickelodeon boom, a network of film exchanges now covers the US.

1908 The nickelodeon boom reaches its height ~ moving pictures are covered by copyright laws ~ Edison licenses the use of his patents to Lubin, Selig Polyscope, Vitagraph, Kalem, Essanay, and importers Mèliés and Pathé, the largest supplier of pictures for the American market ~ negotiations with Biograph lead to the establishment of the Motion Picture Patents Company (MPPC), the first attempt to establish a monopoly over the industry ~ the first safety film is introduced by Eastman Kodak ~ the Cameraphone, combining sound with pictures, plays in vaudeville.

1909 Rival production companies, including Thanhouser, Rex and Carl Laemmle's Independent Motion Picture Company (IMP), are established to contest the MPPC's attempted monopoly ~ the industry establishes the National Board of Censorship to vet movie content ~ Chicago has 400 picture houses ~ Vitagraph begins sending out prepared music scores with its "films de luxe," and releases the first American feature film, *Les Misérables* ~ Kalem is the first production company to put actors' names on posters.

1910   The MPPC forms the General Film Company (GFC) to control national distribution ~ Laemmle establishes the Motion Picture Distributing and Sales Company (MPDSC) as a rival to the GFC ~ access to the American market becomes increasingly difficult for foreign companies ~ Marcus Loew founds Loew's Consolidated Enterprises, with Joseph and Nicholas Schenck ~ Edison demonstrates the Kinetophone, with simultaneous sound ~ D.W. Griffith takes a Biograph film crew to Los Angeles ~ Essanay, Lubin, Kalem, and Nestor also send production units there ~ every major production company except Biograph publicizes their "picture personalities," among them Florence Lawrence and King Baggot.

1911   Los Angeles becomes the second most important production center in the US, after New York ~ Nestor builds the first studio located in Hollywood ~ Selig, Pathé, Biograph, Kalem, and Essanay also build permanent studios in the Los Angeles area ~ Pennsylvania is the first state to establish a board of censorship for moving pictures ~ the first fan magazines, *Motion Picture Story Magazine* and *Photoplay*, are published ~ the Bell and Howell camera is invented ~ Pathé's Weekly is the first American newsreel ~ "picture personalities," including Florence Turner, Mary Pickford, and Francis X. Bushman, become famous.

1912   The US government brings an anti-trust suit against the MPPC and General Film, which controls about 60% of the US market ~ the Majestic Film Company leaves MPDSC and forms Mutual Film ~ Carl Laemmle forms the Universal Film Manufacturing Company, and builds a studio in Hollywood ~ Adolph Zukor founds Famous Players and distributes *Queen Elizabeth*, starring Sarah Bernhardt ~ Mack Sennett establishes the Keystone Company ~ Edison and Keith Albee launch the American Talking Picture Company ~ the first American Kinemacolor production, *La Tosca*, is released ~ US Congress bans pictures of prizefights after Jack Johnson's 1910 defeat of Jim Jeffries makes him the first black heavyweight champion.
From the Manger to the Cross.

1913   The Jesse L. Lasky Feature Play Company is formed ~ Ohio and Kansas establish state censorship ~ 3,000 movie theaters are in operation, and larger and more elaborate movie theaters are built in many American cities ~ Warner's Features Inc. is organized, with Albert Warner as its head ~ Maurice Costello and Alice Joyce are popular stars ~ Selig releases the first serial, *The Adventures of Kathlyn*.
Traffic in Souls ~ *Judith of Bethulia.*

1914   Paramount distribution company is formed by W.W. Hodkinson to distribute multiple-reel features ~ William Fox establishes the Box Office Attractions Film Rental Company, renamed the Fox Film Corporation in 1916 ~ US Senate hearings consider federal regulation of the industry ~ Earl

Williams and Clara Kimball Young are among the most popular stars ~ Pearl White stars in Pathé's serial *The Perils of Pauline*.

1915 The US Supreme Court rules Ohio state censorship is constitutional, and denies movies First Amendment protection ~ protests against the racism of *The Birth of a Nation* do not affect its huge commercial success, but the National Board of Censorship loses credibility for passing the movie ~ Universal City opens for production in Hollywood ~ the US district court finds against the MPPC in its anti-trust suit ~ Vitagraph, Lubin, Selig, and Essanay form V-L-S-E to distribute their features ~ after leaving Mutual, Harry Aitken forms Triangle with Griffith, Sennett, and Thomas Ince, in an early attempt at vertical integration ~ Metro Pictures is formed as a distribution company ~ the Technicolor Corporation is founded ~ the Los Angeles Chamber of Commerce claims 80% of American films are produced there ~ William S. Hart and Mabel Normand are popular stars ~ the Fox Film Corporation begins production, making "vamp" Theda Bara a star in *A Fool There Was*.
The Cheat.

1916 Famous Players merges with the Jesse L. Lasky Feature Play Company to become Famous Players-Lasky (FPL), and takes over Paramount: Zukor president, Lasky in charge of production ~ Samuel Goldfish leaves to form Goldwyn Pictures ~ the National Association of the Motion Picture Industry (NAMPI) is formed ~ New York replaces London as the center of worldwide movie distribution after the British impose tariffs on foreign film trade ~ exports of American movies benefit from the wartime disruption of European industries, and American companies open distribution offices in Latin America, Australia, South Africa, and the Far East as well as Europe ~ average theater seating capacity is 502 seats ~ the Society of Motion Picture Engineers (SMPE) is established ~ *The Gulf Between* is the first two-strip Technicolor picture.
Intolerance.

1917 In cooperation with the government's Committee on Public Information (CPI), NAMPI organizes the industry's contribution to the war effort, through propaganda speeches in theaters and drives to sell Liberty Bonds ~ after Triangle collapses, FPL absorbs Triangle's talent and reorganizes ~ in resistance to FPL's insistence that exhibitors block-book pictures, the First National Exhibitors' Circuit is formed, and signs up Chaplin ~ Metro Pictures enters production ~ Fox's Hollywood studio opens ~ Balaban and Katz's Central Park Theater, Chicago, is the first to have air-conditioning ~ Douglas Fairbanks is the top box-office star.

1918 The War Industries Board declares motion pictures an essential industry ~ MPPC is dissolved ~ American control of the world film market has increased enormously during the war ~ Robertson-Cole Company is formed ~ FPL distributes 220 pictures ~ Mary Pickford and D.W. Griffith join First National ~ Pickford, Marguerite Clark, and Douglas Fairbanks are the most popular stars.
Old Wives for New.

1919 United Artists (UA) is formed by Douglas Fairbanks, Mary Pickford,

Charlie Chaplin, and D.W. Griffith ~ there are over 2,500 US theaters with more than 1,000 seats ~ financed by Wall Street capital, Zukor begins buying theaters, establishing FPL as the first vertically integrated motion picture company ~ General Electric establishes the Radio Corporation of America (RCA) ~ the American Society of Cinematographers (ASC) is founded ~ *Film Daily Yearbook* is first published ~ Wallace Reid is the top box-office draw.
Male and Female ~ True Heart Susie.

1920   American movies earn one third of their gross income from the foreign market ~ Loew's, Inc., acquires Metro Pictures ~ CBC Sales Company (later to become Columbia) is formed ~ Irving Thalberg becomes head of production at Universal ~ tinting is used on 80–90% of pictures.
Way Down East ~ Why Change Your Wife? ~ The Penalty ~ Under Crimson Skies.

1921   The Federal Trade Commission begins an investigation into industry trade practices, and institutes an anti-trust suit against FPL, which now owns over 300 theaters ~ First National merges with Associated Producers to become Associated First National ~ economic recession causes a box-office slump ~ in response to campaigns for state motion picture censorship, NAMPI proposes a code of self-regulation (the Thirteen Points), but New York establishes state censorship ~ *The Four Horsemen of the Apocalypse* launches Rudolph Valentino's career, followed by *The Sheik*.
The Three Musketeers ~ The Conquering Power.

1922   The Motion Picture Producers and Distributors of America, Inc. (MPPDA), is formed to replace NAMPI as the major companies' trade association, with former postmaster-general Will H. Hays as its president ~ Massachusetts state censorship is defeated in referendum ~ in protest at Hollywood's representation of Mexicans, the government of Mexico bans American movies ~ First National builds a studio at Burbank ~ Robertson-Cole is reorganized as Film Booking Offices of America (FBO) ~ average weekly attendance is 40 million ~ 84% of American movie production takes place in Hollywood ~ *The Toll of the Sea* is the first feature to use subtractive Technicolor.
Robin Hood ~ Orphans of the Storm ~ Tess of the Storm Country ~ Blood and Sand ~ Foolish Wives.

1923   Warner Bros. Pictures (WB) is incorporated: Harry Warner president, Jack Warner in charge of production ~ *The Covered Wagon* and Cecil B. DeMille's *The Ten Commandments* are the year's most successful movies ~ the HOLLYWOODLAND sign is erected ~ Walt Disney releases his first cartoon, *Alice in Cartoonland* ~ Thomas Meigham is the top box-office star.
The Hunchback of Notre Dame ~ Safety Last.

1924   Through "the Formula," the MPPDA prohibits its member companies from adapting the most dangerous and censorable books and plays ~ CBC Sales Company becomes Columbia Pictures, with Harry Cohn as head of production ~ Loew's, Inc., acquires Goldwyn Pictures and establishes Metro-Goldwyn-Mayer (MGM) as its production company: Louis B. Mayer head of studio, Irving Thalberg head of production ~ the Association of Motion

Picture Producers (AMPP) is formed as the Hollywood subsidiary of MPPDA ~ Joseph Schenck reorganizes UA after D.W. Griffith leaves ~ average weekly attendance is 45 million ~ Harold Lloyd is the most popular box-office draw ~ Norma Talmadge is the highest-paid star.
The Iron Horse ~ The Sea Hawk ~ The Thief of Bagdad ~ Greed ~ The Navigator ~ Merton of the Movies.

1925 FPL becomes Paramount-Famous-Lasky, buys a controlling interest in Chicago's Balaban and Katz theater chain, and merges its theater interests into Publix Theaters ~ WB takes over Vitagraph ~ Germany imposes a quota on American movie imports ~ Samuel Goldwyn joins UA ~ Fox begins an expansion program, buying West Coast Theaters ~ WB and Western Electric begin sound movie experiments.
The Big Parade ~ The Gold Rush ~ The Freshman ~ The Phantom of the Opera.

1926 AMPP establishes the Studio Relations Committee, and the Central Casting Corporation to regulate employment of extras ~ the Studio Basic Agreement recognizes five major unions ~ Western Electric grants WB exclusive license to the Vitaphone sound process ~ WB's *Don Juan* is the first feature with soundtrack synchronized on discs, with sound effects and recorded music ~ Western Electric forms Electrical Research Products Inc. (ERPI) ~ Fox-Case Corporation is formed to develop sound newsreels ~ Columbia begins distribution ~ Joseph Schenck takes control of UA ~ Joseph Kennedy buys production and distribution company FBO ~ average weekly attendance is 50 million ~ Publix Theaters employs more musicians than any other organization in the world ~ the major companies produce 449 pictures ~ Rudolph Valentino dies.
The Son of the Sheik ~ Ben-Hur ~ What Price Glory? ~ Beau Geste ~ The Black Pirate.

1927 WB's *The Jazz Singer* is the first "talkie," Fox's Movietone the first sound newsreel ~ the Federal Trade Commission orders FPL to cease block-booking, then oversees an industry-wide agreement on trade practices ~ MPPDA establishes a code of "Don'ts and Be Carefuls" covering material liable to censorship in domestic and foreign markets ~ the Department of Commerce establishes a Motion Picture Department to assist the industry's foreign distribution, on the ground that "trade follows the films" ~ in an attempt to prevent the unionization of the production industry, the Academy of Motion Picture Arts and Sciences (AMPAS) is founded to "improve the artistic quality of the film medium, provide a common forum for the various branches and crafts of the industry, [and] foster cooperation in technical research and cultural progress" ~ Marcus Loew dies, Nicholas M. Schenck becomes president of Loew's, Inc. ~ New York's Roxy Theater opens ~ Tom Mix is a top box-office draw.
The King of Kings ~ Wings ~ It ~ Seventh Heaven ~ Sunrise ~ The General ~ The Unknown ~ The Way of All Flesh ~ The Road to Glory ~ Chang.

1928 Paramount, Loew's, and UA adopt Western Electric sound system ~ RCA finances the creation of a new vertically integrated company to exploit its rival Photophone system, and merges FBO with the Keith-Albee-Orpheum theater chain to form Radio-Keith-Orpheum (RKO), with RCA's David Sarnoff as president and William LeBaron in charge of production ~ Fox

attempts a take-over of Loew's, to create the largest company in the industry ~ Darryl Zanuck becomes head of production at WB, which buys Stanley Theaters ~ Britain imposes a quota on American film imports, which make up 80% of the features shown ~ the first Academy Awards ceremony is held ~ average weekly attendance is 65 million ~ *Lights of New York* is the first all-talking feature ~ Walt Disney releases the first cartoon featuring Mickey Mouse, *Steamboat Willie*.
The Singing Fool ~ Steamboat Bill, Jr.

1929   WB takes over First National ~ Universal buys theaters ~ Paramount acquires half of the Columbia Broadcasting System (CBS) ~ Paramount and WB negotiate a merger, to create Paramount-Vitaphone, but are prevented by threats of government anti-trust action ~ the US Justice Department brings an anti-trust suit to dismantle Fox-Loew's merger ~ $24 million is spent on refurbishing theaters for sound ~ Mascot Pictures is established ~ MPPDA suggests that 75% of the audience are women ~ *International Motion Picture Almanac* is first published ~ the majors produce 393 pictures.
Sunny Side Up ~ Broadway Melody ~ Hallelujah!

1930   The MPPDA's Production Code is written, and begins to be administered by the Studio Relations Committee ~ William Fox loses control of the Fox Film Corporation ~ Paramount-Famous-Lasky becomes Paramount-Publix and extends its theater ownership ~ the Academy Research Council is created to coordinate the studios' technical research and encourage technological standardization ~ Fox experiments with the Grandeur widescreen process ~ attendance reaches a peak at 80 million a week ~ Monogram Pictures established ~ *Hollywood Reporter* begins publication ~ Paramount introduces commercials to cinemas ~ Joan Crawford is a top box-office star ~ *Anna Christie* is Greta Garbo's first sound movie.
Min and Bill ~ The Divorcee ~ Hell's Angels ~ All Quiet on the Western Front ~ Morocco ~ Little Caesar.

1931   The Depression begins to affect the industry as theater attendance falls to 70 million a week ~ burdened by their debts from theater purchases, the majors institute production cutbacks ~ Fox divests itself of its shares in Loew's ~ Publix Pictures is the largest movie circuit ever, with 1,200 theaters ~ RKO completes purchase of Pathé, and David O. Selznick takes charge of RKO production ~ Universal inaugurates a horror cycle with *Dracula* and *Frankenstein* ~ double bills become increasingly common ~ the majors produce 324 pictures.
Cimarron ~ Back Street ~ City Lights ~ The Public Enemy ~ The Smiling Lieutenant ~ Alias the Doctor.

1932   Attendance falls to 55 million a week ~ 4,000 theaters have closed ~ Paramount cuts production budgets by 33%, and sells its interest in CBS ~ Jesse Lasky leaves Paramount ~ Sidney Kent leaves Paramount and becomes president of Fox ~ Fox loses $11.5 million ~ RKO opens Radio City Music Hall ~ MGM's weekly payroll is estimated at $250,000 ~ Disney's *Flowers and Trees* is the first to use three-strip Technicolor ~ top stars are Marie Dressler and Janet Gaynor.
Grand Hotel ~ Trouble in Paradise ~ Scarface ~ I Am a Fugitive from a Chain Gang ~ The Champ ~ What Price Hollywood? ~ Scarlet Dawn.

1933   Worst recorded year ~ Paramount's deficit of $20 million prompts its entry into receivership ~ Universal disposes of its theaters ~ both it and RKO are in receivership, Universal until 1936, RKO until 1940 ~ Darryl Zanuck leaves WB, and forms Twentieth Century Pictures with Joseph Schenck, distributing through UA ~ Hal B. Wallis becomes WB head of production ~ the Screen Writers Guild is formed ~ the motion picture industry's National Recovery Administration (NRA) Code of Fair Competition sanctions the Big Five's distribution practices ~ Joe Breen becomes head of the Studio Relations Committee ~ the Screen Actors Guild is formed ~ Joseph Walker receives a patent for the zoom lens ~ the Payne Fund Studies into the effects of motion pictures on youth intensify calls for federal regulation of the industry ~ the majors produce 338 pictures ~ Mae West is the top box-office attraction.
42nd Street ~ King Kong ~ She Done Him Wrong ~ Cavalcade ~ State Fair ~ Little Women.

1934   Attendance, and box-office takings, begin to recover ~ the Legion of Decency is organized by the Catholic church to protest immoral movies ~ the Studio Relations Committee is renamed the Production Code Administration (PCA) and given greater authority to enforce self-regulation in production ~ Will Rogers and Clark Gable are the most popular box-office stars ~ *It Happened One Night* is the first movie to win Academy Awards in the four major categories, and is Columbia's biggest hit to date.
Roman Scandals ~ One Night of Love ~ The Thin Man ~ The Barretts of Wimpole Street ~ Imitation of Life ~ Of Human Bondage ~ A Modern Hero.

1935   Paramount is reorganized, becoming Paramount Pictures, Inc. ~ Twentieth Century merges with Fox to become Twentieth Century-Fox (TCF), with Joseph Schenck as chairman of the board and Darryl Zanuck as head of production ~ Ernst Lubitsch briefly becomes head of production at Paramount ~ David O. Selznick leaves MGM to form Selznick International Pictures, distributing through UA ~ Time Inc. launches *The March of Time* newsreel series ~ Floyd Odlum of Atlas Corporation buys a minority interest in RKO ~ Herbert J. Yates merges Monogram and Mascot to form Republic Pictures ~ the majors produce 356 pictures ~ Shirley Temple becomes the top box-office star ~ *Becky Sharpe* is the first three-strip Technicolor feature.
A Midsummer Night's Dream ~ Lives of a Bengal Lancer ~ Captain Blood ~ Top Hat ~ G-Men ~ Mutiny on the Bounty ~ Bordertown ~ Call of the Wild ~ Dangerous.

1936   Loew's makes a profit of $10.6 million and buys one fifth of Gaumont-British Corporation ~ Irving Thalberg dies ~ Barney Balaban becomes president of Paramount, with Zukor as chairman of the board ~ Carl Laemmle sells Universal to J. Cheever Cowdin's Standard Capital Corporation ~ W. Ray Johnston leaves Republic to reform Monogram ~ the Hollywood Anti-Nazi League is formed ~ James Cagney wins a breach of contract case against WB ~ Deanna Durbin, the economic savior of Universal, first appears in *Three Smart Girls*.
San Francisco ~ Bullets or Ballots ~ The Green Pastures ~ San Francisco ~ Rose

Marie ~ Modern Times ~ The Story of Louis Pasteur ~ My Man Godfrey ~ The Charge of the Light Brigade.

1937   World attendance is 215 million a week ~ movies account for 75% of the money Americans spend on amusements ~ Nathan J. Blumberg becomes president of Universal, Cliff Work head of production ~ studio craft unions strike for recognition, and the Screen Actors Guild is recognized by studios ~ the Screen Directors Guild is formed ~ the majors produce 408 pictures ~ *Snow White and the Seven Dwarfs* is Disney's first feature-length animated movie ~ *A Family Affair* is the first of MGM's Andy Hardy pictures, starring Mickey Rooney.
Stella Dallas ~ They Won't Forget ~ Black Legion ~ The Good Earth ~ Dead End ~ A Star is Born ~ The Hurricane ~ The Life of Emile Zola ~ Marked Woman.

1938   The Department of Justice begins an anti-trust suit (the Paramount suit) against the eight majors ~ the Screen Writers and Directors Guilds are recognized by studios ~ Y. Frank Freeman becomes head of production at Paramount ~ many smaller neighborhood theaters install air-conditioning, and sales of popcorn and candy become an increasingly important source of profit for small exhibitors ~ Shirley Temple, Clark Gable, and ice-skater Sonja Henie are the most popular stars.
The Adventures of Robin Hood ~ Angels with Dirty Faces ~ Blockade ~ You Can't Take It With You ~ Boys Town ~ In Old Chicago ~ Bringing Up Baby ~ Boy Meets Girl.

1939   "Hollywood's greatest year" ~ the industry employs 177,420 people, 33,687 of them in production ~ $187 million is spent on production ~ average weekly attendance is 85 million ~ the majors produce 388 pictures ~ Bette Davis becomes top female star, in *The Private Lives of Elizabeth and Essex*, *The Old Maid*, and *Dark Victory*.
Confessions of a Nazi Spy ~ Mr Smith Goes to Washington ~ Ninotchka ~ Juárez ~ Jesse James ~ Drums Along the Mohawk ~ The Story of Alexander Graham Bell ~ Only Angels Have Wings ~ The Roaring Twenties ~ Stagecoach ~ The Wizard of Oz ~ Gone with the Wind ~ Young Mr Lincoln.

1940   The Paramount suit is temporarily settled by a consent decree, in which the majors agree to restrict the size of the block of movies they require exhibitors to buy ~ investment in the industry exceeds $2 billion ~ the House Committee on Un-American Activities (HUAC) conducts its first brief investigation of Hollywood ~ the Producers Releasing Corporation (PRC) is established ~ *Rebecca* is director Alfred Hitchcock's first American movie, for David O. Selznick ~ Bob Hope and Bing Crosby are teamed with Dorothy Lamour in *Road to Singapore*, the first of a successful series for Paramount ~ WB's *Santa Fe Trail* and *Four Wives* are the first American pictures in stereophonic sound ~ MGM releases the first *Tom and Jerry* cartoon.
Fantasia ~ The Letter ~ The Grapes of Wrath ~ Kitty Foyle ~ The Philadelphia Story ~ The Great Dictator ~ Abe Lincoln in Illinois ~ Our Town ~ The Long Voyage Home ~ Escape ~ The Mortal Storm.

1941   US Senate hearings investigating allegations that Hollywood is producing propaganda in favor of American entry into the war are curtailed by Pearl

Harbor ~ President Roosevelt declares that movies should not be subject to war censorship ~ the industry organizes a War Activities Committee ~ Spyros Skouras becomes president of TCF ~ WB buys one quarter of the Associated British Picture Corporation ~ the Conference of Studio Unions is organized after a strike at the Disney Studios ~ the majors produce 379 pictures ~ Betty Grable begins her career at TCF in *Down Argentine Way* ~ Abbott and Costello begin their series of successful comedies for Universal with *Buck Privates*.
Citizen Kane ~ *The Maltese Falcon* ~ *Back Street* ~ *Sergeant York* ~ *A Yank in the RAF* ~ *Sullivan's Travels* ~ *Meet John Doe* ~ *The Great Lie*.

1942 The Bureau of Motion Pictures is established as part of the government's Office of War Information (OWI), to direct the industry's representation of the war ~ one in four pictures' theme relates to the war effort ~ wartime audiences of 84 million double the previous year's profits ~ the *Why We Fight* propaganda series of documentaries begins ~ Floyd Odlum buys a controlling interest in RKO and appoints Charles M. Koerner as head of production ~ wartime taxes encourage stars and producers to set up independent production companies ~ Abbott and Costello are top box-office draws.
Now Voyager ~ *The Palm Beach Story* ~ *For Me and My Gal* ~ *Yankee Doodle Dandy* ~ *Mrs Miniver* ~ *Casablanca*.

1943 Movie theaters participate in the sale of war bonds, scrap collections, and other war work ~ Hollywood's contributions to the war effort include pro-Russian movies *Mission to Moscow*, *North Star*, and *Song of Russia* ~ Disney makes *Victory through Air Power* ~ Olivia de Havilland wins an important legal victory against WB over players' contracts ~ the majors produce 289 pictures ~ Betty Grable and Bob Hope are top box-office stars.
This is the Army ~ *This is the Navy* ~ *Air Force* ~ *Watch on the Rhine* ~ *Destination Tokyo* ~ *For Whom the Bell Tolls* ~ *Destroyer* ~ *Madame Curie* ~ *Cabin in the Sky* ~ *The Ox-Bow Incident*.

1944 The Department of Justice reactivates the Paramount suit ~ Hal Wallis resigns as head of production at WB to become an independent producer ~ the Motion Picture Alliance for the Preservation of American Ideals is founded ~ top stars are Bing Crosby and Gary Cooper.
Going My Way ~ *Meet Me in St Louis* ~ *Since You Went Away* ~ *The Mask of Dimitrios* ~ *Double Indemnity* ~ *Up in Arms* ~ *Pin Up Girl* ~ *Wilson* ~ *Hollywood Canteen*.

1945 Will Hays retires as president of the MPPDA ~ his replacement, Eric Johnston, changes the name of the industry trade association to the Motion Picture Association of America (MPAA), and establishes its foreign department as the Motion Picture Export Association (MPEA) ~ a strike by the Conference of Studio Unions lasts for 30 weeks ~ the Screen Extras Guild is organized ~ the majors produce 234 pictures ~ Humphrey Bogart and Lauren Bacall appear in *To Have and Have Not*.
The Bells of St Mary's ~ *Mildred Pierce* ~ *The Story of GI Joe* ~ *Pride of the Marines* ~ *Objective Burma* ~ *They Were Expendable* ~ *Anchors Aweigh* ~ *Spellbound*.

1946 The industry's most profitable year, in which it generates 1.5% of US corporate profit, and $232 million in domestic rentals ~ 600 American movies flood the postwar Italian market ~ Universal merges with William Goetz's International Pictures to become Universal-International, with Goetz as head of production ~ the studio's policy concentrates on independent production ~ RKO Theaters is formed ~ producer Howard Hughes is ordered to return the PCA seal after releasing an unauthorized version of *The Outlaw* ~ Bing Crosby and Ingrid Bergman are leading box-office stars.
The Best Years of Our Lives ~ Duel in the Sun ~ The Jolson Story ~ My Darling Clementine ~ Gilda ~ The Big Sleep ~ The Lady in the Lake ~ The Postman Always Rings Twice ~ It's a Wonderful Life ~ Night and Day ~ Notorious ~ Terror by Night.

1947 HUAC resumes its investigations of "Communist infiltration of the motion picture industry" ~ the Hollywood Ten are charged with contempt of Congress, and dismissed by their studios ~ the federal government files an anti-trust suit against Technicolor ~ 90% of theaters sell popcorn, 66% show double bills ~ 742 actors are under studio contract ~ Britain briefly imposes an embargo on American films ~ WB buys RKO-Pathé newsreel ~ Dore Schary becomes head of production at RKO ~ there is a sharp fall in MGM profits.
Gentleman's Agreement ~ Crossfire ~ Body and Soul ~ Forever Amber ~ Dark Passage.

1948 The Paramount case reaches the Supreme Court, which decides that industry practices are in breach of the anti-trust laws, and approves a consent decree that will divorce the majors' theaters from their production and distribution operations ~ Howard Hughes buys RKO ~ Dore Schary leaves RKO to become head of production under Mayer at MGM ~ Eagle-Lion absorbs PRC ~ "Theater television" is initiated ~ 18,000 theaters in the US, but weekly audiences fall to 66 million ~ Burt Lancaster is one of several stars to establish his own production company, Hecht-Lancaster.
Red River ~ The Beautiful Blonde from Bashful Bend ~ Rope ~ The Pirate ~ Letter from an Unknown Woman ~ Easter Parade ~ All the King's Men ~ The Treasure of the Sierra Madre.

1949 Paramount and RKO enter into consent decrees to divorce their theater holdings from production-distribution ~ 20% of movies released by the majors are independent productions ~ one million American homes have television ~ Eastman Kodak introduces single-strip color stock ~ the majors produce 234 pictures, 46 in Technicolor ~ Bob Hope is the top box-office draw ~ Republic Studios has its biggest ever success with *The Sands of Iwo Jima*.
Twelve O'Clock High ~ On the Town ~ Home of the Brave ~ Lost Boundaries ~ Pinky ~ Intruder in the Dust ~ The Snake Pit ~ She Wore a Yellow Ribbon ~ I Married a Communist ~ I Was a Male War Bride ~ Adam's Rib.

1950 The Hollywood Ten are jailed ~ the American Cinema Editors (ACE) organization is founded ~ John Wayne is the top box-office star.
Broken Arrow ~ The Gunfighter ~ Stage Fright ~ White Heat ~ Sunset Boulevard ~ No Way Out ~ Father of the Bride ~ The Asphalt Jungle ~ Samson and Delilah ~ Battleground ~ All About Eve.

1951   TCF and WB sign consent decrees ~ Louis B. Mayer resigns from MGM, and Dore Schary becomes head of the studio ~ Arthur Krim and Robert Benjamin take over UA ~ Krim's Eagle-Lion is absorbed into UA ~ the HUAC "mass hearings" begin ~ Columbia establishes a subsidiary, Screen Gems, to produce telefilms ~ Monogram releases the rights of 300 features to television ~ the Screen Actors Guild demands royalties for showings of all post-1948 movies on television ~ the majors release 320 pictures.
A Streetcar Named Desire ~ Storm Warning ~ Ace in the Hole ~ David and Bathsheba ~ Showboat ~ An American in Paris.

1952   The Supreme Court decision in *The Miracle* case establishes that motion pictures are protected by the First Amendment, making state censorship unconstitutional ~ TCF sells its theaters to National Theaters, Inc. ~ Decca Records buys Universal ~ UA releases the first 3-D movie, *Bwana Devil* ~ Cinerama is launched in New York with *This is Cinerama* ~ Dean Martin and Jerry Lewis become the top box-office draw.
High Noon ~ The Greatest Show on Earth ~ Quo Vadis? ~ Singin' in the Rain ~ The African Queen ~ The Bad and the Beautiful ~ The Road to Bali.

1953   TCF releases the first movie in CinemaScope (*The Robe*) ~ 24 3-D movies are released ~ box-office returns improve for the first time since 1946, but only 32% of theaters make profits on admission income, and attendance is half that of 1946 ~ 46% of American families own a television ~ United Paramount Theaters merges with the American Broadcasting Corporation (ABC) ~ Disney forms its own distribution company, Buena Vista ~ Monogram Pictures is reorganized as Allied Artists ~ WB sells its theaters to the Stanley Warner Corporation ~ the majors release 301 pictures ~ Gary Cooper is the top box-office star ~ UA releases *The Moon is Blue* without a PCA seal, and the movie is a commercial success.
Gentlemen Prefer Blondes ~ How to Marry a Millionaire ~ From Here to Eternity ~ Shane.

1954   Major companies abandon production of 3-D movies ~ the Screen Writers Guild becomes the Writers Guild of America ~ Samuel Z. Arkoff and James Nicholson form the American Releasing Corporation (ARC) ~ 3,000 movie theaters have closed since 1948, but 3,000 drive-ins have opened ~ the majors' production drops to 225 pictures ~ Paramount releases *White Christmas* in VistaVision.
Rear Window ~ A Star is Born ~ The Bridges at Toko-Ri ~ Johnny Guitar ~ The Wild One.

1955   Of all movies released 62% are in color, 38% in widescreen ~ the Todd-AO process debuts with *Oklahoma!* ~ Howard Hughes sells RKO to General Telluride, a subsidiary of the General Tire and Rubber Company ~ *On the Waterfront* wins eight Oscars, including Best Actor for Marlon Brando ~ WB begins producing television programming ~ Nicholas Schenck retires as president of Loew's, Inc. ~ the majors are producing 20% of prime-time television programming, but their production of features drops to 215 pictures ~ John Wayne forms Batjac Productions, Kirk Douglas forms Bryna Productions, Randolph Scott forms Ranown Productions ~ James Stewart and Grace Kelly are top box-office stars.

Blackboard Jungle ~ East of Eden ~ Rebel Without a Cause ~ All That Heaven Allows ~ Bad Day at Black Rock ~ The Seven Year Itch ~ Marty.

1956   The Production Code is revised to permit references to prostitution and drugs ~ Darryl Zanuck resigns as head of production at TCF, replaced by Buddy Adler ~ Harry and Albert Warner sell their interest in WB and retire ~ WB sells television rights to its library of pre-1948 movies ~ 229 actors are under studio contract ~ the last Hollywood serial is produced (*Blazing the Overland Trail*) ~ Dore Schary leaves MGM ~ ARC is reorganized as American-International Pictures (AIP) ~ William Holden and John Wayne are top box-office attractions.
The Ten Commandments ~ Around the World in Eighty Days ~ The Big Knife ~ The Searchers ~ Written on the Wind ~ The Man with the Golden Arm ~ Baby Doll ~ Bigger Than Life ~ Tea and Sympathy ~ Invasion of the Body Snatchers ~ Guys and Dolls ~ The King and I.

1957   Production of movies in color declines to 34% of the total ~ RKO ceases movie production ~ 58% of the movies released by the majors are independent productions ~ UA acquires distribution rights to WB's pre-1948 film library, and is floated on the stock market ~ the majors release 268 pictures ~ 52% of the audience is under 20, 72% under 29 ~ Rock Hudson is the top box-office star.
The Bridge on the River Kwai ~ Peyton Place ~ I Was a Teenage Werewolf ~ The Long Hot Summer ~ Silk Stockings ~ Jailhouse Rock.

1958   The RKO studio is bought by Desilu Productions, producers of the *I Love Lucy* television show ~ RKO's theaters merge with Stanley Warner ~ Republic Pictures closes ~ 4,700 drive-in theaters in the US, accounting for 20% of movie rentals ~ MCA buys Paramount's film library ~ Glenn Ford and Elizabeth Taylor are top box-office stars.
South Pacific ~ Touch of Evil ~ The Defiant Ones ~ Vertigo ~ Cat on a Hot Tin Roof ~ Rio Bravo.

1959   Loew's is the last major company to complete the divorcement of exhibition from production–distribution ~ Decca and MCA merge ~ Y. Frank Freeman retires as Paramount head of production ~ the majors release 189 pictures ~ Rock Hudson and Cary Grant are top box-office stars ~ *Behind the Great Wall* is the first movie in AromaRama.
Ben-Hur ~ Some Like It Hot ~ North by Northwest ~ Imitation of Life ~ Anatomy of a Murder.

1960   The Screen Actors Guild refuses to merge with the American Federation of Radio and Television Artists (AFRTA) ~ *Scent of Mystery* is the first movie in Smell-o-Vision ~ Dalton Trumbo is the first of the Hollywood Ten to receive screen credit, as writer on *Exodus* and *Spartacus* ~ Doris Day and Rock Hudson are top box-office stars.
Psycho ~ The Sundowners ~ The Apartment ~ Comanche Station ~ The Alamo ~ The Magnificent Seven.

1961   Average production costs $1.5 million ~ half of Hollywood's rental revenues come from the foreign market ~ NBC launches "NBC Saturday Night

at the Movies," the first prime-time series of post-1948 movies on television ~ the TCF studio site is sold to Aluminum Corporation of America (ALCOA), and redeveloped as Century City ~ the majors release 167 pictures ~ Elizabeth Taylor is the top box-office star.
West Side Story ~ The Guns of Navarone ~ The Absent-Minded Professor.

1962   Talent agency Music Corporation of America (MCA) completes its takeover of Universal, and Lew Wasserman becomes president ~ Darryl Zanuck returns to TCF as president with Richard Zanuck in charge of production after the studio reports losses of $40 million ~ Doris Day is the top box-office star ~ MGM's *The Wonderful World of the Brothers Grimm* is the first full-length Cinerama feature.
The Longest Day ~ Lawrence of Arabia ~ The Courtship of Eddie's Father ~ The Man Who Shot Liberty Valance ~ The Manchurian Candidate.

1963   *Cleopatra,* produced at a cost of $44 million, is the most expensive movie ever made ~ the majors are producing 70% of prime-time television programming, and earning 30% of their revenue from telefilm production ~ the Parkway Twin, Kansas City, becomes the first two-screen cinema ~ there are 12,652 screens in the US ~ the majors release 142 pictures.
The Birds ~ Irma La Douce ~ It's a Mad Mad Mad Mad World ~ How the West Was Won.

1964   Sidney Poitier becomes the first African-American man to win an Academy Award, as Best Actor in *Lilies of the Field* ~ Barney Balaban retires as president of Paramount ~ *The Pawnbroker* is the first movie featuring a brief scene of female nudity to be passed uncut by the PCA ~ Universal Studios opens as a theme park ~ average weekly audience is half that of 1957 ~ Doris Day and Jack Lemmon are top box-office attractions.
Dr Strangelove ~ Goldfinger ~ Marnie ~ The Best Man ~ The Fall of the Roman Empire ~ Kiss Me, Stupid.

1965   The success of *The Sound of Music* inaugurates a cycle of high-budget productions ~ average cost of admission, $1 ~ the majors release 167 pictures ~ Sean Connery is the top box-office star.
Mary Poppins ~ Thunderball ~ The Agony and the Ecstasy ~ Red Line 7000 ~ The Greatest Story Ever Told ~ Cat Ballou.

1966   Paramount bought by Gulf and Western: Charles Bluhdorn becomes president, Robert Evans head of production ~ Jack Valenti replaces Eric Johnston as president of the MPAA ~ the Production Code is rewritten ~ its new classification, "Suggested for Mature Audiences" (SMA), is first applied to *Who's Afraid of Virginia Woolf?* ~ the National Legion of Decency changes its name to the National Catholic Office for Motion Pictures and liberalizes its ratings ~ Julie Andrews becomes top box-office star ~ ABC pays $2 million to Columbia for the television rights to *The Bridge on the River Kwai.*
El Dorado ~ Grand Prix ~ Dr Zhivago ~ The Chase.

1967   US movie attendances rise for the first time since 1947 ~ UA becomes a subsidiary of the Transamerica Corporation ~ Jack Warner sells his interest in WB, which merges with Seven Arts ~ CBS television buys the Republic Studio lot ~ the success of *The Graduate* and *Bonnie and Clyde* encourages studios to hire younger producers and directors to make movies appealing

to a younger audience ~ the majors release 157 movies ~ Julie Andrews and Lee Marvin are top stars.
Guess Who's Coming to Dinner ~ In the Heat of the Night ~ The Dirty Dozen.

1968   After Supreme Court decisions upholding the constitutional power of states to prevent children being exposed to material permitted for adults, the MPAA abandons the Production Code in favor of a ratings system, with four categories (G, M, R, and X) awarded by the Code and Ratings Administration (CARA) ~ the Avco Corporation takes over Embassy Pictures ~ BBS is formed by Burt Scheider, Bob Rafelson, and Steve Blauner ~ majors' box-office tops $1 billion ~ Sidney Poitier is the top box-office star.
2001: A Space Odyssey ~ Madigan ~ Bullitt ~ Valley of the Dolls.

1969   Overproduction, especially of blockbusters, causes industry recession ~ MGM is bought by financier Kirk Kerkorian ~ WB is bought by the Kinney National Service Corporation, headed by Stephen J. Ross, with Ted Ashley in charge of production ~ TCF incurs record losses of $65 million ~ Universal is close to liquidation ~ UA loses $89 million and comes under new leadership ~ the first major X-rated release, *Midnight Cowboy*, wins Academy Award for Best Picture ~ Francis Ford Coppola founds American Zoetrope ~ the American Film Institute opens the Advanced Study Center in Los Angeles ~ the majors release 154 movies ~ 70% of features are "runaway" productions made outside Hollywood ~ Paul Newman becomes top box-office star.
Butch Cassidy and the Sundance Kid ~ Easy Rider ~ Woodstock ~ The Wild Bunch ~ True Grit ~ The Love Bug ~ Funny Girl.

1970   TCF records a deficit of $77.4 million ~ CARA raises age limits on R and X categories from 16 to 17, and changes M to GP (all ages permitted, parental discretion advised) ~ Ted Ashley takes charge of production at WB ~ Roger Corman forms New World Pictures ~ Sidney Poitier, Paul Newman, and Barbra Streisand form First Artists Production Company ~ there are 14,500 screens in the US ~ IMAX debuts at the Osaka Exposition ~ 94% of movies are produced in color.
Love Story ~ Airport ~ M*A*S*H ~ Rio Lobo ~ Catch-22 ~ Little Big Man ~ Patton.

1971   The "Hollywood Renaissance" begins ~ average weekly audience reaches an all-time low of 16 million ~ the Zanucks resign from TCF, and are replaced by Dennis Stanfill ~ Frank Yablans becomes president of Paramount ~ Columbia loses $29 million ~ DisneyWorld opens in Florida ~ Robert Altman forms Lion's Gate Films ~ many major newspaper syndicates refuse to advertise X-rated movies ~ about 400 non-rated movies are screened in the US ~ the majors release 143 movies ~ only 24% of Screen Actors Guild members' income comes from movies, the rest from television ~ John Wayne is the top box-office star ~ *A Clockwork Orange* is the first picture with Dolby sound.
The French Connection ~ Dirty Harry ~ Klute ~ Carnal Knowledge ~ The Last Picture Show.

1972   Average production costs $2 million ~ industry recession produces 50% unemployment ~ CARA changes GP category to PG (parental guidance

suggested) ~ MGM threatens withdrawal from MPAA ~ Ned Tanen becomes head of production at Universal ~ Columbia sells its studio and
shares studio space and plant with WB ~ Clint Eastwood and George C.
Scott are top box-office stars ~ *The Godfather* takes three times as much
money at the US box-office as its nearest competitor, *Fiddler on the Roof* ~ the
"blaxploitation" cycle, of movies made by white producers aimed at
African-American audiences, peaks with *Superfly*, *Blacula*, and *Blackenstein*.
The Poseidon Adventure ~ *Two Lane Blacktop* ~ *The Candidate* ~ *Deliverance* ~
Cabaret ~ *A Clockwork Orange* ~ *What's Up, Doc?*

1973   73% of ticket sales are to the 12–19 age group ~ the Supreme Court decides
that questions of offensiveness should be judged by local community standards, allowing them to disregard CARA ratings ~ MGM sells off studio
property and abandons distribution after a series of box-office failures,
including *Pat Garrett and Billy the Kid*, and subsequently distributes through
UA ~ WB becomes Warner Communications Inc. (WCI) ~ Alan Hirschfield
and David Begelman take over management at Columbia ~ a bill to limit
runaway production is introduced to Congress ~ the majors release 132
pictures.
The Exorcist ~ *American Graffiti* ~ *The Sting* ~ *The Long Goodbye* ~ *High Plains
Drifter* ~ *The Friends of Eddie Coyle*.

1974   Box-office grosses increase by $150 million ~ 100 new screens open ~
weekly attendance is 18 million ~ Robert Redford is the top box-office star
~ *Earthquake* is the first movie in Sensurround.
Blazing Saddles ~ *Chinatown* ~ *The Eiger Sanction* ~ *The Godfather Part II* ~ *The
Longest Yard* ~ *Death Wish* ~ *The Conversation* ~ *Alice Doesn't Live Here
Anymore*.

1975   Average admission price $2 ~ there are 10,000 indoor theaters in the US,
and a total of 14,000 screens ~ an estimated 10% of production effort is
applied to making sequels ~ Home Box Office (HBO) begins satellite transmission to its cable television networks ~ Industrial Light and Magic is
established to develop special effects for *Star Wars* ~ the majors release 97
movies ~ Robert Redford and Barbra Streisand are top box-office stars ~ *The
Towering Inferno* is the first co-production by two major studios, TCF and
WCI.
Jaws ~ *One Flew Over the Cuckoo's Nest* ~ *Nashville* ~ *Shampoo* ~ *Dog Day
Afternoon*.

1976   VHS and Betamax video-recording systems introduced ~ MCA and Disney
bring suit against Sony, charging that video-recorders infringe copyright ~
the US Congress abolishes tax shelter schemes for financing movies, drastically reducing the volume of independent production ~ HBO wins its
challenge against the Federal Communication Commission's protection of
broadcast television.
Rocky ~ *All the President's Men* ~ *Network* ~ *Taxi Driver* ~ *A Star is Born* ~ *The
Shootist*.

1977   Average production cost $7.5 million ~ CARA is reorganized as the Classi-
fication and Rating Administration, and abandons the practice of vetting
scripts ~ MCA and Paramount form Cinema International Corporation

(CIC) to distribute theatrical pictures outside the US ~ after a dispute with Transamerica corporate managers, Krim and Benjamin resign as UA's management team ~ TCF diversifies by buying a ski resort and a Coca-Cola bottling plant ~ Steadicam is developed ~ MPAA establishes the Office of Film Security to combat piracy ~ TCF releases 50 features to Sony for distribution on video ~ the majors release 78 movies ~ Sylvester Stallone becomes top box-office draw ~ *Star Wars* becomes the highest-grossing movie.
Close Encounters of the Third Kind ~ *Saturday Night Fever* ~ *Annie Hall* ~ *Smokey and the Bandit* ~ *The Hills Have Eyes*.

1978   Krim and Benjamin form Orion Pictures with Mike Madavoy ~ the Washington task force concludes that anti-trust decrees had little effect upon the majors' oligopoly power ~ David Begelman quits as head of Columbia following a financial scandal ~ Burt Reynolds is the most profitable star.
Grease ~ *National Lampoon's Animal House* ~ *Halloween* ~ *The Deer Hunter* ~ *Coming Home* ~ *Jaws 2*.

1979   The average movie earns 80% of its receipts from theatrical release, 20% from video and television ~ Cannon Pictures taken over by Menachem Golan and Yoram Globus ~ *Variety* claims business has doubled since 1971 ~ MGM resumes distribution ~ Cineplex Odeon opens its 18-screen multiplex cinema in Toronto ~ average production cost is $6 million.
Superman ~ *Kramer vs Kramer* ~ *Alien* ~ *Apocalypse Now* ~ *The China Syndrome* ~ *The Jerk* ~ *Star Trek* ~ *Norma Rae* ~ *Manhattan* ~ *Every Which Way But Loose*.

1980   Average production cost rises to $10 million ~ *Heaven's Gate* records a box-office loss of $40 million, leading Transamerica to withdraw from the industry and sell UA ~ Sherry Lansing becomes president of Twentieth Century-Fox, the first woman to head a major Hollywood company ~ ten-week actors' strike ~ video-cassette sales account for 15% of domestic revenue ~ the American Film Marketing Association (AFMA) is formed as the trade association for smaller producers and distributors ~ Clint Eastwood is the top box-office draw.
Ordinary People ~ *The Empire Strikes Back* ~ *Dressed to Kill* ~ *Friday the 13th* ~ *American Gigolo* ~ *The Shining* ~ *Raging Bull*.

1981   TCF is bought by oil tycoon Marvin Davis ~ Kirk Kerkorian buys UA from Transamerica and forms the MGM/UA Entertainment Company ~ MGM/UA joins CIC to form United International Pictures (UIP) to distribute their movies abroad ~ average feature costs $11 million ~ the majors release 112 movies.
Raiders of the Lost Ark ~ *Hell Night* ~ *On Golden Pond* ~ *Body Heat* ~ *Southern Comfort* ~ *Superman II* ~ *Stir Crazy*.

1982   Coca-Cola purchases Columbia ~ Tri-Star Pictures is formed by Columbia, HBO, and CBS ~ drive-ins decline as their sites become valuable as real estate ~ *E.T. – The Extra-Terrestrial* becomes the highest-grossing movie of all time.
Tootsie ~ *Reds* ~ *Blade Runner* ~ *The Thing* ~ *Tender Mercies* ~ *An Officer and a Gentleman* ~ *Evil Under the Sun* ~ *Gandhi*.

1983   WCI abandons its involvement in video games after large losses, and restructures to concentrate on movie and television production and distribution, recorded music and publishing ~ Cannon, now a "mini-major," is California's fastest-growing corporation ~ average weekly audience is 23 million ~ Frank Mancuso becomes president of Paramount ~ the majors release 106 movies ~ Clint Eastwood is top box-office star.
Terms of Endearment ~ Return of the Jedi ~ Zelig ~ Wargames ~ Trading Places.

1984   The Supreme Court decides in favor of Sony in video-tape copyright suit ~ Michael Eisner and Jeffrey Katzenberg take over management at Disney, and establish Touchstone Pictures to make movies for adult audiences ~ after a dispute with producer-director Steven Spielberg over the rating for *Indiana Jones and the Temple of Doom*, CARA introduces a new classification of PG-13 ~ 85% of the audience is under 40 ~ Japan becomes the largest importer of American movies ~ the growth of multiplexes increases the number of screens to 22,000 ~ box-office gross reaches $4.2 billion.
Ghostbusters ~ Indiana Jones and the Temple of Doom ~ Beverly Hills Cop ~ Once Upon a Time in America ~ The Terminator ~ Gremlins ~ Police Academy ~ Romancing the Stone ~ Amadeus.

1985   The legal decision that had required the major companies to sell their theaters after 1948 is reversed, and the majors begin buying theater chains ~ media mogul Rupert Murdoch's News International buys Twentieth Century-Fox, with Barry Diller in charge of production ~ TV magnate Ted Turner buys MGM/UA ~ average ticket price is $3.50 ~ home video business generates more revenue than theatrical rentals ($2.1 billion) ~ Dino de Laurentiis forms De Laurentiis Entertainment and buys Embassy Pictures ~ Cineplex Odeon takes over the Plitt Theater chain and becomes one of the four largest theater chains in the US ~ the majors release 116 movies ~ Sylvester Stallone is the top box-office star.
Rambo: First Blood Part II ~ Out of Africa ~ Back to the Future ~ Desperately Seeking Susan ~ Rocky IV ~ Cocoon ~ Witness.

1986   Ted Turner sells MGM/UA back to Kerkorian, but keeps its film and television library ~ British producer David Putnam briefly becomes chairman of Columbia ~ 50% of American homes have VCRs ~ there are 30,000 video stores in the US ~ MCA buys half of Cineplex Odeon ~ Cannon acquires foreign production and distribution facilities, then collapses after a Securities and Exchange Commission investigation ~ admissions of over-40s rise ~ the majors release 102 pictures, compared to 131 released by independents.
Aliens ~ Peggy Sue Got Married ~ Top Gun ~ Platoon ~ Hannah and Her Sisters ~ Blue Velvet ~ The Color Purple ~ She's Gotta Have It.

1987   Coca-Cola merges Columbia with Tri-Star to form Columbia Pictures Entertainment ~ Universal has 50% equity in Cineplex Odeon cinemas ~ Paramount and Orion have the largest shares of the domestic box-office ~ independents release 25% of the top 100 pictures ~ Eddie Murphy is the top box-office star.

Beverly Hills Cop II ~ Angel Heart ~ Fatal Attraction ~ Wall Street ~ Three Men and a Baby ~ Robocop.

1988 Disney has 20% of the domestic market ~ 50% of US households own VCRs ~ sales of *E.T.* on video generate $150 million for MCA ~ De Laurentiis Entertainment folds ~ writers' strike in Hollywood ~ Tom Cruise is the top box-office star.
Who Framed Roger Rabbit ~ Die Hard ~ Cop ~ Willow ~ Mississippi Burning ~ Rain Man ~ Coming to America ~ Beetlejuice.

1989 Record box-office takings of $5.03 billion ~ Columbia takes over Tri-Star, then is bought by Sony Corporation for $3.4 billion in preparation for a convergence of technologies around high definition television ~ Gulf and Western becomes Paramount Communications Inc., and attempts to take over WCI ~ instead, WCI merges with Time Inc. to create Time-Warner, the world's largest media conglomerate ~ Joe Roth takes charge of production for TCF ~ Disney forms Hollywood Pictures.
Batman ~ Back to the Future Part II ~ Friday the 13th Part VIII ~ Lethal Weapon 2 ~ Do the Right Thing ~ The Little Mermaid ~ Field of Dreams.

1990 Controversy over the content of *Henry and June* causes CARA to introduce the NC-17 category, replacing X ~ Pathé Corporation acquires MGM/UA ~ MCA opens Universal Studios in Orlando, Florida ~ the Matsushita Corporation buys MCA for $6.6 billion in the largest ever Japanese take-over in the US ~ average production cost rises to $24 million ~ 24% of the audience is now over 40 ~ Arnold Schwarzenegger is the top box-office star.
Pretty Woman ~ Total Recall ~ Dances with Wolves ~ Guilty by Suspicion ~ Ghost ~ Home Alone ~ Days of Thunder ~ Kindergarten Cop.

1991 31% of the audience is 12–20, 25% is 21–9, 44% over 30 ~ Sony renames Columbia as Sony Pictures Entertainment ~ Kevin Costner is the top box-office star ~ computer "morphing" special effects are used in *Terminator 2: Judgment Day.*
The Silence of the Lambs ~ Arachnophobia ~ The Prince of Tides ~ The Last of the Mohicans ~ Jungle Fever ~ City Slickers ~ Thelma and Louise ~ Robin Hood, Prince of Thieves ~ The Addams Family ~ Naked Gun 2½ ~ Boyz N The Hood.

1992 Despite a succession of box-office successes, Orion Pictures files for bankruptcy ~ stars' salaries are cut because of the recession ~ EuroDisney opens in Paris ~ videos are issued in widescreen format ~ Tom Cruise is the top box-office star.
Basic Instinct ~ Unforgiven ~ The Player ~ JFK ~ Grand Canyon ~ Bob Roberts.

1993 American theatrical exhibition accounts for 20% of the average movie's earnings, foreign theatrical exhibition 15%, video and television sales the remainder ~ Disney buys Miramax Pictures ~ GATT trade negotiations stall over American access to overseas movie and television markets. *Jurassic Park* becomes the highest grossing movie ever.
Cliffhanger ~ Sleepless in Seattle ~ Groundhog Day ~ The Last Action Hero ~ Falling Down ~ Dave ~ Malcolm X.

Glossary

This glossary provides explanations of the terms emboldened where they are first used or explained in the text. Some of these terms have a sense specific to this book, and are identified as such in the explanation. A page reference to the first or principal occurrence of each term is also provided. Cross-references to other entries in the glossary appear in **bold type**.

180-degree rule The 180-degree rule maintains audience comprehension of figures' relative situations in **represented space** by granting the spectator a relatively stable viewpoint on the action. In filming a scene between two characters, we can draw an imaginary line that connects them. So long as the camera stays on one side of this **center line** or **line of action**, the characters will stay in the same relation to each other in the screen space, and the **movie** can cut between any two images taken from below the line without disturbing the audience. If the camera crosses the line, viewers may lose their sense of spatial position, and this may distract them from following the action. P. 208. The 180-degree rule is illustrated on p. 206.

analogical/digital Analogical media use a continuously variable physical phenomenon, such as **film** emulsion, to describe, imitate, or represent another dynamic phenomenon, such as light. Digital media such as television or video, by contrast, approximate continuous phenomena by recording information as a digital code, which can subsequently be retranslated. Digital media are in one sense more precise, in that they can reproduce exactly the data originally recorded. They are, however, also less complete, in that they can only approximate the variable aspects of a continuous phenomenon. An analogue clock, for instance, can tell you the time with as much precision as you care to interpret into the continuous movement of its hands, but a digital clock insists that it is either one moment in time, or another. The analogical properties of cinema provide the basis for the claims to **realism** or **mimesis** made on its behalf, but they also explain the difficulties involved in adequately describing an image or a performance, which relies for its communication on proportion, relation, and inflection, by means of a digital system such as language, which requires a set of clear-cut distinctions and differences. P. 236.

apparatus of cinema   See **cinematic apparatus**.

apparatus theory   The name given to a body of theoretical writing (see **theory**) by Jean-Louis Baudry, Christian Metz, and others, which credited the **cinematic apparatus** with delivering an impression of reality so charged as to be, like dreams, more than real, engulfing the spectator. P. 430.

artistic motivation   See **motivation**.

aspect ratio   The ratio of the height of the image to its width. The standard aspect ratio in **Classical Hollywood**, the Academy ratio, was 1:1.33. Widescreen ratios vary from 1:1.85 to 1:2.6. P. 154. Aspect ratios are illustrated on p. 155.

auteurism   As a critical method, auteurism (originated in France by the critics of *Cahiers du Cinéma* as the *politique des auteurs*, and translated into Anglo-American criticism by Andrew Sarris as the auteur theory) proposes that an individual, usually the director, has an authorial responsibility for a **movie** that allows it to be identified as his or her work, and studied as the work of an individual creator, in a manner similar to the study of literature. Auteurism is not a **theory** as such; it relies on theoretical principles to evaluate particular movies and rank directors in a hierarchy of worth, rather than achieve a systematic understanding of cinema as a general phenomenon. P. 31.

auteur-structuralism   A version of **auteurism** that incorporated aspects of structuralist criticism (see **structuralism**). It studied the recurring structural features of a body of **movies** "signed" by the same name (for example, those "directed by Alfred Hitchcock"), but it also sought to detach those structures from the cult of personality that auteurism encouraged. Understanding the author as a critical construct rather than a person, auteur-structuralism identified "Hitchcock" as a body of structuring principles that could be divined from a critical examination of films, but bearing no necessary relation to the small, fat, male person who routinely appeared in each of these movies. P. 423.

autonomous performance   A performance within a **movie** offering the audience a source of pleasure largely separable from their engagement with the movie's **story**. An element of performance commonly found in musicals and comedies, it is also an important element in the pleasures offered by star vehicles displaying their stars in as many of their famous postures as possible. P. 249.

biopic   One of Hollywood's biographical pictures. P. 310.

block-booking   This trade practice, imposed by the major, vertically integrated companies (see **vertical integration**), obliged smaller exhibitors to rent **movies** in blocks of between five and fifty. For every expensive production in a block, there would be several lower-budget movies. The system worked in the distributor's interest, by ensuring a wider distribution for lower-budget movies and preventing independent exhibitors from buying only the most successful product. P. 66.

blockbuster   After **divorcement**, the major companies concentrated on producing more lavish and spectacular features which were expected to perform equally spectacularly at the box-office, on the theory that this strategy was more profitable than **Classical Hollywood**'s mass production studio system. The economic logic of the blockbuster phenomenon was demonstrated by the success of *The Sound of Music* in 1965, and the pattern established in the late 1960s, whereby a handful of blockbuster **movies** make very large profits while the majority of movies produced fail to recoup their costs, persisted until video established a more solid second-release system in the 1980s. P. 74.

blocking   The physical placement of characters in a scene. P. 209.

center line   See **180-degree rule**.

cinematic apparatus   A term used in contemporary film **theory** to refer to both the technological and economic components of the cinema and to the psychological operation of cinema's impression of reality on its spectators. In this context, the term "apparatus" adopts Louis Althusser's usage in his analysis of "ideological state apparatuses." In this book, we use the term **apparatus of cinema** to refer specifically to the technological components of cinema. P. 430.

cine-psychoanalysis   In this book, the name given to a disparate body of critical writing about cinema, which takes its theoretical principles from a combination of Marxism, **semiology**, and psychoanalysis. Often called "psychoanalytic film **theory**," it has often also been identified as a "second semiology" or a "second-phase" semiotics. It is more or less synonymous with the term "contemporary film theory." P. 427.

Classical Hollywood   In this book, Classical Hollywood cinema is taken to be a period of Hollywood's history, and refers to the style, the mode of production, and the industrial organization under which **movies** were made from the early 1920s to the late 1950s. P. 6.

clearance   A trade practice by which the major, vertically integrated companies (see **vertical integration**) determined which **movies** were shown in which theaters, by allotting every movie theater in America a position on a scale of priorities that determined how long after its initial release a given theater could show a picture. In any given area, a movie would play in a first-run theater for a period, before becoming available to second-run theaters, and then on down the scale until it eventually reached the neighborhood theaters in America's small towns and rural areas several months after its New York premiere. The system was designed to encourage patrons to pay the highest prices to see a movie at a first-run house, which was in any case most likely to be owned by one of the Big Five companies. P. 66.

close shot   See **shot scale**.

close-up (CU)   See **shot scale**.

commercial aesthetic   In this book, the term used to describe Hollywood's aesthetic system, driven as it is by the existence of entertainment as a commercial commodity. From this perspective, Hollywood's most profound significance lies in its ability to turn pleasure into a product we can buy. An understanding of Hollywood's commercial aesthetic requires a consideration of both the formal conventions of Hollywood **movies** and the external social and cultural pressures that regulate movies as products of a system of mass production and distribution. P. 7.

compositional motivation   See **motivation**.

confrontation   See **resolution**.

continuity system   Hollywood's system of spatial construction, in which action unfolds as a smooth and continuous flow across shots. Within this system the camera remains relatively unobtrusive, seldom drawing attention to its mediating presence. Continuity editing keeps the position, movement, and screen direction of objects within the frame consistent between shots, ensuring audience comprehension of the action. P. 190.

continuous present   The tense in which **movies** take place. Unlike writing, movies do not have a range of tenses at their disposal, because of the physical characteristics through which **film** produces the illusion of movement. At whatever point in a movie's story an event takes place, the audience always experiences it as being in the here and now of a continuous present. P. 304.

coverage   The procedure by which the whole action of a scene is filmed in one shot (the master shot), and then filmed in smaller sections from a variety of camera positions, to provide the editor with enough material to construct the scene as he, or the producer, sees fit. P. 202.

crane shot   The camera is mounted on the arm of a purpose-designed crane, allowing it to move up and down, as well as forward and back and from side to side. P. 160. A camera crane appears on p. 164.

cross-cutting   Editing between two scenes taking place in separate spaces, to suggest the simultaneity of the action occurring in both scenes. P. 165.

cultural verisimilitude   See **verisimilitude**.

cut-away   A brief shot inserted into a longer **take**, showing either a detail of the scene, the reaction of another character to the action in the main shot, or another scene. P. 276.

depth of field   The range of distances from the camera that are in focus. P. 171. Depth of field is illustrated on p. 172.

diegesis   See **mimesis**.

diegetic   Film criticism uses the terms **diegetic** and **non-diegetic** to distinguish between what is included within the imaginary world of the **story**, whether it is visible onscreen or not, and what is outside it. The terms are often used to identify the source of sounds. The background music that sets the emotional tone of a scene is non-diegetic (sometimes the term **extradiegetic** is used to mean the same thing), unless we know that it is coming from an orchestra playing in the ballroom the characters are dancing in, or a radio in the room. Other non-diegetic elements in a **movie** include its credits and other titles. Extradiegetic background music had, of course, always accompanied silent movies, setting the mood of each scene. PP. 165, 186, 327.

diffusion   See **innovation**.

digital   See **analogical/digital**.

dissolve   An optical transition between two shots, in which the second shot is gradually superimposed on the first. In **Classical Hollywood**, a dissolve most commonly implied a relatively short time lapse between the two scenes shown, while a **fade** suggested a longer interval. P. 162.

divorcement   The result of the 1948 US Supreme Court decision in the **Paramount case** that the trade practices of the vertically integrated major companies (see **vertical integration**) constituted a monopoly. The court decided that the production and distribution branches of the major companies should be separated, or divorced, from their exhibition branches. P. 71.

establishing shot   The opening long shot in a scene, which shows the setting in which the scene will take place, and orients the viewer to the spatial relations between the objects and figures in the scene. See **shot scale**. P. 163.

event movie   In the 1970s, the **blockbuster** evolved into the "event movie" such as *Star Wars* (1977), in which as much commercial importance was attached to the merchandizing of ancillary goods – toys, games, books, clothing, bubblegum – as to the **movie**'s performance at the box-office. This merchandizing extended the life of the product and guaranteed the success of its sequels. P. 75.

excess   A Formalist concept (see **Formalism**) referring to the material in a **movie** that is not motivated, and which may distract viewers from their involvement with a movie's **story**. P. 335.

expressive space   Space endowed with meaning beyond the literal, **represented space** in an image. P. 192.

extradiegetic See **diegetic**.

eyeline matching A convention governing the direction of a character's gaze. When a character looks offscreen in one shot, we expect the next shot to show us what the character is looking at. Following characters' eyelines allows us to connect the spaces in separate shots together across a cut. Manuals of continuity editing (see **continuity system**) observe that "the most natural cut is the cut on the look," because "the eyes are the most powerful direction pointer that a human being has to attract or to direct interest." P. 208.

fabula See **story**.

fade In a **fade-out**, the screen is gradually darkened to black. This is followed by a **fade-in**, in which the screen gradually brightens on a new scene. In **Classical Hollywood**, a fade generally implied a longer time lapse between two scenes than was suggested by a **dissolve**. P. 162.

fade-in See **fade**.

fade-out See **fade**.

film Throughout this book, we distinguish between film and **movie**, using film to mean the physical, celluloid material on which images are registered and a soundtrack recorded. Thus, **film time** refers to the amount of time it takes to project a movie, and is a matter of fixed duration, determined by the length of the film and the set speed at which it passes through the projector. The distinction we make between film and movie is broadly comparable to the distinction between print and literature: the material and the experiential forms have different properties. Most other critics, however, use the two terms film and movie as if they were interchangeable. P. 2.

film time See **film**.

flashback A scene set in the past of the **story**, occurring out of chronological order in the **plot**. Flashbacks are most often staged as the memories of characters, or during scenes in which one character explains past events to another. P. 303.

Formalism The name given to the work of a group of Russian literary critics of the 1920s, and to criticism which has made use of the theoretical premises (see **theory**) of their work. In film studies, **neoformalism** has combined these premises with an understanding of viewing activity informed by the branches of psychology concerned with perception and cognition, in contrast to psychoanalysis. Neoformalism defines the viewer as an active figure, responding to cues within the **movie** and forming hypotheses about its progress on the basis of previous experience. P. 440.

framing The composition of an image, which takes place in relation first of all to the borders of its frame. P. 194.

full shot See **shot scale**.

gauge The width of the **film** stock, normally 35 mm. P. 169.

iconography A system of recurring visual motifs, which provides the knowledgeable viewer with a means of gleaning information about characters and situation from the appearance of characters and settings. Genre criticism often uses iconography as a way of distinguishing between genres. P. 117.

identification **Cine-psychoanalysis** argues that, in watching a movie, the spectator's primary identification is not with the characters or performers, but with the camera (we have to look where the camera looks; the camera is the eye/I). It then suggests that in **Classical Hollywood** cinema, the look of the spectator is passed through the camera onto the character, encouraging specta-tors to make a range of secondary identifications within the fiction. P. 212.

"impact" edit   A cut that produces a violent disruption of spatial continuity, designed to have a shock effect on the audience. P. 224.

innovation   Technological change is brought about in three stages. **Invention** requires only a limited financial commitment to fund experimentation and the development of a prototype. In the second stage, innovation, the invention is adapted to meet the requirements of a market, and involves much greater expenditure in developing the market. The final stage, **diffusion**, occurs when the product is adopted as an industry standard, so that the whole industry invests in its exploitation. P. 178.

integrated performance   An acting performance organized in order to further the **movie**'s **story**, rather than to draw attention to itself as a performance. P. 249.

intertextuality   A **movie**'s inheritance from, resemblance to, and relationship with other similarly styled aesthetic objects. P. 41.

intertextual motivation   See **motivation**.

invention   See **innovation**.

legitimate theater   "Legitimate" theater originally described plays with spoken dialogue, distinguishing them from melodramas in which the dialogue was accompanied by music. During the nineteenth century, it gradually acquired overtones of identifying those plays deemed to have poetic quality or literary worth, and by the beginning of the twentieth century it distinguished drama from slapstick and acrobatics, which had by then become separate entertain-ment forms in vaudeville and burlesque. P. 247.

line of action   See **180-degree rule**.

long shot (LS)   See **shot scale**.

long take   A shot that continues uncut for an unusually long time – a minute or more. P. 241.

medium long shot   See **shot scale**.

medium shot (MS)   See **shot scale**.

mimesis   Imitation. The classical Greek philosopher Plato made a distinction between mimesis, in which the poet "makes a speech pretending to be someone else," and diegesis, in which "the poet speaks in his own person"; a distinction, that is, between a performance and a report. (This use of the term **diegesis** should be distinguished from the use of diegetic defined above.) **Analogical** forms of representation, such as photography and cinema, are conventionally considered more mimetic than **digital** forms such as writing. Within a **movie**, an action or situation can be considered mimetic if it provides a recognizable imitation of behavior that we might encounter outside the cinema. P. 327.

mise-en-scène   The arrangement of screen space as a meaningful organization of elements: literally, the "putting into a scene" or staging of a fiction. It is through mise-en-scène that **represented space** becomes **expressive**. **Classical Holly-wood** mise-en-scène balances and fills the frame, avoiding both distracting detail and empty spots in the composition, and using conventional composi-tional principles to focus attention on the main line of action. Some film **theories** draw a distinction between mise-en-scène and editing (montage), on the basis that mise-en-scène takes place on the set, and editing afterwards. However, in practice, **Classical Hollywood** mise-en-scène and continuity editing (see **conti-nuity system**) are closely interrelated. P. 199.

mise-en-temps In this book, the term we have given to the process of construct-ing a coherent sequence of plot events as **movie time**. Mise-en-temps uses temporal conventions similar to those by which Hollywood constructs its spa-tial framework. Like **mise-en-scène**, these conventions are both obvious and virtually invisible to us. P. 301.

monocular perspective The perspective produced when viewing the world through a single lens. This mode of representing the world dominates the central tradition of western European art from the Renaissance until the early twentieth century, and is inherent in the optical arrangement of still and **movie** cameras. P. 170.

motivation The justification given for the inclusion of an object or other element within a scene or **movie**. **Formalism** distinguishes between four kinds of moti-vation. **Compositional motivation** explains the presence of an element in terms of its necessity for **story** comprehension. **Realistic motivation** justifies the pres-ence of a device on the grounds that it makes the movie seem more authentic or plausible. **Intertextual motivation** appeals directly to the audience's familiarity with generic convention. **Artistic motivation** justifies the presence of a device on the grounds of the movie's stylistic pattern. Usually these kinds of motiva-tion operate collaboratively. P. 336.

movie Throughout this book, we distinguish between **film** and movie, using movie to refer to the stream of images that we consume as both **narrative** and spectacle when the material is projected. Thus, **movie time** refers to the time represented within the fiction, and is much more flexible than **film time**, involv-ing **flashbacks**, ellipses, and other conventional devices of temporal construc-tion. The distinction we make between film and movie is broadly comparable to the distinction between print and literature: the material and the experiential forms have different properties. Most other critics, however, use the two terms film and movie as if they were interchangeable. P. 2.

movie time See **movie**.

narration The process by which a **plot** is arranged to permit the telling of a **story**. Where plot and story can both be understood as objects – sequences of events – narration is a process. One part of this process is undertaken by the movie's producers, when they arrange the sequence of events and actions within the plot. The procedures of **mise-en-scène** and editing become the means by which viewers are guided through the plot. While the devices of narration are con-structed on the sound stage and in the editing room, the process of narration is only completed in the movie theater, when viewers use their knowledge of convention and the plot information provided for them to construct the story in their own minds. P. 332.

narrative An ambiguous term, often used as a synonym for **plot**, **story**, and **narration**, and having different connotations as a noun and an adjective. The ambiguous senses of the term narrative become useful if we understand it as identifying the play between senses of plot, story, and narration in our experi-ence of viewing a movie. P. 332.

narratology The general study of **narrative**. P. 324.

naturalism As a critical term, naturalism has a history almost as complex as that of **realism**. Its most common contemporary sense is in describing representa-tions or performances concerned to produce an accurate imitation of external appearances. A naturalistic acting performance, for instance, will be **integrated** into the narrative, and will not draw attention to itself as a performance (see autonomous performance). This "invisible" style of acting tries to imitate the expressions and emotions of the everyday world, since its aim is to create a sense of character for the audience without making them consciously aware of how that sense is created. P. 250.

neoformalism   See **Formalism**.

non-diegetic   See **diegetic**.

oligopoly   Monopoly power exercised by a small group, such as **Classical Hollywood**'s major, vertically integrated companies (see **vertical integration**). P. 63.

ostensiveness   The degree to which a performance (see **autonomous performance**) is visibly marked out as a performance for its audience by its expressive features. Different acting styles display different degrees of ostensiveness: styles considered to be naturalistic (see **naturalism**) are less ostensive than others, and Hollywood has usually required supporting players, ethnic minorities and women to be more broadly expressive than white male stars. P. 257.

pan   Pivoting movement of the camera from left to right or right to left. P. 160.

Paramount case   See **divorcement**.

persistence of vision   A **theory** explaining the perception of the illusion of movement, formalized in 1824 by Peter Mark Roget. Roget suggested that every time we look at something, a brief residual image is stored on the retina of the eye, so that in watching sequences of still images, each individual image is retained until the next one appears to replace it. More recent research into the psychology of perception, however, suggests that the process is much more complicated, and that seeing and hearing are positive mental activities, not involuntary physical processes. Rather than the illusion of movement being created by a deception of the eye, the brain constructs a continuous image from the sequence of stills, filling in the missing parts. This is known as the Phi phenomenon. P. 291.

plan Americain   See **shot scale**.

plot   The order in which events are represented in the **movie**, for which the **Formalists** used the word **syuzhet**, defined as "the structured set of all causal events as we see and hear them presented." P. 331.

plot point   An event or incident in a **plot** that turns the **story** in a new direction. P. 289.

point of view   A shot taken from the approximate **viewpoint** of a character and showing what the character can see is usually called a point-of-view shot. In this book, we distinguish between the literal viewpoint, which is a position in space, determined by its angle, level, height, and distance from its subject; and a point of view, which we use to describe a position of knowledge in relation to the fiction. A character's **narrative** point of view is a matter of the character's relative subjectivity or omniscience. P. 212.

poststructuralism   A critical movement best understood as a reaction to **structuralism**'s attempts to establish broad, incorporative theoretical procedures. Rather than being a **theory** in itself, poststructuralism proposed a mode of inquiry concerned with what had been left out of, or repressed by, structuralism's totalizing systems. Instead, it argued for a "decentering" of the attention paid to the structures of a text, and a deconstruction of textual meaning. Although poststructuralism involved a rejection of the structuralist claim to scientific status, it also evolved out of structuralism's concerns and shared several of its fundamental assumptions. **Cine-psychoanalysis** is in large part a poststructuralist theory. P. 435.

production values   Those elements of a **movie** designed to appeal to an audience independently of the story: the sets, the costumes, the star performances, the "quality" of the product visible on the screen. Production values represent areas of pleasure offered to the viewer incidental to, and separate from, the plausibility of the fiction. P. 26.

public fantasy   See **safe space**.

realism   A term with a complex history and a multiplicity of meanings. In our everyday use of the term "realistic," we invoke realism to evaluate the extent to which a representation or a **narrative** is like some previously established reality – or, in a commonly used critical phrase, the extent of its "adequacy to the real." Many critical propositions about realism in cinema derive from the commonly held assumption that **analogical** media such as photography are inherently more "realist" than other, less mimetic media (see **mimesis**). Literary critic Raymond Williams has suggested that the purpose of realism in art is "to show things as they really are." John Ellis points out that beneath this tautology lie several other tautologies dealing with different ways in which "realism" can be "realistic": it "should have a surface accuracy; it should conform to notions of what we expect to happen; it should explain itself adequately to us as audience; it should conform to particular notions of psychology and character **motivation**." But no account of realism progresses very far before it recognizes that realism, like all other approaches to art, relies on a system of conventions of representation. P. 148.

realistic motivation   See **motivation**.

reception studies   A critical approach which concentrates its attention on the audience, viewer, or reader of a work, rather than on the work as a text. P. 443.

represented space   The area that exists in front of the camera lens and is recorded by it. It is the recognizable space in which actors stand, in which props are placed, and in which things happen. P. 191.

resolution   Contemporary screenwriting manuals declare that "proper structure occurs when the right events occur in the right sequence to elicit maximum emotional involvement in the ... audience ... good plot structure means that the right thing is happening at the right time." To this end, they suggest that a **movie** screenplay should have three acts. Act 1, the **setup**, establishes the **plot** situation in the first quarter of the movie. Act 2, the **confrontation**, builds it during the next half. Act 3, the resolution, brings the **story** to its conclusion in the final quarter. P. 288.

reverse-angle   See **shot/reverse shot**.

rough cut   The first assembly of a **movie**, usually prepared by the editor while shooting continues. P. 87.

runaway production   The practice of producing American-financed **movies** abroad, either to meet quota regulations, to enhance their appeal to the international market, or to take advantage of cheaper production costs outside the US. "Runaway" production reached its height during the late 1960s, when nearly half of the features made by American companies were produced abroad. P. 70.

rushes   The first printing from the day's exposed negative stock, made to be examined before the next day's shooting begins. P. 83.

safe action area   An area marked in the viewfinders of widescreen cameras to identify the dimensions of the television frame, so that cinematographers could ensure that the essential object in each shot was inside the part of the composition that would appear on the television screen. P. 169.

safe space   In this book, safe space identifies an interrelated set of concepts around the presentation of a **movie**. The physical environment of the movie theater operates as a safe space for the audience's engagement in **public fantasy**, the public expression of ideas and actions we must each individually repress in our everyday behavior. The price of admission to this everyday place of refuge from the everyday is our knowledge that what happens inside the movie theater has nothing to do with what happens outside, but takes place only in the trivialized safe space of entertainment. Within the movie, the **continuity system**'s devices of invisible editing, **eyeline matches**, and **shot/reverse shot** patterns secure the viewer's mapping of a movie's spatial topography. By guaranteeing the secure placement of the audience in relation to the fictional world of the movie, safe space allows viewers to enjoy the pleasures of spectacle and **narrative**, and to engage emotionally with the characters, confident that the movie's image stream will avoid any sudden shocks that might abruptly disrupt our involvement in the action. P. 190.

scopophilia   Pleasure, particularly sexual pleasure, in looking. Scopophilia is distinguished from **voyeurism** in that it identifies a general pleasure in looking, while voyeurism is usually understood as a perversion. Scopophilia is a central idea in the account of the **cinematic apparatus** proposed by **cine-psychoanalysis**. P. 340.

semiology   The study of signs, sign systems, and their meanings. In his *Course in General Linguistics*, Ferdinand de Saussure described semiology as a science that would show what constitutes signs, and what laws govern them. He understood linguistics to be part of the general science of semiology. Semiology, sometimes also called semiotics, has been central to structuralist studies of cinema (see **structuralism**), but its claim to scientific status has never been established. P. 422.

set-up   One positioning of the camera and accompanying lighting arrangement. One set-up may yield more than one shot in the final picture: the **close-ups** of one player in a scene may well all be photographed from the same set-up, for instance. P. 203.

setup   See **resolution**.

shot/reverse shot   One of Hollywood's most frequent formal figures, in which two consecutive shots depict complementary spaces. The most common instance of this figure occurs in dialogue scenes presented in over-the-shoulder close **medium shots**, where the looks of the characters at each other and the graphic similarity between the shots help the viewer infer that the spaces in the two shots are contiguous. **Apparatus theory** describes this operation as a process of "**suturing**," by which the viewer perceives gaps in the space represented, only to have these gaps filled in a process which binds the spectator into the coherence of the fiction. Through the suture, the Hollywood **movie** masks both its formal and its ideological operations. P. 211. Shot/reverse shot construction is illustrated on p. 209.

shot scale   The range of different shots used in a **movie**, usually established in terms of the most commonly represented object, the human body. In a **long shot (LS)**, people fill half or three quarters of the height of the screen. In a **full shot**, the height of the frame is filled with the human figure, while a **medium long shot** covers the body from mid-calf or knees up. This shot is sometimes called a

plan Americain or "Hollywood shot," because of the frequency of its use in Hollywood. A **medium shot (MS)**, cuts characters off at the waist, a **close shot** takes in the character from the chest up, and a **close-up (CU)** is a shot of the face. P. 204. Shot scale is illustrated on p. 205.

slow motion   Slow-motion effects are produced by passing the **film** through the camera at a faster rate than normal, so that the film takes longer to project than the duration of the action it records. P. 291.

story   The reconstruction of **plot** events in their chronological order, through which we can establish the chain of causality which links them. **Formalist** criticism designates the story the **fabula**. P. 331.

structuralism   As an intellectual movement, structuralism originated in the proposition, by anthropologist Claude Lévi-Strauss, that kinship relations and primitive myths were structured like language, and could be studied according to the principles of linguistic analysis. Structuralism maintained that the elements within a structure did not possess meaning as independent units, but gained their meaning through their relations to other elements. Meaning is, for instance, often constructed through binary oppositions: "good" means something only in relation to "bad"; "raw" and "cooked" signify opposing states. Applications of the structuralist approach proliferated in European thought in the 1960s, and cultural theorists such as Roland Barthes and Umberto Eco argued that cultural events could be understood by examining the structure that underlay them as if it were a language. P. 422.

suturing   See **shot/reverse shot**.

syuzhet   See **plot**.

take   A version of a shot. Generally, the film crew will shoot several takes of each shot in a **set-up**, selecting the take with the best acting and technical performance for printing. A **long take** refers to the temporal duration of the shot. P. 241.

theory   The word "theory" has its origins in a Greek root, *thea*, meaning sight. It shares a common linguistic point of origin with "theater," and a common point of derivation with ideas of both spectacle and speculation. To formulate a theory is thus to articulate a point of view. Theory, however, often makes rhetorical claims to a degree of objectivity that it denies to other forms of criticism, and it also commonly lays claim to a broader scope than other critical practices. Dudley Andrew, for example, distinguishes between theory and criticism by suggesting that while criticism concentrates on individual **movies** or groups of movies, theory is concerned with the properties of cinema as a whole, or what he calls "the cinematic capability." P. 416.

track, tracking shot   A shot in which the camera physically moves through space. Often the camera will be mounted on a platform that runs on tracks laid on the ground like railroad tracks. A shot in which the camera moves toward the object it is photographing is called a track-in, and one in which it moves away is a track-out. PP. 160, 206.

transparency   A quality of Hollywood's **commercial aesthetic**, often understood as contributing substantially to the particular kind of **realism** that Hollywood offers. Although acting, for instance, can draw attention to itself and function as a separate spectacle (see **autonomous performance**), it more routinely aspires to transparency (see **integrated performance**), in the same way as the **continuity system**'s codes of editing and camerawork seek to render themselves "invisible" by working according to what André Bazin called "the material or dramatic logic of a scene." P. 190.

unsafe space   Post-**Classical Hollywood** cinema has frequently disrupted the audience's sense of the screen as a safe space to look at. The unsafe space of post-*Psycho* "nightmare **movies**" is actively malign, seeking to catch the viewer unawares and stab screen space when the audience least expects it. Movies may assault their audiences physically, stabbing them in the eye with flashes of light, rapid, disjointed cutting, or sudden movement. The frame can be violently penetrated by a murderous implement, at any moment and from any angle. Typically, unsafe space empowers malign characters, capable of moving through screen space in a manner incomprehensible or invisible to the audience, and threatening both sympathetic characters and viewers with their sudden, unpredictable appearance. In such movies, the audience is associated with the fictional victims, even when the camera's **viewpoint** is that of the monster as it attacks. Unsafe space disorients the viewer, emphasizing the power of a movie's image track to control the viewer's look. P. 219.

verisimilitude   In a general sense verisimilitude means truthfulness, and although its meaning overlaps with that of **realism**, in the context in which it is used in this book it implies something that is probable, plausible, or appropriate, rather than realistic. Verisimilitude is also a matter of conventions, and sometimes generic conventions transgress broader social or cultural regimes of verisimilitude: as, for instance, when a character bursts into song while walking down a street. P. 109.

vertical integration   A vertically integrated company is involved in all three branches of its business: manufacture, wholesaling, and retailing; and this position gives it a much greater degree of control over its terms of trade than a company involved in only one branch of the business can exercise. A small number of vertically integrated companies, all pursuing the same business strategies, can between them dominate an industry. The history of American business in the twentieth century has been predominantly a history of the growth of vertically integrated corporations, and with it the growth of **oligopoly** control. P. 62.

viewpoint   See **point of view**.

voice-over   A narrator's voice when the narrator is not seen. P. 305.

voyeurism   See **scopophilia**.

wipe   A transition between shots in which a line moves across the screen, with the image changing behind it from one scene to the next. In **Classical Hollywood**, a wipe usually implied a transition between scenes occurring in different locations in continuous time. P. 162.

Select Bibliography

Adler, Mortimer, *Art and Prudence: A Study in Practical Philosophy* (New York: Longmans, 1937).

Adorno, Theodor, and Max Horkheimer, *Dialectic of Enlightenment* (New York: Herder and Herder, 1972).

Affron, Charles, *Cinema and Sentiment* (Chicago: University of Chicago Press, 1982).

Agee, James, *Agee on Film* (New York: Beacon, 1958).

Allen, Jeanne, "The Film Viewer as Consumer," *Quarterly Review of Film Studies* 5:4 (Fall 1980), pp. 481–97.

Allen, Robert, *Speaking of Soap Opera* (Chapel Hill: University of North Carolina Press, 1985).

Allen, Robert C., *Channels of Discourse* (London: Methuen, 1987).

Allen, Robert C., and Douglas Gomery, *Film History: Theory and Practice* (New York: Knopf, 1985).

Althusser, Louis, *Lenin and Philosophy and Other Essays* (London: NLB, 1971).

Althusser, Louis, *For Marx* (London: NLB, 1977).

Altman, Charles F., "Psychoanalysis and Cinema: The Imaginary Discourse," *Quarterly Review of Film Studies* 2:3 (August 1977), pp. 257–72.

Altman, Rick, ed., *Genre: The Musical* (London: Routledge and Kegan Paul, 1981).

Altman, Rick, *The American Film Musical* (Bloomington: Indiana University Press, 1987).

Altman, Rick, ed., *Sound Theory, Sound Practice* (New York: Routledge, 1992).

Alton, John, *Painting with Light* (New York: Macmillan, 1949).

Alvarado, Manuel, and John O. Thompson, eds, *The Media Reader* (London: British Film Institute, 1990).

Andrew, Dudley, *The Major Film Theories: An Introduction* (New York: Oxford University Press, 1976).

Andrew, Dudley, *Concepts in Film Theory* (New York: Oxford University Press, 1984).

Arijon, Daniel, *Grammar of the Film Language* (Los Angeles: Silman-James Press, 1976).

Armes, Roy, "Entendre, C'est Comprendre: In Defence of Sound Reproduction," *Screen* 29:2 (Spring 1988), pp. 8–22.

Armes, Roy, *On Video* (London: Routledge, 1989).

Austin, Bruce A., *Immediate Seating: A Look at Movie Audiences* (Belmont, CA: Wadsworth, 1989).

Bach, Steven, *Final Cut: Dreams and Disaster in the Making of Heaven's Gate* (London: Faber, 1986).

Balio, Tino, *United Artists: The Company Built by the Stars* (Madison: University of Wisconsin Press, 1976).

Balio, Tino, ed., *The American Film Industry*, 1st edn 1976, revised edn (Madison: University of Wisconsin Press, 1985).

Balio, Tino, *United Artists: The Company that Changed the Film Industry* (Madison: University of Wisconsin Press, 1987).

Balio, Tino, ed., *Hollywood in the Age of Television* (Boston: Unwin Hyman, 1990).

Balio, Tino, *Grand Design: Hollywood as a Modern Business Enterprise 1930–1939* (New York: Scribner's, 1993).

Barthes, Roland, *Mythologies* (London: Paladin, 1973).

Barthes, Roland, *Image Music Text* (London: Fontana, 1977).

Bazin, André, *What is Cinema? Vol. 1*, trans. Hugh Gray (Berkeley, CA: University of California Press, 1967).

Bazin, André, *What is Cinema? Vol. 2*, trans. Hugh Gray (Berkeley, CA: University of California Press, 1971).

Bazin, André, "Will CinemaScope Save the Cinema?," trans. Catherine Jones and Richard Neupert, *The Velvet Light Trap* 21 (Summer 1985), pp. 9–14.

Bego, Mark, ed., *The Best of Modern Screen* (London: Columbus Books, 1986).

Behlmer, Rudy, ed., *Memo from: David O. Selznick* (New York: Avon, 1973; 1st pub. New York: Viking, 1972).

Behlmer, Rudy, *Behind the Scenes* (New York: Samuel French, 1982).

Behlmer, Rudy, ed., *Inside Warner Bros. (1935–1951)* (London: Weidenfeld and Nicolson, 1986).

Bell, Daniel, *The End of Ideology* (New York: Collier Books, 1960).

Bellour, Raymond, "Hitchcock the Enunciator," *Camera Obscura* 2 (Fall 1977), pp. 66–91.

Belsey, Catherine, *Critical Practice* (London: Methuen, 1980).

Belton, John, "CinemaScope: The Economics of Technology," *The Velvet Light Trap* 21 (Summer 1985), pp. 35–43.

Belton, John, "CinemaScope and Historical Methodology," *Cinema Journal* 28:1 (Fall 1988), pp. 22–44.

Belton, John, *Widescreen Cinema* (Cambridge, MA: Harvard University Press, 1992).

Benjamin, Walter, "The Work of Art in the Age of Mechanical Reproduction," in *Illuminations* (London: Cape, 1970), pp. 219–53.

Bennett, Tony, Susan Boyd-Bowman, Colin Mercer, and Janet Woollacott, eds, *Popular Television and Film* (London: British Film Institute, 1981).

Biskind, Peter, *Seeing is Believing: How Hollywood Taught Us to Stop Worrying and Love the Fifties* (London: Pluto Press, 1983).

Blum, Richard A., *American Film Acting: The Stanislavski Heritage* (Ann Arbor: UMI Research Press, 1984).

Bogle, Donald, *Toms, Coons, Mulattoes, Mammies and Bucks: An Interpretive History of Blacks in American Films* (New York: Bantam, 1974).

Bordwell, David, *Narration in the Fiction Film* (London: Methuen, 1985).

Bordwell, David, *Making Meaning: Inference and Rhetoric in the Interpretation of Cinema* (Cambridge, MA: Harvard University Press, 1989).

Bordwell, David, and Kristin Thompson, *Film Art: An Introduction*, 3rd edn (New York: McGraw-Hill, 1990).

Bordwell, David, Janet Staiger, and Kristin Thompson, *The Classical Hollywood Cinema: Film Style and Mode of Production to 1960* (London: Routledge and Kegan Paul, 1985).

Bowser, Eileen, *The Transformation of Cinema: 1907–1915* (New York: Scribner's, 1990).

Branigan, Edward, *Point of View in the Cinema: A Theory of Narration and Subjectivity in Classical Film* (New York: Mouton, 1984).

Branigan, Edward, *Narrative Comprehension and Film* (London: Routledge, 1992).

Brantlinger, Patrick, *Bread and Circuses: Theories of Mass Culture as Social Decay* (Ithaca, NY: Cornell University Press, 1983).

Britton, Andrew, "Blissing Out: The Politics of Reaganite Entertainment," *MOVIE* 31/32 (Winter 1986), pp. 1–42.

Browne, Nick, *The Rhetoric of Filmic Narration* (Ann Arbor: University of Michigan Press, 1982).

Brownstein, Ronald, *The Power and the Glitter: The Hollywood–Washington Connection* (New York: Pantheon, 1990).

Buscombe, Edward, ed., *The BFI Companion to the Western* (London: André Deutsch, 1988).

Butsch, Richard, ed., *For Fun and Profit: The Transformation of Leisure into Consumption* (Philadelphia: Temple University Press, 1990).

Byars, Jackie, *All That Hollywood Allows: Re-reading Gender in 1950s Melodrama* (Chapel Hill: University of North Carolina, 1991).

Carroll, Noel, *Mystifying Movies: Fads and Fallacies in Contemporary Film Theory* (New York: Columbia University Press, 1988).

Caughie, John, *Theories of Authorship* (London: Routledge and Kegan Paul, 1981).

Cavell, Stanley, *The World Viewed: Reflections on the Ontology of Film* (New York: Viking, 1971).

Cavell, Stanley, *Pursuits of Happiness: The Hollywood Comedy of Remarriage* (Cambridge, MA: Harvard University Press, 1981).

Cawelti, John, *The Six-Gun Mystique* (Bowling Green: Bowling Green Popular University Press, 1970).

Ceplair, Larry, and Steven Englund, *The Inquisition in Hollywood: Politics in the Film Community, 1930–1960* (Berkeley, CA: University of California Press, 1983).

Chandler, Alfred D., Jr, *The Visible Hand: The Managerial Revolution in American Business* (Cambridge, MA: Harvard University Press, 1977).

Chatman, Seymour, *Story and Discourse: Narrative Structure in Fiction and Film* (Ithaca, NY: Cornell University Press, 1978).

Christensen, Terry, *Reel Politics: American Political Movies from Birth of a Nation to Platoon* (New York: Blackwell, 1987).

Ciment, Michel, *Kazan on Kazan* (London: Secker and Warburg, 1973).

Clifford, James, *The Predicament of Culture* (Cambridge, MA: Harvard University Press, 1988).

Clover, Carol J., *Men, Women and Chainsaws: Gender in the Modern Horror Film* (London: British Film Institute, 1992).

Cohan, Steven, and Linda M. Shires, *Telling Stories: A Theoretical Analysis of*

Narrative Fiction (London: Routledge, 1988).

Cohen, Steven, and Ina Rae Hark, eds, *Screening the Male: Exploring Masculinities in Hollywood Cinema* (London: Routledge, 1993).

Collins, Jim, Hilary Radner, and Ava Preacher Collins, eds, *Film Theory Goes to the Movies* (London: Routledge, 1993).

Combs, James, ed., *Movies and Politics: The Dynamic Relationship* (New York: Garland, 1993).

Comolli, Jean-Louis, and Jean Narboni, "Cinema/Ideology/Criticism (1)," trans. Susan Bennett, in John Ellis, ed., *Screen Reader 1* (London: Society for Education in Film and Television, 1977). 1st pub. in *Cahiers du Cinéma* (October–November 1969); 1st pub. in English in *Screen* 12:1 (1971).

Cook, David A., *A History of Narrative Film*, 2nd edn (New York: Norton, 1990).

Cook, Pam, ed., *The Cinema Book* (London: British Film Institute, 1985).

Cooke, Alistair, ed., *Garbo and the Night Watchmen*, 1st pub. 1937 (London: Secker and Warburg, 1971).

Corrigan, Timothy, *A Cinema Without Walls: Movies and Culture after Vietnam* (New Brunswick, NJ: Rutgers University Press, 1991).

Craven, Ian, "Alternatives to Narrative in the American Cinema: A Study of Comic Performance,", PhD dissertation, University of Exeter, 1982.

Cripps, Thomas, *Slow Fade to Black: The Negro in American Film* (New York: Oxford University Press, 1977).

Cripps, Thomas, *Making Movies Black: The Hollywood Message Movie from World War II to the Civil Rights Era* (New York: Oxford University Press, 1993).

Curran, James, Michael Gurevich, and Janet Woolacott, eds, *Mass Communication and Society* (London: Edward Arnold, 1977).

Custen, George F., *Bio/Pics: How Hollywood Constructed Public Fiction* (New Brunswick, NJ: Rutgers University Press, 1992).

Czitrom, Daniel, *Media and the American Mind: From Morse to McLuhan* (Chapel Hill: University of North Carolina Press, 1982).

Dardis, Tom, *Some Time in the Sun* (London: André Deutsch, 1976).

Davies, Philip, and Brian Neve, eds, *Cinema, Politics and Society in America* (Manchester: Manchester University Press, 1981).

deCordova, Richard, *Picture Personalities: The Emergence of the Star System in America* (Urbana: University of Illinois Press, 1990).

de Lauretis, Teresa, *Alice Doesn't: Feminism, Semiotics, Cinema* (Bloomington: Indiana University Press, 1984).

de Lauretis, Teresa, *Technologies of Gender: Essays on Theory, Film, and Fiction* (London: Macmillan, 1987).

de Lauretis, Teresa, and Stephen Heath, eds, *The Cinematic Apparatus* (London: Macmillan, 1980).

Deming, Barbara, *Running Away from Myself: A Dream Portrait of America Drawn from the Films of the Forties* (New York: Grossman, 1969).

de Saussure, Ferdinand, *Course in General Linguistics* (London: Fontana, 1974).

Deutelbaum, Marshall, and Leland Poague, eds, *A Hitchcock Reader* (Ames: Iowa State University Press, 1986).

Doane, Mary Ann, *The Desire to Desire: The Woman's Film of the 1940s* (London: Macmillan, 1987).

Doane, Mary Ann, *Femmes Fatales: Feminism, Film Theory, Psychoanalysis* (London: Routledge, 1991).

Doane, Mary Ann, Patricia Mellencamp, and Linda Williams, eds, *Re-Visions:*

Essays in Feminist Film Criticism (Frederick, MD: University Publications of America, 1984).

Doherty, Thomas, *Teenagers and Teenpix: The Juvenilization of American Movies in the 1950s* (Boston: Unwin Hyman, 1988).

Dyer, Richard, "Entertainment and Utopia," *MOVIE* 24 (1977), pp. 2–13.

Dyer, Richard, *Stars* (London: British Film Institute, 1979).

Dyer, Richard, *Heavenly Bodies: Film Stars and Society* (London: Macmillan, 1987).

Dyer, Richard, *Only Entertainment* (London: Routledge, 1992).

Eagleton, Terry, *Literary Theory: An Introduction* (Oxford: Blackwell, 1983).

Eagleton, Terry, *Ideology: An Introduction* (London: Verso, 1991).

Easty, Edward Dwight, *On Method Acting*, 1st edn New York: Allograph Press, 1966 (New York: Ballantine, 1989).

Eco, Umberto, *The Role of the Reader: Explorations in the Semiotics of Texts* (London: Hutchinson, 1979).

Eco, Umberto, *Travels in Hyperreality* (London: Picador, 1987).

Edwards, Christine, *The Stanislavsky Heritage: Its Contribution to the Russian and American Theatre* (New York: New York University Press, 1965).

Ellis, John, ed., *Screen Reader 1* (London: Society for Education in Film and Television, 1977).

Ellis, John, *Visible Fictions* (London: Routledge and Kegan Paul, 1982).

Elsaesser, Thomas, "Why Hollywood?," *Monogram* 1 (1971), pp. 4–10.

Elsaesser, Thomas, *Early Cinema: Space, Frame, Narrative* (London: British Film Institute, 1990).

Farber, Manny, *Negative Space* (London: Studio Vista, 1971).

Fell, John L., ed., *Film Before Griffith* (Berkeley, CA: University of California Press, 1983).

Feuer, Jane, *The Hollywood Musical* (London: British Film Institute, 1982).

Field, Syd, *Screenplay: The Foundations of Screenwriting* (New York: Dell, 1979).

Fine, Richard, *Hollywood and the Profession of Authorship* (Ann Arbor: University of Michigan Press, 1985).

Finler, Joel W., *The Hollywood Story: Everything You Always Wanted to Know about the American Movie Business but Didn't Know Where to Look* (London: Octopus Books, 1988).

Fitzgerald, F. Scott, *The Last Tycoon* (Harmondsworth: Penguin, 1974).

Fordin, Hugh, *The World of Entertainment: Hollywood's Greatest Musicals* (New York: Avon, 1975).

Franklin, Harold B., *Motion Picture Theatre Management* (New York: Doran, 1927).

French, Brandon, *On the Verge of Revolt: Women in American Films of the Fifties* (New York: Ungar, 1978).

French, Philip, *The Movie Moguls: An Informal History of the Hollywood Tycoons* (Harmondsworth: Penguin, 1969).

Friedman, Lester, *Unspeakable Images: Ethnicity and the American Cinema* (Urbana: University of Illinois Press, 1991).

Gabler, Neal, *An Empire of Their Own: How the Jews Invented Hollywood* (New York: Crown, 1988).

Gaines, Jane, ed., *Classical Hollywood Narrative: The Paradigm Wars* (Durham, NC: Duke University Press, 1992).

Gaines, Jane, and Charlotte Herzog, eds, *Fabrications: Costume and the Female Body* (New York: Routledge, 1990).

Gallagher, Tag, *John Ford: The Man and his Films* (Berkeley, CA: University of

California Press, 1986).

Geertz, Clifford, *The Interpretation of Cultures* (New York: Basic Books, 1973).

Genette, Gerard, *Narrative Discourse: An Essay in Method*, trans. Jane E. Lewin (Ithaca, NY: Cornell University Press, 1980).

Gledhill, Christine, ed., *Home Is Where the Heart Is: Studies in Melodrama and the Woman's Film* (London: British Film Institute, 1987).

Gledhill, Christine, ed., *Stardom: Industry of Desire* (London: Routledge, 1991).

Gomery, Douglas, *The Hollywood Studio System* (London: Macmillan, 1986).

Gomery, Douglas, *Shared Pleasures: A History of Movie Presentation in the United States* (Madison: University of Wisconsin Press, 1992).

Goodman, Ezra, *The Fifty-year Decline of Hollywood* (New York: Simon and Schuster, 1961).

Gorbman, Claudia, *Unheard Melodies: Narrative Film Music* (Bloomington: Indiana University Press, 1987).

Grant, Barry Keith, ed., *Film Genre Reader* (Austin: University of Teseas Press, 1986).

Griffith, Richard, ed., *The Talkies: Articles and Illustrations from a Great Fan Magazine, 1928–1940* (New York: Dover, 1971).

Gussow, Mel, *Don't Say Yes Until I've Finished Talking* (New York: Doubleday, 1971).

Hague, Michael, *Writing Screenplays that Sell* (London: Elm Tree Books, 1989).

Hall, Ben M., *The Best Remaining Seats: The Golden Age of the Movie Palace* (New York: DaCapo, 1988).

Halliday, John, *Sirk on Sirk* (London: Secker and Warburg, 1971).

Hamilton, Ian, *Writers in Hollywood* (London: Heinemann, 1990).

Handel, Leo A., *Hollywood Looks at its Audience: A Report of Film Audience Research* (Urbana: University of Illinois Press, 1950).

Hansen, Miriam, *Babel and Babylon: Spectatorship in American Silent Film* (Cambridge, MA: Harvard University Press, 1991).

Harmetz, Aljean, *Round Up the Usual Suspects: The Making of Casablanca – Bogart, Bergman, and World War II* (New York: Hyperion, 1992).

Harvey, Sylvia, *May '68 and Film Culture* (London: British Film Institute, 1978).

Haskell, Molly, *From Reverence to Rape: The Treatment of Women in the Movies* (Chicago: University of Chicago Press, 1973).

Hauge, Michael, *Writing Screenplays that Sell* (New York: McGraw-Hill, 1988).

Haver, Ronald, *David O. Selznick's Hollywood* (New York: Knopf, 1980).

Hayward, Philip, and Tana Wollen, eds, *Future Visions: New Technologies of the Screen* (London: British Film Institute, 1993).

Heath, Stephen, *Questions of Cinema* (London: Macmillan, 1981).

Heath, Stephen, and Patricia Mellencamp, eds, *Cinema and Language* (Frederick, MD: University Publications of America, 1983).

Herman, Lewis, *A Practical Manual of Screen Playwriting for Theater and Television Films* (New York: New English Library, 1974).

Hillier, Jim, *The New Hollywood* (London: Studio Vista, 1992).

Hilmes, Michelle, *Hollywood and Broadcasting: From Radio to Cable* (Urbana: University of Illinois Press, 1990).

Hincha, Richard, "Selling CinemaScope: 1953–1956," *The Velvet Light Trap* 21 (Summer 1985), pp. 44–53.

Hirsch, Foster, *Acting Hollywood Style* (New York: Abrams, 1991).

Huettig, Mae D., *Economic Control of the Motion Picture Industry: A Study in*

Industrial Organization (Philadelphia: University of Pennsylvania Press, 1944).

Hugo, Chris, "The Economic Background," *MOVIE* 27/28 (1981), pp. 43–9.

Inglis, Ruth, *Freedom of the Movies: A Report on Self-regulation from the Commission on Freedom of the Press* (Chicago: University of Chicago Press, 1947).

Izod, John, *Hollywood and the Box Office 1895–1986* (London: Macmillan, 1988).

Jacobs, Lea, "Industry Self-regulation and the Problem of Textual Determination," *The Velvet Light Trap* 23 (Spring 1989), pp. 4–15.

Jacobs, Lea, *The Wages of Sin: Censorship and the Fallen Woman Film, 1928–1942* (Madison: University of Wisconsin Press, 1991).

Jowett, Garth, *Film: The Democratic Art* (Boston: Little, Brown, 1976).

Jowett, Garth, "'A Capacity for Evil': The 1915 Supreme Court *Mutual* Decision," *Historical Journal of Film, Radio and Television* 9:1 (1989), pp. 59–78.

Kahn, Gordon, *Hollywood on Trial: The Story of the Ten who were Indicted* (New York: Boni and Gaer, 1948).

Kaplan, E. Ann, ed., *Women in Film Noir* (London: British Film Institute, 1978).

Kaplan, E. Ann, *Women and Film: Both Sides of the Camera* (New York: Methuen, 1983).

Kaplan, E. Ann, ed., *Psychoanalysis and Cinema* (New York: Routledge, 1990).

Karpis, Robert E., *Hitchcock: The Making of a Reputation* (Chicago: University of Chicago Press, 1992).

Katz, Steven D., *Film Directing Shot by Shot: Visualizing from Concept to Screen* (Los Angeles: Michael Wiese Productions, 1991).

Kawin, Bruce, *How Movies Work* (Berkeley, CA: University of California Press, 1992).

Kennedy, Joseph P., ed., *The Story of the Films* (Chicago: A.W. Shaw, 1927).

Kent, Nicholas, *Naked Hollywood: Money, Power and the Movies* (London: BBC Books, 1991).

Kerr, Paul, ed., *The Hollywood Film Industry* (London: Routledge and Kegan Paul, 1986).

Kiesling, Barrett C., *Talking Pictures* (Richmond, VA: Johnson Publishing Co., 1937).

Kitses, Jim, *Horizons West: Anthony Mann, Budd Boetticher, Sam Peckinpah: Studies of Authorship within the Western* (London: Thames and Hudson, 1969).

Kline, Herbert, ed., *New Theatre and Film, 1934–1937* (New York: Harcourt Brace Jovanovich, 1985).

Klinger, Barbara, "Digressions at the Cinema: Reception and Mass Culture," *Cinema Journal* 28:4 (Summer 1989), pp. 3–19.

Klinger, Barbara, "Much Ado About Excess: Genre, Mise-en-scène and the Woman in *Written on the Wind*," *Wide Angle* 11:4 (1989), pp. 4–21.

Koppes, Clayton R., and Gregory D. Black, *Hollywood Goes to War: How Politics, Profits and Propaganda Shaped World War II Movies* (New York: Macmillan, 1987).

Koszarski, Richard, ed., *Hollywood Directors 1914–1940* (New York: Oxford University Press, 1976).

Koszarski, Richard, *Hollywood Directors, 1941–1976* (New York: Oxford University Press, 1977).

Koszarski, Richard, *An Evening's Entertainment: The Age of the Silent Feature Picture, 1915–1928* (New York: Scribner's, 1990).

Kozloff, Sarah, *Invisible Storytellers: Voice-over Narration in American Fiction Film* (Berkeley, CA: University of California Press, 1988).

Kuhn, Annette, *The Power of the Image: Essays on Representation and Sexuality*

(London: Routledge and Kegan Paul, 1985).

Kuhn, Annette, ed., *Alien Zone: Cultural Theory and Contemporary Science Fiction* (London: Verso, 1990).

Kuleshov, Lev, *Kuleshov on Film: Writings by Lev Kuleshov*, ed. and trans. Ronald Levaco (Berkeley, CA: University of California Press, 1974).

Kuntzel, Thierry, "The Film Work 2," *Camera Obscura* 5 (Spring 1980), pp. 6–69.

Lapsley, Robert, and Michael Westlake, *Film Theory: An Introduction* (Manchester: Manchester University Press, 1988).

Lawrence, Amy, *Echo and Narcissus: Women's Voices in Classical Hollywood Cinema* (Berkeley, CA: University of California Press, 1991).

Leff, Leonard J., and Jerrold R. Simmons, *The Dame in the Kimono: Hollywood, Censorship, and the Production Code from the 1920s to the 1960s* (New York: Grove, Weidenfeld, 1990).

Lehman, Peter, ed., *Close Viewings: An Anthology of New Film Criticism* (Tallahassee: Florida State University Press, 1990).

Leitch, Thomas M., *Find the Director and Other Hitchcock Games* (Athens, GA: University of Georgia Press, 1991).

Lenihan, John L., *Showdown: Confronting Modern America in the Western Film* (Urbana: University of Illinois Press, 1980).

Levin, Martin, ed., *Hollywood and the Great Fan Magazines* (London: Ian Allen, 1970).

Levine, Lawrence W., *Highbrow/Lowbrow: The Emergence of Cultural Hierarchy in America* (Cambridge, MA: Harvard University Press, 1988).

Lévi-Strauss, Claude, *Structural Anthropology*, trans. Claire Jacobson and Brooke Grundfest Schoepf (Garden City, NY: Doubleday, 1967).

Levy, Emanuel, *Small-town America in Film: The Decline and Fall of Community* (New York: Continuum, 1991).

Lewis, Howard T., *The Motion Picture Industry* (New York: Van Nostrand, 1933).

Lovell, Terry, *Pictures of Reality* (London: British Film Institute, 1980).

Lowery, Shearon, and Melvin L. DeFleur, *Milestones in Mass Communication Research: Media Effects* (New York: Longman, 1983).

Lynd, Robert S., and Helen Merrill Lynd, *Middletown: A Study in Modern American Culture* (New York: Harcourt, Brace, and World, 1929).

McArthur, Benjamin, *Actors and American Culture, 1880–1920* (Philadelphia: Temple University Press, 1984).

McBride, Joseph, *Focus on Howard Hawks* (Englewood Cliffs, NJ: Prentice-Hall, 1972).

MacCabe, Colin, "Realism and the Cinema: Notes on Some Brechtian Theses," *Screen* 15:2 (Summer 1974), pp. 7–27.

McCann, Richard Dyer, *Hollywood in Transition* (Boston: Houghton Mifflin, 1962).

McConnell, Frank D., *The Spoken Seen: Film and the Romantic Imagination* (Baltimore: Johns Hopkins University Press, 1975).

McNiven, Roger D., "The Middle-class American Home of the Fifties: The Use of Architecture in Nicholas Ray's *Bigger Than Life* and Douglas Sirk's *All That Heaven Allows*," *Cinema Journal* 22:2 (Summer 1983), pp. 38–57.

McWilliams, Carey, *Southern California: An Island on the Land*, 1st pub. 1946 (Santa Barbara: Peregrine Smith, Inc., 1973).

Maeder, Edward, ed., *Hollywood and History: Costume Design in Film* (London: Thames and Hudson, 1987).

Maltby, Richard, *Harmless Entertainment: Hollywood and the Ideology of Consensus*

(Metuchen, NJ: Scarecrow, 1983).

Maltby, Richard, "Film Noir: The Politics of the Maladjusted Text," *Journal of American Studies* 18:1 (1984), pp. 49–71.

Maltby, Richard, "American Media and the Denial of History," in Dennis Welland, ed., *The United States: A Companion to American Studies*, 2nd edn (London: Methuen, 1987), pp. 490–517.

Maltby, Richard, ed., *Dreams for Sale: Popular Culture in the 20th Century* (London: Harrap, 1989).

Maltby, Richard, " 'To Prevent the Prevalent Type of Book': Censorship and Adaptation in Hollywood, 1924–1934," *American Quarterly* 44:4 (1992), pp. 554–83.

Maltby, Richard, and Kate Bowles, "Hollywood: The Economics of Utopia," in Jeremy Mitchell and Richard Maidment, eds, *The United States in the Twentieth Century: Culture* (London: Hodder and Stoughton, 1994), pp. 99–134.

Marner, Terence St John, *Directing Motion Pictures* (London: Tantivy, 1972).

Mast, Gerald, *Howard Hawks, Storyteller* (New York: Oxford University Press, 1982).

Mast, Gerald, ed., *The Movies in Our Midst: Documents in the Cultural History of Film in America* (Chicago: University of Chicago Press, 1982).

Mast, Gerald, and Marshall Cohen, eds, *Film Theory and Criticism*, 3rd edn (New York: Oxford University Press, 1985).

Matthews, Brander, ed., *Papers on Acting* (New York: Hill and Wang, 1958).

May, Lary, *Screening Out the Past: The Birth of Mass Culture and the Motion Picture Industry* (New York: Oxford University Press, 1980).

Mayer, J.P., *Sociology of Film: Studies and Documents* (London: Faber, 1946).

Mayer, J.P., *British Cinemas and their Audiences: Sociological Studies* (London: Dobson, 1948).

Mellencamp, Patricia, and Philip Rosen, eds, *Cinema Histories, Cinema Practices* (Frederick, MD: University Publications of America, 1984).

Metz, Christian, *Film Language: A Semiotics of the Cinema*, trans. Michael Taylor (New York: Oxford University Press, 1974).

Metz, Christian, *The Imaginary Signifier: Psychoanalysis and the Cinema*, trans. Celia Britton, Annwyl Williams, Ben Brewster, and Alfred Guzzetti (Bloomington: Indiana University Press, 1982).

Miller, Mark Crispin, ed., *Seeing Through Movies* (New York: Pantheon, 1990).

Modleski, Tania, ed., *Studies in Entertainment: Critical Approaches to Mass Culture* (Bloomington: Indiana University Press, 1987).

Modleski, Tania, *The Women Who Knew Too Much: Hitchcock and Feminist Theory* (London: Methuen, 1988).

Moley, Raymond, *The Hays Office* (Indianapolis: Bobbs-Merrill, 1945).

Monaco, James, *How to Read a Film: The Art, Technology, Language, History and Theory of Film and Media* (New York: Oxford University Press, 1977).

Monaco, James, *American Film Now: The People, the Power, the Money, the Movies* (New York: New American Library, 1979).

Mulvey, Laura, *Visual and Other Pleasures* (Bloomington: Indiana University Press, 1989).

Mulvey, Laura, and Jon Halliday, *Douglas Sirk* (Edinburgh: Edinburgh Film Festival, 1972).

Münsterberg, Hugo, *The Photoplay: A Psychological Study* (New York: Appleton, 1916; reprinted New York: Dover, 1970).

Musser, Charles, *The Emergence of Cinema: The American Screen to 1907* (New York: Scribner's, 1990).

Musser, Charles, *Before the Nickelodeon: Edwin S. Porter and the Edison Manufacturing Company* (Berkeley, CA: University of California Press, 1991).

Naremore, James, *Acting in the Cinema* (Berkeley, CA: University of California Press, 1988).

Neale, Steve, *Genre* (London: British Film Institute, 1980).

Neale, Steve, *Cinema and Technology: Image, Sound, Colour* (London: Macmillan, 1985).

Neale, Steve, "Questions of Genre," *Screen* 31:1 (Spring 1990), pp. 45–67.

Neale, Steve, "Melo Talk: On the Meaning and Use of the Term 'Melodrama' in the American Trade Press," *The Velvet Light Trap* 22 (Fall 1993), pp. 66–89.

Neale, Steve, and Frank Krutnik, *Popular Film and Television Comedy* (London: Routledge, 1990).

Neve, Brian, *Film and Politics in America: A Social Tradition* (London: Routledge, 1992).

Nichols, Bill, ed., *Movies and Methods* (Berkeley, CA: University of California Press, 1976).

Nichols, Bill, *Ideology and the Image* (Bloomington: Indiana University Press, 1981).

Nichols, Bill, ed., *Movies and Methods Vol. II* (Berkeley, CA: University of California Press, 1985).

O'Connor, John E., and Martin A. Jackson, eds, *American History/American Film: Interpreting the Hollywood Image* (New York: Ungar, 1980).

Ogle, Patrick J., "Technological and Aesthetic Influences upon the Development of Deep Focus Cinematography in the United States," in John Ellis, ed., *Screen Reader 1: Cinema/Ideology/Politics* (London: Society for Education in Film and Television, 1977), pp. 81–108.

Ohmer, Susan, "Measuring Desire: George Gallup and Audience Research in Hollywood," *Journal of Film and Video* 43:1–2 (Summer 1991), pp. 3–28.

Parrish, Robert, *Growing Up in Hollywood* (London: Bodley Head, 1976).

Patterson, Frances Taylor, *Cinema Craftsmanship: A Book for Photo Playwrights* (New York: Harcourt, Brace, and Howe, 1920).

Penley, Constance, ed., *Feminism and Film Theory* (London: Routledge, 1988).

Perkins, V.F., *Films as Film: Understanding and Judging Movies* (Harmondsworth: Penguin, 1972).

Perkins, V.F., "Must We Say What They Mean? Film Criticism and Interpretation," *MOVIE* 34/5 (Winter 1990), pp. 1–6.

Poague, Leland, *Howard Hawks* (Boston: Twayne, 1982).

Potamkin, Harry Alan, *The Compound Cinema*, ed. Lewis Jacobs (New York: Teachers College Press, 1977).

Powdermaker, Hortense, *Hollywood the Dream Factory: An Anthropologist Looks at the Movie-makers* (Boston: Little, Brown, 1950).

Propp, Vladimir, *Morphology of the Folktale*, trans. Laurence Scott (Austin: University of Texas Press, 1968).

Pudovkin, Vsevolod, *Film Technique and Film Acting: The Cinema Writings of V.I. Pudovkin*, trans. Ivor Montagu (New York: Bonanza, 1949).

Pye, Douglas, "Genre and Movies," *MOVIE* 20 (Spring 1975), pp. 29–43.

Pye, Douglas, "Bordwell and Hollywood," *MOVIE* 33 (Winter 1989), pp. 46–52.

Ramsaye, Terry, *A Million and One Nights: A History of the Motion Picture through 1925* (New York: Simon and Schuster, 1926).

Raubicheck, Walter, and Walter Srebnick, eds, *Hitchcock's Rereleased Films: From Rope to Vertigo* (Detroit: Wayne State University Press, 1991).

Ray, Robert, *A Certain Tendency of the Hollywood Cinema, 1930–1980* (Princeton, NJ: Princeton University Press, 1985).

Rebello, Stephen, *Alfred Hitchcock and the Making of Psycho* (New York: Dembner Books, 1990).

Reid, Mark A., *Redefining Black Film* (Berkeley, CA: University of California Press, 1993).

Rhode, Eric, *A History of the Cinema from its Origins to 1970* (Harmondsworth: Penguin, 1978).

Ribuffo, Leo, *Right, Center, Left: Essays in American History* (New Brunswick, NJ: Rutgers University Press, 1992).

Richards, Jeffrey, *The Age of the Dream Palace: Cinema and Society in Britain, 1930–1939* (London: Routledge and Kegan Paul, 1984).

Richetson, Frank H., *The Management of Motion Pictures* (New York: McGraw-Hill, 1938).

Rimmon-Kenan, Slomith, *Narrative Fiction: Contemporary Poetics* (London: Methuen, 1983).

Roddick, Nick, *A New Deal in Entertainment: Warner Brothers in the 1930s* (London: British Film Institute, 1983).

Rogin, Michael, *Ronald Reagan, the Movie and Other Episodes in Political Demonology* (Berkeley, CA: University of California Press, 1987).

Rollins, Peter C., *Hollywood as Historian: American Film in a Cultural Context* (Lexington: University of Kentucky Press, 1983).

Rosen, Marjorie, *Popcorn Venus* (New York: Avon, 1973).

Rosen, Philip, ed., *Narrative, Apparatus, Ideology: A Film Theory Reader* (New York: Columbia University Press, 1986).

Rosenberg, Bernard, and David Manning White, eds, *Mass Culture: The Popular Arts in America* (New York: Free Press, 1957).

Ross, Murray, *Stars and Strikes: Unionization of Hollywood* (New York: Columbia University Press, 1941).

Rosten, Leo, *Hollywood: The Movie Colony, the Movie Makers* (New York: Harcourt, Brace, 1941).

Rothman, William, *The "I" of the Camera: Essays in Film Criticism, History and Aesthetics* (Cambridge: Cambridge University Press, 1988).

Ryan, Michael, and Douglas Kellner, *Camera Politica: The Politics and Ideology of the Contemporary Hollywood Film* (Bloomington: Indiana University Press, 1988).

Said, Edward, *The World, the Text, and the Critic* (Cambridge, MA: Harvard University Press, 1983).

Salt, Barry, *Film Style and Technology: History and Analysis* (London: Starword, 1983).

Sarris, Andrew, *The American Cinema: Directors and Directions, 1929–1968* (New York: Dutton, 1968).

Schatz, Thomas, *Hollywood Genres: Formulas, Filmmaking, and the Studio System* (New York: Random House, 1981).

Schatz, Thomas, *The Genius of the System: Hollywood Filmmaking in the Studio Era* (New York: Pantheon, 1988).

Schickel, Richard, *D.W. Griffith and the Birth of Film* (London: Pavilion, 1984).

Schickel, Richard, *Brando: A Life in Our Times* (London: Pavilion, 1991).

Seidman, Steve, *Comedian Comedy: A Tradition in Hollywood Film* (Ann Arbor: UMI

Research Press, 1981).

Silva, Fred, ed., *Focus on The Birth of a Nation* (Englewood Cliffs, NJ: Prentice-Hall, 1971).

Sinclair, Upton, *Upton Sinclair Presents William Fox* (Los Angeles: Upton Sinclair, 1933).

Singer, Ben, "Female Power in the Serial-queen Melodrama: The Etiology of an Anomaly," *Camera Obscura* 22 (January 1990), pp. 90–129.

Sklar, Robert, *Movie-made America: A Cultural History of American Movies* (New York: Random House, 1975).

Sklar, Robert, *City Boys: Cagney, Bogart, Garfield* (Princeton, NJ: Princeton University Press, 1992).

Sklar, Robert, and Charles Musser, eds, *Resisting Images: Essays on Cinema and History* (Philadelphia: Temple University Press, 1990).

Slide, Anthony, *The American Film Industry: A Historical Dictionary* (Westport, CT: Greenwood, 1986).

Solomon, Aubrey, *Twentieth Century-Fox: A Corporate and Financial History* (Metuchen, NJ: Scarecrow, 1988).

Spellerberg, James, "CinemaScope and Ideology," *The Velvet Light Trap* 21 (Summer 1985), pp. 26–34.

Spoto, Donald, *The Life of Alfred Hitchcock: The Dark Side of Genius* (London: Collins, 1983).

Staiger, Janet, "The Politics of Film Canons," *Cinema Journal* 24:2 (Spring 1985), pp. 4–25.

Staiger, Janet, *Interpreting Films: Studies in the Historical Reception of American Cinema* (Princeton, NJ: Princeton University Press, 1992).

Stam, Robert, Robert Burgoyne, and Sandy Flitterman-Lewis, *New Vocabularies in Film Semiotics: Structuralism, Post-structuralism and Beyond* (London: Routledge, 1992).

Stebbins, Genevieve, *Delsarte System of Expression* (New York: Edger S. Werner, 1902; reprinted New York: Dance Horizons, 1977).

Studlar, Gaylyn, "Discourses of Gender and Ethnicity: The Construction and De(con)struction of Rudolph Valentino as Other," *Film Criticism* 13:2 (1989), pp. 18–35.

Studlar, Gaylyn, "The Perils of Pleasure? Fan Magazine Discourse as Women's Commodified Culture in the 1920s," *Wide Angle* 13:1 (January 1991), pp. 6–33.

Sweeney, Russell C., *Coming Next Week: A Pictorial History of Film Advertising* (New York: Barnes, 1973).

Talbot, Daniel, ed., *Film: An Anthology* (Berkeley, CA: University of California Press, 1969).

Thompson, Kristin, *Exporting Entertainment: America in the World Film Market, 1907–1934* (London: British Film Institute, 1985).

Thompson, Kristin, *Breaking the Glass Armor: Neoformalist Film Analysis* (Princeton, NJ: Princeton University Press, 1988).

Thorp, Margaret, *America at the Movies* (London: Faber, 1946).

Tibbetts, John C., ed., *Introduction to the Photoplay* (Shawnee Mission, KS: National Film Society, 1977).

Toeplitz, Jerzy, *Hollywood and After: The Changing Face of Movies in America* (London: Allen and Unwin, 1974).

Truffaut, François, *Hitchcock*, revised edn (London: Paladin, 1986).

Tudor, Andrew, *Theories of Film* (London: Secker and Warburg, 1974).

Tudor, Andrew, *Monsters and Mad Scientists: A Cultural History of the Horror Movie* (Oxford: Blackwell, 1989).

Turner, Graeme, *Film as Social Practice* (London: Routledge, 1988).

Twitchell, James, *Dreadful Pleasures: An Anatomy of Modern Horror* (New York: Oxford University Press, 1985).

Tyler, Parker, *The Hollywood Hallucination* (New York: Simon and Schuster, 1944).

Tyler, Parker, *Magic and Myth of the Movies* (New York: Simon and Schuster, 1947).

Vale, Eugene, *The Technique of Screenplay Writing*, 1st pub. 1944 (New York: Grosset and Dunlap, 1973).

Vanderwood, Paul J., ed., *Juárez* (Madison: University of Wisconsin Press, 1983).

Vasey, Ruth, "Foreign Parts: Hollywood's Global Distribution and the Representation of Ethnicity," *American Quarterly* 44:4 (December 1992), pp. 617–42.

Vasey, Ruth, "The Media," in Mick Gidley, ed., *Modern American Culture: An Introduction* (London: Longman, 1993), pp. 213–38.

Vasey, Ruth, *Diplomatic Representations: The World According to Hollywood, 1919–1939* (Madison: University of Wisconsin Press, forthcoming).

Vidal, Gore, *Screening History* (London: Abacus, 1993).

Vineberg, Steve, *Method Actors: Three Generations of an American Acting Style* (New York: Macmillan, 1991).

Vizzard, Jack, *See No Evil: Life Inside a Hollywood Censor* (New York: Simon and Schuster, 1970).

Wagenknecht, Edward, *The Movies in the Age of Innocence* (Norman: University of Oklahoma Press, 1962).

Walker, John, ed., *Halliwell's Film Guide*, 8th edn (London: Grafton, 1992).

Waller, Gregory A., ed., *American Horrors: Essays on the Modern American Horror Film* (Urbana: University of Illinois Press, 1987).

Weales, Gerald, *Canned Goods as Caviar* (Chicago: University of Chicago Press, 1985).

Wenders, Wim, *Emotion Pictures*, trans. Shaun Whiteside and Michael Hoffman (London: Faber, 1989).

Wexman, Virginia Wright, "The Critic as Consumer: Film Study in the University, *Vertigo*, and the Film Canon," *Film Quarterly* 39:3 (Spring 1986), pp. 32–41.

Williams, Raymond, *Keywords: A Vocabulary of Culture and Society* (London: Fontana, 1976).

Williams, Raymond, *The Sociology of Culture* (New York: Schocken, 1982).

Willis, Donald C., *The Films of Howard Hawks* (Metuchen, NJ: Scarecrow, 1975).

Wolfenstein, Martha, and Nathan Leites, *Movies: A Psychological Study* (Glencoe, IL: Free Press, 1950).

Wollen, Peter, *Signs and Meaning in the Cinema* (London: Secker and Warburg, 1972; 1st pub. 1968).

Wollen, Peter, *Readings and Writings: Semiotic Counter-strategies* (London: Verso, 1982).

Wood, Michael, *America in the Movies; or, "Santa Maria, It Had Slipped My Mind!"* (New York: Basic Books, 1975).

Wood, Robin, *Howard Hawks* (London: Secker and Warburg, 1968).

Wood, Robin, *Personal Views: Explorations in Film* (London: Gordon Fraser, 1976).

Wood, Robin, *Hollywood from Vietnam to Reagan* (New York: Columbia University Press, 1986).

Wood, Robin, *Hitchcock's Films Revisited* (New York: Columbia University Press, 1989).

Wright, Will, *Sixguns and Society: A Structural Study of the Western* (Berkeley, CA: University of California Press, 1975).

Zizek, Slavov, ed., *Everything You Always Wanted to Know about Lacan (But Were Afraid to Ask Hitchcock)* (London: Verso, 1992).

Index